Economics Today

THE MICRO VIEW

Economics Today

THE MICRO VIEW

Seventeenth Edition

Roger LeRoy Miller

Research Professor of Economics
University of Texas—Arlington

PEARSON

Boston   Columbus   Indianapolis   New York   San Francisco   Upper Saddle River
Amsterdam   Cape Town   Dubai   London   Madrid   Milan   Munich   Paris   Montréal   Toronto
Delhi   Mexico City   São Paulo   Sydney   Hong Kong   Seoul   Singapore   Taipei   Tokyo

MyEconLab® Provides the Power of Practice

Optimize your study time with **MyEconLab**, the online assessment and tutorial system. When you take a sample test online, **MyEconLab** gives you targeted feedback and a personalized Study Plan to identify the topics you need to review.

Study Plan

The Study Plan shows you the sections you should study next, gives easy access to practice problems, and provides you with an automatically generated quiz to prove mastery of the course material.

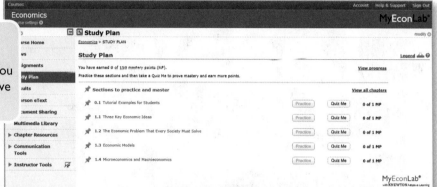

Unlimited Practice

As you work each exercise, instant feedback helps you understand and apply the concepts. Many Study Plan exercises contain algorithmically generated values to ensure that you get as much practice as you need.

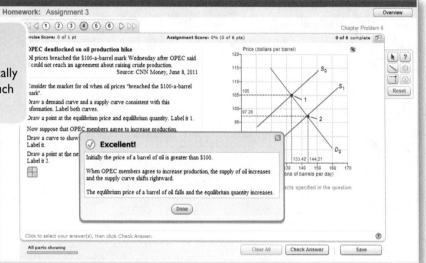

Learning Resources

Study Plan problems link to learning resources that further reinforce concepts you need to master.

- **Help Me Solve This** learning aids help you break down a problem much the same way as an instructor would do during office hours. Help Me Solve This is available for select problems.

- **eText links** are specific to the problem at hand so that related concepts are easy to review just when they are needed.

- A **graphing tool** enables you to build and manipulate graphs to better understand how concepts, numbers, and graphs connect.

Find out more at www.myeconlab.com

Real-Time Data Analysis Exercises

Up-to-date macro data is a great way to engage in and understand the usefulness of macro variables and their impact on the economy. Real-Time Data Analysis exercises communicate directly with the Federal Reserve Bank of St. Louis's FRED site, so every time FRED posts new data, students see new data.

End-of-chapter exercises accompanied by the Real-Time Data Analysis icon include Real-Time Data versions in **MyEconLab**.

Select in-text figures labeled **MyEconLab** Real-Time Data update in the electronic version of the text using FRED data.

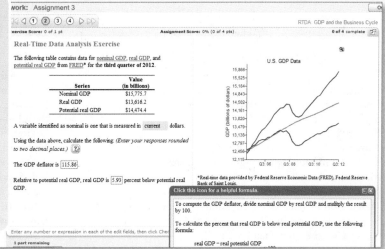

Current News Exercises

Posted weekly, we find the latest microeconomic and macroeconomic news stories, post them, and write auto-graded multi-part exercises that illustrate the economic way of thinking about the news.

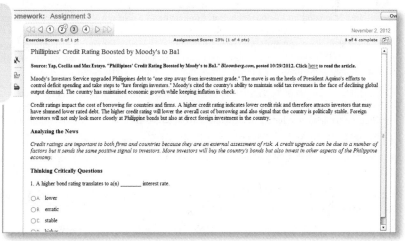

Interactive Homework Exercises

Participate in a fun and engaging activity that helps promote active learning and mastery of important economic concepts.

Pearson's experiments program is flexible and easy for instructors and students to use. For a complete list of available experiments, visit *www.myeconlab.com*.

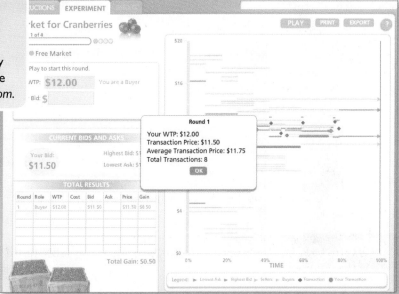

Dedication | To Pam and Joel,

Thanks for always being available
to keep me on top of the world.

—R.L.M.

Editor in Chief: Donna Battista
Executive Editor: David Alexander
Senior Editorial Project Manager: Carolyn Terbush
Editorial Assistant: Emily Brodeur
Director of Marketing: Maggie Moylan
Executive Marketing Manager: Lori DeShazo
Marketing Assistant: Kim Lovato
Managing Editor: Jeff Holcomb
Production Project Manager: Kathryn Dinovo
Senior Manufacturing Buyer: Carol Melville
Cover Designer: Jonathan Boylan
Manager, Visual Research: Rachel Youdelman

Photo Researcher: Jonathan Yonan
Manager, Rights and Permissions: Michael Joyce
Permissions Specialist/Project Manager: Jill C. Dougan
Digital Publisher, Economics: Denise Clinton
MyEconLab Content Media Leads: Noel Lotz, Courtney Kamauf
Executive Media Producer: Melissa Honig
Full-Service Project Management: Cenveo Publishing Services/
Nesbitt Graphics
Printer/Binder: Courier/Kendallville
Cover Printer: Lehigh-Phoenix Color/Hagerstown
Text Font: Janson Text LT Std.

Credits and acknowledgments borrowed from other sources and reproduced, with permission, in this textbook appear on page xxvii.

Library of Congress Cataloging-in-Publication Data is on file.

10 9 8 7 6 5 4 3 2 1

ISBN 10: 0-13-294888-5
ISBN 13: 978-0-13-294888-3

Brief Contents

Preface xviii

PART I Introduction
1 The Nature of Economics 1
2 Scarcity and the World of Trade-Offs 26
3 Demand and Supply 48
4 Extensions of Demand and Supply Analysis 75
5 Public Spending and Public Choice 100
6 Funding the Public Sector 122

IN THIS VOLUME, CHAPTER 6 IS FOLLOWED BY CHAPTER 19

PART 5 Dimensions of Microeconomics
19 Demand and Supply Elasticity 414
20 Consumer Choice 434
21 Rents, Profits, and the Financial Environment of Business 462

PART 6 Market Structure, Resource Allocation, and Regulation
22 The Firm: Cost and Output Determination 483
23 Perfect Competition 507
24 Monopoly 532
25 Monopolistic Competition 555
26 Oligopoly and Strategic Behavior 573
27 Regulation and Antitrust Policy in a Globalized Economy 594

PART 7 Labor Resources and the Environment
28 The Labor Market: Demand, Supply, and Outsourcing 618
29 Unions and Labor Market Monopoly Power 642
30 Income, Poverty, and Health Care 663
31 Environmental Economics 687

PART 8 Global Economics
32 Comparative Advantage and the Open Economy 704
33 Exchange Rates and the Balance of Payments 725

Contents

Preface xviii

PART 1 Introduction

1 The Nature of Economics 1

The Power of Economic Analysis 2
Defining Economics 2
The Three Basic Economic Questions and Two Opposing Answers 3
The Economic Approach: Systematic Decisions 5
Economics as a Science 7

WHAT IF... economists were to base their theories of human behavior on what people *say* they do, rather than on what people *actually* do? 9
Positive versus Normative Economics 10

YOU ARE THERE Why So Many Firms Are Incorporating Outside the United States 11

ISSUES & APPLICATIONS Why So Many Tourists Have Been Giving Birth in Hong Kong 12

Summary: What You Should Know/Where to Go to Practice 13
Problems 14
Economics on the Net 16
Answers to Quick Quizzes 16

APPENDIX A Reading and Working with Graphs 17
Direct and Inverse Relationships 17
Constructing a Graph 18
Graphing Numbers in a Table 19
The Slope of a Line (A Linear Curve) 21
Summary: What You Should Know/Where to Go to Practice 24
Problems 25

EXAMPLE
Hello, Bank Robber, I'll Remember You 6
The Perceived Value of Gifts 7
Getting Directions 8

INTERNATIONAL POLICY EXAMPLE
Cuba Experiments with Mixing It Up 5

POLICY EXAMPLE
The Federal Government Directs New California Train Tracks 4

EXAMPLE
The Opportunity Cost of 17 Minutes of Labor in the United States 30
A Comparative Advantage in Watching Gift-Card Balances 39

INTERNATIONAL POLICY EXAMPLE
A Lower Productive Contribution of Sweltering Japanese Labor 28

INTERNATIONAL EXAMPLE
In China, More Factories Mean Fewer Roads—and More Traffic 33

2 Scarcity and the World of Trade-Offs 26

Scarcity 27
Wants and Needs 29
Scarcity, Choice, and Opportunity Cost 29
The World of Trade-Offs 30
The Choices a Nation's Economy Faces 32

WHAT IF... the U.S. government tries to increase total production of all goods by diverting resources to the manufacture of "green" products? 34
Economic Growth and the Production Possibilities Curve 36
The Trade-Off between the Present and the Future 36
Specialization and Greater Productivity 38
Comparative Advantage and Trade among Nations 40

YOU ARE THERE The Opportunity Cost of Vacation Time in South Korea 41

ISSUES & APPLICATIONS The Rising Opportunity Cost of Airlines' "Block Times" 42

Summary: What You Should Know/Where to Go to Practice 43
Problems 45
Economics on the Net 47
Answers to Quick Quizzes 47

EXAMPLE

Why Sales of Electric Cars Are Stuck in Low
Gear 50

Lower Incomes Boost the Demand for
Reconditioned Cell Phones 55

Why Fewer Wine Bottles Have Natural Cork
Stoppers 56

Steel Producers Reduce Production When the Price
of Steel Falls 59

Cotton Price Movements Squeeze and Stretch
Clothing Supply 63

How Deadly Southern Twisters Pummeled the U.S.
Poultry Supply 64

Production Breakdowns Create a Shortage of a
Life-Saving Drug 67

POLICY EXAMPLE

An Expected Uranium Price Implosion Cuts
Current Uranium Demand 57

Should Shortages in the Ticket Market Be Solved
by Scalpers? 68

3 Demand and Supply 48

Demand 49
The Demand Schedule 51
Shifts in Demand 52
The Law of Supply 58
The Supply Schedule 59
Shifts in Supply 61

WHAT IF... politicians simultaneously oppose a higher price for the current quantity of gasoline supplied yet favor higher taxes on the fuel? 63
Putting Demand and Supply Together 64

YOU ARE THERE Why the Casket Industry Is on Life Support 69

ISSUES & APPLICATIONS Your Higher Education Bills Really Are Increasing 69
Summary: What You Should Know/Where to Go to Practice 70
Problems 72
Economics on the Net 74
Answers to Quick Quizzes 74

EXAMPLE

Linking Businesses to Customers on the Go via
QR Apps 77

An Airline Boarding Lottery 81

INTERNATIONAL POLICY EXAMPLE

Multiple Price Ceilings Lead to Electricity
Rationing in China 83

INTERNATIONAL EXAMPLE

What Accounts for the Rising Price of Shipping
Containers? 79

POLICY EXAMPLE

A Higher Minimum Wage Translates into Fewer
Employed Teens 88

4 Extensions of Demand and Supply Analysis 75

The Price System and Markets 76
Changes in Demand and Supply 77
The Rationing Function of Prices 80
The Policy of Government-Imposed Price Controls 81
The Policy of Controlling Rents 83
Price Floors in Agriculture 85

WHAT IF... the government decides to "help dairy farmers" by imposing a floor price in the market for milk that is above the equilibrium price? 87
Price Floors in the Labor Market 87
Quantity Restrictions 89

YOU ARE THERE Explaining the "Crisis" of Persistent Drug Shortages 89

ISSUES & APPLICATIONS Why Prices of Used Cars Are So High 90
Summary: What You Should Know/Where to Go to Practice 91
Problems 92
Economics on the Net 94
Answers to Quick Quizzes 95

APPENDIX B Consumer Surplus, Producer Surplus, and Gains from Trade within a Price System 96
Consumer Surplus 96
Producer Surplus 97
Gains from Trade within a Price System 98
Price Controls and Gains from Trade 98

EXAMPLE

Private Companies Look to Place Humans in
Orbit—and Beyond 107

INTERNATIONAL POLICY EXAMPLE

Hungary's Tax on Prepackaged Snacks 104

POLICY EXAMPLE

Stop the Presses for Subsidies! 104

The Great Underestimates of Government Health
Care Expenses 111

A Weak Relationship between Spending and
Schooling Results 113

EXAMPLE

State University Tuition Rates Jump—Even at the
Last Moment 123

POLICY EXAMPLE

Is It Time to Replace Gasoline Taxes with Mileage
Taxes? 124

Calculating the Top U.S. Marginal Tax Rate 125

Figuring Out How Much to Pay in Income Taxes Is
Not Cheap 127

States Seek to Apply Sales Taxes to Internet
Retailers' Sales 130

EXAMPLE

The Price Elasticity of Demand for a Tablet
Device 417

Price and Revenue Changes and Price Elasticity
of Demand for Air Travel 420

What Do Real-World Price Elasticities of Demand
Look Like? 424

Are Walmart's Products Inferior Goods? 426

5 Public Spending and Public Choice 100

What a Price System Can and Cannot Do 101
Correcting for Externalities 101
The Other Economic Functions of Government 105
The Political Functions of Government 108
Public Spending and Transfer Programs 109

WHAT IF... the federal government continues reducing the out-of-pocket prices that
consumers must pay for health care services? 112

Collective Decision Making: The Theory of Public Choice 114

YOU ARE THERE The U.S. Government Ensures That an Airport Is "Convenient" 116

ISSUES & APPLICATIONS The Government-Sponsored U.S. Postal Service 116

Summary: What You Should Know/Where to Go to Practice 117

Problems 119
Economics on the Net 121
Answers to Quick Quizzes 121

6 Funding the Public Sector 122

Paying for the Public Sector 123
Systems of Taxation 123
The Most Important Federal Taxes 125
Tax Rates and Tax Revenues 129

WHAT IF... the government seeks to collect higher taxes by increasing capital gains
tax rates? 131

Taxation from the Point of View of Producers and Consumers 132

YOU ARE THERE How to Keep Social Security in Business 134

ISSUES & APPLICATIONS What Determines the U.S. Long-Run Average
Tax Rate? 134

Summary: What You Should Know/Where to Go to Practice 136

Problems 137
Economics on the Net 138
Answers to Quick Quizzes 138

PART 5 Dimensions of Microeconomics

19 Demand and Supply Elasticity 414

Price Elasticity 415
Price Elasticity Ranges 417
Elasticity and Total Revenues 418

WHAT IF... the government offers to pay for higher-priced health care to try to reduce
society's overall health care expenditures? 421

Determinants of the Price Elasticity of Demand 421
Cross Price Elasticity of Demand 424
Income Elasticity of Demand 425
Price Elasticity of Supply 427

YOU ARE THERE Implications of Housing Demand Elasticities in China 429

ISSUES & APPLICATIONS Rock Stars Face High Price Elasticities of Demand 429

Summary: What You Should Know/Where to Go to Practice 430

Problems 432
Economics on the Net 433
Answers to Quick Quizzes 433

EXAMPLE

Newspaper Vending Machines versus Candy
Vending Machines 438

High-Priced Blue Jeans as Part of a Consumer
Optimum 440

INTERNATIONAL EXAMPLE

Inferring Substantial Marginal Utility from an Oil
Change 441

20 Consumer Choice 434

Utility Theory 435
Graphical Analysis 436
Diminishing Marginal Utility 438
Optimizing Consumption Choices 439
How a Price Change Affects Consumer Optimum 442
The Demand Curve Revisited 444
Behavioral Economics and Consumer Choice Theory 445

WHAT IF... the government bans certain products to try to prevent poor decisions? 446

YOU ARE THERE Using a Smartphone to Attain a Consumer Optimum 446

ISSUES & APPLICATIONS Why Are Consumers Making More Healthful Choices? 447

Summary: What You Should Know/Where to Go to Practice 448

Problems 449
Economics on the Net 451
Answers to Quick Quizzes 451

APPENDIX F More Advanced Consumer Choice Theory 452

On Being Indifferent 452
Properties of Indifference Curves 453
The Marginal Rate of Substitution 455
The Indifference Map 455
The Budget Constraint 456
Consumer Optimum Revisited 457
Deriving the Demand Curve 458

Summary: What You Should Know/Where to Go to Practice 459

Problems 460

EXAMPLE

Do Entertainment Superstars Make Super
Economic Rents? 464

Explaining the Allure of "Century Bonds" 475

Can the Hindenburg Omen Detect an Impending
Market Crash? 476

INTERNATIONAL EXAMPLE

Using Artificial Intelligence to Try to Beat the
Market 476

POLICY EXAMPLE

The Government Considers Allowing "Crowd
Funding" of Firms 467

21 Rents, Profits, and the Financial Environment of Business 462

Economic Rent 463
Firms and Profits 465
Interest 470

WHAT IF... the government directs credit to favored industries at artificially low interest rates? 473

Corporate Financing Methods 474
The Markets for Stocks and Bonds 475

YOU ARE THERE College Hunks Hauling Junk Weighs Partnership Pros and Cons 477

ISSUES & APPLICATIONS Shrinking Numbers of New Proprietorships, Partnerships, and Corporations 477

Summary: What You Should Know/Where to Go to Practice 479

Problems 480
Economics on the Net 482
Answers to Quick Quizzes 482

PART 6 Market Structure, Resource Allocation, and Regulation

EXAMPLE

3D Printers Shift from Design to Production 485

Evaluating the Marginal Physical Product of Oil
Drilling 488

Diseconomies of Scale at One of the World's Top
Airlines 500

INTERNATIONAL EXAMPLE

Using Cheap Power from the Sun to Reduce
Average Total Costs 492

POLICY EXAMPLE

How the U.S. Army Uses Virtual Warfare to Cut
Variable Costs 491

22 The Firm: Cost and Output Determination 483

Short Run versus Long Run 484
The Relationship between Output and Inputs 485
Diminishing Marginal Product 487
Short-Run Costs to the Firm 489
The Relationship between Diminishing Marginal Product and Cost Curves 494
Long-Run Cost Curves 497
Why the Long-Run Average Cost Curve Is U-Shaped 498
Minimum Efficient Scale 500

WHAT IF... the government required firms to reduce their long-run scales of operation to cut overall U.S. energy use? 501

YOU ARE THERE Cutting Costs by Replacing Pilot Projects with Simulations 501

ISSUES & APPLICATIONS Can Electric Car Production Attain Minimum Efficient Scale? 502

Summary: What You Should Know/Where to Go to Practice 503
    Problems 504
    Economics on the Net 506
    Answers to Quick Quizzes 506

EXAMPLE
Vets Respond to Higher Market Prices of Treatments for Fido 518
For Many Hamburger Sellers, the Exit Signal Is Flashing 521
Economic Profits Attract Online-Daily-Deals Entrants in Droves 522

23 Perfect Competition 507

Characteristics of a Perfectly Competitive Market Structure 508
The Demand Curve of the Perfect Competitor 509
How Much Should the Perfect Competitor Produce? 509
Using Marginal Analysis to Determine the Profit-Maximizing Rate of Production 510
Short-Run Profits 513
The Short-Run Break-Even Price and the Short-Run Shutdown Price 515
The Supply Curve for a Perfectly Competitive Industry 517
Price Determination under Perfect Competition 519

WHAT IF... the government mandated that prices stay at long-run equilibrium levels? 520
The Long-Run Industry Situation: Exit and Entry 520
Long-Run Equilibrium 524
Competitive Pricing: Marginal Cost Pricing 524

YOU ARE THERE Looking to Enter a Competitive Online Market? Rent a Desk! 526

ISSUES & APPLICATIONS A Decreasing-Cost, "White Gold" Industry 526
Summary: What You Should Know/Where to Go to Practice 528
    Problems 529
    Economics on the Net 531
    Answers to Quick Quizzes 531

EXAMPLE
Trial and Error Yields Profits from Monopoly Time in the Air 542
Why Students Pay Different Prices to Attend College 545

POLICY EXAMPLE
Waging Economic War on Children's Lemonade Stands 535
The U.S. Rail Monopoly That Subsists on Taxpayer Handouts 544

24 Monopoly 532

Definition of a Monopolist 533
Barriers to Entry 533
The Demand Curve a Monopolist Faces 536
Elasticity and Monopoly 538
Costs and Monopoly Profit Maximization 539
Calculating Monopoly Profit 542
On Making Higher Profits: Price Discrimination 544
The Social Cost of Monopolies 546

WHAT IF... governments protect local retailers from "big-box" retailers such as Walmart and Target? 547

YOU ARE THERE Seeking Higher Rents from Souvenir Vendors in Atlanta 548

ISSUES & APPLICATIONS The U.S. Occupational License Explosion 548
Summary: What You Should Know/Where to Go to Practice 549
    Problems 551
    Economics on the Net 552
    Answers to Quick Quizzes 552

APPENDIX G Consumer Surplus and the Deadweight Loss Resulting from Monopoly 553
    Consumer Surplus in a Perfectly Competitive Market 553
    How Society Loses from Monopoly 554

EXAMPLE
A Biodegradable Chips Bag Is Crunchier Than the
Chips 558

INTERNATIONAL EXAMPLE
A Push to Make Electronic Billboards Interactive
in Japan 563

25 Monopolistic Competition 555

Monopolistic Competition 556
Price and Output for the Monopolistic Competitor 558
Comparing Perfect Competition with Monopolistic Competition 560
Brand Names and Advertising 561

WHAT IF... the government were to limit or even ban "excessive" advertising? 564
Information Products and Monopolistic Competition 564

YOU ARE THERE Have You Smelled a Ford Lately? 568

ISSUES & APPLICATIONS Why E-Books Are Upending the Publishing Business 568
Summary: What You Should Know/Where to Go to Practice 569
Problems 570
Economics on the Net 572
Answers to Quick Quizzes 572

EXAMPLE
The Four-Firm Concentration Ratio in the U.S.
Auto Industry 577
The Prisoners' Dilemma 579
Fishing for Date Seekers with Ads Boosts
PlentyOfFish 586

INTERNATIONAL EXAMPLE
The HHI for the Global Internet Browser
Industry 578

26 Oligopoly and Strategic Behavior 573

Oligopoly 574

WHAT IF... the government promoted competition among more firms by prohibiting horizontal mergers? 575
Strategic Behavior and Game Theory 578
The Cooperative Game: A Collusive Cartel 581
Network Effects 583
Two-Sided Markets, Network Effects, and Oligopoly 584
The Old and New of Two-Sided Markets 587
Comparing Market Structures 587

YOU ARE THERE Hyundai Goes Vertical 588

ISSUES & APPLICATIONS Concentration in the Textbook-Publishing Industry 588
Summary: What You Should Know/Where to Go to Practice 590
Problems 591
Economics on the Net 593
Answers to Quick Quizzes 593

EXAMPLE
Learn the Price and Buy from the College
Bookstore in One Step 603

INTERNATIONAL EXAMPLE
A Perceived Monopoly Threat Motivates Net
Neutrality Rules 600

POLICY EXAMPLE
New Nicotine Market Entry? Not If the FDA Can
Help It! 604
The FTC Blocks a Merger in Advance of the Firms'
Bankruptcy 607
A Proposed Wireless Merger Experiences a
Dropped Connection 610

27 Regulation and Antitrust Policy in a Globalized Economy 594

Forms of Industry Regulation 595
Regulating Natural Monopolies 598
Regulating Nonmonopolistic Industries 600
Incentives and Costs of Regulation 603
Antitrust Policy 606

WHAT IF... all U.S. business organizations were subject to antitrust laws? 608
Antitrust Enforcement 609

YOU ARE THERE No Longer in a State of Sticker Shock in Michigan 612

ISSUES & APPLICATIONS More Regulations Breed More Federal Regulatory Jobs 612
Summary: What You Should Know/Where to Go to Practice 613
Problems 615
Economics on the Net 617
Answers to Quick Quizzes 617

PART 7 Labor Resources and the Environment

EXAMPLE
E-Books' Popularity Is Reducing the Demand for Authors' Labor 623
Why Contract Attorneys' Wages Have Plummeted 627

INTERNATIONAL EXAMPLE
China's Declining Status as an Outsourcing Destination 630

POLICY EXAMPLE
A "Reclassification Regulation" Cuts Overall Labor Employment 635

28 The Labor Market: Demand, Supply, and Outsourcing 618

Labor Demand for a Perfectly Competitive Firm 619
The Market Demand for Labor 623
Wage Determination in a Perfectly Competitive Labor Market 625
Labor Outsourcing, Wages, and Employment 628

WHAT IF... the government required U.S. firms to hire only workers who reside in the United States? 631

Monopoly in the Product Market 632
The Utilization of Other Factors of Production 634

YOU ARE THERE Combating U.S. Unemployment via Job-Search Outsourcing 636
ISSUES & APPLICATIONS Will You Be Replaced by an App? 636
Summary: What You Should Know/Where to Go to Practice 637

Problems 639
Economics on the Net 640
Answers to Quick Quizzes 641

EXAMPLE
Symphony Musicians "Win" a Lengthy Strike 646

INTERNATIONAL EXAMPLE
The Global Public-Union Benefits Explosion 651

POLICY EXAMPLE
Can Minimum Wage Laws Ever Boost Employment? 654

29 Unions and Labor Market Monopoly Power 642

Industrialization and Labor Unions 643
Union Goals and Strategies 646

WHAT IF... the government required all workers to be unionized so that they could earn higher wages? 649

Economic Effects of Labor Unions 650
Monopsony: A Buyer's Monopoly 651

YOU ARE THERE A Union Hires a Nonunion Picketer to Protest Nonunion Hiring 656
ISSUES & APPLICATIONS Gauging Labor Lost to Union Disputes Each Year 657
Summary: What You Should Know/Where to Go to Practice 658

Problems 660
Economics on the Net 662
Answers to Quick Quizzes 662

EXAMPLE
U.S. Residents Move among Income Groups over Time 666

INTERNATIONAL POLICY EXAMPLE
In Greece, "Free" Care Now Includes Substantial Implicit Costs 680

POLICY EXAMPLE
Dual Coverage Drives Up Federal Health Care Spending 678

30 Income, Poverty, and Health Care 663

Income 664
Determinants of Income Differences 667
Theories of Desired Income Distribution 670
Poverty and Attempts to Eliminate It 671
Health Care 674

WHAT IF... the government forced lower spending on health care by placing legal limits on prices? 675

YOU ARE THERE A Portuguese Woman Rethinks Her Human Capital Investment 681
ISSUES & APPLICATIONS Why Is the Female Income Gap Shrinking? 682
Summary: What You Should Know/Where to Go to Practice 683

Problems 685
Economics on the Net 686
Answers to Quick Quizzes 686

INTERNATIONAL EXAMPLE

Passengers Help Pay for the Emissions on EU
Airline Routes 696

POLICY EXAMPLE

Increasing the Marginal Cost of U.S. Air Pollution
Abatement 693

California Dreaming: A Western Cap-and-Trade
Pact? 696

INTERNATIONAL POLICY EXAMPLE

African Nations Benefit from Lower U.S. Trade
Barriers 718

INTERNATIONAL EXAMPLE

Comparative Advantage and Specialization in
European Linens 711

POLICY EXAMPLE

A U.S. Agency Subsidizes U.S. Exports—and Also
Foreign Firms 713

Gibson Guitars Confronts a Very Particular Import
Quota 716

INTERNATIONAL POLICY EXAMPLE

Poland's Floating Exchange Rate Protects It from
Euro Ills 741

INTERNATIONAL EXAMPLE

The Most Traded Currencies in Foreign Exchange
Markets 737

31 Environmental Economics 687

Private versus Social Costs 688
Correcting for Externalities 690
Pollution 691
Common Property 693
Reducing Humanity's Carbon Footprint: Restraining Pollution-Causing
Activities 695
Wild Species, Common Property, and Trade-Offs 697

WHAT IF... governments allowed people to own endangered animals as private
property? 697

YOU ARE THERE A Mayor Faces the Grimy Economics of Trash Removal 698

ISSUES & APPLICATIONS The New Sulfur Dioxide "Cap and Fade" Program 698
Summary: What You Should Know/Where to Go to Practice 699

Problems 701
Economics on the Net 703
Answers to Quick Quizzes 703

PART 8 Global Economics

32 Comparative Advantage and the Open Economy 704

The Worldwide Importance of International Trade 705
Why We Trade: Comparative Advantage and Mutual Gains from Exchange 706
The Relationship between Imports and Exports 711

WHAT IF... the government saved U.S. jobs from foreign competition by prohibiting all
imports? 712

International Competitiveness 712
Arguments against Free Trade 712
Ways to Restrict Foreign Trade 715
International Trade Organizations 718

YOU ARE THERE A French Family Bookshop Seeks Protection from U.S. E-Books 720

ISSUES & APPLICATIONS U.S. Flower Growers Induce Congress to Snip Foreign
Imports 720
Summary: What You Should Know/Where to Go to Practice 721

Problems 723
Economics on the Net 724
Answers to Quick Quizzes 724

33 Exchange Rates and the Balance of Payments 725

The Balance of Payments and International Capital Movements 726

WHAT IF... all governments attempted to require their nations to have current account
surpluses? 729

Determining Foreign Exchange Rates 732
The Gold Standard and the International Monetary Fund 738
Fixed versus Floating Exchange Rates 739

YOU ARE THERE An Exchange-Rate-Induced U.S. Shopping *Bagunça* for *Brazilians* 742

ISSUES & APPLICATIONS Items "Made in China" Generate Income Elsewhere 742
Summary: What You Should Know/Where to Go to Practice 743

Problems 745
Economics on the Net 746
Answers to Quick Quizzes 746

Answers to Odd-Numbered Problems A-1

Glossary G-1

Index I-1

One-Semester Course Outline

Macroeconomic Emphasis
The Macro View

1. The Nature of Economics
2. Scarcity and the World of Trade-Offs
3. Demand and Supply
4. Extensions of Demand and Supply Analysis
5. Public Spending and Public Choice
6. Funding the Public Sector
7. The Macroeconomy. Unemployment, Inflation, and Deflation
8. Measuring the Economy's Performance
9. Global Economic Growth and Development
10. Real GDP and the Price Level in the Long Run
11. Classical and Keynesian Macro Analyses
12. Consumption, Real GDP, and the Multiplier
13. Fiscal Policy
14. Deficit Spending and the Public Debt
15. Money, Banking, and Central Banking
16. Domestic and International Dimensions of Monetary Policy
17. Stabilization in an Integrated World Economy
18. Policies and Prospects for Global Economic Growth
32. Comparative Advantage and the Open Economy
33. Exchange Rates and the Balance of Payments

Microeconomic Emphasis
The Micro View

1. The Nature of Economics
2. Scarcity and the World of Trade-Offs
3. Demand and Supply
4. Extensions of Demand and Supply Analysis
5. Public Spending and Public Choice
6. Funding the Public Sector
19. Demand and Supply Elasticity
20. Consumer Choice
21. Rents, Profits, and the Financial Environment of Business
22. The Firm: Cost and Output Determination
23. Perfect Competition
24. Monopoly
25. Monopolistic Competition
26. Oligopoly and Strategic Behavior
27. Regulation and Antitrust Policy in a Globalized Economy
28. The Labor Market: Demand, Supply, and Outsourcing
29. Unions and Labor Market Monopoly Power
30. Income, Poverty, and Health Care
31. Environmental Economics
32. Comparative Advantage and the Open Economy
33. Exchange Rates and the Balance of Payments

Balanced Micro-Macro

1. The Nature of Economics
2. Scarcity and the World of Trade-Offs
3. Demand and Supply
4. Extensions of Demand and Supply Analysis
5. Public Spending and Public Choice
6. Funding the Public Sector
20. Consumer Choice
21. Rents, Profits, and the Financial Environment of Business
22. The Firm: Cost and Output Determination
23. Perfect Competition
24. Monopoly
28. The Labor Market: Demand, Supply, and Outsourcing
29. Unions and Labor Market Monopoly Power
7. The Macroeconomy. Unemployment, Inflation, and Deflation
10. Real GDP and the Price Level in the Long Run
11. Classical and Keynesian Macro Analyses
12. Consumption, Real GDP, and the Multiplier
13. Fiscal Policy
14. Deficit Spending and the Public Debt
15. Money, Banking, and Central Banking
16. Domestic and International Dimensions of Monetary Policy
32. Comparative Advantage and the Open Economy
33. Exchange Rates and the Balance of Payments

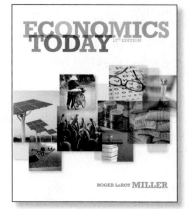

Economics Today—Bringing the Real World to Your Students

How do you compete for students' time and attention when their world is so fast paced? How do you get students to focus? How do you present the topics or principles of economics in a way that is both attention grabbing and meaningful? The best way to do so is through real-world examples. I believe in teaching by example. That is why *Economics Today* has always been a textbook filled with international, policy, and domestic examples. This edition is no exception—a total of 110 topics bring your students into the real world, including why it costs so much to go to college, why you should expect to pay more for what you buy on the Internet, why it will cost $700 million to be able to play 3D movies nationwide, and why e-books are upending the publishing business.

In keeping with this approach, I have changed almost every example as well as every Issues & Applications. This chapter-ending feature forms a "bookend" with the introduction presented on the first page of every chapter. Key Concepts are presented along with two Critical Thinking Questions and a Web Resources Project. The *You Are There* features remain student friendly and illustrate how people in the real world respond to changing economic conditions.

> "I believe in teaching by example. That is why *Economics Today* has always been a textbook filled with international, policy, and domestic examples."

An engaging new feature called *What If . . . ?* can be found in every chapter. Students new to economics sometimes believe that complex problems can be solved by simple government policies or solutions that require instantaneous changes in human behavior. In the new *What If . . .?* features I attempt to dispel some of the current notions about how to solve economic issues facing the nation and also encourage students to think like economists. *What If . . . the government were to limit or even ban excessive advertising? What If . . . the government saved U.S. jobs from foreign competition by prohibiting all exports? What If . . . the government required U.S. firms to hire only workers who reside in the United States?* These are just a few examples of this new feature.

While this edition has been updated throughout, several topics have received special attention. For the macro policy chapters, issues relating to the growing U.S. federal deficit and public debt are covered in even more detail in Chapter 14. This chapter now discusses whether raising taxes on the highest earners can close the deficit gap and whether official measures of the current public debt underestimate promised future benefits. Chapter 16 now provides an analysis of various instruments of credit policy that the Fed appears to have adopted for the foreseeable future as a supplement to traditional monetary policy tools. Along the microeconomic dimension, Chapter 26 extends the coverage of network effects by examining two-sided markets in which intermediary platforms link groups of end users. Finally, Chapter 27 includes discussions of real changes in concentration measures and thresholds used in enforcement of U.S. antitrust policy.

> "That is one of the underlying goals I have always set for myself when I revise *Economics Today*—to help students recognize the value of the concepts they are learning."

Timely and relevant learning continues with MyEconLab, Pearson's online tutorial and assessment system. You can assign homework, quizzes, and tests that are automatically graded. Students have access to a suite of learning aids that help them at the very moment they might be struggling with the concepts. There are weekly news articles, many experiments, and questions that update in real time with data from the Federal Reserve Bank of St. Louis.

The trained economist sees economics everywhere—we observe people responding to changes in incentives all of the time. We economists would all like to have our students not only understand how powerful economics is but also use their newly acquired skills in their daily and professional lives. That is one of the underlying goals I have always set for myself when I revise *Economics Today*—to help students recognize the value of the concepts they are learning.

—Roger LeRoy Miller

New to This Edition

This new edition of *Economics Today* covers leading-edge issues while lowering barriers to student learning. The text relentlessly pursues the fundamental objective of showing students how economics is front and center in *their* own lives while providing them with many ways to evaluate their understanding of key concepts covered in each chapter.

Modern topics in economic theory and policy are spotlighted throughout the text. These include:

- An appraisal of key questions raised by continuing growth of the **U.S. government deficit and the public debt:** Chapter 14 considers whether the federal government can rely on raising taxes to eliminate its budget deficit and whether official measures of *today's* public debt understate total promises of benefits to be paid in the *future*.

- An evaluation of a new aspect of **Federal Reserve policymaking:** Chapter 16 provides an analysis of various tools of *credit policy* adopted by the Federal Reserve in recent years to supplement its traditional monetary policy instruments.

- Coverage of **two-sided markets:** The discussion of network effects in Chapter 26 now includes consideration of oligopoly pricing complications that arise in markets in which intermediary *platforms* link groups of *end users*.

- An updated exposition of **antitrust guidelines:** Chapter 27 has been revised in light of recent changes in concentration measures and thresholds applied by authorities charged with enforcing U.S. *antitrust policy*.

ISSUES & APPLICATIONS

Have Unemployment Benefits Boosted Unemployment?

CONCEPTS APPLIED
- ▶ Unemployment Rate
- ▶ Cyclical Unemployment
- ▶ Structural Unemployment

Between June 2008 and February 2009, the U.S. unemployment rate rose sharply, from 5.6 percent to more than 8 percent. Although the recession officially ended in June 2009, the unemployment rate ultimately reached a peak of 10.1 percent in October 2009. Since then, the unemployment rate has stayed near 8 percent. Thus, the unemployment rate remained above its prior level by at least 2 percentage points for more than three years. Many economists conclude that structural unemployment has risen. One element contributing to this rise, they suggest, was a substantial increase in the length of time the government paid benefits to unemployed workers.

Additional macro analyses include the following:

- Chapter 7 considers the extent to which lengthening the duration of **unemployment benefits** from 26 weeks to 99 weeks may have contributed to a higher U.S. unemployment rate.

- Chapter 11 explains why an index measure of **financial market fear** is often associated with short-term declines in total production of goods and services.

- Chapter 13 examines why most federal tax dollars recently transmitted to states to spend and thereby provide **stimulus to the U.S. economy** have failed to do so.

- Chapter 15 offers an explanation of why many banks no longer desire to expand **deposits** and indeed now actively discourage customers from depositing more funds.

The micro portion of the text now includes the following:

- Chapter 19 discusses how the concept of **price elasticity of demand** explains why many rock musicians have experienced declining revenues from sales of music recordings and concert tickets, even though the prices of recordings and tickets have increased.

- Chapter 24 examines the economic effects of a substantial expansion of **occupational licensing** requirements that many states impose on their citizens.

- Chapter 28 covers how groundbreaking new technology, such as **robotic apps,** might affect the labor market.

- Chapter 30 explains why the **income gap** between males and females has been shrinking and conceivably could eventually disappear.

Making the Connection— from the Classroom to the Real World

Economics Today provides current examples with critical analysis questions that show students how economic theory applies to their diverse interests and lives. For the Seventeenth Edition, **more than 90 percent** of the examples are new.

DOMESTIC TOPICS AND EVENTS are presented through thought-provoking discussions, such as:

- State University Tuition Rates Jump—Even at the Last Moment
- Price and Revenue Changes and Price Elasticity of Demand for Air Travel

EXAMPLE
Going Online for Credit When Bank Loans Dry Up

Today, a growing number of entrepreneurs who fail to receive loans from banks instead obtain credit from Internet-based companies such as Lending Club and Prosper Marketplace. These firms provide online forums for entrepreneurs to post detailed business plans along with the specific amounts of credit desired to try to achieve success. Individual savers can assess these plans and, if they wish, commit some of their own funds to help fund entrepreneurs' projects.

In exchange for service fees, the online firms pool these individual funding commitments into larger loan packages. For example, if an entrepreneur requests $15,000 in credit and 150 savers provide an average amount of $100 each, the online company collects the savers' funds and extends a loan to the entrepreneur. In this way, firms such as Lending Club and Prosper Marketplace act as financial intermediaries.

FOR CRITICAL THINKING
Why do you suppose that default rates on loans arranged by online firms tend to be substantially higher than default rates on bank loans?

IMPORTANT POLICY QUESTIONS help students understand public debates, such as:

- Federal Indebtedness Is Much Higher Than the Net Public Debt
- The Fed Becomes a Lender of Last Resort for Foreign Banks

POLICY EXAMPLE
A Proposed Wireless Merger Experiences a Dropped Connection

Recently, AT&T and T-Mobile sought to merge their wireless operations into a single firm providing cellular phone and broadband Internet services. The proposed merger would have increased the HHI value for the nationwide wireless market—which the Justice Department's Antitrust Division determined to be the relevant market—by nearly 600. The postmerger level of the HHI would have exceeded 2,800. These amounts were well above thresholds sufficient to raise U.S. antitrust authorities' concerns about potential monopoly capability generated by a horizontal merger. Thus, the Antitrust Division filed a lawsuit seeking to block the merger, based on a claim that if the merger occurred, consumers ultimately would face much higher prices for wireless services. A few weeks later, AT&T and T-Mobile abandoned their merger plans rather than combat the lawsuit in court.

FOR CRITICAL THINKING
By definition, any horizontal merger increases industry concentration. Why might some mergers lead to lower prices for consumers? (Hint: Recall that mergers might enable firms to experience economies of scale that reduce long-run average cost.)

INTERNATIONAL EXAMPLE
Why the Value of China's Consumer Price Index Is Rising

In China, food's weight in the CPI is slightly below 35 percent. Food prices have been rising so rapidly, though, that the overall rate of increase in food prices per year has been contributing to 75 percent of China's officially measured annual rate of CPI inflation. Consequently, during a recent 12-month period in which the nation's measured rate of CPI inflation was 6.4 percent, the rate of increase in food prices accounted for 4.8 percentage points

FOR CRITICAL THINKING
Food's weight in the U.S. CPI is about 16 percent. If U.S. food prices rose as rapidly as Chinese food prices, would the U.S. CPI increase as much as the CPI in China? Explain.

INTERNATIONAL POLICY EXAMPLE
African Nations Benefit from Lower U.S. Trade Barriers

In 2000, the U.S. Congress passed the African Growth and Opportunity Act, which reduced substantially the tariffs faced by African companies seeking to export goods and services to the United States. African-U.S. trade has risen considerably since. Earnings that African companies derive from exports are now 500 percent higher than in 2001. Furthermore, estimates indicate that export industries in African nations now employ 300,000 additional workers as a consequence of the increased volume of trade. Thus, slashing trade barriers has generated welfare gains for African residents.

FOR CRITICAL THINKING
How might U.S. residents have benefited from the fact that African countries granted reciprocal reductions in tariffs on imports into their nations from the United States?

GLOBAL AND INTERNATIONAL POLICY EXAMPLES emphasize the continued importance of international perspectives and policy, such as:

- Ireland Experiences Yet Another Big "Brain Drain"
- Utilizing Artificial Intelligence to Try to Beat the Market
- Iran Removes Four Zeroes from Each Unit of Its Currency
- In Greece, "Free" Care Now Includes Substantial Implicit Costs

Helping Students Focus and Think Critically

New and revised pedagogical tools engage students and help them focus on the central ideas in economics today.

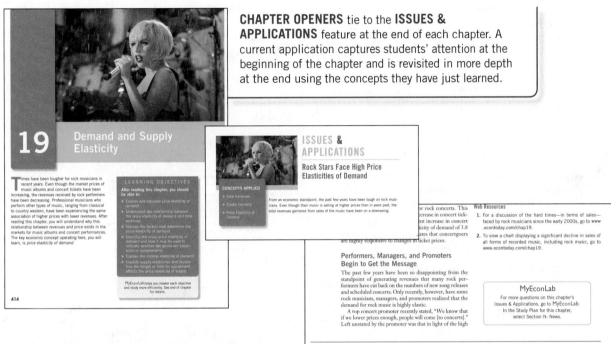

CHAPTER OPENERS tie to the **ISSUES & APPLICATIONS** feature at the end of each chapter. A current application captures students' attention at the beginning of the chapter and is revisited in more depth at the end using the concepts they have just learned.

CRITICAL ANALYSIS QUESTIONS AND WEB RESOURCES provide further opportunities for discussion and exploration. Suggested answers for Critical Analysis questions are in the **INSTRUCTOR'S MANUAL**. Visit MyEconLab for additional practice and assignable questions for each chapter topic.

The **END-OF-CHAPTER SUMMARY** shows students what they need to know and where to go in MyEconLab for more practice.

A VARIETY OF END-OF-CHAPTER PROBLEMS offer students opportunities to test their knowledge and review chapter concepts. Answers for odd-numbered questions are provided in the back of the text, and **ALL QUESTIONS** are assignable in MyEconLab.

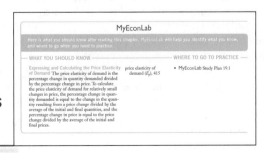

QUICK QUIZZES encourage student interaction and provide an opportunity for them to check their understanding before moving on. Answers are at the end of the chapter, and more practice questions can be found in MyEconLab.

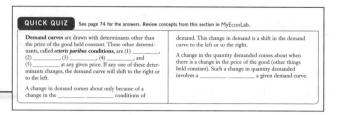

YOU ARE THERE
Implementing a New Patent Framework to Promote Innovation

Senator Patrick Leahy looks on as President Barack Obama signs into law the America Invents Act, a law Leahy had authored with the aim of boosting the rate of U.S. innovation via an overhaul of the nation's patent system. Under the prior law governing patents, property rights to the returns from invention were determined on a "first-to-invent" basis. This meant that if two individuals or companies happened to invent similar products or processes at about the same time, they had to prove in court whose invention was first. Over the years, this requirement had touched off thousands of court fights among patent holders.

The legislation drawn up by Leahy and approved by Congress and the president has established a "first-to-file" rule for patents. Now the property rights associated with any invention are automatically assigned to

the first individual or firm to apply for a patent for that invention. Leahy's expectation is that patent holders who once directed financial resources toward funding court battles now will use them to transform more inventions into market innovations. Speeding along the innovation process, Leahy anticipates, will help to fuel economic growth.

Critical Thinking Questions

1. Why are inventions alone insufficient to help boost economic growth?
2. What role do you think that markets perform in determining whether inventions of new products or processes translate into longer-lasting innovations?

YOU ARE THERE discusses real people making real personal and business decisions. Topics include:

- Why a Federal Stimulus Project Took Time to Provide Stimulus
- Using a Smartphone to Attain a Consumer Optimum

NEW! WHAT IF...? boxes can be found in every chapter. This new feature aims to help students think critically about important real-world questions through the eyes of an economist.

- What If... economists were to base their theories of human behavior on what people say they do, rather than on what people actually do?
- What if... a nation's government tries to head off a recession by pushing down the exchange value of the country's currency?

WHAT IF... governments allowed people to own endangered animals as private property?

If all animals of endangered species could be marked and cataloged as private property, some people undoubtedly would mishandle the animals they owned, just as they misuse other resources in their possession. Nevertheless, by definition, animals of endangered species are scarce resources that would have positive values—and sometimes relatively high dollar values—in private markets. This

fact would give most self-interested people the incentive to preserve such animal life. Indeed, the most successful programs for preventing "too much" fishing, seal hunting, rhino poaching, and so on have been those that assign property rights. These programs motivate the rights holders to rein in such injurious activities and to preserve endangered species.

MyEconLab: The Power of Practice

MyEconLab is a powerful assessment and tutorial system that works hand-in-hand with *Economics Today*. MyEconLab includes comprehensive homework, quiz, test, and tutorial options, allowing instructors to manage all assessment needs in one program.

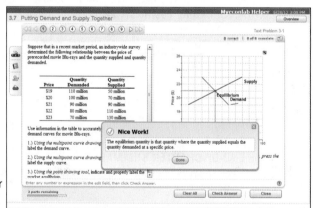

For the Instructor

- Instructors can now select a preloaded course option, which creates a ready-to-go course with homework, quizzes, and tests already set up. Instructors can also choose to create their own assignments and add them to the preloaded course. Or, instructors can start from a blank course

- All end-of-chapter problems are assignable and automatically graded in MyEconLab, and for most chapters, additional algorithmic, draw-graph, and numerical exercises are available to choose among.

- Instructors can also choose questions from the Test Bank and use the Custom Exercise Builder to create their own problems for assignment.

- The powerful Gradebook records each student's performance and time spent on the Tests and Study Plan, and generates reports by student or by chapter.

MyEconLab *Real-Time Data Analysis*

We now offer new real-time data exercises that students can complete in MyEconLab.

- **Real-Time Data Analysis Exercises** are marked with  and allow instructors to assign problems that use up-to-the-minute data. Each RTDA exercise loads the appropriate and most currently available data from FRED, a comprehensive and up-to-date data set maintained by the Federal Reserve Bank of St. Louis. Exercises are graded based on that instance of data, and feedback is provided.

- In the eText available in MyEconLab, select figures labeled MyEconLab Real-Time Data now include a popup graph updated with real-time data from FRED.

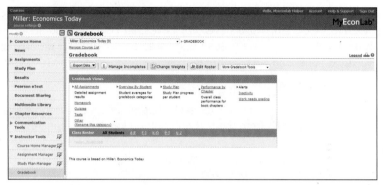

- Current News Exercises, new to this edition of the MyEconLab course, provide a turn-key way to assign gradable news-based exercises in MyEconLab. Every week, Pearson scours the news, finds a current article appropriate for the macroeconomics course, creates an exercise around this news article, and then automatically adds it to MyEconLab. Assigning and grading current news-based exercises that deal with the latest macro events and policy issues has never been more convenient.

- Economics in the News is a turn-key solution to bringing current news into the classroom. Updated weekly during the academic year, this feature posts news articles with questions for further discussion.

- Experiments in MyEconLab are a fun and engaging way to promote active learning and mastery of important economic concepts. Pearson's experiments program is flexible and easy for instructors and students to use.
  - Single-player experiments allow your students to play an experiment against virtual players from anywhere at any time with an Internet connection.
  - Multiplayer experiments allow you to assign and manage a real-time experiment with your class.

  In both cases, pre- and post-questions for each experiment are available for assignment in MyEconLab.

For the Student

Students are in control of their own learning through a collection of tests, practice, and study tools. Highlights include:

- Two Sample Tests per chapter are preloaded in MyEconLab, enabling students to practice what they have learned, test their understanding, and identify areas for further work.

- Based on each student's performance on homework, quizzes, and tests, MyEconLab generates a Study Plan that shows where the student needs further study.

- Learning Aids, such as step-by-step guided solutions, a graphing tool, content-specific links to the eText, animated graphs, and glossary flashcards, help students master the material.

Please visit www.myeconlab.com for more information.

Supplemental Resources

Student and instructor materials provide tools for success.

Test Banks 1, 2, and 3 offer more than 10,000 multiple choice and short answer questions, all of which are available in computerized format in the TestGen software. The significant revision process by author Jim Lee of Texas A&M University–Corpus Christi and accuracy reviewers Ercument Aksoy of Los Angeles Valley College and Fatma Antar of Manchester Community College ensures the accuracy of problems and solutions in these revised and updated Test Banks. The Test Bank author has connected the questions to the general knowledge and skill guidelines found in the Association to Advance Collegiate Schools of Business (AACSB) assurance of learning standards.

The Instructor's Manual, prepared by Jim Lee of Texas A&M University–Corpus Christi, includes lecture-ready examples; chapter overviews, objectives, and outlines; points to emphasize; answers to all critical analysis questions; answers to even-numbered end-of-chapter problems; suggested answers to "You Are There" questions; and selected references.

PowerPoint lecture presentations for each chapter, revised by Debbie Evercloud of University of Colorado–Denver, include graphs from the text and outline key terms, concepts, and figures from the text.

Clicker PowerPoint slides, prepared by Rick Pretzsch of Lonestar College–CyFair, allow professors to instantly quiz students in class and receive immediate feedback through Clicker Response System technology.

The Instructor's Resource Disk offers all instructor supplements conveniently packaged on a disk.

The Instructor Resource Center puts supplements right at instructors' fingertips. Visit www.pearson highered.com/irc to register.

The Study Guide offers the practice and review that students need to excel. Written by Roger LeRoy Miller and updated by David Van Hoose of Baylor University, the Study Guide has been thoroughly revised to take into account changes to the Seventeenth Edition.

The CourseSmart eTextbook for the text is available through www.coursesmart.com. CourseSmart goes beyond traditional expectations by providing instant, online access to the textbooks and course materials you need at a lower cost to students. And, even as students save money, you can save time and hassle with a digital textbook that allows you to search the most relevant content at the very moment you need it. Whether you're evaluating textbooks or creating lecture notes to help students with difficult concepts, CourseSmart can make life a little easier. See how when you visit www.coursesmart.com /instructors.

Acknowledgments

I am the most fortunate of economics textbook writers, for I receive the benefit of literally hundreds of suggestions from those of you who use *Economics Today*. Some professors have been asked by my publisher to participate in a more detailed reviewing process of this edition. I list them below. I hope that each one of you so listed accepts my sincere appreciation for the fine work that you have done.

Hamilton Galloway, *College of Western Idaho*
Frank Garland, *TriCounty Technical College*
Reza G. Hamzaee, *Missouri Western State University*
Ricot Jean, *Valencia College*
Richard W. Kreissle, *Landmark College*
James M. Leaman, *Eastern Mennonite University*
Dr. Larry Olanrewaju, *John Tyler Community College*
Benny E. Overton, *Vance/Granville Community College*

Elizabeth Patch, *Broome Community College*
Van Thi Hong Pham, *Salem State University*
Leila Angelica Rodemann, *Trident Technical College*
Lewis Sage, *Baldwin-Wallace College*
Jonathan Silberman, *Oakland University*
Brian Sommer, *Lynn University*
Manjuri Talukdar, *Northern Illinois University*
Ethel C. Weeks, *Nassau Community College*

I also thank the reviewers of previous editions:

Rebecca Abraham
Cinda J. Adams
Esmond Adams
John Adams
Bill Adamson
Carlos Aguilar
John R. Aidem
Mohammed Akacem
Ercument Aksoy
M. C. Alderfer
John Allen
Ann Al-Yasiri
Charles Anderson
Leslie J. Anderson
Fatma W. Antar
Len Anyanwu
Rebecca Arnold
Mohammad Ashraf
Ali A. Ataiifar
Aliakbar Ataiifar
Leonard Atencio
John Atkins
Glen W. Atkinson
Thomas R. Atkinson
James Q. Aylesworth
John Baffoe-Bonnie
Kevin Baird
Maurice B. Ballabon
Charley Ballard
G. Jeffrey Barbour
Robin L. Barlett
Daniel Barszcz
Kari Battaglia
Robert Becker
Charles Beem
Glen Beeson
Bruce W. Bellner
Daniel K. Benjamin
Emil Berendt
Charles Berry
Abraham Bertisch
John Bethune
R. A. Blewett
Scott Bloom
John Bockino
M. L. Bodnar
Mary Bone
Karl Bonnhi

Thomas W.
 Bonsor
John M. Booth
Wesley F. Booth
Thomas
 Borcherding
Melvin Borland
Tom Boston
Barry Boyer
Maryanna
 Boynton
Ronald Brandolini
Fenton L.
 Broadhead
Elba Brown
William Brown
Michael Bull
Maureen Burton
Conrad P.
 Caligaris
Kevin Carey
James Carlson
Robert Carlsson
Dancy R. Carr
Scott Carson
Doris Cash
Thomas H. Cate
Richard J. Cebula
Catherine
 Chambers
K. Merry
 Chambers
Richard Chapman
Ronald Cherry
Young Back Choi
Marc Chopin
Carol Cies
Joy L. Clark
Curtis Clarke
Gary Clayton
Marsha Clayton
Dale O.
 Cloninger
Warren L. Coats
Ed Coen
Pat Conroy
James Cox
Stephen R. Cox

Eleanor D. Craig
Peggy Crane
Jerry Crawford
Patrick M. Crowley
Joanna Cruse
John P. Cullity
Will Cummings
Thomas Curtis
Margaret M.
 Dalton
Andrew J. Dane
Mahmoud Davoudi
Diana Denison
Edward Dennis
Julia G. Derrick
Sowjanya
 Dharmasankar
Carol Dimamro
William Dougherty
Barry Duman
Diane Dumont
Floyd Durham
G. B. Duwaji
James A. Dyal
Ishita Edwards
Robert P. Edwards
Alan E. Ellis
Miuke Ellis
Steffany Ellis
Frank Emerson
Carl Enomoto
Zaki Eusufzai
Sandy Evans
John L. Ewing-
 Smith
Frank Falero
Frank Fato
Abdollah Ferdowsi
Grant Ferguson
Victoria L. Figiel
Mitchell Fisher
David Fletcher
James Foley
John Foreman
Diana Fortier
Ralph G. Fowler
Arthur Friedberg
Peter Frost

Timothy S. Fuerst
Tom Fullerton
E. Gabriel
James Gale
Byron Gangnes
Peter C. Garlick
Steve Garner
Neil Garston
Alexander Garvin
Joe Garwood
Doug Gehrke
Robert Gentenaar
J. P. Gilbert
Otis Gilley
Frank Glesber
Jack Goddard
Michael G. Goode
Allen C. Goodman
Richard J.
 Gosselin
Paul Graf
Anthony J. Greco
Edward
 Greenberg
Gary Greene
Peter A.
 Groothuis
Philip J. Grossman
Nicholas Grunt
William Gunther
Kwabena Gyimah-
 Brempong
Demos Hadjiyanis
Martin D. Haney
Mehdi Haririan
Ray Harvey
Michael J.
 Haupert
E. L. Hazlett
Sanford B.
 Helman
William
 Henderson
Robert Herman
Gus W. Herring
Charles Hill
John M. Hill
Morton Hirsch

Benjamin
 Hitchner
Charles W.
 Hockert
R. Bradley
 Hoppes
James Horner
Grover Howard
Nancy Howe-
 Ford
Yu-Mong Hsiao
Yu Hsing
James Hubert
George Hughes
Joseph W. Hunt
 Jr.
Scott Hunt
John Ifediora
R. Jack Inch
Christopher Inya
Tomotaka
 Ishimine
E. E. Jarvis
Parvis Jenab
Allan Jenkins
John Jensel
Mark Jensen
S. D. Jevremovic
J. Paul Jewell
Nancy
 Jianakoplos
Frederick
 Johnson
David Jones
Lamar B. Jones
Paul A. Joray
Daniel A. Joseph
Craig Justice
M. James Kahiga
Septimus Kai Kai
Devajyoti Kataky
Timothy R. Keely
Ziad Keilany
Norman F. Keiser
Brian Kench
Randall G.
 Kesselring
Alan Kessler

E. D. Key
Saleem Khan
M. Barbara Killen
Bruce Kimzey
Terrence Kinal
Philip G. King
E. R. Kittrell
David Klingman
Charles Knapp
Jerry Knarr
Tori Knight
Faik Koray
Janet Koscianski
Dennis Lee Kovach
Marie Kratochvil
Peter Kressler
Paul J. Kubik
Michael Kupilik
Margaret Landman
Richard LaNear
Larry Landrum
Keith Langford
Theresa Laughlin
Anthony T. Lee
Jim Lee
Loren Lee
Bozena Leven
Donald Lien
George Lieu
Stephen E. Lile
Lawrence W.
 Lovick
Marty Ludlum
Laura Maghoney
G. Dirk Mateer
Robert McAuliffe
James C. McBrearty
Howard J. McBride
Bruce McClung
John McDowell
E. S. McKuskey
James J. McLain
Kevin McWoodson
John L. Madden
Mary Lou Madden
John Marangos
Dan Marburger
Glen Marston

John M. Martin
Paul J. Mascotti
James D. Mason
Paul M. Mason
Tom Mathew
Warren Matthews
Akbar Marvasti
Pete
    Mavrokordatos
Fred May
G. Hartley Mellish
Mike Melvin
Diego Mendez-
    Carbajo
Dan C.
    Messerschmidt
Michael Metzger
Herbert C.
    Milikien
Joel C. Millonzi
Glenn Milner
Daniel Mizak
Khan Mohabbat
Thomas Molloy
William H. Moon
Margaret D. Moore
William E. Morgan
Stephen Morrell
Irving Morrissett
James W. Moser
Thaddeaus
    Mounkurai
Martin F. Murray
Densel L. Myers
George L. Nagy

Solomon Namala
Ronald M. Nate
Jerome Neadly
James E. Needham
Claron Nelson
Douglas Nettleton
William Nook
Gerald T. O'Boyle
Greg Okoro
Richard E. O'Neill
Lucian T. Orlowski
Diane S. Osborne
Joan Osborne
Melissa A Osborne
James O'Toole
Jan Palmer
Zuohong Pan
Gerald Parker
Ginger Parker
Randall E. Parker
Mohammed
    Partapurwala
Kenneth Parzych
Norm Paul
Wesley Payne
Raymond A. Pepin
Martin M. Perline
Timothy Perri
Jerry Petr
Maurice Pfannesteil
James Phillips
Raymond J. Phillips
I. James Pickl
Bruce Pietrykowski
Dennis Placone

Mannie Poen
William L.
    Polvent
Robert Posatko
Greg Pratt
Leila J. Pratt
Steven Pressman
Rick Pretzsch
Renée Prim
Robert E.
    Pulsinelli
Rod D. Raehsler
Kambriz Raffiee
Sandra Rahman
Jaishankar Raman
John Rapp
Richard Rawlins
Gautam
    Raychaudhuri
Ron Reddall
Mitchell Redlo
Charles Reichhelu
Robert S. Rippey
Charles Roberts
Ray C. Roberts
Richard Romano
Judy Roobian-
    Mohr
Duane Rosa
Richard Rosenberg
Larry Ross
Barbara Ross-
    Pfeiffer
Marina Rosser
Philip Rothman

John Roufagalas
Stephen Rubb
Henry Ryder
Basel Saleh
Patricia Sanderson
Thomas N. Schaap
William A.
    Schaeffer
William Schamoe
David Schauer
A. C. Schlenker
David Schlow
Scott J. Schroeder
William Scott
Dan Segebarth
Paul Seidenstat
Swapan Sen
Augustus
    Shackelford
Richard Sherman
    Jr.
Liang-rong Shiau
Gail Shields
David Shorow
Vishwa Shukla
R. J. Sidwell
David E. Sisk
Alden Smith
Garvin Smith
Howard F. Smith
Lynn A. Smith
Phil Smith
William Doyle
    Smith
Lee Spector

George Spiva
Richard L. Sprinkle
Alan Stafford
Amanda Stallings-Wood
Herbert F. Steeper
Diane L. Stehman
Columbus Stephens
William Stine
Allen D. Stone
Osman Suliman
J. M. Sullivan
Rebecca Summary
Terry Sutton
Joseph L. Swaffar
Thomas Swanke
Frank D. Taylor
Daniel Teferra
Lea Templer
Gary Theige
Dave Thiessen
Robert P. Thomas
Deborah Thorsen
Richard Trieff
George Troxler
William T. Trulove
William N. Trumbull
Arianne K. Turner
Kay Unger
Anthony Uremovic
John Vahaly
Jim Van Beek
David Van Hoose
Lee J. Van Scyoc
Roy Van Til
Sharmila Vishwasrao

Craig Walker
Robert F. Wallace
Henry C. Wallich
Milledge Weathers
Ethel Weeks
Roger E. Wehr
Robert G. Welch
Terence West
James Wetzel
Wylie Whalthall
James H. Wheeler
Everett E. White
Michael D. White
Mark A. Wilkening
Raburn M. Williams
James Willis
George Wilson
Travis Wilson
Mark Wohar
Ken Woodward
Tim Wulf
Peter R. Wyman
Whitney Yamamura
Donald Yankovic
Alex Yguado
Paul Young
Shik Young
Mohammed Zaheer
Ed Zajicek
Charles Zalonka
Sourushe Zandvakili
Paul Zarembka
George K. Zestos
William J. Zimmer
    Jr.

As always, a revision of *Economics Today* requires me to put in the latest data at the last minute. If I did not have such an incredible editorial and production team, I wouldn't be able to do so. I do have a fantastic team both at the publisher—Pearson—and at our production house—Nesbitt (Cenveo Publisher Services), working through them with my long-time Production Manager, John Orr of Orr Book Services. He again did a terrific job. I was fortunate to once more have Kathryn Dinovo, Senior Production Project Manager at Pearson, lead the production team to as perfect a textbook as possible. To be sure, I was pushed hard by my long-time Senior Acquisitions Editor, Noel Seibert, and I was helped greatly by Carolyn Terbush, the Senior Editorial Project Manager on this project. The "pushing" all makes sense now.

I am greatly pleased with the design revision created by Jerilyn Bockorick of Nesbitt Graphics. It is always a challenge to keep the traditional feel of this book, yet make it more exciting for today's students. I think that she succeeded. I am appreciative of the hard work my copy editor, Bonnie Boehme, did. And, of course, the proofreader *par excellence*, Pat Lewis, made sure that everything was perfect. As for the supplements for this edition, I wish to thank the team at Nesbitt for producing them for students and professors. On the marketing side, I appreciate the fine work performed by Lori DeShazo and Kim Lovato.

The online media materials, particularly great improvements in *MyEconLab*, were accomplished by Melissa Honig, Noel Lotz, and Courtney Kamauf.

Jim Lee of Texas A&M University–Corpus Christi, Ercument Aksoy of Los Angeles Valley College, and Fatma Antar of Manchester Community College undertook the vast job of revising and improving the three test banks. David Van Hoose of Baylor University continued to create an accurate *Study Guide*. The *Instructor's Manual* was masterfully revised by Jim Lee of Texas A&M University–Corpus Christi. PowerPoint presentations were updated and improved by Debbie Evercloud of the University of Colorado–Denver. Rick Pretzsch of Lonestar College–Cyfair provided the clicker PowerPoint slides.

As always, my "super reviewer," Professor Dan Benjamin of Clemson University, really kept me honest this time around. And, as always, my long-time assistant, Sue Jasin, did enough typing and retyping to fill a room with paper. I welcome comments and ideas from professors and students alike and hope that you enjoy this latest edition of *Economics Today*.

R. L. M.

Credits

Cover images: Solar power panel array, S.R. Lee Photo Traveller/Shutterstock; Woman riding a bicycle in Vietnam, MJ Prototype/Shutterstock; Eye chart test, Pinkcandy/Shutterstock; Plant sample, Chepko Danil Vitalevich/Shutterstock; Bags in warehouse in shop, Mikhail Zahranichny/Shutterstock; Apple on stack of books and laptop computer, Andreka Photography/Shutterstock; Crowd at a music concert, Alexey Lysenko/Shutterstock; Goalman on the stadium field, Andrey Yurlov/Shutterstock

FRED® is a registered trademark and the FRED® logo and ST. LOUIS FED are trademarks of the Federal Reserve Bank of St Louis, http://research.stlouisfed.org/fred2/

Chapter 1	Alex Hofford/Newscom	1, 12
Chapter 2	Fotolia	26, 42
Chapter 3	Harry Lynch/AP Images	48, 69
Chapter 4	Radius Images/Alamy	75, 90
Chapter 5	Marilyn Humphries/Newscom	100, 116
Chapter 6	Gerald Herbert/AP Images	122, 134
Chapter 19	Gregorio T. Binuya/Everett Collection/Newscom	414, 429
Chapter 20	Corbis Super RF/Alamy	434, 447
Chapter 21	Randy Duchaine/Alamy	462, 477
Chapter 22	PR Newswire/AP Images	483, 502
Chapter 23	Shutterstock	507, 526
Chapter 24	Everett Collection/Alamy	532, 548
Chapter 25	Pixellover RM7/Alamy	555, 568
Chapter 26	Mira/Alamy	573, 588
Chapter 27	Keith Dannemiller/Alamy	594, 612
Chapter 28	Superstock	618, 636
Chapter 29	Jim West/Alamy	642, 657
Chapter 30	Andres Rodriguez/Alamy	663, 682
Chapter 31	AP Images	687, 698
Chapter 32	Gallo Images/Alamy	704, 720
Chapter 33	Fotolia	725, 742

Economics Today

THE MICRO VIEW

The Nature of Economics

1

LEARNING OBJECTIVES

After reading this chapter, you should be able to:

▶ Discuss the difference between microeconomics and macroeconomics

▶ Evaluate the role that rational self-interest plays in economic analysis

▶ Explain why economics is a science

▶ Distinguish between positive and normative economics

MyEconLab helps you master each objective and study more efficiently. See end of chapter for details.

Half of the babies delivered in 2011 in a typical Hong Kong hospital maternity ward were born to non–Hong Kong residents. This fact means that these babies were born to women classified as tourists visiting from the Chinese mainland. Why have nearly half of the babies born in Hong Kong hospitals had mothers who are not residents of Hong Kong? To formulate an answer, you must learn more about principles of economics. In particular, you must learn the key concepts discussed in this chapter, such as self-interest.

the number of college students majoring in economics rose by more than 40 percent during the past decade? One reason that students opt for extensive study of economics is that they find the subject fascinating. Another reason, however, is self-interest. On average, students who major in economics earn 13 percent more than business management majors, 26 percent more than chemistry majors, and 50 percent more than psychology majors. Thus, students have a strong incentive to consider majoring in economics.

In this chapter, you will learn why contemplating the nature of self-interested responses to **incentives** is the starting point for analyzing choices people make in all walks of life. After all, how much time you devote to studying economics in this introductory course depends in part on the incentives established by your instructor's grading system. As you will see, self-interest and incentives are the underpinnings for all the decisions you and others around you make each day.

Incentives
Rewards or penalties for engaging in a particular activity.

The Power of Economic Analysis

Simply knowing that self-interest and incentives are central to any decision-making process is not sufficient for predicting the choices that people will actually make. You also have to develop a framework that will allow you to analyze solutions to each economic problem—whether you are trying to decide how much to study, which courses to take, whether to finish school, or whether the U.S. government should provide more grants to universities or raise taxes. The framework that you will learn in this text is the *economic way of thinking*.

This framework gives you power—the power to reach informed judgments about what is happening in the world. You can, of course, live your life without the power of economic analysis as part of your analytical framework. Indeed, most people do. But economists believe that economic analysis can help you make better decisions concerning your career, your education, financing your home, and other important matters. In the business world, the power of economic analysis can help you increase your competitive edge as an employee or as the owner of a business. As a voter, for the rest of your life you will be asked to make judgments about policies that are advocated by political parties. Many of these policies will deal with questions related to international economics, such as whether the U.S. government should encourage or discourage immigration, prevent foreign residents and firms from investing in port facilities or domestic banks, or restrict other countries from selling their goods here.

Finally, just as taking an art, music, or literature appreciation class increases the pleasure you receive when you view paintings, listen to concerts, or read novels, taking an economics course will increase your understanding and pleasure when watching the news on TV or reading articles on your iPad.

Defining Economics

Economics
The study of how people allocate their limited resources to satisfy their unlimited wants.

Economics is part of the social sciences and, as such, seeks explanations of real events. All social sciences analyze human behavior, as opposed to the physical sciences, which generally analyze the behavior of electrons, atoms, and other nonhuman phenomena.

> *Economics is the study of how people allocate their limited resources in an attempt to satisfy their unlimited wants. As such, economics is the study of how people make choices.*

To understand this definition fully, two other words need explaining: *resources* and *wants*. **Resources** are things that have value and, more specifically, are used to produce goods and services that satisfy people's wants. **Wants** are all of the items that people would purchase if they had unlimited income.

Whenever an individual, a business, or a nation faces alternatives, a choice must be made, and economics helps us study how those choices are made. For example, you have to choose how to spend your limited income. You also have to choose how to spend your limited time. You may have to choose how many of your company's limited resources to allocate to advertising and how many to allocate to new-product

Resources
Things used to produce goods and services to satisfy people's wants.

Wants
What people would buy if their incomes were unlimited.

research. In economics, we examine situations in which individuals choose how to do things, when to do things, and with whom to do them. Ultimately, the purpose of economics is to explain choices.

Microeconomics versus Macroeconomics

Economics is typically divided into two types of analysis: **microeconomics** and **macroeconomics.**

> *Microeconomics is the part of economic analysis that studies decision making undertaken by individuals (or households) and by firms. It is like looking through a microscope to focus on the small parts of our economy.*

> *Macroeconomics is the part of economic analysis that studies the behavior of the economy as a whole. It deals with economywide phenomena such as changes in unemployment, in the general price level, and in national income.*

Microeconomic analysis, for example, is concerned with the effects of changes in the price of gasoline relative to that of other energy sources. It examines the effects of new taxes on a specific product or industry. If the government establishes new health care regulations, how individual firms and consumers would react to those regulations would be in the realm of microeconomics. The effects of higher wages brought about by an effective union strike would also be analyzed using the tools of microeconomics.

In contrast, issues such as the rate of inflation, the amount of economywide unemployment, and the yearly growth in the output of goods and services in the nation all fall into the realm of macroeconomic analysis. In other words, macroeconomics deals with **aggregates,** or totals—such as total output in an economy.

Be aware, however, of the blending of microeconomics and macroeconomics in modern economic theory. Modern economists are increasingly using microeconomic analysis—the study of decision making by individuals and by firms—as the basis of macroeconomic analysis. They do this because even though macroeconomic analysis focuses on aggregates, those aggregates are the result of choices made by individuals and firms.

Microeconomics
The study of decision making undertaken by individuals (or households) and by firms.

Macroeconomics
The study of the behavior of the economy as a whole, including such economywide phenomena as changes in unemployment, the general price level, and national income.

Aggregates
Total amounts or quantities. Aggregate demand, for example, is total planned expenditures throughout a nation.

The Three Basic Economic Questions and Two Opposing Answers

In every nation, three fundamental questions must be addressed irrespective of the form of its government or who heads that government, how rich or how poor the nation may be, or what type of **economic system**—the institutional mechanism through which resources are utilized to satisfy human wants—has been chosen. The three questions concern the problem of how to allocate society's scarce resources:

Economic system
A society's institutional mechanism for determining the way in which scarce resources are used to satisfy human desires.

1. *What and how much will be produced?* Some mechanism must exist for determining which items will be produced while others remain inventors' pipe dreams or individuals' unfulfilled desires.

2. *How will items be produced?* There are many ways to produce a desired item. It is possible to use more labor and less capital, or vice versa. It is possible, for instance, to produce an item with an aim to maximize the number of people employed. Alternatively, an item may be produced with an aim to minimize the total expenses that members of society incur. Somehow, a decision must be made about the mix of resources used in production, the way in which they are organized, and how they are brought together at a particular location.

3. *For whom will items be produced?* Once an item is produced, who should be able to obtain it? People use scarce resources to produce any item, so typically people value access to that item. Thus, determining a mechanism for distributing produced items is a crucial issue for any society.

Now that you know the questions that an economic system must answer, how do current systems actually answer them?

Two Opposing Answers

At any point in time, every nation has its own economic system. How a nation goes about answering the three basic economic questions depends on that nation's economic system.

CENTRALIZED COMMAND AND CONTROL Throughout history, one common type of economic system has been *command and control* (also called *central planning*) by a centralized authority, such as a king or queen, a dictator, a central government, or some other type of authority that assumes responsibility for addressing fundamental economic issues. Under command and control, this authority decides what items to produce and how many, determines how the scarce resources will be organized in the items' production, and identifies who will be able to obtain the items.

For instance, in a command-and-control economic system, a government might decide that particular types of automobiles ought to be produced in certain numbers. The government might issue specific rules for how to marshal resources to produce these vehicles, or it might even establish ownership over those resources so that it can make all such resource allocation decisions directly. Finally, the government will then decide who will be authorized to purchase or otherwise utilize the vehicles.

How is centralized command and control affecting the net cost of constructing a high-speed rail project in California?

POLICY EXAMPLE

The Federal Government Directs New California Train Tracks

The U.S. Department of Transportation recently provided an initial $3 billion in federal tax funds for a 500-mile high-speed rail project stretching between the California cities of Anaheim and San Francisco. Local planners proposed construction of operating rail line segments in phases, starting at the highly populated ends of the route, at a projected total expense of about $18 billion. Planners suggested that opening operating segments at the more heavily populated ends of the line would generate revenues that could assist in financing the building of remaining segments of the multiyear rail construction project.

In reaction, Transportation Department officials mandated the rail line to start in California's less-populated Central Valley region. Of course, train passengers will be far fewer. Why did the U.S. government officials do this? They did so because they consider residents of the Central Valley to be "underserved" by rail transit services. The resulting completion delay will be at least two years and will add more than $1 billion to the project's ultimate net expense to taxpayers.

FOR CRITICAL THINKING
Would Transportation Department officials have made the same decision if they, rather than taxpayers, had to cover the added costs of starting construction in the Central Valley?

THE PRICE SYSTEM The alternative to command and control is the *price system* (also called a *market system*), which is a shorthand term describing an economic system that answers the three basic economic questions via decentralized decision making. Under a pure price system, individuals and families own all of the scarce resources used in production. Consequently, choices about what and how many items to produce are left to private parties to determine on their own initiative, as are decisions about how to go about producing those items. Furthermore, individuals and families choose how to allocate their own incomes to obtain the produced items at prices established via privately organized mechanisms.

In the price system, which you will learn about in considerable detail in Chapters 3 and 4, prices define the terms under which people agree to make exchanges. Prices signal to everyone within a price system which resources are relatively scarce and which resources are relatively abundant. This *signaling* aspect of the price system provides information to individual buyers and sellers about what and how many items should be produced, how production of items should be organized, and who will choose to buy the produced items.

Thus, in a price system, individuals and families own the facilities used to produce automobiles. They decide which types of automobiles to produce, how many of them to produce, and how to bring scarce resources together within their facilities to generate the desired production. Other individuals and families decide how much of their earnings they wish to spend on automobiles.

MIXED ECONOMIC SYSTEMS By and large, the economic systems of the world's nations are mixed economic systems that incorporate aspects of both centralized command and control and a decentralized price system. At any given time, some nations lean toward centralized mechanisms of command and control and allow relatively little scope for decentralized decision making. At the same time, other nations limit the extent to which a central authority dictates answers to the three basic economic questions, leaving people mostly free to utilize a decentralized price system to generate their own answers.

A given country may reach different decisions at different times about how much to rely on command and control versus a price system to answer its three basic economic questions. Until 2008, for instance, the people of the United States preferred to rely mainly on a decentralized price system to decide which and how many automobiles to produce, how to marshal scarce resources to produce those vehicles, and how to decide who should obtain them. Today, the U.S. government owns a substantial fraction of the facilities used to manufacture automobiles and hence has considerable command-and-control authority over U.S. vehicle production.

How has Cuba altered the extent to which it relies on command and control compared with the price system?

INTERNATIONAL POLICY EXAMPLE

Cuba Experiments with Mixing It Up

For more than half of a century, Cuba has been the Western Hemisphere's only Communist nation. The Cuban government sets the prices of most goods and services. For many years, the government also set the wages of about 85 percent of the country's 5.5 million workers who are government-employed. The government permitted the remaining 15 percent of employed individuals to work in 124 "authorized" private occupations, which include farming, teaching music, selling piñatas, and repairing existing items such as furniture and toys.

Today, the government is in the midst of letting go nearly 600,000 public employees, who will have to seek employment at privately determined wages. Although the nation will maintain its heavy reliance on command and control, a larger share of its workers will have their wages determined in the price system. Thus, Cuba's economy is becoming more mixed.

FOR CRITICAL THINKING
When there are fewer public workers and more private workers, will changes in wages be better or worse signals?

The Economic Approach: Systematic Decisions

Economists assume that individuals act *as if* they systematically pursue self-motivated interests and respond predictably to perceived opportunities to attain those interests. This central insight of economics was first clearly articulated by Adam Smith in 1776. Smith wrote in his most famous book, *An Inquiry into the Nature and Causes of the Wealth of Nations*, that "it is not from the benevolence of the butcher, the brewer, or the baker that we expect our dinner, but from their regard to their own interest." Thus, the typical person about whom economists make behavioral predictions is assumed to act *as though* he or she systematically pursues self-motivated interest.

The Rationality Assumption

The **rationality assumption** of economics, simply stated, is as follows:

We assume that individuals do not intentionally make decisions that would leave themselves worse off.

Rationality assumption
The assumption that people do not intentionally make decisions that would leave them worse off.

The distinction here is between what people may think—the realm of psychology and psychiatry and perhaps sociology—and what they do. Economics does *not* involve itself in analyzing individual or group thought processes. Economics looks at what people actually do in life with their limited resources. It does little good to criticize the rationality assumption by stating, "Nobody thinks that way" or "I never think that way" or "How unrealistic! That's as irrational as anyone can get!" In a world in which people can be atypical in countless ways, economists find it useful to concentrate on discovering the baseline. Knowing what happens on average is a good place to start. In this way, we avoid building our thinking on exceptions rather than on reality.

Take the example of driving. When you consider passing another car on a two-lane highway with oncoming traffic, you have to make very quick decisions: You must estimate the speed of the car that you are going to pass, the speed of the oncoming cars, the distance between your car and the oncoming cars, and your car's potential rate of acceleration. If we were to apply a model to your behavior, we would use the rules of calculus. In actual fact, you and most other drivers in such a situation do not actually think of using the rules of calculus, but to predict your behavior, we could make the prediction *as if* you understood those rules.

How are bankers reducing robbery rates by counting on the rationality of would-be thieves?

EXAMPLE

Hello, Bank Robber, I'll Remember You

Until recently, each year since 1979, on average 11 of every 100 U.S. bank branches experienced a robbery. Bankers have worked to bring down this robbery rate by treating prospective robbers as rational people. A would-be bank robber knows that the likelihood of being caught and sentenced to prison increases significantly when someone in the bank gets a good enough look at the robber's face to provide a positive identification.

Consequently, many banks now make a point of having a teller, guard, or branch manager greet each entering customer, look the customer directly in the eye, and say hello. Since banks around the nation have instituted a policy of greeting customers at the doors, the robbery rate has dropped to only 6 of every 100 bank branches.

FOR CRITICAL THINKING
What types of costs and benefits must a prospective criminal rationally weigh before deciding whether to attempt a bank robbery?

Responding to Incentives

If it can be assumed that individuals never intentionally make decisions that would leave them worse off, then almost by definition they will respond to changes in incentives. Indeed, much of human behavior can be explained in terms of how individuals respond to changing incentives over time.

Schoolchildren are motivated to do better by a variety of incentive systems, ranging from gold stars and certificates of achievement when they are young, to better grades with accompanying promises of a "better life" as they get older. Of course, negative incentives affect our behavior, too. Penalties, punishments, and other forms of negative incentives can raise the cost of engaging in various activities.

Defining Self-Interest

Self-interest does not always mean increasing one's wealth measured in dollars and cents. We assume that individuals seek many goals, not just increased wealth measured in monetary terms. Thus, the self-interest part of our economic-person assumption includes goals relating to prestige, friendship, love, power, helping others, creating works of art, and many other matters. We can also think in terms of enlightened self-interest, whereby individuals, in the pursuit of what makes them better off, also achieve the betterment of others around them. In brief, individuals are assumed to want the ability to further their goals by making decisions about how things around them are

YOU ARE THERE

To contemplate how a higher corporate tax rate in the United States relative to other nations is affecting the incentive for U.S. firms to form corporate structures within U.S. borders, take a look at **Why So Many Firms Are Incorporating Outside the United States** on page 11.

used. The head of a charitable organization usually will not turn down an additional contribution, because accepting the funds yields control over how they are used, even though it is for other people's benefit.

Thus, self-interest does not rule out doing charitable acts. Giving gifts to relatives can be considered a form of charity that is nonetheless in the self-interest of the giver. But how efficient is such gift giving?

EXAMPLE

The Perceived Value of Gifts

Every holiday season, aunts, uncles, grandparents, mothers, and fathers give gifts to their college-aged loved ones. Joel Waldfogel, an economist at the University of Minnesota, has surveyed several thousand college students after Christmas to find out the value of holiday gifts. He finds that recorded music and outerwear (coats and jackets) have a perceived intrinsic value about equal to their actual cash equivalent. By the time he gets down the list to socks, underwear, and cosmetics, the students'

valuation is only about 82 percent of the cash value of the gift. He find that aunts, uncles, and grandparents give the "worst" gifts and friends, siblings, and parents give the "best."

FOR CRITICAL ANALYSIS

What argument could you use against the idea of substituting cash or gift cards for physical gifts?

QUICK QUIZ   See page 16 for the answers. Review concepts from this section in MyEconLab.

Economics is a social science that involves the study of how individuals choose among alternatives to satisfy their_____, which are what people would buy if their incomes were_____.

_____, the study of the decision-making processes of individuals (or households) and firms, and _____, the study of the performance of the economy as a whole, are the two main branches into which the study of economics is divided.

The three basic economic questions ask what and how much will be produced, how will items be produced, and for whom will items be produced. The two opposing answers are provided by the type of economic system: either_____ _____ _____ _____ or the_____ _____.

In economics, we assume that people do not intentionally make decisions that will leave them worse off. This is known as the _____ assumption.

Economics as a Science

Economics is a social science that employs the same kinds of methods used in other sciences, such as biology, physics, and chemistry. Like these other sciences, economics uses models, or theories. Economic **models,** or **theories,** are simplified representations of the real world that we use to help us understand, explain, and predict economic phenomena in the real world. There are, of course, differences between sciences. The social sciences—especially economics—make little use of laboratory experiments in which changes in variables are studied under controlled conditions. Rather, social scientists, and especially economists, usually have to test their models, or theories, by examining what has already happened in the real world.

Models, or theories
Simplified representations of the real world used as the basis for predictions or explanations.

Models and Realism

At the outset it must be emphasized that no model in *any* science, and therefore no economic model, is complete in the sense that it captures *every* detail or interrelationship that exists. Indeed, a model, by definition, is an abstraction from reality. It is conceptually impossible to construct a perfectly complete realistic model. For example, in physics we cannot account for every molecule and its position and certainly not for every atom and subatomic particle. Not only is such a model unreasonably expensive to build, but working with it would be impossibly complex.

The nature of scientific model building is that the model should capture only the *essential* relationships that are sufficient to analyze the particular problem or answer the particular question with which we are concerned. *An economic model cannot be faulted as unrealistic simply because it does not represent every detail of the real world.* A map of a city that shows only major streets is not faulty if, in fact, all you need to know is how to pass through the city using major streets. As long as a model is able to shed light on the *central* issue at hand or forces at work, it may be useful.

A map is the quintessential model. It is always a simplified representation. It is always unrealistic. But it is also useful in making predictions about the world. If the model—the map—predicts that when you take Campus Avenue to the north, you always run into the campus, that is a prediction. If a simple model can explain observed behavior in repeated settings just as well as a complex model, the simple model has some value and is probably easier to use.

Assumptions

Every model, or theory, must be based on a set of assumptions. Assumptions define the array of circumstances in which our model is most likely to be applicable. When some people predicted that sailing ships would fall off the edge of the earth, they used the *assumption* that the earth was flat. Columbus did not accept the implications of such a model because he did not accept its assumptions. He assumed that the world was round. The real-world test of his own model refuted the flat-earth model. Indirectly, then, it was a test of the assumption of the flat-earth model.

Is it possible to use our knowledge about assumptions to understand why driving directions sometimes contain very few details?

EXAMPLE

Getting Directions

Assumptions are a shorthand for reality. Imagine that you have decided to drive from your home in San Diego to downtown San Francisco. Because you have never driven this route, you decide to use a travel-planner device such as global-positioning-system equipment.

When you ask for directions, the electronic travel planner could give you a set of detailed maps that shows each city through which you will travel—Oceanside, San Clemente, Irvine, Anaheim, Los Angeles, Bakersfield, Modesto, and so on—with the individual maps showing you exactly how the freeway threads through each of these cities. You would get a nearly complete description of reality because the GPS travel planner will not have used many simplifying assumptions. It is more likely, however, that the travel planner will simply

say, "Get on Interstate 5 going north. Stay on it for about 500 miles. Follow the signs for San Francisco. After crossing the toll bridge, take any exit marked 'Downtown.'" By omitting all of the trivial details, the travel planner has told you all that you really need and want to know. The models you will be using in this text are similar to the simplified directions on how to drive from San Diego to San Francisco—they focus on what is relevant to the problem at hand and omit what is not.

FOR CRITICAL ANALYSIS
In what way do small talk and gossip represent the use of simplifying assumptions?

THE *CETERIS PARIBUS* ASSUMPTION: ALL OTHER THINGS BEING EQUAL Everything in the world seems to relate in some way to everything else in the world. It would be impossible to isolate the effects of changes in one variable on another variable if we always had to worry about the many other variables that might also enter the analysis. Similar to other sciences, economics uses the **ceteris paribus assumption.** *Ceteris paribus* means "other things constant" or "other things equal."

Consider an example taken from economics. One of the most important determinants of how much of a particular product a family buys is how expensive that product is relative to other products. We know that in addition to relative prices, other factors influence decisions about making purchases. Some of them have to do with income, others with tastes, and yet others with custom and religious beliefs. Whatever these other factors are, we hold them constant when we look at the relationship between changes in prices and changes in how much of a given product people will purchase.

Ceteris paribus [KAY-ter-us PEAR-uh-bus] assumption
The assumption that nothing changes except the factor or factors being studied.

Deciding on the Usefulness of a Model

We generally do not attempt to determine the usefulness, or "goodness," of a model merely by evaluating how realistic its assumptions are. Rather, we consider a model "good" if it yields usable predictions that are supported by real-world observations. In other words, can we use the model to predict what will happen in the world around us? Does the model provide useful implications about how things happen in our world?

Once we have determined that the model may be useful in predicting real-world phenomena, the scientific approach to the analysis of the world around us requires that we consider evidence. Evidence is used to test the usefulness of a model. This is why we call economics an **empirical** science. *Empirical* means that evidence (data) is looked at to see whether we are right. Economists are often engaged in empirically testing their models.

Empirical
Relying on real-world data in evaluating the usefulness of a model.

Models of Behavior, Not Thought Processes

Take special note of the fact that economists' models do not relate to the way people *think*. Economic models relate to the way people *act*, to what they do in life with their limited resources. Normally, the economist does not attempt to predict how people will think about a particular topic, such as a higher price of oil products, accelerated inflation, or higher taxes. Rather, the task at hand is to predict how people will behave, which may be quite different from what they *say* they will do (much to the consternation of poll takers and market researchers). Thus, people's *declared* preferences are generally of little use in testing economic theories, which aim to explain and predict people's *revealed* preferences. The people involved in examining thought processes are psychologists and psychiatrists, not typically economists.

WHAT IF... economists were to base their theories of human behavior on what people *say* they do, rather than on what people *actually* do?

The task of economists is to try to predict decisions that people will make given the incentives that they face. Consider how people respond when asked by pollsters about whether they will cut back on charitable giving if the government eliminates tax breaks for such donations. Most people state that they will continue to give as much as before, because they suspect this answer will please those who have posed the question. In fact, studies of actual responses to smaller tax breaks for charitable giving reveal that people pursue their own interest. Whether or not their true action might have pleased a pollster, they reduce donations. Thus, if economists were to rely on polls indicating how people claim that they respond to incentives such as diminished tax breaks, economists would persistently make erroneous predictions about the decisions that people actually make.

Behavioral Economics and Bounded Rationality

In recent years, some economists have proposed paying more attention to psychologists and psychiatrists. They have suggested an alternative approach to economic analysis. Their approach, which is known as **behavioral economics,** examines consumer behavior in the face of psychological limitations and complications that may interfere with rational decision making.

Behavioral economics
An approach to the study of consumer behavior that emphasizes psychological limitations and complications that potentially interfere with rational decision making.

BOUNDED RATIONALITY Proponents of behavioral economics suggest that traditional economic models assume that people exhibit three "unrealistic" characteristics:

1. *Unbounded selfishness.* People are interested only in their own satisfaction.

2. *Unbounded willpower.* Their choices are always consistent with their long-term goals.

3. *Unbounded rationality.* They are able to consider every relevant choice.

Bounded rationality
The hypothesis that people are *nearly*, but not fully, rational, so that they cannot examine every possible choice available to them but instead use simple rules of thumb to sort among the alternatives that happen to occur to them.

As an alternative, advocates of behavioral economics have proposed replacing the rationality assumption with the assumption of **bounded rationality,** which assumes that people cannot examine and think through every possible choice they confront. As a consequence, behavioral economists suggest, people cannot always pursue their best long-term personal interests. From time to time, they must also rely on other people and take into account other people's interests as well as their own.

RULES OF THUMB A key behavioral implication of the bounded rationality assumption is that people should use so-called *rules of thumb:* Because every possible choice cannot be considered, an individual will tend to fall back on methods of making decisions that are simpler than trying to sort through every possibility.

A problem confronting advocates of behavioral economics is that people who *appear* to use rules of thumb may in fact behave *as if* they are fully rational. For instance, if a person faces persistently predictable ranges of choices for a time, the individual may rationally settle into repetitive behaviors that an outside observer might conclude to be consistent with a rule of thumb. According to the bounded rationality assumption, the person should continue to rely on a rule of thumb even if there is a major change in the environment that the individual faces. Time and time again, however, economists find that people respond to altered circumstances by fundamentally changing their behaviors. Economists also generally observe that people make decisions that are consistent with their own self-interest and long-term objectives.

BEHAVIORAL ECONOMICS: A WORK IN PROGRESS It remains to be seen whether the application of the assumption of bounded rationality proposed by behavioral economists will truly alter the manner in which economists construct models intended to better predict human decision making. So far, proponents of behavioral economics have not conclusively demonstrated that paying closer attention to psychological thought processes can improve economic predictions.

As a consequence, the bulk of economic analysis continues to rely on the rationality assumption as the basis for constructing economic models. As you will learn in Chapter 20, advocates of behavioral economics continue to explore ways in which psychological elements might improve analysis of decision making by individual consumers.

Positive versus Normative Economics

Economics uses *positive analysis*, a value-free approach to inquiry. No subjective or moral judgments enter into the analysis. Positive analysis relates to statements such as "If A, then B." For example, "If the price of gasoline goes up relative to all other prices, then the amount of it that people buy will fall." That is a positive economic statement. It is a statement of *what is*. It is not a statement of anyone's value judgment or subjective feelings.

Distinguishing between Positive and Normative Economics

For many problems analyzed in the "hard" sciences such as physics and chemistry, the analyses are considered to be virtually value-free. After all, how can someone's values enter into a theory of molecular behavior? But economists face a different problem. They deal with the behavior of individuals, not molecules. That makes it more difficult to stick to what we consider to be value-free or **positive economics** without reference to our feelings.

Positive economics
Analysis that is *strictly* limited to making either purely descriptive statements or scientific predictions; for example, "If A, then B." A statement of *what is*.

Normative economics
Analysis involving value judgments about economic policies; relates to whether outcomes are good or bad. A statement of *what ought to be*.

When our values are interjected into the analysis, we enter the realm of **normative economics,** involving *normative analysis*. A positive economic statement is "If the price of gas rises, people will buy less." If we add to that analysis the statement "so we should not allow the price to go up," we have entered the realm of normative economics—we have expressed a value judgment. In fact, any time you see the word *should*, you will know that values are entering into the discussion. Just remember that positive statements are concerned with *what is*, whereas normative statements are concerned with *what ought to be*.

Each of us has a desire for different things. That means that we have different values. When we express a value judgment, we are simply saying what we prefer, like, or desire. Because individual values are diverse, we expect—and indeed observe—that people express widely varying value judgments about how the world ought to be.

A Warning: Recognize Normative Analysis

It is easy to define positive economics. It is quite another matter to catch all unlabeled normative statements in a textbook, even though an author goes over the manuscript many times before it is printed or electronically created. Therefore, do not get the impression that a textbook author will be able to keep all personal values out of the book. They will slip through. In fact, the very choice of which topics to include in an introductory textbook involves normative economics. There is no value-free way to decide which topics to use in a textbook. The author's values ultimately make a difference when choices have to be made. But from your own standpoint, you might want to be able to recognize when you are engaging in normative as opposed to positive economic analysis. Reading this text will help equip you for that task.

QUICK QUIZ   See page 16 for the answers. Review concepts from this section in MyEconLab.

A _____, or _____, uses assumptions and is by nature a simplification of the real world. The usefulness of a _____ can be evaluated by bringing empirical evidence to bear on its predictions.

Most models use the _____ _____ assumption that all other things are held constant, or equal.

_____ economics emphasizes psychological constraints and complexities that potentially interfere with rational decision making. This approach utilizes the

_____ _____ hypothesis that people are not quite rational, because they cannot study every possible alternative but instead use simple rules of thumb to decide among choices.

_____ economics is value-free and relates to statements that can be refuted, such as "If A, then B." _____ economics involves people's values and typically uses the word *should*.

YOU ARE THERE
Why So Many Firms Are Incorporating Outside the United States

Willard Taylor, a tax attorney with Sullivan & Cromwell LLP, is contemplating the latest trend among U.S. firms that have been opting to become corporations. Until recently, it was unusual for U.S. family-owned companies or partnerships to "go public" by incorporating in another nation and selling shares of stock to residents of other nations. A decade ago, only about 1 percent of U.S. companies that became corporations did so outside the United States. During each of the past three years, however, more than 20 percent of U.S. firms choosing corporate structures have decided to incorporate abroad.

As a tax lawyer, Taylor pays close attention to tax rates assessed on corporations based abroad as well as those that apply to U.S. corporations. Most countries' governments, Taylor realizes, have slashed their corporate tax rates in recent years, whereas the U.S. corporate tax rate has remained unchanged at 35 percent. The result, Taylor notes, is that the U.S. corporate tax rate is now second highest in the world, which provides a strong incentive to incorporate elsewhere. Taylor asks, "What are the pluses and minuses of being incorporated in the U.S. versus somewhere else?" He deduces that given the strong incentive provided by lower corporate tax rates abroad, "Very often, depending on what the business is, you'll conclude that there are no pluses to being in the United States."

Critical Thinking Questions

1. How have lower foreign tax rates affected the incentive to incorporate abroad?

2. What do you suppose has happened to federal collections of corporate taxes?

ISSUES & APPLICATIONS

Why So Many Tourists Have Been Giving Birth in Hong Kong

CONCEPTS APPLIED

▶ Rationality Assumption

▶ Incentives

▶ Self-Interest

There has been a significant upswing in the number of babies born in Hong Kong to mothers from China's mainland who officially are visiting Hong Kong as tourists. The number of births to this category of mothers rose from about 13,000 in 2004 to more than 40,000 in 2011—almost half of all Hong Kong births in the latter year. It turns out that this substantial increase in Hong Kong "tourist births" is consistent with the rationality assumption.

Incentives for a Mainland Resident to Desire a Hong Kong Birth

Why are so many more women who are officially in Hong Kong as tourists giving birth instead of visiting the city's sites? The answer is that mothers from mainland China are responding to incentives in a manner consistent with self-interested behavior.

Although the $5,000 price of hospital maternity care is several times higher in Hong Kong than in most hospitals on the mainland, the quality of care is considerably better in Hong Kong. In addition, the benefits for a child born in Hong Kong—and hence for the child's mother—are much greater than those available to a child born on the mainland. These benefits of a Hong Kong birth include twelve years of publicly provided education for the child at no explicit cost and close to zero out-of-pocket health care expenses. Furthermore, tourists who give birth in Hong Kong are exempt from China's "one-child policy," which limits women to bearing a single child. Such an exemption gives pregnant women desiring to raise a second child a strong incentive to "visit" Hong Kong.

Why the "Tourist" Fiction Has Been Rational for Hong Kong

Of course, nearly all tourist mothers who travel to Hong Kong to give birth actually plan to remain there. Why does the Hong Kong government permit these women to remain and to obtain publicly provided health care and education for their children? The answer to this second question also relates to the rationality assumption: The Hong Kong government is responding to incentives.

Since the 1990s, the birth rate among Hong Kong residents has declined by more than 33 percent. Early in the 2000s, government officials realized that unless more people immigrated to Hong Kong, its population would begin to shrink—perhaps eventually by about one-third. The city's leaders did not wish to open its borders to all who desired to immigrate, so they decided to permit more expectant mothers to enter under the tourist classification. Thus, it has been rational for the government of Hong Kong to allow numerous "tourist" births, just as it has been consistent with individual self-interest for "tourists" to give birth there.

For Critical Thinking

1. How have recent improvements in maternity care in mainland China likely affected the incentives to become a "tourist" mother in Hong Kong?

2. How are Hong Kong's incentives to allow "tourist" births affected by the fact that the city pays benefits to older residents from taxes paid by younger residents?

Web Resources

1. To contemplate the sources of pressures within Hong Kong to restrict tourist births, go to **www.econtoday.com/chap01**.

2. Read about the 2011 suspension of Hong Kong's tourist births at **www.econtoday.com/chap01**.

MyEconLab

For more questions on this chapter's Issues & Applications, go to MyEconLab. In the Study Plan for this chapter, select Section N: News.

MyEconLab

Here is what you should know after reading this chapter. MyEconLab will help you identify what you know, and where to go when you need to practice.

WHAT YOU SHOULD KNOW

WHERE TO GO TO PRACTICE

Answering the Three Basic Economic Questions Economics is the study of how individuals make choices to satisfy wants. Microeconomics is the study of decision making by individual households and firms, and macroeconomics is the study of nationwide phenomena such as inflation and unemployment. The three basic economic questions ask what and how much will be produced, how items will be produced, and for whom items will be produced. The two opposing answers to these questions are provided by the type of economic system: either centralized command and control or the price system.

incentives, 2
economics, 2
resources, 2
wants, 2
microeconomics, 3
macroeconomics, 3
aggregates, 3
economic system, 3

• MyEconLab Study Plans 1.1, 1.2, 1.3

Self-Interest in Economic Analysis Rational self-interest is the assumption that people never intentionally make decisions that would leave them worse off. Instead, they are motivated mainly by their self-interest, which can relate to monetary and nonmonetary goals, such as love, prestige, and helping others.

rationality
    assumption, 5

• MyEconLab Study Plan 1.3

Economics as a Science Economic models, or theories, are simplified representations of the real world. Economic models are never completely realistic because by definition they are simplifications using assumptions that are not directly testable. Nevertheless, economists can subject the predictions of economic theories to empirical tests in which real-world data are used to decide whether or not to reject the predictions.

models, or theories, 7
ceteris paribus
    assumption, 8
empirical, 9
behavioral
    economics, 9
bounded rationality, 10

• MyEconLab Study Plan 1.5

Positive and Normative Economics Positive economics deals with *what is*, whereas normative economics deals with *what ought to be*. Positive economic statements are of the "if . . . then" variety. They are descriptive and predictive. In contrast, statements embodying values are within the realm of normative economics, or how people think things ought to be.

positive economics, 10
normative
    economics, 10

• MyEconLab Study Plan 1.6

Log in to MyEconLab, take a chapter test, and get a personalized Study Plan that tells you which concepts you understand and which ones you need to review. From there, MyEconLab will give you further practice, tutorials, animations, videos, and guided solutions. For more information, visit www.myeconlab.com

PROBLEMS

All problems are assignable in MyEconLab. Answers to odd-numbered problems appear at the back of the book.

1-1. Define economics. Explain briefly how the economic way of thinking—in terms of rational, self-interested people responding to incentives—relates to each of the following situations. (See pages 2, 5–6.)

   a. A student deciding whether to purchase a textbook for a particular class

   b. Government officials seeking more funding for mass transit through higher taxes

   c. A municipality taxing hotel guests to obtain funding for a new sports stadium

1-2. Some people claim that the "economic way of thinking" does not apply to issues such as health care. Explain how economics does apply to this issue by developing a "model" of an individual's choices. (See pages 7–8.)

1-3. Does the phrase "unlimited wants and limited resources" apply to both a low-income household and a middle-income household? Can the same phrase be applied to a very high-income household? (See page 2.)

1-4. In a single sentence, contrast microeconomics and macroeconomics. Next, categorize each of the following issues as a microeconomic issue, a macroeconomic issue, or not an economic issue. (See page 3.)

   a. The national unemployment rate

   b. The decision of a worker to work overtime or not

   c. A family's choice to have a baby

   d. The rate of growth of the money supply

   e. The national government's budget deficit

   f. A student's allocation of study time across two subjects

1-5. One of your classmates, Sally, is a hardworking student, serious about her classes, and conscientious about her grades. Sally is also involved, however, in volunteer activities and an extracurricular sport. Is Sally displaying rational behavior? Based on what you read in this chapter, construct an argument supporting the conclusion that she is. (See pages 5–7.)

1-6. Recently, a bank was trying to decide what fee to charge for "expedited payments"—payments that the bank would transmit extra-speedily to enable customers to avoid late fees on cable TV bills, electric bills, and the like. To try to determine what fee customers were willing to pay for expedited payments, the bank conducted a survey. It was able to determine that many of the people surveyed already paid fees for expedited payment services that *exceeded* the maximum fees that they said they were willing to pay. How does the bank's finding relate to economists' traditional focus on what people do, rather than what they *say* they will do? (See page 9.)

1-7. Explain, in your own words, the rationality assumption, and contrast it with the assumption of bounded rationality proposed by adherents of behavioral economics. (See pages 5–6, 9–10.)

1-8. Why does the assumption of bounded rationality suggest that people might use rules of thumb to guide their decision making instead of considering every possible choice available to them? (See page 10.)

1-9. Under what circumstances might people appear to use rules of thumb, as suggested by the assumption of bounded rationality, even though they really are behaving in a manner suggested by the rationality assumption? (See page 10.)

1-10. For each of the following approaches that an economist might follow in examining a decision-making process, identify whether the approach relies on the rationality assumption or on the assumption of bounded rationality. (See page 10.)

   a. To make predictions about how many apps a person will download onto her tablet device, an economist presumes that the individual faces limitations that make it impossible for her to examine every possible choice among relevant apps.

   b. In evaluating the price that an individual will be willing to pay for a given quantity of a particular type of health care service, a researcher assumes that the person considers all relevant health care options in pursuit of his own long-term satisfaction with resulting health outcomes.

   c. To determine the amount of time that a person will decide to devote to watching online videos each week, an economist makes the assumption that the individual will feel overwhelmed by the sheer volume of videos available online and will respond by using a rule of thumb.

1-11. For each of the following approaches that an economist might follow in examining a decision-making process, identify whether the approach relies on the rationality assumption or on the assumption of bounded rationality. (See page 10.)

   a. An economic study of the number of online searches that individuals conduct before selecting a particular item to purchase online presumes that people are interested only in their own satisfaction, pursue their ultimate objectives, and consider every relevant option.

b. An economist seeking to predict the effect that an increase in a state's sales tax rate will have on consumers' purchases of goods and services presumes that people are limited in their ability to process information about how the tax-rate increase will influence the after-tax prices those consumers will pay.

c. To evaluate the impact of an increase in the range of choices that an individual confronts when deciding among devices for accessing the Internet, an economic researcher makes the assumption that the individual is unable to take into account every new Internet-access option available to her.

1-12. Which of the following predictions appear(s) to follow from a model based on the assumption that rational, self-interested individuals respond to incentives? (See pages 6–7.)

a. For every 10 exam points Myrna must earn in order to pass her economics course and meet her graduation requirements, she will study one additional hour for her economics test next week.

b. A coin toss will best predict Leonardo's decision about whether to purchase an expensive business suit or an inexpensive casual outfit to wear next week when he interviews for a high-paying job he is seeking.

c. Celeste, who uses earnings from her regularly scheduled hours of part-time work to pay for her room and board at college, will decide to purchase and download a newly released video this week only if she is able to work two additional hours.

1-13. Consider two models for estimating, in advance of an election, the shares of votes that will go to rival candidates. According to one model, pollsters' surveys of a randomly chosen set of registered voters before an election can be used to forecast the percentage of votes that each candidate will receive. This first model relies on the assumption that unpaid survey respondents will give truthful responses about how they will vote and that they will actually cast a ballot in the election. The other model uses prices of financial assets (legally binding

IOUs) issued by the Iowa Electronic Markets, operated by the University of Iowa, to predict electoral outcomes. The final payments received by owners of these assets, which can be bought or sold during the weeks and days preceding an election, depend on the shares of votes the candidates actually end up receiving. This second model assumes that owners of these assets wish to earn the highest possible returns, and it predicts that the market prices of these assets provide an indication of the percentage of votes that each candidate will actually receive on the day of the election. (See pages 8–9.)

a. Which of these two models for forecasting electoral results is more firmly based on the rationality assumption of economics?

b. How would an economist evaluate which is the better model for forecasting electoral outcomes?

1-14. Write a sentence contrasting positive and normative economic analysis. (See pages 10–11.)

1-15. Based on your answer to Problem 1–14, categorize each of the following conclusions as being the result of positive analysis or normative analysis.

a. A higher minimum wage will reduce employment opportunities for minimum wage workers.

b. Increasing the earnings of minimum wage employees is desirable, and raising the minimum wage is the best way to accomplish this.

c. Everyone should enjoy open access to health care at no explicit charge.

d. Heath care subsidies will increase the consumption of health care.

1-16. Consider the following statements, based on a positive economic analysis that assumes that all other things remain constant. For each, list one other thing that might change and thus offset the outcome stated. (See pages 8, 10.)

a. Increased demand for laptop computers will drive up their price.

b. Falling gasoline prices will result in additional vacation travel.

c. A reduction of income tax rates will result in more people working.

ECONOMICS ON THE NET

The Usefulness of Studying Economics This application helps you see how accomplished people benefited from their study of economics. It also explores ways in which these people feel others of all walks of life can gain from learning more about the economics field.

Title: How Taking an Economics Course Can Lead to Becoming an Economist

Navigation: Go to www.econtoday.com/chap01 to visit the Federal Reserve Bank of Minneapolis publication, *The Region*. Select the last article of the issue, "Economists in *The Region* on Their Student Experiences and the Need for Economic Literacy."

Application Read the interviews of the six economists, and answer the following questions.

1. Based on your reading, which economists do you think other economists regard as influential? What educational institutions do you think are the most influential in economics?

2. Which economists do you think were attracted to microeconomics and which to macroeconomics?

For Group Study and Analysis Divide the class into three groups, and assign the groups the Blinder, Yellen, and Rivlin interviews. Have each group use the content of its assigned interview to develop a statement explaining why the study of economics is important, regardless of a student's chosen major.

ANSWERS TO QUICK QUIZZES

p. 7: (i) wants . . . unlimited; (ii) Microeconomics . . . macroeconomics; (iii) centralized command and control . . . price system; (iv) rationality

p. 11: (i) model . . . theory . . . model; (ii) *ceteris paribus;* (iii) Behavioral . . . bounded rationality; (iv) Positive . . . Normative

APPENDIX A

Reading and Working with Graphs

A graph is a visual representation of the relationship between variables. In this appendix, we'll deal with just two variables: an **independent variable,** which can change in value freely, and a **dependent variable,** which changes as a result of changes in the value of the independent variable. For example, even if nothing else is changing in your life, your weight depends on your intake of calories. The independent variable is caloric intake, and the dependent variable is weight.

A table is a list of numerical values showing the relationship between two (or more) variables. Any table can be converted into a graph, which is a visual representation of that list. Once you understand how a table can be converted to a graph, you will understand what graphs are and how to construct and use them.

Consider a practical example. A conservationist may try to convince you that driving at lower highway speeds will help you conserve gas. Table A-1 shows the relationship between speed—the independent variable—and the distance you can go on a gallon of gas at that speed—the dependent variable. This table does show a pattern. As the data in the first column get larger in value, the data in the second column get smaller.

Now let's take a look at the different ways in which variables can be related.

Direct and Inverse Relationships

Two variables can be related in different ways, some simple, others more complex. For example, a person's weight and height are often related. If we measured the height and weight of thousands of people, we would surely find that taller people tend to weigh more than shorter people. That is, we would discover that there is a **direct relationship** between height and weight. By this we simply mean that an *increase* in one variable is usually associated with an *increase* in the related variable. This can easily be seen in panel (a) of Figure A-1 below.

Let's look at another simple way in which two variables can be related. Much evidence indicates that as the price of a specific commodity rises, the amount purchased decreases—there is an **inverse relationship** between the variable's price per unit and quantity purchased. Such a relationship indicates that for higher and higher prices, smaller and smaller quantities will be purchased. We see this relationship in panel (b) of Figure A-1.

Independent variable
A variable whose value is determined independently of, or outside, the equation under study.

Dependent variable
A variable whose value changes according to changes in the value of one or more independent variables.

TABLE A-1

Gas Mileage as a Function of Driving Speed

Miles per Hour	Miles per Gallon
45	25
50	24
55	23
60	21
65	19
70	16
75	13

Direct relationship
A relationship between two variables that is positive, meaning that an increase in one variable is associated with an increase in the other and a decrease in one variable is associated with a decrease in the other.

Inverse relationship
A relationship between two variables that is negative, meaning that an increase in one variable is associated with a decrease in the other and a decrease in one variable is associated with an increase in the other.

FIGURE A-1

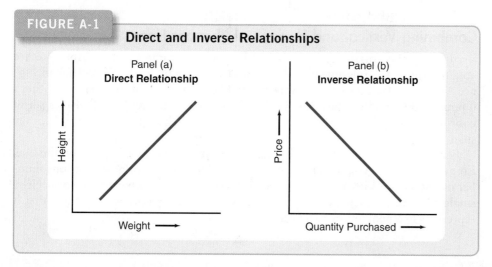

Direct and Inverse Relationships

Panel (a)
Direct Relationship

Panel (b)
Inverse Relationship

FIGURE A-2

Horizontal Number Line

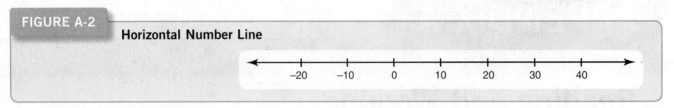

Number line
A line that can be divided into segments of equal length, each associated with a number.

FIGURE A-3

Vertical Number Line

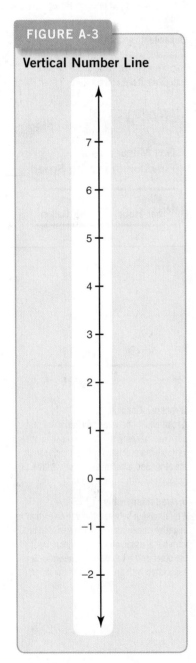

Constructing a Graph

Let us now examine how to construct a graph to illustrate a relationship between two variables.

A Number Line

The first step is to become familiar with what is called a **number line.** One is shown in Figure A-2 above. You should know two things about it:

1. The points on the line divide the line into equal segments.

2. The numbers associated with the points on the line increase in value from left to right. Saying it the other way around, the numbers decrease in value from right to left. However you say it, what you're describing is formally called an *ordered set of points.*

On the number line, we have shown the line segments—that is, the distance from 0 to 10 or the distance between 30 and 40. They all appear to be equal and, indeed, are each equal to $\frac{1}{2}$ inch. When we use a distance to represent a quantity, such as barrels of oil, graphically, we are *scaling* the number line. In the example shown, the distance between 0 and 10 might represent 10 barrels of oil, or the distance from 0 to 40 might represent 40 barrels. Of course, the scale may differ on different number lines. For example, a distance of 1 inch could represent 10 units on one number line but 5,000 units on another. Notice that on our number line, points to the left of 0 correspond to negative numbers and points to the right of 0 correspond to positive numbers.

Of course, we can also construct a vertical number line. Consider the one in Figure A-3 alongside. As we move up this vertical number line, the numbers increase in value; conversely, as we descend, they decrease in value. Below 0 the numbers are negative, and above 0 the numbers are positive. And as on the horizontal number line, all the line segments are equal. This line is divided into segments such that the distance between –2 and –1 is the same as the distance between 0 and 1.

Combining Vertical and Horizontal Number Lines

By drawing the horizontal and vertical lines on the same sheet of paper, we are able to express the relationships between variables graphically. We do this in Figure A-4 on the facing page. We draw them (1) so that they intersect at each other's 0 point and (2) so that they are perpendicular to each other. The result is a set of coordinate axes, where each line is called an *axis.* When we have two axes, they span a *plane.*

For one number line, you need only one number to specify any point on the line. Equivalently, when you see a point on the line, you know that it represents one number or one value. With a coordinate value system, you need two numbers to specify a single point in the plane; when you see a single point on a graph, you know that it represents two numbers or two values.

FIGURE A-4

A Set of Coordinate Axes

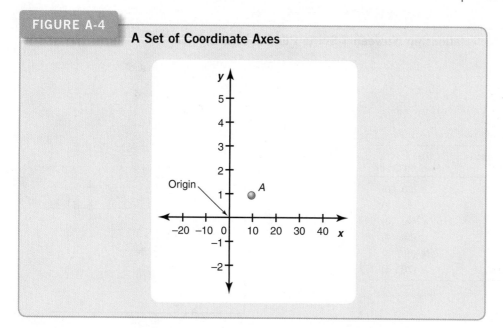

The basic things that you should know about a coordinate number system are that the vertical number line is referred to as the **y axis,** the horizontal number line is referred to as the **x axis,** and the point of intersection of the two lines is referred to as the **origin.**

Any point such as A in Figure A-4 above represents two numbers—a value of x and a value of y. But we know more than that: We also know that point A represents a positive value of y because it is above the x axis, and we know that it represents a positive value of x because it is to the right of the y axis.

Point A represents a "paired observation" of the variables x and y; in particular, in Figure A-4, A represents an observation of the pair of values $x = 10$ and $y = 1$. Every point in the coordinate system corresponds to a paired observation of x and y, which can be simply written (x, y)—the x value is always specified first and then the y value. When we give the values associated with the position of point A in the coordinate number system, we are in effect giving the coordinates of that point. A's coordinates are $x = 10$, $y = 1$, or $(10, 1)$.

y axis
The vertical axis in a graph.

x axis
The horizontal axis in a graph.

Origin
The intersection of the y axis and the x axis in a graph.

Graphing Numbers in a Table

Consider Table A-2 alongside. Column 1 shows different prices for T-shirts, and column 2 gives the number of T-shirts purchased per week at these prices. Notice the pattern of these numbers. As the price of T-shirts falls, the number of T-shirts purchased per week increases. Therefore, an inverse relationship exists between these two variables, and as soon as we represent it on a graph, you will be able to see the relationship. We can graph this relationship using a coordinate number system—a vertical and horizontal number line for each of these two variables. Such a graph is shown in panel (b) of Figure A-5 on the following page.

In economics, it is conventional to put dollar values on the y axis and quantities on the horizontal axis. We therefore construct a vertical number line for price and a horizontal number line, the x axis, for quantity of T-shirts purchased per week. The resulting coordinate system allows the plotting of each of the paired observation points. In panel (a), we repeat Table A-2, with a column added expressing these points in paired-data (x, y) form. For example, point J is the paired observation $(30, 9)$. It indicates that when the price of a T-shirt is $9, 30 will be purchased per week.

TABLE A-2

T-Shirts Purchased

(1) Price of T-Shirts	(2) Number of T-Shirts Purchased per Week
$10	20
9	30
8	40
7	50
6	60
5	70

FIGURE A-5

Graphing the Relationship between T-Shirts Purchased and Price

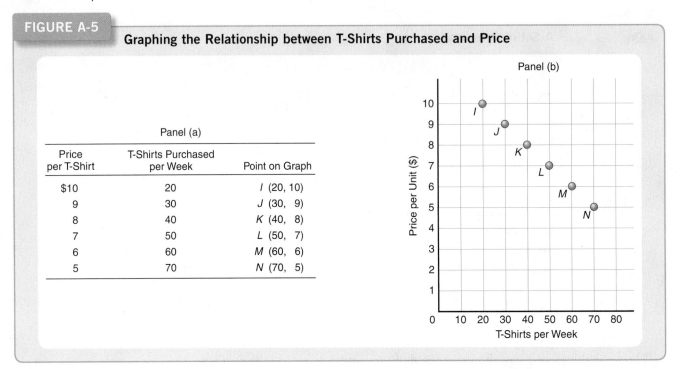

Panel (a)

Price per T-Shirt	T-Shirts Purchased per Week	Point on Graph
$10	20	I (20, 10)
9	30	J (30, 9)
8	40	K (40, 8)
7	50	L (50, 7)
6	60	M (60, 6)
5	70	N (70, 5)

If it were possible to sell parts of a T-shirt ($\frac{1}{2}$ or $\frac{1}{20}$ of a shirt), we would have observations at every possible price. That is, we would be able to connect our paired observations, represented as lettered points. Let's assume that we can make T-shirts perfectly divisible so that the linear relationship shown in Figure A-5 also holds for fractions of dollars and T-shirts. We would then have a line that connects these points, as shown in the graph in Figure A-6 below.

In short, we have now represented the data from the table in the form of a graph. Note that an inverse relationship between two variables shows up on a graph as a line or curve that slopes *downward* from left to right. (You might as well get used to the idea that economists call a straight line a "curve" even though it may not curve at all. Economists' data frequently turn out to be curves, so they refer to everything represented graphically, even straight lines, as curves.)

FIGURE A-6

Connecting the Observation Points

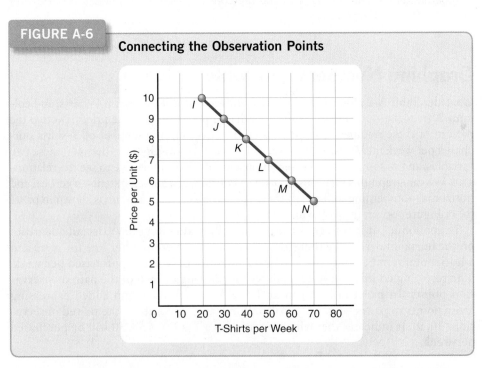

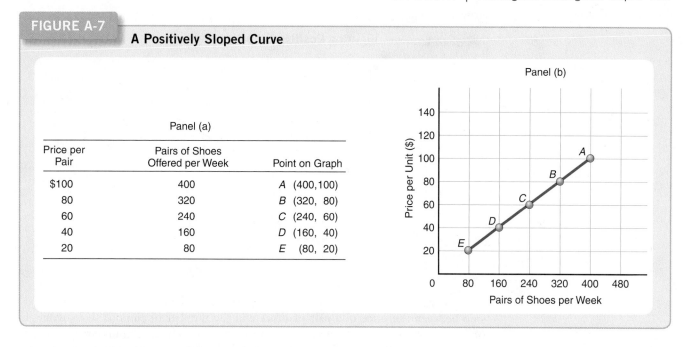

FIGURE A-7

A Positively Sloped Curve

Panel (a)

Price per Pair	Pairs of Shoes Offered per Week	Point on Graph
$100	400	A (400, 100)
80	320	B (320, 80)
60	240	C (240, 60)
40	160	D (160, 40)
20	80	E (80, 20)

The Slope of a Line (A Linear Curve)

An important property of a curve represented on a graph is its *slope*. Consider Figure A-7 above, which represents the quantities of shoes per week that a seller is willing to offer at different prices. Note that in panel (a) of Figure A-7, as in Figure A-5 on page 20, we have expressed the coordinates of the points in parentheses in paired-data form.

The **slope** of a line is defined as the change in the *y* values divided by the corresponding change in the *x* values as we move along the line. Let's move from point *E* to point *D* in panel (b) of Figure A-7. As we move, we note that the change in the *y* values, which is the change in price, is +20, because we have moved from a price of $20 to a price of $40 per pair. As we move from *E* to *D*, the change in the *x* values is +80; the number of pairs of shoes willingly offered per week rises from 80 to 160 pairs. The slope, calculated as a change in the *y* values divided by the change in the *x* values, is therefore

$$\frac{20}{80} = \frac{1}{4}$$

It may be helpful for you to think of slope as a "rise" (movement in the vertical direction) over a "run" (movement in the horizontal direction). We show this abstractly in Figure A-8 on the following page. The slope is the amount of rise divided by the amount of run. In the example in Figure A-8, and of course in Figure A-7 above, the amount of rise is positive and so is the amount of run. That's because it's a direct relationship. We show an inverse relationship in Figure A-9 on the next page. The slope is still equal to the rise divided by the run, but in this case the rise and the run have opposite signs because the curve slopes downward. That means that the slope is negative and that we are dealing with an inverse relationship.

Now let's calculate the slope for a different part of the curve in panel (b) of Figure A-7. We will find the slope as we move from point *B* to point *A*. Again, we note that the slope, or rise over run, from *B* to *A* equals

$$\frac{20}{80} = \frac{1}{4}$$

A specific property of a straight line is that its slope is the same between any two points. In other words, the slope is constant at all points on a straight line in a graph.

Slope
The change in the *y* value divided by the corresponding change in the *x* value of a curve; the "incline" of the curve.

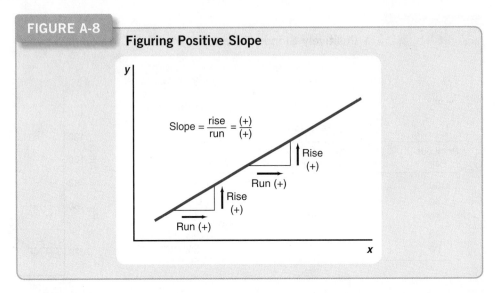

FIGURE A-8

Figuring Positive Slope

We conclude that for our example in Figure A-7 on the previous page, the relationship between the price of a pair of shoes and the number of pairs of shoes willingly offered per week is *linear*, which simply means "in a straight line," and our calculations indicate a constant slope. Moreover, we calculate a direct relationship between these two variables, which turns out to be an upward-sloping (from left to right) curve. Upward-sloping curves have positive slopes—in this case, the slope is $+\frac{1}{4}$.

We know that an inverse relationship between two variables is a downward-sloping curve—rise over run will be negative because the rise and run have opposite signs, as shown in Figure A-9 below. When we see a negative slope, we know that increases in one variable are associated with decreases in the other. Therefore, we say that downward-sloping curves have negative slopes. Can you verify that the slope of the graph representing the relationship between T-shirt prices and the quantity of T-shirts purchased per week in Figure A-6 on page 20 is $-\frac{1}{10}$?

Slopes of Nonlinear Curves

The graph presented in Figure A-10 on the facing page indicates a *nonlinear* relationship between two variables, total profits and output per unit of time. Inspection of this graph indicates that, at first, increases in output lead to increases in total profits; that is, total profits rise as output increases. But beyond some output level, further increases in output cause decreases in total profits.

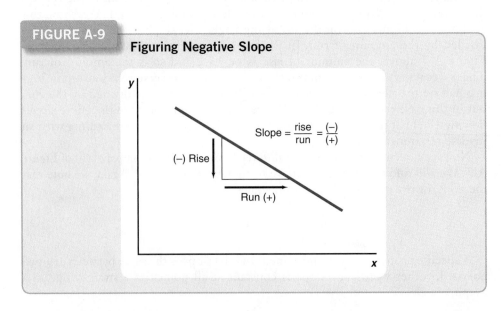

FIGURE A-9

Figuring Negative Slope

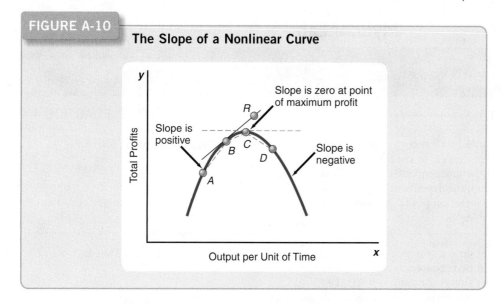

FIGURE A-10

The Slope of a Nonlinear Curve

Can you see how this curve rises at first, reaches a peak at point *C*, and then falls? This curve relating total profits to output levels appears mountain-shaped.

Considering that this curve is nonlinear (it is obviously not a straight line), should we expect a constant slope when we compute changes in *y* divided by corresponding changes in *x* in moving from one point to another? A quick inspection, even without specific numbers, should lead us to conclude that the slopes of lines joining different points in this curve, such as between *A* and *B*, *B* and *C*, or *C* and *D*, will *not* be the same. The curve slopes upward (in a positive direction) for some values and downward (in a negative direction) for other values. In fact, the slope of the line between any two points on this curve will be different from the slope of the line between any two other points. Each slope will be different as we move along the curve.

Instead of using a line between two points to discuss slope, mathematicians and economists prefer to discuss the slope *at a particular point*. The slope at a point on the curve, such as point *B* in the graph in Figure A-10 above, is the slope of a line tangent to that point. A tangent line is a straight line that touches a curve at only one point. For example, it might be helpful to think of the tangent at *B* as the straight line that just "kisses" the curve at point *B*.

To calculate the slope of a tangent line, you need to have some additional information besides the two values of the point of tangency. For example, in Figure A-10, if we knew that the point *R* also lay on the tangent line and we knew the two values of that point, we could calculate the slope of the tangent line. We could calculate rise over run between points *B* and *R*, and the result would be the slope of the line tangent to the one point *B* on the curve.

MyEconLab

Here is what you should know after reading this appendix. MyEconLab will help you identify what you know, and where to go when you need to practice.

─ WHAT YOU SHOULD KNOW ─────────────────────── WHERE TO GO TO PRACTICE ─

Direct and Inverse Relationships In a direct relationship, a dependent variable changes in the same direction as the change in the independent variable. In an inverse relationship, the dependent variable changes in the opposite direction of the change in the independent variable.

independent variable, 17
dependent variable, 17
direct relationship, 17
inverse relationship, 17

• MyEconLab Study Plan 1.7

Constructing a Graph When we draw a graph showing the relationship between two economic variables, we are holding all other things constant (the Latin term for which is *ceteris paribus).*

number line, 18
y axis, 19
x axis, 19
origin, 19

• MyEconLab Study Plan 1.8

Graphing Numbers We obtain a set of coordinates by putting vertical and horizontal number lines together. The vertical line is called the *y* axis; the horizontal line, the *x* axis.

• MyEconLab Study Plan 1.9

The Slope of a Linear Curve The slope of any linear (straight-line) curve is the change in the *y* values divided by the corresponding change in the *x* values as we move along the line. Otherwise stated, the slope is calculated as the amount of rise over the amount of run, where rise is movement in the vertical direction and run is movement in the horizontal direction.

slope, 21

Key Figures
Figure A-8, 22
Figure A-9, 22

• MyEconLab Study Plan 1.10
• Animated Figures A-8, A-9

The Slope of a Nonlinear Curve The slope of a nonlinear curve changes; it is positive when the curve is rising and negative when the curve is falling. At a maximum or minimum point, the slope of the nonlinear curve is zero.

Key Figure
Figure A-10, 23

• MyEconLab Study Plan 1.10
• Animated Figure A-10

Log in to MyEconLab, take an appendix test, and get a personalized Study Plan that tells you which concepts you understand and which ones you need to review. From there, MyEconLab will give you further practice, tutorials, animations, videos, and guided solutions. For more information, visit www.myeconlab.com

PROBLEMS

All problems are assignable in MyEconLab. Answers to odd-numbered problems appear at the back of the book.

A-1. Explain which is the independent variable and which is the dependent variable for each of the following examples. (See page 17.)

   a. Once you determine the price of a notebook at the college bookstore, you will decide how many notebooks to buy.

   b. You will decide how many credit hours to register for this semester once the university tells you how many work-study hours you will be assigned.

   c. You anticipate earning a higher grade on your next economics exam because you studied more hours in the weeks preceding the exam.

A-2. For each of the following items, state whether a direct or an inverse relationship is likely to exist. (See page 17.)

   a. The number of hours you study for an exam and your exam score

   b. The price of pizza and the quantity purchased

   c. The number of games the university basketball team won last year and the number of season tickets sold this year

A-3. Review Figure A-4 on page 19, and then state whether each of the following paired observations is on, above, or below the x axis and on, to the left of, or to the right of the y axis. (See page 19.)

   a. $(-10, 4)$

   b. $(20, -2)$

   c. $(10, 0)$

A-4. State whether each of the following functions specifies a direct or an inverse relationship. (See page 17.)

   a. $y = 5x$

   b. $y = 10 - 2x$

   c. $y = 3 + x$

   d. $y = -3x$

A-5. Given the function $y = 5x$, complete the following schedule and plot the curve. (See page 20.)

y	x
	−4
	−2
	0
	2
	4

A-6. Given the function $y = 8 - 2x$, complete the following schedule and plot the curve. (See page 21.)

y	x
	−4
	−2
	0
	2
	4

A-7. Calculate the slope of the function you graphed in Problem A-5. (See page 21.)

A-8. Calculate the slope of the function you graphed in Problem A-6. (See page 21.)

2

Scarcity and the World of Trade-Offs

The airliner in which you have been flying will land about an hour earlier than indicated by your formal travel itinerary. As the plane taxis to the gate, you contemplate how to use that extra hour. You might eat a more leisurely dinner at a nicer restaurant, grab an extra hour of sleep, or engage in additional income-generating work. Now you find out the bad news: No empty gates are available for your plane, and you will have to wait at least one hour to exit the plane. Nonetheless, the airline can now report your flight as "on time" because it touched down on the ground earlier than officially scheduled. The result is that you must remain on the plane for the hour you thought would be available for another, most-valued use off the plane. Thus, you will have to give up the alternative use of that hour after all. As you will learn in this chapter, you have incurred an *opportunity cost*.

? the U.S. Department of Commerce recently published a report concluding that each year, U.S. consumers spend about $1.2 trillion, or more than 11 percent of total consumer expenditures, on "non-essential items"? Included among these items were candy, gambling, jewelry, liquor, and pleasure boats. During the weeks that followed, media commentators filled newspaper pages, TV airtime, and the blogosphere with laments about U.S. residents making "poor economic decisions" by paying prices that are "too high" to buy goods and services that "they don't really need."

You will discover in this chapter that economists do not rely on the particularly subjective concept of "needs" to explain people's decisions. What influences individuals' economic choices are their *wants*, which, you learned in the previous chapter, are all of the items that people would purchase if they had unlimited income. In reality, of course, people's incomes *are* limited. Irrespective of normative judgments by U.S. government officials to classify some items as "non-essential," *all* of the items among which consumers allocate their limited incomes are *scarce* goods available only at prices greater than zero.

Scarcity

Whenever individuals or communities cannot obtain everything they desire simultaneously, they must make choices. Choices occur because of *scarcity*. **Scarcity** is the most basic concept in all of economics. Scarcity means that we do not ever have enough of everything, including time, to satisfy our *every* desire. Scarcity exists because human wants always exceed what can be produced with the limited resources and time that nature makes available.

Scarcity
A situation in which the ingredients for producing the things that people desire are insufficient to satisfy all wants at a zero price.

What Scarcity Is Not

Scarcity is not a shortage. After a hurricane hits and cuts off supplies to a community, TV newscasts often show people standing in line to get minimum amounts of cooking fuel and food. A news commentator might say that the line is caused by the "scarcity" of these products. But cooking fuel and food are always scarce—we cannot obtain all that we want at a zero price. Therefore, do not confuse the concept of scarcity, which is general and all-encompassing, with the concept of shortages as evidenced by people waiting in line to obtain a particular product.

Scarcity is not the same thing as poverty. Scarcity occurs among the poor and among the rich. Even the richest person on earth faces scarcity. For instance, even the world's richest person has only limited time available. Low income levels do not create more scarcity. High income levels do not create less scarcity.

Scarcity is a fact of life, like gravity. And just as physicists did not invent gravity, economists did not invent scarcity—it existed well before the first economist ever lived. It has existed at all times in the past and will exist at all times in the future.

Scarcity and Resources

Scarcity exists because resources are insufficient to satisfy our every desire. Resources are the inputs used in the production of the things that we want. **Production** can be defined as virtually any activity that results in the conversion of resources into products that can be used in consumption. Production includes delivering items from one part of the country to another. It includes taking ice from an ice tray to put it in your soft-drink glass. The resources used in production are called *factors of production*, and some economists use the terms *resources* and *factors of production* interchangeably. The total quantity of all resources that an economy has at any one time determines what that economy can produce.

Factors of production can be classified in many ways. Here is one such classification:

1. *Land.* **Land** encompasses all the nonhuman gifts of nature, including timber, water, fish, minerals, and the original fertility of land. It is often called the *natural resource*.

2. *Labor.* **Labor** is the *human resource*, which includes productive contributions made by individuals who work, such as Web page designers, iPad applications creators, and professional football players.

Production
Any activity that results in the conversion of resources into products that can be used in consumption.

Land
The natural resources that are available from nature. Land as a resource includes location, original fertility and mineral deposits, topography, climate, water, and vegetation.

Labor
Productive contributions of humans who work.

How has Japan's energy policy reduced the productive contributions of many individuals who provide labor?

INTERNATIONAL POLICY EXAMPLE
A Lower Productive Contribution of Sweltering Japanese Labor

During the past few years, the Japanese government has established rules aimed at reducing the nation's emissions of carbon dioxide (CO_2) by nearly 3 million tons each summer. To attain this goal, Japan's government has effectively declared war on air conditioning. The government has mandated that thermostats in all government offices be set no lower than 82 degrees during the months spanning June to September. Private Japanese businesses have followed suit with a "Cool Biz" program establishing 82 degrees as the "new office norm" for indoor temperatures.

Of course, 82 degrees is above the temperature at which people in enclosed spaces are most effective at producing goods and services. Consequently, the productive contribution of Japanese labor now declines every summer.

FOR CRITICAL THINKING
What do you suppose happened to the productive contribution of labor when Japan's government temporarily raised the summer target office temperature to 86 degrees?

Physical capital
All manufactured resources, including buildings, equipment, machines, and improvements to land that are used for production.

Human capital
The accumulated training and education of workers.

3. *Physical capital.* **Physical capital** consists of the factories and equipment used in production. It also includes improvements to natural resources, such as irrigation ditches.

4. *Human capital.* **Human capital** is the economic characterization of the education and training of workers. How much the nation produces depends not only on how many hours people work but also on how productive they are, and that in turn depends in part on education and training. To become more educated, individuals have to devote time and resources, just as a business has to devote resources if it wants to increase its physical capital. Whenever a worker's skills increase, human capital has been improved.

Entrepreneurship
The component of human resources that performs the functions of raising capital; organizing, managing, and assembling other factors of production; making basic business policy decisions; and taking risks.

5. *Entrepreneurship.* **Entrepreneurship** (actually a subdivision of labor) is the component of human resources that performs the functions of organizing, managing, and assembling the other factors of production to create and operate business ventures. Entrepreneurship also encompasses taking risks that involve the possibility of losing large sums of wealth. It includes new methods of engaging in common activities and generally experimenting with any type of new thinking that could lead to making more income. Without entrepreneurship, hardly any business organizations could continue to operate.

Goods versus Economic Goods

Goods
All things from which individuals derive satisfaction or happiness.

Economic goods
Goods that are scarce, for which the quantity demanded exceeds the quantity supplied at a zero price.

Services
Mental or physical labor or assistance purchased by consumers. Examples are the assistance of physicians, lawyers, dentists, repair personnel, housecleaners, educators, retailers, and wholesalers; items purchased or used by consumers that do not have physical characteristics.

Goods are defined as all things from which individuals derive satisfaction or happiness. Goods therefore include air to breathe and the beauty of a sunset as well as food, cars, and iPhones.

Economic goods are a subset of all goods—they are scarce goods, about which we must constantly make decisions regarding their best use. By definition, the desired quantity of an economic good exceeds the amount that is available at a zero price. Almost every example we use in economics concerns economic goods—cars, Blu-ray disc players, computers, socks, baseball bats, and corn. Weeds are a good example of *bads*—goods for which the desired quantity is much *less* than what nature provides at a zero price.

Sometimes you will see references to "goods and services." **Services** are tasks that are performed by individuals, often for someone else, such as laundry, Internet access, hospital care, restaurant meal preparation, car polishing, psychological counseling, and teaching. One way of looking at services is to think of them as *intangible goods*.

Wants and Needs

Wants are not the same as needs. Indeed, from the economist's point of view, the term *needs* is objectively undefinable. When someone says, "I need some new clothes," there is no way to know whether that person is stating a vague wish, a want, or a lifesaving requirement. If the individual making the statement were dying of exposure in a northern country during the winter, we might conclude that indeed the person does need clothes—perhaps not new ones, but at least some articles of warm clothing. Typically, however, the term *need* is used very casually in conversation. What people mean, usually, is that they desire something that they do not currently have.

Humans have unlimited wants. Just imagine that every single material want that you might have was satisfied. You could have all of the clothes, cars, houses, downloadable movies, yachts, and other items that you want. Does that mean that nothing else could add to your total level of happiness? Undoubtedly, you might continue to think of new goods and services that you could obtain, particularly as they came to market. You would also still be lacking in fulfilling all of your wants for compassion, friendship, love, affection, prestige, musical abilities, sports abilities, and the like.

In reality, every individual has competing wants but cannot satisfy all of them, given limited resources. This is the reality of scarcity. Each person must therefore make choices. Whenever a choice is made to produce or buy something, something else that is also desired is not produced or not purchased. In other words, in a world of scarcity, every want that ends up being satisfied causes one or more other wants to remain unsatisfied or to be forfeited.

QUICK QUIZ See page 47 for the answers. Review concepts from this section in MyEconLab.

_____ is the situation in which human wants always exceed what can be produced with the limited resources and time that nature makes available.

We use scarce resources, such as_____, _____, _____ and _____ capital, and _____, to produce economic goods—goods that are desired but are not directly obtainable from nature to the extent demanded or desired at a zero price.

_____ are unlimited. They include all material desires and all nonmaterial desires, such as love, affection, power, and prestige.

The concept of _____ is difficult to define objectively for every person. Consequently, we simply consider every person's wants to be unlimited. In a world of **scarcity**, satisfaction of one want necessarily means nonsatisfaction of one or more other wants.

Scarcity, Choice, and Opportunity Cost

The natural fact of scarcity implies that we must make choices. One of the most important results of this fact is that every choice made means that some opportunity must be sacrificed. Every choice involves giving up an opportunity to produce or consume something else.

Valuing Forgone Alternatives

Consider a practical example. Every choice you make to study economics for one more hour requires that you give up the opportunity to choose to engage in any one of the following activities: study more of another subject, listen to music, sleep, browse at a local store, read a novel, or work out at the gym. The most highly valued of these opportunities is forgone if you choose to study economics an additional hour.

Because there were so many alternatives from which to choose, how could you determine the value of what you gave up to engage in that extra hour of studying economics? First of all, no one else can tell you the answer because only *you* can put a value on the alternatives forgone. Only you know the value of another hour of sleep or of an hour looking for the latest digital music downloads—whatever one activity *you* would have chosen if you had not opted to study economics for that hour. That means that only you can determine the highest-valued, next-best alternative that you had to sacrifice in order to study economics one more hour. Only you can determine the value of the next-best alternative.

Opportunity Cost

Opportunity cost
The highest-valued, next-best alternative that must be sacrificed to obtain something or to satisfy a want.

The value of the next-best alternative is called **opportunity cost.** The opportunity cost of any action is the value of what is given up—the next-highest-ranked alternative—because a choice was made. What is important is the choice that you would have made if you hadn't studied one more hour. Your opportunity cost is the *next-highest-ranked* alternative, not *all* alternatives.

> *In economics, cost is always a forgone opportunity.*

One way to think about opportunity cost is to understand that when you choose to do something, you lose something else. What you lose is being able to engage in your next-highest-valued alternative. The cost of your chosen alternative is what you lose, which is by definition your next-highest-valued alternative. This is your opportunity cost.

What has a decrease in the daily amount of time spent working by a typical U.S. resident revealed about the opportunity cost of approximately a quarter hour of time?

YOU ARE THERE

To consider why perceived opportunity costs induce residents of South Korea to work more hours each year than workers in many other countries and, hence, take fewer vacation days, read **The Opportunity Cost of Vacation Time in South Korea** on page 41.

EXAMPLE

The Opportunity Cost of 17 Minutes of Labor in the United States

In the aftermath of the significant economic downturn between 2007 and 2009, the average U.S. resident aged 15 years or older found herself working about 17 fewer minutes per day. The U.S. Labor Department has determined that there were no changes in the amounts of time that the typical resident devoted to engaging in pursuits such as education, volunteering, exercise, or religious activities. Instead, the amount of time per day that the average U.S. resident spent watching TV rose by nearly 12 minutes, and the amount of time she spent sleeping increased by more than

5 minutes. Hence, the implied opportunity cost of the 17 minutes per day that previously had been spent working is the value of passive leisure time that otherwise would have been devoted to TV viewing and sleeping.

FOR CRITICAL THINKING
For someone who could otherwise be working but decides to devote an extra hour per day to obtaining education, what is the opportunity cost of that hour of learning?

The World of Trade-Offs

Whenever you engage in any activity using any resource, even time, you are *trading off* the use of that resource for one or more alternative uses. The extent of the trade-off is represented by the opportunity cost. The opportunity cost of studying economics has already been mentioned—it is the value of the next-best alternative. When you think of *any* alternative, you are thinking of trade-offs.

Let's consider a hypothetical example of a trade-off between the results of spending time studying economics and mathematics. For the sake of this argument, we will assume that additional time studying either economics or mathematics will lead to a higher grade in the subject to which additional study time is allocated. One of the best ways to examine this trade-off is with a graph. (If you would like a refresher on graphical techniques, study Appendix A at the end of Chapter 1 before going on.)

Graphical Analysis

In Figure 2-1 on the facing page, the expected grade in mathematics is measured on the vertical axis of the graph, and the expected grade in economics is measured on the horizontal axis. We simplify the world and assume that you have a maximum of

FIGURE 2-1

Production Possibilities Curve for Grades in Mathematics and Economics (Trade-Offs)

We assume that only 12 hours can be spent per week on studying. If the student is at point *x*, equal time (6 hours a week) is spent on both courses, and equal grades of C will be received. If a higher grade in economics is desired, the student may go to point *y*, thereby receiving a B in economics but a D in mathematics. At point *y*, 3 hours are spent on mathematics and 9 hours on economics.

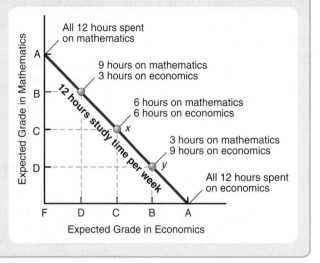

The Production Possibilities Curve (PPC)

The graph in Figure 2-1 above illustrates the relationship between the possible results that can be produced in each of two activities, depending on how much time you choose to devote to each activity. This graph shows a representation of a **production possibilities curve (PPC)**.

Consider that you are producing a grade in economics when you study economics and a grade in mathematics when you study mathematics. Then the line that goes from A on one axis to A on the other axis therefore becomes a production possibilities curve. It is defined as the maximum quantity of one good or service that can be produced, given that a specific quantity of another is produced. It is a curve that shows the possibilities available for increasing the output of one good or service by reducing the amount of another. In the example in Figure 2-1, your time for studying was limited to 12 hours per week. The two possible outputs were your grade in mathematics and your grade in economics. The particular production possibilities curve presented in Figure 2-1 is a graphical representation of the opportunity cost of studying one more hour in one subject. It is a *straight-line production possibilities curve*, which is a special case. (The more general case will be discussed next.)

If you decide to be at point *x* in Figure 2-1, you will devote 6 hours of study time to mathematics and 6 hours to economics. The expected grade in each course will be a C. If you are more interested in getting a B in economics, you will go to point *y* on the production possibilities curve, spending only 3 hours on mathematics but 9 hours on economics. Your expected grade in mathematics will then drop from a C to a D.

Note that these trade-offs between expected grades in mathematics and economics are the result of *holding constant* total study time as well as all other factors that might influence your ability to learn, such as computerized study aids. Quite clearly, if you were able to spend more total time studying, it would be possible to have higher grades in both economics and mathematics. In that case, however, we would no longer be on the specific production possibilities curve illustrated in Figure 2-1. We would have to draw a new curve, farther to the right, to show the greater total study time and a different set of possible trade-offs.

Production possibilities curve (PPC)
A curve representing all possible combinations of maximum outputs that could be produced, assuming a fixed amount of productive resources of a given quality.

12 hours per week to spend studying these two subjects and that if you spend all 12 hours on economics, you will get an A in the course. You will, however, fail mathematics. Conversely, if you spend all of your 12 hours studying mathematics, you will get an A in that subject, but you will flunk economics. Here the trade-off is a special case: one to one. A one-to-one trade-off means that the opportunity cost of receiving one grade higher in economics (for example, improving from a C to a B) is one grade lower in mathematics (falling from a C to a D).

QUICK QUIZ   See page 47 for the answers. Review concepts from this section in MyEconLab.

Scarcity requires us to choose. Whenever we choose, we lose the _____-_____-valued alternative.

Cost is always a forgone _____.

Another way to look at **opportunity cost** is the trade-off that occurs when one activity is undertaken rather than the _____-_____ alternative activity.

A _____ _____ curve graphically shows the trade-off that occurs when more of one output is obtained at the sacrifice of another. This curve is a graphical representation of, among other things, opportunity cost.

The Choices a Nation's Economy Faces

The straight-line production possibilities curve presented in Figure 2-1 on the previous page can be generalized to demonstrate the related concepts of scarcity, choice, and trade-offs that our entire nation faces. As you will see, the production possibilities curve is a simple but powerful economic model because it can demonstrate these related concepts.

A Two-Good Example

The example we will use is the choice between the production of smartphones and tablet devices. We assume for the moment that these are the only two goods that can be produced in the nation.

Panel (a) of Figure 2-2 below gives the various combinations of smartphones and tablet devices, or tablets, that are possible. If all resources are devoted to smartphone production, 50 million per year can be produced. If all resources are devoted to production of tablets, 60 million per year can be produced. In between are various possible combinations.

FIGURE 2-2

The Trade-Off between Smartphones and Tablet Devices

The production of smartphones and tablet devices is measured in millions of units per year. The various combinations are given in panel (a) and plotted in panel (b). Connecting the points *A–G* with a relatively smooth line gives society's production possibilities curve for smartphones and tablets. Point *R* lies outside the production possibilities curve and is therefore unattainable at the point in time for which the graph is drawn. Point *S* lies inside the production possibilities curve and therefore entails unemployed or underemployed resources.

Panel (a)

Combination	Smartphones (millions per year)	Tablets (millions per year)
A	50.0	0
B	48.0	10
C	45.0	20
D	40.0	30
E	33.0	40
F	22.5	50
G	0.0	60

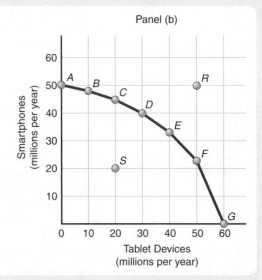

Production Trade-Offs

The nation's production combinations are plotted as points *A, B, C, D, E, F,* and *G* in panel (b) of Figure 2-2 on the previous page. If these points are connected with a smooth curve, the nation's production possibilities curve (PPC) is shown, demonstrating the trade-off between the production of smartphones and tablets. These trade-offs occur *on* the PPC.

Notice the major difference in the shape of the production possibilities curves in Figure 2-1 on page 31 and Figure 2-2. In Figure 2-1, there is a constant trade-off between grades in economics and in mathematics. In Figure 2-2, the trade-off between production of smartphones and tablet production is not constant, and therefore the PPC is a *bowed* curve. To understand why the production possibilities curve is typically bowed outward, you must understand the assumptions underlying the PPC.

How has a trade-off between roads and factories contributed to traffic problems in China?

Go to www.econtoday.com/chap02 for one perspective, offered by the National Center for Policy Analysis, on whether society's production decisions should be publicly or privately coordinated.

INTERNATIONAL EXAMPLE

In China, More Factories Mean Fewer Roads—and More Traffic

Recently, a 62-mile section of highway between the Chinese cities of Beijing and Zhangjiakou became ensnarled in a massive traffic jam that took public safety officers nearly two weeks to break up. Traffic experts agree that this stretch of highway, which covers less than 0.7 square mile of area stretched thinly along the 62 miles, is often overburdened with much more traffic than it was designed to handle.

Most observers agree that this state of affairs has arisen because the people of China have allocated resources away from road construction in favor of building new manufacturing facilities. These facilities,

though, churn out more products to be shipped by trucks that clog roads. Thus, in China the choice to build more factories to produce goods has entailed an opportunity cost: fewer roads for transporting those goods.

FOR CRITICAL THINKING

What is an example of an opportunity cost that a trucker may have incurred by spending a full day traversing the traffic jam between Beijing and Zhangjiakou?

Assumptions Underlying the Production Possibilities Curve

When we draw the curve that is shown in Figure 2-2, we make the following assumptions:

1. Resources are fully employed.

2. Production takes place over a specific time period—for example, one year.

3. The resource inputs, in both quantity and quality, used to produce smartphones or tablets are fixed over this time period.

4. Technology does not change over this time period.

Technology is defined as the total pool of applied knowledge concerning how goods and services can be produced by managers, workers, engineers, scientists, and artisans, using land, physical and human capital, and entrepreneurship. You can think of technology as the formula or recipe used to combine factors of production. (When better formulas are developed, more production can be obtained from the same amount of resources.) The level of technology sets the limit on the amount and types of goods and services that we can derive from any given amount of resources. The production possibilities curve is drawn under the assumption that we use the best technology that we currently have available and that this technology doesn't change over the time period under study.

Technology
The total pool of applied knowledge concerning how goods and services can be produced.

Being off the Production Possibilities Curve

Look again at panel (b) of Figure 2-2 on page 32. Point *R* lies *outside* the production possibilities curve and is *impossible* to achieve during the time period assumed. By definition, the PPC indicates the *maximum* quantity of one good, given the quantity produced of the other good.

It is possible, however, to be at point *S* in Figure 2-2. That point lies beneath the PPC. If the nation is at point *S*, it means that its resources are not being fully utilized. This occurs, for example, during periods of relatively high unemployment. Point *S* and all such points inside the PPC are always attainable but imply unemployed or underemployed resources.

Efficiency

The production possibilities curve can be used to define the notion of efficiency. Whenever the economy is operating on the PPC, at points such as *A*, *B*, *C*, or *D*, we say that its production is efficient. Points such as *S* in Figure 2-2, which lie beneath the PPC, are said to represent production situations that are not efficient.

Efficiency can mean many things to many people. Even in economics, there are different types of efficiency. Here we are discussing *productive efficiency*. An economy is productively efficient whenever it is producing the maximum output with given technology and resources.

A simple commonsense definition of efficiency is getting the most out of what we have. Clearly, we are not getting the most out of what we have if we are at point *S* in panel (b) of Figure 2-2. We can move from point *S* to, say, point *C*, thereby increasing the total quantity of smartphones produced without any decrease in the total quantity of tablets produced. Alternatively, we can move from point *S* to point *E*, for example, and have both more smartphones and more tablets. Point *S* is called an **inefficient point,** which is defined as any point below the production possibilities curve.

Efficiency
The case in which a given level of inputs is used to produce the maximum output possible. Alternatively, the situation in which a given output is produced at minimum cost.

Inefficient point
Any point below the production possibilities curve, at which the use of resources is not generating the maximum possible output.

The Law of Increasing Additional Cost

In the example in Figure 2-1 on page 31, the trade-off between a grade in mathematics and a grade in economics was one to one. The trade-off ratio was constant. That is, the production possibilities curve was a straight line. The curve in Figure 2-2 is a more general case. We have re-created the curve in Figure 2-2 as Figure 2-3 on the facing page. Each combination, *A* through *G*, of smartphones and tablets is represented on the PPC. Starting with the production of zero tablets, the nation can produce 50 million smartphones with its available resources and technology.

INCREASING ADDITIONAL COSTS When we increase production of tablet devices from zero to 10 million per year, the nation has to give up in smartphones an amount shown by that first vertical arrow, *Aa*. From panel (a) of Figure 2-2, you can see that this is 2 million per year (50 million minus 48 million). Again, if we increase production of tablets by another 10 million units per year, we go from *B* to *C*. In order to do so, the nation has to give up the vertical distance *Bb*, or 3 million smartphones per year. By the time we go from 50 million to 60 million tablets, to obtain that 10 million increase, we have to forgo the vertical distance *Ff*, or 22.5 million smartphones.

FIGURE 2-3

The Law of Increasing Additional Cost

Consider equal increments of production of tablets, as measured on the horizontal axis. All of the horizontal arrows—*aB, bC,* and so on—are of equal length (10 million). In contrast, the length of each vertical arrow—*Aa, Bb,* and so on—increases as we move down the production possibilities curve. Hence, the opportunity cost of going from 50 million tablets per year to 60 million (*Ff*) is much greater than going from zero units to 10 million (*Aa*). The opportunity cost of each additional equal increase in production of tablets rises.

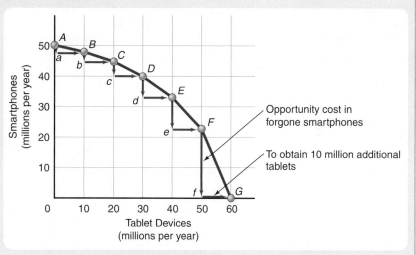

In other words, we see that the opportunity cost of the last 10 million tablets has increased to 22.5 million smartphones, compared to 2 million smartphones for the same increase in tablets when we started with none at all being produced.

What we are observing is called the **law of increasing additional cost.** When people take more resources and applies them to the production of any specific good, the opportunity cost increases for each additional unit produced.

EXPLAINING THE LAW OF INCREASING ADDITIONAL COST The reason that as a nation we face the law of increasing additional cost (shown as a production possibilities curve that is bowed outward) is that certain resources are better suited for producing some goods than they are for other goods. Generally, resources are not *perfectly* adaptable for alternative uses. When increasing the output of a particular good, producers must use less suitable resources than those already used in order to produce the additional output. Hence, the cost of producing the additional units increases.

With respect to our hypothetical example here, at first the computing specialists at smartphone firms would shift over to producing tablet devices. After a while, though, the workers who normally design and produce smartphones would be asked to help design and manufacture tablet components. Typically, they would be less effective at making tablets than the people who previously specialized in this task.

In general, *the more specialized the resources, the more bowed the production possibilities curve.* At the other extreme, if all resources are equally suitable for smartphone production or production of tablets, the curves in Figures 2-2 (p. 32) and 2-3 above would approach the straight line shown in our first example in Figure 2-1 on page 31.

Law of increasing additional cost
The fact that the opportunity cost of additional units of a good generally increases as people attempt to produce more of that good. This accounts for the bowed-out shape of the production possibilities curve.

QUICK QUIZ See page 47 for the answers. Review concepts from this section in MyEconLab.

Trade-offs are represented graphically by a _____ _____ curve showing the maximum quantity of one good or service that can be produced, given a specific quantity of another, from a given set of resources over a specified period of time—for example, one year.

A **production possibilities curve** is drawn holding the quantity and quality of all resources _____ over the time period under study.

Points _____ the **production possibilities curve** are unattainable. Points _____ are attainable but represent an inefficient use or underuse of available resources.

Because many resources are better suited for certain productive tasks than for others, the production possibilities curve is bowed _____, reflecting the **law of increasing additional cost.**

FIGURE 2-4

FIGURE 2-4

Economic Growth Allows for More of Everything

If the nation experiences economic growth, the production possibilities curve between smartphones and tablets will move out as shown. This output increase takes time, however, and it does not occur automatically. This means, therefore, that we can have more of both smartphones and tablets only after a period of time during which we have experienced economic growth.

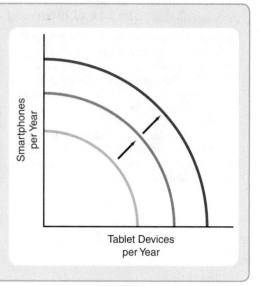

Economic Growth and the Production Possibilities Curve

At any particular point in time, a society cannot be outside the production possibilities curve. *Over time*, however, it is possible to have more of everything. This occurs through economic growth. (An important reason for economic growth, capital accumulation, is discussed next. A more complete discussion of why economic growth occurs appears in Chapter 9.) Figure 2-4 above shows the production possibilities curve for smartphones and tablet devices shifting outward. The two additional curves shown represent new choices open to an economy that has experienced economic growth. Such economic growth occurs for many reasons, including increases in the number of workers and productive investment in equipment.

Scarcity still exists, however, no matter how much economic growth there is. At any point in time, we will always be on some production possibilities curve. Thus, we will always face trade-offs. The more we have of one thing, the less we can have of others.

If economic growth occurs in the nation, the production possibilities curve between smartphones and tablets moves outward, as shown in Figure 2-4. This takes time and does not occur automatically. One reason it will occur involves the choice about how much to consume today.

The Trade-Off between the Present and the Future

Consumption
The use of goods and services for personal satisfaction.

The production possibilities curve and economic growth can be combined to examine the trade-off between present **consumption** and future consumption. When we consume today, we are using up what we call consumption or consumer goods—food and clothes, for example.

Why We Make Capital Goods

Why would we be willing to use productive resources to make things—capital goods—that we cannot consume directly? The reason is that capital goods enable us to produce larger quantities of consumer goods or to produce them less expensively than we otherwise could. Before fish are "produced" for the market, equipment such as fishing boats, nets, and poles is produced first. Imagine how expensive it would be to obtain fish for market without using these capital goods. Catching fish with one's hands is not an easy task. The cost per fish would be very high if capital goods weren't used.

Forgoing Current Consumption

Whenever we use productive resources to make capital goods, we are implicitly forgoing current consumption. We are waiting for some time in the future to consume the rewards that will be reaped from the use of capital goods. In effect, when we forgo current consumption to invest in capital goods, we are engaging in an economic activity that is forward-looking—we do not get instant utility or satisfaction from our activity.

The Trade-Off between Consumption Goods and Capital Goods

To have more consumer goods in the future, we must accept fewer consumer goods today, because resources must be used in producing capital goods instead of consumer goods. In other words, an opportunity cost is involved. Every time we make a choice of more goods today, we incur an opportunity cost of fewer goods tomorrow, and every time we make a choice of more goods in the future, we incur an opportunity cost of fewer goods today. With the resources that we don't use to produce consumer goods for today, we invest in capital goods that will produce more consumer goods for us later. The trade-off is shown in Figure 2-5 below. On the left in panel (a), you can see this trade-off depicted as a production possibilities curve between capital goods and consumption goods.

Assume that we are willing to give up $1 trillion worth of consumption today. We will be at point *A* in the left-hand diagram of panel (a). This will allow the economy to grow. We will have more future consumption because we invested in more capital goods today. In the right-hand diagram of panel (a), we see two consumer goods represented, food and entertainment. The production possibilities

---

FIGURE 2-5

Capital Goods and Growth

In panel (a), people choose not to consume $1 trillion, so they invest that amount in capital goods. As a result, more of all goods may be produced in the future, as shown in the right-hand diagram in panel (a). In panel (b), people choose even more capital goods (point *C*). The result is that the production possibilities curve (PPC) moves even more to the right on the right-hand diagram in panel (b).

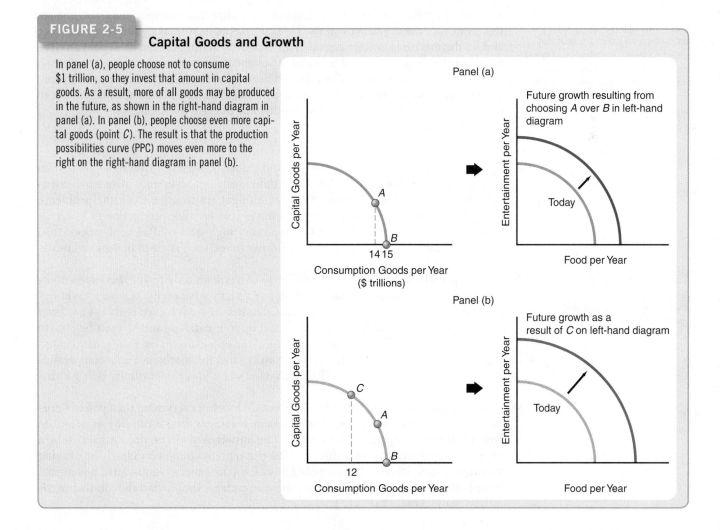

curve will move outward if individuals in the economy decide to restrict consumption now and invest in capital goods.

In panel (b) in Figure 2-5 on the previous page, we show the results of our willingness to forgo even more current consumption. We move from point *A* to point *C* in the left-hand side, where we have many fewer consumer goods today but produce many more capital goods. This leads to more future growth in this simplified model, and thus the production possibilities curve in the right-hand side of panel (b) shifts outward more than it did in the right-hand side of panel (a). In other words, the more we give up today, the more we can have tomorrow, provided, of course, that the capital goods are productive in future periods.

QUICK QUIZ See page 47 for the answers. Review concepts from this section in MyEconLab.

_____ goods are goods that will later be used to produce consumer goods.

A trade-off is involved between current consumption and capital goods or, alternatively, between current consumption and future consumption. The _____ we invest in capital goods today, the greater the amount of consumer goods we can produce in the future and the _____ the amount of consumer goods we can produce today.

Specialization and Greater Productivity

Specialization
The organization of economic activity so that what each person (or region) consumes is not identical to what that person (or region) produces. An individual may specialize, for example, in law or medicine. A nation may specialize in the production of coffee, e-book readers, or digital cameras.

Specialization involves working at a relatively well-defined, limited endeavor, such as accounting or teaching. Most individuals do specialize. For example, you could change the oil in your car if you wanted to. Typically, though, you take your car to a garage and let the mechanic change the oil. You benefit by letting the garage mechanic specialize in changing the oil and in doing other repairs on your car.

The specialist normally will get the job finished sooner than you could and has the proper equipment to make the job go more smoothly. Specialization usually leads to greater productivity, not only for each individual but also for the nation.

Comparative Advantage

Specialization occurs because different individuals experience different costs when they engage in the same activities. Some individuals can accurately solve mathematical problems at lower cost than others who might try to solve the same problems. Thus, those who solve math problems at lower cost sacrifice production of fewer alternative items. Some people can develop more high-quality iPad applications than others while giving up less production of other items, such as clean houses and neatly manicured yards.

Comparative advantage
The ability to produce a good or service at a lower opportunity cost compared to other producers.

Comparative advantage is the ability to perform an activity *at a lower opportunity cost*. You have a comparative advantage in one activity whenever you have a lower opportunity cost of performing that activity. Comparative advantage is always a *relative* concept. You may be able to change the oil in your car. You might even be able to change it faster than the local mechanic. But if the opportunity cost you face by changing the oil exceeds the mechanic's opportunity cost, the mechanic has a comparative advantage in changing the oil. The mechanic faces a lower opportunity cost for that activity.

You may be convinced that everybody can do more of everything than you can during the same period of time and using the same resources. In this extreme situation, do you still have a comparative advantage? The answer is yes. You do not have to be a mathematical genius to figure this out. The market tells you so very clearly by offering you the highest income for the job for which you have a comparative advantage. Stated differently, to find your comparative advantage, simply find the job that maximizes your income.

When contemplating how to keep track of balances remaining on gift cards, some people find that doing their own tabulations entails a higher opportunity cost than others face. How has this increased opportunity cost given entrepreneurs an occasion to profit from providing gift-card tracking services?

EXAMPLE

A Comparative Advantage in Watching Gift-Card Balances

Each year, consumers juggle a total of $100 billion in balances on gift cards. Keeping track of these funds and making certain all funds are spent can require considerable time.

Increasingly, people are deciding that taking the time to keep tabs on their gift-card balances is a next-best alternative. These individuals pay others to make sure they are spending all available funds. For instance, a firm called Tango Card uses software to track gift-card balances and provide periodic reports to consumers. The company also sends e-mails warning consumers when unused cards are about to expire before all funds have been spent. The fact that owners of Tango Card have a comparative advantage in keeping tabs on gift-card balances enables its customers to devote extra time to other activities, such as earning additional income.

FOR CRITICAL THINKING

What is the comparative advantage of customers of Tango Cards who devote time to earning income instead of tracking their card balances?

Absolute Advantage

Suppose that you are the president of a firm and are convinced that you have the ability to do every job in that company faster than everyone else who works there. You might be able to enter data into a spreadsheet program faster than any of the other employees, file documents in order in a file cabinet faster than any of the file clerks, and wash windows faster than any of the window washers. Furthermore, you are able to manage the firm in less time more effectively than any other individual in the company.

If all of these self-perceptions were really true, then you would have an **absolute advantage** in all of these endeavors. In other words, if you were to spend a given amount of time in any one of them, you could produce more than anyone else in the company. Nonetheless, you would not spend your time doing these other activities. Why not? Because your time advantage in undertaking the president's managerial duties is even greater. Therefore, you would find yourself specializing in that particular task even though you have an *absolute* advantage in all these other tasks. Indeed, absolute advantage is irrelevant in predicting how you will allocate your time. Only *comparative advantage* matters in determining how you will allocate your time, because it is the relative cost that is important in making this choice.

The coaches of sports teams often have to determine the comparative advantage of an individual player who has an absolute advantage in every aspect of the sport in question. Babe Ruth, who could hit more home runs and pitch more strikeouts per game than other players on the Boston Red Sox, was a pitcher on that professional baseball team. After he was traded to the New York Yankees, the owner and the manager decided to make him an outfielder, even though he could also pitch more strikeouts per game than other Yankees. They wanted "The Babe" to concentrate on his hitting because a home-run king would bring in more paying fans than a good pitcher would. Babe Ruth had an absolute advantage in both aspects of the game of baseball, but his comparative advantage was clearly in hitting homers rather than in practicing and developing his pitching game.

Absolute advantage
The ability to produce more units of a good or service using a given quantity of labor or resource inputs. Equivalently, the ability to produce the same quantity of a good or service using fewer units of labor or resource inputs.

Scarcity, Self-Interest, and Specialization

In Chapter 1, you learned about the assumption of rational self-interest. To repeat, for the purposes of our analyses we assume that individuals are rational in that they will do what is in their own self-interest. They will not consciously carry out actions that will make them worse off. In this chapter, you learned that scarcity requires people to make choices. We *assume* that they make choices based on their self-interest. When people make choices, they attempt to maximize benefits net of opportunity cost. In so doing, individuals choose their comparative advantage and end up specializing.

The Division of Labor

In any firm that includes specialized human and nonhuman resources, there is a **division of labor** among those resources. The best-known example comes from Adam Smith (1723–1790), who in *The Wealth of Nations* illustrated the benefits of a division of labor in the making of pins, as depicted in the following example:

> One man draws out the wire, another straightens it, a third cuts it, a fourth points it, a fifth grinds it at the top for receiving the head; to make the head requires two or three distinct operations; to put it on is a peculiar business, to whiten the pins is another; it is even a trade by itself to put them into the paper.

Making pins this way allowed 10 workers without very much skill to make almost 48,000 pins "of a middling size" in a day. One worker, toiling alone, could have made perhaps 20 pins a day. Therefore, 10 workers could have produced 200. Division of labor allowed for an increase in the daily output of the pin factory from 200 to 48,000! (Smith did not attribute all of the gain to the division of labor but credited also the use of machinery and the fact that less time was spent shifting from task to task.)

What we are discussing here involves a division of the resource called labor into different uses of labor. The different uses of labor are organized in such a way as to increase the amount of output possible from the fixed resources available. We can therefore talk about an organized division of labor within a firm leading to increased output.

Division of labor
The segregation of resources into different specific tasks. For instance, one automobile worker puts on bumpers, another doors, and so on.

Comparative Advantage and Trade among Nations

Most of our analysis of absolute advantage, comparative advantage, and specialization has dealt with individuals. Nevertheless, it is equally applicable to groups of people.

Trade among Regions

Consider the United States. The Plains states have a comparative advantage in the production of grains and other agricultural goods. Relative to the Plains states, the states to the east tend to specialize in industrialized production, such as automobiles. Not surprisingly, grains are shipped from the Plains states to the eastern states, and automobiles are shipped in the reverse direction. Such specialization and trade allow for higher incomes and standards of living.

If both the Plains states and the eastern states were separate nations, the same analysis would still hold, but we would call it international trade. Indeed, the European Union (EU) is comparable to the United States in area and population, but instead of one nation, the EU has 27. What U.S. residents call *interstate* trade, Europeans call *international* trade. There is no difference, however, in the economic results—both yield greater economic efficiency and higher average incomes.

International Aspects of Trade

Political problems that normally do not occur within a particular nation often arise between nations. For example, if California avocado growers develop a cheaper method of producing avocados than growers in southern Florida use, the Florida growers will lose out. They cannot do much about the situation except try to lower their own costs of production or improve their product.

If avocado growers in Mexico, however, develop a cheaper method of producing avocados, both California and Florida growers can (and likely will) try to raise political barriers that will prevent Mexican avocado growers from freely selling their product in the United States. U.S. avocado growers will use such arguments as "unfair" competition and loss of U.S. jobs. Certainly, avocado-growing jobs may decline in the United States, but there is no reason to believe that U.S. jobs will decline overall. Instead, former U.S. avocado workers will move into alternative employment—something that 1 million people do every *week* in the United States. If the argument of U.S. avocado growers had any validity, every time a region in the United States developed a better way to produce a product manufactured somewhere else in the country, U.S. employment would decline. That has never happened and never will.

When nations specialize in an area of comparative advantage and then trade with the rest of the world, the average standard of living in the world rises. In effect, international trade allows the world to move from inside the global production possibilities curve toward the curve itself, thereby improving worldwide economic efficiency. Thus, all countries that engage in trade can benefit from comparative advantage, just as regions in the United States benefit from interregional trade.

Go to www.econtoday.com/chap02 to find out from the World Trade Organization how much international trade takes place. Under "Resources," click on "Trade statistics" and then click on "International Trade Statistics" for the most recent year.

QUICK QUIZ See page 47 for the answers. Review concepts from this section in MyEconLab.

With a given set of resources, specialization results in _____ output. In other words, there are gains to specialization in terms of greater material well-being.

Individuals and nations specialize in their areas of _____ advantage in order to reap the gains of specialization.

Comparative advantages are found by determining which activities have the _____ opportunity costs—that is,

which activities yield the highest return for the time and resources used.

A _____ of labor occurs when different workers are assigned different tasks. Together, the workers produce a desired product.

YOU ARE THERE
The Opportunity Cost of Vacation Time in South Korea

Lee Charm recently became head of the South Korean government's Korea Tourism Organization (KTO), which develops and promotes vacation tours for South Koreans. Shortly after assuming this position, Charm discovered that the agency's 550 employees were allocating only about five days to vacations each year, one fewer than for the average Korean.

Charm was rebuffed when he tried to convince KTO employees to take more vacation days each year voluntarily. A key reason for the unwillingness of KTO's employees to take off additional days for vacations was that KTO, like other government agencies and private firms in South Korea, rewards both workers and managers with extra pay for unused vacation days. Thus, if KTO employees had expanded their number of vacation days, they would have forgone income that could be

allocated to other purposes. They viewed the opportunity cost of any additional time spent on vacations as too high to justify taking more time off.

Critical Thinking Questions

1. Why do you suppose KTO employees were displeased when Charm required them to take more vacation days each year to "set a good example" for other workers?

2. During his first year as KTO's manager, what did Charm himself gain from taking one less day off than the average KTO employee's five vacation days?

ISSUES & APPLICATIONS

The Rising Opportunity Cost of Airlines' "Block Times"

CONCEPTS APPLIED

▶ Scarcity

▶ Opportunity Cost

▶ Trade-Offs

Average published durations of airline flights increased by about ten minutes between the late 1990s and early 2010s. Time is scarce for everyone, including air travelers, who are experiencing increases in opportunity costs equal to the values of alternative uses for which they could spend these extra minutes now allocated to air travel.

Why Published Flight Times Are Longer Than They Used to Be

For about fifteen years, airlines lengthened their *block times*—intervals of time for flight schedules. Block times include the sum of estimated times required to taxi out onto the runway, to travel in the air, to taxi to the destination terminal, and to pull into a gate. In addition, block times typically include a *buffer*, which is a period that can range from just a few minutes to more than an hour.

Airlines have long built buffer minutes into block times for flights, to allow for contrary winds and other weather-related factors that can lengthen time in the air. Figure 2-6 below displays buffer periods for a number of airlines' flights on a recent day and shows that airlines tend to set longer buffers for flights of greater duration.

Fewer than two of the ten extra minutes that airlines for a time added to the average per-flight block time reflected increased time spent taxiing at airports. What accounted for the additional eight minutes? Airlines lengthened buf-

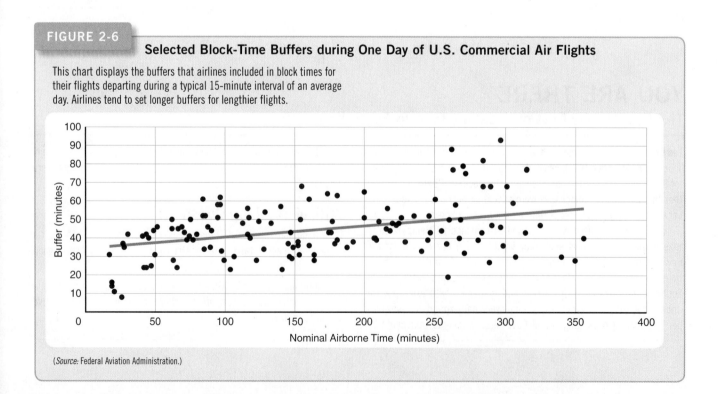

FIGURE 2-6

Selected Block-Time Buffers during One Day of U.S. Commercial Air Flights

This chart displays the buffers that airlines included in block times for their flights departing during a typical 15-minute interval of an average day. Airlines tend to set longer buffers for lengthier flights.

(*Source:* Federal Aviation Administration.)

fers to ensure that many flights that previously would have been marked a few minutes late instead would be listed as "on time." Being classified as consistently "on time" has considerable value to an airline company, because it helps the company sell more tickets.

A Higher Opportunity Cost of Air Travel Time

Traveling by air entails incurring both explicit and implicit costs. The explicit cost is the price of the plane ticket. A key implicit-cost component is the time that a person spends at and between airports instead of being able to allocate the time to the next-highest-valued activity—that is, the opportunity cost of the time.

For everyone who flies, the terms of the trade-off associated with flying worsened slightly between the late 1990s and early 2010s. Consider each individual who otherwise could have been earning the average U.S. hourly wage, for whom ten extra minutes devoted to a flight translates into approximately $3 of lost wages. Suppose that we use this figure to place a dollar value on each passenger's opportunity cost, and consider a "slow day" in which only 500,000 U.S. residents otherwise could have been earning hourly wages fly on airliners. Under these assumptions, the extra ten minutes of block time per passenger yielded an estimated additional $1.5 million total *daily* opportunity cost.

For Critical Thinking

1. Why might it prove difficult to measure the aggregate additional opportunity cost of ten extra minutes of airlines' block time across *all* individuals? (Hint: Not everyone works.)
2. Why did the extra ten minutes of block time constitute an opportunity cost even for an airline passenger who were on vacation from a job that pays hourly wages?

Web Resources

1. Learn about block time and other economic issues that airlines face in scheduling flights at www.econtoday.com /chap02.
2. To contemplate how adding block time can potentially boost airlines' own explicit labor costs, go to www .econtoday.com/chap02.

MyEconLab
For more questions on this chapter's Issues & Applications, go to MyEconLab. In the Study Plan for this chapter, select Section N: News.

MyEconLab

Here is what you should know after reading this chapter. MyEconLab will help you identify what you know, and where to go when you need to practice.

WHAT YOU SHOULD KNOW

The Problem of Scarcity, Even for the Affluent Even the richest people face scarcity because they have to make choices among alternatives. Despite their high levels of income or wealth, affluent people, like everyone else, want more than they can have (in terms of goods, power, prestige, and so on).

scarcity, 27
production, 27
land, 27
labor, 27
physical capital, 28
human capital, 28
entrepreneurship, 28
goods, 28
economic goods, 28
services, 28

WHERE TO GO TO PRACTICE

• MyEconLab Study Plan 2.1

Why Economists Consider Individuals' Wants but Not Their "Needs" Goods are all things from which individuals derive satisfaction. Economic goods are those for which the desired quantity exceeds the amount that is available at a zero price. The term *need* is undefinable, whereas humans have unlimited *wants*, which are the items on which we place a positive value.

• MyEconLab Study Plan 2.2

MyEconLab *continued*

WHAT YOU SHOULD KNOW — WHERE TO GO TO PRACTICE —

Why Scarcity Leads People to Evaluate Opportunity Costs Opportunity cost is the highest-valued alternative that one must give up to obtain an item. The trade-offs people face can be represented by a production possibilities curve (PPC). Moving along a PPC from one point to another entails incurring an opportunity cost of allocating scarce resources toward the production of one good instead of another good.

opportunity cost, 30
production possibilities curve (PPC), 31

Key Figure
Figure 2-1, 31

- MyEconLab Study Plans 2.3, 2.4

Why Obtaining Increasing Increments of a Good Requires Giving Up More and More Units of Other Goods When people allocate additional resources to producing more units of a good, it must increasingly employ resources that would be better suited for producing other goods. As a result, the law of increasing additional cost holds. Each additional unit of a good can be obtained only by giving up more and more of other goods. Hence, the production possibilities curve is bowed outward.

technology, 33
efficiency, 34
inefficient point, 34
law of increasing additional cost, 35

Key Figures
Figure 2-3, 35
Figure 2-4, 36

- MyEconLab Study Plan 2.5
- Animated Figures 2-3, 2-4

The Trade-Off between Consumption Goods and Capital Goods If we allocate more resources to producing capital goods today, then the production possibilities curve will shift outward by more in the future, which means that we can have additional future consumption goods. The trade-off is that producing more capital goods today entails giving up consumption goods today.

consumption, 36

- MyEconLab Study Plans 2.6, 2.7

Absolute Advantage versus Comparative Advantage A person has an absolute advantage if she can produce more of a good than someone else who uses the same amount of resources. An individual can gain from specializing in producing a good if she has a comparative advantage in producing that good, meaning that she can produce the good at a lower opportunity cost than someone else.

specialization, 38
comparative advantage, 38
absolute advantage, 39
division of labor, 40

- MyEconLab Study Plans 2.8, 2.9

Log in to MyEconLab, take a chapter test, and get a personalized Study Plan that tells you which concepts you understand and which ones you need to review. From there, MyEconLab will give you further practice, tutorials, animations, videos, and guided solutions. For more information, visit www.myeconlab.com

PROBLEMS

All problems are assignable in MyEconLab. *Answers to odd-numbered problems appear at the back of the book.*

2-1. Define opportunity cost. What is your opportunity cost of attending a class at 11:00 a.m.? How does it differ from your opportunity cost of attending a class at 8:00 a.m.? (See page 30.)

2-2. If you receive a ticket to a concert at no charge, what, if anything, is your opportunity cost of attending the concert? How does your opportunity cost change if miserable weather on the night of the concert requires you to leave much earlier for the concert hall and greatly extends the time it takes to get home afterward? (See page 30.)

2-3. You and a friend decide to spend $100 each on concert tickets. Each of you alternatively could have spent the $100 to purchase a textbook, a meal at a highly rated local restaurant, or several Internet movie downloads. As you are on the way to the concert, your friend tells you that if she had not bought the concert ticket, she would have opted for a restaurant meal, and you reply that you otherwise would have downloaded several movies. Identify the relevant opportunity costs for you and your friend of the concert tickets that you purchased. Explain briefly. (See page 30.)

2-4. After the concert discussed in Problem 2-3 is over and you and your friend are traveling home, you discuss how each of you might otherwise have used the four hours devoted to attending the concert. The four hours could have been used to study, to watch a sporting event on TV, or to get some extra sleep. Your friend decides that if she had not spent four hours attending the concert, she would have chosen to study, and you reply that you otherwise would have watched the televised sporting event. Identify the relevant opportunity costs for you and your friend for allocating your four hours to attending the concert. Explain briefly. (See page 30.)

2-5. Recently, a woman named Mary Krawiec attended an auction in Troy, New York. At the auction, a bank was seeking to sell a foreclosed property: a large Victorian house suffering from years of neglect in a neighborhood in which many properties had been on the market for years yet remained unsold. Her $10 offer was the highest bid in the auction, and she handed over a $10 bill for a title to ownership. Once she acquired the house, however, she became responsible for all taxes on the property and for an overdue water bill of $2,000. In addition, to make the house habitable, she and her husband devoted months of time and unpaid

labor to renovating the property. In the process, they incurred explicit expenses totaling $65,000. Why do you suppose that the bank was willing to sell the house to Ms. Krawiec for only $10? (Hint: Contemplate the bank's expected gain, net of all explicit and opportunity costs, if it had attempted to make the house habitable. See page 30.)

2-6. The following table illustrates the points a student can earn on examinations in economics and biology if the student uses all available hours for study.

Economics	Biology
100	40
90	50
80	60
70	70
60	80
50	90
40	100

Plot this student's production possibilities curve. Does the PPC illustrate the law of increasing additional cost? (See page 31.)

2-7. Based on the information provided in Problem 2-6, what is the opportunity cost to this student of allocating enough additional study time on economics to move her grade up from a 90 to a 100?

2-8. Consider a change in the table in Problem 2-6. The student's set of opportunities is now as follows:

Economics	Biology
100	40
90	60
80	75
70	85
60	93
50	98
40	100

Does the PPC illustrate the law of increasing additional cost? What is the opportunity cost to this student for the additional amount of study time on economics required to move her grade from 60 to 70? From 90 to 100? (See page 35.)

2-9. Construct a production possibilities curve for a nation facing increasing opportunity costs for producing food and video games. Show how the PPC changes given the following events. (See page 37.)

a. A new and better fertilizer is invented.

b. Immigration occurs, and immigrants' labor can be employed in both the agricultural sector and the video game sector.

c. People invent a new programming language that is much less costly to code and is more memory-efficient.

d. A heat wave and drought result in a 10 percent decrease in usable farmland.

Consider the following diagram when answering Problems 2-10, 2-11, and 2-12.

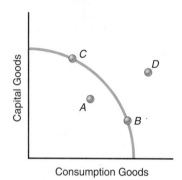

2-10. During a debate on the floor of the U.S. Senate, Senator Creighton states, "Our nation should not devote so many of its fully employed resources to producing capital goods because we already are not producing enough consumption goods for our citizens." Compared with the other labeled points on the diagram, which one could be consistent with the *current* production combination choice that Senator Creighton believes the nation has made? (See page 34.)

2-11. In response to Senator Creighton's statement reported in Problem 2-10, Senator Long replies, "We must remain at our current production combination if we want to be able to produce more consumption goods in the future." Of the labeled points on the diagram, which one could depict the *future* production combination Senator Long has in mind? (See page 34.)

2-12. Senator Borman interjects the following comment after the statements by Senators Creighton and Long reported in Problems 2-10 and 2-11: "In fact, both of my esteemed colleagues are wrong, because an unacceptably large portion of our nation's resources is currently unemployed." Of the labeled points on the diagram, which one is consistent with Senator Borman's position? (See page 34.)

2-13. A nation's residents can allocate their scarce resources either to producing consumption goods or to producing human capital—that is, providing themselves with training and education. (See page 35.) The table at the top of next column displays the production possibilities for this nation:

Production Combination	Units of Consumption Goods	Units of Human Capital
A	0	100
B	10	97
C	20	90
D	30	75
E	40	55
F	50	30
G	60	0

a. Suppose that the nation's residents currently produce combination A. What is the opportunity cost of increasing production of consumption goods by 10 units? By 60 units?

b. Does the law of increasing additional cost hold true for this nation? Why or why not?

2-14. Like physical capital, human capital produced in the present can be applied to the production of future goods and services. Consider the table in Problem 2-13, and suppose that the nation's residents are trying to choose between combination C and combination F. Other things being equal, will the future production possibilities curve for this nation be located farther outward if the nation chooses combination F instead of combination C? Explain. (See page 35.)

2-15. You can wash, fold, and iron a basket of laundry in two hours and prepare a meal in one hour. Your roommate can wash, fold, and iron a basket of laundry in three hours and prepare a meal in one hour. Who has the absolute advantage in laundry, and who has an absolute advantage in meal preparation? Who has the comparative advantage in laundry, and who has a comparative advantage in meal preparation? (See page 38.)

2-16. Based on the information in Problem 2-15, should you and your roommate specialize in a particular task? Why? And if so, who should specialize in which task? Show how much labor time you save if you choose to "trade" an appropriate task with your roommate as opposed to doing it yourself. (See page 38.)

2-17. Using only the concept of comparative advantage, evaluate this statement: "A professor with a Ph.D. in physics should never mow his or her own lawn, because this would fail to take into account the professor's comparative advantage." (See page 38.)

2-18. Country A and country B produce the same consumption goods and capital goods and currently have *identical* production possibilities curves. They also have the same resources at present, and they have access to the same technology. (See page 38.)

a. At present, does either country have a comparative advantage in producing capital goods? Consumption goods?

b. Currently, country A has chosen to produce more consumption goods, compared with country B. Other things being equal, which country will experience the larger outward shift of its PPC during the next year?

ECONOMICS ON THE NET

Opportunity Cost and Labor Force Participation Many students choose to forgo full-time employment to concentrate on their studies, thereby incurring a sizable opportunity cost. This application explores the nature of this opportunity cost.

Title: College Enrollment and Work Activity of High School Graduates

Navigation: Go to www.econtoday.com/chap02 to visit the Bureau of Labor Statistics (BLS) home page. Select A–Z Index and then click on *Educational attainment (Statistics)*. Under "School Enrollment," click on *Recent High School Graduates and Labor Force Participation*.

Application Read the abbreviated report on college enrollment and work activity of high school graduates. Then answer the following questions.

1. Based on the article, explain who the BLS considers to be in the labor force and who it does not view as part of the labor force.

2. What is the difference in labor force participation rates between high school students entering four-year universities and those entering two-year universities? Using the concept of opportunity cost, explain the difference.

3. What is the difference in labor force participation rates between part-time college students and full-time college students? Using the concept of opportunity cost, explain the difference.

For Group Study and Analysis Read the last paragraph of the article. Then divide the class into two groups. The first group should explain, based on the concept of opportunity cost, the difference in labor force participation rates between youths not in school but with a high school diploma and youths not in school and without a high school diploma. The second group should explain, based on opportunity cost, the difference in labor force participation rates between men and women not in school but with a high school diploma and men and women not in school and without a high school diploma.

ANSWERS TO QUICK QUIZZES

p. 29: (i) Scarcity; (ii) land . . . labor . . . physical . . . human . . . entrepreneurship; (iii) Wants; (iv) need

p. 32: (i) next-highest; (ii) opportunity; (iii) next-best; (iv) production possibilities

p. 35: (i) production possibilities; (ii) fixed; (iii) outside . . . inside; (iv) outward

p. 38: (i) Capital; (ii) more . . . smaller

p. 41: (i) higher; (ii) comparative; (iii) lowest; (iv) division

3

Demand and Supply

At the time that your parents might have attended college, average tuition and fees were more than 90 percent lower than their current levels. In addition, the prices of textbooks and supplies were more than 80 percent lower than current prices. For example, in comparison with a college student who pays $20,000 in annual tuition and fees today, a student in the 1980s would have paid not much over $1,600 in inflation-adjusted dollars. Compared with a student who spends $1,000 per year for textbooks and other supplies, a student in the 1980s would have spent about $110 in inflation-adjusted dollars. Why have these prices risen so much? In this chapter, you will learn the answer.

? DID YOU KNOW THAT...

after truck freight-hauling prices jumped substantially in the early 2010s, rail shipments of freight containers rose by more than 10 percent? Higher truck-transportation prices induced many companies to substitute away from having their products moved by trucks in favor of rail transportation.

If we use the economist's primary set of tools, *demand* and *supply*, we can develop a better understanding of why we sometimes observe relatively large increases in the purchase, or consumption, of items such as rail freight services. We can also better understand why a persistent increase in the price of an item such as truck-hauling services ultimately induces an increase in consumption of rail freight services. Demand and supply are two ways of categorizing the influences on the prices of goods that you buy and the quantities available. Indeed, demand and supply characterize much economic analysis of the world around us.

As you will see throughout this text, the operation of the forces of demand and supply takes place in *markets*. A **market** is an abstract concept summarizing all of the arrangements individuals have for exchanging with one another. Goods and services are sold in markets, such as the automobile market, the health care market, and the market for high-speed Internet access. Workers offer their services in the labor market. Companies, or firms, buy workers' labor services in the labor market. Firms also buy other inputs to produce the goods and services that you buy as a consumer. Firms purchase machines, buildings, and land. These markets are in operation at all times. One of the most important activities in these markets is the determination of the prices of all of the inputs and outputs that are bought and sold in our complicated economy. To understand the determination of prices, you first need to look at the law of demand.

Market
All of the arrangements that individuals have for exchanging with one another. Thus, for example, we can speak of the labor market, the automobile market, and the credit market.

Demand

Demand has a special meaning in economics. It refers to the quantities of specific goods or services that individuals, taken singly or as a group, will purchase at various possible prices, other things being constant. We can therefore talk about the demand for microprocessor chips, french fries, multifunction digital devices, children, and criminal activities.

Demand
A schedule showing how much of a good or service people will purchase at any price during a specified time period, other things being constant.

The Law of Demand

Associated with the concept of demand is the **law of demand,** which can be stated as follows:

> *When the price of a good goes up, people buy less of it, other things being equal.*
> *When the price of a good goes down, people buy more of it, other things being equal.*

The law of demand tells us that the quantity demanded of any commodity is inversely related to its price, other things being equal. In an inverse relationship, one variable moves up in value when the other moves down. The law of demand states that a change in price causes a change in the quantity demanded in the *opposite* direction.

Notice that we tacked on to the end of the law of demand the statement "other things being equal." We referred to this in Chapter 1 as the *ceteris paribus* assumption. It means, for example, that when we predict that people will buy fewer digital devices if their price goes up, we are holding constant the price of all other goods in the economy as well as people's incomes. Implicitly, therefore, if we are assuming that no other prices change when we examine the price behavior of digital devices, we are looking at the *relative* price of digital devices.

The law of demand is supported by millions of observations of people's behavior in the marketplace. Theoretically, it can be derived from an economic model based on rational behavior, as was discussed in Chapter 1. Basically, if nothing else changes and the price of a good falls, the lower price induces us to buy more because we can enjoy additional net gains that were unavailable at the higher price. If you examine your own behavior, you will see that it generally follows the law of demand.

Law of demand
The observation that there is a negative, or inverse, relationship between the price of any good or service and the quantity demanded, holding other factors constant.

Relative Prices versus Money Prices

The **relative price** of any commodity is its price in terms of another commodity. The price that you pay in dollars and cents for any good or service at any point in time is called its **money price.** You might hear from your grandparents, "My first new car cost only

Relative price
The money price of one commodity divided by the money price of another commodity; the number of units of one commodity that must be sacrificed to purchase one unit of another commodity.

Money price
The price expressed in today's dollars; also called the *absolute* or *nominal price*.

Table 3-1

Money Price versus Relative Price

The money prices of both 350-gigabyte flash memory drives and 350-gigabyte external hard drives have fallen. But the relative price of external hard drives has risen (or conversely, the relative price of flash memory drives has fallen).

	Money Price		Relative Price	
	Price Last Year	Price This Year	Price Last Year	Price This Year
Flash memory drives	$300	$210	$\frac{\$300}{\$150} = 2.0$	$\frac{\$210}{\$140} = 1.50$
External hard drives	$150	$140	$\frac{\$150}{\$300} = 0.50$	$\frac{\$140}{\$210} = 0.67$

fifteen hundred dollars." The implication, of course, is that the price of cars today is outrageously high because the average new car may cost $32,000. But that is not an accurate comparison. What was the price of the average house during that same year? Perhaps it was only $12,000. By comparison, then, given that the average price of houses today is close to $180,000, the price of a new car today doesn't sound so far out of line, does it?

The point is that money prices during different time periods don't tell you much. You have to calculate relative prices. Consider an example of the price of 350-gigabyte flash memory drives versus the price of 350-gigabyte external hard drives from last year and this year. In Table 3-1 above, we show the money prices of flash memory drives and external hard drives for two years during which they have both gone down.

That means that in today's dollars we have to pay out less for both flash memory drives and external hard drives. If we look, though, at the relative prices of flash memory drives and external hard drives, we find that last year, flash memory drives were twice as expensive as external hard drives, whereas this year they are only one and a half times as expensive. Conversely, if we compare external hard drives to flash memory drives, last year the price of external hard drives was 50 percent of the price of external hard drives, but today the price of external hard drives is about 67 percent of the price of flash memory drives. In the one-year period, although both prices have declined in money terms, the relative price of external hard drives has risen in relation to that of flash memory drives.

Sometimes relative price changes occur because the quality of a product improves, thereby bringing about a decrease in the item's effective *price per constant-quality unit*. Or the price of an item may decrease simply because producers have reduced the item's quality. Thus, when evaluating the effects of price changes, we must always compare *price per constant-quality unit*.

Why is it that for most drivers, the quality-adjusted price of electric vehicles is higher than the posted price?

EXAMPLE

Why Sales of Electric Cars Are Stuck in Low Gear

Prices of solely battery-operated, "electric" autos exceed prices of hybrid (combined gasoline and battery-powered) versions of the same vehicles by at least 30 percent and of all-gasoline-powered versions by at least 50 percent. Nevertheless, the quality-adjusted prices of electric vehicles are even higher.

Not everyone uses an auto just for traveling short, local distances between home and schools, retail stores, and places of employment. Many people commonly desire to drive vehicles farther out than the roughly 250-mile range beyond which the batteries in electric autos

cease to function. The absence of networks of battery-charging or battery-swapping stations limits the usefulness of the vehicles, thereby increasing their quality-adjusted prices. This fact helps to explain why purchases of these vehicles have been trivial since the early 2010s.

FOR CRITICAL THINKING
As the prices of digital devices have declined over time—even as these devices have performed more functions—what has happened to their quality-adjusted prices?

The **law of demand** posits an _____ relationship between the quantity demanded of a good and its price, other things being equal.	The law of _____ applies when other things, such as income and the prices of all other goods and services, are held constant.

The Demand Schedule

Let's take a hypothetical demand situation to see how the inverse relationship between the price and the quantity demanded looks (holding other things equal). We will consider the quantity of magneto optical (MO) disks—utilized for digital data storage—demanded *per year*. Without stating the *time dimension*, we could not make sense out of this demand relationship because the numbers would be different if we were talking about the quantity demanded per month or the quantity demanded per decade.

In addition to implicitly or explicitly stating a time dimension for a demand relationship, we are also implicitly referring to *constant-quality units* of the good or service in question. Prices are always expressed in constant-quality units in order to avoid the problem of comparing commodities that are in fact not truly comparable.

In panel (a) of Figure 3-1 below, we see that if the price is $1 apiece, 50 magneto optical (MO) disks will be bought each year by our representative individual, but if the price is $5 apiece, only 10 MO disks will be bought each year. This reflects the law of demand. Panel (a) is also called simply demand, or a *demand schedule*, because it gives a schedule of alternative quantities demanded per year at different possible prices.

FIGURE 3-1

The Individual Demand Schedule and the Individual Demand Curve

In panel (a), we show combinations *A* through *E* of the quantities of magneto optical disks demanded, measured in constant-quality units at prices ranging from $5 down to $1 apiece. These combinations are points on the demand schedule. In panel (b), we plot combinations *A* through *E* on a grid. The result is the individual demand curve for MO disks.

Panel (a)

Combination	Price per Constant-Quality Magneto Optical Disk	Quantity of Constant-Quality Titanium Batteries per Year
A	$5	10
B	4	20
C	3	30
D	2	40
E	1	50

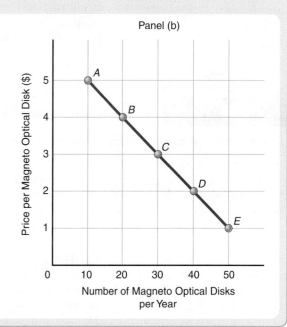

The Demand Curve

Tables expressing relationships between two variables can be represented in graphical terms. To do this, we need only construct a graph that has the price per constant-quality magneto optical disk on the vertical axis and the quantity measured in constant-quality MO disks per year on the horizontal axis. All we have to do is take combinations *A* through *E* from panel (a) of Figure 3-1 on the previous page and plot those points in panel (b). Now we connect the points with a smooth line, and *voilà*, we have a **demand curve.** It is downward sloping (from left to right) to indicate the inverse relationship between the price of MO disks and the quantity demanded per year.

Our presentation of demand schedules and curves applies equally well to all commodities, including dental floss, bagels, textbooks, credit, and labor. Remember, the demand curve is simply a graphical representation of the law of demand.

Demand curve

A graphical representation of the demand schedule. It is a negatively sloped line showing the inverse relationship between the price and the quantity demanded (other things being equal).

Market demand

The demand of all consumers in the marketplace for a particular good or service. The summation at each price of the quantity demanded by each individual.

Individual versus Market Demand Curves

The demand schedule shown in panel (a) of Figure 3-1 and the resulting demand curve shown in panel (b) are both given for an individual. As we shall see, the determination of price in the marketplace depends on, among other things, the **market demand** for a particular commodity. The way in which we measure a market demand schedule and derive a market demand curve for magneto optical disks or any other good or service is by summing (at each price) the individual quantities demanded by all buyers in the market. Suppose that the market demand for MO disks consists of only two buyers: buyer 1, for whom we've already shown the demand schedule, and buyer 2, whose demand schedule is displayed in column 3 of panel (a) of Figure 3-2 on the facing page. Column 1 shows the price, and column 2 shows the quantity demanded by buyer 1 at each price. These data are taken directly from Figure 3-1. In column 3, we show the quantity demanded by buyer 2. Column 4 shows the total quantity demanded at each price, which is obtained by simply adding columns 2 and 3. Graphically, in panel (d) of Figure 3-2, we add the demand curves of buyer 1 [panel (b)] and buyer 2 [panel (c)] to derive the market demand curve.

There are, of course, numerous potential consumers of MO disks. We'll simply assume that the summation of all of the consumers in the market results in a demand schedule, given in panel (a) of Figure 3-3 on page 54, and a demand curve, given in panel (b). The quantity demanded is now measured in millions of units per year. Remember, panel (b) in Figure 3-3 shows the market demand curve for the millions of buyers of MO disks. The "market" demand curve that we derived in Figure 3-2 on the facing page was undertaken assuming that there were only two buyers in the entire market. That's why we assume that the "market" demand curve for two buyers in panel (d) of Figure 3-2 is not a smooth line, whereas the true market demand curve in panel (b) of Figure 3-3 is a smooth line with no kinks.

QUICK QUIZ See page 74 for the answers. Review concepts from this section in MyEconLab.

We measure the **demand schedule** in terms of a time dimension and in _____-quality units.

The _____ _____ curve is derived by summing the quantity demanded by individuals at each price.

Graphically, we add the individual demand curves horizontally to derive the total, or market, demand curve.

Shifts in Demand

Assume that the federal government gives every student registered in a college, university, or technical school in the United States a magneto optical disk drive. The demand curve presented in panel (b) of Figure 3-3 on page 54 would no longer

FIGURE 3-2

The Horizontal Summation of Two Demand Curves

Panel (a) shows how to sum the demand schedule for one buyer with that of another buyer. In column 2 is the quantity demanded by buyer 1, taken from panel (a) of Figure 3-1 on page 51. Column 4 is the sum of columns 2 and 3. We plot the demand curve for buyer 1 in panel (b) and the demand curve for buyer 2 in panel (c). When we add those two demand curves horizontally, we get the market demand curve for two buyers, shown in panel (d).

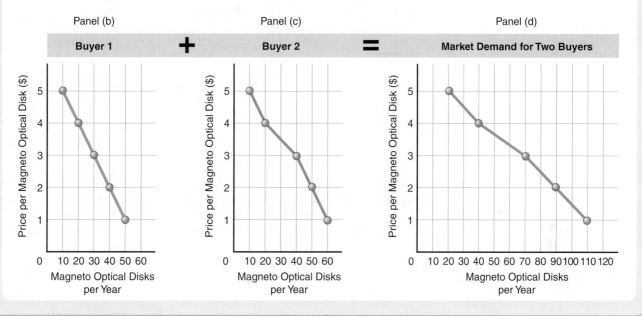

Panel (a)

(1) Price per Magneto Optical Disk	(2) Buyer 1's Quantity Demanded	(3) Buyer 2's Quantity Demanded	(4) = (2) + (3) Combined Quantity Demanded per Year
$5	10	10	20
4	20	20	40
3	30	40	70
2	40	50	90
1	50	60	110

be an accurate representation of total market demand for MO disks. What we have to do is shift the curve outward, or to the right, to represent the rise in demand that would result from this program. There will now be an increase in the number of MO disks demanded at *each and every possible price*. The demand curve shown in Figure 3-4 on the following page will shift from D_1 to D_2. Take any price, say, $3 per MO disk. Originally, before the federal government giveaway of MO disk drives, the amount demanded at $3 was 6 million MO disks per year. After the government giveaway of MO disk drives, however, the new amount demanded at the $3 price is 10 million MO disks per year. What we have seen is a shift in the demand for MO disks.

Under different circumstances, the shift can also go in the opposite direction. What if colleges uniformly prohibited the use of magneto optical disk drives by any of their students? Such a regulation would cause a shift inward—to the left—of the demand curve for MO disks. In Figure 3-4 on the following page, the demand curve would shift to D_3. The quantity demanded would now be less at each and every possible price.

FIGURE 3-3

The Market Demand Schedule for Magneto Optical Disks

In panel (a), we add up the existing demand schedules for magneto optical disks. In panel (b), we plot the quantities from panel (a) on a grid. Connecting them produces the market demand curve for MO disks.

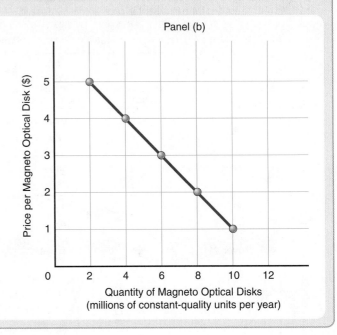

Panel (a)

Price per Constant-Quality Magneto Optical Disk	Total Quantity Demanded of Constant-Quality Magneto Optical Disks per Year (millions)
$5	2
4	4
3	6
2	8
1	10

The Other Determinants of Demand

The demand curve in panel (b) of Figure 3-3 above is drawn with other things held constant, specifically all of the other factors that determine how many magneto optical disks will be bought. There are many such determinants. We refer to these determinants as *ceteris paribus* **conditions,** and they include consumers' income; tastes and preferences; the prices of related goods; expectations regarding future prices and future incomes; and market size (number of potential buyers). Let's examine each of these determinants more closely.

Ceteris paribus **conditions**
Determinants of the relationship between price and quantity that are unchanged along a curve. Changes in these factors cause the curve to shift.

FIGURE 3-4

Shifts in the Demand Curve

If some factor other than price changes, we can show its effect by moving the entire demand curve, say, from D_1 to D_2. We have assumed in our example that this move was precipitated by the government's giving a magneto optical disk drive to every registered college student in the United States. Thus, at *all* prices, a larger number of MO disks would be demanded than before. Curve D_3 represents reduced demand compared to curve D_1, caused by a prohibition of MO disk drives on campus.

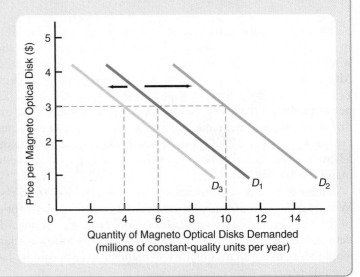

INCOME For most goods, an increase in income will lead to an increase in demand. That is, an increase in income will lead to a rightward shift in the position of the demand curve from, say, D_1 to D_2 in Figure 3-4 on the facing page. You can avoid confusion about shifts in curves by always relating a rise in demand to a rightward shift in the demand curve and a fall in demand to a leftward shift in the demand curve. Goods for which the demand rises when consumer income rises are called **normal goods.** Most goods, such as shoes, computers, and flash memory drives, are "normal goods." For some goods, however, demand *falls* as income rises. These are called **inferior goods.** Beans might be an example. As households get richer, they tend to purchase fewer and fewer beans and purchase more and more fish. (The terms *normal* and *inferior* are merely part of the economist's lexicon. No value judgments are associated with them.)

Remember, a shift to the left in the demand curve represents a decrease in demand, and a shift to the right represents an increase in demand.

How have recent declines in incomes for a large share of U.S. consumers affected the demand for used cell phones that specialty firms recondition and resell?

Normal goods
Goods for which demand rises as income rises. Most goods are normal goods.

Inferior goods
Goods for which demand falls as income rises.

EXAMPLE

Lower Incomes Boost the Demand for Reconditioned Cell Phones

The more than 15 percent of U.S. residents who either have been out of work or are classified by the government as discouraged workers who have given up looking for jobs. These people are earning much lower incomes than they did a few years ago. Many of these people are customers of companies such as ReCellular and Second Rotation, firms that obtain used cell phones from previous owners, recondition the devices, and resell them. Since the economy slipped into its dampened state, sales of reconditioned cell phones have increased by more than 150 percent. Thus, as incomes have fallen for a significant percentage of U.S. consumers, the amount of reconditioned cell phones demanded has increased, indicating that reconditioned cell phones are an inferior good.

FOR CRITICAL THINKING
What is your prediction about the likely effect on the amount of reconditioned cell phones demanded if the U.S. economy were to rebound?

TASTES AND PREFERENCES A change in consumer tastes in favor of a good can shift its demand curve outward to the right. When Pokémon trading cards became the rage, the demand curve for them shifted outward to the right. When the rage died out, the demand curve shifted inward to the left. Fashions depend to a large extent on people's tastes and preferences. Economists have little to say about the determination of tastes. That is, they don't have any "good" theories of taste determination or why people buy one brand of product rather than others. (Advertisers, however, have various theories that they use to try to make consumers prefer their products over those of competitors.)

PRICES OF RELATED GOODS: SUBSTITUTES AND COMPLEMENTS Demand schedules are always drawn with the prices of all other commodities held constant. That is to say, when deriving a given demand curve, we assume that only the price of the good under study changes. For example, when we draw the demand curve for laptop computers, we assume that the price of tablet devices is held constant. When we draw the demand curve for home cinema speakers, we assume that the price of surround-sound amplifiers is held constant. When we refer to *related goods*, we are talking about goods for which demand is interdependent. If a change in the price of one good shifts the demand for another good, those two goods have interdependent demands.

There are two types of demand interdependencies: those in which goods are *substitutes* and those in which goods are *complements*. We can define and distinguish between substitutes and complements in terms of how the change in price of one commodity affects the demand for its related commodity.

YOU ARE THERE

To contemplate how a widening spread between the price of an item and the price of another good that is a close substitute can affect the industry producing the item, take a look at **Why the Casket Industry Is on Life Support**, on page 69.

Substitutes

Two goods are substitutes when a change in the price of one causes a shift in demand for the other in the same direction as the price change.

Butter and margarine are **substitutes.** Either can be consumed to satisfy the same basic want. Let's assume that both products originally cost $2 per pound. If the price of butter remains the same and the price of margarine falls from $2 per pound to $1 per pound, people will buy more margarine and less butter. The demand curve for butter shifts inward to the left. If, conversely, the price of margarine rises from $2 per pound to $3 per pound, people will buy more butter and less margarine. The demand curve for butter shifts outward to the right. In other words, an increase in the price of margarine will lead to an increase in the demand for butter, and an increase in the price of butter will lead to an increase in the demand for margarine. For substitutes, a change in the price of a substitute will cause a change in demand *in the same direction.*

How has the availability of lower-priced plastic substitutes affected the market demand for natural cork stoppers for wine bottles?

EXAMPLE

Why Fewer Wine Bottles Have Natural Cork Stoppers

In the late 1600s, a French monk discovered that natural cork bottle stoppers seal wine into a bottle while allowing the wine to indirectly "breathe" air via the porous characteristics of natural cork's cell structure. Nevertheless, many of today's wine sellers utilize plastic stoppers. These plastic stoppers add to the overall price of a bottle of wine an amount ranging from $0.02 for screw-on stoppers to $0.20 for stoppers composed of extruded plastic that replicates the sponginess of natural cork.

Since the early 2000s, prices of natural cork stoppers have risen above those of plastic stoppers, to levels from about $0.03 for low-quality stoppers to as much as $2 for stoppers of the highest quality. Wine consumers have responded to higher prices of wines bottled with natural cork stoppers by substituting in favor of wines bottled with plastic stoppers. During the past decade, purchases of wine bottled with plastic stoppers have increased by more than 50 percent.

FOR CRITICAL THINKING

Natural cork producers advertise that plastic stoppers harm the environment. If such ads shift the preferences of wine producers and consumers back in favor of natural cork stoppers, what will happen to the market demand for plastic stoppers?

Complements

Two goods are complements when a change in the price of one causes an opposite shift in the demand for the other.

For **complements,** goods typically consumed together, the situation is reversed. Consider digital devices and online applications (apps). We draw the demand curve for apps with the price of digital devices held constant. If the price per constant-quality unit of digital devices decreases from, say, $500 to $300, that will encourage more people to purchase apps. They will now buy more apps, at any given app price, than before. The demand curve for apps will shift outward to the right. If, by contrast, the price of digital devices increases from $250 to $450, fewer people will purchase downloadable applications. The demand curve for apps will shift inward to the left.

To summarize, a decrease in the price of digital devices leads to an increase in the demand for apps. An increase in the price of digital devices leads to a decrease in the demand for apps. Thus, for complements, a change in the price of a product will cause a change in demand *in the opposite direction* for the other good.

EXPECTATIONS Consumers' expectations regarding future prices and future incomes will prompt them to buy more or less of a particular good without a change in its current money price. For example, consumers getting wind of a scheduled 100 percent increase in the price of magneto optical disks next month will buy more of them today at today's prices. Today's demand curve for MO disks will shift from D_1 to D_2 in Figure 3-4 on page 54. The opposite would occur if a decrease in the price of MO disks was scheduled for next month (from D_1 to D_3).

Expectations of a rise in income may cause consumers to want to purchase more of everything today at today's prices. Again, such a change in expectations of higher future income will cause a shift in the demand curve from D_1 to D_2 in Figure 3-4.

Finally, expectations that goods will not be available at any price will induce consumers to stock up now, increasing current demand.

In what ways did recent policy actions by several nations' governments regarding the use of nuclear power affect expectations of the future price of uranium and, as a result, the current market demand for uranium?

POLICY EXAMPLE

An Expected Uranium Price Implosion Cuts Current Uranium Demand

Following the meltdown of a Japanese nuclear reactor in the wake of that nation's disastrous earthquake and tsunami in 2011, governments of a number of countries announced that they planned to decrease their reliance on nuclear power as a source of energy. These policy actions led participants in the uranium market to anticipate a decrease in the future price of uranium. In turn, this expectation of a lower *future* uranium price induced consumers of the nuclear fuel to postpone *current* purchases to the future, when they expected lower

prices to prevail. As a consequence, the expected drop in the future price of uranium generated a nearly 10 percent decrease in the contemporaneous market demand for uranium.

FOR CRITICAL THINKING
What would happen to the market demand for uranium if a different current event induced people to anticipate higher future uranium prices?

MARKET SIZE (NUMBER OF POTENTIAL BUYERS) An increase in the number of potential buyers (holding buyers' incomes constant) at any given price shifts the market demand curve outward. Conversely, a reduction in the number of potential buyers at any given price shifts the market demand curve inward.

Changes in Demand versus Changes in Quantity Demanded

We have made repeated references to demand and to quantity demanded. It is important to realize that there is a difference between a *change in demand* and a *change in quantity demanded*.

Demand refers to a schedule of planned rates of purchase and depends on a great many *ceteris paribus* conditions, such as incomes, expectations, and the prices of substitutes or complements. Whenever there is a change in a *ceteris paribus* condition, there will be a change in demand—a shift in the entire demand curve to the right or to the left.

A *quantity demanded* is a specific quantity at a specific price, represented by a single point on a demand curve. When price changes, quantity demanded changes according to the law of demand, and there will be a movement from one point to another along the same demand curve. Look at Figure 3-5 on the following page. At a price of $3 per magneto optical disk, 6 million MO disks per year are demanded. If the price falls to $1, quantity demanded increases to 10 million per year. This movement occurs because the current market price for the product changes. In Figure 3-5, you can see the arrow pointing down the given demand curve *D*.

When you think of demand, think of the entire curve. Quantity demanded, in contrast, is represented by a single point on the demand curve.

*A change or shift in demand is a movement of the entire curve. The **only** thing that can cause the entire curve to move is a change in a determinant **other than** the good's own price.*

In economic analysis, we cannot emphasize too much the following distinction that must constantly be made:

*A change in a good's own price leads to a change in quantity demanded for any given demand curve, other things held constant. This is a movement **along** the curve.*

*A change in any of the **ceteris paribus** conditions for demand leads to a change in demand. This causes a **shift** of the curve.*

FIGURE 3-5

Movement along a Given Demand Curve

A change in price changes the quantity of a good demanded. This can be represented as movement along a given demand schedule. If, in our example, the price of magneto optical disks falls from $3 to $1 apiece, the quantity demanded will increase from 6 million to 10 million MO disks per year.

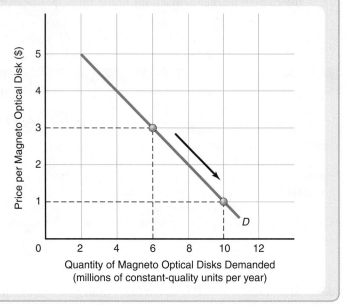

Quantity of Magneto Optical Disks Demanded
(millions of constant-quality units per year)

QUICK QUIZ See page 74 for the answers. Review concepts from this section in MyEconLab.

Demand curves are drawn with determinants other than the price of the good held constant. These other determinants, called *ceteris paribus* conditions, are (1) _____, (2) _____, (3) _____, (4) _____, and (5) _____ at any given price. If any one of these determinants changes, the demand curve will shift to the right or to the left.

A change in demand comes about only because of a change in the _____ _____ conditions of

demand. This change in demand is a shift in the demand curve to the left or to the right.

A change in the quantity demanded comes about when there is a change in the price of the good (other things held constant). Such a change in quantity demanded involves a _____ _____ a given demand curve.

The Law of Supply

Supply
A schedule showing the relationship between price and quantity supplied for a specified period of time, other things being equal.

Law of supply
The observation that the higher the price of a good, the more of that good sellers will make available over a specified time period, other things being equal.

The other side of the basic model in economics involves the quantities of goods and services that firms will offer for sale to the market. The **supply** of any good or service is the amount that firms will produce and offer for sale under certain conditions during a specified time period. The relationship between price and quantity supplied, called the **law of supply,** can be summarized as follows:

> *At higher prices, a larger quantity will generally be supplied than at lower prices, all other things held constant. At lower prices, a smaller quantity will generally be supplied than at higher prices, all other things held constant.*

There is generally a direct relationship between price and quantity supplied. As the price rises, the quantity supplied rises. As the price falls, the quantity supplied also falls. Producers are normally willing to produce and sell more of their product at a higher price than at a lower price, other things being constant. At $5 per magneto optical disk, manufacturers would almost certainly be willing to supply a larger quantity than at $1 per MO disk, assuming, of course, that no other prices in the economy had changed.

As with the law of demand, millions of instances in the real world have given us confidence in the law of supply. On a theoretical level, the law of supply is based on a model in which producers and sellers seek to make the most gain possible from their activities. For example, as a manufacturer attempts to produce more and more MO disks over the same time period, it will eventually have to hire more workers, pay overtime wages (which are higher), and overutilize its machines. Only if offered a higher price per MO disk will the manufacturer be willing to incur these higher costs. That is why the law of supply implies a direct relationship between price and quantity supplied.

Have steel manufacturers' responses to a decline in the price of steel been consistent with the law of supply?

EXAMPLE

Steel Producers Reduce Production When the Price of Steel Falls

Recently, the market price of steel declined from $660 per ton to below $625 per ton. Steel-producing firms responded by cutting back on their production of steel. Thus, as predicted by the law of supply, a decrease in the price of steel resulted in a decrease in the quantity of steel supplied. This direct relationship between price and quantity supplied is consistent with an upward-sloping supply curve for steel.

FOR CRITICAL THINKING
After the price of steel declined, which direction did each steel manufacturer move along its supply curve?

The Supply Schedule

Just as we were able to construct a demand schedule, we can construct a *supply schedule*, which is a table relating prices to the quantity supplied at each price. A supply schedule can also be referred to simply as *supply*. It is a set of planned production rates that depends on the price of the product. We show the individual supply schedule for a hypothetical producer in panel (a) of Figure 3-6 below. At a price of $1 per MO disk, for example, this producer will supply 20,000 MO disks per year. At a price of $5 per MO disk, this producer will supply 55,000 MO disks per year.

FIGURE 3-6

The Individual Producer's Supply Schedule and Supply Curve for Magneto Optical Disks

Panel (a) shows that at higher prices, a hypothetical supplier will be willing to provide a greater quantity of magneto optical disks. We plot the various price-quantity combinations in panel (a) on the grid in panel

(b). When we connect these points, we create the individual supply curve for MO disks. It is positively sloped.

Panel (a)

Combination	Price per Constant-Quality Magneto Optical Disk	Quantity of Magneto Optical Disks Supplied (thousands of constant-quality units per year)
F	$5	55
G	4	40
H	3	35
I	2	25
J	1	20

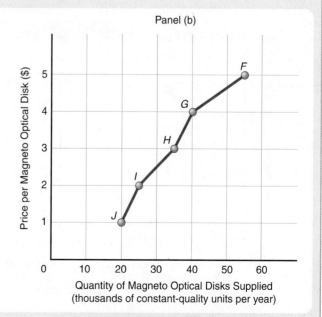

Panel (b)

The Supply Curve

Supply curve
The graphical representation of the supply schedule; a line (curve) showing the supply schedule, which generally slopes upward (has a positive slope), other things being equal.

We can convert the supply schedule from panel (a) of Figure 3-6 on the previous page into a **supply curve,** just as we earlier created a demand curve in Figure 3-1 on page 51. All we do is take the price-quantity combinations from panel (a) of Figure 3-6 and plot them in panel (b). We have labeled these combinations *F* through *J.* Connecting these points, we obtain an upward-sloping curve that shows the typically direct relationship between price and quantity supplied. Again, we have to remember that we are talking about quantity supplied *per year*, measured in constant-quality units.

The Market Supply Curve

Just as we summed the individual demand curves to obtain the market demand curve, we sum the individual producers' supply curves to obtain the market supply curve. Look at Figure 3-7 below, in which we horizontally sum two typical supply curves for manufacturers of magneto optical disks. Supplier 1's data are taken from Figure 3-6 on the previous page. Supplier 2 is added. The numbers are presented in panel (a). The graphical representation of supplier 1 is in panel (b), of supplier 2 in panel (c), and of the summation in panel (d). The result, then, is the supply curve for magneto optical

---

FIGURE 3-7

Horizontal Summation of Supply Curves

In panel (a), we show the data for two individual suppliers of magneto optical disks. Adding how much each is willing to supply at different prices, we come up with the combined quantities supplied in column 4. When we plot the values in columns 2 and 3 on grids from panels (b) and (c) and add them horizontally, we obtain the combined supply curve for the two suppliers in question, shown in panel (d).

Panel (a)

(1) Price per Magneto Optical Disk	(2) Supplier 1's Quantity Supplied (thousands)	(3) Supplier 2's Quantity Supplied (thousands)	(4) = (2) + (3) Combined Quantity Supplied per Year (thousands)
$5	55	35	90
4	40	30	70
3	35	20	55
2	25	15	40
1	20	10	30

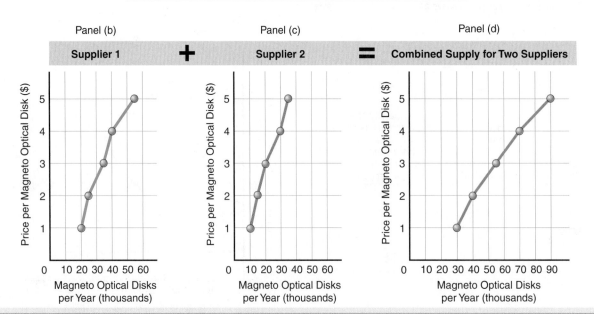

Panel (b)

Supplier 1 **+**

Panel (c)

Supplier 2 **=**

Panel (d)

Combined Supply for Two Suppliers

disks for suppliers 1 and 2. We assume that there are more suppliers of MO disks, however. The total market supply schedule and total market supply curve for MO disks are represented in Figure 3-8 below, with the curve in panel (b) obtained by adding all of the supply curves, such as those shown in panels (b) and (c) of Figure 3-7 on the facing page. Notice the difference between the market supply curve with only two suppliers in Figure 3-7 and the one with many suppliers—the entire true market—in panel (b) of Figure 3-8. (For simplicity, we assume that the true total market supply curve is a straight line.)

Note what happens at the market level when price changes. If the price is $3, the quantity supplied is 6 million. If the price goes up to $4, the quantity supplied increases to 8 million per year. If the price falls to $2, the quantity supplied decreases to 4 million per year. Changes in quantity supplied are represented by movements along the supply curve in panel (b) of Figure 3-8.

QUICK QUIZ See page 74 for the answers. Review concepts from this section in MyEconLab.

There is normally a _____ relationship between price and quantity of a good supplied, other things held constant.

The _____ curve normally shows a direct relationship between price and quantity supplied. The _____ _____ curve is obtained by horizontally adding individual supply curves in the market.

Shifts in Supply

When we looked at demand, we found out that any change in anything relevant besides the price of the good or service caused the demand curve to shift inward or outward. The same is true for the supply curve. If something besides price changes and alters the willingness of suppliers to produce a good or service, we will see the entire supply curve shift.

FIGURE 3-8

The Market Supply Schedule and the Market Supply Curve for Magneto Optical Disks

In panel (a), we show the summation of all the individual producers' supply schedules. In panel (b), we graph the resulting supply curve. It represents the market supply curve for MO disks and is upward sloping.

Panel (a)

Price per Constant-Quality Magneto Optical Disk	Quantity of Magneto Optical Disks Supplied (millions of constant-quality units per year)
$5	10
4	8
3	6
2	4
1	2

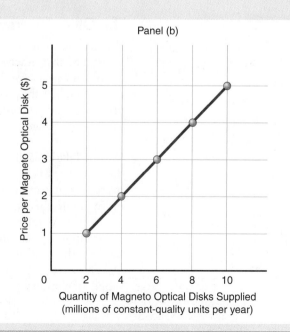

Panel (b)

FIGURE 3-9

Shifts in the Supply Curve

If the cost of producing magneto optical disks were to fall dramatically, the supply curve would shift rightward from S_1 to S_2 such that at all prices, a larger quantity would be forthcoming from suppliers. Conversely, if the cost of production rose, the supply curve would shift leftward to S_3.

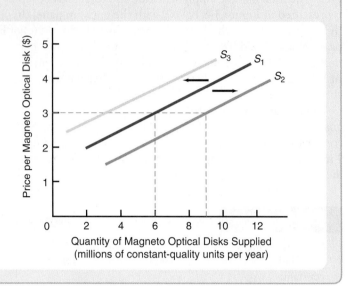

Consider an example. There is a new method of manufacturing magneto optical disks that significantly reduces the cost of production. In this situation, producers of MO disks will supply more product at *all* prices because their cost of so doing has fallen dramatically. Competition among manufacturers to produce more at each and every price will shift the supply curve outward to the right from S_1 to S_2 in Figure 3-9 above. At a price of $3, the number supplied was originally 6 million per year, but now the amount supplied (after the reduction in the costs of production) at $3 per MO disk will be 9 million a year. (This is similar to what has happened to the supply curve of digital devices in recent years as memory chip prices have fallen.)

Consider the opposite case. If the price of raw materials used in manufacturing magneto optical disks increases, the supply curve in Figure 3-9 will shift from S_1 to S_3. At each and every price, the quantity of MO disks supplied will fall due to the increase in the price of raw materials.

The Other Determinants of Supply

When supply curves are drawn, only the price of the good in question changes, and it is assumed that other things remain constant. The other things assumed constant are the *ceteris paribus* conditions of supply. They include the prices of resources (inputs) used to produce the product, technology and productivity, taxes and subsidies, producers' price expectations, and the number of firms in the industry. If *any* of these *ceteris paribus* conditions changes, there will be a shift in the supply curve.

COST OF INPUTS USED TO PRODUCE THE PRODUCT If one or more input prices fall, production costs fall, and the supply curve will shift outward to the right. That is, more will be supplied at each and every price. The opposite will be true if one or more inputs become more expensive. For example, when we draw the supply curve of new tablet devices, we are holding the price of microprocessors (and other inputs) constant. When we draw the supply curve of blue jeans, we are holding the cost of cotton fabric fixed.

Why have large swings in the price of cotton generated variations in the market supply of clothing?

EXAMPLE

Cotton Price Movements Squeeze and Stretch Clothing Supply

Between 2009 and 2010, the price of cotton, a key input cost in the production of many articles of clothing, increased by 55 percent. Clothing manufacturers responded by reducing the amount of clothing supplied at any given price of clothing, so the market supply of clothing decreased.

During 2011, the price of cotton decreased by 53 percent, to nearly its 2009 level. This cotton-price reversal induced clothing-producing firms to increase the amount of clothing supplied at each possible clothing price. Thus, the market supply of clothing increased.

FOR CRITICAL THINKING
What do you think happened to the market supply of clothing when cotton prices rose somewhat again in 2012?

TECHNOLOGY AND PRODUCTIVITY Supply curves are drawn by assuming a given technology, or "state of the art." When the available production techniques change, the supply curve will shift. For example, when a better production technique for magneto optical disks becomes available, production costs decrease, and the supply curve will shift to the right. A larger quantity will be forthcoming at each and every price because the cost of production is lower.

TAXES AND SUBSIDIES Certain taxes, such as a per-unit tax, are effectively an addition to production costs and therefore reduce the supply. If the supply curve is S_1 in Figure 3-9 on the facing page, a per-unit tax increase would shift it to S_3. A per-unit **subsidy** would do the opposite. Every producer would get a "gift" from the government for each unit produced. This per-unit subsidy would shift the curve to S_2.

Subsidy
A negative tax; a payment to a producer from the government, usually in the form of a cash grant per unit.

WHAT IF... politicians simultaneously oppose a higher price for the current quantity of gasoline supplied yet favor higher taxes on the fuel?

A decrease in the market supply of gasoline implies that producers require a higher price to continue providing the same quantity of this fuel. When this occurs, media reports typically feature members of Congress complaining about gasoline sellers insisting on prices that are "too high." Voting records, though, often reveal that many of the politicians who make these complaints have voted to boost federal fuel taxes. Such tax hikes generate decreases in the supply of gasoline and hence contribute to sellers' desires to receive a higher price for any given quantity. Thus, when politicians join congressional majorities to impose higher federal gasoline taxes, what results is the fuel supply reductions that these politicians criticize.

PRICE EXPECTATIONS A change in the expectation of a future relative price of a product can affect a producer's current willingness to supply, just as price expectations affect a consumer's current willingness to purchase. For example, suppliers of magneto optical disks may withhold from the market part of their current supply if they anticipate higher prices in the future. The current amount supplied at each and every price will decrease.

NUMBER OF FIRMS IN THE INDUSTRY In the short run, when firms can change only the number of employees they use, we hold the number of firms in the industry constant. In the long run, the number of firms may change. If the number of firms increases, supply will increase, and the supply curve will shift outward to the right. If the number of firms decreases, supply will decrease, and the supply curve will shift inward to the left.

How did a rash of tornadoes affect the supply curve in the U.S. poultry market?

EXAMPLE

How Deadly Southern Twisters Pummeled the U.S. Poultry Supply

During the course of the deadliest U.S. tornado season in decades, 278 tornadoes swept across the United States between April 26 and 28, 2011. Most of the twisters struck southern states. Particularly hard hit was Alabama, whose farmers typically contribute just over 1 billion chickens to the nation's production of poultry—about 12 percent of the total. Tornadoes damaged numerous feed mills and chicken-processing plants so severely that many poultry-producing companies were unable to supply poultry for a few months. This reduction in the number of chicken-producing firms in operation caused a decrease in the amount of poultry supplied at any given poultry price. That is, the U.S. market poultry supply decreased temporarily in 2011.

FOR CRITICAL THINKING
How did the outright destruction of millions of chickens by the April 2011 tornadoes affect the position of the market poultry supply curve?

Changes in Supply versus Changes in Quantity Supplied

We cannot overstress the importance of distinguishing between a movement along the supply curve—which occurs only when the price changes for a given supply curve—and a shift in the supply curve—which occurs only with changes in *ceteris paribus* conditions. A change in the price of the good in question always (and only) brings about a change in the quantity supplied along a given supply curve. We move to a different point on the existing supply curve. This is specifically called a *change in quantity supplied*. When price changes, quantity supplied changes—there is a movement from one point to another along the same supply curve.

When you think of *supply*, think of the entire curve. Quantity supplied is represented by a single point on the supply curve.

> *A change, or shift, in supply is a movement of the entire curve. The **only** thing that can cause the entire curve to move is a change in one of the **ceteris paribus** conditions.*

Consequently,

> *A change in price leads to a change in the quantity supplied, other things being constant. This is a movement **along** the curve.*

> *A change in any **ceteris paribus** condition for supply leads to a change in supply. This causes a **shift** of the curve.*

QUICK QUIZ See page 74 for the answers. Review concepts from this section in MyEconLab.

If the price changes, we _____ _____ a curve—there is a change in quantity demanded or supplied. If some other determinant changes, we _____ a curve—there is a change in demand or supply.

The **supply curve** is drawn with other things held constant. If these *ceteris paribus* conditions of supply change, the supply curve will shift. The major *ceteris paribus* conditions are (1) _____, (2) _____, (3) _____, (4) _____, and (5) _____.

Putting Demand and Supply Together

In the sections on demand and supply, we tried to confine each discussion to demand or supply only. But you have probably already realized that we can't view the world just from the demand side or just from the supply side. There is interaction between the two. In this section, we will discuss how they interact and how that interaction determines the prices that prevail in our economy and other economies in which the forces of demand and supply are allowed to work.

Let's first combine the demand and supply schedules and then combine the curves.

Go to www.econtoday.com/chap03 to see how the U.S. Department of Agriculture seeks to estimate demand and supply conditions for major agricultural products.

Demand and Supply Schedules Combined

Let's place panel (a) from Figure 3-3 (the market demand schedule) on page 54 and panel (a) from Figure 3-8 (the market supply schedule) on page 61 together in panel (a) of Figure 3-10 on the following page. Column 1 displays the price. Column 2 shows the quantity supplied per year at any given price. Column 3 displays the quantity demanded. Column 4 is the difference between columns 2 and 3, or the difference between the quantity supplied and the quantity demanded. In column 5, we label those differences as either excess quantity supplied (called a *surplus*, which we shall discuss shortly) or excess quantity demanded (commonly known as a *shortage*, also discussed shortly). For example, at a price of $1, only 2 million magneto optical disks would be supplied, but the quantity demanded would be 10 million. The difference would be −8 million, which we label excess quantity demanded (a shortage). At the other end, a price of $5 would elicit 10 million in quantity supplied. Quantity demanded would drop to 2 million, leaving a difference of +8 million units, which we call excess quantity supplied (a surplus).

Now, do you notice something special about the price of $3? At that price, both the quantity supplied and the quantity demanded per year are 6 million. The difference then is zero. There is neither excess quantity demanded (shortage) nor excess quantity supplied (surplus). Hence the price of $3 is very special. It is called the **market clearing price**—it clears the market of all excess quantities demanded or supplied. There are no willing consumers who want to pay $3 per MO disk but are turned away by sellers, and there are no willing suppliers who want to sell MO disks at $3 who cannot sell all they want at that price. Another term for the market clearing price is the **equilibrium price,** the price at which there is no tendency for change. Consumers are able to get all they want at that price, and suppliers are able to sell all they want at that price.

Market clearing, or equilibrium, price
The price that clears the market, at which quantity demanded equals quantity supplied; the price where the demand curve intersects the supply curve.

Equilibrium

We can define **equilibrium** in general as a point at which quantity demanded equals quantity supplied at a particular price. There tends to be no movement of the price or the quantity away from this point unless demand or supply changes. Any movement away from this point will set into motion forces that will cause movement back to it. Therefore, equilibrium is a stable point. Any point that is not an equilibrium is unstable and will not persist.

Equilibrium
The situation when quantity supplied equals quantity demanded at a particular price.

The equilibrium point occurs where the supply and demand curves intersect. The equilibrium price is given on the vertical axis directly to the left of where the supply and demand curves cross. The equilibrium quantity is given on the horizontal axis directly underneath the intersection of the demand and supply curves.

Panel (b) in Figure 3-3 (p. 54) and panel (b) in Figure 3-8 (p. 61) are combined as panel (b) in Figure 3-10 on the next page. The demand curve is labeled *D*, the supply curve *S*. We have labeled the intersection of the supply curve with the demand curve as point *E*, for equilibrium. That corresponds to a market clearing price of $3, at which both the quantity supplied and the quantity demanded are 6 million units per year. There is neither excess quantity supplied nor excess quantity demanded. Point *E*, the equilibrium point, always occurs at the intersection of the supply and demand curves. This is the price *toward which* the market price will automatically tend to gravitate, because there is no outcome more advantageous than this price for both consumers and producers.

FIGURE 3-10

Putting Demand and Supply Together

In panel (a), we see that at the price of $3, the quantity supplied and the quantity demanded are equal, resulting in neither an excess quantity demanded nor an excess quantity supplied. We call this price the equilibrium, or market clearing, price. In panel (b), the intersection of the supply and demand curves is at *E*, at a price of $3 and a quantity of 6 million per year. At point *E*, there is neither an excess quantity demanded nor an excess quantity supplied. At a price of $1, the quantity supplied will be only 2 million per year, but the quantity demanded will be 10 million. The difference is excess quantity demanded at a price of $1. The price will rise, so we will move from point *A* up the supply curve and from point *B* up the demand curve to point *E*. At the other extreme, a price of $5 elicits a quantity supplied of 10 million but a quantity demanded of only 2 million. The difference is excess quantity supplied at a price of $5. The price will fall, so we will move down the demand curve and the supply curve to the equilibrium price, $3 per magneto optical disk.

Panel (a)

(1) Price per Constant-Quality Magneto Optical Disk	(2) Quantity Supplied (magneto optical disks per year)	(3) Quantity Demanded (magneto optical disks per year)	(4) Difference (2) − (3) (magneto optical disks per year)	(5) Condition
$5	10 million	2 million	8 million	Excess quantity supplied (surplus)
4	8 million	4 million	4 million	Excess quantity supplied (surplus)
3	6 million	6 million	0	Market clearing price—equilibrium (no surplus, no shortage)
2	4 million	8 million	−4 million	Excess quantity demanded (shortage)
1	2 million	10 million	−8 million	Excess quantity demanded (shortage)

Panel (b)

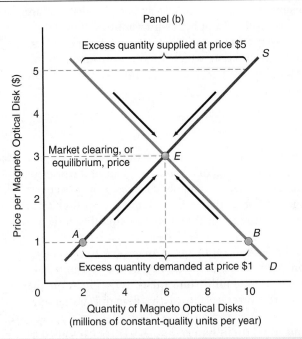

Shortages

The price of $3 depicted in Figure 3-10 above represents a situation of equilibrium. If there were a non-market-clearing, or disequilibrium, price, this price would put into play forces that would cause the price to change toward the market clearing price, at which equilibrium would again be sustained. Look again at panel (b) in Figure 3-10. Suppose that instead of being at the equilibrium price of $3, for some reason the market price is $1. At this price, the quantity demanded of 10 million per year exceeds the quantity supplied of 2 million per year. We have a situation of excess quantity demanded at the price of $1. This is usually called a **shortage.** Consumers of magneto optical disks would find that they could not buy all that they wished at $1 apiece. But forces will cause the price to rise: Competing consumers will bid up the price, and suppliers will increase output in response. (Remember, some buyers would pay $5 or more rather than do without MO disks.) We would move from points *A* and *B* toward point *E*. The process would stop when the price again reached $3 per MO disk.

At this point, it is important to recall a distinction made in Chapter 2:

Shortages and scarcity are not the same thing.

A shortage is a situation in which the quantity demanded exceeds the quantity supplied at a price that is somehow kept *below* the market clearing price. Our definition of scarcity was much more general and all-encompassing: a situation in which the resources available for producing output are insufficient to satisfy all wants. Any choice necessarily costs an opportunity, and the opportunity is lost. Hence, we will always live in a world of scarcity because we must constantly make choices, but we do not necessarily have to live in a world of shortages.

What has caused a shortage of a key drug used to treat victims of a common form of leukemia?

Shortage
A situation in which quantity demanded is greater than quantity supplied at a price below the market clearing price.

EXAMPLE

Production Breakdowns Create a Shortage of a Life-Saving Drug

Each year, physicians diagnose more than 20,000 new cases of acute lymphoblastic leukemia. Recently, all of the companies that manufacture cytarabine, a drug commonly used in treatment regimens for this disease, experienced problems that slowed or halted production of the drug. As a consequence, the quantity of cytarabine supplied fell well below the quantity demanded for treatments at the prevailing price.

In response to the shortage, hospitals and clinics began limiting available cytarabine doses to children and to only a few adults judged most likely to benefit from treatment with that drug. Other adults had to switch to different drugs even if they were unlikely to be as effective. Physicians hope that eventually more adults will be able to undergo treatment with this drug, after resolution of production problems, albeit at a market clearing price that probably will be higher.

FOR CRITICAL THINKING
Why is the market clearing price of cytarabine likely to increase, and why might an increase in that price be required to eliminate the shortage of the drug?

Surpluses

Now let's repeat the experiment with the market price at $5 rather than at the market clearing price of $3. Clearly, the quantity supplied will exceed the quantity demanded at that price. The result will be an excess quantity supplied at $5 per unit. This excess quantity supplied is often called a **surplus.** Given the curves in panel (b) in Figure 3-10 on the facing page, however, there will be forces pushing the price back down toward $3 per magneto optical disk. Competing suppliers will cut prices and reduce output, and consumers will purchase more at these new lower prices. If the two forces of supply and demand are unrestricted, they will bring the price back to $3 per MO disk.

Shortages and surpluses are resolved in unfettered markets—markets in which price changes are free to occur. The forces that resolve them are those of competition: In the case of shortages, consumers competing for a limited quantity supplied drive up the price; in the case of surpluses, sellers compete for the limited quantity demanded, thus driving prices down to equilibrium. The equilibrium price is the only stable price, and the (unrestricted) market price tends to gravitate toward it.

What happens when the price is set below the equilibrium price? Here come the scalpers.

Surplus
A situation in which quantity supplied is greater than quantity demanded at a price above the market clearing price.

POLICY EXAMPLE

Should Shortages in the Ticket Market Be Solved by Scalpers?

If you have ever tried to get tickets to a playoff game in sports, a popular Broadway play, or a superstar's rap concert, you know about "shortages." The standard Super Bowl ticket situation is shown in Figure 3-11 below. At the face-value price of Super Bowl tickets ($800), the quantity demanded (175,000) greatly exceeds the quantity supplied (80,000). Because shortages last only as long as prices and quantities do not change, markets tend to exhibit a movement out of this disequilibrium toward equilibrium. Obviously, the quantity of Super Bowl tickets cannot change, but the price can go as high as $6,000.

Enter the scalper. This colorful term is used because when you purchase a ticket that is being resold at a price higher than face value, the seller is skimming profit off the top ("taking your scalp"). If an event sells out and people who wished to purchase tickets at current prices were unable to do so, ticket prices by definition were lower than market clearing prices. People without tickets may be willing to buy high-priced tickets because they place a greater value on the entertainment event than the face value of the ticket. Without scalpers, those individuals would not be able to attend the event. In the case of the Super Bowl, various forms of scalping occur nationwide. Tickets for a seat on the 50-yard line have been sold for as much as $6,000 apiece. In front of every Super Bowl arena, you can find ticket scalpers hawking their wares.

In most states, scalping is illegal. In Pennsylvania, convicted scalpers are either fined $5,000 or sentenced to two years behind bars. For an economist, such legislation seems strange. As one New York ticket broker said, "I look at scalping like working as a stockbroker, buying low and selling high. If people are willing to pay me the money, what kind of problem is that?"

FOR CRITICAL ANALYSIS

What happens to ticket scalpers who are still holding tickets after an event has started?

FIGURE 3-11

Shortages of Super Bowl Tickets

The quantity of tickets for a Super Bowl game is fixed at 80,000. At the price per ticket of $800, the quantity demanded is 175,000. Consequently, there is an excess quantity demanded at the below-market clearing price. In this example, prices can go as high as $6,000 in the scalpers' market.

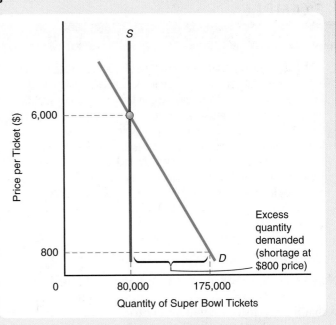

QUICK QUIZ See page 74 for the answers. Review concepts from this section in MyEconLab.

The market clearing price occurs at the _____ of the market demand curve and the market supply curve. It is also called the _____ price, the price from which there is no tendency to change unless there is a change in demand or supply.

Whenever the price is _____ than the equilibrium price, there is an excess quantity supplied (a **surplus**).

Whenever the price is _____ than the equilibrium price, there is an excess quantity demanded (a **shortage**).

YOU ARE THERE
Why the Casket Industry Is on Life Support

Ken Camp, the chief executive officer of Hillenbrand, Inc., has succinctly summed up his company's situation: "We are a very significant player in an industry that isn't growing." Hillenbrand is part of the casket industry, which is facing tough times as a consequence of the falling price of cremations, which are substitutes for casket burials of deceased individuals. The overall price of a traditional casket burial exceeds $7,200. In contrast, the price of a cremation service has recently fallen to about $1,300.

The widening differential between the price of traditional casket burials and the price of cremation services has induced many people to substitute away from purchasing caskets. Today, nearly 400,000 fewer caskets are purchased per year in the United States than were purchased

in 2008. Thus, the demand for caskets has declined in response to a decrease in the price of an already lower-priced substitute—cremation. This fact explains why Camp has concluded that the casket industry "isn't growing."

Critical Thinking Questions

1. What impact do you think that the decline in demand for caskets has had on sellers' total revenues, which equal price multiplied by quantity sold?

2. How have technological improvements in the cremation-services industry likely affected the supply curve for these services?

ISSUES & APPLICATIONS

Your Higher Education Bills Really Are Increasing

CONCEPTS APPLIED

▶ Money Price

▶ Relative Price

▶ Market Clearing Price

Undoubtedly, you have noticed that your college expenses have been rising. The reason is that the prices of goods and services that students must purchase to obtain higher education have been increasing persistently for more than three decades.

A Tale of Upward Trends in Two Sets of Money Prices

Figure 3-12 on the following page displays index measures of two sets of money prices that are important to current U.S. college students. One is an index measure of U.S. college tuition and fees. The other is an index measure of the prices of U.S. educational books and supplies.

Clearly, the figure indicates that both indexes of these money prices have increased substantially in recent years. The money value of tuition and fees that college students pay is about thirteen times greater today than in the late 1970s, and the money prices of educational books and supplies are more than nine times higher.

Relative Prices of Higher Education Are Also Rising

Have prices of higher education been rising faster than the average level of prices of all good and services? Figure 3-12 also shows an index measure of the level of prices of all goods and services purchased in the United States. Taking into account the significant increase in the prices of all goods and services during the past four decades indicates that *relative* prices of educational books and supplies have more than doubled. *Relative* tuition-and-fee prices have more than tripled.

Continuing increases in the relative prices of tuition and fees and of educational books and supplies reflect higher market clearing prices of college enrollment, books, and

FIGURE 3-12

Indexes of Prices for Higher-Education-Related Items and All Goods and Services since 1978

The rise in the index of U.S. tuition and fees from 100 in 1978 to the current level of just over 1,300 indicates that the money price of college enrollment is now thirteen times higher. Money prices of educational books and supplies are now more than nine times higher, and money prices of all goods and services are about four times higher.

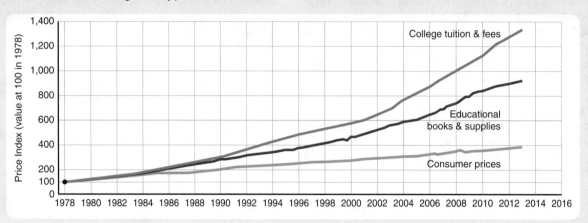

Sources: Bureau of Labor Statistics; author's estimates.

supplies. These are the prices at which the demand and supply curves for these items cross in the relevant markets—prices at intersections that have continued drifting upward over time.

For Critical Thinking

1. In relation to higher education, what has happened to the relative prices of other goods and services?

2. Given that market supply has increased steadily during the past four decades, what must account for rising money and relative prices of higher education?

Web Resources

1. Review a list of the highest-priced U.S. colleges at **www .econtoday.com/chap03**.

2. Compare the money prices of college enrollment in the United States to the lower money prices prevailing in the United Kingdom at **www.econtoday.com/chap03**.

MyEconLab

— WHAT YOU SHOULD KNOW —

— WHERE TO GO TO PRACTICE —

The Law of Demand Other things being equal, individuals will purchase fewer units of a good at a higher price and will purchase more units at a lower price.

market, 49
demand, 49
law of demand, 49

• MyEconLab Study Plan 3.1

WHAT YOU SHOULD KNOW	MyEconLab *continued*	WHERE TO GO TO PRACTICE
Relative Prices versus Money Prices The relative price is the price of the good in terms of other goods. In a world of generally rising prices, people compare the price of one good with the general level of prices of other goods in order to decide whether the relative price of that one good has gone up, gone down, or stayed the same.	relative price, 49 money price, 49	• MyEconLab Study Plan 3.1
A Change in Quantity Demanded versus a Change in Demand The demand schedule shows quantities purchased per unit of time at various possible prices. Graphically, the demand schedule is a downward-sloping demand curve. A change in the price of the good generates a change in the quantity demanded, which is a movement along the demand curve. Factors other than the price of the good that affect the amount demanded are (1) income, (2) tastes and preferences, (3) the prices of related goods, (4) expectations, and (5) market size (the number of potential buyers). If any of these *ceteris paribus* conditions of demand changes, there is a change in demand, and the demand curve shifts to a new position.	demand curve, 52 market demand, 52 *ceteris paribus* conditions, 54 normal goods, 55 inferior goods, 55 substitutes, 56 complements, 56 **Key Figures** Figure 3-2, 53 Figure 3-4, 54 Figure 3-5, 58	• MyEconLab Study Plans 3.2, 3.3 • Animated Figures 3-2, 3-4, 3-5
The Law of Supply According to the law of supply, sellers will produce and offer for sale more units of a good at a higher price, and they will produce and offer for sale fewer units of the good at a lower price.	supply, 58 law of supply, 58	• MyEconLab Study Plan 3.4
A Change in Quantity Supplied versus a Change in Supply The supply schedule shows quantities produced and sold per unit of time at various possible prices. On a graph, the supply schedule is a supply curve that slopes upward. A change in the price of the good generates a change in the quantity supplied, which is a movement along the supply curve. Factors other than the price of the good that affect the amount supplied are (1) input prices, (2) technology and productivity, (3) taxes and subsidies, (4) price expectations, and (5) the number of sellers. If any of these *ceteris paribus* conditions changes, there is a change in supply, and the supply curve shifts to a new position.	supply curve, 60 subsidy, 63 **Key Figures** Figure 3-6, 59 Figure 3-7, 60 Figure 3-9, 62	• MyEconLab Study Plans 3.5, 3.6 • Animated Figures 3-6, 3-7, 3-9

MyEconLab *continued*

┌─ **WHAT YOU SHOULD KNOW** ───────────────── **WHERE TO GO TO PRACTICE** ─

**Determining the Market Price and the
Equilibrium Quantity** The equilibrium price
of a good and the equilibrium quantity of the
good that is produced and sold are determined
by the intersection of the demand and supply
curves. At this intersection point, the quantity
demanded by buyers of the good just equals
the quantity supplied by sellers, so there is neither an excess quantity of the good supplied
(surplus) nor an excess quantity of the good
demanded (shortage).

market clearing, or
    equilibrium, price, 65
equilibrium, 65
shortage, 67
surplus, 67

Key Figure
Figure 3-11, 68

- MyEconLab Study Plan 3.7
- Animated Figure 3-11

Log in to MyEconLab, take a chapter test, and get a personalized Study Plan that tells you which concepts you understand and
which ones you need to review. From there, MyEconLab will give you further practice, tutorials, animations, videos,
and guided solutions. For more information, visit www.myeconlab.com

PROBLEMS

All problems are assignable in MyEconLab. *Answers to
odd-numbered problems appear at the back of the book.*

3-1. Suppose that in a recent market period, the following relationship existed between the price of
tablet devices and the quantity supplied and quantity demanded.

Price	Quantity Demanded	Quantity Supplied
$390	100 million	40 million
$400	90 million	60 million
$410	80 million	80 million
$420	70 million	100 million
$430	60 million	120 million

Graph the supply and demand curves for tablet
devices using the information in the table. What
are the equilibrium price and quantity? If the
industry price is $400, is there a shortage or sur-
plus of tablet devices? How much is the shortage
or surplus? (See pages 66–67.)

3-2. Suppose that in a later market period, the quantities supplied in the table in Problem 3-1 are
unchanged. The amount demanded, however, has
increased by 30 million at each price. Construct
the resulting demand curve in the illustration you
made for Problem 3-1. Is this an increase or a
decrease in demand? What are the new equilibrium quantity and the new market price? Give two

examples of changes in *ceteris paribus* conditions
that might cause such a change. (See page 54.)

3-3. Consider the market for cable-based Internet
access service, which is a normal good. Explain
whether the following events would cause an increase or a decrease in demand or an increase or a
decrease in the quantity demanded. (See page 57.)

a. Firms providing wireless (an alternative to cable)
Internet access services reduce their prices.

b. Firms providing cable-based Internet access
services reduce their prices.

c. There is a decrease in the incomes earned by
consumers of cable-based Internet access
services.

d. Consumers' tastes shift away from using
wireless Internet access in favor of cable-based
Internet access services.

3-4. In the market for flash memory drives (a normal
good), explain whether the following events would
cause an increase or a decrease in demand or an
increase or a decrease in the quantity demanded.
Also explain what happens to the equilibrium quantity and the market clearing price. (See page 54.)

a. There are increases in the prices of storage racks
for flash memory drives.

b. There is a decrease in the price of computer
drives that read the information contained on
flash memory drives.

c. There is a dramatic increase in the price of secure digital cards that, like flash memory drives, can be used to store digital data.

d. A booming economy increases the income of the typical buyer of flash memory drives.

e. Consumers of flash memory drives anticipate that the price of this good will decline in the future.

3-5. Give an example of a complement and a substitute in consumption for each of the following items. (See pages 55–56.)

a. Bacon

b. Tennis racquets

c. Coffee

d. Automobiles

3-6. For each of the following shifts in the demand curve and associated price change of a complement or substitute item, explain whether the change in the price of the complement or substitute must have been an increase or a decrease. (See page 56.)

a. A rise in the demand for a dashboard global-positioning-system device follows a change in the price of automobiles, which are complements.

b. A fall in the demand for e-book readers follows a change in the price of e-books, which are complements.

c. A rise in the demand for tablet devices follows a change in the price of ultrathin laptop computers, which are substitutes.

d. A fall in the demand for physical books follows a change in the price of e-books, which are substitutes.

3-7. Identify which of the following would generate an increase in the market demand for tablet devices, which are a normal good. (See pages 54–57.)

a. A decrease in the incomes of consumers of tablet devices

b. An increase in the price of ultrathin computers, which are substitutes

c. An increase in the price of online apps, which are complements

d. An increase in the number of consumers in the market for tablet devices

3-8. Identify which of the following would generate a decrease in the market demand for e-book readers, which are a normal good. (See pages 54–57.)

a. An increase in the price of downloadable apps utilized to enhance the e-book reading experience, which are complements

b. An increase in the number of consumers in the market for e-book readers

c. A decrease in the price of tablet devices, which are substitutes

d. A reduction in the incomes of consumers of e-book readers

3-9. Consider the following diagram of a market for one-bedroom rental apartments in a college community. (See pages 66–67.)

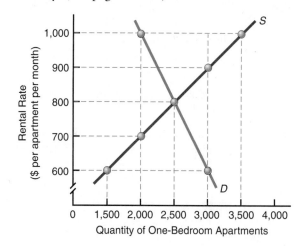

a. At a rental rate of $1,000 per month, is there an excess quantity supplied, or is there an excess quantity demanded? What is the amount of the excess quantity supplied or demanded?

b. If the present rental rate of one-bedroom apartments is $1,000 per month, through what mechanism will the rental rate adjust to the equilibrium rental rate of $800?

c. At a rental rate of $600 per month, is there an excess quantity supplied, or is there an excess quantity demanded? What is the amount of the excess quantity supplied or demanded?

d. If the present rental rate of one-bedroom apartments is $600 per month, through what mechanism will the rental rate adjust to the equilibrium rental rate of $800?

3-10. Consider the market for paperbound economics textbooks. Explain whether the following events would cause an increase or a decrease in supply or an increase or a decrease in the quantity supplied. (See page 64.)

a. The market price of paper increases.

b. The market price of economics textbooks increases.

c. The number of publishers of economics textbooks increases.

d. Publishers expect that the market price of economics textbooks will increase next month.

3-11. Consider the market for smartphones. Explain whether the following events would cause an increase or a decrease in supply or an increase or a decrease in the quantity supplied. Illustrate each, and show what would happen to the equilibrium quantity and the market price. (See page 64.)

    a. The price of touch screens used in smartphones declines.

    b. The price of machinery used to produce smartphones increases.

    c. The number of manufacturers of smartphones increases.

    d. There is a decrease in the market demand for smartphones.

3-12. If the price of flash memory chips used in manufacturing smartphones decreases, what will happen in the market for smartphones? How will the equilibrium price and equilibrium quantity of smartphones change? (See page 56.)

3-13. Assume that the cost of aluminum used by soft-drink companies increases. Which of the following correctly describes the resulting effects in the market for soft drinks distributed in aluminum cans? (More than one statement may be correct. See page 56.)

    a. The demand for soft drinks decreases.

    b. The quantity of soft drinks demanded decreases.

    c. The supply of soft drinks decreases.

    d. The quantity of soft drinks supplied decreases.

ECONOMICS ON THE NET

The U.S. Nursing Shortage For some years media stories have discussed a shortage of qualified nurses in the United States. This application explores some of the factors that have caused the quantity of newly trained nurses demanded to tend to exceed the quantity of newly trained nurses supplied.

Title: Nursing Shortage Resource Web Link

Navigation: Go to the Nursing Shortage Resource Web Link at **www.econtoday.com/chap03**, and click on *Nursing Shortage Fact Sheet*.

Application Read the discussion, and answer the following questions.

    1. What has happened to the demand for new nurses in the United States? What has happened to the supply of new nurses? Why has the result been a shortage?

    2. If there is a free market for the skills of new nurses, what can you predict is likely to happen to the wage rate earned by individuals who have just completed their nursing training?

For Group Study and Analysis Discuss the pros and cons of high schools and colleges trying to factor predictions about future wages into student career counseling. How might this potentially benefit students? What problems might high schools and colleges face in trying to assist students in evaluating the future earnings prospects of various jobs?

ANSWERS TO QUICK QUIZZES

p. 51: (i) inverse; (ii) demand

p. 52: (i) constant; (ii) market demand

p. 58: (i) income . . . tastes and preferences . . . prices of related goods . . . expectations about future prices and incomes . . . market size (the number of potential buyers in the market); (ii) *ceteris paribus;* (iii) movement along

p. 61: (i) direct; (ii) supply; (iii) market supply

p. 64: (i) move along . . . shift; (ii) input prices . . . technology and productivity . . . taxes and subsidies . . . expectations of future relative prices . . . the number of firms in the industry

p. 68: (i) intersection . . . equilibrium; (ii) greater; (iii) less

Extensions of Demand and Supply Analysis

4

LEARNING OBJECTIVES

After reading this chapter, you should be able to:

▶ Discuss the essential features of the price system

▶ Evaluate the effects of changes in demand and supply on the market price and equilibrium quantity

▶ Understand the rationing function of prices

▶ Explain the effects of price ceilings

▶ Explain the effects of price floors

▶ Describe various types of government-imposed quantity restrictions on markets

MyEconLab helps you master each objective and study more efficiently. See end of chapter for details.

uring the past couple of years, people shopping for cars have confronted an unusual type of "sticker shock": As the prices of new vehicles have increased, the prices of used models have risen even faster. Today, the prices of a number of used vehicles are only a few hundred dollars lower than those of newly produced versions of the same cars. To understand why this situation exists in the used-car market, you must learn more about the effects of changes in market demand and supply on equilibrium prices and quantities—one key topic of this chapter. Indeed, you must develop an ability to consider the effects of *simultaneous* changes in market demand and supply, because such variations have occurred in the market for used cars.

in Venezuela, in which substantial quantities of coffee once were produced and consumed year after year, so little coffee is now produced that persistent coffee *shortages* exist? As you learned in Chapter 3, normally we would anticipate that in the face of a shortage in which quantity supplied is less than the quantity demanded, the price of coffee would increase. A rise in the price to its market clearing level, you learned, would bring quantities demanded and supplied back into equality. Since 2003, however, Venezuela's government has maintained a *price ceiling* in the coffee market. This means that it is illegal in Venezuela for the price of coffee to increase in order to eliminate a shortage.

What effects can a price ceiling have on the availability and consumption of a good or service? As you will learn in this chapter, we can use the supply and demand analysis developed in Chapter 3 to answer this question. You will find that when a government sets a ceiling below the equilibrium price, the result will be a shortage. Similarly, you will learn how we can use supply and demand analysis to examine the "surplus" of various agricultural products, the "shortage" of apartments in certain cities, and many other phenomena. All of these examples are part of our economy, which we characterize as a *price system*.

The Price System and Markets

Price system

An economic system in which relative prices are constantly changing to reflect changes in supply and demand for different commodities. The prices of those commodities are signals to everyone within the system as to what is relatively scarce and what is relatively abundant.

In a **price system,** otherwise known as a *market system*, relative prices are constantly changing to reflect changes in supply and demand for different commodities. The prices of those commodities are the signals to everyone within the price system as to what is relatively scarce and what is relatively abundant. In this sense, prices provide information.

Indeed, it is the *signaling* aspect of the price system that provides the information to buyers and sellers about what should be bought and what should be produced. In a price system, there is a clear-cut chain of events in which any changes in demand and supply cause changes in prices that in turn affect the opportunities that businesses and individuals have for profit and personal gain. Such changes influence our use of resources.

Exchange and Markets

Voluntary exchange

An act of trading, done on an elective basis, in which both parties to the trade expect to be better off after the exchange.

The price system features **voluntary exchange,** acts of trading between individuals that make both parties to the trade subjectively better off. The prices we pay for the desired items are determined by the interaction of the forces underlying supply and demand. In our economy, exchanges take place voluntarily in markets. A market encompasses the exchange arrangements of both buyers and sellers that underlie the forces of supply and demand. Indeed, one definition of a market is that it is a low-cost institution for facilitating exchange. A market increases incomes by helping resources move to their highest-valued uses.

Transaction Costs

Transaction costs

All of the costs associated with exchange, including the informational costs of finding out the price and quality, service record, and durability of a product, plus the cost of contracting and enforcing that contract.

Individuals turn to markets because markets reduce the cost of exchanges. These costs are sometimes referred to as **transaction costs,** which are broadly defined as the costs associated with finding out exactly what is being transacted as well as the cost of enforcing contracts. If you were Robinson Crusoe and lived alone on an island, you would never incur a transaction cost. For everyone else, transaction costs are just as real as the costs of production. Today, high-speed computers have allowed us to reduce transaction costs by increasing our ability to process information and keep records.

Consider some simple examples of transaction costs. A club warehouse such as Sam's Club or Costco reduces the transaction costs of having to go to numerous specialty stores to obtain the items you desire. Financial institutions, such as commercial banks, have reduced the transaction costs of directing funds from savers to borrowers. In general, the more organized the market, the lower the transaction costs. Among those who constantly attempt to lower transaction costs are the much maligned middlemen.

The Role of Middlemen

As long as there are costs of bringing together buyers and sellers, there will be an incentive for intermediaries linking ultimate sellers and buyers, normally called middlemen, to lower those costs. This means that middlemen specialize in lowering transaction costs. Whenever producers do not sell their products directly to the final consumer, by definition, one or more middlemen are involved. Farmers typically sell their output to distributors, who are usually called wholesalers, who then sell those products to retailers such as supermarkets.

How have companies that offer downloadable apps altered the transaction costs of firms seeking to sell products to mobile consumers?

EXAMPLE

Linking Businesses to Customers on the Go via QR Apps

In recent years, firms seeking to simplify the process of selling their products to busy customers have been turning to online apps, or Web-based application programs. One increasingly useful type of app for many small businesses is the quick-response (QR) app. These apps are offered by middlemen companies, such as Kaywa AT and Scanbuy, Inc. The apps enable sellers to create codes that they can place on poster ads. Consumers can scan the ads with their smartphones to place orders for the firms' products.

For instance, an individual who is about to board a commuter train can use a smartphone to scan a code from the ad of a coffee shop near the train's destination. The code enables the smartphone to acquire the QR app, which in turn displays the coffee shop's menu, from which the individual can choose items to purchase remotely. The individual can then pick up those items at the coffee shop upon arrival—hence completing a mobile purchase made possible by a middlemen company that offers the QR app linking the individual to the coffee shop.

FOR CRITICAL THINKING

Why do you suppose that firms such as coffee shops are willing to pay fees to middlemen for ad codes to be used with QR apps?

Changes in Demand and Supply

A key function of middlemen is to reduce transaction costs of buyers and sellers in markets for goods and services, and it is in markets that we see the results of changes in demand and supply. Market equilibrium can change whenever there is a *shock* caused by a change in a *ceteris paribus* condition for demand or supply. A shock to the supply and demand system can be represented by a shift in the supply curve, a shift in the demand curve, or a shift in both curves. Any shock to the system will result in a new set of supply and demand relationships and a new equilibrium. Forces will come into play to move the system from the old price-quantity equilibrium (now a disequilibrium situation) to the new equilibrium, where the new demand and supply curves intersect.

Effects of Changes in Either Demand or Supply

In many situations, it is possible to predict what will happen to both equilibrium price and equilibrium quantity when demand or supply changes. Specifically, whenever one curve is stable while the other curve shifts, we can tell what will happen to both price and quantity. Consider the possibilities in Figure 4-1 on the following page. In panel (a), the supply curve remains unchanged, but demand increases from D_1 to D_2. Note that the results are an increase in the market clearing price from P_1 to P_2 and an increase in the equilibrium quantity from Q_1 to Q_2.

In panel (b) in Figure 4-1, there is a decrease in demand from D_1 to D_3. This results in a decrease in both the equilibrium price of the good and the equilibrium quantity. Panels (c) and (d) show the effects of a shift in the supply curve while the demand curve is unchanged. In panel (c), the supply curve has shifted rightward. The equilibrium price of the product falls, and the equilibrium quantity increases. In panel (d), supply has shifted leftward—there has been a supply decrease. The product's equilibrium price increases, and the equilibrium quantity decreases.

FIGURE 4-1

Shifts in Demand and in Supply: Determinate Results

In panel (a), the supply curve is unchanged at S. The demand curve shifts outward from D_1 to D_2. The equilibrium price and quantity rise from P_1, Q_1 to P_2, Q_2, respectively. In panel (b), again the supply curve is unchanged at S. The demand curve shifts inward to the left, showing a decrease in demand from D_1 to D_3. Both equilibrium price and equilibrium quantity fall. In panel (c), the demand curve now remains unchanged at D. The supply curve shifts from S_1 to S_2. The equilibrium price falls from P_1 to P_2. The equilibrium quantity increases, however, from Q_1 to Q_2. In panel (d), the demand curve is unchanged at D. Supply decreases as shown by a leftward shift of the supply curve from S_1 to S_3. The market clearing price increases from P_1 to P_3. The equilibrium quantity falls from Q_1 to Q_3.

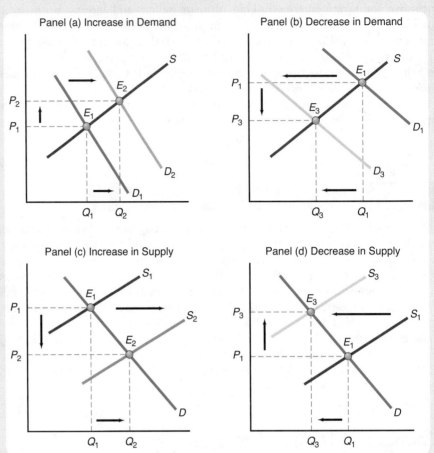

Situations in Which Both Demand and Supply Shift

The examples in Figure 4-1 above show a theoretically determinate outcome of a shift either in the demand curve, holding the supply curve constant, or in the supply curve, holding the demand curve constant. When both the supply and demand curves change, the outcome is indeterminate for either equilibrium price or equilibrium quantity.

When both demand and supply increase, the equilibrium quantity unambiguously rises, because the increase in demand and the increase in supply *both* tend to generate a rise in quantity. The change in the equilibrium price is uncertain without more information, because the increase in demand tends to increase the equilibrium price, whereas the increase in supply tends to decrease the equilibrium price.

Decreases in both demand and supply tend to generate a fall in quantity, so the equilibrium quantity falls. Again, the effect on the equilibrium price is uncertain without additional information, because a decrease in demand tends to reduce the equilibrium price, whereas a decrease in supply tends to increase the equilibrium price.

We can be certain that when demand decreases and supply increases at the same time, the equilibrium price will fall, because *both* the decrease in demand and the increase in supply tend to push down the equilibrium price. The change in the equilibrium quantity is uncertain without more information, because the decrease in demand tends to reduce the equilibrium quantity, whereas the increase in supply tends to increase the equilibrium quantity. If demand increases and supply decreases at the same time, both occurrences tend to push up the equilibrium price, so the equilibrium price definitely rises. The change in the equilibrium quantity cannot be determined without more information, because the increase in demand tends to raise the equilibrium quantity, whereas the decrease in supply tends to reduce the equilibrium quantity.

How have simultaneous shifts in demand and supply affected the equilibrium global price of shipping containers?

INTERNATIONAL EXAMPLE

What Accounts for the Rising Price of Shipping Containers?

Since 2011, shipping-container prices have surged. Several reasons account for the jump in the equilibrium price. One is that companies using the containers, which typically last no longer than 8 to 10 years, bought large quantities during a five-year period that began in 2001, and many of these containers now must be replaced to maintain shipping volumes. Hence, as shown in Figure 4-2 below, the demand curve for shipping containers has shifted rightward.

In addition, the massive tsunami that struck Japan in 2011 washed thousands of containers out to sea. Furthermore, the price of steel that serves as the primary input for the containers has increased by 7 percent. These events have contributed to a reduction in the supply of shipping containers. On net, the equilibrium quantity of shipping containers produced and purchased has risen, and the market clearing price of shipping containers has increased.

FOR CRITICAL THINKING

How do you suppose that a rise in the price of truck trailers that are substitutes for shipping containers has affected the market clearing price of shipping containers?

FIGURE 4-2

The Effects of a Simultaneous Decrease in Shipping-Container Supply and Increase in Shipping-Container Demand

Since 2011, various factors have contributed to a reduction in the supply of shipping containers, depicted by the leftward shift in the supply curve from S_1 to S_2. At the same time, there was an increase in the demand for shipping containers, as shown by the shift in the demand curve from D_1 to D_2. On net, the equilibrium quantity of shipping containers produced and purchased rose, from 750,000 containers per year at point E_1 to 900,000 containers per year at point E_2, and the equilibrium price of shipping containers increased from about $3,000 per container to about $3,500 per container.

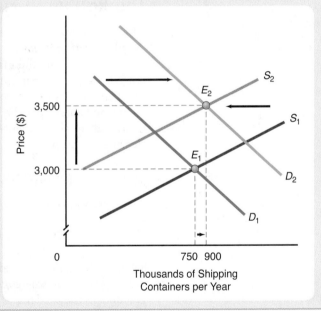

Price Flexibility and Adjustment Speed

We have used as an illustration for our analysis a market in which prices are quite flexible. Some markets are indeed like that. In others, however, price flexibility may take the form of subtle adjustments such as hidden payments or quality changes. For example, although the published price of bouquets of flowers may stay the same, the freshness of the flowers may change, meaning that the price per constant-quality unit changes. The published price of French bread might stay the same, but the quality could go up or down, perhaps through use of a different recipe, thereby changing the price per constant-quality unit. There are many ways to implicitly change prices without actually changing the published price for a *nominal* unit of a product or service.

We must also note that markets do not always return to equilibrium immediately. There may be a significant adjustment time. A shock to the economy in the form of an oil embargo, a drought, or a long strike will not be absorbed overnight. This means that even in unfettered market situations, in which there are no restrictions on changes in prices and quantities, temporary excess quantities supplied or excess quantities demanded may appear. Our analysis simply indicates what the market clearing price and equilibrium quantity ultimately will be, given a demand curve and a supply curve.

Nowhere in the analysis is there any indication of the speed with which a market will get to a new equilibrium after a shock. The price may even temporarily overshoot the new equilibrium level. Remember this warning when we examine changes in demand and in supply due to changes in their *ceteris paribus* conditions.

QUICK QUIZ See page 95 for the answers. Review concepts from this section in MyEconLab.

When the _____ curve shifts outward or inward with an unchanged _____ curve, equilibrium price and quantity increase or decrease, respectively. When the _____ curve shifts outward or inward given an unchanged _____ curve, equilibrium price moves in the direction opposite to equilibrium quantity.

When there is a shift in demand or supply, the new equilibrium price is not obtained _____. Adjustment takes _____.

The Rationing Function of Prices

The synchronization of decisions by buyers and sellers that leads to equilibrium is called the *rationing function of prices*. Prices are indicators of relative scarcity. An equilibrium price clears the market. The plans of buyers and sellers, given the price, are not frustrated. It is the free interaction of buyers and sellers that sets the price that eventually clears the market. Price, in effect, rations a good to demanders who are willing and able to pay the highest price. Whenever the rationing function of prices is frustrated by government-enforced price ceilings that set prices below the market clearing level, a prolonged shortage results.

Methods of Nonprice Rationing

There are ways other than price to ration goods. *First come, first served* is one method. *Political power* is another. *Physical force* is yet another. Cultural, religious, and physical differences have been and are used as rationing devices throughout the world.

RATIONING BY WAITING Consider first come, first served as a rationing device. We call this *rationing by queues*, where *queue* means "line." Whoever is willing to wait in line the longest obtains the good that is being sold at less than the market clearing price. All who wait in line are paying a higher *total outlay* than the money price paid for the good. Personal time has an opportunity cost. To calculate the total outlay expended on the good, we must add up the money price plus the opportunity cost of the time spent waiting.

Rationing by waiting may occur in situations in which entrepreneurs are free to change prices to equate quantity demanded with quantity supplied but choose not to do so. This results in queues of potential buyers. It may seem that the price in the market is being held below equilibrium by some noncompetitive force. That is not true, however. Such queuing may arise in a free market when the demand for a good is subject to large or unpredictable fluctuations, and the additional costs to firms (and ultimately to consumers) of constantly changing prices or of holding sufficient inventories or providing sufficient excess capacity to cover peak demands are greater than the costs to consumers of waiting for the good.

Common examples are waiting in line to purchase a fast-food lunch and queuing to purchase a movie ticket a few minutes before the next showing.

RATIONING BY RANDOM ASSIGNMENT OR COUPONS *Random assignment* is another way to ration goods. You may have been involved in a rationing-by-random-assignment scheme in college if you were assigned a housing unit. Sometimes rationing by random assignment is used to fill slots in popular classes.

Rationing by *coupons* has also been used, particularly during wartime. In the United States during World War II, families were allotted coupons that allowed them to purchase specified quantities of rationed goods, such as meat and gasoline. To purchase such goods, they had to pay a specified price *and* give up a coupon.

Why has American Airlines been randomly assigning its coach passengers to boarding groups?

EXAMPLE

An Airline Boarding Lottery

For several years now, U.S. airlines have charged coach passengers to transport bags as separate cargo. This practice has induced many passengers to pack more items into carry-on bags that they stuff under seats or into overhead compartments.

American Airlines has been assigning coach boarding-group numbers randomly, rather than by groups of rows starting with the rear of the plane and ending with the front coach rows. Under the latter boarding method, many people with seats at the rear of a plane tend to place their carry-on bags in compartments near the front of the plane. Then people arriving in the front at the end of the boarding process spend time scrambling to find places to stow their carry-ons. In contrast, under a randomized boarding process that ignores row locations, coach passengers are more likely to stow their bags near their seats. This mode of passenger behavior speeds the overall boarding process by several minutes, thereby ensuring that more flights depart on time.

FOR CRITICAL THINKING
Suppose the airline has established a system of boarding fees in which passengers wishing to be among the first to board a plane pay the highest fees. Would such a system likely reduce or lengthen boarding times? Why?

The Essential Role of Rationing

In a world of scarcity, there is, by definition, competition for what is scarce. After all, any resources that are not scarce can be obtained by everyone at a zero price in as large a quantity as everyone wants, such as air to burn in internal combustion engines. Once scarcity arises, there has to be some method to ration the available resources, goods, and services. The price system is one form of rationing. The others that we mentioned are alternatives. Economists cannot say which system of rationing is "best." They can, however, say that rationing via the price system leads to the most efficient use of available resources. As explained in Appendix B, this means that generally in a freely functioning price system, all of the gains from mutually beneficial trade will be captured.

QUICK QUIZ See page 95 for the answers. Review concepts from this section in MyEconLab.

Prices in a market economy perform a rationing function because they reflect relative scarcity, allowing the market to clear. Other ways to ration goods include _____ _____, _____ _____, _____ _____, _____ _____, and _____.

Even when businesspeople can change prices, some rationing by waiting may occur. Such _____ arises when there are large changes in demand coupled with high costs of satisfying those changes immediately.

The Policy of Government-Imposed Price Controls

The rationing function of prices is prevented when governments impose price controls. **Price controls** often involve setting a **price ceiling**—the maximum price that may be allowed in an exchange. The world has had a long history of price ceilings

Price controls
Government-mandated minimum or maximum prices that may be charged for goods and services.

Price ceiling
A legal maximum price that may be charged for a particular good or service.

Price floor

A legal minimum price below which a good or service may not be sold. Legal minimum wages are an example.

YOU ARE THERE

To learn about how government controls of prices of life-saving medications are creating situations in which quantities demanded exceed quantities supplied year after year, read **Explaining the "Crisis" of Persistent Drug Shortages** on page 89.

Nonprice rationing devices

All methods used to ration scarce goods that are price-controlled. Whenever the price system is not allowed to work, nonprice rationing devices will evolve to ration the affected goods and services.

Black market

A market in which goods are traded at prices above their legal maximum prices or in which illegal goods are sold.

applied to product prices, wages, rents, and interest rates. Occasionally, a government will set a **price floor**—a minimum price below which a good or service may not be sold. Price floors have most often been applied to wages and agricultural products. Let's first consider price ceilings.

Price Ceilings and Black Markets

As long as a price ceiling is below the market clearing price, imposing a price ceiling creates a shortage, as can be seen in Figure 4-3 below. At any price below the market clearing, or equilibrium, price of $1,000, there will always be a larger quantity demanded than quantity supplied—a shortage, as you will recall from Chapter 3. Normally, whenever quantity demanded exceeds quantity supplied—that is, when a shortage exists—there is a tendency for the price to rise to its equilibrium level. But with a price ceiling, this tendency cannot be fully realized because everyone is forbidden to trade at the equilibrium price.

The result is fewer exchanges and **nonprice rationing devices.** Figure 4-3 shows the situation for portable electric generators after a natural disaster: The equilibrium quantity of portable generators demanded and supplied (or traded) would be 10,000 units, and the market clearing price would be $1,000 per generator. But, if the government essentially imposes a price ceiling by requiring the price of portable generators to remain at the predisaster level, which the government determines was a price of $600, the equilibrium quantity offered is only 5,000.

Because frustrated consumers will be able to purchase only 5,000 units, there is a shortage. The most obvious nonprice rationing device to help clear the market is queuing, or physical lines, which we have already discussed. To avoid physical lines, waiting lists may be established.

Typically, an effective price ceiling leads to a **black market.** A black market is a market in which the price-controlled good is sold at an illegally high price through various methods. For example, if the price of gasoline is controlled at lower than the market clearing price, drivers who wish to fill up their cars may offer the gas station attendant a cash payment on the side (as happened in the United States in the 1970s and in China and India in the mid-2000s during price controls on gasoline). If the price of beef is controlled at below its market clearing price, a customer who offers the butcher tickets for good seats to an upcoming football game may be allocated otherwise

---

FIGURE 4-3

Black Markets for Portable Electric Generators

The demand curve is *D*. The supply curve is *S*. The equilibrium price is $1,000. The government, however, steps in and imposes a maximum price of $600. At that lower price, the quantity demanded will be 15,000, but the quantity supplied will be only 5,000. There is a "shortage." The implicit price (including time costs) tends to increase to $1,400. If black markets arise, as they generally will, the equilibrium black market price will end up somewhere between $600 and $1,400. The actual quantity transacted will be between 5,000 and 10,000.

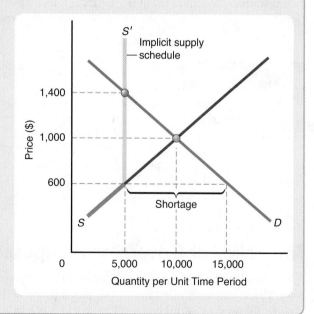

unavailable beef. Indeed, the true implicit price of a price-controlled good or service can be increased in an infinite number of ways, limited only by the imagination. (Black markets also occur when goods are made illegal.)

How have multiple price ceilings magnified electricity shortages in China?

INTERNATIONAL POLICY EXAMPLE

Multiple Price Ceilings Lead to Electricity Rationing in China

In China, two key sources of electricity are coal and diesel fuel that power generators. Sellers of both items, however, confront ceiling prices that are below market clearing levels. Hence, firms operating power generators often struggle to obtain enough coal and diesel fuel to provide as much electricity as they wish to produce. Power companies do not desire to sell as much electricity as many Chinese residents want to use, though, because China's government has also placed ceilings on electricity prices in a number of regional electricity markets.

These multiple price ceilings help to explain why most of the nation commonly faces electricity rationing in the form of "brownouts," or reductions in power flow. Shortages created by the ceiling prices also explain why businesses in more than one-third of China's provinces often have their power completely shut off for days at a time during the coldest weeks of winter and the warmest weeks of summer.

FOR CRITICAL THINKING

Given that China's electricity demand is growing at 13 percent per year, why do you suppose that electricity shortages likely will worsen in the future?

QUICK QUIZ   See page 95 for the answers. Review concepts from this section in MyEconLab.

Governments sometimes impose **price controls** in the form of price _____ and price _____.

An effective price _____ is one that sets the legal price below the market clearing price and is enforced.

Effective price _____ lead to nonprice rationing devices and black markets.

The Policy of Controlling Rents

More than 200 U.S. cities and towns, including Berkeley, California, and New York City, operate under some kind of rent control. **Rent control** is a system under which the local government tells building owners how much they can charge their tenants for rent. In the United States, rent controls date back to at least World War II. The objective of rent control is to keep rents below levels that would be observed in a freely competitive market.

Rent control
Price ceilings on rents.

The Functions of Rental Prices

In any housing market, rental prices serve three functions: (1) to promote the efficient maintenance of existing housing and to stimulate the construction of new housing, (2) to allocate existing scarce housing among competing claimants, and (3) to ration the use of existing housing by current demanders. Rent controls interfere with all of these functions.

RENT CONTROLS AND CONSTRUCTION Rent controls discourage the construction of new rental units. Rents are the most important long-term determinant of profitability, and rent controls artificially depress them. Consider some examples. In a recent year in Dallas, Texas, with a 16 percent rental vacancy rate but no rent control laws, 11,000 new rental housing units were built. In the same year in San Francisco, California, only 2,000 units were built, despite a mere 1.6 percent vacancy rate. The major difference? San Francisco has had stringent rent control laws. In New York City, most rental units being built are luxury units, which are exempt from controls.

EFFECTS ON THE EXISTING SUPPLY OF HOUSING When rental rates are held below equilibrium levels, property owners cannot recover the cost of maintenance, repairs, and capital improvements through higher rents. Hence, they curtail these activities. In the extreme situation, taxes, utilities, and the expenses of basic repairs exceed rental receipts. The result has been abandoned buildings from Santa Monica, California, to New York City. Some owners have resorted to arson, hoping to collect the insurance on their empty buildings before the city claims them to pay back taxes.

RATIONING THE CURRENT USE OF HOUSING Rent controls also affect the current use of housing because they restrict tenant mobility. Consider a family whose children have gone off to college. That family might want to live in a smaller apartment. But in a rent-controlled environment, giving up a rent-controlled unit can entail a substantial cost. In most rent-controlled cities, rents can be adjusted only when a tenant leaves. That means that a move from a long-occupied rent-controlled apartment to a smaller apartment can involve a hefty rent hike. In New York, this artificial preservation of the status quo came to be known as "housing gridlock."

Go to www.econtoday.com/chap04 to learn more about New York City's rent controls from Tenant.net.

Attempts to Evade Rent Controls

The distortions produced by rent controls lead to efforts by both property owners and tenants to evade the rules. These efforts lead to the growth of expensive government bureaucracies whose job it is to make sure that rent controls aren't evaded. In New York City, because rent on a rent-controlled apartment can be raised only if the tenant leaves, property owners have had an incentive to make life unpleasant for tenants in order to drive them out or to evict them on the slightest pretext. The city has responded by making evictions extremely costly for property owners. Eviction requires a tedious and expensive judicial proceeding.

Tenants, for their part, routinely try to sublet all or part of their rent-controlled apartments at fees substantially above the rent they pay to the owner. Both the city and the property owners try to prohibit subletting and often end up in the city's housing courts—an entire judicial system developed to deal with disputes involving rent-controlled apartments. The overflow and appeals from the city's housing courts sometimes clog the rest of New York's judicial system.

Who Gains and Who Loses from Rent Controls?

The big losers from rent controls are clearly property owners. But there is another group of losers—low-income individuals, especially single mothers, trying to find apartments. Some observers now believe that rent controls have worsened the problem of homelessness in cities such as New York.

Often, owners of rent-controlled apartments charge "key money" before allowing a new tenant to move in. This is a large up-front cash payment, usually illegal but demanded nonetheless—just one aspect of the black market in rent-controlled apartments. Poor individuals have insufficient income to pay the hefty key money payment, nor can they assure the owner that their rent will be on time or even paid each month.

Because controlled rents are usually below market clearing levels, apartment owners have little incentive to take any risk on low-income individuals as tenants. This is particularly true when a prospective tenant's chief source of income is a welfare check. Indeed, a large number of the litigants in the New York housing courts are welfare mothers who have missed their rent payments due to emergency expenses or delayed welfare checks. Their appeals often end in evictions and a new home in a temporary public shelter—or on the streets.

Who benefits from rent control? Ample evidence indicates that upper-income professionals benefit the most. These people can use their mastery of the bureaucracy and their large network of friends and connections to exploit the rent control system. Consider that in New York, actresses Mia Farrow and Cicely Tyson live in rent-controlled apartments, paying well below market rates. So do the former director of the Metropolitan Museum of Art and singer and children's book author Carly Simon.

_____ prices perform three functions: (1) allocating existing scarce housing among competing claimants, (2) promoting efficient maintenance of existing houses and stimulating new housing construction, and (3) rationing the use of existing houses by current demanders.

Effective rent _____ impede the functioning of rental prices. Construction of new rental units is discouraged.

Rent _____ decrease spending on maintenance of existing ones and also lead to "housing gridlock."

There are numerous ways to evade rent controls. _____ _____ is one.

Price Floors in Agriculture

Another way that government can affect markets is by imposing price floors or price supports. In the United States, price supports are most often associated with agricultural products.

Price Supports

During the Great Depression, the federal government swung into action to help farmers. In 1933, it established a system of price supports for many agricultural products. Since then, there have been price supports for wheat, feed grains, cotton, rice, soybeans, sorghum, and dairy products, among other foodstuffs. The nature of the supports is quite simple: The government simply chooses a *support price* for an agricultural product and then acts to ensure that the price of the product never falls below the support level. Figure 4-4 below shows the market demand for and supply of milk. Without a price-support program, competitive forces would yield an equilibrium price of $0.08 per pound and an equilibrium quantity of 15.4 billion pounds per year. Clearly, if the government were to set the support price at or below $0.08 per pound, the quantity of milk demanded would equal the quantity of milk supplied at point E, because farmers could sell all they wanted at the market clearing price of $0.08 per pound.

FIGURE 4-4

Agricultural Price Supports

Free market equilibrium occurs at *E*, with an equilibrium price of $0.08 per pound and an equilibrium quantity of 15.4 billion pounds. When the government sets a support price at $0.10 per pound, the quantity demanded is 15 billion pounds and the quantity supplied is 16 billion pounds. The difference is the surplus, which the government buys. Farmers' income from consumers equals $0.10 per pound × 1 billion pounds = $100 million.

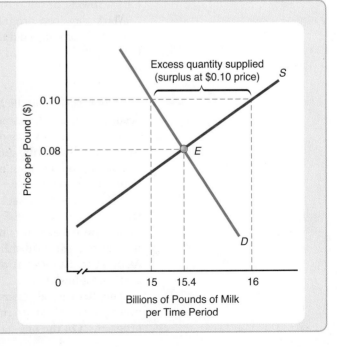

But what happens when the government sets the support price *above* the market clearing price, at $0.10 per pound? At a support price of $0.10 per pound, the quantity demanded is only 15 billion pounds, but the quantity supplied is 16 billion pounds. The 1-billion-pound difference between them is called the *excess quantity supplied*, or *surplus*. As simple as this program seems, its existence creates a fundamental question: How can the government agency charged with administering the price-support program prevent market forces from pushing the actual price down to $0.08 per pound?

If production exceeds the amount that consumers want to buy at the support price, what happens to the surplus? Quite simply, if the price-support program is to work, the government has to buy the surplus—the 1-billion-pound difference. As a practical matter, the government acquires the 1-billion-pound surplus indirectly through a government agency. The government either stores the surplus or sells it to foreign countries at a greatly reduced price (or gives it away free of charge) under the Food for Peace program.

Who Benefits from Agricultural Price Supports?

Although agricultural price supports have traditionally been promoted as a way to guarantee "decent" earnings for low-income farmers, most of the benefits have in fact gone to the owners of very large farms. Price-support payments are made on a per-pound basis, not on a per-farm basis. Thus, traditionally, the larger the farm, the bigger the benefit from agricultural price supports. In addition, *all* of the benefits from price supports ultimately accrue to *landowners* on whose land price-supported crops grow.

KEEPING PRICE SUPPORTS ALIVE UNDER A NEW NAME Back in the early 1990s, Congress indicated an intention to phase out most agricultural subsidies by the early 2000s. What Congress actually *did* throughout the 1990s, however, was to pass a series of "emergency laws" keeping farm subsidies alive. Some of these laws aimed to replace agricultural price supports with payments to many farmers for growing no crops at all, thereby boosting the market prices of crops by reducing supply. Nevertheless, the federal government and several state governments have continued to support prices of a number of agricultural products, such as peanuts, through "marketing loan" programs. These programs advance funds to farmers to help them finance the storage of some or all of their crops. The farmers can then use the stored produce as collateral for borrowing or sell it to the government and use the proceeds to repay debts.

Marketing loan programs raise the effective price that farmers receive for their crops and commit federal and state governments to purchasing surplus production. Consequently, they lead to outcomes similar to those of traditional price-support programs.

THE MAIN BENEFICIARIES OF AGRICULTURAL SUBSIDIES In 2002, Congress enacted the Farm Security Act, which has perpetuated marketing loan programs and other subsidy and price-support arrangements for such farm products as wheat, corn, rice, peanuts, and soybeans. All told, the more than $9 billion in U.S. government payments for these and other products amounts to about 25 percent of the annual market value of all U.S. farm production.

The government seeks to cap the annual subsidy payment that an individual farmer can receive at $360,000 per year, but some farmers are able to garner higher annual amounts by exploiting regulatory loopholes. The greatest share of total agricultural subsidies goes to the owners of the largest farming operations. At present, 10 percent of U.S. farmers receive more than 70 percent of agricultural subsidies.

The 2008 Food, Conservation, and Energy Act expanded on the 2002 legislation by giving farmers raising any of a number of crops a choice between subsidy programs. On the one hand, farmers can opt to participate in traditional programs involving a mix of direct payments and marketing loan programs. On the other hand, farmers can choose a program offering guaranteed revenues. If market clearing crop prices end up higher than those associated with the government's revenue guarantee, farmers sell their crops at the higher prices instead of collecting government subsidies. But if equilibrium crop prices end up below a level consistent with the government guarantee, farmers receive direct subsidies to bring their total revenues up to the guaranteed level.

WHAT IF... the government decides to "help dairy farmers" by imposing a floor price in the market for milk that is above the equilibrium price?

The floor price above the equilibrium level would cause the quantity of milk supplied by dairy farmers to rise above the quantity demanded by consumers. The government would have to purchase the surplus milk, which would indeed "help" the dairy farmers from whom the milk would be purchased. As a result, consumers, such as parents of young children, would have to pay a higher price for each unit of the smaller quantity of milk that they will choose to buy. Thus, the government's price-support program would necessarily "help dairy farmers" at the expense of milk consumers.

Price Floors in the Labor Market

The **minimum wage** is the lowest hourly wage rate that firms may legally pay their workers. Proponents favor higher minimum wages to ensure low-income workers a "decent" standard of living. Opponents counter that higher minimum wages cause increased unemployment, particularly among unskilled minority teenagers.

Minimum wage
A wage floor, legislated by government, setting the lowest hourly rate that firms may legally pay workers.

Minimum Wages in the United States

The federal minimum wage started in 1938 at 25 cents an hour, about 40 percent of the average manufacturing wage at the time. Typically, its level has stayed at about 40 to 50 percent of average manufacturing wages. After holding the minimum wage at $5.15 per hour from 1997 to 2007, Congress enacted a series of phased increases in the hourly minimum wage, effective on July 24 of each year, to $5.85 in 2007, $6.55 in 2008, and $7.25 in 2009.

Many states and cities have their own minimum wage laws that exceed the federal minimum. A number of municipalities refer to their minimum wage rules as "living wage" laws. Governments of these municipalities seek to set minimum wages consistent with living standards they deem to be socially acceptable—that is, overall wage income judged to be sufficient to purchase basic items such as housing and food.

Go to www.econtoday.com/chap04 for information from the U.S. Department of Labor about recent developments concerning the federal minimum wage.

Economic Effects of a Minimum Wage

What happens when the government establishes a floor on wages? The effects can be seen in Figure 4-5 on the following page. We start off in equilibrium with the equilibrium wage rate of W_e and the equilibrium quantity of labor equal to Q_e. A minimum wage, W_m, higher than W_e, is imposed. At W_m, the quantity demanded for labor is reduced to Q_d, and some workers now become unemployed. Certain workers will become unemployed as a result of the minimum wage, but others will move to sectors where minimum wage laws do not apply. Wages will be pushed down in these uncovered sectors.

Note that the reduction in employment from Q_e to Q_d, or the distance from B to A, is less than the excess quantity of labor supplied at wage rate W_m. This excess quantity supplied is the distance between A and C, or the distance between Q_d and Q_s. The reason the reduction in employment is smaller than the excess quantity of

FIGURE 4-5

The Effect of Minimum Wages

The market clearing wage rate is W_e. The market clearing quantity of employment is Q_e, determined by the intersection of supply and demand at point E. A minimum wage equal to W_m is established. The quantity of labor demanded is reduced to Q_d. The reduction in employment from Q_e to Q_d is equal to the distance between B and A. That distance is smaller than the excess quantity of labor supplied at wage rate W_m. The distance between B and C is the increase in the quantity of labor supplied that results from the higher minimum wage rate.

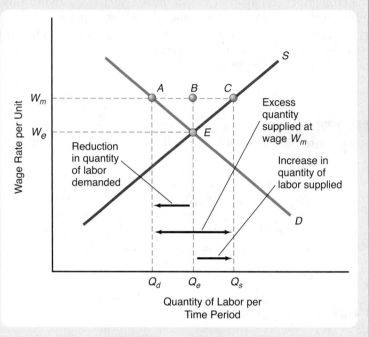

labor supplied at the minimum wage is that the excess quantity of labor supplied also includes the *additional* workers who would like to work more hours at the new, higher minimum wage.

In the long run (a time period that is long enough to allow for full adjustment by workers and firms), some of the reduction in the quantity of labor demanded will result from a reduction in the number of firms, and some will result from changes in the number of workers employed by each firm. Economists estimate that a 10 percent increase in the inflation-adjusted minimum wage decreases total employment of those affected by 1 to 2 percent.

We can conclude from the application of demand and supply analysis that a minimum wage established above the equilibrium wage rate typically has two fundamental effects. On the one hand, it boosts the wage earnings of those people who obtain employment. On the other hand, the minimum wage results in unemployment for other individuals. Thus, demand and supply analysis implies that the minimum wage makes some people better off while making others worse off.

How have teenagers fared following successive increases in the minimum wage in 2007, 2008, and 2009?

POLICY EXAMPLE

A Higher Minimum Wage Translates into Fewer Employed Teens

In three steps between 2007 and 2009, the federal government boosted the minimum wage rate faced by all employers in the 50 states from $5.15 per hour to $7.25 per hour. The legislation had almost no effects in 18 states in which market wages were generally already higher than $7.25 per hour. In the other 32 states, though, the three-stage hike in the minimum wage reduced total employment of teens by an estimated 2.5 percentage points. The result for these states was an estimated reduction in the number of employed teens totaling more than 114,000 teens, who consequently joined the ranks of the nation's unemployed.

FOR CRITICAL THINKING

What do you suppose has happened to the teen unemployment rate as the demand for labor has fallen and remained dampened since the 2008–2009 economic downturn?

Quantity Restrictions

Governments can impose quantity restrictions on a market. The most obvious restriction is an outright ban on the ownership or trading of a good. It is currently illegal to buy and sell human organs. It is also currently illegal to buy and sell certain psychoactive drugs such as cocaine, heroin, and methamphetamine. In some states, it is illegal to start a new hospital without obtaining a license for a particular number of beds to be offered to patients. This licensing requirement effectively limits the quantity of hospital beds in some states. From 1933 to 1973, it was illegal for U.S. citizens to own gold except for manufacturing, medicinal, or jewelry purposes.

Some of the most common quantity restrictions exist in the area of international trade. The U.S. government, as well as many foreign governments, imposes import quotas on a variety of goods. An **import quota** is a supply restriction that prohibits the importation of more than a specified quantity of a particular good in a one-year period. The United States has had import quotas on tobacco, sugar, and immigrant labor. For many years, there were import quotas on oil coming into the United States. There are also "voluntary" import quotas on certain goods. For instance, since the mid-2000s, the Chinese government has agreed to "voluntarily" restrict the amount of textile products China sends to the United States and the European Union.

Import quota
A physical supply restriction on imports of a particular good, such as sugar. Foreign exporters are unable to sell in the United States more than the quantity specified in the import quota.

QUICK QUIZ   See page 95 for the answers. Review concepts from this section in MyEconLab.

With a price-_____ system, the government sets a minimum price at which, say, qualifying farm products can be sold. Any farmers who cannot sell at that price in the market can "sell" their surplus to the government. The only way a price-_____ system can survive is for the government or some other entity to buy up the excess quantity supplied at the support price.

When a _____ is placed on wages at a rate that is above market equilibrium, the result is an excess quantity of labor supplied at that minimum wage.

Quantity restrictions may take the form of _____ _____, which are limits on the quantity of specific foreign goods that can be brought into the United States for resale purposes.

YOU ARE THERE
Explaining the "Crisis" of Persistent Drug Shortages

According to Bona Benjamin of the American Society of Health-System Pharmacists, "We are in a crisis situation" in terms of shortages of many drugs used to treat a variety of diseases, including cancer. In 2006, the U.S. Food and Drug Administration (FDA) identified persistent shortages of 55 drugs. Today, there are shortages of about 300 drugs.

Benjamin and others involved in the markets for pharmaceuticals suggest that the persistent shortages of many drugs result from government price restrictions. The FDA can place limits on the percentage increase in a drug's price during a given year. Such a limitation often causes the allowed level of a drug's price in a given year to be lower than the market clearing price. Thus, the FDA's restraint on allowed price growth creates a shortage. If the FDA continues imposing limits on annual percentage increases in the price that are too low in relation to the rate of increase in the market clearing price, then the result is a persistent shortage.

Each year, the FDA has also broadened the list of medications for which limits on annual rates of allowed percentage price increases apply. This is why the number of drugs experiencing persistent shortages has increased.

Critical Thinking Questions

1. What would happen to the magnitudes of drug shortages if the FDA allowed higher annual price increases?

2. Would drug shortages be likely to persist if price controls were lifted? Explain.

ISSUES & APPLICATIONS

Why Prices of Used Cars Are So High

CONCEPTS APPLIED

▶ Supply

▶ Demand

▶ Market Clearing Price

Since 2009, the average price of a used car has increased by nearly 10 percent. Prices of a number of used models have risen by more than 30 percent. In some cases, prices of used cars are within a few hundred dollars of the prices of newly produced versions of the same models. These significant price increases can be explained by simultaneous changes in the supply of and demand for used cars.

"Cash for Clunkers" and a Decreased Supply of Used Cars

During the summer of 2009, the federal government implemented a program that became widely known as "cash for clunkers." Under this program, the government provided owners of specific low-fuel-economy vehicles with vouchers that the owners could apply toward purchases of new, more fuel-efficient vehicles. Ultimately, the government expended nearly $3 billion to purchase and crush (or shred) almost 700,000 used vehicles.

In the years since 2009, many of the vehicles destroyed under the program would have been available for sale in the used-car market. Their absence reduced the market supply of used vehicles: Fewer used vehicles were offered for sale at any given used-car price. Consequently, as shown in Figure 4-6 below, the market supply curve for used cars shifted leftward.

FIGURE 4-6

The Effects of a Decrease in the Supply of Used Cars in Conjunction with an Increase in the Demand for Used Cars

The federal government's cash-for-clunkers program removed hundreds of thousands of used cars from the used-car market, resulting in a decrease in supply, depicted by the leftward shift in the supply curve from S_1 to S_2. In addition, higher new-car prices induced consumers to substitute in favor of used cars, resulting in an increase in demand, shown by the rightward shift in the demand curve from D_1 to D_2. The market clearing price of used cars increased, from P_1 to P_2, and the equilibrium quantity of used cars decreased, from Q_1 to Q_2.

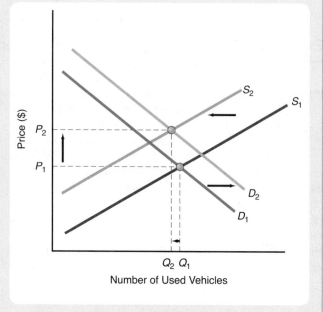

Higher Prices of New Cars Boost the Demand for Used Cars

Then, in 2011, northeastern Japan was struck both by destructive earthquakes and by a massive tsunami. Manufacturers based in Japan supply one of every four newly produced autos sold in the United States. For months following the disaster, exports of vehicles produced in Japan and shipments of Japanese-produced vehicle parts to U.S.-based assembly facilities of Japanese automakers were halted or delayed. The result was a fall in the supply of *new* vehicles, which led to an increase in the market clearing price of *new* cars.

Because new cars are a substitute for used vehicles, the rise in the price of new cars generated an increase in the demand for *used* vehicles: People desired to purchase more used vehicles at any given used-car price. Thus, as shown in Figure 4-6, the demand curve for used cars shifted rightward.

Taken together, the reduction in the supply of used cars caused by the cash-for-clunkers program and the increase in demand caused by higher new-car prices generated an increase in the market clearing price of used cars. The observed equilibrium-quantity outcome in the used-car market has been a slight decrease, as displayed in the figure.

For Critical Thinking

1. If used cars are a normal good and consumers' incomes were to fall during the next few years, what would happen to the market clearing price of used cars?
2. If the price change discussed in Question 1 were to occur, would this cause a change in the supply of used cars or in the quantity supplied? Explain.

Web Resources

1. Learn more about the federal government's cash-for-clunkers program at www.econtoday.com/chap04.
2. For a discussion of the lengthy production delays faced by Japanese automakers for an extended period following the earthquake and tsunami disaster, go to www.econtoday.com/chap04.

MyEconLab

For more questions on this chapter's Issues & Applications, go to MyEconLab. In the Study Plan for this chapter, select Section N: News.

MyEconLab

Here is what you should know after reading this chapter. MyEconLab will help you identify what you know, and where to go when you need to practice.

WHAT YOU SHOULD KNOW		WHERE TO GO TO PRACTICE
Essential Features of the Price System In the price system, prices respond to changes in supply and demand. Decisions on resource use depend on what happens to prices. Middlemen reduce transaction costs by bringing buyers and sellers together.	price system, 76 voluntary exchange, 76 transaction costs, 76	• MyEconLab Study Plan 4.1
How Changes in Demand and Supply Affect the Market Price and Equilibrium Quantity With a given supply curve, an increase in demand causes increases in the market price and equilibrium quantity, and a decrease in demand induces decreases in the market price and equilibrium quantity. With a given demand curve, an increase in supply causes a fall in the market price and an increase in the equilibrium quantity, and a decrease in supply causes a rise in the market price and a decline in the equilibrium quantity. When both demand and supply shift at the same time, we must know the direction and amount of each shift in order to predict changes in the market price and the equilibrium quantity.	Key Figure Figure 4-1, 78	• MyEconLab Study Plan 4.2 • Animated Figure 4-1

MyEconLab *continued*

WHAT YOU SHOULD KNOW ——————————————————————— WHERE TO GO TO PRACTICE —

The Rationing Function of Prices In the price system, prices ration scarce goods and services. Other ways of rationing include first come, first served; political power; physical force; random assignment; and coupons.

- MyEconLab Study Plan 4.3

The Effects of Price Ceilings Government-imposed price controls that require prices to be no higher than a certain level are price ceilings. If a government sets a price ceiling below the market price, then at the ceiling price the quantity of the good demanded will exceed the quantity supplied. There will be a shortage at the ceiling price. Price ceilings can lead to nonprice rationing devices and black markets.

price controls, 81
price ceiling, 81
price floor, 82
nonprice rationing
  devices, 82
black market, 82
rent control, 83

Key Figure
Figure 4-3, 82

- MyEconLab Study Plans 4.4, 4.5
- Animated Figure 4-3

The Effects of Price Floors Government-mandated price controls that require prices to be no lower than a certain level are price floors. If a government sets a price floor above the market price, then at the floor price the quantity of the good supplied will exceed the quantity demanded. There will be a surplus at the floor price.

minimum wage, 87

Key Figures
Figure 4-4, 85
Figure 4-5, 88

- MyEconLab Study Plans 4.6, 4.7
- Animated Figures 4-4, 4-5

Government-Imposed Restrictions on Market Quantities Quantity restrictions can take the form of outright government bans on the sale of certain goods. They can also arise from licensing and import restrictions that limit the number of sellers and thereby restrict the amount supplied.

import quota, 89

- MyEconLab Study Plan 4.8

Log in to MyEconLab, take a chapter test, and get a personalized Study Plan that tells you which concepts you understand and which ones you need to review. From there, MyEconLab will give you further practice, tutorials, animations, videos, and guided solutions. For more information, visit www.myeconlab.com

PROBLEMS

All problems are assignable in MyEconLab. Answers to odd-numbered problems appear at the back of the book.

4-1. In recent years, technological improvements have greatly reduced the costs of producing basic cell phones, and a number of new firms have entered the cell phone industry. At the same time, prices of substitutes for cell phones, such as smartphones and some tablet devices, have declined considerably. Construct a supply and demand diagram of the market for cell phones. Illustrate the impacts of these developments, and evaluate the effects on the market price and equilibrium quantity. (See page 78.)

4-2. Advances in research and development in the pharmaceutical industry have enabled manufacturers to identify potential cures more quickly and therefore at lower cost. At the same time, the aging of our society has increased the demand for new drugs. Construct a supply and demand diagram of the market for pharmaceutical drugs. Illustrate the impacts of these developments, and evaluate the effects on the market price and the equilibrium quantity. (See page 78.)

4-3. There are simultaneous changes in the demand for and supply of global-positioning-system (GPS) devices, with the consequences being an unambiguous increase in the market clearing price of these devices but no change in the equilibrium quantity. What changes in the demand for and supply of GPS devices could have generated these outcomes? Explain. (See pages 78–79.)

4-4. There are simultaneous changes in the demand for and supply of tablet devices, with the consequences being an unambiguous decrease in the equilibrium quantity of these devices but no change in the market clearing price. What changes in the demand for and supply of tablet devices could have generated these outcomes? Explain. (See pages 78–79.)

4-5. The following table depicts the quantity demanded and quantity supplied of studio apartments in a small college town.

Monthly Rent	Quantity Demanded	Quantity Supplied
$600	3,000	1,600
$650	2,500	1,800
$700	2,000	2,000
$750	1,500	2,200
$800	1,000	2,400

What are the market price and equilibrium quantity of apartments in this town? If this town imposes a rent control of $650 per month, how many studio apartments will be rented? (See pages 83–84.)

4-6. Suppose that the government places a ceiling on the price of a medical drug below the equilibrium price. (See page 82.)

a. Show why there is a shortage of the medical drug at the new ceiling price.

b. Suppose that a black market for the medical drug arises, with pharmaceutical firms secretly selling the drug at higher prices. Illustrate the black market for this medical drug, including the implicit supply schedule, the ceiling price, the black market supply and demand, and the highest feasible black market price.

4-7. The table below illustrates the demand and supply schedules for seats on air flights between two cities:

Price	Quantity Demanded	Quantity Supplied
$200	2,000	1,200
$300	1,800	1,400
$400	1,600	1,600
$500	1,400	1,800
$600	1,200	2,000

What are the market price and equilibrium quantity in this market? Now suppose that federal authorities limit the number of flights between the two cities to ensure that no more than 1,200 passengers can be flown. Evaluate the effects of this quota if price adjusts. (Hint: What price per flight are the 1,200 passengers willing to pay? See page 89.)

4-8. The consequences of decriminalizing illegal drugs have long been debated. Some claim that legalization will lower the price of these drugs and reduce related crime and that more people will use these drugs. Suppose that some of these drugs are legalized so that anyone may sell them and use them. Now consider the two claims—that price will fall and quantity demanded will increase. Based on positive economic analysis, are these claims sound? (See page 89.)

4-9. In recent years, the government of Pakistan has established a support price for wheat of about $0.20 per kilogram of wheat. At this price, consumers are willing to purchase 10 billion kilograms of wheat per year, while Pakistani farmers are willing to grow and harvest 18 billion kilograms of wheat per year. The government purchases and stores all surplus wheat. (See page 85.)

a. What are annual consumer expenditures on the Pakistani wheat crop?

b. What are annual government expenditures on the Pakistani wheat crop?

c. How much, in total, do Pakistani wheat farmers receive for the wheat they produce?

4-10. Consider the information in Problem 4-9 and your answers to that question. Suppose that the market clearing price of Pakistani wheat in the absence of price supports is equal to $0.10 per kilogram. At this price, the quantity of wheat demanded is 12 billion kilograms. Under the government wheat price-support program, how much more is spent each year on wheat harvested in Pakistan than otherwise would have been spent in an unregulated market for Pakistani wheat? (See page 85.)

4-11. Consider the diagram below, which depicts the labor market in a city that has adopted a "living wage law" requiring employers to pay a minimum wage rate of $11 per hour. Answer the questions that follow. (See page 88.)

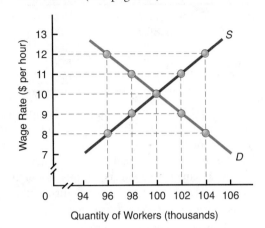

a. What condition exists in this city's labor market at the present minimum wage of $11 per hour? How many people are unemployed at this wage?

b. A city councilwoman has proposed amending the living wage law. She suggests reducing the minimum wage to $9 per hour. Assuming that the labor demand and supply curves were to remain in their present positions, how many people would be unemployed at a new $9 minimum wage?

c. A councilman has offered a counterproposal. In his view, the current minimum wage is too low and should be increased to $12 per hour. Assuming that the labor demand and supply curves remain in their present positions, how many people would be unemployed at a new $12 minimum wage?

4-12. A city has decided to impose rent controls, and it has established a rent ceiling below the previous equilibrium rental rate for offices throughout the city. How will the quantity of offices leased by building owners change? (See page 83.)

4-13. In 2011, the government of a nation established a price support for wheat. The government's support price has been above the equilibrium price each year since, and the government has purchased all wheat over and above the amounts that consumers have bought at the support price. Every year since 2011, there has been an increase in the number of wheat producers in the market. No other factors affecting the market for wheat have changed. Predict what has happened every year since 2011, to each of the following (see page 85):

a. Amount of wheat supplied by wheat producers

b. Amount of wheat demanded by all wheat consumers

c. Amount of wheat purchased by the government

4-14. In advance of the recent increase in the U.S. minimum wage rate, the government of the state of Arizona decided to boost its own minimum wage by an additional $1.60 per hour. This pushed the wage rate earned by Arizona teenagers above the equilibrium wage rate in the teen labor market. What is the predicted effect of this action by Arizona's government on each of the following? (See page 88.)

a. The quantity of labor supplied by Arizona teenagers

b. The quantity of labor demanded by employers of Arizona teenagers

c. The number of unemployed Arizona teenagers

ECONOMICS ON THE NET

The Floor on Milk Prices At various times, the U.S. government has established price floors for milk. This application gives you an opportunity to apply what you have learned in this chapter to this real-world issue.

Title: Northeast Dairy Compact Commission

Navigation: Go to **www.econtoday.com/chap04** to visit the Web site of the Northeast Dairy Compact Commission.

Application Read the contents and answer these questions.

1. Based on the government-set price control concepts discussed in Chapter 4, explain the Northeast Dairy Compact that was once in place in the northeastern United States.

2. Draw a diagram illustrating the supply of and demand for milk in the Northeast Dairy Compact and the supply of and demand for milk outside the Northeast

Dairy Compact. Illustrate how the compact affected the quantities demanded and supplied for participants in the compact. In addition, show how this affected the market for milk produced by those producers outside the dairy compact.

3. Economists have found that while the Northeast Dairy Compact functioned, midwestern dairy farmers lost their dominance of milk production and sales.

In light of your answer to Question 2, explain how this occurred.

For Group Discussion and Analysis Discuss the impact of congressional failure to reauthorize the compact based on your above answers. Identify which arguments in your debate are based on positive economic analysis and which are normative arguments.

ANSWERS TO QUICK QUIZZES

p. 80: (i) demand . . . supply . . . supply . . . demand; (ii) immediately . . . time

p. 81: (i) first come, first served . . . political power . . . physical force . . . random assignment . . . coupons; (ii) queuing

p. 83: (i) ceilings . . . floors; (ii) ceiling . . . controls

p. 85: (i) Rental; (ii) controls . . . controls; (iii) Key money

p. 89: (i) support . . . support; (ii) floor; (iii) import quotas

APPENDIX B

Consumer Surplus, Producer Surplus, and Gains from Trade within a Price System

A key principle of economics is that the price system enables people to benefit from the voluntary exchange of goods and services. Economists measure the benefits from trade by applying the concepts of *consumer surplus* and *producer surplus*, which are defined in the sections that follow.

Consumer Surplus

Let's first examine how economists measure the benefits that consumers gain from engaging in market transactions in the price system. Consider Figure B-1 below, which displays a market demand curve, D. We begin by assuming that consumers face a per-unit price of this item given by P_A. Thus, the quantity demanded of this particular product is equal to Q_A at point A on the demand curve.

FIGURE B-1

Consumer Surplus

If the per-unit price is P_A, then at point A on the demand curve D, consumers desire to purchase Q_A units. To purchase Q_1 units of this item, consumers would have been willing to pay the price P_1 for the last unit purchased, but they have to pay only the per-unit price P_A, so they gain a surplus equal to $P_1 - P_A$ for the last of the Q_1 units purchased. Likewise, to buy the last of the Q_2 units, consumers would have been willing to pay the price P_2, so they gain the surplus equal to $P_2 - P_A$ for the last of the Q_2 units purchased. Summing these and all other surpluses that consumers receive from purchasing each of the Q_A units at the price P_A yields the total consumer surplus at this price, shown by the blue-shaded area.

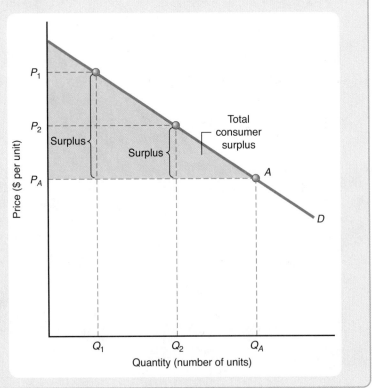

Typically, we visualize the market demand curve as indicating the quantities that all consumers are willing to purchase at each possible price. But the demand curve also tells us the price that consumers are willing to pay for a unit of output at various possible quantities. For instance, if consumers buy Q_1 units of this good, they will be willing to pay a price equal to P_1 for the last unit purchased. If they have to pay only the price P_A for each unit they buy, however, consumers gain an amount equal to $P_1 - P_A$ for the last of the Q_1 units purchased. This benefit to consumers equals the vertical distance between the demand curve and the level of the market clearing price. Economists call this vertical distance a *surplus* value to consumers from being able to consume the last of the Q_1 units at the lower, market clearing price.

Likewise, if consumers purchase Q_2 units of this good, they will be willing to pay a price equal to P_2 for the last unit. Nevertheless, because they have to pay only the price P_A for each unit purchased, consumers gain an amount equal to $P_2 - P_A$. Hence, this is the surplus associated with the last of the Q_2 units that consumers buy.

Of course, when consumers pay the same per-unit price P_A for every unit of this product that they purchase at point A, they obtain Q_A units. Thus, consumers gain surplus values—all of the vertical distances between the demand curve and the level of the market clearing price—for each unit consumed, up to the total of Q_A units. Graphically, this is equivalent to the blue-shaded *area under the demand curve but above the market clearing price* in Figure B-1 on the facing page. This entire area equals the total **consumer surplus,** which is the difference between the total amount that consumers *would have been willing to pay* for an item and the total amount that they actually pay.

Consumer surplus
The difference between the total amount that consumers would have been willing to pay for an item and the total amount that they actually pay.

Producer Surplus

Consumers are not the only ones who gain from exchange. Producers (suppliers) gain as well. To consider how economists measure the benefits to producers from supplying goods and services in exchange, look at Figure B-2 below, which displays a market supply curve, S. Let's begin by assuming that suppliers face a per-unit price of this item given by P_B. Thus, the quantity supplied of this particular product is equal to Q_B at point B on the supply curve.

FIGURE B-2

Producer Surplus

If the per-unit price is P_B, then at point B on the supply curve S, producers are willing to supply Q_B units. To sell Q_3 units of this item, producers would have been willing to receive the price P_3 for the last unit sold, but instead they accept the higher per-unit price P_B, so they gain a surplus equal to $P_B - P_3$ for the last of the Q_3 units sold. Similarly, producers would have been willing to accept P_4 to provide Q_4 units, so they gain the surplus equal to $P_B - P_4$ for the last of the Q_4 units sold. Summing these and all other surpluses that producers receive from supplying each of the Q_B units at the price P_B yields the total producer surplus at this price, shown by the red-shaded area.

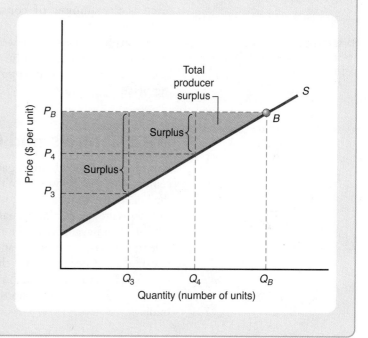

The market supply curve tells us the quantities that all producers are willing to to sell at each possible price. At the same time, the supply curve also indicates the price that producers are willing to accept to sell a unit of output at various possible quantities. For example, if producers sell Q_3 units of this good, they will be willing to accept a price equal to P_3 for the last unit sold. If they receive the price P_B for each unit that they supply, however, producers gain an amount equal to $P_B - P_3$ for the last of the Q_3 units sold. This benefit to producers equals the vertical distance between the supply curve and the market clearing price, which is a *surplus* value from being able to provide the last of the Q_3 units at the higher, market clearing price.

Similarly, if producers supply Q_4 units of this good, they will be willing to accept a price equal to P_4 for the last unit. Producers actually receive the price P_B for each unit supplied, however, so they gain an amount equal to $P_B - P_4$. Hence, this is the surplus gained from supplying the last of the Q_4 units.

Naturally, when producers receive the same per-unit price P_B for each unit supplied at point B, producers sell Q_B units. Consequently, producers gain surplus values—all of the vertical distances between the level of the market clearing price and the supply curve—for each unit supplied, up to the total of Q_B units. In Figure B-2 on the previous page, this is equivalent to the red-shaded *area above the supply curve but below the market clearing price*. This area is the total **producer surplus,** which is the difference between the total amount that producers actually receive for an item and the total amount that they *would have been willing to accept* for supplying that item.

Producer surplus
The difference between the total amount that producers actually receive for an item and the total amount that they would have been willing to accept for supplying that item.

Gains from Trade within a Price System

The concepts of consumer surplus and producer surplus can be combined to measure the gains realized by consumers and producers from engaging in voluntary exchange. To see how, take a look at Figure B-3 on the facing page. The market demand and supply curves intersect at point E, and as you have learned, at this point, the equilibrium quantity is Q_E. At the market clearing price P_E, this is both the quantity that consumers are willing to purchase and the quantity that producers are willing to supply.

In addition, at the market clearing price P_E and the equilibrium quantity Q_E, the blue-shaded area under the demand curve but above the market clearing price is the amount of consumer surplus. Furthermore, the red-shaded area under the market clearing price but above the supply curve is the amount of producer surplus. The sum of *both* areas is the total value of the **gains from trade**—the sum of consumer surplus and producer surplus—generated by the mutually beneficial voluntary exchange of the equilibrium quantity Q_E at the market clearing price P_E.

Gains from trade
The sum of consumer surplus and producer surplus.

Price Controls and Gains from Trade

How do price controls affect gains from trade? Consider first the effects of imposing a ceiling price that is lower than the market clearing price. As you learned in Chapter 4, the results are an increase in quantity demanded and a decrease in quantity supplied, so a shortage occurs. The smaller quantity supplied by firms is the amount actually produced and available in the market for the item in question. Thus, consumers are able to purchase fewer units, and this means that consumer surplus may be lower than it would have been without the government's price ceiling. Furthermore, because firms sell fewer units at the lower ceiling price, producer surplus definitely decreases. Thus, the government's imposition of the price ceiling tends to reduce gains from trade.

Consumer Surplus, Producer Surplus, and Gains from Trade

At point E, the demand and supply curves intersect at the equilibrium quantity Q_E and the market clearing price P_E. Total consumer surplus at the market clearing price is the blue-shaded area under the demand curve but above the market clearing price. Total producer surplus is the red-shaded area below the market clearing price but above the supply curve. The sum of consumer surplus and producer surplus at the market clearing price constitutes the total gain to society from voluntary exchange of the quantity Q_E at the market clearing price P_E.

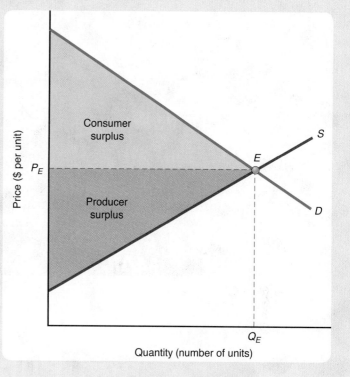

Now consider the effects of the establishment of a price floor above the market clearing price of a good. As discussed in Chapter 4, the effects of imposing such a floor price are an increase in the quantity supplied and a decrease in the quantity demanded. The smaller quantity demanded by consumers is the amount actually traded in the market. Thus, consumers purchase fewer units of the good, resulting in a reduction in consumer surplus. In addition, firms sell fewer units, so producer surplus may decrease. Thus, the establishment of a price floor also tends to reduce gains from trade.

5

Public Spending and Public Choice

The U.S. Postal Service (USPS) delivers nearly 40 percent of the world's mail. Nevertheless, its annual volume of delivered mail has declined by more than 20 percent since 2006. Even though the USPS commonly refers to itself as a private enterprise, economists classify it as *government-sponsored*. Government sponsorship of the USPS is evidenced by the fact that the USPS now receives more than $15 billion in U.S. government loans. Without these funds, the USPS would have to shut down many of its operations. Why does the government sponsor the provision of certain items, such as mail delivery services, even though private firms otherwise could provide them? This is among the several questions relating to government's economic role that are addressed in the present chapter.

LEARNING OBJECTIVES

After reading this chapter, you should be able to:

▶ Explain how market failures such as externalities might justify economic functions of government

▶ Distinguish between private goods and public goods and explain the nature of the free-rider problem

▶ Describe political functions of government that entail its involvement in the economy

▶ Analyze how Medicare affects the incentives to consume medical services

▶ Explain why increases in government spending on public education have not been associated with improvements in measures of student performance

▶ Discuss the central elements of the theory of public choice

MyEconLab helps you master each objective and study more efficiently. See end of chapter for details.

a 75-year-old woman accidentally managed to halt all Internet traffic to the entire country of Armenia? The woman was shoveling for scrap metal in the Eastern European nation of Georgia, when she sliced through the single fiber optic cable routing all of Armenia's Web transmissions. In her defense, the woman stated that a jump in the market price of scrap metals had induced her to search beneath the ground for old, unused wires that might contain copper. She was only pursuing her own self-interest with an aim to profit from selling items in the scrap-metals market, she contended. She had not, she insisted, intended to cut off Internet access for thousands of people. This event was an example of how people interacting in markets, including the market for scrap metal, can create negative spillovers, such as interrupted Internet traffic, for people outside those markets. As you will learn in this chapter, economists classify such third-party spillovers, which they refer to as *externalities*, among flaws in the price system called *market failures*.

What a Price System Can and Cannot Do

Throughout the book so far, we have alluded to the advantages of a price system. High on the list is economic efficiency. In its ideal form, a price system allows all resources to move from lower-valued uses to higher-valued uses via voluntary exchange, by which mutually advantageous trades take place. In a price system, consumers are sovereign. That is to say, they have the individual freedom to decide what they wish to purchase. Politicians and even business managers do not ultimately decide what is produced. Consumers decide. Some proponents of the price system argue that this is its most important characteristic. Competition among sellers protects consumers from coercion by one seller, and sellers are protected from coercion by one consumer because other consumers are available.

Sometimes, though, the price system does not generate these results, and too few or too many resources go to specific economic activities. Such situations are **market failures.** Market failures prevent the price system from attaining economic efficiency and individual freedom. Market failures offer one of the strongest arguments in favor of certain economic functions of government, which we now examine.

Market failure
A situation in which the market economy leads to too few or too many resources going to a specific economic activity.

Correcting for Externalities

In a pure market system, competition generates economic efficiency only when individuals know and must bear the true opportunity cost of their actions. In some circumstances, the price that someone actually pays for a resource, good, or service is higher or lower than the opportunity cost that all of society pays for that same resource, good, or service.

Externalities

Consider a hypothetical world in which there is no government regulation against pollution. You are living in a town that until now has had clean air. A steel mill moves into town. It produces steel and has paid for the inputs—land, labor, capital, and entrepreneurship. The price the mill charges for the steel reflects, in this example, only the costs that it incurs. In the course of production, however, the mill utilizes one input— clean air—by simply using it. This is indeed an input because in making steel, the furnaces emit smoke. The steel mill doesn't have to pay the cost of dirtying the air. Rather, it is the people in the community who incur that cost in the form of dirtier clothes, dirtier cars and houses, and more respiratory illnesses.

The effect is similar to what would happen if the steel mill could take coal or oil or workers' services without paying for them. There is an **externality,** an external cost. Some of the costs associated with the production of the steel have "spilled over" to affect **third parties,** parties other than the buyer and the seller of the steel.

Externality
A consequence of an economic activity that spills over to affect third parties. Pollution is an externality.

Third parties
Parties who are not directly involved in a given activity or transaction.

Property rights
The rights of an owner to use and to exchange property.

A fundamental reason that air pollution creates external costs is that the air belongs to everyone and hence to no one in particular. Lack of clearly assigned **property rights,** or the rights of an owner to use and exchange property, prevents market prices from reflecting all the costs created by activities that generate spillovers onto third parties.

External Costs in Graphical Form

To consider how market prices fail to take into account external costs in situations in which third-party spillovers exist without a clear assignment of property rights, look at panel (a) in Figure 5-1 below. Here we show the demand curve for steel as D. The supply curve is S_1. The supply curve includes only the costs that the firms in the market have to pay. Equilibrium occurs at point E, with a price of $800 per ton and a quantity equal to 110 million tons per year.

But producing steel also involves externalities—the external costs that you and your neighbors pay in the form of dirtier clothes, cars, and houses and increased respiratory disease due to the air pollution emitted from the steel mill. In this case, the producers of steel use clean air without having to pay for it. Let's include these external costs in our graph to find out what the full cost of steel production would really be if property rights to the air around the steel mill could generate payments for "owners" of that air. We do this by imagining that steel producers have to pay the "owners" of the air for the input—clean air—that the producers previously used at a zero price.

Recall from Chapter 3 that an increase in input prices shifts the supply curve up and to the left. Thus, in panel (a) of the figure, the supply curve shifts from S_1 to S_2. External costs equal the vertical distance between A and E_1. In this example, if steel firms had to take into account these external costs, the equilibrium quantity would

FIGURE 5-1

External Costs and Benefits

Panel (a) shows a situation in which production of steel generates external costs. If the steel mills ignore pollution, at equilibrium the quantity of steel will be 110 million tons. If the steel mills had to pay external costs caused by the mills' production but currently borne by nearby residents, the supply curve would shift the vertical distance $A–E_1$, to S_2. If consumers of steel were forced to pay a price that reflected the spillover costs, the quantity demanded would fall to 100 million tons. Panel (b) shows a situation in which inoculations against communicable diseases generate

external benefits to those individuals who may not be inoculated but who will benefit because epidemics will not occur. If each individual ignores the external benefit of inoculations, the market clearing quantity will be 150 million. If external benefits were taken into account by purchasers of inoculations, however, the demand curve would shift to D_2. The new equilibrium quantity would be 200 million inoculations, and the price of an inoculation would rise from $10 to $15.

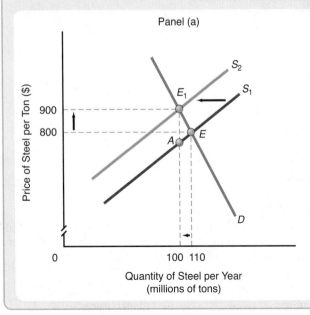

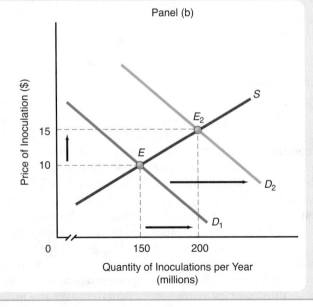

fall to 100 million tons per year, and the price would rise to $900 per ton. Equilibrium would shift from E to E_1. In contrast, if the price of steel does not account for external costs, third parties bear those costs—represented by the distance between A and E_1—in the form of dirtier clothes, houses, and cars and increased respiratory illnesses.

External Benefits in Graphical Form

Externalities can also be positive. To demonstrate external benefits in graphical form, we will use the example of inoculations against communicable disease. In panel (b) of Figure 5-1 on the facing page, we show the demand curve as D_1 (without taking account of any external benefits) and the supply curve as S. The equilibrium price is $10 per inoculation, and the equilibrium quantity is 150 million inoculations.

We assume, however, that inoculations against communicable diseases generate external benefits to individuals who may not be inoculated but will benefit nevertheless because epidemics will not break out. If such external benefits were taken into account by those who purchase inoculations, the demand curve would shift from D_1 to D_2.

As a consequence of this shift in demand at point E_2, the new equilibrium quantity would be 200 million inoculations, and the new equilibrium price would be $15 per inoculation. If people who consider getting inoculations fail to take external benefits into account, individuals in society are not devoting enough resources to inoculations against communicable diseases.

Resource Misallocations of Externalities

When there are external costs, the market will tend to *overallocate* resources to the production of the good or service in question, for those goods or services are implicitly priced deceptively low. In the steel example, too many resources will be allocated to steel production, because the steel mill owners and managers are not required to take account of the external cost that steel production is imposing on other individuals. In essence, the full cost of production is not borne by the owners and managers, so the price they charge the public for steel is lower than it would otherwise be. And, of course, the lower price means that buyers are willing and able to buy more. More steel is produced and consumed than if the sellers and buyers were to bear external costs.

In contrast, when there are external benefits, the price is too low to induce suppliers to allocate resources to the production of that good or service (because the demand, which fails to reflect the external benefits, is relatively too low). Thus, the market *underallocates* resources to producing the good or service. Hence, in a market system, too many of the goods that generate external costs are produced, and too few of the goods that generate external benefits are produced.

How the Government Can Correct Negative Externalities

In theory, the government can take action to try to correct situations in which a lack of property rights allows third-party spillovers to create an externality. In the case of negative externalities, at least two avenues are open to the government: special taxes and legislative regulation or prohibition.

SPECIAL TAXES In our example of the steel mill, the externality problem arises because using the air for waste disposal is costless to the firm but not to society. The government could attempt to tax the steel mill commensurate with the cost to third parties from smoke in the air. This, in effect, would be a pollution tax or an **effluent fee**. The ultimate effect would be to reduce the supply of steel and raise the price to consumers, ideally making the price equal to the full cost of production to society.

Why has Hungary's government imposed taxes on foods that it has determined to be detrimental to the health of that nation's residents?

Effluent fee
A charge to a polluter that gives the right to discharge into the air or water a certain amount of pollution; also called a *pollution tax*.

INTERNATIONAL POLICY EXAMPLE

Hungary's Tax on Prepackaged Snacks

The government of Hungary has determined that the nation's health care system experiences external spillovers from the snack food market. People who consume too many chips, salted nuts, sweets, ice creams, instant soups, and energy drinks are, the government has concluded, experiencing worse health. As these people seek treatment for their health problems, they are clogging the nation's physicians' offices and hospitals. Thus, Hungary's government is seeking to induce producers of certain snack foods and beverages to cut back on an overallocation of resources that the government perceives to be creating a negative externality.

Toward this end, the government is placing special taxes on foodstuffs with high sugar, salt, and carbohydrate content and on fluid products containing more than 20 milligrams of caffeine per 100 milliliters. By imposing these taxes, it intends to reduce the supply of each of these items and thereby raise its price toward equality with the full cost of its production to society as a whole.

FOR CRITICAL THINKING
If untaxed bakery sweets and fast food are close substitutes for snack foods, could Hungary's tax on snack foods boost consumption of the untaxed items? Explain.

Go to www.econtoday.com/chap05 to learn more about how the Environmental Protection Agency uses regulations to try to protect the environment.

REGULATION Alternatively, to correct a negative externality arising from steel production, the government could specify a maximum allowable rate of pollution. This regulation would require that the steel mill install pollution abatement equipment at its facilities, reduce its rate of output, or some combination of the two. Note that the government's job would not be simple, for it would have to determine the appropriate level of pollution, which would require extensive knowledge of both the benefits and the costs of pollution control.

How the Government Can Correct Positive Externalities

What can the government do when the production of one good spills *benefits* over to third parties? It has several policy options: financing the production of the good or producing the good itself, subsidies (negative taxes), and regulation.

GOVERNMENT FINANCING AND PRODUCTION If the positive externalities seem extremely large, the government has the option of financing the desired additional production facilities so that the "right" amount of the good will be produced. Again consider inoculations against communicable diseases. The government could—and often does—finance campaigns to inoculate the population. It could (and does) even produce and operate inoculation centers where inoculations are given at no charge.

SUBSIDIES A subsidy is a negative tax. A subsidy is a per-unit payment made either to a business or to a consumer when the business produces or the consumer buys a good or a service. To generate more inoculations against communicable diseases, the government could subsidize everyone who obtains an inoculation by directly reimbursing those inoculated or by making per-unit payments to private firms that provide inoculations. Subsidies reduce the net price to consumers, thereby causing a larger quantity to be demanded.

How are some state governments seeking to help society capture external benefits that the governments suggest society derives from being kept informed?

POLICY EXAMPLE

Stop the Presses for Subsidies!

Since the late 2000s, total physical newspaper circulation to paid subscribers has declined by more than 5 percent per year. The cumulative reduction in readership of paper editions since 2000 has exceeded 50 percent.

Some state government officials suggest that local newspapers provide positive externalities. Making readers better informed, they argue, improves people's lives and in some cases saves lives. On the basis of this logic, several state governments are now providing subsidies to newspapers. For example, Minnesota's state government has provided hundreds of thousands

of dollars to newspapers in Duluth and St. Paul. These newspapers have used the funds to train their staffs to post content and ads online instead of relying solely on physical print editions to generate revenues. In this way, the Minnesota state government seeks to help local newspapers keep operating.

FOR CRITICAL THINKING
How does the provision of subsidies to local newspapers likely affect the supply of news content at each possible price?

REGULATION In some cases involving positive externalities, the government can require by law that individuals in the society undertake a certain action. For example, regulations require that all school-age children be inoculated before entering public and private schools. Some people believe that a basic school education itself generates positive externalities. Perhaps as a result of this belief, we have regulations—laws—that require all school-age children to be enrolled in a public or private school.

QUICK QUIZ See page 121 for the answers. Review concepts from this section in MyEconLab.

External _____ lead to an overallocation of resources to the specific economic activity. Two possible ways of correcting these spillovers are _____ and _____.

External _____ result in an underallocation of resources to the specific activity. Three possible government corrections are _____ the production of the activity, _____ private firms or consumers to engage in the activity, and _____.

The Other Economic Functions of Government

Besides correcting for externalities, the government performs many other economic functions that affect the way exchange is carried out. In contrast, the political functions of government have to do with deciding how income should be redistributed among households and selecting which goods and services have special merits and should therefore be treated differently. The economic and political functions of government can and do overlap.

Let's look at four more economic functions of government.

Providing a Legal System

The courts and the police may not at first seem like economic functions of government. Their activities nonetheless have important consequences for economic activities in any country. You and I enter into contracts constantly, whether they be oral or written, expressed or implied. When we believe that we have been wronged, we seek redress of our grievances through our legal institutions. Moreover, consider the legal system that is necessary for the smooth functioning of our economic system. Our system has defined quite explicitly the legal status of businesses, the rights of private ownership, and a method of enforcing contracts. All relationships among consumers and businesses are governed by the legal rules of the game.

In its judicial function, then, the government serves as the referee for settling disputes in the economic arena. In this role, the government often imposes penalties for violations of legal rules.

Much of our legal system is involved with defining and protecting property rights. One might say that property rights are really the rules of our economic game. When property rights are well defined, owners of property have an incentive to use that property efficiently. Any mistakes in their decisions about the use of property have negative consequences that the owners suffer. Furthermore, when property rights are well defined, owners of property have an incentive to maintain that property so that if they ever desire to sell it, it will fetch a better price.

What happens when the government fails to establish clear rights to private property and fails to enforce owners' rights fully? In such situations, individuals and firms are more likely to be willing to engage in activities that create spillover effects for other individuals. Thus, externalities will result. In such cases, however, these externalities result from ambiguously assigned and weakly enforced property rights. The government, rather than the market, is at fault.

Promoting Competition

Many economists argue that the only way to attain economic efficiency is through competition. One of the roles of government is to serve as the protector of a competitive economic system. Congress and the various state governments have passed **antitrust legislation.** Such legislation makes illegal certain (but not all) economic activities that might restrain trade—that is, that might prevent free competition among actual and potential rival firms in the marketplace. The avowed aim of antitrust legislation is to reduce the power of **monopolies**—firms that can determine the market price of the goods they sell. A large number of antitrust laws have been passed that prohibit specific anticompetitive actions. Both the Antitrust Division of the U.S. Department of Justice and the Federal Trade Commission attempt to enforce these antitrust laws. Various state judicial agencies also expend efforts at maintaining competition.

Providing Public Goods

The goods used in our examples up to this point have been **private goods.** When I eat a cheeseburger, you cannot eat the same one. So you and I are rivals for that cheeseburger, just as much as contenders for the title of world champion are. When I use the services of an auto mechanic, that person cannot work at the same time for you. That is the distinguishing feature of private goods—their use is exclusive to the people who purchase them. The **principle of rival consumption** applies to most private goods. Rival consumption is easy to understand. Either you use such a private good or I use it.

Of course, private firms provide some goods and services that are not fully subject to the principle of rival consumption. For instance, you and a friend can both purchase tickets providing the two of you with the right to sit in a musical facility and listen to a concert during a specified period of time. Your friend's presence does not prohibit you from enjoying the music, nor does your presence prevent him from appreciating the concert. Nevertheless, the owner of the musical facility can prevent others who have not purchased tickets from entering the facility during the concert. Consequently, as long as nonpayers can be excluded from consuming an item, that item can also be produced and sold as a private good.

There is an entire class of goods that are not private goods. These are called **public goods.** Like musical concerts, public goods are items to which the principle of rival consumption does not apply. Hence, many individuals simultaneously can consume public goods *jointly*. What truly distinguishes public goods from all private goods is that the costs required to exclude nonpayers from consuming public goods are so high that doing so is infeasible. National defense and police protection are examples. Suppose that your next-door neighbor were to pay for protection from a terrorist effort to explode a large bomb. If so, your neighbor's life and property could not be defended from such a threat without your life and property also receiving the same defense, even if you had failed to provide any payment for protection. Finding a way to avoid protecting you while still protecting your neighbor would be so expensive that such exclusion of defense for you and your property would be difficult.

CHARACTERISTICS OF PUBLIC GOODS Two fundamental characteristics of public goods set them apart from all other goods:

1. *Public goods can be used by more and more people at no additional opportunity cost and without depriving others of any of the services of the goods.* Once funds have been spent on national defense, the defense protection you receive does not reduce the amount of protection bestowed on anyone else. The opportunity cost of your receiving national defense once it is in place is zero because once national defense is in place to protect you, it also protects others.

2. *It is difficult to design a collection system for a public good on the basis of how much individuals use it.* Nonpayers can often utilize a public good without incurring any monetary cost, because the cost of excluding them from using the good is so high. Those

---

Antitrust legislation
Laws that restrict the formation of monopolies and regulate certain anticompetitive business practices.

Monopoly
A firm that can determine the market price of a good. In the extreme case, a monopoly is the only seller of a good or service.

Private goods
Goods that can be consumed by only one individual at a time. Private goods are subject to the principle of rival consumption.

Principle of rival consumption
The recognition that individuals are rivals in consuming private goods because one person's consumption reduces the amount available for others to consume.

Public goods
Goods for which the principle of rival consumption does not apply and for which exclusion of nonpaying consumers is too costly to be feasible. They can be jointly consumed by many individuals simultaneously at no additional cost and with no reduction in quality or quantity. Furthermore, no one who fails to help pay for the good can be denied the benefit of the good.

who provide the public good find that it is not cost-effective to prevent nonpayers from utilizing it. For instance, taxpayers who pay to provide national defense typically do not incur the costs that would be entailed in excluding nonpayers from benefiting from national defense.

The fundamental problem of public goods is that the private sector has a difficult, if not impossible, time providing them. Individuals in the private sector have little or no incentive to offer public goods. It is difficult for them to make a profit doing so, because it is too costly and, hence, infeasible to exclude nonpayers. Consequently, true public goods must necessarily be provided by government. (Note, though, that economists do not categorize something as a public good simply because the government provides it.)

Governments traditionally have operated facilities for space flight, so why are private firms now involved in placing humans beyond the earth's atmosphere?

EXAMPLE

Private Companies Look to Place Humans in Orbit—and Beyond

Would you like to live in earth orbit, or would you prefer landing on the moon? If you wish to go no farther than 228 miles above the earth, Bigelow Aerospace has developed, constructed, and tested low-cost inflatable space stations in which humans can reside. The company has already established a rental rate of $28,750,000 per astronaut per month. If your objective is to go to the moon—say, to mine platinum—then you could contact another firm called Moon Express. That company has developed a new technology for landing people on the moon at a cost 90 percent below that at which the U.S. government could manage to do it.

In both cases, the only catch is that you would have to find another company that could send you into orbit about the earth or take you to the moon. In fact, several private firms are working on developing rocket propulsion systems for transporting humans to and beyond earth orbit.

FOR CRITICAL THINKING
Do the services of transporting people to or beyond the earth's orbit or providing them with places to reside in space possess the characteristics of public or private goods?

FREE RIDERS The nature of public goods leads to the **free-rider problem,** a situation in which some individuals take advantage of the fact that others will assume the burden of paying for public goods such as national defense. Suppose that citizens were taxed directly in proportion to how much they tell an interviewer that they value national defense. Some people who actually value national defense will probably tell interviewers that it has no value to them—they don't want any of it. Such people are trying to be free riders. We may all want to be free riders if we believe that someone else will provide the commodity in question that we actually value.

The free-rider problem often arises in connection with sharing the burden of international defense. A country may choose to belong to a multilateral defense organization, such as the North Atlantic Treaty Organization (NATO), but then consistently attempt to avoid contributing funds to the organization. The nation knows it would be defended by others in NATO if it were attacked but would rather not pay for such defense. In short, it seeks a free ride.

Free-rider problem
A problem that arises when individuals presume that others will pay for public goods so that, individually, they can escape paying for their portion without causing a reduction in production.

Ensuring Economywide Stability

Our economy sometimes faces the problems of undesired unemployment and rising prices. The government, especially the federal government, has made an attempt to solve these problems by trying to stabilize the economy by smoothing out the ups and downs in overall business activity. The notion that the federal government should undertake actions to stabilize business activity is a relatively new idea in the United States, encouraged by high unemployment rates during the Great Depression of the 1930s and subsequent theories about possible ways that government could reduce unemployment. In 1946, Congress passed the Full-Employment Act, a landmark law concerning government responsibility for economic performance. It established three goals for government stabilization policy: full employment, price stability, and economic growth. These goals have provided the justification for many government economic programs during the post–World War II period.

The Political Functions of Government

At least two functions of government are political or normative functions rather than economic ones like those discussed in the first part of this chapter. These two areas are (1) the provision and regulation of government-sponsored and government-inhibited goods and (2) income redistribution.

Government-Sponsored and Government-Inhibited Goods

Government-sponsored good

A good that has been deemed socially desirable through the political process. Museums are an example.

Through political processes, governments often determine that certain goods possess special merit and seek to promote their production and consumption. A **government-sponsored good** is defined as any good that the political process has deemed socially desirable. (Note that nothing inherent in any particular good makes that item a government-sponsored good. The designation is entirely subjective.) Examples of government-sponsored goods in our society are sports stadiums, museums, ballets, plays, and concerts. In these areas, the government's role is the provision of these goods to the people in society who would not otherwise purchase them at market clearing prices or who would not purchase an amount of them judged to be sufficient. This provision may take the form of government production and distribution of the goods. It can also take the form of reimbursement for spending on government-sponsored goods or subsidies to producers or consumers for part of the goods' costs.

Governments do indeed subsidize such goods as professional sports, concerts, ballets, museums, and plays. In most cases, those goods would not be so numerous without subsidization.

Government-inhibited good

A good that has been deemed socially undesirable through the political process. Heroin is an example.

Government-inhibited goods are the opposite of government-sponsored goods. They are goods that, through the political process, have been deemed socially undesirable. Heroin, cigarettes, gambling, and cocaine are examples. The government exercises its role with respect to these goods by taxing, regulating, or prohibiting their manufacture, sale, and use. Governments justify the relatively high taxes on alcohol and tobacco by declaring that they are socially undesirable. The best-known example of governmental exercise of power in this area is the stance against certain psychoactive drugs. Most psychoactives (except nicotine, caffeine, and alcohol) are either expressly prohibited, as is the case for heroin, cocaine, and opium, or heavily regulated, as in the case of prescription psychoactives.

Income Redistribution

Transfer payments

Money payments made by governments to individuals for which no services or goods are rendered in return. Examples are Social Security old-age and disability benefits and unemployment insurance benefits.

Transfers in kind

Payments that are in the form of actual goods and services, such as food stamps, subsidized public housing, and medical care, and for which no goods or services are rendered in return.

Another relatively recent political function of government has been the explicit redistribution of income. This redistribution uses two systems: the progressive income tax (described in Chapter 6) and transfer payments. **Transfer payments** are payments made to individuals for which no services or goods are rendered in return. The two primary money transfer payments in our system are Social Security old-age and disability benefits and unemployment insurance benefits. Income redistribution also includes a large amount of income **transfers in kind,** rather than money transfers. Some income transfers in kind are food stamps, Medicare and Medicaid, government health care services, and subsidized public housing.

The government has also engaged in other activities as a form of redistribution of income. For example, the provision of public education is at least in part an attempt to redistribute income by making sure that the poor have access to education.

QUICK QUIZ   See page 121 for the answers. Review concepts from this section in MyEconLab.

The economic activities of government include (1) correcting for _____, (2) providing a _____ _____, (3) promoting _____, (4) producing _____ goods, and (5) ensuring _____ _____.

The principle of _____ _____ does not apply to public goods as it does to private goods.

Public goods have two characteristics: (1) Once they are produced, there is no additional _____ _____

when additional consumers use them, because your use of a public good does not deprive others of its simultaneous use; and (2) consumers cannot conveniently be _____ on the basis of use.

Political, or normative, activities of the government include the provision and regulation of _____-_____ and _____-_____ goods and _____ redistribution.

Public Spending and Transfer Programs

The size of the public sector can be measured in many different ways. One way is to count the number of public employees. Another is to look at total government outlays. Government outlays include all government expenditures on employees, rent, electricity, and the like. In addition, total government outlays include transfer payments, such as welfare and Social Security. In Figure 5-2 below, you see that government outlays prior to World War I did not exceed 10 percent of annual national income. There was a spike during World War I, a general increase during the Great Depression, and then a huge spike during World War II. After World War II, government outlays as a percentage of total national income rose steadily before dropping in the 1990s, rising again in the early 2000s, and then jumping sharply beginning in 2008.

How do federal and state governments allocate their spending? A typical federal government budget is shown in panel (a) of Figure 5-3 on the following page. The three largest categories are Medicare and other health-related spending, Social Security and other income-security programs, and national defense, which together constitute 79.7 percent of the total federal budget.

The makeup of state and local expenditures is quite different. As panel (b) shows, education is the biggest category, accounting for 34.3 percent of all expenditures.

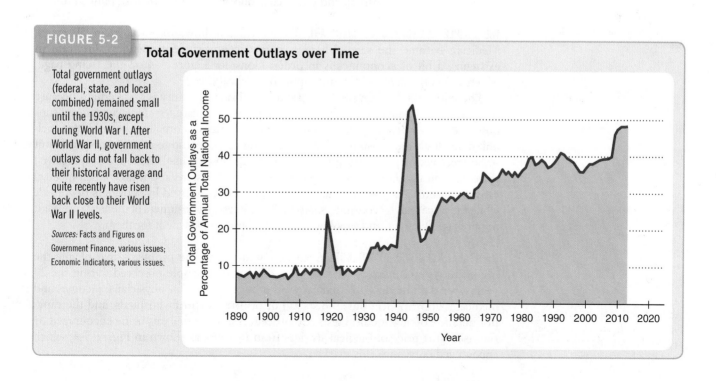

FIGURE 5-2

Total Government Outlays over Time

Total government outlays (federal, state, and local combined) remained small until the 1930s, except during World War I. After World War II, government outlays did not fall back to their historical average and quite recently have risen back close to their World War II levels.

Sources: Facts and Figures on Government Finance, various issues; Economic Indicators, various issues.

FIGURE 5-3
Federal Government Spending Compared to State and Local Spending

The federal government's spending habits are quite different from those of the states and cities. In panel (a), you can see that the most important categories in the federal budget are Medicare and other health-related spending, Social Security and other income-security programs, and national defense, which make up 79.7 percent. In panel (b), the most important category at the state and local level is education, which makes up 34.3 percent. "Other" includes expenditures in such areas as waste treatment, garbage collection, mosquito abatement, and the judicial system.

Sources: Economic Report of the President, Economic Indicators.

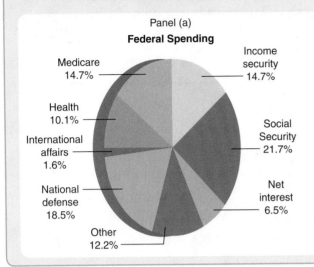

Panel (a)
Federal Spending

Medicare 14.7%
Income security 14.7%
Health 10.1%
International affairs 1.6%
Social Security 21.7%
National defense 18.5%
Net interest 6.5%
Other 12.2%

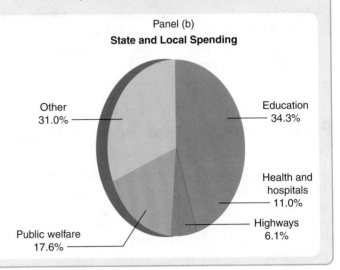

Panel (b)
State and Local Spending

Other 31.0%
Education 34.3%
Health and hospitals 11.0%
Highways 6.1%
Public welfare 17.6%

Publicly Subsidized Health Care: Medicare

Figure 5-3 above shows that health-related spending is a significant portion of total government expenditures. Certainly, medical expenses are a major concern for many elderly people. Since 1965, that concern has been reflected in the existence of the Medicare program, which pays hospital and physicians' bills for U.S. residents over the age of 65 (and for those younger than 65 in some instances). In return for paying a tax on their earnings while in the workforce (2.9 percent of wages and salaries, plus 3.8 percent on certain income for high-income households), retirees are assured that the majority of their hospital and physicians' bills will be paid for with public monies.

Go to www.econtoday.com/chap05 to visit the U.S. government's official Medicare Web site.

THE SIMPLE ECONOMICS OF MEDICARE To understand how, in fewer than 50 years, Medicare became the second-biggest domestic government spending program in existence, a bit of economics is in order. Consider Figure 5-4 on the facing page, which shows the demand for and supply of medical care.

The initial equilibrium price is P_0 and equilibrium quantity is Q_0. Perhaps because the government believes that Q_0 is not enough medical care for these consumers, suppose that the government begins paying a subsidy that eventually is set at M for each unit of medical care consumed. This will simultaneously tend to raise the price per unit of care received by providers (physicians, hospitals, and the like) and lower the perceived price per unit that consumers see when they make decisions about how much medical care to consume. As presented in the figure, the price received by providers rises to P_s, while the price paid by consumers falls to P_d. As a result, consumers of medical care want to purchase Q_m units, and suppliers are quite happy to provide it for them.

MEDICARE INCENTIVES AT WORK We can now understand the problems that plague the Medicare system today. First, one of the things that people observed during the 20 years after the founding of Medicare was a huge upsurge in physicians' incomes and medical school applications, the spread of private for-profit hospitals, and the rapid proliferation of new medical tests and procedures. All of this was being encouraged by the rise in the price of medical services from P_0 to P_s, as shown in Figure 5-4, which encouraged entry into this market.

FIGURE 5-4

The Economic Effects of Medicare Subsidies

When the government pays a per-unit subsidy M for medical care, consumers pay the price of services P_d for the quantity of services Q_m. Providers receive the price P_s for supplying this quantity. Originally, the federal government projected that its total spending on Medicare would equal an amount such as the area $Q_0 \times (P_0 - P_d)$. Because actual consumption equals Q_m, however, the government's total expenditures equal $Q_m \times M$.

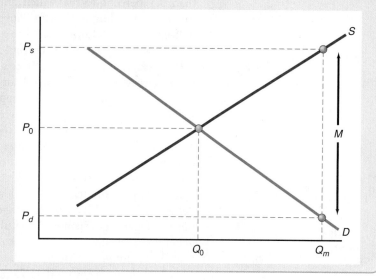

Second, government expenditures on Medicare have routinely turned out to be far in excess of the expenditures forecast at the time the program was put in place or was expanded. The reasons for this are easy to see. Bureaucratic planners often fail to recognize the incentive effects of government programs. On the demand side, they fail to account for the huge increase in consumption (from Q_0 to Q_m) that will result from a subsidy like Medicare. On the supply side, they fail to recognize that the larger number of services can only be extracted from suppliers at a higher price, P_s. Consequently, original projected spending on Medicare was an area like $Q_0 \times (P_0 - P_d)$, because original plans for the program only contemplated consumption of Q_0 and assumed that the subsidy would have to be only $P_0 - P_d$ per unit. In fact, consumption rises to Q_m, and the additional cost per unit of service rises to P_s, implying an increase in the per-unit subsidy to M. Hence, actual expenditures turn out to be the far larger number $Q_m \times M$. Every expansion of the program, including the 2004 broadening of Medicare to cover obesity as a new illness eligible for coverage and the extension of Medicare to cover patients' prescription drug expenses beginning in 2006, has followed the same pattern.

Third, total spending on medical services has soared, consuming far more income than initially expected. Originally, total spending on medical services was $P_0 \times Q_0$. In the presence of Medicare, spending rises to $P_s \times Q_m$.

In the past, why have government officials considerably underestimated taxpayers' actual expenses for health care programs such as Medicare?

POLICY EXAMPLE

The Great Underestimates of Government Health Care Expenses

When the federal government launched Medicare in 1965, officials estimated that its one-year inflation-adjusted cost in 1990 would turn out to be $12 billion, but the actual program cost in 1990 was $110 billion. When it initiated the Medicaid health-care-subsidy program for lower-income individuals in 1966, the government projected that its annual inflation-adjusted cost for 1990 would be about $7 billion, but that program's true expense in 1990 exceeded $45 billion. One reason for these underestimates was that as time passed, Congress expanded the number of people eligible for both programs. Another reason was that Congress assumed that creating the programs would not increase the quantity of health care demanded.

Of course, when the government offered per-unit subsidies that significantly pushed down the out-of-pocket price, people *did* raise their consumption. These increases in quantities of health care services consumed under Medicare and Medicaid dramatically raised the programs' actual expenses.

FOR CRITICAL THINKING

Why do you suppose that even though Medicare was supposed to be self-sustaining indefinitely, Medicare taxes will fail to cover program costs by 2024?

HEALTH CARE SUBSIDIES CONTINUE TO GROW Just how fast are Medicare subsidies growing? Medicare's cost has risen from 0.7 percent of U.S. national income in 1970 to more than 3.5 percent today, which amounts to nearly $550 billion per year. Because Medicare spending is growing much faster than total employer and employee contributions, future spending guarantees far outstrip the taxes to be collected in the future to pay for the system. (The current Medicare tax rate is 2.9 percent on all wages, with 1.45 percent paid by the employee and 1.45 percent paid by the employer. For certain income earned above $200,000 for individuals and $250,000 for married couples, a 3.8 percent Medicare tax rate applies.) Today, unfunded guarantees of Medicare spending in the future are estimated at more than $25 trillion (in today's dollars).

These amounts fail to reflect the costs of another federal health program called Medicaid. The Medicaid program is structured similarly to Medicare, in that the government also pays per-unit subsidies for health care to qualifying patients. Medicaid, however, provides subsidies only to people who qualify because they have lower incomes. At present, about 50 million people, or about one out of every six U.S. residents, qualify for Medicaid coverage. Medicaid is administered by state governments, but the federal government pays about 60 percent of the program's total cost from general tax revenues. The current cost of the program is more than $400 billion per year. In recent years, Medicaid spending has grown even faster than expenditures on Medicare, rising by more than 75 percent since 2000 alone.

Of course, in legislation enacted in 2010, the U.S. Congress further expanded by more than $100 billion per year the rate of growth of government health care spending, which already has been growing at an average pace of 8 percent per year.

WHAT IF... the federal government continues reducing the out-of-pocket prices that consumers must pay for health care services?

Persistent reductions in out-of-pocket prices of health care services would lead to higher quantities of services demanded by consumers. Providers of health care would be willing to supply these higher quantities only if they receive higher prices. Thus, to continue pushing downward the out-of-pocket price of health care services toward an explicit price of zero, the federal government would have to keep raising the per-unit subsidies that it pays health care providers. Multiplying the increased quantities of health care services consumed and provided times the higher per-unit subsidies would yield larger total subsidies that taxpayers would have to fund. Overall, the total expenses that society would incur for health care services would continue to climb.

Economic Issues of Public Education

In the United States, government involvement in health care is a relatively recent phenomenon. In contrast, state and local governments have assumed primary responsibility for public education for many years. Currently, these governments spend more than $900 billion on education—in excess of 6 percent of total U.S. national income. State and local sales, excise, property, and income taxes finance the bulk of these expenditures. In addition, each year the federal government provides tens of billions of dollars of support for public education through grants and other transfers to state and local governments.

THE NOW-FAMILIAR ECONOMICS OF PUBLIC EDUCATION State and local governments around the United States have developed a variety of complex mechanisms for funding public education. What all public education programs have in common, however, is the provision of educational services to primary, secondary, and college students at prices well below those that would otherwise prevail in the marketplace for these services.

So how do state and local governments accomplish this? The answer is that they operate public education programs that share some of the features of government-subsidized health care programs such as Medicare. Analogously to Figure 5-4 on page 111, public schools provide educational services at a price below the market price. They are willing to produce the quantity of educational services demanded at this below-market price as long as they receive a sufficiently high per-unit subsidy from state and local governments.

THE INCENTIVE PROBLEMS OF PUBLIC EDUCATION Since the 1960s, various measures of the performance of U.S. primary and secondary students have failed to increase even as public spending on education has risen. Some measures of student performance have even declined.

Many economists argue that the incentive effects that have naturally arisen with higher government subsidies for public education help to explain this lack of improvement in student performance. A higher per-pupil subsidy creates a difference between the relatively high per-unit costs of providing the number of educational services that parents and students are willing to purchase and lower valuations of those services. As a consequence, some schools have provided services, such as after-school babysitting and various social services, that have contributed relatively little to student learning.

A factor that complicates efforts to assess the effects of education subsidies is that the public schools often face little or no competition from unsubsidized providers of educational services. In addition, public schools rarely compete against each other. In most locales, therefore, parents who are unhappy with the quality of services provided at the subsidized price cannot transfer their child to a different public school.

Are higher school subsidies associated with improved learning outcomes?

YOU ARE THERE

To consider another setting in which government per-unit subsidies are important, read **The U.S. Government Ensures That an Airport Is "Convenient"** on page 116.

POLICY EXAMPLE

A Weak Relationship between Spending and Schooling Results

In a recent year, the five U.S. states with highest annual per-pupil spending were Alaska, New Jersey, New York, Vermont, and Washington, in which an average level of per-student expenditures was $16,106. This amount was more than twice as much as the average per-student expenditures of $7,409 in Arizona, Idaho, Oklahoma, Tennessee, and Utah, the five lowest-spending states. The differences in measurable outcomes were only minor, however.

For instance, in the five states with highest spending, an average of 25.2 percent of students failed to meet basic goals for math and reading. In the five states with lowest spending, this figure was only slightly higher at 30.6 percent. New York, the state with highest per-student expenditures, spent nearly three times as much per pupil as lowest-spending Utah, yet both states had just over 26 percent of students who failed to satisfy basic math and reading objectives. By virtually every measure of schooling outcomes, studies consistently find at best a weak relationship—and often find no relationship—between per-pupil expenditures and educational results.

FOR CRITICAL THINKING

Could the fact that the valuation of the last unit of services falls as the per-student subsidy rises help to explain why higher spending is not closely related to learning outcomes?

QUICK QUIZ See page 121 for the answers. Review concepts from this section in MyEconLab.

Medicare subsidizes the consumption of medical care by the elderly, thus increasing the amount of such care consumed. People tend to purchase large amounts of _____-value, _____-cost services in publicly funded health care programs such as Medicare, because they do not directly bear the full cost of their decisions.

Basic economic analysis indicates that higher subsidies for public education have widened the differential between parents' and students' relatively _____ per-unit valuations of the educational services of public schools and the _____ costs that schools incur in providing those services.

Collective Decision Making: The Theory of Public Choice

Governments consist of individuals. No government actually thinks and acts. Instead, government actions are the result of decision making by individuals in their roles as elected representatives, appointed officials, and salaried bureaucrats. Therefore, to understand how government works, we must examine the incentives of the people in government as well as those who would like to be in government—avowed or would-be candidates for elective or appointed positions—and special-interest lobbyists attempting to get government to do something. At issue is the analysis of **collective decision making.**

Collective decision making involves the actions of voters, politicians, political parties, interest groups, and many other groups and individuals. The analysis of collective decision making is usually called the **theory of public choice.** It has been given this name because it involves hypotheses about how choices are made in the public sector, as opposed to the private sector. The foundation of public-choice theory is the assumption that individuals will act within the political process to maximize their *individual* (not collective) well-being. In that sense, the theory is similar to our analysis of the market economy, in which we also assume that individuals act as though they are motivated by self-interest.

To understand public-choice theory, it is necessary to point out other similarities between the private market sector and the public, or government, sector. Then we will look at the differences.

Collective decision making
How voters, politicians, and other interested parties act and how these actions influence nonmarket decisions.

Theory of public choice
The study of collective decision making.

Similarities in Market and Public-Sector Decision Making

In addition to the assumption of self-interest being the motivating force in both sectors, there are other similarities.

OPPORTUNITY COST Everything that is spent by all levels of government plus everything that is spent by the private sector must add up to the total income available at any point in time. Hence, every government action has an opportunity cost, just as in the market sector.

COMPETITION Although we typically think of competition as a private market phenomenon, it is also present in collective action. Given the scarcity constraint government faces, bureaucrats, appointed officials, and elected representatives will always be in competition for available government funds. Furthermore, the individuals within any government agency or institution will act as individuals do in the private sector: They will try to obtain higher wages, better working conditions, and higher job-level classifications. We assume that they will compete and act in their own interest, not society's.

SIMILARITY OF INDIVIDUALS Contrary to popular belief, the types of individuals working in the private sector and working in the public sector are not inherently different. The difference, as we shall see, is that the individuals in government face a different **incentive structure** than those in the private sector. For example, the costs and benefits of being efficient or inefficient differ in the private and public sectors.

One approach to predicting government bureaucratic behavior is to ask what incentives bureaucrats face. Take the U.S. Postal Service (USPS) as an example. The bureaucrats running that government corporation are human beings with IQs not dissimilar to those possessed by workers in similar positions at Google or Apple. Yet the USPS does not function like either of these companies. The difference can be explained in terms of the incentives provided for managers in the two types of institutions. When the bureaucratic managers and workers at Google make incorrect decisions, work slowly, produce shoddy programs, and are generally "inefficient," the profitability of the company declines. The owners—millions of shareholders—express their displeasure by selling some of their shares of company stock. The market value, as tracked on the stock exchange, falls. This induces owners of shares of stock to pressure managers to pursue strategies more likely to boost revenues and reduce costs.

Incentive structure
The system of rewards and punishments individuals face with respect to their own actions.

But what about the USPS? If a manager, a worker, or a bureaucrat in the USPS gives shoddy service, the organization's owners—the taxpayers—have no straightforward mechanism for expressing their dissatisfaction. Despite the postal service's status as a "government corporation," taxpayers as shareholders do not really own shares of stock in the organization that they can sell.

Thus, to understand purported inefficiency in the government bureaucracy, we need to examine incentives and institutional arrangements—not people and personalities.

Differences between Market and Collective Decision Making

There are probably more dissimilarities between the market sector and the public sector than there are similarities.

GOVERNMENT GOODS AND SERVICES AT ZERO PRICE The majority of goods that governments produce are furnished to the ultimate consumers without payment required. **Government, or political, goods** can be either private or public goods. The fact that they are furnished to the ultimate consumer free of charge does *not* mean that the cost to society of those goods is zero, however. It only means that the price *charged* is zero. The full opportunity cost to society is the value of the resources used in the production of goods produced and provided by the government.

For example, none of us pays directly for each unit of consumption of defense or police protection. Rather, we pay for all these items indirectly through the taxes that support our governments—federal, state, and local. This special feature of government can be looked at in a different way. There is no longer a one-to-one relationship between consumption of government-provided goods and services and payment for these items. Indeed, most taxpayers will find that their tax bill is the same whether or not they consume government-provided goods.

Government, or political, goods
Goods (and services) provided by the public sector; they can be either private or public goods.

USE OF FORCE All governments can resort to using force in their regulation of economic affairs. For example, governments can use *expropriation*, which means that if you refuse to pay your taxes, your bank account and other assets may be seized by the Internal Revenue Service. In fact, you have no choice in the matter of paying taxes to governments. Collectively, we decide the total size of government through the political process, but individually, we cannot determine how much service we pay for during any one year.

VOTING VERSUS SPENDING In the private market sector, a dollar voting system is in effect. This dollar voting system is not equivalent to the voting system in the public sector. There are at least three differences:

1. In a political system, one person gets one vote, whereas in the market system, each dollar a person spends counts separately.

2. The political system is run by **majority rule,** whereas the market system is run by **proportional rule.**

3. The spending of dollars can indicate intensity of want, whereas because of the all-or-nothing nature of political voting, a vote cannot.

Majority rule
A collective decision-making system in which group decisions are made on the basis of more than 50 percent of the vote. In other words, whatever more than half of the electorate votes for, the entire electorate has to accept.

Proportional rule
A decision-making system in which actions are based on the proportion of the "votes" cast and are in proportion to them. In a market system, if 10 percent of the "dollar votes" are cast for blue cars, 10 percent of automobile output will be blue cars.

Political outcomes often differ from economic outcomes. Remember that economic efficiency is a situation in which, given the prevailing distribution of income, consumers obtain the economic goods they want. There is no corresponding situation when political voting determines economic outcomes. Thus, a political voting process is unlikely to lead to the same decisions that a dollar voting process would yield in the marketplace.

Indeed, consider the dilemma every voter faces. Usually, a voter is not asked to decide on a single issue (although this happens). Rather, a voter is asked to choose among candidates who present a large number of issues and state a position on each of them. Just consider the average U.S. senator, who has to vote on several thousand different issues during a six-year term. When you vote for that senator, you are voting for a person who must make thousands of decisions during the next six years.

The theory of _____ _____ examines how voters, politicians, and other parties collectively reach decisions in the public sector of the economy.

As in private markets, _____ _____ and _____ have incentive effects that influence

public-sector decision making. In contrast to private market situations, however, there is not a one-to-one relationship between consumption of a publicly provided good and the payment for that good.

YOU ARE THERE
The U.S. Government Ensures That an Airport Is "Convenient"

Phil Ridenour, director of Hagerstown Regional Airport, in Hagerstown, Maryland, surveys the surroundings: free parking, short security lines for departing passengers, and plenty of space for passengers at the baggage carousel. "The convenience of it all is just phenomenal compared to going to any major airport," Ridenour remarks. Indeed, a flight to Baltimore takes only 40 minutes in the air, compared with an 80-minute automobile drive via highways, and each passenger's out-of-pocket ticket price is less than $60.

Nonetheless, all of this convenience comes at considerable expense to U.S. taxpayers. Each time a passenger boards a nine-seat plane providing the airline service connecting Hagerstown to Baltimore, the cost to taxpayers is $191. This is the additional per-passenger payment required to

induce Cape Air to provide its daily flights to and from Baltimore. Summing all of the subsidies that the federal government provides to keep the Hagerstown Regional Airport operating at its current pace requires an amount exceeding $1.2 million per year.

Critical Thinking Questions

1. What is the total subsidy paid by U.S. taxpayers each time a full Cape Air flight departs from Hagerstown for Baltimore?

2. Why do you suppose that 109 regional airports receiving federal support require about $175 million per year in total subsidies to provide current service flows?

ISSUES & APPLICATIONS

The Government-Sponsored U.S. Postal Service

CONCEPTS APPLIED

▶ Government-Sponsored Goods

▶ Monopoly

▶ Subsidies

Since 1971, the legal classification of the U.S. Postal Service (USPS) has been as a private enterprise. That is, the USPS officially is a nongovernmental business. *Economic* functions of the USPS remain government-sponsored, however.

Implicit Government Sponsorship via Regulatory Controls

The USPS operates a network of more than 31,000 post offices. The majority of these post offices do not generate revenues sufficiently high in relation to costs to justify keeping them in operation. If the USPS were

truly a private firm, many of these post offices would be closed.

Until recently, what has enabled the USPS to keep these post offices operating in spite of their meager rates of profitability has been the receipt of an implicit subsidy in the form of protection from competition. The USPS is the only institution in the United States authorized to make regular deliveries of "non-urgent letters" to mailboxes of households, businesses, and government offices. Thus, the USPS faces no threat of being undersold by competitors in its primary business of delivering non-urgent mail.

Government Sponsorship Becomes Much More Explicit

In spite of these government protections of the USPS, the annual volume of mail handled by the USPS has fallen from 213 billion items per year in 2006 to about 165 billion items per year today. As a consequence, postage revenues at USPS have plummeted even as its labor expenses have remained nearly unchanged. Since 2007, the USPS has experienced average annual *losses* from its operations exceeding *$7 billion* per year.

What allows the USPS to continue operating without employee layoffs in spite of annual losses exceeding $120,000 per USPS worker per year? The answer is the sponsorship of U.S. taxpayers. The federal government continues lending funds to the USPS to enable it to keep providing the same level of services with an unchanged workforce. Few observers anticipate that the USPS will ever repay the loans, which likely will become explicit subsidies to this government-sponsored institution.

For Critical Thinking

1. Why would a non-government-sponsored firm have difficulty remaining in operation incurring $7 billion in losses per year?
2. Why might a government-sponsored firm such as the USPS be more willing than a non-government-sponsored firm to agree to non-layoff contracts for workers?

Web Resources

1. For a discussion of the deteriorating situation at the USPS, go to **www.econtoday.com/chap05**.
2. Take a look at a list of contemplated USPS post office closings—but no planned employee layoffs at **www.econtoday.com/chap05**.

MyEconLab

For more questions on this chapter's Issues & Applications, go to MyEconLab. In the Study Plan for this chapter, select Section N: News.

MyEconLab

Here is what you should know after reading this chapter. MyEconLab will help you identify what you know, and where to go when you need to practice.

WHAT YOU SHOULD KNOW

How Market Failures Such as Externalities Might Justify Economic Functions of Government A market failure occurs when too many or too few resources are directed to a specific form of economic activity. One type of market failure is an externality, which is a spillover effect on third parties not directly involved in producing or purchasing a good or service. In the case of a negative externality, firms do not pay for the costs arising from spillover effects that their production of a good imposes on others, so they produce too much of the good in question. In the case of a positive externality, buyers fail to take into account the benefits that their consumption of a good yields to others, so they purchase too little of the good.

market failure, 101
externality, 101
third parties, 101
property rights, 102
effluent fee, 103
antitrust legislation, 106
monopoly, 106

Key Figure
Figure 5-1, 102

WHERE TO GO TO PRACTICE

- MyEconLab Study Plans 5.1, 5.2
- Animated Figure 5-1

MyEconLab *continued*

Private Goods versus Public Goods and the Free-Rider Problem Private goods are subject to the principle of rival consumption, meaning that one person's consumption of such a good reduces the amount available for another person to consume. In contrast, public goods can be consumed by many people simultaneously at no additional opportunity cost and with no reduction in quality or quantity. In addition, no individual can be excluded from the benefits of a public good even if that person fails to help pay for it.

private goods, 106
principle of rival
  consumption, 106
public goods, 106
free-rider problem, 107

• MyEconLab Study Plan 5.3

Political Functions of Government That Lead to Its Involvement in the Economy As a result of the political process, government may seek to promote the production and consumption of government-sponsored goods. The government may also seek to restrict the production and sale of goods that have been deemed socially undesirable, called government-inhibited goods. In addition, the political process may determine that income redistribution is socially desirable.

government-sponsored
  good, 108
government-inhibited
  good, 108
transfer payments, 108
transfers in kind, 108

• MyEconLab Study Plan 5.4

The Effect of Medicare on the Incentives to Consume Medical Services Medicare subsidizes the consumption of medical services. As a result, the quantity consumed is higher, as is the price sellers receive per unit of those services. Medicare also encourages people to consume medical services that are very low in per-unit value relative to the cost of providing them.

Key Figures
Figure 5-2, 109
Figure 5-4, 111

• MyEconLab Study Plan 5.5
• Animated Figures 5-2, 5-4

Why Bigger Subsidies for Public Schools Do Not Necessarily Translate into Improved Student Performance When governments subsidize public schools, the last unit of educational services provided by public schools costs more than its valuation by parents and students. Thus, public schools provide services in excess of those best suited to promoting student learning.

• MyEconLab Study Plan 5.5

Central Elements of the Theory of Public Choice The theory of public choice applies to collective decision making, or the process through which voters and politicians interact to influence nonmarket choices. Certain aspects of public-sector decision making, such as scarcity and competition, are similar to those that affect private-sector choices. Others, however, such as legal coercion and majority-rule decision making, differ from those involved in the market system.

collective decision
  making, 114
theory of public choice, 114
incentive structure, 114
government, or political,
  goods, 115
majority rule, 115
proportional rule, 115

• MyEconLab Study Plan 5.6

Log in to MyEconLab, take a chapter test, and get a personalized Study Plan that tells you which concepts you understand and which ones you need to review. From there, MyEconLab will give you further practice, tutorials, animations, videos, and guided solutions. For more information, visit www.myeconlab.com

PROBLEMS

All problems are assignable in MyEconLab. Answers to odd-numbered problems appear at the back of the book.

5-1. Many people who do not smoke cigars are bothered by the odor of cigar smoke. If private contracting is impossible, will too many or too few cigars be produced and consumed? Taking *all* costs into account, is the market price of cigars too high or too low? (See page 102.)

5-2. Suppose that repeated application of a pesticide used on orange trees causes harmful contamination of groundwater. The pesticide is applied annually in almost all of the orange groves throughout the world. Most orange growers regard the pesticide as a key input in their production of oranges. (See page 102.)

    a. Use a diagram of the market for the pesticide to illustrate the implications of a failure of orange producers' costs to reflect the social costs of groundwater contamination.

    b. Use your diagram from part (a) to explain a government policy that might be effective in achieving the amount of orange production that fully reflects all social costs.

5-3. Now draw a diagram of the market for oranges. Explain how the government policy you discussed in part (b) of Problem 5-2 is likely to affect the market price and equilibrium quantity in the orange market. In what sense do consumers of oranges now "pay" for dealing with the spillover costs of pesticide production? (See page 102.)

5-4. Suppose that the U.S. government determines that cigarette smoking creates social costs not reflected in the current market price and equilibrium quantity of cigarettes. A study has recommended that the government can correct for the externality effect of cigarette consumption by paying farmers *not* to plant tobacco used to manufacture cigarettes. It also recommends raising the funds to make these payments by increasing taxes on cigarettes. Assuming that the government is correct that cigarette smoking creates external costs, evaluate whether the study's recommended policies might help correct this negative externality. (See page 102.)

5-5. A nation's government has determined that mass transit, such as bus lines, helps alleviate traffic congestion, thereby benefiting both individual auto commuters and companies that desire to move products and factors of production speedily along streets and highways. Nevertheless, even though several private bus lines are in service, the country's commuters are failing to take into account the social benefits of the use of mass transit. (See pages 102–103.)

    a. Discuss, in the context of demand-supply analysis, the essential implications of commuters' failure to take into account the social benefits associated with bus ridership.

    b. Explain a government policy that might be effective in achieving the socially efficient use of bus services.

5-6. Draw a diagram of this nation's market for automobiles, which are a substitute for buses. Explain how the government policy you discussed in part (b) of Problem 5-5 is likely to affect the market price and equilibrium quantity in the country's auto market. How are auto consumers affected by this policy to attain the spillover benefits of bus transit? (See pages 102–103.)

5-7. Consider a nation with a government that does not provide people with property rights for a number of items and that fails to enforce the property rights it does assign for remaining items. Would externalities be more or less common in this nation than in a country such as the United States? Explain. (See page 105.)

5-8. Many economists suggest that our nation's legal system is an example of a public good. Does the legal system satisfy the key properties of a public good? Explain your reasoning. (See page 106.)

5-9. Displayed in the diagram below are conditions in the market for residential Internet access in a U.S. state. The government of this state has determined that access to the Internet improves the learning skills of children, which it has concluded is an external benefit of Internet access. The government has also concluded that if these external benefits were to be taken into account, 3 million residences would have Internet access. Suppose that the state government's judgments about the

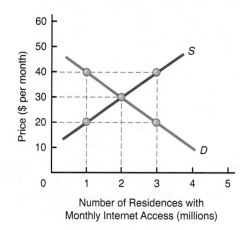

benefits of Internet access are correct and that it wishes to offer a per-unit subsidy just sufficient to increase total Internet access to 3 million residences. What per-unit subsidy should it offer? Use the diagram to explain how providing this subsidy would affect conditions in the state's market for residential Internet access. (See pages 102–103.)

5-10. The French government recently allocated the equivalent of more than $120 million in public funds to *Quaero* (Latin for "I search"), an Internet search engine analogous to Google or Yahoo. Does an Internet search engine satisfy the key characteristics of a public good? Why or why not? Based on your answer, is a publicly funded Internet search engine a public good or a government-sponsored good? (See page 106.)

5-11. A government offers to let a number of students at a public school transfer to a private school under two conditions: It will transmit to the private school the same per-pupil subsidy it provides the public school, and the private school will be required to admit the students at a below-market net tuition rate. Will the economic outcome be the same as the one that would have arisen if the government instead simply provided students with grants to cover the current market tuition rate at the private school? (Hint: Does it matter if schools receive payments directly from the government or from consumers? See pages 111–113.)

5-12. After a government implements a voucher program, granting funds that families can spend at schools of their choice, numerous students in public schools switch to private schools. Parents' and students' valuations of the services provided at both private and public schools adjust to equality with the true market price of educational services. Is anyone likely to lose out nonetheless? If so, who? (See page 113.)

5-13. Suppose that the current price of a tablet device is $300 and that people are buying 1 million drives per year. The government decides to begin subsidizing the purchase of new tablet devices. The government believes that the appropriate price is $260 per tablet, so the program offers to send people cash for the difference between $260 and whatever the people pay for each tablet they buy. (See page 111.)

a. If no consumers change their tablet-buying behavior, how much will this program cost the taxpayers?

b. Will the subsidy cause people to buy more, fewer, or the same number of tablets? Explain.

c. Suppose that people end up buying 1.5 million tablets once the program is in place. If the market price of tablets does not change, how much will this program cost the taxpayers?

d. Under the assumption that the program causes people to buy 1.5 million tablets and also causes the market price of tablets to rise to $320, how much will this program cost the taxpayers?

5-14. Scans of internal organs using magnetic resonance imaging (MRI) devices are often covered by subsidized health insurance programs such as Medicare. Consider the following table illustrating hypothetical quantities of individual MRI testing procedures demanded and supplied at various prices, and then answer the questions that follow. (See page 111.)

Price	Quantity Demanded	Quantity Supplied
$100	100,000	40,000
$300	90,000	60,000
$500	80,000	80,000
$700	70,000	100,000
$900	60,000	120,000

a. In the absence of a government-subsidized health plan, what is the equilibrium price of MRI tests? What is the amount of society's total spending on MRI tests?

b. Suppose that the government establishes a health plan guaranteeing that all qualified participants can purchase MRI tests at an effective price (that is, out-of-pocket cost) to the individual of $100 per test. How many MRI tests will people consume?

c. What is the per-unit price that induces producers to provide the number of MRI tests demanded at the government-guaranteed price of $100? What is society's total spending on MRI tests?

d. Under the government's coverage of MRI tests, what is the per-unit subsidy it provides? What is the total subsidy that the government pays to support MRI testing at its guaranteed price?

5-15. Suppose that, as part of an expansion of its State Care health system, a state government decides to offer a $50 subsidy to all people who, according to their physicians, should have their own blood pressure monitoring devices. Prior to this governmental decision, the market clearing price of blood pressure monitors in this state was $50, and the equilibrium quantity purchased was 20,000 per year. (See page 111.)

a. After the government expands its State Care plan, people in this state desire to purchase 40,000 devices each year. Manufacturers of blood pressure monitors are willing to provide 40,000 devices at a price of $60 per device. What out-of-pocket price does each consumer pay for a blood pressure monitor?

b. What is the dollar amount of the increase in total expenditures on blood pressure monitors in this state following the expansion in the State Care program?

   c. Following the expansion of the State Care program, what *percentage* of total expenditures on blood pressure monitors is paid by the government? What percentage of total expenditures is paid by consumers of these devices?

5-16. A government agency is contemplating launching an effort to expand the scope of its activities. One rationale for doing so is that another government agency might make the same effort and, if successful, receive larger budget allocations in future years. Another rationale for expanding the agency's activities is that this will make the jobs of its workers more interesting, which may help the government agency attract better-qualified employees. Nevertheless, to broaden its legal mandate, the agency will have to convince more than half of the House of Representatives and the Senate to approve a formal proposal to expand its activities. In addition, to expand its activities, the agency must have the authority to force private companies it does not currently regulate to be officially licensed by agency personnel. Identify which aspects of this problem are similar to those faced by firms that operate in private markets and which aspects are specific to the public sector. (See pages 114–115.)

ECONOMICS ON THE NET

Putting Tax Dollars to Work In this application, you will learn about how the U.S. government allocates its expenditures. This will enable you to conduct an evaluation of the current functions of the federal government.

Title: Historical Tables: Budget of the United States Government

Navigation: Go to www.econtoday.com/chap05 to visit the home page of the U.S. Government Printing Office. Click on "Browse the FY Budget" for the applicable year, and then click on "PDF" next to *Historical Tables*.

Application After the document downloads, examine Section 3, Federal Government Outlays by Function, and in particular Table 3.1, Outlays by Superfunction and Function. Then answer the following questions.

1. What government functions have been capturing growing shares of government spending in recent years? Which of these do you believe are related to the problem of addressing externalities, providing public goods, or dealing with other market failures? Which appear to be related to political functions instead of economic functions?

2. Which government functions are receiving declining shares of total spending? Are any of these related to the problem of addressing externalities, providing public goods, or dealing with other market failures? Are any related to political functions instead of economic functions?

For Group Study and Analysis Assign groups to the following overall categories of government functions: national defense, health, income security, and Social Security. Have each group prepare a brief report concerning long-term and recent trends in government spending on its category. Each group should take a stand on whether specific spending on items in its category is likely to relate to resolving market failures, public funding of government-sponsored goods, regulating the sale of government-inhibited goods, and so on.

ANSWERS TO QUICK QUIZZES

p. 105: (i) costs . . . taxation . . . regulation; (ii) benefits . . . financing . . . subsidizing . . . regulation

p. 109: (i) externalities . . . legal system . . . competition . . . public . . . economywide stability; (ii) rival consumption; (iii) opportunity cost . . . charged; (iv) government-sponsored . . . government-inhibited . . . income

p. 113: (i) low . . . high; (ii) low . . . higher

p. 116: (i) public choice; (ii) opportunity cost . . . competition

6

Funding the Public Sector

During the past few years, federal government spending as a percentage of total national income rose to about 25 percent before declining slightly. At the same time, total federal revenues from taxes and other sources fell to approximately 15 percent of national income before recovering somewhat. To cover expenditures out of national income not directly funded by revenues, the federal government resorted to borrowing. As you will learn in this chapter, however, the *government budget constraint* faced by the federal government dictates that ultimately spending and revenues must balance. As a consequence, eventually federal spending as a percentage of national income will have to equalize with federal revenues as a percentage of national income, which you will also learn is a measure of the nation's average federal tax rate.

governments of more than a dozen states have sold bonds promising annual payments based on more than $100 billion in projected shares of revenues from a legal settlement with the tobacco industry? The state governments have sold these "tobacco bonds" to raise funds for financing their operations now, rather than waiting for the streams of payments to arrive in future years. Of course, many state governments also have been selling more traditional bonds offering annual payments they plan to cover with future taxation. State and local governments assess sales taxes, property taxes, income taxes, hotel occupancy taxes, and electricity, gasoline, water, and sewage taxes. At the federal level, there are income taxes, Social Security taxes, Medicare taxes, and so-called excise taxes. When a person dies, state and federal governments also collect estate taxes. Clearly, governments give considerable attention to their roles as tax collectors.

Paying for the Public Sector

There are three sources of funding available to governments. One source is explicit fees, called user *charges*, for government services. The second and main source of government funding is taxes. Nevertheless, sometimes federal, state, and local governments spend more than they collect in taxes. To do this, they must rely on a third source of financing, which is borrowing. A government cannot borrow unlimited amounts, however. After all, a government, like an individual or a firm, can convince others to lend it funds only if it can provide evidence that it will repay its debts. A government must ultimately rely on taxation and user charges, the sources of its own current and future revenues, to repay its debts.

Over the long run, therefore, taxes and user charges are any government's *fundamental* sources of revenues. The **government budget constraint** states that each dollar of public spending on goods, services, transfer payments, and repayments of borrowed funds during a given period must be provided by tax revenues and user charges collected by the government. This long-term constraint indicates that the total amount a government plans to spend and transfer today and into the future cannot exceed the total taxes and user charges that it currently earns and can reasonably anticipate collecting in future years. Taxation dwarfs user charges as a source of government resources, so let's begin by looking at taxation from a government's perspective.

How has the fact that states must satisfy government budget constraints impinged directly on the personal budgets of students at a number of state universities?

YOU ARE THERE

To consider a real-world application regarding government budget constraints, take a look at **How to Keep Social Security in Business** on page 134.

Government budget constraint
The limit on government spending and transfers imposed by the fact that every dollar the government spends, transfers, or uses to repay borrowed funds must ultimately be provided by the user charges and taxes it collects.

EXAMPLE

State University Tuition Rates Jump—Even at the Last Moment

Spending on public education is one of the larger components of most states' budgets. Dampened economic activity since 2008 has led to lower tax revenues throughout the fifty states. To continue operating within their government budget constraints, more than half of the states have cut their spending on higher education. State universities face their own budget constraints, and in response to reduced funding from state governments, they have raised tuition rates charged to enrolled students.

At a number of state universities, tuition rates have jumped as late as the time of final course registration. In a few instances, state universities have even raised tuition after completion of the first semester of the academic year, before the start of the second semester. Students affected by such last-minute tuition increases have first-hand experience with government budget constraints.

FOR CRITICAL THINKING
How does the fact that government budget constraints must be satisfied help explain why many states have taken back scholarships that they initially offered to university enrollees?

Systems of Taxation

In light of the government budget constraint, a major concern of any government is how to collect taxes. Jean-Baptiste Colbert, the seventeenth-century French finance minister, said the art of taxation was in "plucking the goose so as to obtain the largest amount of feathers with the least possible amount of hissing." In the United States, governments have designed a variety of methods of plucking the private-sector goose.

The Tax Base and the Tax Rate

Tax base
The value of goods, services, wealth, or incomes subject to taxation.

Tax rate
The proportion of a tax base that must be paid to a government as taxes.

To collect a tax, a government typically establishes a **tax base,** which is the value of goods, services, wealth, or incomes subject to taxation. Then it assesses a **tax rate,** which is the proportion of the tax base that must be paid to the government as taxes.

As we discuss shortly, for the federal government and many state governments, incomes are key tax bases. Therefore, to discuss tax rates and the structure of taxation systems in more detail, let's focus for now on income taxation.

Marginal and Average Tax Rates

Marginal tax rate
The change in the tax payment divided by the change in income, or the percentage of *additional* dollars that must be paid in taxes. The marginal tax rate is applied to the highest tax bracket of taxable income reached.

Tax bracket
A specified interval of income to which a specific and unique marginal tax rate is applied.

Average tax rate
The total tax payment divided by total income. It is the proportion of total income paid in taxes.

If somebody says, "I pay 28 percent in taxes," you cannot really tell what that person means unless you know whether he or she is referring to average taxes paid or the tax rate on the last dollars earned. The latter concept refers to the **marginal tax rate,** with the word *marginal* meaning "incremental."

The marginal tax rate is expressed as follows:

$$\text{Marginal tax rate} = \frac{\text{change in taxes due}}{\text{change in taxable income}}$$

It is important to understand that the marginal tax rate applies only to the income in the highest **tax bracket** reached, with a tax bracket defined as a specified range of taxable income to which a specific and unique marginal tax rate is applied.

The marginal tax rate is not the same thing as the **average tax rate,** which is defined as follows:

$$\text{Average tax rate} = \frac{\text{total taxes due}}{\text{total taxable income}}$$

Why are governments contemplating a change in the tax base for the gasoline taxes that currently ring up at the pumps?

POLICY EXAMPLE

Is It Time to Replace Gasoline Taxes with Mileage Taxes?

A main source of revenues used by federal, state, and local governments to finance road construction and repair is taxation of gasoline purchases. As more vehicles that partly or fully rely on battery power have hit the road, gasoline purchases have been declining at any given price of gasoline. Thus, the gasoline tax base has been shrinking, so gasoline tax collections are dropping.

Battery-powered vehicles continue to subject roadways to wear and tear, so governments somehow must still obtain funds to finance road maintenance. Recently, the Congressional Budget Office has proposed a *mileage* tax base. Under a mileage-based taxation system, governments would require

vehicles to be equipped with special mileage meters. Government agencies would periodically tally the number of miles traveled by each vehicle, which would constitute a tax base. Then application of mileage tax rates to the new mileage tax base would determine the total mileage taxes owed by the vehicle's owner. In this way, governments could collect taxes on miles driven as well as on the gasoline that fuels the vehicle down the road.

FOR CRITICAL THINKING
Why would a mileage tax constitute "double taxation"?

Taxation Systems

No matter how governments raise revenues—from income taxes, sales taxes, or other taxes—all of those taxes fit into one of three types of taxation systems: proportional, progressive, or regressive, according to the relationship between the tax rate and income. To determine whether a tax system is proportional, progressive, or regressive, we simply ask, What is the relationship between the average tax rate and the marginal tax rate?

Proportional taxation
A tax system in which, regardless of an individual's income, the tax bill comprises exactly the same proportion.

PROPORTIONAL TAXATION **Proportional taxation** means that regardless of an individual's income, taxes comprise exactly the same proportion. In a proportional taxation system, the marginal tax rate is always equal to the average tax rate. If every dollar is taxed at 20 percent, then the average tax rate is 20 percent, and so is the marginal tax rate.

Under a proportional system of taxation, taxpayers at all income levels end up paying the same *percentage* of their income in taxes. With a proportional tax rate of 20 percent, an individual with an income of $10,000 pays $2,000 in taxes, while an individual making $100,000 pays $20,000. Thus, the identical 20 percent rate is levied on both taxpayers.

PROGRESSIVE TAXATION Under **progressive taxation,** as a person's taxable income increases, the percentage of income paid in taxes increases. In a progressive system, the marginal tax rate is above the average tax rate. If you are taxed 5 percent on the first $10,000 you earn, 10 percent on the next $10,000 you earn, and 30 percent on the last $10,000 you earn, you face a progressive income tax system. Your marginal tax rate is always above your average tax rate.

What is the marginal income tax rate faced by the highest U.S. income earners?

Go to www.econtoday.com/chap06 to learn from the National Center for Policy Analysis about what distinguishes recent flat tax proposals from a truly proportional income tax system. Click on "Flat Tax Proposals."

Progressive taxation
A tax system in which, as income increases, a higher percentage of the additional income is paid as taxes. The marginal tax rate exceeds the average tax rate as income rises.

POLICY EXAMPLE

Calculating the Top U.S. Marginal Tax Rate

Because the income tax systems of the federal government and of most state governments are progressive, the highest-income earners pay the highest overall income tax rates. The top federal income tax rate is at least 35 percent. In addition, the highest-income earners face the 2.9 percent Medicare payroll tax rate plus a "higher-earners surcharge" of 0.9 percent. Finally, the highest-income earners are hit with a 3.8 percent surcharge on investment and royalty earnings to fund the new national health care system. After taking into account allowed federal tax deductions based on state tax payments, the effective marginal state

income tax rate for the average high earner is approximately 4 percent. Summing these rates yields a current top marginal income tax rate for U.S. high-income earners with investment and royalty earnings of about 46.2 percent. Thus, the highest-income earners can keep for their own use just over half of the last dollar they earn.

FOR CRITICAL THINKING
How does the fact that a number of cities and counties also have their own income taxes affect the top marginal tax rate for some high earners?

REGRESSIVE TAXATION With **regressive taxation,** a smaller percentage of taxable income is taken in taxes as taxable income increases. The marginal rate is *below* the average rate. As income increases, the marginal tax rate falls, and so does the average tax rate. The U.S. Social Security tax is regressive. Once the legislative maximum taxable wage base is reached, no further Social Security taxes are paid. Consider a simplified hypothetical example: Suppose that every dollar up to $100,000 is taxed at 10 percent. After $100,000 there is no Social Security tax. Someone making $200,000 still pays only $10,000 in Social Security taxes. That person's average Social Security tax is 5 percent. The person making $100,000, by contrast, effectively pays 10 percent. The person making $1 million faces an average Social Security tax rate of only 1 percent in our simplified example.

Regressive taxation
A tax system in which as more dollars are earned, the percentage of tax paid on them falls. The marginal tax rate is less than the average tax rate as income rises.

QUICK QUIZ
See page 138 for the answers. Review concepts from this section in MyEconLab.

Governments collect taxes by applying a tax _____ to a tax _____, which refers to the value of goods, services, wealth, or incomes. Income tax rates are applied to tax brackets, which are ranges of income over which the tax rate is constant.

The _____ tax rate is the total tax payment divided by total income, and the _____ tax rate is the change

in the tax payment divided by the change in income.

Tax systems can be _____, _____, or _____, depending on whether the marginal tax rate is the same as, greater than, or less than the average tax rate as income rises.

The Most Important Federal Taxes

What types of taxes do federal, state, and local governments collect? The two pie charts in Figure 6-1 on the following page show the percentages of receipts from various taxes obtained by the federal government and by state and local governments. For the federal government, key taxes are individual income taxes, corporate income taxes, Social

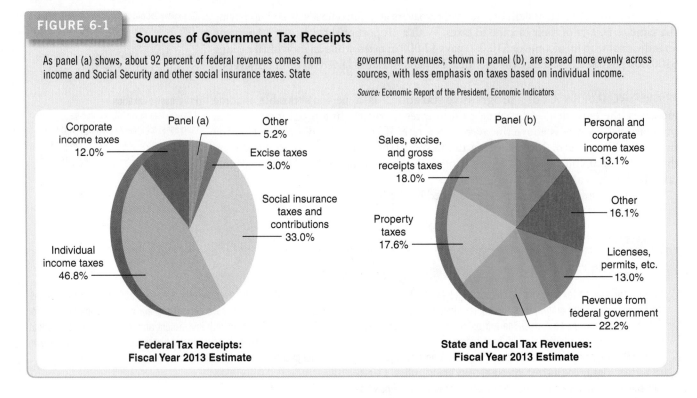

FIGURE 6-1

Sources of Government Tax Receipts

As panel (a) shows, about 92 percent of federal revenues comes from income and Social Security and other social insurance taxes. State government revenues, shown in panel (b), are spread more evenly across sources, with less emphasis on taxes based on individual income.

Source: Economic Report of the President, Economic Indicators

Security taxes, and excise taxes on items such as gasoline and alcoholic beverages. For state and local governments, sales taxes, property taxes, and personal and corporate income taxes are the main types of taxes.

The Federal Personal Income Tax

The most important tax in the U.S. economy is the federal personal income tax, which, as Figure 6-1 above indicates, accounts for almost 47 percent of all federal revenues. All U.S. citizens, resident aliens, and most others who earn income in the United States are required to pay federal income taxes on all taxable income, including income earned abroad.

The rates that are paid rise as income increases, as can be seen in Table 6-1 below. Marginal income tax rates at the federal level have ranged from as low as 1 percent after the 1913 passage of the Sixteenth Amendment, which made the individual income tax constitutional, to as high as 94 percent (reached in 1944). There were 14 separate tax brackets prior to the Tax Reform Act of 1986, which reduced the number to three (now six, as shown in Table 6-1).

TABLE 6-1

Federal Marginal Income Tax Rates

These rates applied in 2012.

Single Persons		Married Couples	
Marginal Tax Bracket	Marginal Tax Rate	Marginal Tax Bracket	Marginal Tax Rate
$0–$8,700	10%	$0–$17,400	10%
$8,701–$35,350	15%	$17,401–$70,700	15%
$35,351–$85,650	25%	$70,701–$142,700	25%
$85,651–$178,650	28%	$142,701–$217,450	28%
$178,651–$388,350	33%	$217,451–$388,350	33%
$388,351 and up	35%	$388,351 and up	35%

Source: U.S. Department of the Treasury.

What is the annual cost to U.S. taxpayers of determining how much they owe in income taxes?

POLICY EXAMPLE

Figuring Out How Much to Pay in Income Taxes Is Not Cheap

The Internal Revenue Service's Taxpayer Advocate Service has estimated that U.S. taxpayers spend nearly $200 billion per year to determine how much they owe in income taxes. In the process, taxpayers also devote 7.6 billion hours, or the equivalent of time that otherwise could have been spent in 3.8 million full-time jobs. The average hourly wage earned by a U.S. resident exceeds $16 per hour, so the opportunity cost of calculating U.S. income taxes is about $125 billion. Thus, the combined explicit and opportunity costs of complying with the U.S. income tax code amount to roughly $325 billion per year, which is about 20 percent of all federal income taxes collected.

FOR CRITICAL THINKING

What professions benefit from the nearly $200 billion per year spent on preparing tax returns?

The Treatment of Capital Gains

The difference between the purchase price and sale price of an asset, such as a share of stock or a plot of land, is called a **capital gain** if it is a profit and a **capital loss** if it is not. The federal government taxes capital gains, and as of 2013, there were several capital gains tax rates.

What appear to be capital gains are not always real gains. If you pay $100,000 for a financial asset in one year and sell it for 50 percent more 10 years later, your nominal capital gain is $50,000. But what if during those 10 years inflation has driven average asset prices up by 50 percent? Your *real* capital gain would be zero, but you would still have to pay taxes on that $50,000. To counter this problem, many economists have argued that capital gains should be indexed to the rate of inflation. This is exactly what is done with the marginal tax brackets in the federal income tax code. Tax brackets for the purposes of calculating marginal tax rates each year are expanded at the rate of inflation, that is, the rate at which the average of all prices is rising. So, if the rate of inflation is 10 percent, each tax bracket is moved up by 10 percent. The same concept could be applied to capital gains and financial assets. So far, Congress has refused to enact such a measure.

Capital gain
A positive difference between the purchase price and the sale price of an asset. If a share of stock is bought for $5 and then sold for $15, the capital gain is $10.

Capital loss
A negative difference between the purchase price and the sale price of an asset.

The Corporate Income Tax

Figure 6-1 on the facing page shows that corporate income taxes account for 12 percent of all federal taxes collected. They also make up about 2 percent of all state and local taxes collected. Corporations are generally taxed on the difference between their total revenues and their expenses. The federal corporate income tax structure is given in Table 6-2 below.

TABLE 6-2

Federal Corporate Income Tax Schedule

These corporate tax rates were in effect through 2013.

Corporate Taxable Income	Corporate Tax Rate
$0–$50,000	15%
$50,001–$75,000	25%
$75,001–$100,000	34%
$100,001–$335,000	39%
$335,001–$10,000,000	34%
$10,000,001–$15,000,000	35%
$15,000,001–$18,333,333	38%
$18,333,334 and up	35%

Source: Internal Revenue Service.

DOUBLE TAXATION Because individual stockholders must pay taxes on the dividends they receive, and those dividends are paid out of *after-tax* profits by the corporation, corporate profits are taxed twice. If you receive $1,000 in dividends, you have to declare them as income, and you must normally pay taxes on them. Before the corporation was able to pay you those dividends, it had to pay taxes on all its profits, including any that it put back into the company or did not distribute in the form of dividends. Eventually, the new investment made possible by those **retained earnings**—profits not given out to stockholders—along with borrowed funds will be reflected in the value of the stock in that company. When you sell your stock in that company, you will have to pay taxes on the difference between what you paid for the stock and what you sold it for. In both cases, dividends and retained earnings (corporate profits) are taxed twice. In 2003, Congress reduced the double taxation effect somewhat by enacting legislation that allowed most dividends to be taxed at lower rates than are applied to regular income through 2012.

Retained earnings
Earnings that a corporation saves, or retains, for investment in other productive activities; earnings that are not distributed to stockholders.

WHO REALLY PAYS THE CORPORATE INCOME TAX? Corporations can function only as long as consumers buy their products, employees make their goods, stockholders (owners) buy their shares, and bondholders buy their bonds. Corporations per se do not do anything. We must ask, then, who really pays the tax on corporate income? This is a question of **tax incidence.** (The question of tax incidence applies to all taxes, including sales taxes and Social Security taxes.) The incidence of corporate taxation is the subject of considerable debate. Some economists suggest that corporations pass their tax burdens on to consumers by charging higher prices.

Tax incidence
The distribution of tax burdens among various groups in society.

Other economists argue that it is the stockholders who bear most of the tax. Still others contend that employees pay at least part of the tax by receiving lower wages than they would otherwise. Because the debate is not yet settled, we will not hazard a guess here as to what the correct conclusion may be. Suffice it to say that you should be cautious when you advocate increasing corporation income taxes. *People,* whether owners, consumers, or workers, end up paying all of the increase—just as they pay all of any tax.

Social Security and Unemployment Taxes

Each year, taxes levied on payrolls account for an increasing percentage of federal tax receipts. These taxes, which are distinct from personal income taxes, are for Social Security, retirement, survivors' disability, and old-age medical benefits (Medicare). The Social Security tax is imposed on earnings up to roughly $110,100 at a rate of 6.2 percent on employers and 6.2 percent on employees. That is, the employer matches your "contribution" to Social Security. (The employer's contribution is really paid by the employees, at least in part, in the form of a reduced wage rate.) As Chapter 5 explained, a Medicare tax is imposed on all wage earnings at a combined rate of 2.9 percent. The 2010 federal health care law also added a 3.8 percent Medicare tax on certain income above $200,000.

Social Security taxes came into existence when the Federal Insurance Contributions Act (FICA) was passed in 1935. At that time, many more people paid into the Social Security program than the number who received benefits. Currently, however, older people drawing benefits make up a much larger share of the population. Consequently, in recent years, outflows of Social Security benefit payments have sometimes exceeded inflows of Social Security taxes. Various economists have advanced proposals to raise Social Security tax rates on younger workers or to reduce benefit payouts to older retirees and disabled individuals receiving Social Security payments. So far, however, the federal government has failed to address Social Security's deteriorating funding situation.

There is also a federal unemployment tax, which helps pay for unemployment insurance. This tax rate is 0.6 percent on the first $7,000 of annual wages of each employee who earns more than $1,500. Only the employer makes this tax payment. This tax covers the costs of the unemployment insurance system. In addition to this federal tax, some states with an unemployment system impose their own tax of up to about

3 percent, depending on the past record of the particular employer. An employer who frequently lays off workers typically will have a slightly higher state unemployment tax rate than an employer who never lays off workers.

QUICK QUIZ See page 138 for the answers. Review concepts from this section in MyEconLab.

The federal government raises most of its revenues through _____ taxes and social insurance taxes and contributions. State and local governments raise most of their tax revenues from _____ taxes, _____ taxes, and income taxes.

Because corporations must first pay an income tax on most earnings, the personal income tax shareholders pay on dividends received (or realized capital gains) constitutes _____ taxation.

Both employers and employees must pay _____ _____ taxes and contributions at rates of 6.2 percent on roughly the first $110,100 in wage earnings, and a 2.9 percent _____ tax rate is applied to all wage earnings. The federal government and some state governments also assess taxes to pay for _____ insurance systems.

Tax Rates and Tax Revenues

For most state and local governments, income taxes yield fewer revenues than taxes imposed on sales of goods and services. Figure 6-1 on page 126 shows that sales taxes, gross receipts taxes, and excise taxes generate almost one-fifth of the total funds available to state and local governments. Thus, from the perspective of many state and local governments, a fundamental issue is how to set tax rates on sales of goods and services to extract desired total tax payments.

Sales Taxes

Governments levy **sales taxes** on the prices that consumers pay to purchase each unit of a broad range of goods and services. Sellers collect sales taxes and transmit them to the government. Sales taxes are a form of **ad valorem taxation,** which means that the tax is applied "to the value" of the good. Thus, a government using a system of *ad valorem* taxation charges a tax rate equal to a fraction of the market price of each unit that a consumer buys. For instance, if the tax rate is 8 percent and the market price of an item is $100, then the amount of the tax on the item is $8.

A sales tax is therefore a proportional tax with respect to purchased items. The total amount of sales taxes a government collects equals the sales tax rate times the sales tax base, which is the market value of total purchases.

Sales taxes
Taxes assessed on the prices paid on most goods and services.

***Ad valorem* taxation**
Assessing taxes by charging a tax rate equal to a fraction of the market price of each unit purchased.

Static Tax Analysis

There are two approaches to evaluating how changes in tax rates affect government tax collections. **Static tax analysis** assumes that changes in the tax rate have no effect on the tax base. Thus, this approach implies that if a state government desires to increase its sales tax collections, it can simply raise the tax rate. Multiplying the higher tax rate by the tax base thereby produces higher tax revenues.

Governments often rely on static tax analysis. Sometimes this yields unpleasant surprises. Consider, for instance, what happened in 1992 when Congress implemented a federal "luxury tax" on purchases of new pleasure boats priced at $100,000 or more. Applying the 10 percent luxury tax rate to the anticipated tax base—sales of new boats during previous years—produced a forecast of hundreds of millions of dollars in revenues from the luxury tax. What actually happened, however, was an 80 percent plunge in sales of new luxury boats. People postponed boat purchases or bought used boats instead. Consequently, the tax base all but disappeared, and the federal government collected only a few tens of millions of dollars in taxes on boat sales. Congress repealed the tax a year later.

Static tax analysis
Economic evaluation of the effects of tax rate changes under the assumption that there is no effect on the tax base, meaning that there is an unambiguous positive relationship between tax rates and tax revenues.

Have recent efforts by several state governments to include cyberspace-generated sales in their tax bases paid off?

POLICY EXAMPLE

States Seek to Apply Sales Taxes to Internet Retailers' Sales

In recent years, U.S. states have collected too few taxes to fund their expenditures. State governments have responded by seeking new sources of tax revenues. Several states, such as Arkansas, Hawaii, North Carolina, and Rhode Island, have cast their sights on sales programs operated by Internet retailers such as Amazon and Overstock. Under these programs, sellers—called "affiliates"—post links on their own Web sites. When the affiliates' customers click on those links and purchase items, the affiliates receive referral fees from the Internet retailers. The states listed above have declared such affiliate programs to constitute the "physical presences" of Internet retailers. This means that Internet retailers would have to collect sales taxes on *all* of their companies' sales.

Each time that state governments have passed such sales tax laws, Internet retailers have responded by eliminating affiliate programs within those states. Thus, these efforts to expand sales tax bases to include Internet retailers have failed thus far.

FOR CRITICAL THINKING

What do you suppose has happened to state income taxes collected from Internet retailers' former affiliates in Arkansas, Hawaii, North Carolina, and Rhode Island?

Dynamic Tax Analysis

Dynamic tax analysis
Economic evaluation of tax rate changes that recognizes that the tax base eventually declines with ever-higher tax rates, so that tax revenues may eventually decline if the tax rate is raised sufficiently.

The problem with static tax analysis is that it ignores incentive effects created by new taxes or hikes in existing tax rates. According to **dynamic tax analysis**, a likely response to an increase in a tax rate is a *decrease* in the tax base. When a government pushes up its sales tax rate, for example, consumers have an incentive to cut back on their purchases of goods and services subjected to the higher rate, perhaps by buying them in a locale where there is a lower sales tax rate or perhaps no tax rate at all. As shown in Figure 6-2 below, the maximum sales tax rate varies considerably from state to state.

Consider someone who lives in a state bordering Oregon. In such a border state, the sales tax rate can be as high as 8 percent, so a resident of that state has a strong incentive to buy higher-priced goods and services in Oregon, where there is no sales tax. Someone who lives in a high-tax county in Alabama has an incentive to buy an item online from an out-of-state firm to avoid paying sales taxes. Such shifts in expenditures in response to higher relative tax rates will reduce a state's sales tax base and thereby result in lower sales tax collections than the levels predicted by static tax analysis.

FIGURE 6-2

States with the Highest and Lowest Sales Tax Rates

A number of states allow counties and cities to collect their own sales taxes in addition to state sales taxes. This figure shows the maximum sales tax rates for selected states, including county and municipal taxes. Delaware, Montana, New Hampshire, and Oregon have no sales taxes.

Source: U.S. Department of Commerce.

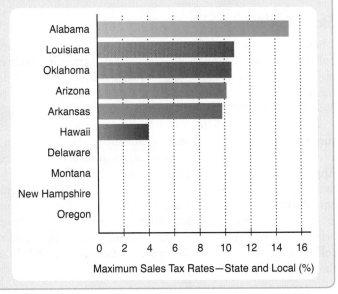

Dynamic tax analysis recognizes that increasing the tax rate could actually cause the government's total tax collections to *decline* if a sufficiently large number of consumers react to the higher sales tax rate by cutting back on purchases of goods and services included in the state's tax base. Some residents who live close to other states with lower sales tax rates might, for instance, drive across the state line to do more of their shopping. Other residents might place more orders with catalog companies or online firms located in other legal jurisdictions where their state's sales tax does not apply.

WHAT IF... the government seeks to collect higher taxes by increasing capital gains tax rates?

People who own assets the sale of which would generate capital gains subject to taxation have considerable discretion over when to sell assets and realize capital gains from such sales. When people learn about upcoming increases in tax rates that apply to capital gains, they can attempt to sell their assets immediately, before the higher tax rate goes into effect. Alternatively, they can indefinitely postpone sales of the assets in the hope that the tax rate will be cut in the future. Either response reduces capital gains subject to taxation when the higher tax rate becomes effective.

Indeed, the evidence for an inverse relationship between capital gains tax rates and realized capital gains is considerable. That is, when capital gains tax rates increase, taxable realized capital gains decline, and tax collections fail to rise as much as expected. Thus, as predicted by dynamic tax analysis, raising the tax rate causes an offsetting decline in the tax base, resulting in fewer tax collections than the government anticipates.

Maximizing Tax Revenues

Dynamic tax analysis indicates that whether a government's tax revenues ultimately rise or fall in response to a tax rate increase depends on exactly how much the tax base declines in response to the higher tax rate. On the one hand, the tax base may decline by a relatively small amount following an increase in the tax rate, or perhaps even imperceptibly, so that tax revenues rise. For instance, in the situation we imagine a government facing in Figure 6-3 below, a rise in the tax rate from 5 percent to 6 percent causes tax revenues to increase. Along this range, static tax analysis can provide a good approximation of the revenue effects of an increase in the tax rate. On the other hand, the tax base may decline so much that total tax revenues decrease. In Figure 6-3, for example, increasing the tax rate from 6 percent to 7 percent causes tax revenues to *decline*.

What is most likely is that when the tax rate is already relatively low, increasing the tax rate causes relatively small declines in the tax base. Within a range of relatively low sales tax rates, therefore, increasing the tax rate generates higher sales tax revenues, as illustrated along the upward-sloping portion of the curve depicted in Figure 6-3. If the government

FIGURE 6-3

Maximizing the Government's Sales Tax Revenues

Dynamic tax analysis predicts that ever-higher tax rates bring about declines in the tax base, so that at sufficiently high tax rates the government's tax revenues begin to fall off. This implies that there is a tax rate, 6 percent in this example, at which the government can collect the maximum possible revenues, T_{max}.

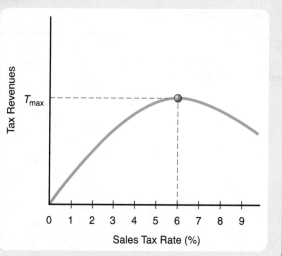

continues to push up the tax rate, however, people increasingly have an incentive to find ways to avoid purchasing taxable goods and services. Eventually, the tax base decreases sufficiently that the government's tax collections decline with ever-higher tax rates.

Consequently, governments that wish to maximize their tax revenues should not necessarily assess a high tax rate. In the situation illustrated in Figure 6-3, on the previous page, the government maximizes its tax revenues at T_{max} by establishing a sales tax rate of 6 percent. If the government were to raise the rate above 6 percent, it would induce a sufficient decline in the tax base that its tax collections would decline. If the government wishes to collect more than T_{max} in revenues to fund various government programs, it must somehow either expand its sales tax base or develop another tax.

QUICK QUIZ See page 138 for the answers. Review concepts from this section in MyEconLab.

The _____ view of the relationship between tax rates and tax revenues implies that higher tax rates always generate increased government tax collections.

According to _____ tax analysis, higher tax rates cause the tax base to decrease. Tax collections will rise less than predicted by _____ tax analysis.

Dynamic tax analysis indicates that there is a tax rate that maximizes the government's tax collections. Setting the tax rate any higher would cause the tax base to _____ sufficiently that the government's tax revenues will _____.

Taxation from the Point of View of Producers and Consumers

Governments collect taxes on product sales at the source. They require producers to charge these taxes when they sell their output. This means that taxes on sales of goods and services affect market prices and quantities. Let's consider why this is so.

Taxes and the Market Supply Curve

Imposing taxes on final sales of a good or service affects the position of the market supply curve. To see why, consider panel (a) of Figure 6-4 on the facing page, which shows a gasoline market supply curve S_1 in the absence of taxation. At a price of $3.35 per gallon, gasoline producers are willing and able to supply 180,000 gallons of gasoline per week. If the price increases to $3.45 per gallon, firms increase production to 200,000 gallons of gasoline per week.

Both federal and state governments assess **excise taxes**—taxes on sales of particular commodities—on sales of gasoline. They levy gasoline excise taxes as a **unit tax,** or a constant tax per unit sold. On average, combined federal and state excise taxes on gasoline are about $0.40 per gallon.

Let's suppose, therefore, that a gasoline producer must transmit a total of $0.40 per gallon to federal and state governments for each gallon sold. Producers must continue to receive a net amount of $3.35 per gallon to induce them to supply 180,000 gallons each week, so they must now receive $3.75 per gallon to supply that weekly quantity. Likewise, gasoline producers now will be willing to supply 200,000 gallons each week only if they receive $0.40 more per gallon, or a total amount of $3.85 per gallon.

As you can see, imposing the combined $0.40 per gallon excise taxes on gasoline shifts the supply curve vertically by exactly that amount to S_2 in panel (a). Thus, the effect of levying excise taxes on gasoline is to shift the supply curve vertically by the total per-unit taxes levied on gasoline sales. Hence, there is a decrease in supply. (In the case of an *ad valorem* sales tax, the supply curve would shift vertically by a proportionate amount equal to the tax rate.)

Excise tax
A tax levied on purchases of a particular good or service.

Unit tax
A constant tax assessed on each unit of a good that consumers purchase.

FIGURE 6-4

The Effects of Excise Taxes on the Market Supply and Equilibrium Price and Quantity of Gasoline

Panel (a) shows what happens if the government requires gasoline sellers to collect and transmit a $0.40 unit excise tax on gasoline. To be willing to continue supplying a given quantity, sellers must receive a price that is $0.40 higher for each gallon they sell, so the market supply curve shifts vertically

by the amount of the tax. As illustrated in panel (b), this decrease in market supply causes a reduction in the equilibrium quantity of gasoline produced and purchased. It also causes a rise in the market clearing price, to $3.75, so that consumers pay part of the tax. Sellers pay the rest in lower profits.

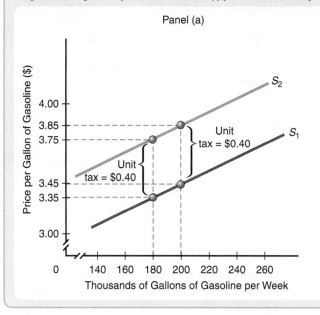

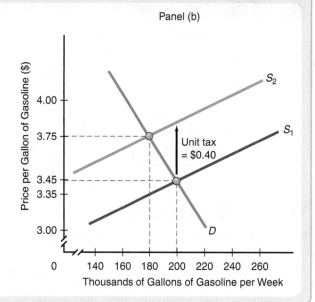

How Taxes Affect the Market Price and Equilibrium Quantity

Panel (b) of Figure 6-4 above shows how imposing $0.40 per gallon in excise taxes affects the market price of gasoline and the equilibrium quantity of gasoline produced and sold. In the absence of excise taxes, the market supply curve S_1 crosses the demand curve D at a market price of $3.45 per gallon. At this market price, the equilibrium quantity of gasoline is 200,000 gallons of gasoline per week.

The excise tax levy of $0.40 per gallon shifts the supply curve to S_2. At the original $3.45 per gallon price, there is now an excess quantity of gasoline demanded, so the market price of gasoline rises to $3.75 per gallon. At this market price, the equilibrium quantity of gasoline produced and consumed each week is 180,000 gallons.

What factors determine how much the equilibrium quantity of a good or service declines in response to taxation? The answer to this question depends on how responsive quantities demanded and supplied are to changes in price.

Who Pays the Tax?

In our example, imposing excise taxes of $0.40 per gallon of gasoline causes the market price to rise to $3.75 per gallon from $3.45 per gallon. Thus, the price that each consumer pays is $0.30 per gallon higher. Consumers pay three-fourths of the excise tax levied on each gallon of gasoline produced and sold in our example.

Gasoline producers must pay the rest of the tax. Their profits decline by $0.10 per gallon because costs have increased by $0.40 per gallon while consumers pay $0.30 more per gallon.

In the gasoline market, as in other markets for products subject to excise taxes and other taxes on sales, the shapes of the market demand and supply curves determine who pays most of a tax. The reason is that the shapes of these curves reflect the responsiveness to price changes of the quantity demanded by consumers and of the quantity supplied by producers.

In the example illustrated in Figure 6-4 on the previous page, the fact that consumers pay most of the excise taxes levied on gasoline reflects a relatively low responsiveness of quantity demanded by consumers to a change in the price of gasoline. Consumers pay most of the excise taxes on each gallon produced and sold because in this example the amount of gasoline they desire to purchase is relatively (but not completely) unresponsive to a change in the market price induced by excise taxes.

QUICK QUIZ See page 138 for the answers. Review concepts from this section in MyEconLab.

When the government levies a tax on sales of a particular product, firms must receive a higher price to continue supplying the same quantity as before, so the supply curve shifts _____. If the tax is a unit excise tax, the supply curve shifts _____ by the amount of the tax.

Imposing a tax on sales of an item _____ the equilibrium quantity produced and consumed and _____ the market price.

When a government assesses a unit excise tax, the market price of the good or service typically rises by an amount _____ than the per-unit tax. Hence, consumers pay a portion of the tax, and firms pay the remainder.

YOU ARE THERE
How to Keep Social Security in Business

Nancy Altman is the co-director of Social Security Works, a group dedicated to preserving the Social Security programs that provide benefits to the elderly and disabled. Altman's view is that these programs are "of crucial importance to every working American and his or her family." Nevertheless, the programs face eventual shortfalls of taxes in relation to promised benefits. Projections indicate that the government will be unable to fund promised benefits to the elderly sometime during the 2030s. The disability program will break down by the end of the 2010s.

Altman proposes two ways of preserving both Social Security programs. One is to combine the programs, so that tax dollars originally intended to fund only benefits for the elderly would begin covering disability benefits. Choosing this option would leave fewer tax funds to pay

for elderly benefits and cause that program to fail even sooner. The other option Altman suggests is to finance the disability program by increasing the Social Security tax rate.

One other approach could keep the disability program in operation. This option, which Altman opposes, would be to reduce disability benefits.

Critical Thinking Questions

1. Could borrowing help to finance Social Security benefits indefinitely? Explain.

2. What will be the effects of Social Security shortfalls on the overall U.S. government budget constraint, which sums all programs' constraints?

ISSUES & APPLICATIONS

What Determines the U.S. Long-Run Average Tax Rate?

CONCEPTS APPLIED

▶ Tax Rate

▶ Average Tax Rate

▶ Government Budget Constraint

If we view the overall tax base as the income earned by all residents during a given year, then the average tax rate equals all tax payments divided by income. This average tax rate is the proportion of total national income paid in taxes.

FIGURE 6-5

The Overall Average Federal Tax Rate and Its Components and Federal Spending as a Percentage of National Income

The overall average tax rate exhibits short-term volatility mainly because of changes in marginal tax rates and tax collections of individual income taxes. Ultimately, this overall tax rate must equal the ratio of federal spending to national income, but currently the government is making up the difference via borrowing.

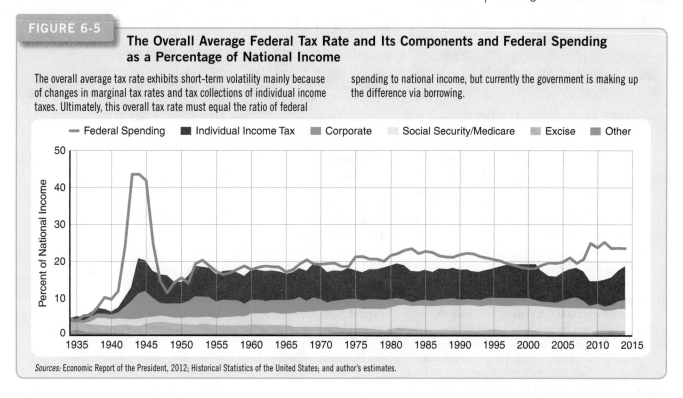

Sources: Economic Report of the President, 2012; Historical Statistics of the United States; and author's estimates.

The Overall Average U.S. Tax Rate and Its Components

Figure 6-5 above displays the average U.S. federal tax rate each year since 1934. Since the early 1950s, this overall average tax rate has ranged between 15 and 21 percent. The shaded regions show how this rate has been split among various forms of taxation.

The greater instability of the average individual income tax rate largely reflects two factors: changes in marginal income tax rates assessed by the federal government and variations in individual income subject to taxation. For instance, the gradual increase in the average individual income tax rate during the 1990s reflects higher marginal tax rates imposed in 1993. Drops in this average tax rate in the early 1980s and early 2000s help to account for declines in the average individual income rate during these intervals. Another key determinant, however, was declines in taxes collected during economic downturns. Since 2007, the significant dropoff in tax collections has been the primary reason for the fall in the average individual income tax rate.

The Role of the Government Budget Constraint

Recall that government spending ultimately must equal all revenues derived from taxes and fees. Thus, the average rate of federal spending out of national income eventually must be equalized with the overall average federal tax rate.

Plotted separately in the figure is federal spending as a percentage of national income. The current ratio of federal spending to national income of about 24 percent is well above the overall average tax rate of just over 15 percent. The federal government has had to make up the difference by borrowing, but it cannot do so indefinitely. If spending as a percentage of national income were to remain close to 24 percent, the overall average federal tax rate would have to rise to 24 percent as well. Ultimately, the average federal tax rate must adjust to equality with government spending's share of national income.

For Critical Thinking

1. If citizens were to decide that the overall average federal tax rate should not be greater than 18 percent, what must happen to the long-term rate of federal expenditures in relation to national income?

2. If citizens were to decide that in the long run, federal expenditures should be 28 percent of national income, what must be the required overall average federal tax rate?

Web Resources

1. Take a look at average federal tax rates for people in different income categories at www.econtoday.com/chap06.

2. Figure 6-5 displays only official "on-budget" federal spending as a percentage of national income. For a look at total—the sum of on-budget and unofficial "off-budget"—spending as a percentage of national income, go to www.econtoday.com/chap06.

> **MyEconLab**
>
> For more questions on this chapter's Issues & Applications, go to MyEconLab. In the Study Plan for this chapter, select Section N: News.

MyEconLab

Here is what you should know after reading this chapter. MyEconLab will help you identify what you know, and where to go when you need to practice.

WHAT YOU SHOULD KNOW — WHERE TO GO TO PRACTICE

Average Tax Rates versus Marginal Tax Rates The average tax rate is the ratio of total tax payments to total income. In contrast, the marginal tax rate is the change in tax payments induced by a change in total taxable income. Thus, the marginal tax rate applies to the last dollar that a person earns.

government budget constraint, 123
tax base, 124
tax rate, 124
marginal tax rate, 124
tax bracket, 124
average tax rate, 124

- MyEconLab Study Plans 6.1, 6.2

The U.S. Income Tax System The U.S. income tax system assesses taxes against both personal and business income. It is designed to be a progressive tax system, in which the marginal tax rate increases as income rises, so that the marginal tax rate exceeds the average tax rate. This contrasts with a regressive tax system, in which higher-income people pay lower marginal tax rates, resulting in a marginal tax rate that is less than the average tax rate. The marginal tax rate equals the average tax rate only under proportional taxation, in which the marginal tax rate does not vary with income.

proportional taxation, 124
progressive taxation, 125
regressive taxation, 125
capital gain, 127
capital loss, 127
retained earnings, 128
tax incidence, 128

- MyEconLab Study Plan 6.3

The Relationship between Tax Rates and Tax Revenues Static tax analysis assumes that the tax base does not respond significantly to an increase in the tax rate, so it seems to imply that a tax rate hike must always boost a government's total tax collections. Dynamic tax analysis reveals, however, that increases in tax rates cause the tax base to decline. Thus, there is a tax rate that maximizes the government's tax revenues. If the government pushes the tax rate higher, tax collections decline.

sales taxes, 129
ad valorem taxation, 129
static tax analysis, 129
dynamic tax analysis, 130

Key Figure
Figure 6-3, 131

- MyEconLab Study Plan 6.4
- Animated Figure 6-3

How Taxes on Purchases of Goods and Services Affect Market Prices and Quantities When a government imposes a per-unit tax on a good or service, a seller is willing to supply any given quantity only if the seller receives a price that is higher by exactly the amount of the tax. Hence, the supply curve shifts vertically by the amount of the tax per unit. In a market with typically shaped demand and supply curves, this results in a fall in the equilibrium quantity and an increase in the market price. To the extent that the market price rises, consumers pay a portion of the tax on each unit they buy. Sellers pay the remainder in lower profits.

excise tax, 132
unit tax, 132

Key Figure
Figure 6-4, 133

- MyEconLab Study Plan 6.5
- Animated Figure 6-4

Log in to MyEconLab, take a chapter test, and get a personalized Study Plan that tells you which concepts you understand and which ones you need to review. From there, MyEconLab will give you further practice, tutorials, animations, videos, and guided solutions. For more information, visit www.myeconlab.com

PROBLEMS

All problems are assignable in MyEconLab. Answers to odd-numbered problems appear at the back of the book.

6-1. A senior citizen gets a part-time job at a fast-food restaurant. She earns $8 per hour for each hour she works, and she works exactly 25 hours per week. Thus, her total pretax weekly income is $200. Her total income tax assessment each week is $40, but she has determined that she is assessed $3 in taxes for the final hour she works each week. (See page 124.)

  a. What is this person's average tax rate each week?

  b. What is the marginal tax rate for the last hour she works each week?

6-2. For purposes of assessing income taxes, there are three official income levels for workers in a small country: high, medium, and low. For the last hour on the job during a 40-hour workweek, a high-income worker pays a marginal income tax rate of 15 percent, a medium-income worker pays a marginal tax rate of 20 percent, and a low-income worker is assessed a 25 percent marginal income tax rate. Based only on this information, does this nation's income tax system appear to be progressive, proportional, or regressive? (See page 125.)

6-3. Consider the table below, in which each person's marginal tax rate is constant but differs from others' marginal tax rates, when answering the questions that follow. Show your work, and explain briefly. (See page 127.)

Christino		Jarius		Meg	
Income	Taxes Paid	Income	Taxes Paid	Income	Taxes Paid
$1,000	$200	$1,000	$200	$1,000	$200
$2,000	$300	$2,000	$400	$2,000	$500
$3,000	$400	$3,000	$600	$3,000	$800

  a. What is Christino's marginal tax rate?

  b. What is Jarius's marginal tax rate?

  c. What is Meg's marginal tax rate?

6-4. Refer to the table in Problem 6-3 when answering the following questions. Show your work, and explain briefly. (See pages 124–125.)

  a. Does Christino experience progressive, proportional, or regressive taxation?

  b. Does Jarius experience progressive, proportional, or regressive taxation?

  c. Does Meg experience progressive, proportional, or regressive taxation?

6-5. Suppose that a state has increased its sales tax rate every other year since 2005. Assume that the state collected all sales taxes that residents legally owed. The table below summarizes its experience. What were total taxable sales in this state during each year displayed in the table? (See page 129.)

Year	Sales Tax Rate	Sales Tax Collections
2005	0.03 (3 percent)	$9.0 million
2007	0.04 (4 percent)	$14.0 million
2009	0.05 (5 percent)	$20.0 million
2011	0.06 (6 percent)	$24.0 million
2013	0.07 (7 percent)	$29.4 million

6-6. The sales tax rate applied to all purchases within a state was 0.04 (4 percent) throughout 2012 but increased to 0.05 (5 percent) during all of 2013. The state government collected all taxes due, but its tax revenues were equal to $40 million each year. What happened to the sales tax base between 2012 and 2013? What could account for this result? (See pages 130–131.)

6-7. The British government recently imposed a unit excise tax of about $154 per ticket on airline tickets applying to flights to or from London airports. In answering the following questions, assume normally shaped demand and supply curves. (See page 133.)

  a. Use an appropriate diagram to predict effects of the ticket tax on the market clearing price of London airline tickets and on the equilibrium number of flights into and out of London.

  b. What do you predict is likely to happen to the equilibrium price of tickets for air flights into and out of cities that are in close proximity to London but are not subject to the new ticket tax? Explain your reasoning.

6-8. To raise funds aimed at providing more support for public schools, a state government has just imposed a unit excise tax equal to $4 for each monthly unit of wireless phone services sold by each company operating in the state. The following diagram depicts the positions of the demand and supply curves for wireless phone services *before* the unit excise tax was imposed. Use this diagram to determine the position of the new market supply curve now that the tax hike has gone into effect. (See pages 132–133.)

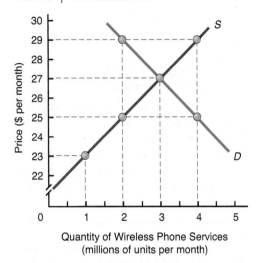

Quantity of Wireless Phone Services
(millions of units per month)

Price ($ per unit)	Quantity Supplied	Quantity Demanded
4	50	200
5	75	175
6	100	150
7	125	125
8	150	100
9	175	75

a. Does imposing the $4-per-month unit excise tax cause the market price of wireless phone services to rise by $4 per month? Why or why not?

b. What portion of the $4-per-month unit excise tax is paid by consumers? What portion is paid by providers of wireless phone services?

6-9. The following information applies to the market for a particular item in the *absence* of a unit excise tax (see pages 132–133):

a. According to the information in the table, in the *absence* of a unit excise tax, what is the market price? What is the equilibrium quantity?

b. Suppose that the government decides to subject producers of this item to a unit excise tax equal to $2 per unit sold. What is the new market price? What is the new equilibrium quantity?

c. What portion of the tax is paid by producers? What portion of the tax is paid by consumers?

ECONOMICS ON THE NET

Social Security Reform There are many proposals for reforming Social Security. The purpose of this exercise is to learn more about why changing Social Security is so often under discussion.

Title: Social Security Privatization

Navigation: Go to www.econtoday.com/chap06 to learn about Social Security privatization. Under "Recent Social Security Publications," click on "*Social Security, Ponzi Schemes, and the Need for Reform.*"

Application For each of the three entries noted here, read the entry and answer the question.

1. According to this article, when will the system begin to experience difficulties? Why?

2. Why does this article contend that Social Security is similar to a "Ponzi scheme"?

3. Why does this article argue that simply adding personal accounts will not solve Social Security's problems?

For Group Study and Analysis Go to www.econtoday.com/chap06 to read a proposal for Social Security reform. Accept or rebut the proposal, depending on the side to which you have been assigned. Be prepared to defend your reasons with more than just your feelings. At a minimum, be prepared to present arguments that are logical, if not entirely backed by facts.

ANSWERS TO QUICK QUIZZES

p. 125: (i) rate . . . base; (ii) average . . . marginal; (iii) proportional . . . progressive . . . regressive

p. 129: (i) income . . . sales . . . property; (ii) double; (iii) Social Security . . . Medicare . . . unemployment

p. 132: (i) static; (ii) dynamic . . . static; (iii) fall . . . decline

p. 134: (i) vertically . . . vertically; (ii) reduces . . . raises; (iii) less

19

Demand and Supply Elasticity

Times have been tougher for rock musicians in recent years. Even though the market prices of music albums and concert tickets have been increasing, the revenues received by rock performers have been decreasing. Professional musicians who perform other types of music, ranging from classical to country western, have been experiencing the same association of higher prices with lower revenues. After reading this chapter, you will understand why this relationship between revenues and price exists in the markets for music albums and concert performances. The key economic concept operating here, you will learn, is *price elasticity of demand*.

Federal Reserve economists have estimated that when bank debit-card transaction fees increase by 10 percent, the number of debit-card transactions that people wish to utilize declines by nearly 67 percent? Thus, an increase as small as 1 percent in the price of debit-card usage generates a significant proportionate reduction in the quantity of transactions demanded by debit-card users.

Businesses must constantly take into account consumers' response to changing fees and prices. If Apple reduces its prices by 10 percent, will consumers respond by buying so many more digital devices that the company's revenues rise? At the other end of the spectrum, can Ferrari dealers "get away" with a 2 percent increase in prices? That is, will Ferrari purchasers respond so little to the relatively small increase in price that the total revenues received for Ferrari sales will not fall and may actually rise? The only way to answer these questions is to know how responsive consumers in the real world will be to changes in prices. Economists have a special name for quantity responsiveness—*elasticity*, which is the subject of this chapter.

Price Elasticity

To begin to understand what elasticity is all about, just keep in mind that it means "responsiveness." Here we are concerned with the price elasticity of demand. We wish to know the extent to which a change in the price of, say, petroleum products will cause the quantity demanded to change, other things held constant. We want to determine the percentage change in quantity demanded in response to a percentage change in price.

Price Elasticity of Demand

We will formally define the **price elasticity of demand,** which we will label E_p, as follows:

$$E_p = \frac{\text{percentage change in quantity demanded}}{\text{percentage change in price}}$$

What will price elasticity of demand tell us? It will tell us the *relative* amount by which the quantity demanded will change in response to a change in the price of a particular good.

Consider an example in which a 10 percent rise in the price of oil leads to a reduction in quantity demanded of only 1 percent. Putting these numbers into the formula, we find that the price elasticity of demand for oil in this case equals the percentage change in quantity demanded divided by the percentage change in price, or

$$E_p = \frac{-1\%}{+10\%} = -0.1$$

An elasticity of −0.1 means that a 1 percent *increase* in the price would lead to a mere 0.1 percent *decrease* in the quantity demanded. If you were now told, in contrast, that the price elasticity of demand for oil was −1, you would know that a 10 percent increase in the price of oil would lead to a 10 percent decrease in the quantity demanded.

RELATIVE QUANTITIES ONLY Notice that in our elasticity formula, we talk about *percentage* changes in quantity demanded divided by *percentage* changes in price. We focus on relative amounts of price changes, because percentage changes are independent of the units chosen. This means that it doesn't matter if we measure price changes in terms of cents, dollars, or hundreds of dollars. It also doesn't matter whether we measure quantity changes in ounces, grams, or pounds.

Price elasticity of demand (E_p)
The responsiveness of the quantity demanded of a commodity to changes in its price; defined as the percentage change in quantity demanded divided by the percentage change in price.

Go to www.econtoday.com/chap19 for additional review of the price elasticity of demand.

ALWAYS NEGATIVE The law of demand states that quantity demanded is *inversely* related to the relative price. An *increase* in the price of a good leads to a *decrease* in the quantity demanded. If a *decrease* in the relative price of a good should occur, the quantity demanded would *increase* by some percentage. The point is that price elasticity of demand will always be negative. By convention, however, *we will ignore the minus sign in our discussion from this point on.*

Basically, the greater the *absolute* price elasticity of demand (disregarding the sign), the greater the demand responsiveness to relative price changes—a small change in price has a great impact on quantity demanded. Conversely, the smaller the absolute price elasticity of demand, the smaller the demand responsiveness to relative price changes—a large change in price has little effect on quantity demanded.

Calculating Elasticity

To calculate the price elasticity of demand, we must compute percentage changes in quantity demanded and in price. To calculate the percentage change in quantity demanded, we might divide the absolute change in the quantity demanded by the original quantity demanded:

$$\frac{\text{change in quantity demanded}}{\text{original quantity demanded}}$$

To find the percentage change in price, we might divide the change in price by the original price:

$$\frac{\text{change in price}}{\text{original price}}$$

There is an arithmetic problem, though, when we calculate percentage changes in this manner. The percentage change, say, from 2 to 3—50 percent—is not the same as the percentage change from 3 to 2—$33\frac{1}{3}$ percent. In other words, it makes a difference where you start. One way out of this dilemma is simply to use average values.

To compute the price elasticity of demand, we take the *average* of the two prices and the two quantities over the range we are considering and compare the change with these averages. Thus, the formula for computing the price elasticity of demand is as follows:

$$E_p = \frac{\text{change in quantity}}{\text{sum of quantities}/2} \div \frac{\text{change in price}}{\text{sum of prices }/2}$$

We can rewrite this more simply if we do two things: (1) We can let Q_1 and Q_2 equal the two different quantities demanded before and after the price change and let P_1 and P_2 equal the two different prices. (2) Because we will be dividing a percentage by a percentage, we simply use the ratio, or the decimal form, of the percentages. Therefore,

$$E_p = \frac{\Delta Q}{(Q_1 + Q_2)/2} \div \frac{\Delta P}{(P_1 + P_2)/2}$$

where the Greek letter Δ (delta) stands for "change in."

How can we use actual changes in the price of a particular brand of tablet device and associated changes in the quantity of tablet devices demanded to calculate the price elasticity of demand with this formula?

EXAMPLE

The Price Elasticity of Demand for a Tablet Device

During a two-month period, the price of Hewlett-Packard's TouchPad tablet device decreased from $499.99 to $99.99. As a consequence, during this two-month period the total quantity of tablet devices demanded increased from 25,000 per month to 425,000 per month.

Assuming other things were equal, we can calculate the price elasticity of demand for TouchPad tablets during this period:

$$E_p = \frac{\text{change in } Q}{\text{sum of quantities}/2} \div \frac{\text{change in } P}{\text{sum of prices}/2}$$

$$= \frac{425,000 - 25,000}{(425,000 + 25,000)/2} \div \frac{\$499.99 - \$99.99}{(\$499.99 + \$99.99)/2}$$

$$= \frac{400,000}{450,000/2} \div \frac{\$400.00}{\$599.98/2} = 1.33$$

The price elasticity of 1.33 means that each 1 percent decrease in price generated a 1.33 percent increase in the quantity of TouchPad tablet devices demanded. Thus, the quantity of tablets demanded was relatively responsive to a reduction in the price of the devices.

FOR CRITICAL THINKING

Would the estimated price elasticity of demand for TouchPad tablets have been different if we had not *used the average-values formula? How?*

Price Elasticity Ranges

We have names for the varying ranges of price elasticities, depending on whether a 1 percent change in price elicits more or less than a 1 percent change in the quantity demanded.

- We say that a good has an **elastic demand** whenever the price elasticity of demand is greater than 1. A change in price of 1 percent causes a greater than 1 percent change in the quantity demanded.

- In a situation of **unit elasticity of demand,** a change in price of 1 percent causes exactly a 1 percent change in the quantity demanded.

- In a situation of **inelastic demand,** a change in price of 1 percent causes a change of less than 1 percent in the quantity demanded.

When we say that a commodity's demand is elastic, we are indicating that consumers are relatively responsive to changes in price. When we say that a commodity's demand is inelastic, we are indicating that its consumers are relatively unresponsive to price changes. When economists say that demand is inelastic, it does not necessarily mean that quantity demanded is *totally* unresponsive to price changes. Remember, the law of demand implies that there will almost always be some responsiveness in quantity demanded to a price change. The question is how much. That's what elasticity attempts to determine.

Elastic demand
A demand relationship in which a given percentage change in price will result in a larger percentage change in quantity demanded.

Unit elasticity of demand
A demand relationship in which the quantity demanded changes exactly in proportion to the change in price.

Inelastic demand
A demand relationship in which a given percentage change in price will result in a less-than-proportionate percentage change in the quantity demanded.

Extreme Elasticities

There are two extremes in price elasticities of demand. One extreme represents total unresponsiveness of quantity demanded to price changes, which is referred to as **perfectly inelastic demand,** or zero elasticity. The other represents total responsiveness, which is referred to as infinitely or **perfectly elastic demand.**

We show perfect inelasticity in panel (a) of Figure 19-1 on the following page. Notice that the quantity demanded per year is 8 million units, no matter what the price. Hence, for any price change, the quantity demanded will remain the same, and thus the change in the quantity demanded will be zero. Look back at our formula for computing elasticity. If the change in the quantity demanded is zero, the numerator is also zero, and a nonzero number divided into zero results in a value of zero too. This is true at any point along the demand curve. Hence, there is perfect inelasticity.

Perfectly inelastic demand
A demand that exhibits zero responsiveness to price changes. No matter what the price is, the quantity demanded remains the same.

Perfectly elastic demand
A demand that has the characteristic that even the slightest increase in price will lead to zero quantity demanded.

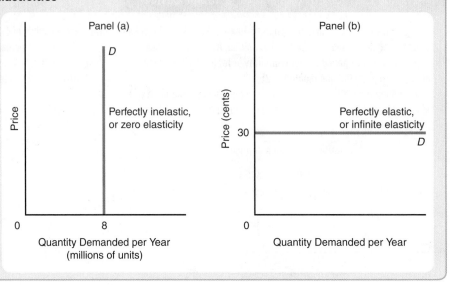

FIGURE 19-1

Extreme Price Elasticities

In panel (a), we show complete price unresponsiveness. The demand curve is vertical at the quantity of 8 million units per year. This means that the price elasticity of demand is zero. In panel (b), we show complete price responsiveness. At a price of 30 cents, in this example, consumers will demand an unlimited quantity of the particular good in question, over the relevant range of quantities. This is a case of infinite price elasticity of demand.

At the opposite extreme is the situation depicted in panel (b) of Figure 19-1 above. Here we show that at a price of 30 cents, an unlimited quantity will be demanded over the relevant range of quantities. At a price that is only slightly above 30 cents, no quantity will be demanded. There is perfect, or infinite, responsiveness at each point along this curve, and hence we call the demand schedule in panel (b) perfectly elastic.

QUICK QUIZ See page 433 for the answers. Review concepts from this section in MyEconLab.

The **price elasticity of demand** is equal to the percentage change in _____ _____ divided by the percentage change in _____.

Price elasticity of demand is calculated in terms of _____ changes in quantity demanded and in price. Thus, it is expressed as a unitless, dimensionless number that is _____ of units of measurement.

The price elasticity of demand is always _____, because an increase in price will lead to a _____ in quantity demanded and a decrease in price will lead to an

_____ in quantity demanded. By convention, we ignore the negative sign in discussions of the price elasticity of demand.

One extreme elasticity occurs when a demand curve is vertical. It has _____ price elasticity of demand. It is completely _____. Another extreme elasticity occurs when a demand curve is horizontal. It has completely _____ demand. Its price elasticity of demand is _____.

Elasticity and Total Revenues

Suppose that you are an employee of a firm in the cellular phone service industry. How would you know when a rise in the market clearing price of cellular phone services will result in an increase in the total revenues, or the total receipts, of firms in the industry? It is commonly thought that the way for total receipts to rise is for the price per unit to increase. But is it possible that a rise in price per unit could lead to a decrease in total revenues? The answer to this question depends on the price elasticity of demand.

Let's look at Figure 19-2 on the facing page. In panel (a), column 1 shows the price of cellular phone service in cents per minute, and column 2 represents billions of minutes per year. In column 3, we multiply column 1 times column 2 to derive total revenue because total revenue is always equal to the number of units (quantity) sold times

FIGURE 19-2

The Relationship between Price Elasticity of Demand and Total Revenues for Cellular Phone Service

In panel (a), we show the elastic, unit-elastic, and inelastic sections of a straight-line demand schedule according to whether a reduction in price increases total revenues, causes them to remain constant, or causes them to decrease, respectively. In panel (b), we show these regions graphically on the demand curve. In panel (c), we show them on the total revenue curve.

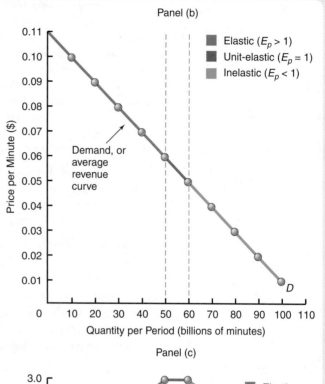

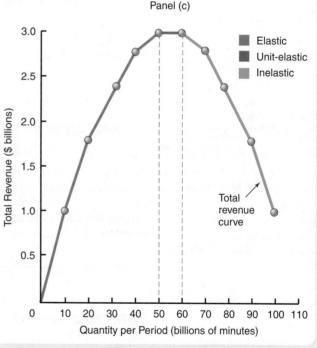

Panel (a)

(1) Price, P, per Minute of Cellular Phone Service	(2) Quantity Demanded, D (billions of minutes)	(3) Total Revenue ($ billions) = (1) x (2)	(4) Elasticity, $E_p = \dfrac{\text{Change in } Q}{(Q_1 + Q_2)/2} \div \dfrac{\text{Change in } P}{(P_1 + P_2)/2}$
$0.11	0	0	
0.10	10	1.0	21.000
0.09	20	1.8	6.330
0.08	30	2.4	3.400 } Elastic
0.07	40	2.8	2.143
0.06	50	3.0	1.144
0.05	60	3.0	1.000 } Unit-elastic
0.04	70	2.8	.692
0.03	80	2.4	.467 } Inelastic
0.02	90	1.8	.294
0.01	100	1.0	.158

the price per unit. In column 4, we calculate values of elasticity. Notice what happens to total revenues throughout the schedule. They rise steadily as the price rises from 1 cent to 5 cents per minute. When the price rises further to 6 cents per minute, total revenues remain constant at $3 billion. At prices per minute higher than 6 cents, total revenues fall as price increases. Indeed, if prices are above 6 cents per minute, total revenues will increase only if the price *declines*, not if the price rises.

Labeling Elasticity

The relationship between price and quantity on the demand schedule is given in columns 1 and 2 of panel (a) in Figure 19-2 on the previous page. In panel (b), the demand curve, *D*, representing that schedule is drawn. In panel (c), the total revenue curve representing the data in column 3 is drawn. Notice first the level of these curves at small quantities. The demand curve is at a maximum height, but total revenue is zero, which makes sense according to this demand schedule—at a price of 11 cents per minute and above, no units will be purchased, and therefore total revenue will be zero. As price is lowered, we travel down the demand curve, and total revenues increase until price is 6 cents per minute, remain constant from 6 cents to 5 cents per minute, and then fall at lower unit prices. Corresponding to those three sections, demand is elastic, unit-elastic, and inelastic. Hence, we have three relationships among the three types of price elasticity and total revenues.

- *Elastic demand.* A negative relationship exists between changes in price and changes in total revenues. That is to say, along the elastic range of market demand for an item, total revenues will rise if the market price decreases. Total revenues will fall if the market price increases.

- *Unit-elastic demand.* Changes in price do not change total revenues. When price increases along the unit-elastic range of market demand, total revenues will not change, nor will total revenues change if the market price decreases.

- *Inelastic demand.* A positive relationship exists between changes in price and total revenues. When price increases along the inelastic range of market demand, total revenues will go up. When the market price decreases, total revenues will fall. We therefore conclude that if demand is inelastic, price and total revenues move in the *same* direction.

How can we use information about price and revenue changes at U.S. airlines to infer whether the demand for air travel is price-elastic, unit-elastic, or price-inelastic?

EXAMPLE

Price and Revenue Changes and Price Elasticity of Demand for Air Travel

During a recent period, the per-mile price that passengers paid to fly on U.S. airlines rose by 14 percent. Associated with this proportionate price increase was a 17 percent rise in total revenues received by airlines. Thus, within the time interval in which the price increase occurred but other determinants of demand for the services of U.S. airlines did not change, demand was inelastic.

FOR CRITICAL THINKING
If a rise in the per-mile price of flying instead had generated no change in airlines' revenues, what would have been true of the price elasticity of demand for air travel?

GRAPHIC PRESENTATION The elastic, unit-elastic, and inelastic areas of the demand curve are shown in Figure 19-2, in panel (a). For prices from 11 cents per minute of cellular phone time to 6 cents per minute, as price decreases, total revenues rise from zero to $3 billion. Demand is elastic. When price changes from 6 cents to 5 cents, however, total revenues remain constant at $3 billion. Demand is unit-elastic. Finally, when price falls from 5 cents to 1 cent, total revenues decrease from $3 billion to $1 billion. Demand is inelastic. In panels (b) and (c) of Figure 19-2, we have labeled the sections of the demand curve accordingly, and we have also shown how total revenues first rise, then remain constant, and finally fall.

THE ELASTICITY-REVENUE RELATIONSHIP The relationship between price elasticity of demand and total revenues brings together some important microeconomic concepts.

TABLE 19-1

Relationship between Price Elasticity of Demand and Total Revenues	Price Elasticity of Demand (E_p)		Effect of Price Change on Total Revenues (TR)	
			Price Decrease	Price Increase
	Inelastic	($E_p < 1$)	TR ↓	TR ↑
	Unit-elastic	($E_p = 1$)	No change in TR	No change in TR
	Elastic	($E_p > 1$)	TR ↑	TR ↓

Total revenues, as we have noted, are the product of price per unit times number of units purchased. The law of demand states that along a given demand curve, price and quantity changes will move in opposite directions: One increases as the other decreases. Consequently, what happens to the product of price times quantity depends on which of the opposing changes exerts a greater force on total revenues. But this is just what price elasticity of demand is designed to measure—responsiveness of quantity demanded to a change in price. The relationship between price elasticity of demand and total revenues is summarized in Table 19-1 above.

WHAT IF... the government offers to pay for higher-priced health care to try to reduce society's overall health care expenditures?

Estimates of the price elasticity of demand for most health care services vary between 0.2 and 0.6. These low elasticity values indicate that the demand for health care is inelastic. Thus, whenever health care prices increase, total revenues of health care providers will rise, which means that total expenditures by health care consumers must also increase. Suppose that the government were to step into the market to pay for health care in response to an observed increase in prices. The government's expenditures on health care would increase. Taken together, the private sector and the government together constitute "society." Thus, total health care expenditures for society as a whole would be higher—not lower—after the government's interventions.

QUICK QUIZ See page 433 for the answers. Review concepts from this section in MyEconLab.

Price elasticity of demand is related to total _____.

When demand is *elastic*, the change in price elicits a change in total revenues in the _____ direction from the price change.

When demand is *unit-elastic*, a change in price elicits _____ change in total revenues (or in total consumer expenditures).

When demand is *inelastic*, a change in price elicits a change in total revenues in the _____ direction as the price change.

Determinants of the Price Elasticity of Demand

We have learned how to calculate the price elasticity of demand. We know that theoretically it ranges numerically from zero (completely inelastic) to infinity (completely elastic). What we would like to do now is to come up with a list of the determinants of the price elasticity of demand. The price elasticity of demand for a particular commodity at any price depends, at a minimum, on the following factors:

- The existence, number, and quality of substitutes
- The share of a consumer's total budget devoted to purchases of that commodity
- The length of time allowed for adjustment to changes in the price of the commodity

Existence of Substitutes

The closer the substitutes for a particular commodity and the more substitutes there are, the greater will be its price elasticity of demand. At the limit, if there is a perfect substitute, the elasticity of demand for the commodity will be infinity. Thus, even the slightest increase in the commodity's price will cause a dramatic reduction in the quantity demanded: Quantity demanded will fall to zero.

Keep in mind that in this extreme example, we are really talking about two goods that the consumer believes are exactly alike and equally desirable, like dollar bills whose only difference is their serial numbers. When we talk about less extreme examples, we can speak only in terms of the number and the similarity of substitutes that are available.

Thus, we will find that the more narrowly we define a good, the closer and greater will be the number of substitutes available. For example, the demand for diet soft drinks may be relatively elastic because consumers can switch to other low-calorie liquid refreshments. The demand for diet drinks (as a single group), however, is relatively less elastic because there are fewer substitutes.

Share of Budget

We know that the greater the share of a person's total budget that is spent on a commodity, the greater that person's price elasticity of demand is for that commodity. A key reason that the demand for pepper is very inelastic is because individuals spend so little on it relative to their total budgets. In contrast, the demand for items such as transportation and housing is far more elastic because they occupy a large part of people's budgets—changes in their prices cannot easily be ignored without sacrificing a lot of other alternative goods that could be purchased.

Consider a numerical example. A household spends $40,000 a year. It purchases $4 of pepper per year and $4,000 of transportation services. Now consider the spending power of this family when the price of pepper and the price of transportation both double. If the household buys the same amount of pepper, it will now spend $8. It will thus have to reduce other expenditures by $4. This $4 represents only 0.01 percent of the entire household budget. By contrast, if transportation costs double, the family will have to spend $8,000, or $4,000 more on transportation, if it is to purchase the same quantity. That increased expenditure on transportation of $4,000 represents 10 percent of total expenditures that must be switched from other purchases.

We would therefore predict that the household will react differently if the price of pepper doubles than it will if transportation prices double. It will reduce its transportation purchases by a proportionately greater amount.

Time for Adjustment

When the price of a commodity changes and that price change persists, more people will learn about it. Further, consumers will be better able to revise their consumption patterns the longer the time period they have to do so. And in fact, the longer the time they do take, the less costly it will be for them to engage in this revision of consumption patterns. Consider a price decrease. The longer the price decrease persists, the greater will be the number of new uses that consumers will discover for the particular commodity, and the greater will be the number of new users of that particular commodity.

It is possible to make a very strong statement about the relationship between the price elasticity of demand and the time allowed for adjustment:

The longer any price change persists, the greater the elasticity of demand, other things held constant. Elasticity of demand is greater in the long run than in the short run.

SHORT-RUN VERSUS LONG-RUN ADJUSTMENTS Let's consider an example. Suppose that the price of electricity goes up 50 percent. How do you adjust in the short run? You can turn the lights off more often, you can stop using your personal computer as much as you usually do, and similar measures. Otherwise it's very difficult to cut back on your consumption of electricity.

In the long run, though, you can devise other methods to reduce your consumption. Instead of using only electric heaters, the next time you have a house built you will install solar panels. You will purchase fluorescent bulbs because they use less electricity. The more time you have to think about it, the more ways you will find to cut your electricity consumption.

DEMAND ELASTICITY IN THE SHORT RUN AND IN THE LONG RUN We would expect, therefore, that the short-run demand curve for electricity would be relatively less elastic (in the price range around P_e), as demonstrated by D_1 in Figure 19-3 below. The long-run demand curve, however, will exhibit more elasticity (in the neighborhood of P_e), as demonstrated by D_3. Indeed, we can think of an entire family of demand curves such as those depicted in the figure. The short-run demand curve is for the period when there is little time for adjustment. As more time is allowed, the demand curve goes first to D_2 and then all the way to D_3. Thus, in the neighborhood of P_e, elasticity differs for each of these curves. It is greater for the less steep curves (but slope alone does not measure elasticity for the entire curve). What are short- and long-run price elasticities of demand for actual goods?

FIGURE 19-3

Short-Run and Long-Run Price Elasticity of Demand

Consider a situation in which the market price is P_e and the quantity demanded is Q_e. Then there is a price increase to P_1. In the short run, as evidenced by the demand curve D_1, we move from equilibrium quantity demanded, Q_e, to Q_1. After more time is allowed for adjustment, the demand curve rotates at original price P_e to D_2. Quantity demanded falls again, now to Q_2. After even more time is allowed for adjustment, the demand curve rotates at price P_e to D_3. At the higher price P_1 in the long run, the quantity demanded falls all the way to Q_3.

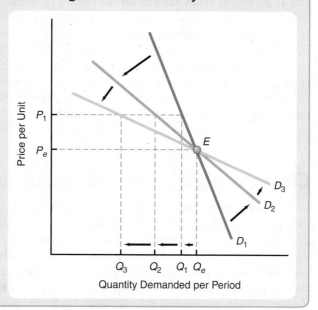

EXAMPLE

What Do Real-World Price Elasticities of Demand Look Like?

In Table 19-2 A below, we present demand elasticities for selected goods. None of them is zero, and the largest is 4.6. Remember that even though we are omitting the negative sign, there is an inverse relationship between price and quantity demanded. Also remember that these elasticities are measured over given price ranges. Recall from the example of the demand curve in Figure 19-2 on page 419 that choosing different price ranges could yield different elasticity estimates for these goods.

Economists have consistently found that estimated price elasticities of demand are greater in the long run than in the short run, as seen in

Table 19-2. There you see that all available estimates indicate that the long-run price elasticity of demand for vacation air travel is 2.7, whereas the estimate for the short run is 1.1. Throughout the table, you see that all estimates of long-run price elasticities of demand exceed their short-run counterparts.

FOR CRITICAL THINKING
Explain the intuitive reasoning behind the difference between long-run and short-run price elasticity of demand.

TABLE 19-2

Price Elasticities of Demand for Selected Goods

Here are estimated demand elasticities for selected goods. All of them are negative, although we omit the minus sign. We have given some estimates of the long-run price elasticities of demand. The long run is associated with the time necessary for consumers to adjust fully to any given price change. (Note: "N.A." indicates that no estimate is available.)

Category	Estimated Elasticity	
	Short Run	Long Run
Air travel (business)	0.4	1.2
Air travel (vacation)	1.1	2.7
Beef	0.6	N.A.
Cheese	0.3	N.A.
Electricity	0.1	1.7
Fresh tomatoes	4.6	N.A.
Gasoline	0.2	0.5
Hospital services	0.1	0.7
Intercity bus service	0.6	2.2
Physician services	0.1	0.6
Private education	1.1	1.9
Restaurant meals	2.3	N.A.
Tires	0.9	1.2

HOW TO DEFINE THE SHORT RUN AND THE LONG RUN We've mentioned the short run and the long run. Is the short run one week, two weeks, one month, two months? Is the long run three years, four years, five years? There is no single answer. The long run is the period of time necessary for consumers to make a full adjustment to a given price change, all other things held constant. In the case of the demand for electricity, the long run will be however long it takes consumers to switch over to cheaper sources of heating, to buy houses and appliances that are more energy-efficient, and so on. The long-run price elasticity of demand for electricity therefore relates to a period of at least several years. The short run—by default—is any period less than the long run.

Cross Price Elasticity of Demand

In Chapter 3, we discussed the effect of a change in the price of one good on the demand for a related good. We defined substitutes and complements in terms of whether a reduction in the price of one caused a decrease or an increase, respectively, in the demand for the other. If the price of Blu-ray discs is held constant, the number of discs purchased (at any price) will certainly be influenced by the price of a close substitute such as Internet digital movie downloads. If the price of digital apps is held constant, the amount of apps demanded (at any price) will certainly be affected by changes in the price of digital devices. (These goods are complements.)

Measuring the Cross Price Elasticity of Demand

What we now need to do is come up with a numerical measure of the responsiveness of the amount of an item demanded to the prices of related goods. This is called the **cross price elasticity of demand (E_{xy})**, which is defined as the percentage change in the amount of a particular item demanded at the item's current price (a shift in the demand curve) divided by the percentage change in the price of the related good. In equation form, the cross price elasticity of demand between good X and good Y is

$$E_{xy} = \frac{\text{percentage change in the amount of good X demanded}}{\text{percentage change in price of good Y}}$$

Alternatively, the cross price elasticity of demand between good Y and good X would use the percentage change in the amount of good Y demanded as the numerator and the percentage change in the price of good X as the denominator.

Cross price elasticity of demand (E_{xy})
The percentage change in the amount of an item demanded (holding its price constant) divided by the percentage change in the price of a related good.

Substitutes and Complements

When two goods are substitutes, the cross price elasticity of demand will be positive. For example, when the price of portable hard drives goes up, the amount of flash memory drives demanded at their current price will rise—the demand curve for flash drives will shift horizontally rightward—in response as consumers shift away from the now relatively more expensive portable hard drives to flash memory drives. A producer of flash memory drives could benefit from a numerical estimate of the cross price elasticity of demand between portable hard drives and flash memory drives. For example, if the price of portable hard drives goes up by 10 percent and the producer of flash memory drives knows that the cross price elasticity of demand is 1, the flash drive producer can estimate that the amount of flash memory drives demanded will also go up by 10 percent at any given price of flash memory drives. Plans for increasing production of flash memory drives can then be made.

When two related goods are complements, the cross price elasticity of demand will be negative (and we will *not* disregard the minus sign). For example, when the price of personal computers declines while all other determinants of demand are unchanged, the amount of computer printers demanded will rise. This is because as prices of computers decrease, the number of printers purchased at any given price of printers will naturally increase, because computers and printers are often used together. Any manufacturer of computer printers must take this into account in making production plans.

If goods are completely unrelated, their cross price elasticity of demand will, by definition, be zero.

Income Elasticity of Demand

In Chapter 3, we discussed the determinants of demand. One of those determinants was income. We can apply our understanding of elasticity to the relationship between changes in income and changes in the amount of a good demanded at that good's current price.

Measuring the Income Elasticity of Demand

We measure the responsiveness of the amount of an item demanded at that item's current price to a change in income by the **income elasticity of demand (E_i):**

$$E_i = \frac{\text{percentage change in amount of a good demanded}}{\text{percentage change in income}}$$

holding relative price constant.

Income elasticity of demand refers to a *horizontal shift* in the demand curve in response to changes in income, whereas price elasticity of demand refers to a *movement along* the curve in response to price changes. Thus, income elasticity of demand is calculated at a given price, and price elasticity of demand is calculated at a given income.

Income elasticity of demand (E_i)
The percentage change in the amount of a good demanded, holding its price constant, divided by the percentage change in income. The responsiveness of the amount of a good demanded to a change in income, holding the good's relative price constant.

TABLE 19-3

How Income Affects Quantity of Digital Apps Demanded

Period	Number of Digital Apps Demanded per Month	Income per Month
1	6	$4,000
2	8	6,000

Calculating the Income Elasticity of Demand

To get the same income elasticity of demand over the same range of values regardless of the direction of change (increase or decrease), we can use the same formula that we used in computing the price elasticity of demand. When doing so, we have

$$E_i = \frac{\text{change in quantity}}{\text{sum of quantities}/2} \div \frac{\text{change in income}}{\text{sum of incomes}/2}$$

YOU ARE THERE

To contemplate how to apply the concepts of income elasticity of demand and price elasticity of demand in a real-world market, take a look at **Implications of Housing Demand Elasticities in China** on page 429.

A simple example will demonstrate how income elasticity of demand can be computed. Table 19-3 above gives the relevant data. The product in question is digital apps. We assume that the price of digital apps remains constant relative to other prices. In period 1, six apps per month are purchased. Income per month is $4,000. In period 2, monthly income increases to $6,000, and the number of apps demanded per month increases to eight. We can apply the following calculation:

$$E_i = \frac{2/[(6 + 8)/2]}{\$2,000/[(\$4,000 + \$6,000)/2]} = \frac{2/7}{2/5} = 0.71$$

Hence, measured income elasticity of demand for digital apps for the individual represented in this example is 0.71.

What retailer sells a line of products that taken together constitute an inferior good (see page 55 in Chapter 3)?

EXAMPLE

Are Walmart's Products Inferior Goods?

Since the economic downturn of 2008–2009, Walmart's sales have outpaced those of other retailers. Retailing experts have suggested the reason is that consumers buy a larger amount of items at Walmart when their incomes decline. To evaluate this hypothesis, Emek Basker of the University of Missouri at Columbia has estimated the income elasticity of demand for products sold by Walmart. He estimated that this income elasticity of demand is equal to −0.7, which indicates that when consumers' incomes fall by 1 percent, purchases from Walmart increase by 0.7 percent. Thus, an inverse relationship exists between income and the amount of Walmart products demanded, indicating that Walmart's retail product line constitutes an inferior good.

FOR CRITICAL THINKING
Would you guess that the income elasticity of demand for high-quality jewelry is positive or negative? Based on your guess, is jewelry an inferior or normal good?

You have just been introduced to three types of elasticities. All three elasticities are important in influencing the consumption of most goods. Reasonably accurate estimates of these elasticities can go a long way toward making accurate forecasts of demand for goods or services.

Some determinants of price elasticity of demand are (1) the existence, number, and quality of _____, (2) the _____ of the total budget spent on the good in question, and (3) the length of time allowed for _____ to a change in prices.

_____ price elasticity of demand measures the responsiveness of the amount of one good demanded to another's price changes. For substitutes, the cross price elasticity of demand is _____. For complements, it is _____.

Income elasticity of demand tells you by what percentage the amount of a good _____ will change for a particular percentage change in _____.

Price Elasticity of Supply

The **price elasticity of supply (E_s)** is defined similarly to the price elasticity of demand. Supply elasticities are generally positive. The reason is that at higher prices, larger quantities will generally be forthcoming from suppliers. The definition of the price elasticity of supply is as follows:

$$E_s = \frac{\text{percentage change in quantity supplied}}{\text{percentage change in price}}$$

Price elasticity of supply (E_s)
The responsiveness of the quantity supplied of a commodity to a change in its price—the percentage change in quantity supplied divided by the percentage change in price.

Classifying Supply Elasticities

Just as with demand, there are different ranges of supply elasticities. They are similar in definition to the ranges of demand elasticities.

If a 1 percent increase in price elicits a greater than 1 percent increase in the quantity supplied, we say that at the particular price in question on the supply schedule, *supply is elastic*. The most extreme elastic supply is called **perfectly elastic supply**—the slightest reduction in price will cause quantity supplied to fall to zero.

If, conversely, a 1 percent increase in price elicits a less than 1 percent increase in the quantity supplied, we refer to that as an *inelastic supply*. The most extreme inelastic supply is called **perfectly inelastic supply**—no matter what the price, the quantity supplied remains the same.

If the percentage change in the quantity supplied is just equal to the percentage change in the price, we call this *unit-elastic supply*.

Figure 19-4 on the next page shows two supply schedules, S and S'. You can tell at a glance, even without reading the labels, which one is perfectly elastic and which one is perfectly inelastic. As you might expect, most supply schedules exhibit elasticities that are somewhere between zero and infinity.

Perfectly elastic supply
A supply characterized by a reduction in quantity supplied to zero when there is the slightest decrease in price.

Perfectly inelastic supply
A supply for which quantity supplied remains constant, no matter what happens to price.

Price Elasticity of Supply and Length of Time for Adjustment

We pointed out earlier that the longer the time period allowed for adjustment, the greater the price elasticity of demand. It turns out that the same proposition applies to supply. The longer the time for adjustment, the more elastic the supply curve. Consider why this is true:

1. The longer the time allowed for adjustment, the more resources can flow into (or out of) an industry through expansion (or contraction) of existing firms. As an example, suppose that there is a long-lasting, significant increase in the demand for gasoline. The result is a sustained rise in the market price of gasoline. Initially, gasoline refiners will be hampered in expanding their production with the operating refining equipment available to them. Over time, however, some refining companies might be able to recondition old equipment that had fallen into disuse. They can

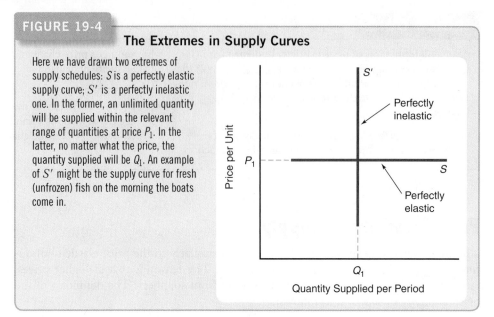

FIGURE 19-4

The Extremes in Supply Curves

Here we have drawn two extremes of supply schedules: S is a perfectly elastic supply curve; S' is a perfectly inelastic one. In the former, an unlimited quantity will be supplied within the relevant range of quantities at price P_1. In the latter, no matter what the price, the quantity supplied will be Q_1. An example of S' might be the supply curve for fresh (unfrozen) fish on the morning the boats come in.

also place orders for construction of new gasoline-refining equipment, and once the equipment arrives, they can also put it into place to expand their gasoline production. Given sufficient time, therefore, existing gasoline refiners can eventually respond to higher gasoline prices by adding new refining operations.

2. The longer the time allowed for adjustment, the entry (or exit) of firms increases (or decreases) production in an industry. Consider what happens if the price of gasoline remains higher than before as a result of a sustained rise in gasoline demand. Even as existing refiners add to their capability to produce gasoline by retooling old equipment, purchasing new equipment, and adding new refining facilities, additional businesses may seek to earn profits at the now-higher gasoline prices. Over time, the entry of new gasoline-refining companies adds to the productive capabilities of the entire refining industry, and the quantity of gasoline supplied increases.

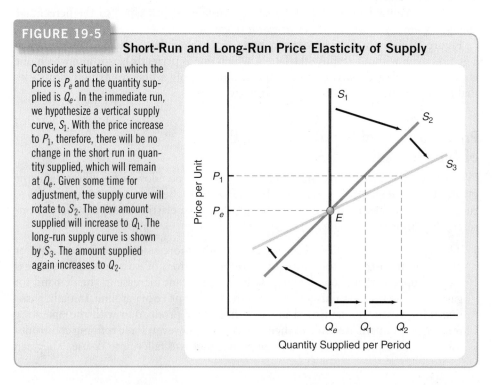

FIGURE 19-5

Short-Run and Long-Run Price Elasticity of Supply

Consider a situation in which the price is P_e and the quantity supplied is Q_e. In the immediate run, we hypothesize a vertical supply curve, S_1. With the price increase to P_1, therefore, there will be no change in the short run in quantity supplied, which will remain at Q_e. Given some time for adjustment, the supply curve will rotate to S_2. The new amount supplied will increase to Q_1. The long-run supply curve is shown by S_3. The amount supplied again increases to Q_2.

We therefore talk about short-run and long-run price elasticities of supply. The short run is defined as the time period during which full adjustment has not yet taken place. The long run is the time period during which firms have been able to adjust fully to the change in price.

A GRAPHIC PRESENTATION We can show a whole set of supply curves similar to the ones we generated for demand. As Figure 19-5 on the facing page shows, when nothing can be done in the immediate run, the supply curve is vertical, S_1. As more time is allowed for adjustment, the supply curve rotates to S_2 and then to S_3, becoming more elastic as it rotates.

QUICK QUIZ   See page 433 for the answers. Review concepts from this section in MyEconLab.

Price elasticity of supply is calculated by dividing the percentage change in the _____ _____ by the percentage change in _____.

Usually, price elasticities of supply are _____—higher prices yield _____ quantities supplied.

Long-run supply curves are _____ elastic than short-run supply curves because the _____ the time allowed, the more resources can flow into or out of an industry when price changes.

YOU ARE THERE
Implications of Housing Demand Elasticities in China

During the past few years, housing prices in China have been rising at a rate of about 10 percent per year. To assess how responsive China's housing demand and supply are to changes in housing prices, Gregory Chow of Princeton University and Linlin Niu of Xiamen University have estimated housing demand and supply elasticities. Chow and Niu estimate that the income elasticity of housing demand is about 0.7. Average Chinese household income has been increasing at an annual pace of close to 10 percent, which implies that, with other things (including housing prices) being equal, the amount of housing demanded rises by almost 7 percent per year. This steady increase in the demand for housing helps to explain the persistent rise in the price of housing.

Chow and Niu's estimate for the price elasticity of demand is about 0.3. Consequently, each 10 percent annual increase in the price of housing

in China results in only a 3 percent reduction in the quantity of housing demanded. Thus, Chow and Niu conclude that higher incomes in China have generated increases in the demand for housing that have pushed up the market price of housing substantially. This increase in the price of housing has then generated a less-than-proportionate decrease in desired housing purchases.

Critical Thinking Questions

1. Is housing a normal good in China? Explain. (See page 55 in Chapter 3.)
2. As the market price of housing has been rising each year, what has happened to the revenues received by suppliers of housing?

ISSUES & APPLICATIONS

Rock Stars Face High Price Elasticities of Demand

CONCEPTS APPLIED

▶ Total Revenues

▶ Elastic Demand

▶ Price Elasticity of Demand

From an economic standpoint, the past few years have been tough on rock musicians. Even though their music is selling at higher prices than in years past, the total revenues garnered from sales of the music have been on a downswing.

Price Increases for Digital Music Translate into Revenue Dips

Most rock musicians earn revenues from sales of recorded music and from concerts. When prices of digital albums increased by 5 percent during a recent 12-month period, revenues derived from sales of digital albums declined by 13 percent. This inverse relationship between the price change and total digital-music revenues suggests that the demand for recorded music is elastic.

During the same interval, prices of tickets to live performances by top rock acts increased by 3.9 percent, and concert revenues fell by 12 percent. This negative relationship between the price change and total concert revenues is consistent with an elastic demand for rock concerts. This fact is borne out by the 15 percent decrease in concert tickets sold in response to the 3.9 percent increase in concert ticket prices. The implied price elasticity of demand of 3.8 (15 percent/3.9 percent = 3.8) indicates that concertgoers are highly responsive to changes in ticket prices.

Performers, Managers, and Promoters Begin to Get the Message

The past few years have been so disappointing from the standpoint of generating revenues that many rock performers have cut back on the numbers of new song releases and scheduled concerts. Only recently, however, have some rock musicians, managers, and promoters realized that the demand for rock music is highly elastic.

A top concert promoter recently stated, "We know that if we lower prices enough, people will come [to concerts]." Left unstated by the promoter was that in light of the high price elasticities of demand that rock musicians confront, lower prices of recorded music and live performances should also generate higher revenues.

For Critical Thinking

1. If the position of the demand curve for digital rock music albums has remained unchanged, what can account for a continuing rise in the market clearing price? (See page 78 in Chapter 4.)

2. If your answer to Question 1 explains why album prices have been rising, what can you predict is likely to happen to revenues from albums in the near future?

Web Resources

1. For a discussion of the hard times—in terms of sales—faced by rock musicians since the early 2000s, go to www.econtoday.com/chap19.

2. To view a chart displaying a significant decline in sales of all forms of recorded music, including rock music, go to www.econtoday.com/chap19.

MyEconLab

For more questions on this chapter's Issues & Applications, go to MyEconLab. In the Study Plan for this chapter, select Section N: News.

MyEconLab

Here is what you should know after reading this chapter. MyEconLab will help you identify what you know, and where to go when you need to practice.

— WHAT YOU SHOULD KNOW —

Expressing and Calculating the Price Elasticity of Demand The price elasticity of demand is the percentage change in quantity demanded divided by the percentage change in price. To calculate the price elasticity of demand for relatively small changes in price, the percentage change in quantity demanded is equal to the change in the quantity resulting from a price change divided by the average of the initial and final quantities, and the percentage change in price is equal to the price change divided by the average of the initial and final prices.

price elasticity of demand (E_p), 415

— WHERE TO GO TO PRACTICE —

• MyEconLab Study Plan 19.1

WHAT YOU SHOULD KNOW   WHERE TO GO TO PRACTICE

The Relationship between the Price Elasticity of Demand and Total Revenues Demand is elastic when the price elasticity of demand exceeds 1, and over the elastic range of a demand curve, an increase in price reduces total revenues. Demand is inelastic when the price elasticity of demand is less than 1, and over this range of a demand curve, an increase in price raises total revenues. Finally, demand is unit-elastic when the price elasticity of demand equals 1, and over this range of a demand curve, an increase in price does not affect total revenues.

elastic demand, 417
unit elasticity of demand, 417
inelastic demand, 417
perfectly inelastic demand, 417
perfectly elastic demand, 417

Key Figures
Figure 19-1, 418
Figure 19-2, 419

• MyEconLab Study Plans 19.2, 19.3
• Animated Figures 19-1, 19-2

Factors That Determine the Price Elasticity of Demand If there are more close substitutes, the price elasticity of demand increases. The price elasticity of demand also tends to be higher when a larger portion of a person's budget is spent on the good. In addition, if people have a longer period of time to adjust to a price change, the price elasticity of demand tends to be higher.

Key Figure
Figure 19-3, 423

• MyEconLab Study Plan 19.4
• Animated Figure 19-3

The Cross Price Elasticity of Demand and Using It to Determine Whether Two Goods Are Substitutes or Complements The cross price elasticity of demand for a good is the percentage change in the amount of that good demanded divided by the percentage change in the price of a related good. If two goods are substitutes, the cross price elasticity of demand is positive. In contrast, if two goods are complements, the cross price elasticity of demand is negative.

cross price elasticity of demand (E_{xy}), 425

• MyEconLab Study Plan 19.5

The Income Elasticity of Demand The income elasticity of demand is equal to the percentage change in the amount of a good demanded divided by the percentage change in income, holding the good's relative price unchanged.

income elasticity of demand (E_i), 425

• MyEconLab Study Plan 19.6

Classifying Supply Elasticities and How the Length of Time for Adjustment Affects the Price Elasticity of Supply The price elasticity of supply equals the percentage change in quantity supplied divided by the percentage change in price. If the price elasticity of supply exceeds 1, supply is elastic, and if the price elasticity of supply is less than 1, supply is inelastic. Supply is unit-elastic if the price elasticity of supply equals 1. Supply is more likely to be elastic when sellers have more time to adjust to price changes.

price elasticity of supply (E_s), 427
perfectly elastic supply, 427
perfectly inelastic supply, 427

Key Figure
Figure 19-5, 428

• MyEconLab Study Plan 19.7
• Animated Figure 19-5

Log in to MyEconLab, take a chapter test, and get a personalized Study Plan that tells you which concepts you understand and which ones you need to review. From there, MyEconLab will give you further practice, tutorials, animations, videos, and guided solutions. For more information, visit www.myeconlab.com

PROBLEMS

All problems are assignable in MyEconLab. *Answers to odd–numbered problems appear at the back of the book.*

19-1. When the price of shirts emblazoned with a college logo is $20, consumers buy 150 per week. When the price declines to $19, consumers purchase 200 per week. Based on this information, calculate the price elasticity of demand for logo-emblazoned shirts. (See page 416.)

19-2. Table 19-2 on page 424 indicates that the short-run price elasticity of demand for tires is 0.9. If an increase in the price of petroleum (used in producing tires) causes the market prices of tires to rise from $50 to $60, by what percentage would you expect the quantity of tires demanded to change? (See page 416.)

19-3. The diagram below depicts the demand curve for "miniburgers" in a nationwide fast-food market. Use the information in this diagram to answer the questions that follow. (See pages 416–418.)

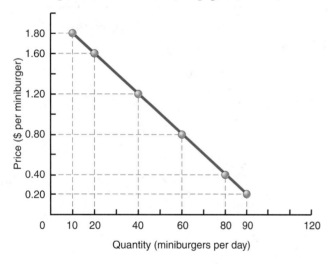

a. What is the price elasticity of demand along the range of the demand curve between a price of $0.20 per miniburger and a price of $0.40 per miniburger? Is demand elastic or inelastic over this range?

b. What is the price elasticity of demand along the range of the demand curve between a price of $0.80 per miniburger and a price of $1.20 per miniburger? Is demand elastic or inelastic over this range?

c. What is the price elasticity of demand along the range of the demand curve between a price of $1.60 per miniburger and a price of $1.80 per miniburger? Is demand elastic or inelastic over this range?

19-4. In a local market, the monthly price of Internet access service decreases from $20 to $10, and the total quantity of monthly accounts across all Internet access providers increases from 100,000 to 200,000. What is the price elasticity of demand? Is demand elastic, unit-elastic, or inelastic? (See page 417.)

19-5. At a price of $57.50 to play 18 holes on local golf courses, 1,200 consumers pay to play a game of golf each day. A rise in the price to $62.50 causes the number of consumers to decline to 800. What is the price elasticity of demand? Is demand elastic, unit-elastic, or inelastic? (See page 417.)

19-6. It is very difficult to find goods with perfectly elastic or perfectly inelastic demand. We can, however, find goods that lie near these extremes. Characterize demands for the following goods as being near perfectly elastic or near perfectly inelastic. (See pages 417–418.)

    a. Corn grown and harvested by a small farmer in Iowa

    b. Heroin for a drug addict

    c. Water for a desert hiker

    d. One of several optional textbooks in a pass-fail course

19-7. In the market for hand-made guitars, when the price of guitars is $800, annual revenues are $640,000. When the price falls to $700, annual revenues decline to $630,000. Over this range of guitar prices, is the demand for hand-made guitars elastic, unit-elastic, or inelastic? (See page 419.)

19-8. Suppose that over a range of prices, the price elasticity of demand varies from 15.0 to 2.5. Over another range of prices, the price elasticity of demand varies from 1.5 to 0.75. What can you say about total revenues and the total revenue curve over these two ranges of the demand curve as price falls? (See page 419.)

19-9. Based solely on the information provided below, characterize the demands for the following goods as being more elastic or more inelastic. (See page 422.)

    a. A 45-cent box of salt that you buy once a year

    b. A type of high-powered ski boat that you can rent from any one of a number of rental agencies

    c. A specific brand of bottled water

    d. Automobile insurance in a state that requires autos to be insured but has only a few insurance companies

    e. A 75-cent guitar pick for the lead guitarist of a major rock band

19-10. The value of cross price elasticity of demand between goods X and Y is 1.25, while the cross price elasticity of demand between goods X and Z is −2.0. Characterize X and Y and X and Z as substitutes or complements. (See page 425.)

19-11. Suppose that the cross price elasticity of demand between eggs and bacon is -0.5. What would you expect to happen to purchases of bacon if the price of eggs rises by 10 percent? (See page 425.)

19-12. A 5 percent increase in the price of digital apps reduces the amount of tablet devices demanded by 3 percent. What is the cross price elasticity of demand? Are tablet devices and digital apps complements or substitutes? (See page 425.)

19-13. An individual's income rises from $80,000 per year to $84,000 per year, and as a consequence the person's purchases of movie downloads rise from four per month to six per month. What is this individual's income elasticity of demand? Are movie downloads a normal or inferior good? (See page 426. Hint: You may want to refer to the discussion of normal and inferior goods on page 55 in Chapter 3.)

19-14. Assume that the income elasticity of demand for hot dogs is −1.25 and that the income elasticity of demand for lobster is 1.25. Based on the fact that the measure for hot dogs is negative while that for lobster is positive, are these normal or inferior goods? (See page 426.)

19-15. At a price of $25,000, producers of midsized automobiles are willing to manufacture and sell 75,000 cars per month. At a price of $35,000, they are willing to produce and sell 125,000 a month. Using the same type of calculation method used to compute the price elasticity of demand, what is the price elasticity of supply? Is supply elastic, unit-elastic, or inelastic? (See page 427.)

19-16. An increase in the market price of men's haircuts, from $15 per haircut to $25 per haircut, initially causes a local barbershop to have its employees work overtime to increase the number of daily haircuts provided from 35 to 45. When the $25 market price remains unchanged for several weeks and all other things remain equal as well, the barbershop hires additional employees and provides 65 haircuts per day. What is the short-run price elasticity of supply? What is the long-run price elasticity of supply? (See pages 427–428.)

ECONOMICS ON THE NET

Price Elasticity and Consumption of Illegal Drugs Making the use of certain drugs illegal drives up their market prices, so the price elasticity of demand is a key factor affecting the use of illegal drugs. This application applies concepts from this chapter to analyze how price elasticity of demand affects drug consumption.

Title: The Demand for Illicit Drugs

Navigation: Go to **www.econtoday.com/chap19**, and follow the link to the summary of this paper published by the National Bureau of Economic Research.

Application Read the summary of the results of this study of price elasticities of participation in use of illegal drugs, and answer the following questions.

1. Based on the results of the study, is the demand for cocaine more or less price elastic than the demand for heroin? For which drug, therefore, will quantity demanded fall by a greater percentage in response to a proportionate increase in price?

2. The study finds that decriminalizing currently illegal drugs would bring about sizable increases both in overall consumption of heroin and cocaine and in the price elasticity of demand for both drugs. Why do you suppose that the price elasticity of demand would rise? (Hint: At present, users of cocaine and heroin are restricted to only a few illegal sources of the drugs, but if the drugs could legally be produced and sold, there would be many more suppliers providing a variety of different types of both drugs.)

For Group Study and Analysis Discuss ways that government officials might use information about the price elasticities of demand for illicit drugs to assist in developing policies intended to reduce the use of these drugs. Which of these proposed policies might prove most effective? Why?

ANSWERS TO QUICK QUIZZES

p. 418: (i) quantity demanded . . . price; (ii) percentage . . . independent; (iii) negative . . . decrease . . . increase; (iv) zero . . . inelastic . . . elastic . . . infinite

p. 421: (i) revenues; (ii) opposite; (iii) zero; (iv) same

p. 427: (i) substitutes . . . share . . . adjustment; (ii) Cross . . . positive . . . negative; (iii) demanded . . . income

p. 429: (i) quantity supplied . . . price; (ii) positive . . . greater; (iii) more . . . longer

20 Consumer Choice

For years, a number of U.S. households have allocated significant portions of expenditures out of their money incomes to purchases of unhealthful items, such as alcohol, high-fat meals at restaurants, and tobacco products. Many households also have consumed relatively small amounts of more healthful items, such as vegetables. Recently, spending on alcoholic beverages, restaurant meals, and tobacco products has decreased considerably, and expenditures on vegetables have increased. Some public officials attribute this shift to governmental efforts to provide consumers with product information, but economists suggest that other determinants of consumers' choices likely have proved more important. Before you can understand why households' spending allocations among healthful and unhealthful products have changed, you must first learn how people make choices intended to maximize their levels of satisfaction. That is the main topic of this chapter.

a consumer who shops at a typical U.S. supermarket chooses among 48,750 different items, more than five times as many as in 1975? The largest among these supermarkets commonly stock more than 80 brands of shampoo, about 90 varieties of toothpaste, and at least 100 types of household cleaning products. Of course, the vast array of goods and services among which individuals make consumption decisions from week to week and from month to month extends far beyond supermarket aisles.

In Chapter 3, you learned that a determinant of the quantity demanded of any particular item is the price of that item. The law of demand implies that at a lower overall price, there will be a higher quantity demanded. Understanding the derivation of the law of demand is useful because it allows us to examine the relevant variables, such as price, income, and tastes, in such a way as to make better sense of the world and even perhaps generate predictions about it. One way of deriving the law of demand involves an analysis of the logic of consumer choice in a world of limited resources. In this chapter, therefore, we discuss what is called *utility analysis*.

Utility Theory

When you buy something, you do so because of the satisfaction you expect to receive from having and using that good. For everything that you like to have, the more you have of it, the higher the level of total satisfaction you receive. Another term that can be used for satisfaction is **utility,** or want-satisfying power. This property is common to all goods that are desired. The concept of utility is purely subjective, however. There is no way that you or I can measure the amount of utility that a consumer might be able to obtain from a particular good, for utility does not imply "useful" or "utilitarian" or "practical." Thus, there can be no accurate scientific assessment of the utility that someone might receive by consuming a fast-food dinner or a movie relative to the utility that another person might receive from that same good or service.

Utility
The want-satisfying power of a good or service.

The utility that individuals receive from consuming a good depends on their tastes and preferences. These tastes and preferences are normally assumed to be given and stable for a particular individual. An individual's tastes determine how much utility that individual derives from consuming a good, and this in turn determines how that individual allocates his or her income to purchases of that good. But we cannot explain why tastes are different between individuals. For example, we cannot explain why some people like yogurt but others do not.

We can analyze in terms of utility the way consumers decide what to buy, just as physicists have analyzed some of their problems in terms of what they call force. No physicist has ever seen a unit of force, and no economist has ever seen a unit of utility. In both cases, however, these concepts have proved useful for analysis.

Throughout this chapter, we will be discussing **utility analysis,** which is the analysis of consumer decision making based on utility maximization—that is, making choices with the aim of attaining the highest feasible satisfaction.

Utility analysis
The analysis of consumer decision making based on utility maximization.

Utility and Utils

Economists once believed that utility could be measured. In fact, there is a philosophical school of thought based on utility theory called *utilitarianism*, developed by the English philosopher Jeremy Bentham (1748–1832). Bentham held that society should seek the greatest happiness for the greatest number. He sought to apply an arithmetic formula for measuring happiness. He and his followers developed the notion of measurable utility and invented the **util** to measure it. For the moment, we will also assume that we can measure satisfaction using this representative unit. Our assumption will allow us to quantify the way we examine consumer behavior.

Util
A representative unit by which utility is measured.

Thus, the first chocolate bar that you eat might yield you 4 utils of satisfaction. The first peanut cluster, might yield 6 utils, and so on. Today, no one really believes that we can actually measure utils, but the ideas forthcoming from such analysis will prove useful in understanding how consumers choose among alternatives.

Total and Marginal Utility

Consider the satisfaction, or utility, that you receive each time that you download and utilize digital apps. To make the example straightforward, let's say that there are thousands of apps to choose from each year and that each of them is of the same quality. Let's say that you normally download and utilize one app per week. You could, of course, download two, or three, or four per week. Presumably, each time you download and utilize another app per week, you will get additional satisfaction, or utility. The question that we must ask, though, is, given that you are already downloading and using one app per week, will the next one downloaded and utilized during that week give you the same amount of additional utility?

That additional, or incremental, utility is called **marginal utility,** where *marginal* means "incremental" or "additional." (Marginal changes also refer to decreases, in which cases we talk about *decremental* changes.) The concept of marginality is important in economics because we can think of people comparing additional (marginal) benefits with additional (marginal) costs.

Marginal utility
The change in total utility due to a one-unit change in the quantity of a good or service consumed.

Applying Marginal Analysis to Utility

The example in Figure 20-1 on the facing page will clarify the distinction between total utility and marginal utility. The table in panel (a) shows the total utility and the marginal utility of downloading and using digital apps each week. Marginal utility is the difference between total utility derived from one level of consumption and total utility derived from another level of consumption within a given time interval. A simple formula for marginal utility is this:

$$\text{Marginal utility} = \frac{\text{change in total utility}}{\text{change in number of units consumed}}$$

In our example, when a person has already downloaded and utilized two digital apps in one week and then downloads and uses another, total utility increases from 16 utils to 19 utils. Therefore, the marginal utility (of downloading and utilizing one more app after already having downloaded and used two in one week) is equal to 3 utils.

Graphical Analysis

We can transfer the information in panel (a) onto a graph, as we do in panels (b) and (c) of Figure 20-1 on the next page. Total utility, which is represented in column 2 of panel (a), is transferred to panel (b).

Total utility continues to rise until four digital apps are downloaded and utilized per week. This measure of utility remains at 20 utils through the fifth app, and at the sixth app per week it falls to 18 utils. We assume that at some quantity consumed per unit time period, boredom with consuming more digital apps begins to set in. Thus, at some quantity consumed, the additional utility from consuming an additional app begins to fall, so total utility first rises and then declines in panel (b).

Marginal Utility

If you look carefully at panels (b) and (c) of Figure 20-1, the notion of marginal utility becomes clear. In economics, the term *marginal* always refers to a *change* in the total. The marginal utility of consuming three downloaded digital apps per week instead of two apps per week is the increment in total utility and is equal to 3 utils per week. All of the points in panel (c) are taken from column 3 of the table in panel (a). Notice that marginal utility falls throughout the graph. A special point occurs after four apps are downloaded and used per week because the total utility curve in panel (b) is unchanged after the consumption of the fourth app. That means that the consumer receives no additional (marginal) utility from downloading and using five apps rather than four.

FIGURE 20-1

Total and Marginal Utility of Downloading and Utilizing Digital Apps

If we were able to assign specific values to the utility derived from downloading and utilizing digital apps each week, we could obtain a marginal utility schedule similar in pattern to the one shown in panel (a). In column 1 is the number of apps downloaded and used per week. Column 2 is the total utility derived from each quantity. Column 3 shows the marginal utility derived from each additional quantity, which is defined as the change in total utility due to a change of one unit of using downloaded apps per week. Total utility from panel (a) is plotted in panel (b). Marginal utility is plotted in panel (c), where you see that it reaches zero where total utility hits its maximum at between 4 and 5 units.

Panel (a)

(1) Number of Digital Apps Downloaded and Utilized per Week	(2) Total Utility (utils per week)	(3) Marginal Utility (utils per week)
0	0	
		10 (10 − 0)
1	10	
		6 (16 − 10)
2	16	
		3 (19 − 16)
3	19	
		1 (20 − 19)
4	20	
		0 (20 − 20)
5	20	
		−2 (18 − 20)
6	18	

Panel (b)

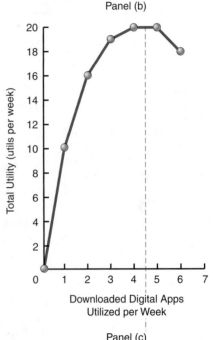

Panel (c)

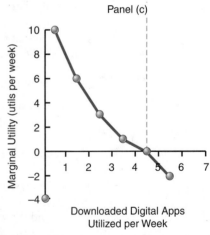

This is shown in panel (c) as *zero* marginal utility. After that point, marginal utility becomes negative.

In our example, when marginal utility becomes negative, it means that the consumer is tired of consuming digital apps and would require some form of compensation to consume any more. When marginal utility is negative, an additional unit consumed actually lowers total utility by becoming a nuisance. Rarely does a consumer face a situation of negative marginal utility. Whenever this point is reached, goods in effect become "bads." Consuming more units actually causes total utility to *fall* so that marginal utility is negative. A rational consumer will stop consuming at the point at which marginal utility becomes negative, even if the good is available at a price of zero.

QUICK QUIZ   See page 451 for the answers. Review concepts from this section in MyEconLab.

_____ is defined as want-satisfying power. It is a characteristic common to all desired goods and services.

We arbitrarily measure **utility** in units called _____.

It is important to distinguish between **total utility** and **marginal utility**. _____ utility is the total satisfaction

derived from the consumption of a given quantity of a good or service. _____ utility is the *change* in total utility due to a one-unit change in the consumption of the good or service.

Diminishing Marginal Utility

Diminishing marginal utility
The principle that as more of any good or service is consumed, its *extra* benefit declines. Otherwise stated, increases in total utility from the consumption of a good or service become smaller and smaller as more is consumed during a given time period.

Notice that in panel (c) of Figure 20-1 on the previous page, marginal utility is continuously declining. This property has been named the principle of **diminishing marginal utility**. There is no way that we can prove diminishing marginal utility. Nevertheless, diminishing marginal utility has even been called a law. This supposed law concerns a psychological, or subjective, utility that you receive as you consume more and more of a particular good.

The Law of Diminishing Marginal Utility

Stated formally, the law of diminishing marginal utility is as follows:

As an individual consumes more of a particular commodity, the total level of utility, or satisfaction, derived from that consumption usually increases. Eventually, however, the rate at which it increases diminishes as more is consumed.

Take a hungry individual at a dinner table. The first serving is greatly appreciated, and the individual derives a substantial amount of utility from it. Consumption of the second serving does not have quite as much pleasurable impact as the first one, and consumption of the third serving is likely to be even less satisfying. This individual experiences diminishing marginal utility of food until he or she stops eating, and this is true for most people. All-you-can-eat restaurants count on this fact. A second helping of ribs may provide some marginal utility, but the third helping would have only a little or even negative marginal utility.

Marginal Utility Cannot Persistently Increase

Consider for a moment the opposite possibility—increasing marginal utility. Under such a situation, the marginal utility after consuming, say, one hamburger would increase. Consuming the second hamburger would yield more utility to you, and consuming the third would yield even more.

Thus, if increasing marginal utility existed, each of us would consume only one good or service! Rather than observing that "variety is the spice of life," we would see that monotony in consumption was preferred. We do not observe such single-item consumption, and therefore we have great confidence in the concept of diminishing marginal utility.

Can diminishing marginal utility explain why newspaper vending machines rarely prevent people from taking more than the one current issue they have paid to purchase?

EXAMPLE

Newspaper Vending Machines versus Candy Vending Machines

Have you ever noticed that newspaper vending machines nearly everywhere in the United States allow you to put in the correct change, lift up the door, and—if you were willing to violate the law—take as many newspapers as you want? Contrast this type of vending machine with candy machines. They are securely locked at all times. You must designate the candy that you wish, normally by using some type of keypad. The candy then drops down so that you can retrieve it, but you cannot grab any other candy.

The difference between these two types of vending machines is explained by diminishing marginal utility. Newspaper companies dispense newspapers from coin-operated boxes that allow dishonest people to take more copies than they pay for. What would a dishonest person do with more than one copy of a newspaper, however? The marginal utility of reading a second newspaper is normally zero. The benefit of storing excessive newspapers is usually nil because yesterday's news has no value. But the same analysis does not hold for candy. The marginal utility of consuming a second candy bar is certainly less than the marginal utility of consuming the first, but it is normally not zero. Moreover, one can store candy for relatively long periods of time at relatively low cost. Consequently, food vending machine companies have to worry about dishonest users of their equipment and must make that equipment more theft-proof than newspaper vending machines.

FOR CRITICAL THINKING

Can you think of a circumstance under which a substantial number of newspaper purchasers might be inclined to take more than one newspaper out of a vending machine?

Optimizing Consumption Choices

Every consumer has a limited income, so choices must be made. When a consumer has made all of his or her choices about what to buy and in what quantities, and when the total level of satisfaction, or utility, from that set of choices is as great as it can be, we say that the consumer has *optimized*. When the consumer has attained an optimum consumption set of goods and services, we say that he or she has reached **consumer optimum.**

Consumer optimum
A choice of a set of goods and services that maximizes the level of satisfaction for each consumer, subject to limited income.

A Two-Good Example

Consider a simple two-good example. During a given period, the consumer has to choose between spending income on downloads of digital apps at $5 per app and on purchasing cappuccinos at $3 each. Let's say that when the consumer has spent all income on digital apps and cappuccinos, the last dollar spent on a cappuccino yields 3 utils of utility but the last dollar spent on apps yields 10 utils. Wouldn't this consumer increase total utility if some dollars were taken away from consumption of cappuccinos and allocated to apps? The answer is yes. More dollars spent downloading apps will reduce marginal utility per last dollar spent, whereas fewer dollars spent on consumption of cappuccinos will increase marginal utility per last dollar spent. The loss in utility from spending fewer dollars purchasing fewer cappuccinos is more than made up by spending additional dollars on more digital apps. As a consequence, total utility increases.

The consumer optimum—where total utility is maximized—occurs when the satisfaction per last dollar spent on both cappuccinos and digital apps per week is equal for the two goods. Thus, the amount of goods consumed depends on the prices of the goods, the income of the consumer, and the marginal utility derived from the amounts of each good consumed.

Table 20-1 below presents information on utility derived from consuming various quantities of digital apps and cappuccinos. Columns 4 and 8 show the marginal utility per dollar spent on apps and cappuccinos, respectively. If the prices of both goods are

TABLE 20-1

Total and Marginal Utility from Consuming Digital Apps and Cappuccinos on an Income of $26

(1) Digital Apps per Period	(2) Total Utility of Digital Apps per Period (utils)	(3) Marginal Utility (utils) MU_d	(4) Marginal Utility Per Dollars Spent (MU_d/P_d) (price = $5)	(5) Cappuccinos per Period	(6) Total Utility of Cappuccinos per Period (utils)	(7) Marginal Utility (utils) MU_c	(8) Marginal Utility per Dollar Spent (MU_c/P_c) (price = $3)
0	0	–	–	0	0	–	–
1	50.0	50.0	10.0	1	25	25	8.3
2	95.0	45.0	9.0	2	47	22	7.3
3	135.0	40.0	8.0	3	65	18	6.0
4	171.5	36.5	7.3	4	80	15	5.0
5	200.0	28.5	5.7	5	89	9	3.0

zero, individuals will consume each as long as their respective marginal utility is positive (at least five units of each and probably much more). It is also true that a consumer with unlimited income will continue consuming goods until the marginal utility of each is equal to zero. When the price is zero or the consumer's income is unlimited, there is no effective constraint on consumption.

Why do some people pay a price as high as $665 for a pair of blue jeans?

EXAMPLE

High-Priced Blue Jeans as Part of a Consumer Optimum

Only about 1 percent of the nearly $14 billion in annual U.S. expenditures on blue jeans goes toward pairs of jeans priced above $50. Among jeans with prices exceeding $200 per pair are J Brand's Maria jeans, Seven for All Mankind's Men's Aidan jeans, and True Religion's Phantom jeans. Certain styles of Gucci jeans have prices as high as $665 per pair.

The theory of the consumer optimum explains why some people are willing to pay such high prices for jeans. For these individuals, it must be the case that the last dollar spent on the pair of, say, Gucci jeans generates the same amount of marginal utility as a dollar spent on any other item. Because these consumers allocate so many dollars of their money income to a pair of Gucci jeans, the marginal utility they derive from buying and wearing the jeans must be substantial. Thus, consuming Gucci jeans must add considerably to these individuals' levels of satisfaction.

FOR CRITICAL THINKING
What condition must be satisfied for the last dollar of money income that a consumer of Gucci jeans spends on chewing gum?

A Two-Good Consumer Optimum

Consumer optimum is attained when the marginal utility of the last dollar spent on each good yields the same utility and income is completely exhausted. In the situation in Table 20-1 on the previous page, the individual's income is $26. From columns 4 and 8 of Table 20-1, equal marginal utilities per dollar spent occur at the consumption level of four digital apps and two cappuccinos (the marginal utility per dollar spent equals 7.3). Notice that the marginal utility per dollar spent for both goods is also (approximately) equal at the consumption level of three apps and one cappuccino, but here total income is not completely exhausted. Likewise, the marginal utility per dollar spent is (approximately) equal at five apps and three cappuccinos, but the expenditures necessary for that level of consumption ($34) exceed the individual's income.

Table 20-2 on the facing page shows the steps taken to arrive at consumer optimum. Using the first digital app would yield a marginal utility per dollar of 10 (50 units of utility divided by $5 per digital app), while consuming the first cappuccino would yield a marginal utility of only 8.3 per dollar (25 units of utility divided by $3 per cappuccino). Because it yields the higher marginal utility per dollar, the app is purchased. This leaves $21 of income. Consuming the second digital app yields a higher marginal utility per dollar (9, versus 8.3 for a cappuccino), so this app is also purchased, leaving an unspent income of $16. Purchasing and consuming the first cappuccino now yield a higher marginal utility per dollar than the next digital app (8.3 versus 8), so the first cappuccino is purchased. This leaves income of $13 to spend. The process continues until all income is exhausted and the marginal utility per dollar spent is equal for both goods.

To restate, consumer optimum requires the following:

> *A consumer's money income should be allocated so that the last dollar spent on each good purchased yields the same amount of marginal utility (when all income is spent), because this rule yields the largest possible total utility.*

A Little Math

We can state the rule of consumer optimum in algebraic terms by examining the ratio of marginal utilities and prices of individual products. The rule simply states that a consumer maximizes personal satisfaction when allocating money income in such a

YOU ARE THERE

To contemplate a real-world example of an individual reaching a consumer optimum, take a look at **Using a Smartphone to Attain a Consumer Optimum** on page 446.

TABLE 20-2

Steps to Consumer Optimum

In each purchase situation described here, the consumer always purchases the good with the higher marginal utility per dollar spent (*MU/P*). For example, at the time of the third purchase, the marginal utility per last dollar spent on digital apps is 8, but it is 8.3 for cappuccinos, and $16 of income remains, so the next purchase will be a cappuccino. Here the price of digital apps is $P_d = \$5$, the price of cappuccinos is $P_c = \$3$, MU_d is the marginal utility of consumption of digital apps, and MU_c is the marginal utility of consumption of cappuccinos.

	Choices					
	Digital Apps		Cappuccinos			
Purchase	Unit	MU_d/P_d	Unit	MU_c/P_c	Buying Decision	Remaining Income
1	First	10.0	First	8.3	First digital app	$26 − \$5 = \$21$
2	Second	9.0	First	8.3	Second digital app	$21 − \$5 = \$16$
3	Third	8.0	First	8.3	First cappuccino	$16 − \$3 = \$13$
4	Third	8.0	Second	7.3	Third digital app	$13 − \$5 = \$8$
5	Fourth	7.3	Second	7.3	Fourth digital app and second cappuccino	$8 − \$5 = \$3$ / $\$3 − \$3 = \$0$

way that the last dollars spent on good A, good B, good C, and so on, yield equal amounts of marginal utility. Marginal utility (*MU*) from good A is indicated by "*MU* of good A." For good B, it is "*MU* of good B." Our algebraic formulation of this rule, therefore, becomes

$$\frac{MU \text{ of good A}}{\text{Price of good A}} = \frac{MU \text{ of good B}}{\text{price of good B}} = \cdots = \frac{MU \text{ of good Z}}{\text{price of good Z}}$$

The letters A, B, . . . , Z indicate the various goods and services that the consumer might purchase.

We know, then, that in order for the consumer to maximize utility, the marginal utility of good A divided by the price of good A must equal the marginal utility of any other good divided by its price. Note, though, that the application of the rule of equal marginal utility per dollar spent does not necessarily describe an explicit or conscious act on the part of consumers. Rather, this is a *model* of consumer optimum.

What does a consumer's willingness to pay a relatively high price for an item indicate about the marginal utility that the consumer derives from the good or service?

INTERNATIONAL EXAMPLE

Inferring Substantial Marginal Utility from an Oil Change

Recently, a resident of Qatar decided to purchase an oil change for the Lamborghini Murciélago LP640 sports car that he had bought at an earlier date at a price of $376,000. He decided to have the lubrication work done in London, which required airlifting the auto to London's Heathrow Airport. Inclusive of transportation costs, the price of obtaining the vehicle's oil change exceeded $45,000.

According to the rule for a consumer optimum, this Qatar resident viewed the marginal utility per dollar spent on the oil change as equal to the marginal utility per dollar spent on other goods and services. This amount would have been his marginal utility from the oil change divided by more than $45,000, which suggests that he derived substantial marginal utility from the work that London mechanics performed on his sports car.

FOR CRITICAL THINKING

What must have been true about the Qatar consumer's marginal utility per dollar spent on fuel for his vehicle compared with the marginal utility per dollar spent on the London oil change?

The principle of **diminishing marginal utility** tells us that each successive marginal unit of a good consumed adds _____ extra utility.

The consumer maximizes total utility by _____ the marginal utility of the last dollar spent on one good with the marginal utility per last dollar spent on all other goods. That is the state of consumer _____.

When a consumer optimum has been reached, _____ additional income is available to spend, and total utility is _____.

How a Price Change Affects Consumer Optimum

Consumption decisions are summarized in the law of demand, which states that the amount purchased is inversely related to price. We can now see why by using utility analysis.

A Consumer's Response to a Price Change

When a consumer has optimally allocated all her income to purchases, the marginal utility per dollar spent at current prices of goods and services is the same for each good or service she buys. No consumer will, when optimizing, buy 10 units of a good per unit of time when the marginal utility per dollar spent on the tenth unit of that good is less than the marginal utility per dollar spent on a unit of some other item.

A PRICE CHANGE AND THE CONSUMER OPTIMUM If we start out at a consumer optimum and then observe a good's price decrease, we can predict that consumers will respond to the price decrease by consuming more of that good. This is because before the price change, the marginal utility per dollar spent on each good or service consumed was the same. Now, when a specific good's price is lower, it is possible to consume more of that good while continuing to equalize the marginal utility per dollar spent on that good with the marginal utility per dollar spent on other goods and services.

The purchase and consumption of additional units of the lower-priced good will cause the marginal utility from consuming the good to fall. Eventually, it will fall to the point at which the marginal utility per dollar spent on the good is once again equal to the marginal utility per dollar spent on other goods and services. At this point, the consumer will stop buying additional units of the lower-priced good.

A hypothetical demand curve for digital apps for a typical consumer during a specific time interval is presented in Figure 20-2 on the facing page. Suppose that at point A, at which the price per digital app is $5, the marginal utility of the last app consumed during the period is MU_A. At point B, at which the price is $4 per app, the marginal utility is represented by MU_B. With the consumption of more digital apps, the marginal utility of the last unit of these additional digital apps is lower—MU_B must be less than MU_A. What has happened is that at a lower price, the number of digital app downloads per week increased from four to five. Marginal utility must have fallen. At a higher consumption rate, the marginal utility falls in response to the rise in digital app consumption so that the marginal utility per dollar spent is equalized across all purchases.

The Substitution Effect

Substitution effect
The tendency of people to substitute cheaper commodities for more expensive commodities.

What is happening as the price of digital app downloads falls is that consumers are substituting the now relatively cheaper digital apps for other goods and services, such as restaurant meals and live concerts. We call this the **substitution effect** of a change in the price of a good because it occurs when consumers substitute relatively cheaper goods for relatively more expensive ones.

Digital App Prices and Marginal Utility

When consumers respond to a reduction in the price of digital app from $5 per app to $4 per app by increasing consumption, marginal utility falls. The movement is from point A, at which marginal utility is MU_A, to point B, at which marginal utility is MU_B, which is less than MU_A. This brings about the equalization of the marginal utility per dollar spent across all purchases.

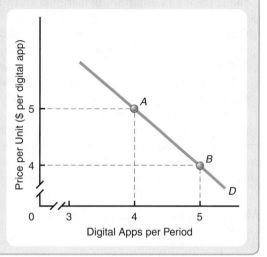

We assume that people desire a variety of goods and pursue a variety of goals. That means that few, if any, goods are irreplaceable in meeting demand. We are generally able to substitute one product for another to satisfy demand. This is commonly referred to as the **principle of substitution**.

AN EXAMPLE Let's assume now that there are several goods, not exactly the same, and perhaps even very different from one another, but all contributing to consumers' total utility. If the relative price of one particular good falls, individuals will substitute in favor of the now lower-priced good and against the other goods that they might have been purchasing. Conversely, if the price of that good rises relative to the price of the other goods, people will substitute in favor of them and not buy as much of the now higher-priced good. An example is the growth in purchases of tablet devices, or digital tablets, since the early 2010s. As the relative price of tablets has plummeted, people have substituted away from other, now relatively more expensive goods in favor of purchasing additional digital tablets.

PURCHASING POWER AND REAL INCOME If the price of some item that you purchase goes down while your money income and all other prices stay the same, your ability to purchase goods goes up. That is to say, your effective **purchasing power** has increased, even though your money income has stayed the same. If you purchase 20 gallons of gas a week at $5 per gallon, your total outlay for gas is $100. If the price goes down by 50 percent, to $2.50 per gallon, you would have to spend only $50 a week to purchase the same number of gallons of gas. If your money income and the prices of other goods remain the same, it would be possible for you to continue purchasing 20 gallons of gas a week *and* to purchase more of other goods. You will feel richer and will indeed probably purchase more of a number of goods, including perhaps even more gasoline.

The converse will also be true. When the price of one good you are purchasing goes up, without any other change in prices or income, the purchasing power of your income drops. You will have to reduce your purchases of either the now higher-priced good or other goods (or a combination).

In general, this **real-income effect** is usually quite small. After all, unless we consider broad categories, such as housing or food, a change in the price of one particular item that we purchase will have a relatively small effect on our total purchasing power. Thus, we anticipate that the substitution effect will be more important than the real-income effect in causing us to purchase more of goods that have become cheaper and less of goods that have become more expensive.

Principle of substitution
The principle that consumers shift away from goods and services that become priced relatively higher in favor of goods and services that are now priced relatively lower.

Purchasing power
The value of money for buying goods and services. If your money income stays the same but the price of one good that you are buying goes up, your effective purchasing power falls, and vice versa.

Real-income effect
The change in people's purchasing power that occurs when, other things being constant, the price of one good that they purchase changes. When that price goes up, real income, or purchasing power, falls, and when that price goes down, real income increases.

The Demand Curve Revisited

Linking the law of diminishing marginal utility and the rule of equal marginal utilities per dollar gives us a negative relationship between the quantity demanded of a good or service and its price. As the relative price of digital apps goes up, for example, the quantity demanded will fall, and as the relative price of digital apps goes down, the quantity demanded will rise. Figure 20-2 on the previous page showed this demand curve for digital apps. As the price of digital apps falls, the consumer can maximize total utility only by purchasing more apps, and vice versa.

In other words, the relationship between price and quantity desired is simply a downward-sloping demand curve. Note, though, that this downward-sloping demand curve (the law of demand) is derived under the assumption of constant tastes and incomes. You must remember that we are keeping these important determining variables constant when we look at the relationship between price and quantity demanded.

Marginal Utility, Total Utility, and the Diamond-Water Paradox

Even though water is essential to life and diamonds are not, water is relatively cheap and diamonds are relatively expensive. The economist Adam Smith in 1776 called this the "diamond-water paradox."

UNDERSTANDING THE PARADOX The diamond-water paradox is easily understood when we make the distinction between total utility and marginal utility. The total utility of water greatly exceeds the total utility derived from diamonds. What determines the price, though, is what happens on the margin. We have relatively few diamonds, so the marginal utility of the last diamond consumed is relatively high. The opposite is true for water. Total utility does not determine what people are willing to pay for a unit of a particular commodity—marginal utility does.

Look at the situation graphically in Figure 20-3 below. We show the demand curve for diamonds, labeled D_{diamonds}. The demand curve for water is labeled D_{water}. We plot quantity in terms of kilograms per unit time period on the horizontal axis. On the vertical axis, we plot price in dollars per kilogram. We use kilograms as our common unit of measurement for water and for diamonds. We could just as well have used pounds or liters.

FIGURE 20-3

The Diamond-Water Paradox

We pick kilograms as a common unit of measurement for both water and diamonds. To demonstrate that the demand for and supply of water are immense, we have put a break in the horizontal quantity axis. Although the demand for water is much greater than the demand for diamonds, the marginal valuation of water is given by the marginal value placed on the *last* unit of water consumed. To find that, we must know the supply of water, which is given as S_1. At that supply, the price of water is P_{water}. But the supply for diamonds is given by S_2. At that supply, the price of diamonds is P_{diamonds}. The total valuation that consumers place on water is tremendous relative to the total valuation consumers place on diamonds. What is important for price determination, however, is the marginal valuation, or the marginal utility received.

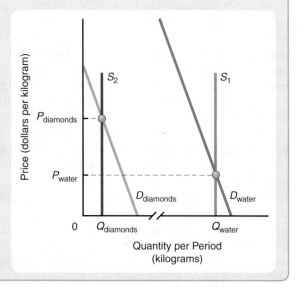

WHY THE PRICE OF DIAMONDS EXCEEDS THE PRICE OF WATER Notice in Figure 20-3 on the facing page that the demand for water is many, many times the demand for diamonds (even though we really can't show this in the diagram). We draw the supply curve of water as S_1 at a quantity of Q_{water}. The supply curve for diamonds is given as S_2 at quantity $Q_{diamonds}$.

At the intersection of the supply curve of water with the demand curve of water, the price per kilogram is P_{water}. The intersection of the supply curve of diamonds with the demand curve of diamonds is at $P_{diamonds}$. Notice that $P_{diamonds}$ exceeds P_{water}. Diamonds sell at a higher price than water.

Behavioral Economics and Consumer Choice Theory

Utility analysis has long been appealing to economists because it makes clear predictions about how individuals will adjust their consumption of different goods and services based on the prices of those items and their incomes. Traditionally, another attraction of utility analysis to many economists has been its reliance on the assumption that consumers behave *rationally*, or that they do not intentionally make decisions that would leave them worse off. As we discussed in Chapter 1, proponents of behavioral economics have doubts about the rationality assumption, which causes them to question the utility-based theory of consumer choice.

Does Behavioral Economics Better Predict Consumer Choices?

Advocates of behavioral economics question whether utility theory is supported by the facts, which they argue are better explained by applying the assumption of *bounded rationality*. Recall from Chapter 1 that this assumption states that human limitations prevent people from examining every possible choice available to them and thereby thwart their efforts to effectively pursue long-term personal interests.

As evidence favoring the bounded rationality assumption, proponents of behavioral economics point to real-world examples that they claim violate rationality-based utility theory. For instance, economists have found that when purchasing electric appliances such as refrigerators, people sometimes buy the lowest-priced, energy-inefficient models even though the initial purchase-price savings often fail to compensate for higher future energy costs. There is also evidence that people who live in earthquake- or flood-prone regions commonly fail to purchase sufficient insurance against these events. In addition, experiments have shown that when people are placed in situations in which strong emotions come into play, they may be willing to pay different amounts for items than they would pay in calmer settings.

These and other observed behaviors, behavioral economists suggest, indicate that consumers do not behave as if they are rational. If the rationality assumption does not apply to actual behavior, they argue, it follows that utility-based consumer choice theory cannot, either.

Consumer Choice Theory Remains Alive and Well

In spite of the doubts expressed by proponents of behavioral economics, most economists continue to apply the assumption that people behave *as if* they act rationally with an aim to maximize utility. These economists continue to utilize utility theory because of a fundamental strength of this approach: It yields clear-cut predictions regarding consumer choices that receive support from real-world evidence.

In contrast, if the rationality assumption is rejected, any number of possible human behaviors might be considered. To proponents of behavioral economics, ambiguities about actual outcomes make the bounded rationality approach to consumer choice more realistic than utility-based consumer choice theory. Nevertheless, a major drawback is that no clearly testable predictions emerge from the many alternative behaviors that people might exhibit if they fail to behave *as if* they are rational.

Certainly, arguments among economists about the "reasonableness" of rational consumers maximizing utility are likely to continue. So far, however, the use of utility-based consumer choice theory has allowed economists to make a wide array of predictions about how consumers respond to changes in prices, incomes, and other factors. In general, these key predictions continue to be supported by the actual choices that consumers make.

WHAT IF... the government bans certain products to try to prevent poor decisions?

The U.S. government limits choices for certain products. Often, government officials say that such limitations aim to prevent ill-informed consumers from making bad decisions. U.S. Secretary of Energy Steven Chu offered such a rationale for banning the sale of incandescent light bulbs. "We are taking away a choice that lets you waste your own money," Chu suggested. The market price of the alternative fluorescent bulb is about six times higher, but the government determined that the fluorescent bulb lasts about six times longer and requires less energy. Hence, the government judged the quality-adjusted price of fluorescent bulbs to be lower. This determination was based on the assumption that consumers leave bulbs lighted for lengthy intervals. In fact, though, consumers who turn lights off and on many times each day would achieve greater energy savings from using incandescent bulbs. Thus, outlawing incandescent bulbs undoubtedly makes many of these consumers worse off than they would have been without the ban. Government limits on the range of choices of other products likewise reduce utility for at least some consumers.

QUICK QUIZ   See page 451 for the answers. Review concepts from this section in MyEconLab.

To remain in consumer optimum, a price decrease requires an _____ in consumption. A price increase requires a _____ in consumption.

Each change in price has a **substitution effect.** When the price of a good _____, the consumer _____ in favor of that relatively cheaper good.

Each change in price also has a **real-income effect.** When price _____, the consumer's real purchasing power increases, causing the consumer to purchase _____ of most goods. Assuming that the principle of diminishing marginal utility holds, the demand curve must slope downward.

The price of water is lower than the price of diamonds because people consume _____ water than diamonds, which results in a _____ marginal utility of water compared with the marginal utility of diamonds.

YOU ARE THERE
Using a Smartphone to Attain a Consumer Optimum

Tri Tang walks into a Sunnyvale, California, Best Buy store and spots what he regards as a perfect gift for his girlfriend: a GPS device with exactly the features he is certain she will desire to use. The Best Buy price for the item is $200 inclusive of sales taxes, which is a higher price than Tang wishes to pay. At that price, his marginal utility per dollar spent would be too low in relation to other items that he consumes to justify purchasing the GPS device. Tang's desired quantity is zero.

Tang pulls out his smartphone and types the model number of the GPS device into a price-comparison app he recently downloaded onto the phone. The app informs him that the item is available for online purchase from Amazon at a no-tax, no-shipping-fee price of about $100. Tang orders the GPS device on the spot. At that price, his marginal utility per dollar spent is sufficiently high in relation to other goods and services he buys to justify purchasing the device. Using his smartphone has enabled Tang to attain a consumer optimum that includes the GPS device for his girlfriend.

Critical Thinking Questions

1. By about what percentage did Tang's anticipated marginal utility per dollar spent increase after he consulted his smartphone app?

2. If Tang decided to buy a second GPS device at the lower price, did his marginal utility per dollar spent on the second unit rise or fall? Explain.

ISSUES & APPLICATIONS

Why Are Consumers Making More Healthful Choices?

CONCEPTS APPLIED

▶ Bounded Rationality

▶ Consumer Optimum

▶ Marginal Utility

Proponents of behavioral economics argue that *bounded rationality* prevents people from acting in their own best interests. For instance, they suggest that people may "underconsume" healthful foods and "overconsume" unhealthful items.

The Tide Turns in Favor of "Eating Your Vegetables"

For years, a number of government agencies have advertised the unhealthful properties of alcohol, tobacco, and fatty foods, in contrast to the healthful characteristics of vegetables.

Recently, government officials have taken heart from the changes in consumer expenditures depicted in Figure 20-4 below. The figure shows substantial decreases in a typical U.S. consumer's inflation-adjusted purchases of alcoholic beverages, restaurant meals, and tobacco products since 2008. During the same period, a significant rise in spending on vegetables has occurred. According to officials at government agencies that have sought to better educate consumers, the data in Figure 20-4 provide evidence of success in easing informational limits that have "bound" consumers in the past.

Another Key Element: Altered Relative Prices

Further consideration of the data indicates that an additional element has played a key role in explaining the consumption shift depicted in Figure 20-4—significant changes in relative prices. Since 2008, average relative prices of vegetables have decreased by 1 percent. During the same period, average relative prices have risen by 4 percent for restaurant food, by more than 6 percent for alcoholic beverages, and by nearly 40 percent for tobacco products.

FIGURE 20-4

Changes in Spending on Selected Items by the Typical U.S. Consumer since 2008

Examination of changes in U.S. consumer spending on healthful vegetables versus less healthful items such as alcoholic beverages, restaurant food, and tobacco products appears to indicate a shift in consumer preferences. Key elements influencing the spending shift were changes in relative prices, which fell for vegetables but rose for the other items.

Source: Bureau of Labor Statistics.

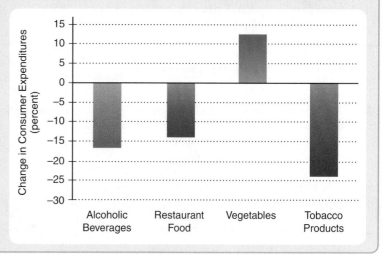

A rational consumer evaluating the marginal utility per dollar spent on vegetables, compared with less healthful items, following changes in relative prices has responded by buying more vegetables. The consumer also has purchased fewer of the less healthful items. Thus, rational consumer responses to relative price changes surely help to explain the spending shift displayed in Figure 20-4.

For Critical Thinking

1. How could the receipt of new information about health implications of foods, alcohol, and tobacco affect a consumer optimum?

2. Other things being equal, would a consumer optimum change if the prices of all items consumed rise at an identical rate? Explain.

Web Resources

1. Track changes in the prices of food items in relation to the overall price level at www.econtoday.com/chap20.

2. For detailed information on consumer food expenditures, go to www.econtoday.com/chap20.

MyEconLab

For more questions on this chapter's Issues & Applications, go to **MyEconLab**. In the Study Plan for this chapter, select Section N: News.

MyEconLab

Here is what you should know after reading this chapter. MyEconLab will help you identify what you know, and where to go when you need to practice.

WHAT YOU SHOULD KNOW		WHERE TO GO TO PRACTICE
Total Utility versus Marginal Utility Total utility is the total satisfaction that an individual derives from consuming a given amount of a good or service during a given period. Marginal utility is the additional satisfaction that a person gains by consuming an additional unit of the good or service.	utility, 435 utility analysis, 435 util, 435 marginal utility, 436 Key Figure Figure 20-1, 437	• MyEconLab Study Plans 20.1, 20.2 • Animated Figure 20-1
The Law of Diminishing Marginal Utility For at least the first unit of consumption of a good or service, a person's total utility increases with increased consumption. Eventually, however, the rate at which an individual's utility rises with greater consumption tends to fall. Thus, marginal utility ultimately declines as the person consumes more and more of the good or service.	diminishing marginal utility, 438	• MyEconLab Study Plan 20.3
The Consumer Optimum An individual optimally allocates available income to consumption of all goods and services when the marginal utility per dollar spent on the last unit consumed of each good is equalized. Thus, a consumer optimum occurs when (1) the ratio of the marginal utility derived from an item to the price of that item is equal across all items that the person consumes and (2) when the person spends all available income.	consumer optimum, 439	• MyEconLab Study Plan 20.4

WHAT YOU SHOULD KNOW		WHERE TO GO TO PRACTICE
The Substitution Effect of a Price Change One effect of a change in the price of a good or service is that the price change induces people to substitute among goods. For example, if the price of a good rises, the individual will tend to consume some other good that has become relatively less expensive as a result. In addition, the individual will tend to reduce consumption of the good whose price increased.	substitution effect, 442 principle of substitution, 443 **Key Figure** Figure 20-2, 443	• MyEconLab Study Plan 20.5 • Animated Figure 20-2
The Real-Income Effect of a Price Change If the price of a good increases, a person responds to the loss of purchasing power of available income by reducing purchases of either the now higher-priced good or other goods (or a combination of both of these responses). Normally, we anticipate that the real-income effect is smaller than the substitution effect, so that when the price of a good or service increases, people will purchase more of goods or services that have lower relative prices as a result.	purchasing power, 443 real-income effect, 443 **Key Figures** Figure 20-2, 443 Figure 20-3, 444	• MyEconLab Study Plan 20.5 • Animated Figures 20-2, 20-3

Log in to MyEconLab, take a chapter test, and get a personalized Study Plan that tells you which concepts you understand and which ones you need to review. From there, MyEconLab will give you further practice, tutorials, animations, videos, and guided solutions. For more information, visit www.myeconlab.com

PROBLEMS

All problems are assignable in MyEconLab. Answers to odd-numbered problems appear at the back of the book.

20-1. The campus pizzeria sells a single pizza for $12. If you order a second pizza, however, the pizzeria charges a price of only $5 for the additional pizza. Explain how an understanding of marginal utility helps to explain the pizzeria's pricing strategy. (See pages 437–438.)

20-2. As an individual consumes more units of an item, the person eventually experiences diminishing marginal utility. This means that to increase marginal utility, the person must consume less of an item. Explain the logic of this behavior using the example in Problem 20-1. (See pages 437–438.)

20-3. Where possible, complete the missing cells in the table in the next column. (See page 439.)

Number of Cheese-burgers	Total Utility of Cheese-burgers	Marginal Utility of Cheese-burgers	Bags of French Fries	Total Utility of French Fries	Marginal Utility of French Fries
0	0	—	0	0	—
1	20	—	1	—	10
2	36	—	2	—	8
3	—	12	3	—	2
4	—	8	4	21	—
5	—	4	5	21	—

20-4. From the data in Problem 20-3, if the price of a cheeseburger is $2, the price of a bag of french fries is $1, and you have $6 to spend (and you spend all of it), what is the utility-maximizing combination of cheeseburgers and french fries? (See page 441.)

20-5. Return to Problem 20-4 on page 449. Suppose that the price of cheeseburgers falls to $1. Determine the new utility-maximizing combination of cheeseburgers and french fries. (See pages 439–441.)

20-6. Suppose that you observe that total utility rises as more of an item is consumed. What can you say for certain about marginal utility? Can you say for sure that it is rising or falling or that it is positive or negative? (See page 437.)

20-7. You determine that your daily consumption of soft drinks is 3 and your daily consumption of tacos is 4 when the prices per unit are 50 cents and $1, respectively. Explain what happens to your consumption bundle, and, after your consumption choices adjust, to the marginal utility of soft drinks and the marginal utility of tacos, when the price of soft drinks rises to 75 cents. (See page 442.)

20-8. At a consumer optimum, for all goods purchased, marginal utility per dollar spent is equalized. A high school student is deciding between attending Western State University and Eastern State University. The student cannot attend both universities simultaneously. Both are fine universities, but the reputation of Western is slightly higher, as is the tuition. Use the rule of consumer optimum to explain how the student will go about deciding which university to attend. (See page 441.)

20-9. Consider the movements that take place from one point to the next (*A* to *B* to *C* and so on) along the total utility curve below as the individual successively increases consumption by one more unit, and answer the questions that follow. (See page 437.)

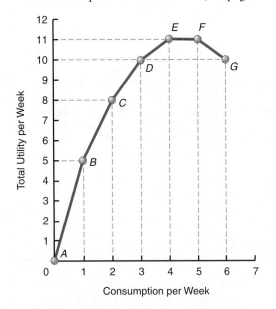

a. Which one-unit increase in consumption from one point to the next along the total utility curve generates the highest marginal utility?

b. Which one-unit increase in consumption from one point to the next along the total utility curve generates zero marginal utility?

c. Which one-unit increase in consumption from one point to the next along the total utility curve generates negative marginal utility?

20-10. Draw a marginal utility curve corresponding to the total utility curve depicted in Problem 20-9. (See page 437.)

20-11. Refer to the table below. If the price of a fudge bar is $2, the price of a Popsicle is $1, and a student has $9 to spend, what quantities will she purchase at a consumer optimum? (See pages 439–441.)

Quantity of Fudge Bars per Week	Marginal Utility (utils)	Quantity of Popsicles per Week	Marginal Utility (utils)
1	1,200	1	1,700
2	1,000	2	1,400
3	800	3	1,100
4	600	4	800
5	400	5	500
6	100	6	200

20-12. Refer to the following table for a different consumer, and assume that each week this consumer buys only hot dogs and tickets to baseball games. The price of a hot dog is $2, and the price of a baseball game is $60. If the consumer's income is $128 per week, what quantity of each item will he purchase each week at a consumer optimum? (See pages 439–441.)

Quantity of Hot Dogs per Week	Total Uility (utils)	Quantity of Baseball Games per Week	Total Utility (utils)
1	40	1	400
2	60	2	700
3	76	3	850
4	86	4	950
5	91	5	1,000
6	93	6	1,025

20-13. In Problem 20–12, if the consumer's income rises to $190 per week, what new quantities characterize the new consumer optimum? (See page 442.)

20-14. At a consumer optimum involving goods A and B, the marginal utility of good A is twice the marginal utility of good B. The price of good B is $3.50. What is the price of good A? (See page 441.)

20-15. At a consumer optimum involving goods X and Y, the marginal utility of good X equals 3 utils. The price of good Y is three times the price of good X. What is the marginal utility of good Y? (See page 441.)

20-16. At a consumer optimum involving goods A and B, the marginal utility of good A is 2 utils, and the marginal utility of good B is 8 utils. How much greater or smaller is the price of good B compared with the price of good A? (See page 441.)

20-17. At a consumer optimum involving goods X and Y, the price of good X is $3 per unit, and the price of good Y is $9 per unit. How much greater or smaller is the marginal utility of good Y than the marginal utility of good X? (See page 441.)

ECONOMICS ON THE NET

Book Prices and Consumer Optimum This application helps you see how a consumer optimum can be attained when one engages in Internet shopping.

Title: Amazon.com Web site

Navigation: Go to www.econtoday.com/chap20 to start at Amazon.com's home page. In the pull-down menu, click on *Books*.

Application

1. Type "top sellers" in the search box, and then search for "Hardbacks." Record the price of the number one book. Then locate the Search window. Type in *Economics Today*. Scroll down until you find your class text listed. Record the price.

2. Suppose you are an individual who has purchased both the number one book and *Economics Today*

through Amazon.com. Describe how economic analysis would explain this choice.

3. Using the prices you recorded for the two books, write an equation that relates the prices and your marginal utilities of the two books. Use this equation to explain verbally how you might quantify the magnitude of your marginal utility for the number one book relative to your marginal utility for your class text.

For Group Study and Analysis Discuss what changes might occur if the price of the number one book were lowered but the student remains enrolled in this course. Discuss what changes might take place regarding the consumer optimum if the student were not enrolled in this course.

ANSWERS TO QUICK QUIZZES

p. 438: (i) Utility; (ii) utils; (iii) Total . . . Marginal

p. 442: (i) less; (ii) equating . . . optimum; (iii) no . . . maximized

p. 446: (i) increase . . . decrease; (ii) falls . . . substitutes; (iii) falls . . . more; (iv) more . . . lower

APPENDIX F

More Advanced Consumer Choice Theory

It is possible to analyze consumer choice verbally, as we did for the most part in Chapter 20. The theory of diminishing marginal utility can be fairly well accepted on intuitive grounds and by introspection. If we want to be more formal and perhaps more elegant in our theorizing, however, we can translate our discussion into a graphical analysis with what we call *indifference curves* and the *budget constraint*. Here we discuss these terms and their relationship and demonstrate consumer equilibrium in geometric form.

On Being Indifferent

What does it mean to be indifferent? It usually means that you don't care one way or the other about something—you are equally disposed to either of two alternatives. With this interpretation in mind, we will turn to two choices, viewing films at theaters and consuming fast-food meals. In panel (a) of Figure F-1 below, we show several combinations of fast food and movie tickets per week that a representative consumer considers equally satisfactory. That is to say, for each combination, *A, B, C,* and *D,* this consumer will have exactly the same level of total utility.

The simple numerical example that we have used happens to concern the consumption of fast-food meals and visits to movie theaters (both of which we assume this consumer enjoys) per week. This example is used to illustrate general features of

FIGURE F-1

Combinations That Yield Equal Levels of Satisfaction

A, B, C, and *D* represent combinations of fast-food meals and movie tickets per week that give an equal level of satisfaction to this consumer. In other words, the consumer is indifferent among these four combinations.

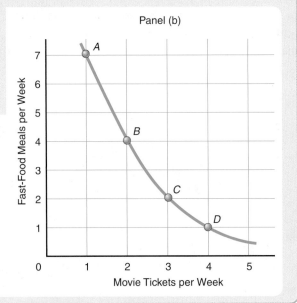

Panel (a)		
Combination	Fast-Food Meals per Week	Movie Tickets per Week
A	7	1
B	4	2
C	2	3
D	1	4

452

indifference curves and related analytical tools that are necessary for deriving the demand curve. Obviously, we could have used any two commodities. Just remember that we are using a *specific* example to illustrate a *general* analysis.

We plot these combinations graphically in panel (b) of Figure F-1 on the facing page, with movie tickets per week on the horizontal axis and fast-food meals per week on the vertical axis. These are our consumer's indifference combinations—the consumer finds each combination as acceptable as the others. These combinations lie along a smooth curve that is known as the consumer's **indifference curve.** Along the indifference curve, every combination of the two goods in question yields the same level of satisfaction. Every point along the indifference curve is equally desirable to the consumer. For example, one fast-food meal per week and four movie tickets per week will give our representative consumer exactly the same total satisfaction as consuming four fast-food meals per week and viewing two movies per week.

Indifference curve
A curve composed of a set of consumption alternatives, each of which yields the same total amount of satisfaction.

Properties of Indifference Curves

Indifference curves have special properties relating to their slope and shape.

Downward Slope

The indifference curve shown in panel (b) of Figure F-1 on the preceding page slopes downward. That is, the indifference curve has a negative slope. Now consider Figure F-2 below. Here we show two points, *A* and *B*. Point *A* represents four fast-food meals per week and two movie tickets per week. Point *B* represents five fast-food meals per week and six movie viewings per week. Clearly, *B* is always preferred to *A* for a consumer who enjoys both fast-food meals and movies, because *B* represents more of everything. If *B* is always preferred to *A*, it is impossible for points *A* and *B* to be on the same indifference curve because the definition of the indifference curve is a set of combinations of two goods that are preferred equally.

FIGURE F-2

Point *B* represents a consumption of more movie tickets per week and more fast-food meals per week than point *A*. *B* is always preferred to *A*. Therefore, *A* and *B* cannot be on the same *positively* sloped indifference curve. An indifference curve shows *equally preferred* combinations of the two goods.

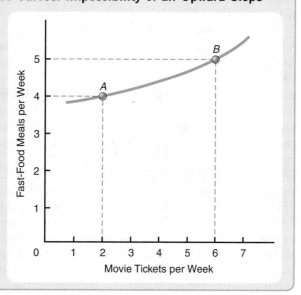

Indifference Curves: Impossibility of an Upward Slope

Implications of a Straight-Line Indifference Curve

This straight-line indifference curve indicates that the consumer will always be willing to give up the same number of fast-food meals to get one more movie ticket per week. For example, the consumer at point *A* consumes five fast-food meals and views no movies at theaters per week. She is willing to give up one fast-food meal in order to get one movie ticket per week. At point *C*, however, the consumer has only one fast-food meal and views four movies per week. Because of the straight-line indifference curve, this consumer is willing to give up the last fast-food meal in order to get one more movie ticket per week, even though she already has four.

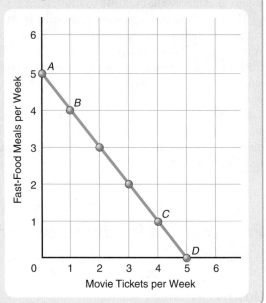

Curvature

The indifference curve that we have drawn in panel (b) of Figure F-1 on page 452 is special. Notice that it is curved. Why didn't we just draw a straight line, as we have usually done for a demand curve?

IMAGINING A STRAIGHT-LINE INDIFFERENCE CURVE   To find out why we don't posit straight-line indifference curves, consider the implications. We show such a straight-line indifference curve in Figure F-3 above. Start at point *A*. The consumer has no movie tickets and five fast-food meals per week. Now the consumer wishes to go to point *B*. She is willing to give up only one fast-food meal in order to get one ticket to a movie. Now let's assume that the consumer is at point *C*, consuming one fast-food meal per week and viewing four movies at a theater per week. If the consumer wants to go to point *D*, she is again willing to give up one fast-food meal in order to get one more movie ticket per week.

In other words, no matter how many times the consumer consumes a fast-food meal, she is willing to give up one fast-food meal to get one movie viewing per week—which does not seem plausible. Doesn't it make sense to hypothesize that the more times the consumer consumes fast-food meals per week, the less she will value an *additional* fast-food meal that week? Presumably, when the consumer has five fast-food meals and no movie tickets per week, she should be willing to give up *more than* one fast-food meal in order to get one movie ticket. Therefore, a straight-line indifference curve as shown in Figure F-3 above no longer seems plausible.

CONVEXITY OF THE INDIFFERENCE CURVE   In mathematical jargon, an indifference curve is convex with respect to the origin. Let's look at this in panel (a) of Figure F-1 on page 452. Starting with combination *A*, the consumer has one movie ticket but seven fast-food meals per week. To remain indifferent, the consumer would have to be willing to give up three fast-food meals to obtain one more ticket to a movie (as shown in combination *B*). To go from combination *C* to combination *D*, however, notice that the consumer would have to be willing to give up only one fast-food meal for an additional movie ticket per week. The quantity of the substitute considered acceptable changes as the rate of consumption of the original item changes.

TABLE F-1

Calculating the Marginal Rate of Substitution

As we move from combination A to combination B, we are still on the same indifference curve. To stay on that curve, the number of fast-food meals decreases by three and the number of movie tickets increases by one. The marginal rate of substitution is 3:1. A three-unit decrease in fast-food meals requires an increase in one movie ticket to leave the consumer's total utility unaltered.

(1) Combination	(2) Fast-Food Meals per Week	(3) Movie Tickets per Week	(4) Marginal Rate of Substitution of Fast-Food Meals for Movie Tickets
A	7	1	3:1
B	4	2	2:1
C	2	3	1:1
D	1	4	

Consequently, the indifference curve in panel (b) of Figure F-1 on page 452 will be convex when viewed from the origin.

The Marginal Rate of Substitution

Instead of using marginal utility, we can talk in terms of the *marginal rate of substitution* between fast-food meals and movie tickets per week. We can formally define the consumer's marginal rate of substitution as follows:

The marginal rate of substitution is equal to the change in the quantity of one good that just offsets a one-unit change in the consumption of another good, such that total satisfaction remains constant.

We can see numerically what happens to the marginal rate of substitution in our example if we rearrange panel (a) of Figure F-1 on page 452 into Table F-1 above. Here we show fast-food meals in the second column and movie tickets in the third. Now we ask the question, what change in the number of movie tickets per week will just compensate for a three-unit change in the consumption of fast-food meals per week and leave the consumer's total utility constant? The movement from A to B increases the number of weekly movie tickets by one. Here the marginal rate of substitution is 3:1—a three-unit decrease in fast-food meals requires an increase of one movie ticket to leave the consumer's total utility unaltered. Thus, the consumer values the three fast-food meals as the equivalent of one movie ticket.

We do this for the rest of the table and find that as fast-food meals decrease, the marginal rate of substitution goes from 3:1 to 2:1 to 1:1. The marginal rate of substitution of fast-food meals for movie tickets per week falls as the consumer views more films at theaters. That is, the consumer values successive movie viewings less and less in terms of fast-food meals. The first movie ticket is valued at three fast-food meals. The last (fourth) movie ticket is valued at only one fast-food meal. The fact that the marginal rate of substitution falls is sometimes called the *law of substitution*.

In geometric language, the slope of the consumer's indifference curve (actually, the negative of the slope of the indifference curve) measures the consumer's marginal rate of substitution.

The Indifference Map

Let's now consider the possibility of having both more movie tickets *and* more fast-food meals per week. When we do this, we can no longer stay on the same indifference curve that we drew in Figure F-1. That indifference curve was drawn for

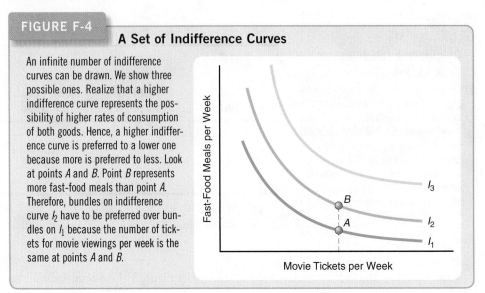

FIGURE F-4

A Set of Indifference Curves

An infinite number of indifference curves can be drawn. We show three possible ones. Realize that a higher indifference curve represents the possibility of higher rates of consumption of both goods. Hence, a higher indifference curve is preferred to a lower one because more is preferred to less. Look at points A and B. Point B represents more fast-food meals than point A. Therefore, bundles on indifference curve I_2 have to be preferred over bundles on I_1 because the number of tickets for movie viewings per week is the same at points A and B.

equally satisfying combinations of movie tickets and fast-food meals per week. If the individual can now obtain more of both, a new indifference curve will have to be drawn, above and to the right of the one shown in panel (b) of Figure F-1 on page 452. Alternatively, if the individual faces the possibility of having less of both movie tickets and fast-food meals per week, an indifference curve will have to be drawn below and to the left of the one in panel (b) of Figure F-1. We can map out a whole set of indifference curves corresponding to these possibilities.

Figure F-4 above shows three possible indifference curves. Indifference curves that are higher than others necessarily imply that for every given quantity of one good, more of the other good can be obtained on a higher indifference curve. Looked at one way, if one goes from curve I_1 to I_2, it is possible to view the same number of movies *and* be able to consume more fast-food meals each week. This is shown as a movement from point A to point B in Figure F-4. We could do it the other way. When we move from a lower to a higher indifference curve, it is possible to consume the same number of fast-food meals *and* to view more movies each week. Thus, the higher an indifference curve is for a consumer, the greater that consumer's total level of satisfaction.

The Budget Constraint

Budget constraint
All of the possible combinations of goods that can be purchased (at fixed prices) with a specific budget.

Our problem here is to find out how to maximize consumer satisfaction. To do so, we must consult not only our *preferences*—given by indifference curves—but also our *market opportunities*, which are given by our available income and prices, called our **budget constraint.** We might want more of everything, but for any given budget constraint, we have to make choices, or trade-offs, among possible goods. Everyone has a budget constraint. That is, everyone faces a limited consumption potential. How do we show this graphically? We must find the prices of the goods in question and determine the maximum consumption of each allowed by our budget.

For example, let's assume that there is a $5 price for each fast-food meal and that a ticket to a movie costs $10. Let's also assume that our representative consumer has a total budget of $30 per week. What is the maximum number of fast-food meals this individual can consume? Six. And the maximum number of films per week she can view? Three. So now, as shown in Figure F-5 on the facing page, we have two points on our budget line, which is sometimes called the *consumption possibilities curve.* These anchor points of the budget line are obtained by dividing money income by the price of each product. The first point is at *b* on the vertical axis.

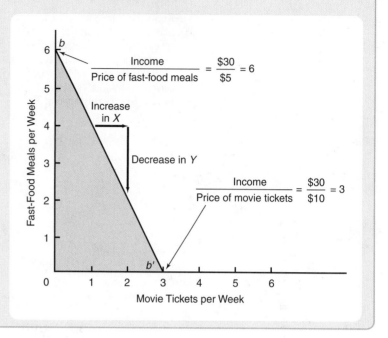

The Budget Constraint

The line *bb'* represents this individual's budget constraint. Assuming that meals at fast-food restaurants cost $5 each, movie tickets cost $10 each, and the individual has a budget of $30 per week, a maximum of six fast-food meals or three movie tickets can be bought each week. These two extreme points are connected to form the budget constraint. All combinations within the colored area and on the budget constraint line are feasible.

The second point is at *b'* on the horizontal axis. The budget line is linear because prices are constant.

Any combination along line *bb'* is possible; in fact, any combination in the colored area is possible. We will assume, however, that there are sufficient goods available that the individual consumer completely uses up the available budget, and we will consider as possible only those points along *bb'*.

Slope of the Budget Constraint

The budget constraint is a line that slopes downward from left to right. The slope of that line has a special meaning. Look carefully at the budget line in Figure F-5 above. Remember from our discussion of graphs in Appendix A on page 21 that we measure a negative slope by the ratio of the decrease in Y over the run in X. In this case, Y is fast-food meals per week and X is movie tickets per week. In Figure F-5, the decrease in Y is −2 fast-food meals per week (a drop from 4 to 2) for an increase in X of one movie ticket per week (an increase from 1 to 2). Therefore, the slope of the budget constraint is −2/1 or −2. This slope of the budget constraint represents the *rate of exchange* between meals at fast-food restaurants and tickets to movies.

Now we are ready to determine how the consumer achieves the optimum consumption rate.

Consumer Optimum Revisited

Consumers will try to attain the highest level of total utility possible, given their budget constraints. How can this be shown graphically? We draw a set of indifference curves similar to those in Figure F-4 on the facing page, and we bring in reality—the budget constraint *bb'*. Both are drawn in Figure F-6 on the following page. Because a higher level of total satisfaction is represented by a higher indifference curve, we know that the consumer will strive to be on the highest indifference curve possible.

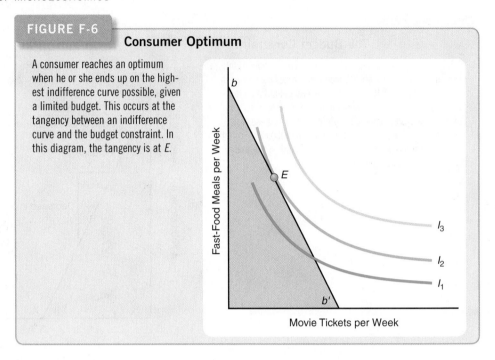

FIGURE F-6

Consumer Optimum

A consumer reaches an optimum when he or she ends up on the highest indifference curve possible, given a limited budget. This occurs at the tangency between an indifference curve and the budget constraint. In this diagram, the tangency is at *E*.

Go to www.econtoday.com/chap20 for a numerical example illustrating the consumer optimum.

The consumer cannot get to indifference curve I_3, however, because the budget will be exhausted before any combination of fast-food meals and movie tickets represented on indifference curve I_3 is attained. This consumer can maximize total utility, subject to the budget constraint, only by being at point *E* on indifference curve I_2 because here the consumer's income is just being exhausted. Mathematically, point *E* is called the *tangency point* of the curve I_2 to the straight line *bb'*.

Consumer optimum is achieved when the marginal rate of substitution (which is subjective) is just equal to the feasible rate of exchange between meals at fast-food restaurants and tickets to movies. This rate is the ratio of the two prices of the goods involved. It is represented by the absolute value of the slope of the budget constraint (i.e., ignoring the negative signs). At point *E*, the point of tangency between indifference curve I_2 and budget constraint *bb'*, the rate at which the consumer wishes to substitute fast-food meals for movie tickets (the numerical value of the slope of the indifference curve) is just equal to the rate at which the consumer *can* substitute fast-food meals for tickets to movies (the slope of the budget line).

Deriving the Demand Curve

We are now in a position to derive the demand curve using indifference curve analysis. In panel (a) of Figure F-7 on the facing page, we show what happens when the price of tickets to movies decreases, holding both the price of meals at fast-food restaurants and income constant. If the price of movie tickets decreases, the budget line rotates from *bb'* to *bb"*.

The two optimum points are given by the tangency at the highest indifference curve that just touches those two budget lines. This is at *E* and *E'*. But those two points give us two price-quantity pairs. At point *E*, the price of movie tickets is $10; the quantity demanded is 2. Thus, we have one point that we can transfer to panel (b) of Figure F-7. At point *E'*, we have another price-quantity pair. The price has fallen to $5, and the quantity demanded has increased to 5. We therefore transfer this other point to panel (b). When we connect these two points (and all the others in between), we derive the demand curve for tickets to movies, which slopes downward.

Deriving the Demand Curve

In panel (a), we show the effects of a decrease in the price of movie tickets from $10 to $5. At $10, the highest indifference curve touches the budget line *bb'* at point *E*. The number of movies viewed is two. We transfer this combination—price, $10; quantity demanded, 2—down to panel (b). Next we decrease the price of movie tickets to $5. This generates a new budget line, or constraint, which is *bb"*. Consumer optimum is now at *E'*. The optimum quantity of movie tickets demanded at a price of $5 is five. We transfer this point—price, $5; quantity demanded, 5—down to panel (b). When we connect these two points, we have a demand curve, *D*, for tickets to movies.

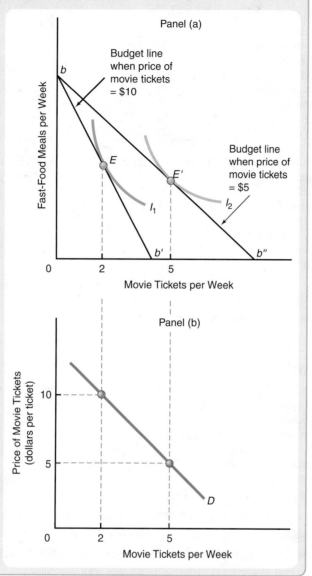

MyEconLab

Here is what you should know after reading this appendix. MyEconLab will help you identify what you know, and where to go when you need to practice.

WHAT YOU SHOULD KNOW		WHERE TO GO TO PRACTICE
On Being Indifferent Along an indifference curve, the consumer experiences equal levels of satisfaction. That is to say, along any indifference curve, every combination of the two goods in question yields exactly the same level of satisfaction.	indifference curve, 453	• MyEconLab Study Plan 20.8
Properties of Indifferent Curves Indifference curves typically slope downward and are usually convex to the origin.		• MyEconLab Study Plan 20.9

MyEconLab *continued*

WHAT YOU SHOULD KNOW ————————————————————————— WHERE TO GO TO PRACTICE

The Marginal Rate of Substitution To measure the marginal rate of substitution, we find out how much of one good has to be given up in order to allow the consumer to consume one more unit of the other good while still remaining on the same indifference curve. The marginal rate of substitution falls as one moves down an indifference curve.	Key Figure Figure F-1, 452	• MyEconLab Study Plan 20.10
The Budget Constraint Indifference curves represent preferences. A budget constraint represents opportunities—how much can be purchased with a given level of income. Consumer optimum is obtained when the highest feasible indifference curve is just tangent to the budget constraint line. At that point, the consumer reaches the highest feasible indifference curve.	budget constraint, 456 Key Figure Figure F-5, 457	• MyEconLab Study Plans 20.9, 20.10, 20.11, 20.12
Slope of the Budget Constraint The slope of the budget constraint is the rate of exchange between two goods, which is the ratio of their dollar prices.	Key Figure Figure F-5, 457	• MyEconLab Study Plan 20.10
Deriving the Demand Curve A decrease in the price of an item causes the budget line to rotate outward. This generates a new consumer optimum, at which the individual chooses to consume more units of the item. Hence, a decrease in price generates an increase in quantity demanded, or a movement down along a derived demand curve.	Key Figure Figure F-7, 459	• MyEconLab Study Plan 20.13

Log in to MyEconLab, take an appendix test, and get a personalized Study Plan that tells you which concepts you understand and which ones you need to review. From there, MyEconLab will give you further practice, tutorials, animations, videos, and guided solutions. For more information, visit www.myeconlab.com

PROBLEMS

All problems are assignable in MyEconLab. *Answers to odd-numbered problems appear at the back of the book.*

F-1. Consider the indifference curve illustrated in Figure F-1 on page 452. Explain, in economic terms, why the curve is convex to the origin. (See page 454.)

F-2. Your classmate tells you that he is indifferent between three soft drinks and two hamburgers or two soft drinks and three hamburgers. (See page 454.)

    a. Draw a rough diagram of an indifference curve containing your classmate's consumption choices.

    b. Suppose that your classmate states that he is also indifferent between two soft drinks and three hamburgers or one soft drink and four hamburgers, but that he prefers three soft drinks and two hamburgers to one soft drink and four hamburgers. Use your diagram from part (a) to reason out whether he can have these preferences.

F-3. The table at the top of the facing page represents Sue's preferences for bottled water and soft drinks, the combination of which yields the same level of utility.

Combination of Bottled Water and Soft Drinks	Bottled Water per Month	Soft Drinks per Month
A	5	11
B	10	7
C	15	4
D	20	2
E	25	1

Calculate Sue's marginal rate of substitution of soft drinks for bottled water at each rate of consumption of water (or soft drinks). Relate the marginal rate of substitution to marginal utility. (See pages 455–456.)

F-4. Using the information provided in Problem F-3, illustrate Sue's indifference curve, with water on the horizontal axis and soft drinks on the vertical axis. (See pages 455–456.)

F-5. Sue's monthly budget for bottled water and soft drinks is $23. The price of bottled water is $1 per bottle, and the price of soft drinks is $2 per bottle. Calculate the slope of Sue's budget constraint. Given this information and the information provided in Problem F-3, find the combination of goods that satisfies Sue's utility maximization problem in light of her budget constraint. (See page 458.)

F-6. Using the indifference curve diagram you constructed in Problem F-4, add in Sue's budget constraint using the information in Problem F-5.

Illustrate the utility-maximizing combination of bottled water and soft drinks. (See page 458.)

F-7. Suppose that at a higher satisfaction level than in Problem F-3, Sue's constant-utility preferences are as shown in the table below. Calculate the slope of Sue's new budget constraint using the information provided in Problem F-5. Supposing now that the price of a soft drink falls to $1, find the combination of goods that satisfies Sue's utility maximization problem in light of her budget constraint. (See page 458.)

Combination of Bottled Water and Soft Drinks	Bottled Water per Month	Soft Drinks per Month
A	5	22
B	10	14
C	15	8
D	20	4
E	25	2

F-8. Illustrate Sue's new budget constraint and indifference curve in a diagram from the data in Problem F-3. Illustrate also the utility-maximizing combination of goods. (See page 458.)

F-9. Given your answers to Problems F-5 and F-7, are Sue's preferences for soft drinks consistent with the law of demand? (See pages 458–459.)

F-10. Using your answer to Problem F-8, draw Sue's demand curve for soft drinks. (See page 459.)

21

Rents, Profits, and the Financial Environment of Business

Since the mid-2000s, in the United States fewer individually owned or co-owned business establishments have opened each year than in prior years. In addition, since the early 2000s, fewer new firms have been formed as U.S. corporations. How can economists explain these recent declines in new business formation in the United States? Why do some firms choose to conduct business with individual owners or a few co-owners while others operate as corporations? In this chapter, you will learn the answers.

U.S. residents have borrowed more funds to finance their educations than the total amount of debt that all residents owe on their credit cards? The student loan debt in the United States now totals more than $1 trillion, which exceeds by $200 billion the amount that U.S. households currently owe on all of their credit cards.

A typical individual with student loans owes about $25,000 in outstanding debts. In addition to amounts borrowed, however, a person with these loans also must eventually pay interest. The interest payments on a student loan depend on the interest rate—the annual amount of interest to be paid as a percentage of the amount borrowed—specified by the student loan contracts.

What is the economic role of interest? What are alternative ways of measuring interest rates? In this chapter, you will learn the answers. First, however, you must learn about the important function of *economic rent*.

Economic Rent

When you hear the term *rent*, you are accustomed to having it mean the payment made to property owners for the use of land or dwellings. The term *rent* has a different meaning in economics. **Economic rent** is payment to the owner of a resource in excess of its *opportunity cost*—that is, the minimum payment that would be necessary to call forth production of that amount (and quality) of the resource.

Economic rent
A payment for the use of any resource over and above its opportunity cost.

Determining Land Rent

Economists originally used the term *rent* to designate payment for the use of land. What was thought to be important about land was that its supply was completely inelastic. That is, the supply curve for land was thought to be a vertical line, so that no matter what the prevailing market price for land, the quantity supplied would remain the same.

The concept of economic rent is associated with the British economist David Ricardo (1772–1823). Here is how Ricardo analyzed economic rent for land. He first simplified his model by assuming that all land is equally productive. Then Ricardo assumed that the quantity of land in a country is *fixed* so that land's opportunity cost is equal to zero. Graphically, then, in terms of supply and demand, we draw the supply curve for land vertically (zero price elasticity). In Figure 21-1 below, the supply curve of land is represented by S. If the demand curve is D_1, it intersects the supply curve, S, at price P_1. The entire

FIGURE 21-1

Economic Rent

If indeed the supply curve of land were completely price-inelastic in the long run, it would be depicted by S. The opportunity cost of land is zero, so the same quantity of land is forthcoming at any constant-quality price. Thus, at the quantity in existence, Q_1, any and all revenues are economic rent. If demand is D_1, the price will be P_1. If demand is D_2, price will rise to P_2. Economic rent would be $P_1 \times Q_1$ and $P_2 \times Q_1$, respectively.

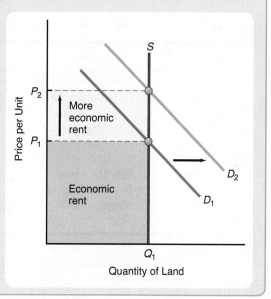

amount of revenues obtained, $P_1 \times Q_1$, is labeled "Economic rent." If the demand for land increases to D_2, the equilibrium price will rise to P_2. Additions to economic rent are labeled "More economic rent." Notice that the quantity of land remains insensitive to the change in price. Another way of stating this is that the supply curve is perfectly inelastic.

Economic Rent to Labor

Land and natural resources are not the only factors of production to which the analysis of economic rent can be applied. In fact, the analysis is probably more often applicable to labor. Here is a list of people who provide different labor services, some of whom probably receive large amounts of economic rent:

- Professional sports superstars

- Hip-hop stars

- Movie stars

- World-class models

- Successful inventors and innovators

- World-famous opera stars

Just apply the definition of economic rent to the phenomenal earnings that these people make. They would undoubtedly work for considerably less than they earn. Therefore, much of their earnings constitutes economic rent (but not all, as we shall see). Economic rent occurs because specific resources cannot be replicated exactly. No one can duplicate today's most highly paid entertainment figures, and therefore they receive economic rent. How much do top performers earn?

EXAMPLE

Do Entertainment Superstars Make Super Economic Rents?

Superstars certainly do well financially. Table 21-1 below shows the one-year earnings of selected individuals in the entertainment industry as estimated by *Forbes* magazine. How much of these earnings can be called economic rent? The question is not easy to answer, because an entertainment newcomer would almost certainly work for much less than she or he earns, implying that the newcomer is making high economic rent. The same cannot necessarily be said for entertainers who have been raking in millions for years. They probably have very high accumulated wealth and also a more jaded outlook about their work. It is therefore not clear how much they would work if they were not offered those huge sums of income.

FOR CRITICAL THINKING

Even if some superstar entertainers would work for less, what forces cause them to earn so much income anyway?

TABLE 21-1

Superstar Earnings

Name	Occupation	One-Year Earnings
Oprah Winfrey	Talk show host and owner, author	$165,000,000
Michael Bay	Director, producer	160,000,000
Steven Spielberg	Director, producer	130,000,000
Jerry Bruckheimer	Director, producer	115,000,000
Dr. Dre	Musician, producer	110,000,000
Tyler Perry	Writer, director, producer	105,000,000
Howard Stern	Talk show host	95,000,000
George Lucas	Director, producer	90,000,000
Elton John	Musician	80,000,000
Tom Cruise	Actor	75,000,000

Source: Forbes, 2012.

Economic Rent and the Allocation of Resources

Suppose that a highly paid movie star would make the same number of movies at half his or her current annual earnings. Why, then, does the superstar receive a higher income? Look again at Figure 21-1 on page 463, but substitute *entertainment activities of the superstars* for the word *land*. The high "price" received by the superstar is due to the demand for his or her services. If Anne Hathaway announces that she will work for a million dollars per movie and do two movies a year, how is she going to know which production company values her services the most highly? Hathaway and other movie stars let the market decide where their resources should be used. In this sense, we can say the following:

Economic rent allocates resources to their highest-valued use.

Otherwise stated, economic rent directs resources to the people who can use them most efficiently.

> **QUICK QUIZ** See page 482 for the answers. Review concepts from this section in MyEconLab.
>
> | **Economic rent** is defined as payment for a factor of production that is completely _____ in supply. | Economic rent _____ resources to their _____-valued use. |
> | --- | --- |

Firms and Profits

Firms or businesses, like individuals, seek to earn the highest possible returns. We define a **firm** as follows:

A firm is an organization that brings together factors of production—labor, land, physical capital, human capital, and entrepreneurial skill—to produce a product or service that it hopes to sell at a profit.

Firm
A business organization that employs resources to produce goods or services for profit. A firm normally owns and operates at least one "plant" or facility in order to produce.

A typical firm will have an organizational structure consisting of an entrepreneur, managers, and workers. The entrepreneur is the person who takes the risks, mainly of losing his or her personal wealth. In compensation, the entrepreneur will get any profits that are made. Recall from Chapter 2 that entrepreneurs take the initiative in combining land, labor, and capital to produce a good or a service. Entrepreneurs are the ones who innovate in the form of new production and new products. The entrepreneur also decides whom to hire to manage the firm. Some economists maintain that the true quality of an entrepreneur becomes evident with his or her selection of managers.

Managers, in turn, decide who else should be hired and fired and how the business should be operated on a day-to-day basis. The workers ultimately use the other inputs to produce the products or services that are being sold by the firm. Workers and managers are paid contractual wages. They receive a specified amount of income for a specified time period. Entrepreneurs are not paid contractual wages. They receive no reward specified in advance. The entrepreneurs make profits if there are any, for profits accrue to those who are willing to take risks. (Because the entrepreneur gets only what is left over after all expenses are paid, she or he is often referred to as a *residual claimant*. The entrepreneur lays claim to the residual—whatever is left.)

The Legal Organization of Firms

We all know that firms differ from one another. Some sell frozen yogurt, others make automobiles. Some advertise. Some do not. Some have annual sales of a few thousand dollars. Others have sales in the billions of dollars. The list of differences is probably endless. Yet for all this diversity, the basic organization of *all* firms can be thought of

TABLE 21-2

Forms of Business Organization

Type of Firm	Percentage of U.S. Firms	Average Size (annual sales in dollars)	Percentage of Total Business Revenues
Proprietorship	71.3	57,000	4.0
Partnership	9.7	1,389,000	13.0
Corporation	19.0	4,501,000	83.0

Sources: U.S. Bureau of the Census. *Statistical Abstract.*

in terms of a few simple structures, the most important of which are the proprietorship, the partnership, and the corporation.

PROPRIETORSHIP The most common form of business organization is the **proprietorship.** As shown in Table 21-2 above, about 71 percent of all firms in the United States are proprietorships. Each is owned by a single individual who makes the business decisions, receives all the profits, and is legally responsible for all the debts of the firm. Although proprietorships are numerous, they are generally rather small businesses, with annual sales averaging about $57,000. For this reason, even though there are more than 22 million proprietorships in the United States, they account for only 4 percent of all business revenues.

Advantages of Proprietorships. Proprietorships offer several advantages as a form of business organization. First, they are *easy to form and to dissolve*. In the simplest case, all one must do to start a business is to start working. To dissolve the firm, one simply stops working. Second, *all decision-making power resides with the sole proprietor*. No partners, shareholders, or board of directors need be consulted. The third advantage is that its *profit is taxed only once*. All profit is treated by law as the net income of the proprietor and as such is subject only to personal income taxation.

Disadvantages of Proprietorships. The most important disadvantage of a proprietorship is that the proprietor faces **unlimited liability** *for the debts of the firm*. This means that the owner is personally responsible for all of the firm's debts. The second disadvantage is that many lenders are reluctant to lend large (or any) sums to a proprietorship. Consequently, a proprietorship may have a *limited ability to raise funds*, to expand the business or even simply to help it survive bad times. The third disadvantage of proprietorships is that they normally *end with the death of the proprietor*, which creates added uncertainty for prospective lenders or employees.

PARTNERSHIP The second important form of business organization is the **partnership.** As shown in Table 21-2 above, partnerships are far less numerous than proprietorships but tend to be larger businesses—about 24 times greater on average. A partnership differs from a proprietorship chiefly in that there are two or more co-owners, called partners. They share the responsibilities of operating the firm and its profits, and they are *each* legally responsible for *all* of the debts incurred by the firm. In this sense, a partnership may be viewed as a proprietorship with more than one owner.

Advantages of Partnerships. The first advantage of a partnership is that it is *easy to form*. In fact, it is almost as easy to form as a proprietorship. Second, partnerships, like proprietorships, often help *reduce the costs of monitoring job performance*. This is particularly true when interpersonal skills are important for successful performance and in lines of business in which, even after the fact, it is difficult to measure performance objectively. Thus, attorneys and physicians often organize themselves as partnerships. A third advantage of the partnership is that it *permits more effective specialization* in

Proprietorship
A business owned by one individual who makes the business decisions, receives all the profits, and is legally responsible for the debts of the firm.

Unlimited liability
A legal concept whereby the personal assets of the owner of a firm can be seized to pay off the firm's debts.

Partnership
A business owned by two or more joint owners, or partners, who share the responsibilities and the profits of the firm and are individually liable for all the debts of the partnership.

occupations in which, for legal or other reasons, the multiple talents required for success are unlikely to be uniform across individuals. Finally, the income of the partnership is treated as personal income and thus is *subject only to personal taxation*.

Disadvantages of Partnerships. Partnerships also have their disadvantages. First, the *partners each have unlimited liability*. Thus, the personal assets of *each* partner are at risk due to debts incurred on behalf of the partnership by *any* of the partners. Second, *decision making is generally more costly* in a partnership than in a proprietorship. More people are involved in making decisions, and they may have differences of opinion that must be resolved before action is possible. Finally, *dissolution of the partnership* often occurs when a partner dies or voluntarily withdraws or when one or more partners wish to remove someone from the partnership. This creates potential uncertainty for creditors and employees.

CORPORATION A **corporation** is a legal entity that may conduct business in its own name just as an individual does. The owners of a corporation are called *shareholders* because they own shares of the profits earned by the firm. By law, shareholders have **limited liability,** meaning that if the corporation incurs debts that it cannot pay, the shareholders' personal property is shielded from claims by the firm's creditors. As shown in Table 21-2 on the facing page, corporations are far less numerous than proprietorships, but because of their large size, they are responsible for 83 percent of all business revenues in the United States.

Advantages of Corporations. Perhaps the greatest advantage of corporations is that their owners (the shareholders) have *limited liability*. The liability of shareholders is limited to the value of their shares. The second advantage is that, legally, the corporation *continues to exist* even if one or more owners cease to be owners. A third advantage of the corporation stems from the first two: Corporations are well positioned to *raise large sums of financial capital*. People are able to buy ownership shares or lend funds to the corporation knowing that their liability is limited to the amount of funds they invest and confident that the corporation's existence does not depend on the life of any one of the firm's owners.

Disadvantages of Corporations. The chief disadvantage of the corporation is that corporate income is subject to *double taxation*. The profits of the corporation are subject first to corporate taxation. Then, if any of the after-tax profits are distributed to shareholders as **dividends,** such payments are treated as personal income to the shareholders and subject to personal taxation. Because the corporate income is also taxed at the corporate level, owners of corporations generally pay higher taxes on corporate income than on other forms of income.

A second disadvantage of the corporation is that corporations are potentially subject to problems associated with the *separation of ownership and control*. The owners and managers of a corporation are typically different persons and may have different incentives. The problems that can result are discussed later in the chapter.

Could a policy decision to permit "crowd funding" of businesses reduce the incentive for partnerships to become corporations?

Corporation
A legal entity that may conduct business in its own name just as an individual does. The owners of a corporation, called shareholders, own shares of the firm's profits and have the protection of limited liability.

Limited liability
A legal concept in which the responsibility, or liability, of the owners of a corporation is limited to the value of the shares in the firm that they own.

YOU ARE THERE

To consider the partnership-versus-corporation advantages and disadvantages faced by two former college students who established a junk-hauling business, take a look at **College Hunks Hauling Junk Weighs Partnership Pros and Cons,** on page 477.

Dividends
Portion of a corporation's profits paid to its owners (shareholders).

POLICY EXAMPLE

The Government Considers Allowing "Crowd Funding" of Firms

Under past federal rules administered by the Securities and Exchange Commission (SEC), a firm could have no more than 499 investing partners before it had to subject itself to regulation as a corporation. The Jumpstart Our Business Startups Act, however, instructs the SEC to develop rules to permit firms organized as private partnerships to raise financial capital on social networks such as Facebook and Twitter. Under this proposal, noncorporate enterprises would be allowed to engage in so-called crowd funding by inviting numerous investors to buy partnership shares valued at no more than $100 per investor. Furthermore, the total amount of partnership shares that a small firm could sell would be capped at $100,000. If the SEC approves this proposal, an advantage of corporations over partnerships would be reduced, which could result in fewer partnerships opting for corporate structures.

FOR CRITICAL THINKING
Even if the SEC approves the crowd-funding proposal, why might a number of partnerships nonetheless decide eventually to become publicly held corporations?

The Profits of a Firm

Most people think of a firm's profit as the difference between the amount of revenues the firm takes in and the amount it spends for wages, materials, and so on. In a bookkeeping sense, the following formula could be used:

$$\text{Accounting profit} = \text{total revenues} - \text{explicit costs}$$

Explicit costs
Costs that business managers must take account of because they must be paid. Examples are wages, taxes, and rent.

Accounting profit
Total revenues minus total explicit costs.

Implicit costs
Expenses that managers do not have to pay out of pocket and hence normally do not explicitly calculate, such as the opportunity cost of factors of production that are owned. Examples are owner-provided capital and owner-provided labor.

where **explicit costs** are expenses that must actually be paid out by the firm. This definition of profit is known as **accounting profit.** It is appropriate when used by accountants to determine a firm's taxable income. Economists are more interested in how firm managers react not just to changes in explicit costs but also to changes in **implicit costs,** defined as expenses that business managers do not have to pay out of pocket but are costs to the firm nonetheless because they represent an opportunity cost. They do not involve any direct cash outlay by the firm and must therefore be measured by the *opportunity cost principle.* That is to say, they are measured by what the resources (land, capital) currently used in producing a particular good or service could earn in other uses. Consequently, a better definition of implicit cost is the opportunity cost of using factors that a producer does not buy or hire but already owns.

Economists use the full opportunity cost of all resources (including both explicit and implicit costs) as the figure to subtract from revenues to obtain a definition of profit.

Opportunity Cost of Capital

Normal rate of return
The amount that must be paid to an investor to induce investment in a business. Also known as the *opportunity cost of capital.*

Firms enter or remain in an industry if they earn, at minimum, a **normal rate of return.** People will not invest their wealth in a business unless they obtain a positive normal (competitive) rate of return—that is, unless their invested wealth pays off. Any business wishing to attract capital must expect to pay at least the same rate of return on that capital as all other businesses (of similar risk) are willing to pay. Put another way, when a firm requires the use of a resource in producing a particular product, it must bid against alternative users of that resource. Thus, the firm must offer a price that is at least as much as other potential users are offering to pay.

Opportunity cost of capital
The normal rate of return, or the available return on the next-best alternative investment. Economists consider this a cost of production, and it is included in our cost examples.

For example, if individuals can invest their wealth in almost any publishing firm and get a rate of return of 10 percent per year, each firm in the publishing industry must *expect* to pay 10 percent as the normal rate of return to present and future investors. This 10 percent is a *cost to the firm,* the **opportunity cost of capital.** The opportunity cost of capital is the amount of income, or yield, that could have been earned by investing in the next-best alternative. Capital will not stay in firms or industries in which the expected rate of return falls below its opportunity cost—that is, what could be earned elsewhere. If a firm owns some capital equipment, it can either use it or lease it out and earn a return. If the firm uses the equipment for production, part of the cost of using that equipment is the forgone revenue that the firm could have earned had it leased out that equipment.

Opportunity Cost of Owner-Provided Labor and Capital

Single-owner proprietorships often grossly exaggerate their profit rates because they understate the opportunity cost of the labor that the proprietor provides to the business. Here we are referring to the opportunity cost of labor. For example, you may know people who run a small grocery store. These people will sit down at the end of the year and figure out what their "profits" are. They will add up all their sales and subtract what they had to pay to other workers, what they had to pay to their suppliers, what they had to pay in taxes, and so on. The end result they will call "profit." They normally will not, however, have figured into their costs the salary that they could have made if they had worked for somebody else in a similar type of job.

By working for themselves, they become residual claimants—they receive what is left after all explicit costs have been accounted for. Part of the costs, however, should include the salary the owner-operator could have received working for someone else.

Consider a simple example of a skilled auto mechanic working 14 hours a day at his own service station, six days a week. Compare this situation to how much he could earn working 84 hours a week as a trucking company mechanic. This self-employed auto mechanic might have an opportunity cost of about $35 an hour. For his 84-hour week in his own service station, he is forfeiting $2,940. Unless his service station shows accounting profits of more than that per week, he is incurring losses in an economic sense.

Another way of looking at the opportunity cost of running a business is that opportunity cost consists of all explicit and implicit costs. Accountants only take account of explicit costs. Therefore, accounting profit ends up being the residual after only explicit costs are subtracted from total revenues.

This same analysis can apply to owner-provided capital, such as land or buildings. The fact that the owner owns the building or the land with which he or she operates a business does not mean that it is "free." Rather, use of the building and land still has an opportunity cost—the value of the next-best alternative use for those assets.

Go to www.econtoday.com/chap21 for a link to Internal Revenue Service reports on U.S. annual revenues and expenses of proprietorships, partnerships, and corporations based on tax returns. Click on recent quarters and choose relevant reports.

Accounting Profits versus Economic Profits

The term *profits* in economics means the income that entrepreneurs earn, over and above all costs including their own opportunity cost of time, plus the opportunity cost of the capital they have invested in their business. Profits can be regarded as total revenues minus total costs—which is how accountants think of them—but we must now include *all* costs. Our definition of **economic profits** will be the following:

> Economic profits = total revenues − total opportunity cost of all inputs used

or

> Economic profits = total revenues − (explicit + implicit costs)

Remember that implicit costs include a normal rate of return on invested capital. We show this relationship in Figure 21-2 below.

Economic profits
Total revenues minus total opportunity costs of all inputs used, or the total of all implicit and explicit costs.

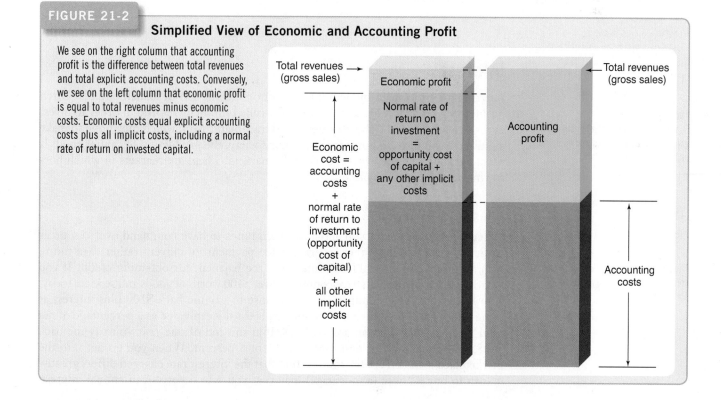

FIGURE 21-2

Simplified View of Economic and Accounting Profit

We see on the right column that accounting profit is the difference between total revenues and total explicit accounting costs. Conversely, we see on the left column that economic profit is equal to total revenues minus economic costs. Economic costs equal explicit accounting costs plus all implicit costs, including a normal rate of return on invested capital.

The Goal of the Firm: Profit Maximization

When we examined the theory of consumer demand, utility (or satisfaction) maximization by the individual provided the basis for the analysis. In the theory of the firm and production, *profit maximization* is the underlying hypothesis of our predictive theory. The goal of the firm is to maximize economic profits, and the firm is expected to make the positive difference between total revenues and total costs as large as it can.

Our justification for assuming profit maximization by firms is similar to our assumption concerning utility maximization by individuals (see Chapter 20). To obtain labor, capital, and other resources required to produce commodities, firms must first obtain financing from investors. Although investors typically monitor managers' performances to ensure that the funds they provide are not misused, they are most interested in the earnings on these funds and the risk of obtaining lower returns or losing the funds they have invested. Firms that can provide relatively higher risk-corrected returns will therefore have an advantage in obtaining the financing needed to continue or expand production. Over time, we would expect a policy of profit maximization to become the dominant mode of behavior for firms that survive.

QUICK QUIZ   See page 482 for the answers. Review concepts from this section in MyEconLab.

_____ are the most common form of business organization, comprising about 71 percent of all firms. Each is owned by a single individual who makes all business decisions, receives all the profits, and has _____ liability for the firm's debts.

_____ are much like **proprietorships,** except that two or more individuals, or partners, share the decisions and the profits of the firm. In addition, each partner has _____ liability for the debts of the firm.

Corporations are responsible for the largest share of business revenues. The owners, called _____, share in the firm's profits but normally have little responsibility for the firm's day-to-day operations. They enjoy _____ liability for the debts of the firm.

Accounting profits differ from **economic profits,** which are defined as total revenues minus total costs, where costs include the full _____ cost of all of the factors of production plus all other implicit costs.

The full opportunity cost of capital invested in a business is generally not included as a cost when accounting profits are calculated. Thus, accounting profits often are _____ than economic profits. We assume throughout that the goal of the firm is to _____ economic profits.

Interest

Financial capital
Funds used to purchase physical capital goods, such as buildings and equipment, and patents and trademarks.

Interest is the price paid by debtors to creditors for the use of loanable funds. Often businesses go to credit markets to obtain so-called **financial capital** in order to invest in physical capital and rights to patents and trademarks from which they hope to make a satisfactory return. In other words, in our society, the production of capital goods is often facilitated by the existence of credit markets. These are markets in which borrowing and lending take place.

Interest and Credit

Interest
The payment for current rather than future command over resources; the cost of obtaining credit.

When you obtain credit, you actually obtain funds to have command over resources today. We can say, then, that **interest** is the payment for current rather than future command over resources. Thus, interest is the payment for obtaining credit. If you borrow $100 from me, you have command over $100 worth of goods and services today. I no longer have that command. You promise to pay me back $100 plus interest at some future date. The interest that you pay is usually expressed as a percentage of the total loan, calculated on an annual basis. If at the end of one year you pay me back $105, the annual interest rate is $5 ÷ $100, or 5 percent. When you go out into the marketplace to obtain credit, you will find that the interest rate charged differs greatly. A loan to buy a house (a mortgage) may cost you 4 to 6 percent in annual interest.

An installment loan to buy an automobile may cost you 6 to 8 percent in annual interest. The federal government, when it wishes to obtain credit (issue U.S. Treasury securities), may have to pay only 0.2 to 4 percent in annual interest. Variations in the rate of annual interest that must be paid for credit depend on the following factors.

1. *Length of loan.* In many (but not all) cases, the longer the loan will be outstanding, other things being equal, the greater will be the interest rate charged.

2. *Risk.* The greater the risk of nonrepayment of the loan, other things being equal, the greater the interest rate charged. Risk is assessed on the basis of the creditworthiness of the borrower and whether the borrower provides collateral for the loan. Collateral consists of any asset that will automatically become the property of the lender should the borrower fail to comply with the loan agreement.

3. *Handling charges.* It takes resources to set up a loan. Papers have to be filled out and filed, credit references have to be checked, collateral has to be examined, and so on. The larger the amount of the loan, the smaller the handling (or administrative) charges as a percentage of the total loan. Therefore, we would predict that, other things being equal, the larger the loan, the lower the interest rate.

Go to www.econtoday.com/chap21 for Federal Reserve data on U.S. interest rates.

Real versus Nominal Interest Rates

We have been assuming that there is no inflation. In a world of inflation—a persistent rise in an average of all prices—the **nominal rate of interest** will be higher than it would be in a world with no inflation. Nominal, or market, rates of interest rise to take account of the anticipated rate of inflation. If, for example, no inflation is expected, the nominal rate of interest might be 5 percent for home mortgages. If the rate of inflation goes to 4 percent a year and stays there, everybody will anticipate that inflation rate. The nominal rate of interest will rise to about 9 percent to take account of the anticipated rate of inflation. If the interest rate did not rise to 9 percent, the principal plus interest earned at 5 percent would have lower purchasing power in the future because inflation would have eroded its real value.

Nominal rate of interest
The market rate of interest expressed in today's dollars.

We can therefore say that the nominal, or market, rate of interest is approximately equal to the real rate of interest plus the anticipated rate of inflation, or

$$i_n = i_r + \text{anticipated rate of inflation}$$

where i_n equals the nominal rate of interest and i_r equals the real rate of interest. In short, you can expect to see high nominal rates of interest in periods of high inflation rates. The **real rate of interest** may not necessarily be high, though. We must first correct the nominal rate of interest for the anticipated rate of inflation before determining whether the real interest rate is in fact higher than normal.

Real rate of interest
The nominal rate of interest minus the anticipated rate of inflation.

The Allocative Role of Interest

In Chapter 4, we talked about the price system and the role that prices play in the allocation of resources. Interest is a price that allocates loanable funds (credit) to consumers and to businesses. Within the business sector, interest allocates funds to different firms and therefore to different investment projects. An investment, or capital, project with a rate of return—an annual payoff as a percentage of the investment—higher than the market rate of interest in the credit market will be undertaken, given an unrestricted market for loanable funds.

For example, if the expected rate of return on the purchase of a new factory or of intellectual property—patents or copyrights—in some industry is 10 percent and funds can be acquired for 6 percent, the investment project will proceed. If, however, that same project had an expected rate of return of only 4 percent, it would not be undertaken. In sum, the interest rate allocates funds to industries whose investments yield the highest (risk-adjusted) returns—where resources will be the most productive.

It is important to realize that the interest rate performs the function of allocating financial capital and that this ultimately allocates real physical capital to various firms for investment projects.

Interest Rates and Present Value

Businesses make investments in which they often incur large costs today but don't make any profits until some time in the future. Somehow they have to be able to compare their investment cost today with a stream of future profits. How can they relate present cost to future benefits?

Interest rates are used to link the present with the future. After all, if you have to pay $105 at the end of the year when you borrow $100, that 5 percent interest rate gives you a measure of the premium on the earlier availability of goods and services. If you want to have things today, you have to pay the 5 percent interest rate in order to have current purchasing power.

The question could be put this way: What is the present value (the value today) of $105 that you could receive one year from now? That depends on the market rate of interest, or the rate of interest that you could earn in some appropriate savings institution, such as in a savings account. To make the arithmetic simple, let's assume that the rate of interest is 5 percent. Now you can figure out the **present value** of $105 to be received one year from now. You figure it out by asking, What sum must I put aside today at the market interest rate of 5 percent to receive $105 one year from now? Mathematically, we represent this equation as

$$(1 + 0.05)PV_1 = \$105$$

where PV_1 is the sum that you must set aside now.

Let's solve this simple equation to obtain PV_1:

$$PV_1 = \frac{\$105}{1.05} = \$100$$

That is, $100 will accumulate to $105 at the end of one year with a market rate of interest of 5 percent. Thus, the present value of $105 one year from now, using a rate of interest of 5 percent, is $100. The formula for present value of any sums to be received one year from now thus becomes

$$PV_1 = \frac{FV_1}{1 + i}$$

where

$$PV_1 = \text{present value of a sum one year hence}$$
$$FV_1 = \text{future sum paid or received one year hence}$$
$$i = \text{market rate of interest}$$

PRESENT VALUES FOR MORE DISTANT PERIODS The present-value formula for figuring out today's worth of dollars to be received at a future date can now be determined. How much would have to be put in the same savings account today to have $105 *two years* from now if the account pays a rate of 5 percent per year compounded annually?

After one year, the sum that would have to be set aside, which we will call PV_2, would have grown to $PV_2 \times 1.05$. This amount during the second year would increase to $PV_2 \times 1.05 \times 1.05$, or $PV_2 \times (1.05)^2$. To find the PV_2 that would grow to $105 over two years, let

$$PV_2 \times (1.05)^2 = \$105$$

and solve for PV_2:

$$PV_2 = \frac{\$105}{(1.05)^2} = \$95.24$$

Present value
The value of a future amount expressed in today's dollars; the most that someone would pay today to receive a certain sum at some point in the future.

Go to www.econtoday.com/chap21 to utilize an MFM Communication Software, Inc., manual providing additional review of present value.

TABLE 21-3

Present Value of a Future Dollar

This table shows how much a dollar received at the end of a certain number of years in the future is worth today. For example, at 5 percent a year, a dollar to be received 20 years in the future is worth 37.7 cents today. If received in 50 years, it isn't even worth a dime today. To find out how much $10,000 would be worth a certain number of years from now, just multiply the figures in the table by 10,000. For example, $10,000 received at the end of 10 years discounted at a 5 percent rate of interest would have a present value of $6,140.

	Discounted Present Values of $1				
Year	3%	5%	8%	10%	20%
1	.971	.952	.926	.909	.833
2	.943	.907	.857	.826	.694
3	.915	.864	.794	.751	.578
4	.889	.823	.735	.683	.482
5	.863	.784	.681	.620	.402
6	.838	.746	.630	.564	.335
7	.813	.711	.583	.513	.279
8	.789	.677	.540	.466	.233
9	.766	.645	.500	.424	.194
10	.744	.614	.463	.385	.162
15	.642	.481	.315	.239	.0649
20	.554	.377	.215	.148	.0261
25	.478	.295	.146	.0923	.0105
30	.412	.231	.0994	.0573	.00421
40	.307	.142	.0460	.0221	.000680
50	.228	.087	.0213	.00852	.000109

Thus, the present value of $105 to be paid or received two years hence, discounted at an interest rate of 5 percent per year compounded annually, is equal to $95.24. In other words, $95.24 put into a savings account yielding 5 percent per year compounded interest would accumulate to $105 in two years.

THE GENERAL FORMULA FOR DISCOUNTING The general formula for **discounting** becomes

$$PV_t = \frac{FV_t}{(1 + i)^t}$$

where t refers to the number of periods in the future the money is to be paid or received.

Table 21-3 above gives the present value of $1 to be received in future years at various interest rates. The interest rate used to derive the present value is called the **rate of discount**.

Discounting
The method by which the present value of a future sum or a future stream of sums is obtained.

Rate of discount
The rate of interest used to discount future sums back to present value.

WHAT IF... the government directs credit to favored industries at artificially low interest rates?

In recent years, government officials have used tax dollars to extend public credit to selected firms, such as green energy companies, at below-market rates of interest. A common argument advanced by these officials is that private savers who otherwise might lend to these companies would require an interest rate that is "too high." Consequently, the discounted present value of future annual payoffs that investments in the officials' favored industries would have to yield is too low for private investors to be willing to direct funds to those industries. Of course, a relatively high market interest rate reflects a greater rate at which people in the private sector discount future sums. Thus, when government officials say that the market interest rate is too high, this means that they think private investors discount the future "too much." In other words, the rate of time discount of the government officials who arrange to redirect taxpayers' funds to the officials' preferred investments must be lower than private investors' rate of time discount. Thus, public officials desire to spend more on certain industries than do private investors.

QUICK QUIZ See page 482 for the answers. Review concepts from this section in MyEconLab.

Interest is the price of obtaining credit. In the credit market, the rate of interest paid depends on the _____ of the loan, the _____, and the handling charges, among other things.

Nominal interest rates include a factor to take account of the _____ rate of inflation. Therefore, during periods of high _____ inflation, nominal interest rates will be relatively high.

Payments received or costs incurred in the future are worth less than those received or incurred today. The _____ _____ of any future sum is lower the further it occurs in the future and the greater the discount rate used.

Corporate Financing Methods

When the Dutch East India Company was founded in 1602, it raised financial capital by selling shares of its expected future profits to investors. The investors thus became the owners of the company, and their ownership shares eventually became known as "shares of stock," or simply *stocks*. The company also issued notes of indebtedness, which involved borrowing funds in return for interest paid on the funds, plus eventual repayment of the principal amount borrowed. In modern parlance, these notes of indebtedness are called *bonds*. As the company prospered over time, some of its revenues were used to pay lenders the interest and principal owed them. Of the profits that remained, some were paid to shareholders in the form of dividends. Some were retained by the company for reinvestment in further enterprises.

The methods of financing used by the Dutch East India Company four centuries ago—stocks, bonds, and reinvestment—remain the principal methods of financing for today's corporations.

Stocks

Share of stock
A legal claim to a share of a corporation's future profits. If it is *common stock*, it incorporates certain voting rights regarding major policy decisions of the corporation. If it is *preferred stock*, its owners are accorded preferential treatment in the payment of dividends but do not have any voting rights.

A **share of stock** in a corporation is simply a legal claim to a share of the corporation's future profits. If there are 100,000 shares of stock in a company and you own 1,000 of them, you own the right to 1 percent of that company's future profits. If the stock you own is *common stock*, you also have the right to vote on major policy decisions affecting the company, such as the selection of the corporation's board of directors. Your 1,000 shares would entitle you to cast 1 percent of the votes on such issues.

If the stock you own is *preferred stock*, you own a share of the future profits of the corporation but do *not* have regular voting rights. You do, however, get something in return for giving up your voting rights: preferential treatment in the payment of dividends. Specifically, the owners of preferred stock generally must receive at least a certain amount of dividends in each period before the owners of common stock can receive *any* dividends.

Bonds

Bond
A legal claim against a firm, usually entitling the owner of the bond to receive a fixed annual coupon payment, plus a lump-sum payment at the bond's maturity date. Bonds are issued in return for funds lent to the firm.

A **bond** is a legal claim against a firm, entitling the owner of the bond to receive a fixed annual *coupon* payment, plus a lump-sum payment at the maturity date of the bond. Bonds are issued in return for funds lent to the firm. The coupon payments represent interest on the amount borrowed by the firm, and the lump-sum payment at maturity of the bond generally equals the amount originally borrowed by the firm.

Bonds are *not* claims on the future profits of the firm. Legally, bondholders must be paid whether the firm prospers or not. To help ensure this, bondholders generally receive their coupon payments each year, along with any principal that is due, before *any* shareholders can receive dividend payments.

Why are a number of U.S. companies contemplating the issuance of bonds with 100-year maturities?

Explaining the Allure of "Century Bonds"

One special type of bond is a perpetual bond that pays a fixed annual coupon payment every year forever. The maximum price that people are willing to pay for a perpetual bond is the sum of discounted present values of all years' coupon payments from next year into the infinite future. Mathematically, this sum—that is, the maximum feasible price of the bond—turns out to equal the annual coupon payment divided by the interest rate.

Bonds with 100-year maturities, called century bonds, have finite maturities. Nevertheless, the discounted present value of coupon payments to be received 100 years from now is so small that the maximum feasible price of a century bond is close to being equal to the coupon payment divided by the interest rate. Today, market interest rates are so low that the implied maximum prices buyers are willing to pay for a century bond with a fixed annual coupon payment are substantial. This fact gives firms a stronger incentive to issue century bonds during the next few years, which explains why a number of U.S. firms have been considering this option.

FOR CRITICAL THINKING
If market interest rates were to rise in the future, what would happen to the prices of century bonds?

Reinvestment

Reinvestment takes place when the firm uses some of its profits to purchase new capital equipment rather than paying the profits out as dividends to shareholders. Although sales of stock are an important source of financing for new firms, reinvestment and borrowing are the primary means of financing for existing firms. Indeed, reinvestment by established firms is such an important source of financing that it dominates the other two sources of corporate finance, amounting to roughly 75 percent of new financial capital for corporations in recent years. Also, small businesses, which are the source of much current growth, commonly cannot rely on the stock market to raise investment funds.

Reinvestment
Profits (or depreciation reserves) used to purchase new capital equipment.

The Markets for Stocks and Bonds

Economists often refer to the "market for wheat" or the "market for labor," but these are concepts rather than actual places. For **securities** (stocks and bonds), however, there really are markets—centralized, physical locations where exchange takes place. The most prestigious of these markets are the New York Stock Exchange (NYSE) and the New York Bond Exchange, both located in New York City. More than 2,500 stocks are traded on the NYSE, which is sometimes called the "Big Board." Numerous other stock and bond markets, or exchanges, exist throughout the United States and in various financial capitals of the world, such as London and Tokyo.

Securities
Stocks and bonds.

Although the exact process by which exchanges are conducted in these markets varies slightly from one to another, the process used on the NYSE is representative of the principles involved. Essentially, brokers earn commissions from volumes of shares traded, while dealers attempt to profit from "buying low and selling high."

Even though the NYSE is traditionally the most prestigious of U.S. stock exchanges, it is no longer the largest. Since the mid-2000s, this title has belonged to the National Association of Securities Dealers Automated Quotations (NASDAQ), which began in 1971 as a tiny electronic network linking about 100 securities firms. Today, the NASDAQ market links about 500 dealers, and NASDAQ is home to nearly 4,000 stocks, including those of such companies as Amazon, Apple, Facebook, and Google.

The Theory of Efficient Markets

At any point in time, there are tens of thousands, even millions, of persons looking for any bit of information that will enable them to forecast correctly the future prices of stocks. Responding to any information that seems useful, these people try to buy low and sell high. The result is that all publicly available information that might be used to forecast stock prices gets taken into account by those with access to the information and the knowledge and ability to learn from it, leaving no predictable profit opportunities. And because so many people are involved in this process, it occurs quite swiftly. Indeed, there is some evidence that *all* information entering the market is fully incorporated into stock prices within less than a minute of its arrival. One view is that any information about specific stocks will prove to have little value by the time it reaches you.

Random walk theory

The theory that there are no predictable trends in securities prices that can be used to "get rich quick."

Consequently, stock prices tend to drift upward following a *random walk*, which is to say that the best forecast of tomorrow's price is today's price plus the effect of any upward drift. This is called the **random walk theory.** Although large values of the random component of stock price changes are less likely than small values, nothing else about the magnitude or direction of a stock price change can be predicted.

Could artificial intelligences allow humans to "get rich quick"?

INTERNATIONAL EXAMPLE

Utilizing Artificial Intelligence to Try to Beat the Market

Some global investment firms have developed artificial intelligence (AI) systems to manage their portfolios of stocks and bonds. These AI systems are designed to avoid predictable errors that humans are prone to make, according to the firms. A few financial firms now regularly utilize AI systems, which they claim can create portfolios of internationally issued securities that yield returns higher than those predicted by the random walk theory.

Teams of humans highly trained in mathematics and computer programming oversee these AI systems. The teams often substitute their own judgment for the AI systems' decisions whenever those choices appear likely to yield losses for the firms. To critics of the idea that AI systems can conduct trades in global stocks and bonds that can beat the market, regular interventions by human management teams reveal that AI systems cannot enable people to "get rich quick."

FOR CRITICAL THINKING

How might faster machine processing of information make the random walk theory more likely to hold true in global securities markets?

Inside Information

Inside information

Information that is not available to the general public about what is happening in a corporation.

Go to www.econtoday.com/chap21 to explore how the U.S. Securities and Exchange Commission seeks to prevent the use of inside information.

Isn't there any way to "beat the market"? The answer is yes—but normally only if you have **inside information** that is not available to the public. Suppose that your best friend is in charge of new product development at Google, the world's largest digital-information firm. Your friend tells you that the company's smartest programmer has just come up with major new software that millions of computer users will want to buy. No one but your friend and the programmer—and now you—is aware of this. You could indeed make a killing using this information by purchasing shares of Google and then selling them (at a higher price) as soon as the new product is publicly announced.

There is one problem: Stock trading based on inside information such as this is illegal, punishable by substantial fines and even imprisonment. So, unless you happen to have a stronger-than-average desire for a long vacation in a federal prison, you might be better off investing in Google after the new program is publicly announced.

Can the "Hindenburg Omen" prevent losses from stock market crashes?

EXAMPLE

Can the Hindenburg Omen Detect an Impending Market Crash?

In advance of a substantial stock market downturn in 1987, three events occurred. First, stock prices of 2.5 percent of firms on the New York Stock Exchange (NYSE) hit 52-week highs, while share prices of 2.5 percent of NYSE firms achieved new 52-week lows. Second, these events followed a long interval of increases in an average measure of all prices of NYSE stocks. Third, the value of a measure of stock price fluctuations became negative. Stock traders call these coinciding events the Hindenburg Omen—a signal of an impending stock market crash.

In August 2010, the Hindenburg Omen events occurred, so many traders responded by selling stocks. Their sales pushed share prices lower. By the end of the following September, stock prices had more than regained their earlier average—resulting in losses for traders who sold stocks based on the "omen." In fact, careful study of the Hindenburg Omen suggests that the omen precedes substantial average stock price declines only about 25 percent of the time.

FOR CRITICAL THINKING
Is the Hindenburg Omen consistent with the random walk theory? Explain.

QUICK QUIZ   See page 482 for the answers. Review concepts from this section in MyEconLab.

The three primary sources of corporate funds are _____, _____, and _____ of profits.

A **share of stock** is a share of _____ providing a legal claim to a corporation's future profits. A _____ is a legal claim entitling the owner to a fixed annual coupon payment and to a lump-sum payment on the date it matures.

Many economists believe that asset markets, especially the stock market, are _____, meaning that one cannot

make a higher-than-normal rate of return without having inside information (information that the general public does not possess). Stock prices normally drift upward following a _____ _____, meaning that you cannot predict changes in future stock prices based on information about stock price behavior in the past.

YOU ARE THERE
College Hunks Hauling Junk Weighs Partnership Pros and Cons

In 2003, college students Nick Friedman and Omar Soliman earned income by removing old furniture and other items from people's homes. After they graduated and worked in the corporate world, they established a junk-removal business called College Hunks Hauling Junk. The two partners hired college students to carry out the same tasks they had undertaken in 2003, using trucks and other equipment the two had purchased and leased.

By 2011, Friedman and Soliman's partnership owned three U.S. offices and had 38 franchises that paid fees to use the company's trademarks and participate in a nationwide network of junk-hauling operations. At that time, some experts argued that the partners should form a corporation to gain the advantage of limited liability. Friedman and Soliman worried, however, about possible problems arising from separation

of ownership and control. In their view, a partnership allowed them to specialize in tasks to which each was best suited and offered lower costs of monitoring job performances. Thus, instead of organizing the growing business as a corporation, they instead merged it into another company called 1-800-Junk-USA—a business that the two continue to operate as a partnership.

Critical Thinking Questions

1. What tax advantage does a partnership offer to Friedman and Soliman, compared with tax issues confronted by a corporation?
2. What possible disadvantages might this business partnership face?

CONCEPTS APPLIED

▶ Firms

▶ Proprietorships

▶ Partnerships

ISSUES & APPLICATIONS

Shrinking Numbers of New Proprietorships, Partnerships, and Corporations

In the United States, fewer new proprietorships and partnerships are now opening for business each year than was true in previous years. In addition, fewer firms per year are opting to become publicly held corporations.

FIGURE 21-3

Declining Numbers of New Proprietorships, Partnerships, and Corporations in the United States

Panel (a) shows that the number of newly formed business proprietorships or partnerships has dropped significantly since the mid-2000s. Panel (b) indicates that initial public offerings of stock to form new

U.S. corporations also have decreased substantially since the early 2000s.

Sources: U.S. Department of Labor, Securities and Exchange Commission, and author's estimates.

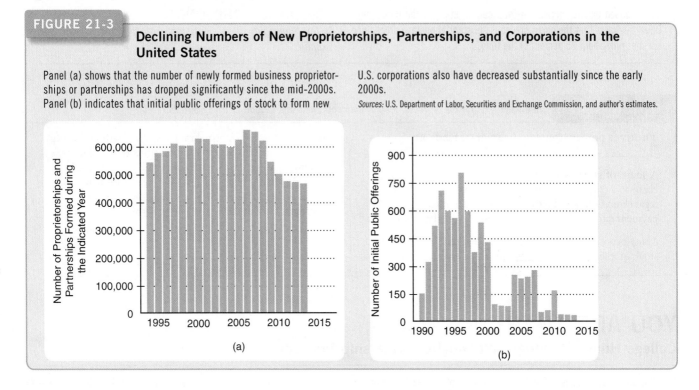

(a)

(b)

Fewer New Firms Are Setting Up Shop

Panel (a) of Figure 21-3 above shows that through the mid-2000s, at least 600,000 new U.S. proprietorships and partnerships began operations each year. Since 2008, however, substantially smaller numbers of these firms have opened for business.

In addition, panel (b) shows that between 1991 and 1999, at least 300 proprietorships or partnerships reorganized annually as corporations via initial public offerings (IPOs) of stock. Since then, there have been many fewer IPOs.

Explaining the Shrinking Numbers of Each Type of Business

A fall in the number of proprietorships and partnerships opening their doors for the first time typically reflects low anticipation that brand-new businesses will be able to succeed. Consequently, the drop-off in formation of new business partnerships and proprietorships depicted in panel (a) of Figure 21-3 likely mainly reflects the dampened state of U.S. economic activity since 2008.

Something that Figure 21-3 does *not* show is that dozens of existing U.S. proprietorships and partnerships *have* chosen to incorporate in recent years. They have done so *outside* the United States. One reason to incorporate abroad is tougher regulations imposed on public corporations based in the United States. These regulations give some existing proprietorships and partnerships an incentive to incorporate abroad to avoid the costs of abiding by those

regulations. Another reason is that U.S. corporate tax rates are among the highest in the world, and undoubtedly a number of U.S. firms incorporate abroad to avoid paying these substantial tax rates.

For Critical Thinking

1. Why do you suppose that a brand-new firm rarely begins as a publicly held corporation?

2. How might tougher regulations and higher tax rates dissuade establishment of new business proprietorships and partnerships?

Web Resources

1. To learn about how a business can incorporate in your state, go to **www.econtoday.com/chap21**.

2. For information about why and how a U.S. firm might incorporate in the Virgin Islands, go to **www.econtoday .com/chap21**.

MyEconLab

For more questions on this chapter's Issues & Applications, go to MyEconLab. In the Study Plan for this chapter, select Section N: News.

MyEconLab

Here is what you should know after reading this chapter. MyEconLab will help you identify what you know, and where to go when you need to practice.

WHAT YOU SHOULD KNOW		WHERE TO GO TO PRACTICE
Economic Rent and Resource Allocation Owners of a resource with a perfectly inelastic supply curve, are paid economic rent, which is a payment for the use of any resource that exceeds the opportunity cost of the resource. The economic rents received by the owners of such a resource reflect the maximum market valuation of the resource's value.	economic rent, 463 **Key Figure** Figure 21-1, 463	• MyEconLab Study Plan 21.1 • Animated Figure 21-1
The Main Organizational Forms of Business and the Chief Advantages and Disadvantages of Each A proprietorship is owned by a single person, who makes the business decisions, is entitled to all the profits, and is subject to unlimited liability. A partnership has two or more owners, who share the responsibility for decision making, share the firm's profits, and individually bear unlimited liability for the firm's debts. Owners of corporations have limited liability, so their responsibility for the debts of the corporation is limited to the value of their ownership shares.	firm, 465 proprietorship, 466 unlimited liability, 466 partnership, 467 corporation, 467 limited liability, 467 dividends, 467	• MyEconLab Study Plan 21.2
Accounting Profits versus Economic Profits A firm's accounting profits equal its total revenues minus its total explicit costs, which are expenses directly paid out by the firm. Economic profits equal accounting profits minus implicit costs, which are expenses that managers do not have to pay out of pocket, such as the opportunity cost of factors of production dedicated to the firm's production process. Owners of a firm seek to maximize the firm's economic profits to ensure that they earn at least a normal rate of return, meaning that the firm's total revenues at least cover explicit costs and implicit opportunity costs.	explicit costs, 468 accounting profit, 468 implicit costs, 468 normal rate of return, 468 opportunity cost of capital, 468 economic profits, 469 **Key Figure** Figure 21-2, 469	• MyEconLab Study Plan 21.2 • Animated Figure 21-2
Interest Rates Interest is a payment for the ability to use resources today instead of in the future. The nominal interest rate includes a factor that takes into account the anticipated inflation rate, so during periods of high anticipated inflation, current market (nominal) interest rates are high. The interest rate allocates funds to investments that yield the highest (risk-adjusted) returns. Hence, resources are put to their most productive uses.	financial capital, 470 interest, 470 nominal rate of interest, 471 real rate of interest, 471	• MyEconLab Study Plan 21.3

MyEconLab *continued*

—— WHAT YOU SHOULD KNOW ————————————————————————— WHERE TO GO TO PRACTICE ——

Calculating the Present Discounted Value of a Payment to Be Received at a Future Date The present value of a future payment is the value of the future amount expressed in today's dollars. It is equal to the most that someone would pay today to receive that amount in the future. The present value of a sum to be received a year from now is equal to the future amount divided by 1 plus the appropriate rate of interest, which is called the *rate of discount*.

present value, 472
discounting, 473
rate of discount, 473

• MyEconLab Study Plan 21.3

The Main Sources of Corporate Funds Stocks are ownership shares, promising a share of profits, sold to investors. Common stocks embody voting rights regarding the major decisions of the firm. Preferred stocks typically have no voting rights but enjoy priority status in the payment of dividends. Bonds are notes of indebtedness that pay interest in the form of annual coupon payments, plus repayment of the original principal amount upon maturity.

share of stock, 474
bond, 475
reinvestment, 475
securities, 475
random walk theory, 476
inside information, 476

• MyEconLab Study Plans 21.4, 21.5

Log in to MyEconLab, take a chapter test, and get a personalized Study Plan that tells you which concepts you understand and which ones you need to review. From there, MyEconLab will give you further practice, tutorials, animations, videos, and guided solutions. For more information, visit www.myeconlab.com

PROBLEMS

All problems are assignable in MyEconLab. Answers to odd-numbered problems appear at the back of the book.

21-1. Which of the following individuals would you expect to have a high level of economic rent, and which would you expect to have a low level of economic rent? Explain why for each. (See page 464.)

　　a. Bob has a highly specialized medical skill shared by very few individuals.

　　b. Sally has never attended school. She is 25 years old and is an internationally known supermodel.

　　c. Tim is a high school teacher and sells insurance part time.

21-2. Which of the following individuals would you expect to have a high level of economic rent, and which would you expect to have a low level of economic rent? Explain why for each. (See page 464.)

　　a. Emily quit high school at age 17, and she has since worked for several years as a waitress in fast-food restaurants.

　　b. Demetrius earned a Ph.D. in financial economics, and he is among a handful of experts who specialize in assessing the values of highly complex securities traded in bond markets.

　　c. Xin was a child prodigy on the violin, and after years of developing her skills, she is now rated among the most talented performing violinists in the world.

21-3. In which of the following situation(s) will owners who supply factors of production be most likely to earn economic rents? (See pages 463–464.)

　　a. Highly elastic supply of the factor; highly elastic demand for the factor

　　b. Highly elastic supply of the factor; highly inelastic demand for the factor

　　c. Highly inelastic supply of the factor; highly inelastic demand for the factor

21-4. A British pharmaceutical company spent several years and considerable funds on the development of a treatment for HIV patients. Now, with the protection afforded by patent rights, the company has the potential to reap enormous gains. The government, in response, has threatened to tax away any economic rents the company may earn. Is this an advisable policy? Why or why not? (See page 464. Hint: Contrast the short-run and long-run effects of taxing away the economic rents.)

21-5. Write a brief explanation of the differences among a sole proprietorship, a partnership, and a corporation. In addition, list one advantage and one disadvantage of a proprietorship, a partnership, and a corporation. (See pages 465–467.)

21-6. After graduation, you face a choice. One option is to work for a multinational consulting firm and earn a starting salary (benefits included) of $40,000. The other option is to use $5,000 in savings to start your own consulting firm. You could earn an interest return of 5 percent on your savings. You choose to start your own consulting firm. At the end of the first year, you add up all of your expenses and revenues. Your total includes $12,000 in rent, $1,000 in office supplies, $20,000 for office staff, and $4,000 in telephone expenses. What are your total explicit costs and total implicit costs? (See page 468.)

21-7. Suppose, as in Problem 21-6, that you have now operated your consulting firm for a year. At the end of the first year, your total revenues are $77,250. Based on the information in Problem 21-6, what is the accounting profit, and what is your economic profit? (See pages 468–469.)

21-8. An individual leaves a college faculty, where she was earning $80,000 a year, to begin a new venture. She invests her savings of $20,000, which were earning 10 percent annually. She then spends $40,000 renting office equipment, hires two students at $60,000 a year each, rents office space for $24,000, and has other variable expenses of $80,000. At the end of the year, her revenues are $400,000. What are her accounting profit and her economic profit for the year? (See pages 468–469.)

21-9. Classify the following items as either financial capital or physical capital. (See page 470.)

   a. A computer server owned by an information-processing company

   b. $100,000 set aside in an account to purchase a computer server

   c. Funds raised through a bond offer to expand plant and equipment

   d. A warehouse owned by a shipping company

21-10. Explain the difference between the dividends of a corporation and the profits of a proprietorship or partnership, particularly in their tax treatment. (See pages 465–467.)

21-11. The owner of WebCity is trying to decide whether to remain a proprietorship or to incorporate. Suppose that the corporate tax rate on profits is 20 percent and the personal income tax rate is 30 percent. For simplicity, assume that all corporate profits (after corporate taxes are paid) are distributed as dividends in the year they are earned and that such dividends are subject to tax at the personal income tax rate. (See pages 465–467.)

   a. If the owner of WebCity expects to earn $100,000 in before-tax profits this year, regardless of whether the firm is a proprietorship or a corporation, which method of organization should be chosen?

   b. What is the dollar value of the after-tax advantage of the form of organization determined in part (a)?

   c. Suppose that the corporate form of organization has cost advantages that will raise before-tax profits by $50,000. Should the owner of WebCity incorporate?

   d. Based on parts (a) and (c), by how much will after-tax profits change due to incorporation?

   e. Suppose that tax policy is changed to completely exempt from personal taxation the first $40,000 per year in dividends. Would this change in policy affect the decision made in part (a)?

   f. How can you explain the fact that even though corporate profits are subject to double taxation, most business in the United States is conducted by corporations rather than by proprietorships or partnerships?

21-12. Explain how the following events would likely affect the relevant interest rate. (See page 471.)

   a. A major bond-rating agency has improved the risk rating of a developing nation.

   b. The government has passed legislation requiring bank regulators to significantly increase the paperwork required when a bank makes a loan.

21-13. Suppose that the interest rate in Japan is only 2 percent, while the comparable rate in the United States is 4 percent. Japan's rate of inflation is 0.5 percent, while the U.S. inflation rate is 3 percent. Which economy has the higher real interest rate? (See page 471.)

21-14. You expect to receive a payment of $104 one year from now. (See pages 472–473.)

   a. Your discount rate is 4 percent. What is the present value of the payment to be received?

   b. Suppose that your discount rate rises to 5 percent. What is the present value of the payment to be received?

21-15. Outline the differences between common stock and preferred stock. (See page 474.)

21-16. Explain the basic differences between a share of stock and a bond. (See page 474.)

21-17. Suppose that one of your classmates informs you that he has developed a method of forecasting stock market returns based on past trends. With a monetary investment from you, he claims that the two of you could profit handsomely from this forecasting method. How should you respond to your classmate? (See pages 475–476.)

21-18. Suppose that you are trying to decide whether to spend $1,000 on stocks issued by WildWeb or on bonds issued by the same company. There is a 50 percent chance that the value of the stock will rise to $2,200 at the end of the year and a 50 percent chance that the stock will be worthless at the end of

the year. The bonds promise an interest rate of 20 percent per year, and it is certain that the bonds and interest will be repaid at the end of the year. (See page 474.)

a. Assuming that your time horizon is exactly one year, will you choose the stocks or the bonds?

b. By how much is your expected end-of-year wealth reduced if you make the wrong choice?

c. Suppose the odds of success improve for WildWeb: Now there is a 60 percent chance that the value of the stock will be $2,200 at year's end and only a 40 percent chance that it will be worthless. Should you now choose the stocks or the bonds?

d. By how much did your expected end-of-year wealth rise as a result of the improved outlook for WildWeb?

ECONOMICS ON THE NET

How the New York Stock Exchange Operates This application gives you the chance to learn about the New York Stock Exchange.

Title: The New York Stock Exchange: Stocks

Navigation: Follow the link at **www.econtoday.com/chap21** to visit the New York Stock Exchange. Click on "About us" in the left margin for a pop-up menu, and then click on *Education.* Select the tab named *Educational Materials.* Click on "All about Investing" and then "Stocks." Read the article.

Application Answer the following questions.

1. Why might growth stocks have been issued by firms that just recently became corporations?

2. Discuss why the industries listed as likely issuers of cyclical stocks and defensive stocks typically satisfy these classifications.

For Group Study and Analysis Go back to the NYSE homepage. Under "Information," click on "For Individual Investors," and then click on "Indices," followed by "Index Directory"; click on *NYSE Indexes,* and read the article. Divide the class into groups, and assign each group to examine one among the five sets of indexes listed. Ask each group to evaluate how stock traders might use an index as a "benchmark" when evaluating whether to buy or sell stocks.

ANSWERS TO QUICK QUIZZES

p. 465: (i) inelastic; (ii) allocates . . . highest

p. 470: (i) Proprietorships . . . unlimited;
(ii) Partnerships . . . unlimited; (iii) shareholders . . . limited; (iv) opportunity; (v) greater . . . maximize

p. 474: (i) length . . . risk; (ii) anticipated . . . anticipated; (iii) present value

p. 477: (i) stocks . . . bonds . . . reinvestment;
(ii) ownership . . . bond; (iii) efficient . . . random walk

The Firm: Cost and Output Determination

22

LEARNING OBJECTIVES

After reading this chapter, you should be able to:

▶ Discuss the difference between the short run and the long run from the perspective of a firm

▶ Understand why the marginal physical product of labor eventually declines as more units of labor are employed

▶ Explain the short-run cost curves a typical firm faces

▶ Describe the long-run cost curves a typical firm faces

▶ Identify situations of economies and diseconomies of scale and define a firm's minimum efficient scale

MyEconLab helps you master each objective and study more efficiently. See end of chapter for details.

The most expensive component of a hybrid or all-electric passenger vehicle is its set of battery packs. For many all-electric cars, battery packs account for more than half of the per-unit cost of producing the vehicles. Automakers have found that a way to reduce expenses on battery packs is to increase the overall rate of their production. For this reason, several firms are in the process of building facilities that produce battery packs in large numbers each year. They face a critical problem, however: Annual production of hybrid and all-electric passenger vehicles is much lower than the scales of operations at which these facilities are intended to operate. Reading this chapter will enable you to understand why the per-unit cost of producing battery packs for hybrid and all-electric vehicles varies with the scale of production of these items. Doing so will also help you to see why a low scale of vehicle production may interfere with the automakers' plans to reduce the cost of making battery packs—and hence of producing vehicles.

although consumers download the largest percentage of applications—"apps"—used in digital devices, utilization of apps is growing at a more rapid pace in the business world? Firms are employing apps in a variety of contexts, such as managing travel plans, tracking equipment, and monitoring time that employees spend working on the road. Business apps are more costly than those most commonly purchased by consumers, with prices typically ranging between $10 and $30 per month. Nevertheless, firms that have integrated apps into their operations have discovered that utilizing digital apps enables them to better organize their diverse resources in producing and distributing goods and services. The resulting managerial coordination gains yield cost reductions much greater than the costs of the apps.

What are the determinants of a company's expenses? To understand the answer to this question, you must learn about the nature of the costs that firms incur in their productive endeavors, which in turn requires contemplating how firms employ inputs in the production of goods and services. This chapter considers each of these important topics.

Short Run versus Long Run

In Chapter 19, we discussed short-run and long-run price elasticities of supply and demand. As you will recall, for consumers, the long run means the time period during which all adjustments to a change in price can be made, and anything shorter than that is considered the short run. For suppliers, the long run is the time in which all adjustments can be made, and anything shorter than that is the short run. Now that we are discussing firms only, we will maintain a similar distinction between the short and the long run, but we will be more specific.

The Short Run

Short run
The time period during which at least one input, such as plant size, cannot be changed.

Plant size
The physical size of the factories that a firm owns and operates to produce its output. Plant size can be defined by square footage, maximum physical capacity, and other physical measures.

In the theory of the firm, the **short run** is defined as any time period so short that there is at least one input, such as current **plant size,** that the firm cannot alter. In other words, during the short run, a firm makes do with whatever big machines and factory size it already has, no matter how much more it wants to produce because of increased demand for its product. We consider the plant and heavy equipment, the size or amount of which cannot be varied in the short run, as *fixed* resources. In agriculture and in some other businesses, land may be a fixed resource.

There are, of course, variable resources that the firm can alter when it wants to change its rate of production. These are called *variable inputs* or *variable factors of production.* Typically, the variable inputs of a firm are its labor and its purchases of raw materials. In the short run, in response to changes in demand, the firm can, by definition, change only the amounts of its variable inputs.

The Long Run

Long run
The time period during which all factors of production can be varied.

The **long run** can now be considered the period of time in which *all* inputs can be varied. Specifically, in the long run, the firm can alter its plant size. How long is the long run? That depends on each individual industry. For Wendy's or McDonald's, the long run may be four or five months, because that is the time it takes to add new franchises. For a steel company, the long run may be several years, because that's how long it takes to plan and build a new plant. An electric utility might need more than a decade to build a new plant.

Short run and *long run* in our discussion are terms that apply to planning decisions made by managers. Managers routinely take account of both the short-run and the long-run consequences of their behavior. While always making decisions about what to do today, tomorrow, and next week—the short run as it were—they keep an eye on the long-run net benefits of all short-run actions. As an individual, you have long-run plans, such as going to graduate school or having a successful career, and you make a series of short-run decisions with these long-run plans in mind.

The Relationship between Output and Inputs

A firm takes numerous inputs, combines them using a technological production process, and ends up with an output. There are, of course, a great many factors of production, or inputs. Keeping the quantity of land fixed, we classify production inputs into two broad categories—capital and labor. The relationship between output and these two inputs is as follows:

Output per time period = some function of capital and labor inputs

We have used the word *production* but have not defined it. **Production** is any process by which resources are transformed into goods or services. Production includes not only making things but also transporting them, retailing, repackaging them, and so on. Notice that the production relationship tells nothing about the worth or value of the inputs or the output.

Production
Any activity that results in the conversion of resources into products.

The Production Function: A Numerical Example

The relationship between maximum physical output and the quantity of capital and labor used in the production process is sometimes called the **production function.** The production function is a technological relationship between inputs and output.

Production function
The relationship between inputs and maximum physical output. A production function is a technological, not an economic, relationship.

PROPERTIES OF THE PRODUCTION FUNCTION The production function specifies the maximum possible output that can be produced with a given amount of inputs. It also specifies the minimum amount of inputs necessary to produce a given level of output. Firms that are inefficient or wasteful in their use of capital and labor will obtain less output than the production function will show. No firm can obtain more output than the production function allows, however. The production function also depends on the technology available to the firm. It follows that an improvement in technology that allows the firm to produce more output with the same amount of inputs (or the same output with fewer inputs) results in a new production function.

How is three-dimensional printing technology allowing firms to produce more output using the same inputs?

EXAMPLE

3D Printers Shift from Design to Production

Engineers and designers have used three-dimensional (3D) printers since the late 1990s. The printers deposit materials in successive, thin layers until a solid 3D model emerges. Printing physical models of products from two-dimensional computer designs has enabled companies to reduce considerably the expenses entailed in paying skilled workers to construct models by hand.

In recent years, many firms have shifted away from using 3D printers solely to design products. These firms now utilize modified versions of 3D printers to produce goods in their *final* forms. Products now "printed" include highly specialized gloves, airline parts, dental crowns, and body

parts for racecars. Materials used in 3D-print production include nylons, plastic, carbon fiber, stainless steel, and titanium. Because the modified form of 3D printing constructs a product in fine layers, the production process entails much less waste of raw materials. Thus, modified 3D printing makes it possible to produce either the same output with fewer inputs or more output with the same quantities of inputs.

FOR CRITICAL THINKING
What happens when managers do not use the best available production procedures?

Panel (a) of Figure 22-1 on the next page shows a production function relating maximum output in column 2 to the quantity of labor in column 1. Zero workers per week produce no output. Five workers per week of input produce a total output of 50 computer servers per week. (Ignore for the moment the rest of that panel.) Panel (b) of Figure 22-1 displays this production function. It relates to the short run, because plant size is fixed, and it applies to a single firm.

FIGURE 22-1

The Production Function and Marginal Product: A Hypothetical Case

Marginal product is the addition to the total product that results when one additional worker is hired (for a week in this example). Thus, in panel (a), the marginal product of adding the fourth worker is eight computer servers. With four workers, 44 servers are produced, but with three workers, only 36 are produced. The difference is 8. In panel (b), we plot the numbers from columns 1 and 2 of panel (a). In panel (c), we plot the numbers from columns 1 and 4 of panel (a). When we go from 0 to 1,

marginal product is 10. When we go from one worker to two workers, marginal product increases to 16. After two workers, marginal product declines, but it is still positive. Total product (output) reaches its peak at about seven workers, so after seven workers, marginal product is negative. When we move from seven to eight workers, marginal product becomes −1 computer server per week.

Panel (a)

(1) Input of Labor (number of worker-weeks)	(2) Total Product (output in computer servers per week)	(3) Average Physical Product (total product ÷ number of worker-weeks) [servers per week]	(4) Marginal Physical Product (output in servers per week)
0	—	—	
			10
1	10	10.00	
			16
2	26	13.00	
			10
3	36	12.00	
			8
4	44	11.00	
			6
5	50	10.00	
			4
6	54	9.00	
			2
7	56	8.00	
			−1
8	55	6.88	
			−2
9	53	5.89	
			−3
10	50	5.00	
			−4
11	46	4.18	

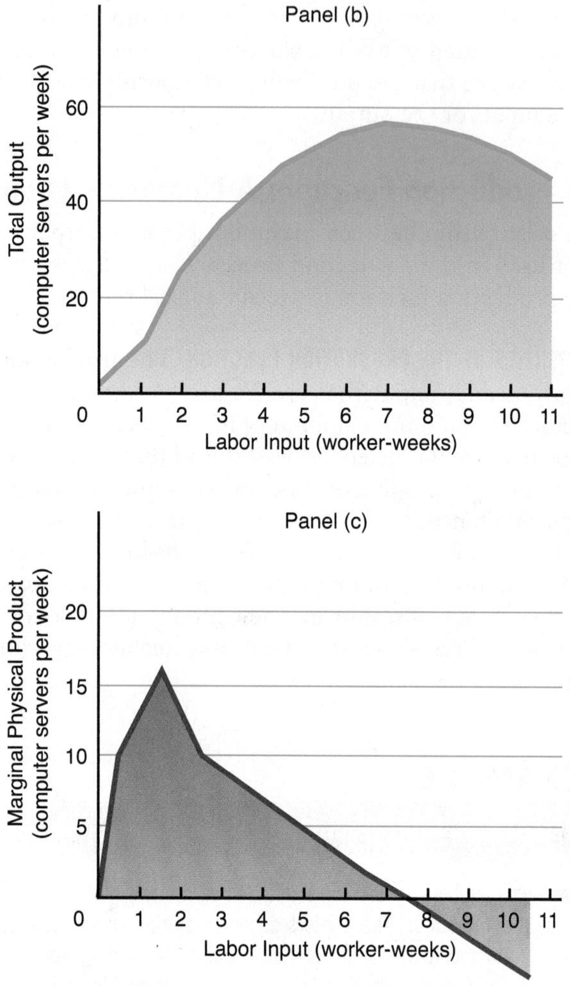

TOTAL PHYSICAL PRODUCT Panel (b) shows a total physical product curve, or the maximum feasible output when we add successive equal-sized units of labor while holding all other inputs constant. The graph of the production function in panel (b) is not a straight line. It peaks at about seven workers per week and then starts to go down.

Average and Marginal Physical Product

To understand the shape of the total physical product curve, let's examine columns 3 and 4 of panel (a) of Figure 22-1 above—that is, average and marginal physical products. **Average physical product** is the total product divided by the number of worker-weeks. You can see in column 3 of panel (a) of Figure 22-1 that the average physical product of labor first rises and then steadily falls after two workers are hired.

Average physical product
Total product divided by the variable input.

Marginal means "additional," so the **marginal physical product** of labor is the *change in total product* that occurs when a worker is added to a production process for a given interval. (The term *physical* here emphasizes the fact that we are measuring in terms of material quantities of goods or tangible amounts of services, not in dollar terms.) The marginal physical product of labor therefore refers to the *change in output caused by a one-unit change in the labor input* as shown in column 4 of panel (a) of Figure 22-1 on the facing page. (Marginal physical product is also referred to as *marginal product*.)

Marginal physical product
The physical output that is due to the addition of one more unit of a variable factor of production. The change in total product occurring when a variable input is increased and all other inputs are held constant. It is also called *marginal product*.

Diminishing Marginal Product

Note that in Figure 22-1, when three workers instead of two are employed each week, marginal product declines. The concept of diminishing marginal product applies to many situations. If you put a seat belt across your lap, a certain amount of safety is obtained. If you add another seat belt over your shoulder, some additional safety is obtained, but less than when the first belt was secured. When you use three seat belts rather than two over the other shoulder, the amount of *additional* safety obtained is even smaller.

Measuring Diminishing Marginal Product

How do we measure diminishing marginal product? First, we limit the analysis to only one variable factor of production (or input)—let's say the factor is labor. Every other factor of production, such as machines, must be held constant. Only in this way can we calculate the marginal product from utilizing more workers with the fixed factors, including machines, and know when we reach the point of diminishing marginal product.

INITIALLY INCREASING MARGINAL PRODUCT The marginal product of labor may increase rapidly at the very beginning. Suppose that a firm starts with no workers, and only two machines. When the firm hires one worker instead of zero, that individual can use both of the firm's machines for producing output, so production jumps. Then, when the firm hires two workers instead of just one, each of the two individuals can utilize a machine to produce output, and production leaps upward again. Indeed, the marginal product from hiring two workers instead of one may be greater than hiring one worker instead of zero. This is the situation displayed Figure 22-1, in which hiring two workers instead of one yields a marginal product of 16 units of output, which exceeds the 10 units of output gained when one worker is hired instead of zero.

DIMINISHING MARGINAL PRODUCT Beyond some point, marginal product must begin to diminish as more workers are hired—*not* because additional workers are less qualified but because each worker has, on average, fewer machines with which to work (remember, all other inputs are fixed). In Figure 22-1, when three workers instead of two are hired to use two machines, the third worker must perform subsidiary tasks, such as moving raw materials or boxing up completed units of output. Total production rises as a consequence, but not by as much as was the case when two workers rather than one were hired. Consequently, the marginal product when three workers instead of two are hired drops to 10 units, which is lower than the 16 units of output gained when two workers are hired instead of one. In fact, eventually the firm's plant will become so crowded that workers will start to get in each other's way. At that point, marginal physical product becomes negative, and total production declines.

Using these ideas, we can define the **law of diminishing marginal product:**

As successive equal increases in a variable factor of production are added to fixed factors of production, there will be a point beyond which the extra, or marginal, product that can be attributed to each additional unit of the variable factor of production will decline.

Law of diminishing marginal product
The observation that after some point, successive equal-sized increases in a variable factor of production, such as labor, added to fixed factors of production will result in smaller increases in output.

Note that the law of diminishing marginal product is a statement about the *physical* relationships between inputs and outputs that we have observed in many firms. If the law of diminishing marginal product were not a fairly accurate statement about the world, what would stop firms from hiring additional workers forever?

An Example of the Law of Diminishing Marginal Product

Production of computer servers provides an example of the law of diminishing marginal product. With a fixed amount of factory space, assembly equipment, and quality-control diagnostic software, the addition of more workers eventually yields successively smaller increases in output. After a while, when all the assembly equipment and quality-control diagnostic software are being used, additional workers will have to start assembling and troubleshooting quality problems manually. Output will not rise as much as when workers were added before this point, because the assembly equipment and diagnostic software are all in use. The marginal physical product of adding a worker, given a specified amount of capital, must eventually be less than that for the previous workers.

GRAPHING THE MARGINAL PRODUCT OF LABOR A hypothetical set of numbers illustrating the law of diminishing marginal product is presented in panel (a) of Figure 22-1 on page 486. The numbers are presented graphically in panel (c). Marginal productivity (additional output from adding more workers during a week) first increases, then decreases, and finally becomes negative.

When one worker is hired, total output goes from 0 to 10. Thus, marginal physical product is 10 computer servers per week. When two workers instead of one are hired, total product goes from 10 to 26 servers per week. Marginal physical product therefore increases to 16 servers per week. When three workers rather than two are hired, total product again increases, from 26 to 36 servers per week. This represents a marginal physical product of only 10 servers per week. Therefore, the point of diminishing marginal product occurs after two workers are hired.

THE POINT OF SATURATION Notice that after seven workers per week, marginal physical product becomes negative. That means that eight workers instead of seven would reduce total product. Sometimes this is called the *point of saturation*, indicating that given the amount of fixed inputs, there is no further positive use for more of the variable input. We have entered the region of negative marginal product.

How are oil companies determining which rock formations beneath the Gulf of Mexico will yield the highest feasible levels of marginal physical product?

EXAMPLE

Evaluating the Marginal Physical Product of Oil Drilling

Chevron has been contemplating more than 100 prospective locations for oil drilling in the Gulf of Mexico. To decide which areas are likely to offer the largest increases in the company's oil output—that is, the highest levels of marginal physical product—Chevron's staff of geophysicists aims sonic booms onto the Gulf's floor. On the basis of data gathered by sensors indicating energy shifts within different areas, the firm's scientists can distinguish between geologic formations containing solid rock and those with ridges of rock lining pools of oil. In this way, the geophysicists can estimate levels of marginal physical product

from efforts to extract oil in differing areas beneath the Gulf of Mexico. The company is using these estimates in planning where it initially should put employees to work extracting oil with underwater drilling equipment.

FOR CRITICAL THINKING
As Chevron adds more units of labor to the extraction of oil in different areas beneath the Gulf, what ultimately must happen to marginal physical product?

Short-Run Costs to the Firm

You will see that costs are the extension of the production ideas just presented. Let's consider the costs the firm faces in the short run. To make this example simple, assume that there are only two factors of production, capital and labor. Our definition of the short run will be the time during which capital is fixed but labor is variable.

In the short run, a firm incurs certain types of costs. We label all costs incurred **total costs.** Then we break total costs down into total fixed costs and total variable costs, which we will explain shortly. Therefore,

Total costs (TC) = total fixed costs (TFC) + total variable costs (TVC)

Remember that these total costs include both explicit and implicit costs, including the normal rate of return on investment.

After we have looked at the elements of total costs, we will find out how to compute average and marginal costs.

Total costs
The sum of total fixed costs and total variable costs.

Total Fixed Costs

Let's look at an ongoing business such as Apple. The decision makers in that corporate giant can look around and see big machines, thousands of parts, huge buildings, and a multitude of other components of plant and equipment that have already been acquired and are in place. Apple has to take into account expenses to replace some worn-out equipment, no matter how many digital devices it produces. The opportunity costs of any fixed resources that Apple owns will all be the same regardless of the rate of output. In the short run, these costs are the same for Apple no matter how many digital devices it produces.

We also have to point out that the opportunity cost (or normal rate of return) of capital must be included along with other costs. Remember that we are dealing in the short run, during which capital is fixed. This leads us to a very straightforward definition of fixed costs: All costs that do not vary—that is, all costs that do not depend on the rate of production—are called **fixed costs.**

Let's now take as an example the fixed costs incurred by a producer of magneto optical (MO) disks used with digital devices. This firm's total fixed costs will usually include the cost of the rent for its plant and equipment and the insurance it has to pay. We see in panel (a) of Figure 22-2 on the next page that total fixed costs per hour are $10. In panel (b), these total fixed costs are represented by the horizontal line at $10 per hour. They are invariant to changes in the daily output of MO disks—no matter how many are produced, fixed costs will remain at $10 per hour.

Fixed costs
Costs that do not vary with output. Fixed costs typically include such expenses as rent on a building. These costs are fixed for a certain period of time (in the long run, though, they are variable).

Total Variable Costs

Total **variable costs** are costs whose magnitude varies with the rate of production. Wages are an obvious variable cost. The more the firm produces, the more labor it has to hire. Therefore, the more wages it has to pay. Parts are another variable cost. To manufacture MO disks, for example, ferromagnetic material must be bought. The more MO disks that are made, the more ferromagnetic material that must be bought. A portion of

Variable costs
Costs that vary with the rate of production. They include wages paid to workers and purchases of materials.

Cost of Production: An Example

In panel (a), the derivations of columns 4 through 9 are given in parentheses in each column heading. For example, in column 6, average variable costs are derived by dividing column 3, total variable costs, by column 1, total output per hour. Note that marginal cost (MC) in panel (c) intersects average variable costs (AVC) at the latter's minimum point. Also, MC intersects average total costs (ATC) at that latter's minimum point. It is a little more difficult to see that MC equals AVC and ATC at their respective minimum points in panel (a) because we are using discrete one-unit changes. You can see, though, that the marginal cost of going from 4 units per hour to 5 units per hour is $2 and increases to $3 when we move to 6 units per hour. Somewhere in between it equals AVC of $2.60, which is in fact the minimum average variable cost. The same analysis holds for ATC, which hits its respective minimum at 7 units per day at $4.28 per unit. MC goes from $4 to $5 and just equals ATC somewhere in between.

Panel (a)

(1) Total Output (Q/hour)	(2) Total Fixed Costs (TFC)	(3) Total Variable Costs (TVC)	(4) Total Costs (TC) $(4) = (2) + (3)$	(5) Average Fixed Costs (AFC) $(5) = (2) \div (1)$	(6) Average Variable Costs (AVC) $(6) = (3) \div (1)$	(7) Average Total Costs (ATC) $(7) = (4) \div (1)$	(8) Total Costs (TC) (4)	(9) Marginal Cost (MC) $(9) = \dfrac{\text{Change in (8)}}{\text{Change in (1)}}$
0	$10	$ 0	$10	—	—	—	$10	
								$5
1	10	5	15	$10.00	$5.00	$15.00	15	
								3
2	10	8	18	5.00	4.00	9.00	18	
								2
3	10	10	20	3.33	3.33	6.67	20	
								1
4	10	11	21	2.50	2.75	5.25	21	
								2
5	10	13	23	2.00	2.60	4.60	23	
								3
6	10	16	26	1.67	2.67	4.33	26	
								4
7	10	20	30	1.43	2.86	4.28	30	
								5
8	10	25	35	1.25	3.12	4.38	35	
								6
9	10	31	41	1.11	3.44	4.56	41	
								7
10	10	38	48	1.00	3.80	4.80	48	
								8
11	10	46	56	.91	4.18	5.09	56	

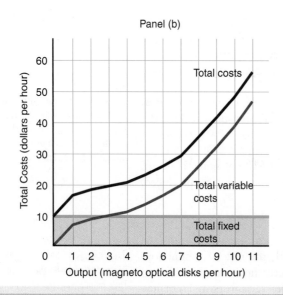

Panel (b)

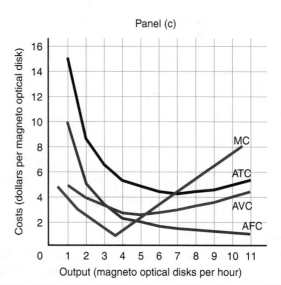

Panel (c)

the rate of depreciation (wear and tear) on machines that are used in the assembly process can also be considered a variable cost if depreciation depends partly on how long and how intensively the machines are used. Total variable costs are given in column 3 in panel (a) of Figure 22-2 on the facing page. These are translated into the total variable cost curve in panel (b). Notice that the total variable cost curve lies below the total cost curve by the vertical distance of $10. This vertical distance of course, represents, total fixed costs.

What new training methods are allowing the U.S. Army to reduce its total variable costs?

YOU ARE THERE

To consider how a trucking firm is using software simulations to reduce its total fixed and variable costs, take a look at **Cutting Costs by Replacing Pilot Projects with Simulations** on page 501.

POLICY EXAMPLE

How the U.S. Army Uses Virtual Warfare to Cut Variable Costs

For the U.S. Army, keeping soldiers in top training form for fighting actual battles has long required the conduct of war games. Every practice battle, though, has entailed costly wear and tear on equipment, used up ammunition, and caused inadvertent injuries to personnel. As a result, the variable costs of training soldiers in the art of warfare have been substantial.

To reduce its training expenses, the Army is turning to digital devices such as smartphones and tablet devices. For training exercises intended mainly to reinforce individual responsibilities and principles of unit coordination, the Army is keeping most equipment in storage and reducing physical demands on soldiers. Instead, it is arming soldiers with digital

devices on which they can simulate field exercises via electronic games, apps, and avatars. This approach has enabled the Army to decrease considerably the number of war games conducted with fully equipped forces and, hence, the expenses of training its soldiers. In this way, the Army has slashed its variable costs.

FOR CRITICAL THINKING

Why is it that in the short run, military leaders view mechanized equipment as fixed inputs but regard soldiers as variable inputs that generate variable costs?

Short-Run Average Cost Curves

In panel (b) of Figure 22-2, we see total costs, total variable costs, and total fixed costs. Now we want to look at average cost. With the average cost concept, we are measuring cost per unit of output. It is a matter of simple arithmetic to figure the averages of these three cost concepts. We can define them as follows:

$$\text{Average total costs (ATC)} = \frac{\text{total costs (TC)}}{\text{output } (Q)}$$

$$\text{Average variable costs (AVC)} = \frac{\text{total variable costs (TVC)}}{\text{output } (Q)}$$

$$\text{Average fixed costs (AFC)} = \frac{\text{total fixed costs (TFC)}}{\text{output } (Q)}$$

The arithmetic is done in columns 5, 6, and 7 in panel (a) of Figure 22-2. The numerical results are translated into a graphical format in panel (c). Because total costs (TC) equal variable costs (TVC) plus fixed costs (TFC), the difference between average total costs (ATC) and average variable costs (AVC) will always be identical to average fixed costs (AFC). That means that average total costs and average variable costs move together as output expands.

Now let's see what we can observe about the three average cost curves in Figure 22-2.

AVERAGE FIXED COSTS (AFC) **Average fixed costs** continue to fall throughout the output range. In fact, if we were to continue panel (c) of Figure 22-2 farther to the right, we would find that average fixed costs would get closer and closer to the horizontal axis. That is because total fixed costs remain constant. As we divide this fixed number by a larger and larger number of units of output, the resulting AFC becomes smaller and smaller. In business, this is called "spreading the overhead."

Average fixed costs
Total fixed costs divided by the number of units produced.

Average variable costs
Total variable costs divided by the number of units produced.

AVERAGE VARIABLE COSTS (AVC) We assume a particular form of the curve for **average variable costs.** The form that it takes is U-shaped: First it falls; then it starts to rise. (It is possible for the AVC curve to take other shapes in the long run.)

Average total costs
Total costs divided by the number of units produced; sometimes called *average per-unit total costs.*

AVERAGE TOTAL COSTS (ATC) This curve has a shape similar to that of the AVC curve. Nevertheless, it falls even more dramatically in the beginning and rises more slowly after it has reached a minimum point. It falls and then rises because **average total costs** are the vertical summation of the AFC curve and the AVC curve. Thus, when AFC and AVC are both falling, ATC must fall too. At some point, however, AVC starts to increase while AFC continues to fall. Once the increase in the AVC curve outweighs the decrease in the AFC curve, the ATC curve will start to increase and will develop a U shape, just like the AVC curve.

How are oil companies around the globe reducing the average total cost of removing leftover oil in aging oil fields?

INTERNATIONAL EXAMPLE

Using Cheap Power from the Sun to Reduce Average Total Costs

From the oil fields of Texas to the sands of Saudi Arabia, extracting small pools of oil that remain after completion of traditional drilling operations could be accomplished only at a very high average total cost. To reduce these per-unit costs of removing oil from old sites throughout the world, a number of firms are now utilizing the power of reflected heat waves from the sun.

The companies use inexpensive aluminum mirrors to reflect and focus energy waves from the sun into networks of pipes. The solar waves heat water within the pipes, which gushes out as steam into pockets containing remaining pools of oil. The steam, in turn, pushes the oil out of these pockets, and other equipment collects the oil and transfers it to barrels for transport to refining facilities. Because this oil collection method is much less costly than sinking drills into old fields time and time again, it greatly reduces the average total cost of extracting oil from the fields.

FOR CRITICAL THINKING

If using solar energy to heat steam reduces the per-unit cost of extracting each possible quantity of oil, what happens to the average total cost curve?

Marginal Cost

We have stated repeatedly that the basis of decisions is always on the margin—movement in economics is always determined at the margin. This dictum also holds true within the firm. Firms, according to the analysis we use to predict their behavior, are very concerned with their **marginal costs.** Because the term *marginal* means "additional" or "incremental" (or "decremental," too) here, *marginal costs* refer to costs that result from a one-unit change in the production rate. For example, if the production of 10 magneto optical (MO) disks per hour costs a firm $48 and the production of 11 MO disks costs $56 per hour, the marginal cost of producing 11 rather than 10 MO disks per hour is $8.

Marginal costs
The change in total costs due to a one-unit change in production rate.

Marginal costs can be measured by using the formula

$$\text{Marginal cost} = \frac{\text{change in total cost}}{\text{change in output}}$$

We show the marginal costs of production of MO disks per hour in column 9 of panel (a) in Figure 22-2 on page 490, computed according to the formula just given. In our example, we have changed output by one unit every time, so the denominator in that particular formula always equals one.

This marginal cost schedule is shown graphically in panel (c) of Figure 22-2. Just as average variable costs and average total costs initially decrease with rising output and then increase, it must also be true that marginal cost first falls with greater output and then rises. The U shape of the marginal cost curve is a result of increasing and then diminishing marginal product. At lower levels of output, the marginal cost curve declines.

The reasoning is that as marginal physical product increases with each addition of output, the marginal cost of this last unit of output must fall.

Conversely, when diminishing marginal product sets in, marginal physical product decreases (and eventually becomes negative). It follows that the marginal cost must rise when the marginal product begins its decline. These relationships are clearly reflected in the geometry of panels (b) and (c) of Figure 22-2 on page 490.

In summary:

> *Over the range of output along which marginal physical product rises, marginal cost will fall. At the output at which marginal physical product starts to fall (after reaching the point of diminishing marginal product), marginal cost will begin to rise.*

The Relationship between Average and Marginal Costs

Let us now examine the relationship between average costs and marginal costs. There is always a definite relationship between averages and marginals. Consider the example of 10 football players with an average weight of 250 pounds. An eleventh player is added. His weight is 300 pounds. That represents the marginal weight. What happens now to the average weight of the team? It must increase. That is, when the marginal player weighs more than the average, the average must increase. Likewise, if the marginal player weighs less than 250 pounds, the average weight will decrease.

AVERAGE VARIABLE COSTS AND MARGINAL COSTS There is a similar relationship between average variable costs and marginal costs. As shown in Figure 22-2, when marginal costs are less than average costs, the latter must fall. Conversely, when marginal costs are greater than average costs, the latter must rise.

When you think about it, the relationship makes sense. The only way average variable costs can fall is if the extra cost of the marginal unit produced is less than the average variable cost of all the preceding units. For example, if the average variable cost for two units of production is $4.00 a unit, the only way for the average variable cost of three units to be less than that of two units is for the variable costs attributable to the last unit—the marginal cost—to be less than the average of the past units. In this particular case, if average variable cost falls to $3.33 a unit, total variable cost for the three units would be three times $3.33, or almost exactly $10.00. Total variable cost for two units is two times $4.00 (average variable cost), or $8.00. The marginal cost is therefore $10.00 minus $8.00, or $2.00, which is less than the average variable cost of $3.33.

A similar type of computation can be carried out for rising average variable costs. The only way average variable costs can rise is if the average variable cost of additional units is more than that for units already produced. But the incremental cost is the marginal cost. In this particular case, the marginal costs have to be higher than the average variable costs.

AVERAGE TOTAL COSTS AND MARGINAL COSTS There is also a relationship between marginal costs and average total costs. Remember that average total cost is equal to total costs divided by the number of units produced. Also remember that marginal cost does not include any fixed costs. Fixed costs are, by definition, fixed and cannot influence marginal costs. Our example can therefore be repeated substituting *average total costs* for *average variable costs.*

These rising and falling relationships can be seen in panel (c) of Figure 22-2, where MC intersects AVC and ATC at their respective minimum points.

Minimum Cost Points

At what rate of output of MO disks per hour does our representative firm experience the minimum average total costs? Column 7 in panel (a) of Figure 22-2 shows that the minimum average total cost is $4.28, which occurs at an output rate of seven MO disks per hour. We can also find this minimum cost by finding the point in panel (c) of

Figure 22-2 on page 490 where the marginal cost curve intersects the average total cost curve. This should not be surprising. When marginal cost is below average total cost, average total cost falls. When marginal cost is above average total cost, average total cost rises. At the point where average total cost is neither falling nor rising, marginal cost must then be equal to average total cost. When we represent this graphically, the marginal cost curve will intersect the average total cost curve at the latter's minimum.

The same analysis applies to the intersection of the marginal cost curve and the average variable cost curve. When are average variable costs at a minimum? According to panel (a) of Figure 22-2, average variable costs are at a minimum of $2.60 at an output rate of five MO disks per hour. This is where the marginal cost curve intersects the average variable cost curve in panel (c) of Figure 22-2.

QUICK QUIZ   See page 506 for the answers. Review concepts from this section in MyEconLab.

Total costs equal total _____ costs plus total _____ costs. Fixed costs are those that do not vary with the rate of production. Variable costs are those that do vary with the rate of production.

_____ total costs equal total costs divided by output (_____ = TC/Q).

Average _____ costs equal total variable costs divided by output (_____ = TVC/Q).

Average _____ costs equal total fixed costs divided by output (_____ = TVC/Q).

_____ cost equals the change in _____ cost divided by the change in output (_____ = Δ_____/ΔQ, where the Greek letter Δ, delta, means "change in").

The marginal cost curve intersects the _____ point of the average total cost curve and the _____ point of the average variable cost curve.

The Relationship between Diminishing Marginal Product and Cost Curves

There is a unique relationship between output and the shape of the various cost curves we have drawn. Let's consider mobile wireless account services and the relationship between marginal cost and diminishing marginal physical product shown in panel (a) of Figure 22-3 on the facing page. It turns out that if wage rates are constant, the shape of the marginal cost curve in panel (d) of Figure 22-3 is both a reflection of and a consequence of the law of diminishing marginal product.

Marginal Cost and Marginal Physical Product

Let's assume that each unit of labor can be purchased at a constant price. Further assume that labor is the only variable input. We see that as more workers are hired, marginal physical product first rises and then falls. The marginal cost of each extra unit of output will first fall as long as marginal physical product is rising, and then it will rise as long as marginal physical product is falling. Recall that marginal cost is defined as

$$MC = \frac{\text{change in total cost}}{\text{change in output}}$$

Because the price of labor is assumed to be constant, the change in total cost depends solely on the unchanged price of labor, W. The change in output is simply the marginal physical product (MPP) of the one-unit increase in labor. Therefore, we see that

$$\text{Marginal cost} = \frac{W}{\text{MPP}}$$

Panel (a)

(1) Labor Input	(2) Total Product (number of mobile wireless accounts serviced per week)	(3) Average Physical Product (accounts per technician) (3) = (2) ÷ (1)	(4) Marginal Physical Product	(5) Average Variable Cost (5) = W ($1,000) ÷ (3)	(6) Marginal Cost (6) = W ($1,000) ÷ (4)
0	0	—	—	—	—
1	50	50	50	$20.00	$20.00
2	110	55	60	18.18	16.67
3	180	60	70	16.67	14.29
4	240	60	60	16.67	16.67
5	290	58	50	17.24	20.00
6	330	55	40	18.18	25.00
7	360	51	30	19.61	33.33

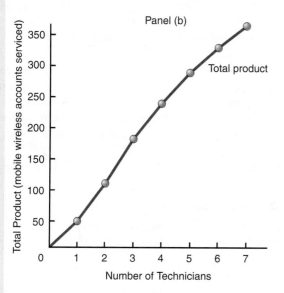

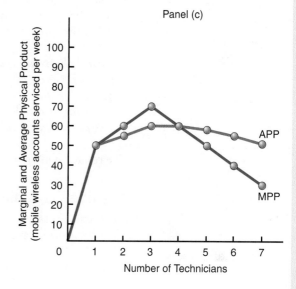

FIGURE 22-3

The Relationship between Output and Costs

As the number of skilled technicians increases, the total number of mobile wireless accounts serviced each week rises, as shown in panels (a) and (b). In panel (c), marginal physical product (MPP) first rises and then falls. Average physical product (APP) follows. The near mirror image of panel (c) is shown in panel (d), in which MC and AVC first fall and then rise.

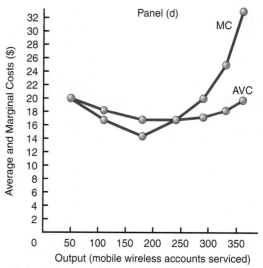

This means that initially, when marginal physical product is increasing, marginal cost falls (we are dividing W by increasingly larger numbers), and later, when marginal product is falling, marginal cost must increase (we are dividing W by smaller numbers). So, as marginal physical product increases, marginal cost decreases, and as marginal physical product decreases, marginal cost must increase. Thus, when marginal physical product reaches its maximum, marginal cost necessarily reaches its minimum.

An Illustration

To illustrate this, let's return to Figure 22-1 on page 486 and consider specifically panel (a). Assume that a skilled worker assembling computer servers is paid $1,000 a week. When we go from zero labor input to one unit, output increases by 10 computer servers. Each of those 10 servers has a marginal cost of $100. Now the second unit of labor is hired, and this individual costs $1,000 per week. Output increases by 16. Thus, the marginal cost is $1,000 \div 16 = \$62.50$. We continue the experiment. We see that adding another unit of labor yields only 10 additional computer servers, so marginal cost starts to rise again back to $100. The following unit of labor yields a marginal physical product of only 8, so marginal cost becomes $1,000 \div 8 = \$125$.

All of the foregoing can be restated in relatively straightforward terms:

> *Firms' short-run cost curves are a reflection of the law of diminishing marginal product. Given any constant price of the variable input, marginal costs decline as long as the marginal physical product of the variable resource is rising. At the point at which marginal product begins to diminish, marginal costs begin to rise as the marginal physical product of the variable input begins to decline.*

The result is a marginal cost curve that slopes down, hits a minimum, and then slopes up.

Average Costs and Average Physical Product

Of course, average total costs and average variable costs are affected. The ATC and AVC curves will have their familiar U shape in the short run. Recall that

$$\text{AVC} = \frac{\text{total variable costs}}{\text{total output}}$$

As we move from zero labor input to one unit in panel (a) of Figure 22-1 on page 486, output increases from zero to 10 computer servers. The total variable costs are the price per worker, W ($1,000), times the number of workers (1). Because the average product (AP) of one worker (column 3) is 10, we can write the total product, 10, as the average product, 10, times the number of workers, 1. Thus, we see that

$$\text{AVC} = \frac{\$1,000 \times 1}{10 \times 1} = \frac{\$1,000}{10} = \frac{W}{\text{AP}}$$

From column 3 in panel (a) of Figure 22-1, we see that the average product increases, reaches a maximum, and then declines. Because AVC = W/AP, average variable cost decreases as average product increases, and increases as average product decreases. AVC reaches its minimum when average product reaches its maximum. Furthermore, because ATC = AVC + AFC, the average total cost curve inherits the relationship between the average variable cost and diminishing marginal product.

To illustrate, consider a firm that employs skilled technicians to provide mobile wireless services within a given geographic area. In panel (a) of Figure 22-3 on the previous page, column 2 shows the total number of mobile wireless accounts serviced as the number of technicians increases. Notice that the total product first increases at an increasing rate and later increases at a decreasing rate. This is reflected in column 4, which shows that the marginal physical product increases at first and then falls. The average physical product too first rises and then falls. The marginal and average physical products are graphed in panel (c) of Figure 22-3 on page 495.

Our immediate interest here is the average variable and marginal costs. Because we can define average variable cost as $1,000/AP (assuming that the wage paid is constant at $1,000), as the average product rises from 50 to 55 to 60 mobile wireless accounts, the average variable cost falls from $20.00 to $18.18 to $16.67. Conversely, as average product falls from 60 to 51, average variable cost rises from $16.67 to $19.61. Likewise, because marginal cost can also be defined as W/MPP, we see that as marginal physical product rises from 50 to 70, marginal cost falls from $20.00 to $14.29. As marginal physical product falls to 30, marginal cost rises to $33.33. These relationships are also expressed in panels (b), (c), and (d) of Figure 22-3.

Long-Run Cost Curves

The long run is defined as a time period during which full adjustment can be made to any change in the economic environment. Thus, in the long run, *all* factors of production are variable. Long-run curves are sometimes called *planning curves*, and the long run is sometimes called the **planning horizon.** We start our analysis of long-run cost curves by considering a single firm contemplating the construction of a single plant. The firm has three alternative plant sizes from which to choose on the planning horizon. Each particular plant size generates its own short-run average total cost curve. Now that we are talking about the difference between long-run and short-run cost curves, we will label all short-run curves with an S and long-run curves with an L. Short-run average (total) costs will be labeled SAC. Long-run average cost curves will be labeled LAC.

Panel (a) of Figure 22-4 on the following page shows short-run average cost curves for three successively larger plants. Which is the optimal size to build, if we can only choose among these three? That depends on the anticipated normal, sustained rate of output per time period. Assume for a moment that the anticipated normal, sustained rate is Q_1. If a plant of size 1 is built, average cost will be C_1. If a plant of size 2 is built, we see on SAC_2 that average cost will be C_2, which is greater than C_1. Thus, if the anticipated rate of output is Q_1, the appropriate plant size is the one from which SAC_1 was derived.

If the anticipated sustained rate of output per time period increases from Q_1 to a higher level such as Q_2, however, and a plant of size 1 is selected, average cost will be C_4. If a plant of size 2 is chosen, average cost will be C_3, which is clearly less than C_4.

In choosing the appropriate plant size for a single-plant firm during the planning horizon, the firm will pick the size whose short-run average cost curve generates an average cost that is lowest for the expected rate of output.

Long-Run Average Cost Curve

If we now assume that the entrepreneur faces an infinite number of choices of plant sizes in the long run, we can conceive of an infinite number of SAC curves similar to the three in panel (a) of Figure 22-4. We are not able, of course, to draw an infinite number, but we have drawn quite a few in panel (b) of Figure 22-4. We then draw the "envelope" to all these various short-run average cost curves. The resulting envelope is the **long-run average cost curve.** This long-run average cost curve is sometimes called the **planning curve,** for it represents the various average costs attainable at the planning stage of the firm's decision making. It represents the locus (path) of points giving the least unit cost of producing any given rate of output.

Note that the LAC curve is *not* tangent to each individual SAC curve at the latter's minimum points, except at the minimum point of the LAC curve. Then and only then are minimum long-run average costs equal to minimum short-run average costs.

Planning horizon
The long run, during which all inputs are variable.

Long-run average cost curve
The locus of points representing the minimum unit cost of producing any given rate of output, given current technology and resource prices.

Planning curve
The long-run average cost curve.

FIGURE 22-4

Preferable Plant Size and the Long-Run Average Cost Curve

If the anticipated sustained rate of output per unit time period is Q_1, the optimal plant to build is the one corresponding to SAC_1 in panel (a) because average cost is lower, at C_1. If the sustained rate of output increases toward the higher level Q_2, however, it will be more profitable to have a plant size corresponding to SAC_2 at $AC = C_3$. If we draw all the possible short-run average cost curves that correspond to different plant sizes and then draw the envelope (a curve tangent to each member of a set of curves) to these various curves, SAC_1–SAC_8, we obtain the long-run average cost (LAC) curve as shown in panel (b).

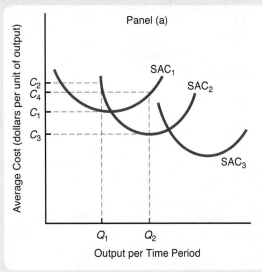
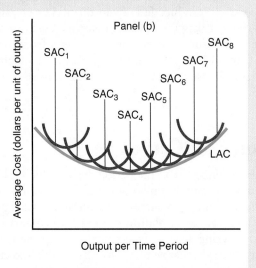

Why the Long-Run Average Cost Curve Is U-Shaped

Notice that the long-run average cost curve, LAC, in panel (b) of Figure 22-4 above is U-shaped, similar to the U shape of the short-run average cost curve developed earlier in this chapter. The reason behind the U shape of the two curves is not the same, however. The short-run average cost curve is U-shaped because of the law of diminishing marginal product. But the law cannot apply to the long run, because in the long run, all factors of production are variable. There is no point of diminishing marginal product because there is no fixed factor of production.

Why, then, do we see the U shape in the long-run average cost curve? The reasoning has to do with economies of scale, constant returns to scale, and diseconomies of scale. When the firm is experiencing **economies of scale,** the long-run average cost curve slopes downward—an increase in scale and production leads to a fall in unit costs. When the firm is experiencing **constant returns to scale,** the long-run average cost curve is at its minimum point, such that an increase in scale of production does not change unit costs. When the firm is experiencing **diseconomies of scale,** the long-run average cost curve slopes upward—an increase in scale and production increases unit costs. These three sections of the long-run average cost curve are broken up into panels (a), (b), and (c) in Figure 22-5 on the facing page.

Reasons for Economies of Scale

We shall examine three of the many reasons why a firm might be expected to experience economies of scale: specialization, the dimensional factor, and improvements in productive equipment.

Economies of scale
Decreases in long-run average costs resulting from increases in output.

Constant returns to scale
No change in long-run average costs when output increases.

Diseconomies of scale
Increases in long-run average costs that occur as output increases.

FIGURE 22-5

Economies of Scale, Constant Returns to Scale, and Diseconomies of Scale Shown with the Long-Run Average Cost Curve

The long-run average cost curve will fall when there are economies of scale, as shown in panel (a). It will be constant (flat) when the firm is experiencing constant returns to scale, as shown in panel (b). It will rise when the firm is experiencing diseconomies of scale, as shown in panel (c).

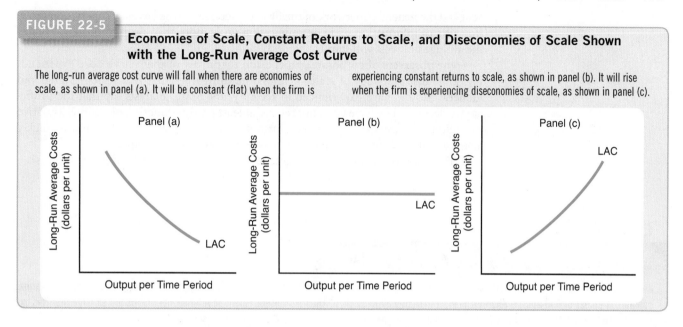

SPECIALIZATION As a firm's scale of operation increases, the opportunities for specialization in the use of resource inputs also increase. This is sometimes called *increased division of tasks* or *operations*. Cost reductions generated by productivity enhancements from such division of labor or increased specialization are well known. When we consider managerial staffs, we also find that larger enterprises may be able to put together more highly specialized staffs.

DIMENSIONAL FACTOR Large-scale firms often require proportionately less input per unit of output simply because certain inputs do not have to be physically doubled in order to double the output. Consider an oil-storage firm's cost of storing oil. The cost of storage is related to the cost of steel that goes into building the storage container. The amount of steel required, however, goes up less than in proportion to the volume (storage capacity) of the container (because the volume of a container increases more than proportionately with its surface area).

IMPROVEMENTS IN PRODUCTIVE EQUIPMENT The larger the scale of the enterprise, the more the firm is able to take advantage of larger-volume (output capacity) types of machinery. Small-scale operations may not be able to profitably use large-volume machines that can be more efficient per unit of output. Also, smaller firms often cannot use technologically more advanced machinery because they are unable to spread out the high cost of such sophisticated equipment over a large output.

For any of these three reasons, the firm may experience economies of scale, which means that equal percentage increases in output result in a decrease in average cost. Thus, output can double, but total costs will less than double. Hence, average cost falls. Note that the factors listed for causing economies of scale are all *internal* to the firm. They do not depend on what other firms are doing or what is happening in the economy.

Why a Firm Might Experience Diseconomies of Scale

One of the basic reasons that a firm can expect to run into diseconomies of scale is that there are limits to the efficient functioning of management. This is so because larger levels of output imply successively larger *plant* size, which in turn implies successively larger *firm* size. Thus, as the level of output increases, more people must be hired, and the firm gets bigger. As this happens, however, the support, supervisory, and administrative staff and the general paperwork of the firm all increase. As the layers of supervision grow, the costs of information and communication grow more than proportionately. Hence, the average unit cost will start to increase.

Some observers of corporate giants claim that many of them have been experiencing some diseconomies of scale. Witness the difficulties that firms such as Dell and General Motors have experienced in recent years. Some analysts say that the profitability declines they have encountered are at least partly a function of their size relative to their smaller, more flexible competitors, which can make decisions more quickly and then take advantage of changing market conditions more rapidly.

Why is American Airlines seeking to shrink the long-run scale of its operations?

EXAMPLE

Diseconomies of Scale at One of the World's Top Airlines

American Airlines is the world's fourth largest airline company. The firm operates in excess of 650 aircraft and flies to more than 650 airports. It also operates at a higher long-run cost per passenger-mile flown than most other airlines. The reason is that its scale is so large. This fact explains why the company is contemplating the sell-off of regional airline routes operated by its American Eagle subsidiary. Furthermore, the airline is working toward reducing the number of routes flown by its fleet of remaining aircraft—a fleet whose size the firm also aims to shrink. Thus, at present American Airlines' operations are so large that it is experiencing diseconomies of scale.

FOR CRITICAL THINKING
Is American Airlines currently operating to the left or right of the minimum point of its long-run average cost curve?

Minimum Efficient Scale

Economists and statisticians have obtained actual data on the relationship between changes in all inputs and changes in average cost. It turns out that for many industries, the long-run average cost curve does not resemble the curve shown in panel (b) of Figure 22-4 on page 498. Rather, it more closely resembles Figure 22-6 below. What you observe there is a small portion of declining long-run average costs (economies of scale) and then a wide range of outputs over which the firm experiences relatively constant economies of scale.

FIGURE 22-6

Minimum Efficient Scale

This long-run average cost curve reaches a minimum point at *A*. After that point, long-run average costs remain horizontal, or constant, and then rise at some later rate of output. Point *A* is called the minimum efficient scale for the firm because that is the point at which it reaches minimum costs. It is the lowest rate of output at which average long-run costs are minimized. At point *B*, diseconomies of scale arise, so long-run average cost begins to increase with further increases in output.

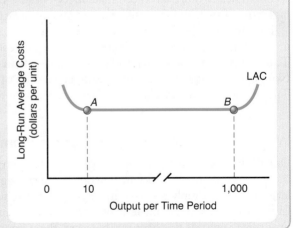

At the output rate when economies of scale end and constant economies of scale start, the **minimum efficient scale (MES)** for the firm is encountered. It occurs at point *A*. The minimum efficient scale is defined as the lowest rate of output at which long-run average costs are minimized. In any industry with a long-run average cost curve similar to the one in Figure 22-6 on the facing page, larger firms will have no cost-saving advantage over smaller firms as long as the smaller firms have at least obtained the minimum efficient scale at point *A*.

Minimum efficient scale (MES)
The lowest rate of output per unit time at which long-run average costs for a particular firm are at a minimum.

WHAT IF... the government required firms to reduce their long-run scales of operation to cut overall U.S. energy use?

Requiring companies to cut back on the scales at which they produce goods and services over their planning horizons would compel each firm to operate at a long-run output rate below its minimum efficient scale. As a consequence, each company's average total cost of producing its product would rise above the minimum feasible average total cost. Effectively, therefore, requiring U.S. companies to reduce their long-run operating scales to save energy would force all firms to manufacture goods and provide services at higher costs per unit.

QUICK QUIZ   See page 506 for the answers. Review concepts from this section in MyEconLab.

The _____ run is often called the **planning horizon.** The _____-run average cost curve is the planning curve. It is found by drawing a curve tangent to points on a series of _____-run average cost curves, each corresponding to a different plant size.

The firm can experience **economies of scale, disecono-mies of scale,** or **constant returns to scale,** all according to whether the long-run average cost curve slopes _____, slopes _____, or is _____. Economies of scale refer to what happens to average cost when all factors of production are increased.

We observe economies of scale for a number of reasons, including specialization, improved productive equipment, and the _____ factor, because large-scale firms require proportionately less input per unit of output. The firm may experience _____ of scale primarily because of limits to the efficient functioning of management.

The **minimum efficient scale** occurs at the _____ rate of output at which long-run average costs are _____.

YOU ARE THERE
Cutting Costs by Replacing Pilot Projects with Simulations

For about 70 years, Schneider National, one of the largest U.S. trucking firms, relied on what its managers called pilot projects to evaluate new ideas for methods to cut costs. Such experiments in cost cutting typically required the company to dedicate dozens or even hundreds of drivers to groups that functioned as separate businesses. The company would then evaluate whether pilot projects succeeded in uncovering cost-saving methods of operation. In many cases, however, the company found that costs were higher. As a consequence, efforts to search for means of cutting costs often *raised* the firm's overall expenses.

Ted Gifford, an operations research scientist, has spent two years developing a method of replacing pilot projects. Gifford has faced a daunting task. At any given moment, Schneider has about 10,000 trucks on the road and about 33,000 freight-hauling trailers available for pickup. Its 13,000 drivers work between four days and three weeks at a time, and their schedules require them to spend specified periods on breaks from work. Gifford has succeeded in developing simulation software to replace pilot projects. His work, which required two years to complete, has reduced Schneider's total costs by tens of millions of dollars per year.

Critical Thinking Questions

1. If Gifford's simulations recommend fewer drivers, would this reduce fixed or variable costs?

2. If the simulations recommend fewer truck depots, would this cut fixed or variable costs?

ISSUES & APPLICATIONS

Can Electric Car Production Attain Minimum Efficient Scale?

CONCEPTS APPLIED

▶ Economies of Scale

▶ Long-Run Average Cost Curve

▶ Minimum Efficient Scale

Automakers are actively seeking to reduce the average cost of producing hybrid and all-electric passenger vehicles. Hindering their efforts is the currently high average cost of producing battery packs to power the vehicles.

Ramping Up Battery-Pack Production Scale

The prices of the least expensive hybrid and all-electric vehicles are above $30,000. A significant portion of the per-vehicle cost is the expense of producing battery packs. For the lowest-priced all-electric autos, battery packs account for more than half the expense of producing each vehicle.

To try to reduce the average expense of powering hybrid and all-electric vehicles, auto companies are seeking economies of scale in production of battery packs. The firms are expanding their productive capabilities in hopes of making larger numbers of battery packs per year. They desire to move downward along their long-run average cost curves to the minimum efficient scale of annual production. Toward this end, Nissan is building a battery pack facility in Smyrna, Tennessee, that will be able to produce 200,000 battery packs per year.

An Unattainable Minimum Efficient Scale?

A fundamental problem stands in the way of achieving economies of scale in production of battery packs: A low scale of production of vehicles using the battery packs. Of the more than 12 million U.S. vehicles produced each year, only about 200,000 are hybrid cars, and fewer than 9,000 per year are all-electric autos. Nor are there many existing vehicles with battery packs requiring replacement. Of the more than 250 million registered passenger vehicles in the United States, only about 2.5 million are hybrid cars. Fewer than 40,000 are all-electric autos.

These figures suggest that fewer than 400,000 vehicles per year will require new battery packs. Hence, only two plants of the size of Nissan's Smyrna, Tennessee, plant would be required to produce a sufficient number of auto battery packs for the entire nation. At least five auto companies plan to operate their own battery pack–producing plants, though, suggesting that on average each company would produce only about 80,000 battery packs per year. Thus, no company will likely be able to produce battery packs at the minimum efficient scale. The long-run average cost of producing a battery pack for use in passenger vehicles is likely to remain higher than the minimum feasible level for many years to come.

For Critical Thinking

1. Other things being equal, what will happen to automakers' profits if they are able to sell more vehicles using battery packs and thereby scale up battery production?

2. Why do you suppose that some automakers support the payment of government subsidies to consumers who purchase hybrid and all-electric passenger vehicles?

Web Resources

1. For data on vehicles powered by alternative energy sources, go to www.econtoday.com/chap22.

2. Learn about tax subsidies available to buyers of vehicles that use battery packs at www.econtoday.com/chap22.

MyEconLab

For more questions on this chapter's Issues & Applications, go to MyEconLab. In the Study Plan for this chapter, select Section N: News.

MyEconLab

Here is what you should know after reading this chapter. MyEconLab will help you identify what you know, and where to go when you need to practice.

— WHAT YOU SHOULD KNOW —

— WHERE TO GO TO PRACTICE —

The Short Run versus the Long Run from a Firm's Perspective The short run for a firm is a period during which at least one input, such as plant size, cannot be altered. Inputs that cannot be changed in the short run are fixed inputs, whereas inputs that may be adjusted in the short run are variable inputs. The long run is a period in which a firm may vary all inputs.

short run, 484
plant size, 484
long run, 484

- MyEconLab Study Plan 22.1

The Law of Diminishing Marginal Product The production function is the relationship between inputs and the maximum physical output, or total product, that a firm can produce. Typically, a firm's marginal physical product—the physical output resulting from the addition of one more unit of a variable factor of production—increases with the first few units of the variable input that it employs. Eventually, as the firm adds more and more units of the variable input, the marginal physical product begins to decline. This is the law of diminishing marginal product.

production, 485
production function, 485
average physical product, 486
marginal physical product, 487
law of diminishing marginal product, 487

Key Figure
Figure 22-1, 486

- MyEconLab Study Plans 22.2, 22.3
- Animated Figure 22-1

A Firm's Short-Run Cost Curves The expenses for a firm's fixed inputs are its fixed costs, and the expenses for its variable inputs are variable costs. The total costs of a firm are the sum of its fixed costs and variable costs. Average fixed cost equals total fixed cost divided by total product. Average variable cost equals total variable cost divided by total product, and average total cost equals total cost divided by total product. Finally, marginal cost is the change in total cost resulting from a one-unit change in production.

total costs, 489
fixed costs, 489
variable costs, 489
average fixed costs, 491
average variable costs, 492
average total costs, 492
marginal costs, 492

Key Figure
Figure 22-2, 490

- MyEconLab Study Plans 22.4, 22.5
- Animated Figure 22-2

A Firm's Long-Run Cost Curves Over a firm's long-run, or planning, horizon, it can choose all inputs, including plant size. Thus, it can choose a long-run scale of production along a long-run average cost curve. The long-run average cost curve, which for most firms is U-shaped, is traced out by the short-run average cost curves corresponding to various plant sizes.

planning horizon, 497
long-run average cost curve, 497
planning curve, 497

Key Figures
Figure 22-3, 495
Figure 22-4, 498

- MyEconLab Study Plans 22.6, 22.7
- Animated Figures 22-3, 22-4

MyEconLab continued

WHAT YOU SHOULD KNOW ─────────────────────────── WHERE TO GO TO PRACTICE ───

Economies and Diseconomies of Scale and a Firm's Minimum Efficient Scale Along the downward-sloping range of a firm's long-run average cost curve, the firm experiences economies of scale, meaning that its long-run production costs decline as it raises its output scale. In contrast, along the upward-sloping portion of the long-run average cost curve, the firm encounters diseconomies of scale, so that its long-run costs of production rise as it increases its output scale. The minimum point of the long-run average cost curve occurs at the firm's minimum efficient scale, which is the lowest rate of output at which the firm can achieve minimum long-run average cost.

economies of scale, 498
constant returns to scale, 498
diseconomies of scale, 498
minimum efficient scale
 (MES), 501

Key Figures
Figure 22-5, 499
Figure 22-6, 500

- MyEconLab Study Plans 22.7, 22.8
- Animated Figures 22-5, 22-6

Log in to MyEconLab, take a chapter test, and get a personalized Study Plan that tells you which concepts you understand and which ones you need to review. From there, MyEconLab will give you further practice, tutorials, animations, videos, and guided solutions. For more information, visit www.myeconlab.com

PROBLEMS

All problems are assignable in MyEconLab. Answers to odd-numbered problems appear at the back of the book.

22-1. The academic calendar for a university is August 15 through May 15. A professor commits to a contract that binds her to a teaching position at this university for this period. Based on this information, explain the short run and long run that the professor faces. (See page 484.)

22-2. The short-run production function for a manufacturer of flash memory drives is shown in the table below. Based on this information, answer the following questions. (See pages 486–487.)

Input of Labor (workers per week)	Total Output of Flash Memory Drives
0	0
1	25
2	60
3	85
4	105
5	115
6	120

a. Calculate the average physical product at each quantity of labor.

b. Calculate the marginal physical product of labor at each quantity of labor.

c. At what point does marginal product begin to diminish?

22-3. During the past year, a firm produced 10,000 laptop computers. Its total costs were $5 million, and its fixed costs were $2 million. What are the average variable costs of this firm? (See page 491.)

22-4. During the previous month, a firm produced 250 tablet devices at an average variable cost of $40 and at an average fixed cost of $10. What were the firm's total costs during the month? (See page 491.)

22-5. Just before the firm discussed in Problem 22-4 produced its last tablet device in the previous month, its total costs were $12,425. What was the marginal cost incurred by the firm in producing the final tablet device that month? (See page 492.)

22-6. The cost structure of a manufacturer of microchips is described in the table on the facing page. The firm's fixed costs equal $10 per day. Calculate the average variable cost, average fixed cost, and average total cost at each output level. (See pages 489–492.)

Output (microchips per day)	Total Cost of Output ($ thousands)
0	10
25	60
50	95
75	150
100	220
125	325
150	465

22-7. The diagram below displays short-run cost curves for a facility that produces liquid crystal display (LCD) screens for cell phones: (See page 491.)

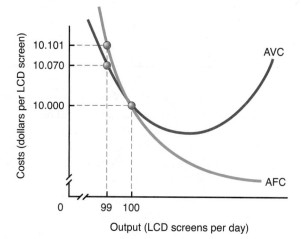

a. What are the daily total fixed costs of producing LCD screens?

b. What are the total variable costs of producing 100 LCD screens per day?

c. What are the total costs of producing 100 LCD screens per day?

d. What is the marginal cost of producing 100 LCD screens instead of 99? (Hint: To answer this question, you must first determine the total costs—or, alternatively, the total variable costs—of producing 99 LCD screens.)

22-8. A watch manufacturer finds that at 1,000 units of output, its marginal costs are below average total costs. If it produces an additional watch, will its average total costs rise, fall, or stay the same? (See page 493.)

22-9. At its current short-run level of production, a firm's average variable costs equal $20 per unit, and its average fixed costs equal $30 per unit. Its total costs at this production level equal $2,500. (See page 491.)

a. What is the firm's current output level?

b. What are its total variable costs at this output level?

c. What are its total fixed costs?

22-10. In an effort to reduce their total costs, many companies are now replacing paychecks with payroll cards, which are stored-value cards onto which the companies can download employees' wages and salaries electronically. If the only factor of production that a company varies in the short run is the number of hours worked by people already on its payroll, would shifting from paychecks to payroll cards reduce the firm's total fixed costs or its total variable costs? Explain your answer. (See page 489.)

22-11. During autumn months, passenger railroads across the globe deal with a condition called slippery rail. It results from a combination of water, leaf oil, and pressure from the train's weight, which creates a slippery black ooze that prevents trains from gaining traction. (See page 489.)

a. One solution for slippery rail is to cut back trees from all of a rail firm's rail network on a regular basis, thereby helping prevent the problem from developing. If incurred, would this railroad expense be a better example of a fixed cost or a variable cost? Why?

b. Another way of addressing slippery rail is to wait until it begins to develop. Then the company purchases sand and dumps it on the slippery tracks so that trains already en route within the rail network can proceed. If incurred, would this railroad expense be a better example of a fixed cost or a variable cost? Why?

22-12. In the short run, a firm's total costs of producing 100 units of output equal $10,000. If it produces one more unit, its total costs will increase to $10,150. (See pages 491–492.)

a. What is the marginal cost of the 101st unit of output?

b. What is the firm's average total cost of producing 100 units?

c. What is the firm's average total cost of producing 101 units?

22-13. Suppose that a firm's only variable input is labor, and the constant hourly wage rate is $20 per hour. The last unit of labor hired enabled the firm to increase its hourly production from 250 units to 251 units. What was the marginal cost of producing 251 units of output instead of 250? (See page 492.)

22-14. Suppose that a firm's only variable input is labor. The firm increases the number of employees from four to five, thereby causing weekly output to rise by two units and total costs to increase from $3,000 per week to $3,300 per week. (See page 492.)

a. What is the marginal physical product of hiring five workers instead of four?

b. What is the weekly wage rate earned by the fifth worker?

22-15. Suppose that a company currently employs 1,000 workers and produces 1 million units of output per month. Labor is its only variable input, and the company pays each worker the same monthly wage. The company's current total variable costs equal $2 million. (See pages 493–494.)

a. What are average variable costs at this firm's current output level?

b. What is the average physical product of labor?

c. What monthly wage does the firm pay each worker?

22-16. A manufacturing firm with a single plant is contemplating changing its plant size. It must choose from among seven alternative plant sizes. In the table, plant size A is the smallest it might build, and size G is the largest. Currently, the firm's plant size is B. (See page 498.)

Plant Size	Average Total Cost ($)
A (smallest)	4,250
B	3,600
C	3,100
D	3,100
E	3,100
F	3,250
G (largest)	4,100

a. At plant site B, is this firm currently experiencing economies of scale or diseconomies of scale?

b. What is the firm's minimum efficient scale?

22-17. An electricity-generating company confronts the following long-run average total costs associated with alternative plant sizes. It is currently operating at plant size G. (See page 498.)

Plant Size	Average Total Cost ($)
A (smallest)	2,000
B	1,800
C	1,600
D	1,550
E	1,500
F	1,500
G (largest)	1,500

a. What is this firm's minimum efficient scale?

b. If damage caused by a powerful hurricane generates a reduction in the firm's plant size from its current size to B, would there be a leftward or rightward movement along the firm's long-run average total cost curve?

ECONOMICS ON THE NET

Industry-Level Capital Expenditures In this chapter, you learned about the explicit and implicit costs that firms incur in the process of producing goods and services. This Internet application gives you an opportunity to consider one type of cost—expenditures on capital goods.

Title: U.S. Census Bureau's Annual Capital Expenditures Survey

Navigation: Follow the link at **www.econtoday.com /chap22**, and select the most recent *Annual Capital Spending Report*.

Application Read the introductory summary of the report, and then answer the following questions.

1. What types of business expenditures does the Census Bureau include in this report?

2. Are the inputs that generate these business expenditures more likely to be inputs that firms can vary in the short run or in the long run?

3. Which inputs account for the largest portion of firms' capital expenditures? Why do you suppose this is so?

For Group Discussion and Analysis Review reports for the past several years. Do capital expenditures vary from year to year? What factors might account for such variations? Are there noticeable differences in capital expenditures from industry to industry?

ANSWERS TO QUICK QUIZZES

p. 489: (i) production . . . output; (ii) product; (iii) decreasing . . . output

p. 499: (i) fixed . . . variable; (ii) Average . . . ATC; (iii) variable . . . AVC; (iv) fixed . . . AFC; (v) Marginal . . . total . . . MC . . . TC; (vi) minimum . . . minimum

p. 501: (i) long . . . long . . . short; (ii) downward . . . upward . . . horizontal; (iii) dimensional . . . diseconomies; (iv) lowest . . . minimized

Perfect Competition

23

LEARNING OBJECTIVES

After reading this chapter, you should be able to:

▶ Identify the characteristics of a perfectly competitive market structure

▶ Discuss the process by which a perfectly competitive firm decides how much output to produce

▶ Understand how the short-run supply curve for a perfectly competitive firm is determined

▶ Explain how the equilibrium price is determined in a perfectly competitive market

▶ Describe what factors induce firms to enter or exit a perfectly competitive industry

▶ Distinguish among constant-, increasing-, and decreasing-cost industries based on the shape of the long-run industry supply curve

MyEconLab helps you master each objective and study more efficiently. See end of chapter for details.

ithium has become an increasingly useful input in the production of batteries used to power popular consumer electronics products and digital devices. Consequently, the market demand for this naturally occurring element has increased. Nevertheless, its inflation-adjusted price has generally declined over time. Thus, the term "white gold," commonly used to refer to lithium, is something of a misnomer. What accounts for the falling relative price of lithium in spite of the rising market demand for the element? In this chapter, you will see that in the market for lithium, input prices have trended downward as more firms producing lithium have entered the market. As you will learn, these events, together with the fact that the market for lithium is *perfectly competitive,* explain why the price of lithium has decreased even as demand for the element has increased.

DID YOU KNOW THAT... the world's oldest company that makes wooden pencils recently celebrated its 350th year of operations? In 1662, pencil craftsman Friedrich Staedtler began making pencils in Nuremberg, Germany. This pencil-making firm has been in operation since the market came into existence. During the three and a half centuries since the pencil market's first beginnings, however, many other manufacturers have come and gone. Very low costs of entering and exiting the pencil market made this possible. Combining this fact with others, such as close similarity among most wooden pencils, large numbers of pencil firms, and widely known information about market conditions, suggests that the market for pencils is *perfectly competitive*. In this chapter, you will learn why this is so. In addition, you will learn what perfect competition in the pencil market implies about the determination of the market price and equilibrium quantity of pencils, and the production, costs, revenues, and profits of individual pencil manufacturers.

Characteristics of a Perfectly Competitive Market Structure

Perfect competition
A market structure in which the decisions of *individual* buyers and sellers have no effect on market price.

Perfectly competitive firm
A firm that is such a small part of the total *industry* that it cannot affect the price of the product it sells.

Price taker
A perfectly competitive firm that must take the price of its product as given because the firm cannot influence its price.

We are interested in studying how a firm acting within a perfectly competitive market structure makes decisions about how much to produce. In a situation of **perfect competition,** each firm is such a small part of the total industry that it cannot affect the price of the product in question. That means that each **perfectly competitive firm** in the industry is a **price taker**—the firm takes price as a given, something determined *outside* the individual firm.

What It Means for a Firm to Be a Price Taker

The definition of a competitive firm is obviously idealized, for in one sense the individual firm *has* to set prices. How can we ever have a situation in which firms regard prices as set by forces outside their control? The answer is that even though every firm sets its own prices, a firm in a perfectly competitive situation will find that it will eventually have no customers at all if it sets its price above the competitive price.

The best example is in agriculture. Although the individual farmer can set any price for a bushel of wheat, if that price doesn't coincide with the market price of a bushel of similar-quality wheat, no one will purchase the wheat at a higher price. Nor would the farmer be inclined to reduce revenues by selling below the market price.

Characteristics of Perfect Competition

Let's examine why a firm in a perfectly competitive industry is a price taker.

1. *There are large numbers of buyers and sellers.* When this is the case, the quantity demanded by one buyer or the quantity supplied by one seller is negligible relative to the market quantity. No one buyer or seller has any influence on price.

2. *The product sold by the firms in the industry is homogeneous—that is, indistinguishable across firms.* The product sold by each firm in the industry is a perfect substitute for the product sold by every other firm. Buyers are able to choose from a large number of sellers of a product that the buyers regard as being the same.

3. *Both buyers and sellers have access to all relevant information.* Consumers are able to find out about lower prices charged by competing firms. Firms are able to find out about cost-saving innovations that can lower production costs and prices, and they are able to learn about profitable opportunities in other industries.

4. *Any firm can enter or leave the industry without serious impediments.* Firms in a competitive industry are not hampered in their ability to get resources or reallocate resources. In pursuit of profit-making opportunities, they move labor and capital to whatever business venture gives them their highest expected rate of return on their investment.

The Demand Curve of the Perfect Competitor

When we discussed substitutes in Chapter 19, we pointed out that the more substitutes there are and the more similar they are to the commodity in question, the greater is the price elasticity of demand. Here we assume that the perfectly competitive firm is producing a homogeneous (indistinguishable across all of the industry's firms) commodity that has perfect substitutes. That means that if the individual firm raises its price one penny, it will lose all of its business. This, then, is how we characterize the demand schedule for a perfectly competitive firm: It is the going market price as determined by the forces of market supply and market demand—that is, where the market demand curve intersects the market supply curve. The demand curve for the product of an individual firm in a perfectly competitive industry is perfectly elastic at the going market price. Remember that with a perfectly elastic demand curve, any increase in price leads to zero quantity demanded.

We show the market demand and supply curves in panel (a) of Figure 23-1 below. Their intersection occurs at the price of $5. The commodity in question is magneto optical (MO) disks. Assume for the purposes of this exposition that all of these MO disks are perfect substitutes for all others. At the going market price of $5 apiece, the demand curve for MO disks produced by an individual firm that sells a very, very small part of total industry production is shown in panel (b). At the market price, this firm can sell all the output it wants. At the market price of $5 each, which is where the demand curve for the individual producer lies, consumer demand for the MO disks of that one producer is perfectly elastic.

This can be seen by noting that if the firm raises its price, consumers, who are assumed to know that this supplier is charging more than other producers, will buy elsewhere, and the producer in question will have no sales at all. Thus, the demand curve for that producer is perfectly elastic. We label the individual producer's demand curve *d*, whereas the *market* demand curve is always labeled *D*.

How Much Should the Perfect Competitor Produce?

As we have shown, from the perspective of a perfectly competitive firm deciding how much to produce, the firm has to accept the price of the product as a given. If the firm raises its price, it sells nothing. If it lowers its price, it earns lower revenues per unit

YOU ARE THERE

To contemplate how features of perfect competition often apply to markets for services provided online, take a look at **Looking to Enter a Competitive Online Market? Rent a Desk!** on page 526.

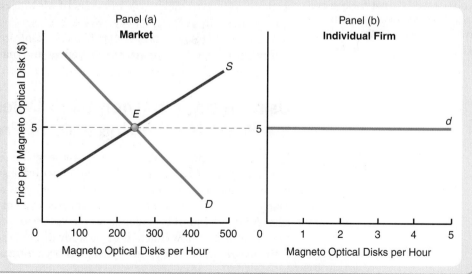

FIGURE 23-1

The Demand Curve for a Producer of Magneto Optical Disks

At $5—where market demand, *D*, and market supply, *S*, intersect—the individual firm faces a perfectly elastic demand curve, *d*. If the firm raises its price even one penny, it will sell no magneto optical disks, measured from its point of view in hourly production, at all. (Notice the difference in the quantities of MO disks represented on the horizontal axes of panels (a) and (b).)

sold than it otherwise could. The firm has one decision left: How much should it produce? We will apply our model of the firm to this question to come up with an answer. We'll use the *profit-maximization model*, which assumes that firms attempt to maximize their total profits—the positive difference between total revenues and total costs. This also means that firms seek to minimize any losses that arise in times when total revenues may be less than total costs.

Total Revenues

Total revenues
The price per unit times the total quantity sold.

Every firm has to consider its *total revenues*. **Total revenues** are defined as the quantity sold multiplied by the price per unit. (They are the same as total receipts from the sale of output.) The perfect competitor must take the price as a given.

Look at Figure 23-2 on the facing page. The information in panel (a) comes from panel (a) of Figure 22-2 on page 490, but we have added some essential columns for our analysis. Column 3 is the market price, *P*, of $5 per MO disk. Column 4 shows the total revenues, or TR, as equal to the market price, *P*, times the total output per hour, or *Q*. Thus, TR = *PQ*.

We are assuming that the market supply and demand schedules intersect at a price of $5 and that this price holds for all the firm's production. We are also assuming that because our maker of MO disks is a small part of the market, it can sell all that it produces at that price. Thus, panel (b) of Figure 23-2 shows the total revenue curve as a straight green line. For every additional MO disk sold, total revenue increases by $5.

Comparing Total Costs with Total Revenues

Total costs are given in column 2 of panel (a) of Figure 23-2 and plotted in panel (b). Remember, the firm's costs always include a normal rate of return on investment. So, whenever we refer to total costs, we are talking *not* about accounting costs but about economic costs. When the total cost curve is above the total revenue curve, the firm is experiencing losses. When total costs are less than total revenues, the firm is making profits.

By comparing total costs with total revenues, we can figure out the number of magneto optical disks the individual competitive firm should produce per hour. Our analysis rests on the assumption that the firm will attempt to maximize total profits. In panel (a) of Figure 23-2, we see that total profits reach a maximum at a production rate of between seven and eight MO disks per hour. We can see this graphically in panel (b) of the figure. The firm will maximize profits where the total revenue curve lies above the total cost curve by the greatest amount. That occurs at a rate of output and sales of between seven and eight MO disks per hour. This rate is called the **profit-maximizing rate of production.** (If output were continuously divisible or there were extremely large numbers of MO disks, we would get a unique profit-maximizing output.)

Profit-maximizing rate of production
The rate of production that maximizes total profits, or the difference between total revenues and total costs. Also, it is the rate of production at which marginal revenue equals marginal cost.

We can also find the profit-maximizing rate of production for the individual competitive firm by looking at marginal revenues and marginal costs.

Using Marginal Analysis to Determine the Profit-Maximizing Rate of Production

It is possible—indeed, preferable—to use marginal analysis to determine the profit-maximizing rate of production. We end up with the same results derived in a different manner, one that focuses more on where decisions are really made—on the margin. Managers examine changes in costs and relate them to changes in revenues. In fact, whether the question is how much more or less to produce, how many more workers to hire or fire, or how much more to study or not study, we compare changes in costs with changes in benefits, where change is occurring at the margin.

Panel (a)

(1) Total Output per Hour (Q)	(2) Total Costs (TC)	(3) Market Price (P)	(4) Total Revenues (TR) (4) = (3) x (1)	(5) Total Profit (TR − TC) (5) = (4) − (2)	(6) Average Total Cost (ATC) (6) = (2) ÷ (1)	(7) Average Variable Cost (AVC)	(8) Marginal Cost (MC) (8) = Change in (2) / Change in (1)	(9) Marginal Revenue (MR) (9) = Change in (4) / Change in (1)
0	$10	$5	$ 0	−$10	—	—		
1	15	5	5	−10	$15.00	$5.00	$5	$5
2	18	5	10	−8	9.00	4.00	3	5
3	20	5	15	−5	6.67	3.33	2	5
4	21	5	20	−1	5.25	2.75	1	5
5	23	5	25	2	4.60	2.60	2	5
6	26	5	30	4	4.33	2.67	3	5
7	30	5	35	**5**	4.28	2.86	4	5
8	35	5	40	**5**	4.38	3.12	5	5
9	41	5	45	4	4.56	3.44	6	5
10	48	5	50	2	4.80	3.80	7	5
11	56	5	55	−1	5.09	4.18	8	5

FIGURE 23-2

Profit Maximization

Profit maximization occurs where marginal revenue equals marginal cost. Panel (a) indicates that this point occurs at a rate of sales of between seven and eight magneto optical disks per hour. In panel (b), we find maximum profits where total revenues exceed total costs by the largest amount. This occurs at a rate of production and sales per hour of seven or eight MO disks. In panel (c), the marginal cost curve, MC, intersects the marginal revenue curve at the same rate of output and sales of somewhere between seven and eight MO disks per hour.

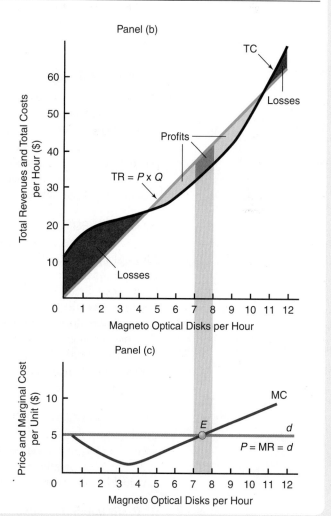

Marginal Revenue

Marginal revenue
The change in total revenues resulting from a one-unit change in output (and sale) of the product in question.

Marginal revenue represents the change in total revenues attributable to changing production of an item by one unit. Hence, a more formal definition of marginal revenue is

$$\text{Marginal revenue} = \frac{\text{change in total revenues}}{\text{change in output}}$$

In a perfectly competitive market, the marginal revenue curve is exactly equivalent to the price line, which is the individual firm's demand curve. Each time the firm produces and sells one more unit, total revenues rise by an amount equal to the (constant) market price of the good. Thus, in Figure 23-1 on page 509, the demand curve, d, for the individual producer is at a price of $5—the price line is coincident with the demand curve. But so is the marginal revenue curve, for marginal revenue in this case also equals $5.

The marginal revenue curve for our competitive producer of MO disks is shown as a line at $5 in panel (c) of Figure 23-2 on the previous page. Notice again that the marginal revenue curve is the price line, which is the firm's demand, or average revenue, curve, d. This equality of MR, P, and d for an individual firm is a general feature of a perfectly competitive industry. The price line shows the quantity that consumers desire to purchase from this firm at each price—which is *any* quantity that the firm provides at the market price—and hence is the demand curve, d, faced by the firm. The market clearing price per unit does not change as the firm varies its output, so the average revenue and marginal revenue also are equal to this price. Thus, MR is identically equal to P along the firm's demand curve.

When Are Profits Maximized?

Now we add the marginal cost curve, MC, taken from column 8 in panel (a) of Figure 23-2. As shown in panel (c) of that figure, because of the law of diminishing marginal product, the marginal cost curve first falls and then starts to rise, eventually intersecting the marginal revenue curve and then rising above it. Notice that the numbers for both the marginal cost schedule, column 8 in panel (a), and the marginal revenue schedule, column 9 in panel (a), are printed *between* the rows on which the quantities appear. This indicates that we are looking at a *change* between one rate of output and the next rate of output.

EQUALIZING MARGINAL REVENUE AND MARGINAL COST In panel (c) of Figure 23-2, the marginal cost curve intersects the marginal revenue curve somewhere between seven and eight MO disks per hour. The firm has an incentive to produce and sell until the amount of the additional revenue received from selling one more MO disk just equals the additional costs incurred for producing and selling that MO disk. This is how the firm maximizes profit. Whenever marginal cost is less than marginal revenue, the firm will always make more profit by increasing production.

Now consider the possibility of producing at an output rate of 10 MO disks per hour. The marginal cost at that output rate is higher than the marginal revenue. The firm would be spending more to produce that additional output than it would be receiving in revenues. It would be foolish to continue producing at this rate.

THE PROFIT-MAXIMIZING OUTPUT RATE But how much should the firm produce? It should produce at point E in panel (c) of Figure 23-2, where the marginal cost curve intersects the marginal revenue curve from below. The firm should continue production until the cost of increasing output by one more unit is just equal to the revenues obtainable from that extra unit. This is a fundamental rule in economics:

Profit maximization occurs at the rate of output at which marginal revenue equals marginal cost.

For a perfectly competitive firm, this rate of output is at the intersection of the demand schedule, d, which is identical to the MR curve, and the marginal cost curve, MC. When MR exceeds MC, each additional unit of output adds more to total revenues than to total costs, so the additional unit should be produced. When MC is greater than MR, each unit produced adds more to total cost than to total revenues, so this unit should not be produced. Therefore, profit maximization occurs when MC equals MR. In our particular example, our profit-maximizing, perfectly competitive producer of MO disks will produce at a rate of between seven and eight MO disks per hour.

QUICK QUIZ See page 531 for the answers. Review concepts from this section in MyEconLab.

Four fundamental characteristics of the market in **perfect competition** are (1) _____ numbers of buyers and sellers, (2) a _____ product, (3) good information in the hands of both buyers and sellers, and (4) _____ exit from and entry into the industry by other firms.

A perfectly competitive firm is a **price taker.** It has _____ control over price and consequently has to take price as a given, but it can sell _____ that it wants at the going market price.

The demand curve for a perfect competitor is perfectly elastic at the going market price. The demand curve is

also the perfect competitor's _____ revenue curve because _____ revenue is defined as the change in total revenue due to a one-unit change in output.

Profit is maximized at the rate of output at which the positive difference between total revenues and total costs is the greatest. This is the same level of output at which marginal _____ equals marginal _____. The perfectly competitive firm produces at an output rate at which marginal cost equals the _____ per unit of output, because MR is always equal to P.

Short-Run Profits

To find what our competitive individual producer of magneto optical disks is making in terms of profits in the short run, we have to add the average total cost curve to panel (c) of Figure 23-2 on page 511. We take the information from column 6 in panel (a) and add it to panel (c) to get Figure 23-3 below. Again the profit-maximizing rate of output is

---

FIGURE 23-3

Measuring Total Profits

Profits are represented by the blue-shaded area. The height of the profit rectangle is given by the difference between average total costs and price ($5), where price is also equal to average revenue. This is found by the vertical difference between the ATC curve and the price, or average revenue, line *d*, at the profit-maximizing rate of output of between seven and eight MO disks per hour.

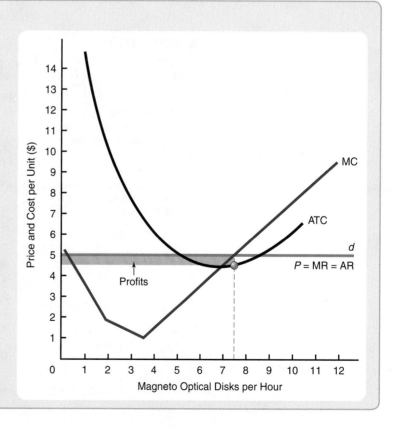

between seven and eight magneto optical disks per hour. If we have production and sales of seven per hour, total revenues will be $35 per hour. Total costs will be $30 MO disks per hour, leaving a profit of $5 per hour. If the rate of output and sales is eight MO disks per hour, total revenues will be $40 and total costs will be $35, again leaving a profit of $5 per hour.

A Graphical Depiction of Maximum Profits

In Figure 23-3 on the previous page, the lower boundary of the rectangle labeled "Profits" is determined by the intersection of the profit-maximizing quantity line represented by vertical dashes and the average total cost curve. Why? Because the ATC curve gives us the cost per unit, whereas the price ($5), represented by d, gives us the revenue per unit, or average revenue. The difference is profit per unit.

Thus, the height of the rectangular box representing profits equals profit per unit, and the length equals the amount of units produced. When we multiply these two quantities, we get total profits. Note, as pointed out earlier, that we are talking about *economic profits* because a normal rate of return on investment plus all opportunity costs is included in the average total cost curve, ATC.

A Graphical Depiction of Minimum Losses

It is also certainly possible for the competitive firm to make short-run losses. We give an example in Figure 23-4 below, where we show the firm's demand curve shifting from d_1 to d_2. The going market price has fallen from $5 to $3 per MO disk because of changes in market demand conditions. The firm will still do the best it can by producing where marginal revenue equals marginal cost.

We see in Figure 23-4 that the marginal revenue (d_2) curve is intersected (from below) by the marginal cost curve at an output rate of about $5\frac{1}{2}$ MO disks per hour. The firm is clearly not making profits because average total costs at that output rate are greater than the price of $3 per MO disk. The losses are shown in the shaded area. By producing where marginal revenue equals marginal cost, however, the firm is minimizing its losses. That is, losses would be greater at any other output.

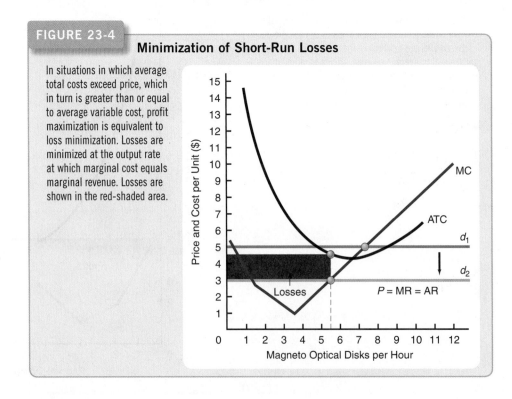

FIGURE 23-4

Minimization of Short-Run Losses

In situations in which average total costs exceed price, which in turn is greater than or equal to average variable cost, profit maximization is equivalent to loss minimization. Losses are minimized at the output rate at which marginal cost equals marginal revenue. Losses are shown in the red-shaded area.

The Short-Run Break-Even Price and the Short-Run Shutdown Price

In Figure 23-4 on the facing page, the firm is sustaining economic losses. Will it go out of business? In the long run it will, but in the short run the firm will not necessarily go out of business. In the short run, as long as the total revenues from continuing to produce output exceed the associated total variable costs, the firm will remain in business and continue to produce. A firm *goes out of business* when the owners sell its assets to someone else. A firm temporarily *shuts down* when it stops producing, but it still is in business.

Now how can a firm that is sustaining economic losses in the short run tell whether it is still worthwhile *not* to shut down? The firm must compare the total revenues that it receives if it continues producing with the resulting total variable costs that it thereby incurs. Looking at the problem on a per-unit basis, as long as average variable cost (AVC) is covered by average revenues (price), the firm is better off continuing to produce. If average variable costs are exceeded even a little bit by the price of the product, staying in production produces some revenues in excess of variable costs. The logic is fairly straightforward:

> *As long as the price per unit sold exceeds the average variable cost per unit produced, the earnings of the firm's owners will be higher if it continues to produce in the short run than if it shuts down.*

Calculating the Short-Run Break-Even Price

Look at demand curve d_1 in Figure 23-5 on the following page. It just touches the minimum point of the average total cost curve, which is exactly where the marginal cost curve intersects the average total cost curve. At that price, which is about $4.30, the firm will be making exactly zero short-run *economic* profits. That price is called the **short-run break-even price,** and point E_1 therefore occurs at the short-run break-even price for a competitive firm. It is the point at which marginal revenue, marginal cost, and average total cost are all equal (that is, at which $P = MC$ and $P = ATC$). The break-even price is the one that yields zero short-run *economic* profits or losses.

Short-run break-even price
The price at which a firm's total revenues equal its total costs. At the break-even price, the firm is just making a normal rate of return on its capital investment. (It is covering its explicit and implicit costs.)

Calculating the Short-Run Shutdown Price

To calculate the firm's shutdown price, we must introduce the average variable cost (AVC) to our graph. In Figure 23-5, we have plotted the AVC values from column 7 in panel (a) of Figure 23-2 on page 511. For the moment, consider two possible demand curves, d_1 and d_2, which are also the firm's respective marginal revenue curves. If demand is d_1, the firm will produce at E_1, where that curve intersects the marginal cost curve. If demand falls to d_2, the firm will produce at E_2. The special feature of the hypothetical demand curve, d_2, is that it just touches the average variable cost curve at the latter's minimum point, which is also where the marginal cost curve intersects it. This price is the **short-run shutdown price.** Why? Below this price, the firm would be paying out more in variable costs than it is receiving in revenues from the sale of its product. Each unit it sold would generate losses that could be avoided if it shut down operations.

The intersection of the price line, the marginal cost curve, and the average variable cost curve is labeled E_2. The resulting short-run shutdown price is valid only for the short run because, of course, in the long run the firm will not stay in business if it is earning less than a normal rate of return (zero economic profits).

Short-run shutdown price
The price that covers average variable costs. It occurs just below the intersection of the marginal cost curve and the average variable cost curve.

The Meaning of Zero Economic Profits

The fact that we labeled point E_1 in Figure 23-5 on page 516, the break-even point may have disturbed you. At point E_1, price is just equal to average total cost. If this is the case, why would a firm continue to produce if it were making no profits whatsoever? If

FIGURE 23-5

Short-Run Break-Even and Shutdown Prices

We can find the short-run break-even price and the short-run shutdown price by comparing price with average total costs and average variable costs. If the demand curve is d_1, profit maximization occurs at output E_1, where MC equals marginal revenue (the d_1 curve). Because the ATC curve includes all relevant opportunity costs, point E_1 is the break-even point, and zero economic profits are being made. The firm is earning a normal rate of return. If the demand curve falls to d_2, profit maximization (loss minimization) occurs at the intersection of MC and MR (the d_2 curve), or E_2. Below this price, it does not pay for the firm to continue in operation because its average variable costs are not covered by the price of the product.

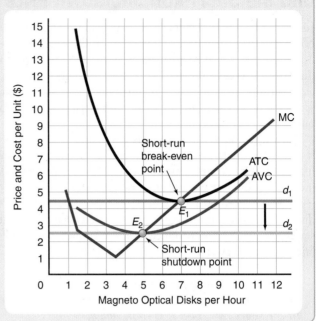

we again make the distinction between accounting profits and economic profits, you will realize that at that price, the firm has zero economic profits but positive accounting profits. Recall that accounting profits are total revenues minus total explicit costs. But such accounting ignores the reward offered to investors—the opportunity cost of capital—plus all other implicit costs.

In economic analysis, the average total cost curve includes the full opportunity cost of capital. Indeed, the average total cost curve includes the opportunity cost of *all* factors of production used in the production process. At the short-run break-even price, economic profits are, by definition, zero. Accounting profits at that price are not, however, equal to zero. They are positive. Consider an example. A manufacturer of homogeneous flash memory chips sells chips at some price. The owners of the firm have supplied all the funds in the business. They have not borrowed from anyone else, and they explicitly pay the full opportunity cost to all factors of production, including any managerial labor that they themselves contribute to the business. Their salaries show up as a cost in the books and are equal to what they could have earned in the next-best alternative occupation.

At the end of the year, the owners find that after they subtract all explicit costs from total revenues, accounting profits are $100,000. If their investment was $1 million, the rate of return on that investment is 10 percent per year. We will assume that this turns out to be equal to the market rate of return.

This $100,000, or 10 percent rate of return, is actually, then, a competitive, or normal, rate of return on invested capital in all industries with similar risks. If the owners had made only $50,000, or 5 percent on their investment, they would have been able to make higher profits by leaving the industry. The 10 percent rate of return is the opportunity cost of capital. Accountants show it as a profit. Economists call it a cost. We include that cost in the average total cost curve, similar to the one shown in Figure 23-5 above. At the short-run break-even price, average total cost, including this opportunity cost of capital, will just equal that price. The firm will be making zero economic profits but a 10 percent *accounting profit*.

The Supply Curve for a Perfectly Competitive Industry

As you learned in Chapter 3, the relationship between a product's price and the quantity produced and offered for sale is a supply curve. Let's now examine the supply curve for a perfectly competitive industry.

The Perfect Competitor's Short-Run Supply Curve

What does the supply curve for the individual firm look like? Actually, we have been looking at it all along. We know that when the price of magneto optical disks is $5, the firm will supply seven or eight of them per hour. If the price falls to $3, the firm will supply five or six MO disks per hour. And if the price falls close to $2, the firm will shut down. Hence, in Figure 23-6 below, the firm's supply curve is the marginal cost curve above the short-run shutdown point. This is shown as the solid part of the marginal cost curve.

> *By definition, then, a firm's short-run supply curve in a competitive industry is its marginal cost curve at and above the point of intersection with the average variable cost curve.*

The Short-Run Industry Supply Curve

In Chapter 3, we indicated that the market supply curve was the summation of individual supply curves. At the beginning of this chapter, we drew a market supply curve in Figure 23-1 on page 509. Now we want to derive more precisely a market, or industry, supply curve to reflect individual producer behavior in that industry. First we must ask, What is an industry? It is merely a collection of firms producing a particular product. Therefore, we have a way to figure out the total supply curve of any industry: As discussed in Chapter 3, we add the quantities that each firm will supply at every possible price. In other words, we sum the individual supply curves of all the competitive firms *horizontally*. The individual supply curves, as we just saw, are simply the marginal cost curves of each firm.

Consider doing this for a hypothetical world in which there are only two producers of magneto optical disks in the industry, firm A and firm B. These two firms' marginal cost curves are given in panels (a) and (b) of Figure 23-7 on the following page. The marginal cost curves for the two separate firms are presented as MC$_A$ in panel (a)

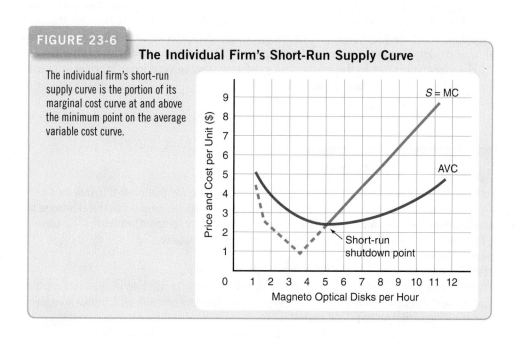

FIGURE 23-6

The Individual Firm's Short-Run Supply Curve

The individual firm's short-run supply curve is the portion of its marginal cost curve at and above the minimum point on the average variable cost curve.

FIGURE 23-7

Deriving the Industry Supply Curve

Marginal cost curves at and above minimum average variable cost are presented in panels (a) and (b) for firms A and B. We horizontally sum the two quantities supplied, 7 units by firm A and 10 units by firm B, at a price of $6. This gives us point *F* in panel (c). We do the same thing for the quantities supplied at a price of $10. This gives us point *G*. When we connect those points, we have the industry supply curve, *S*, which is the horizontal summation—represented by the Greek letter sigma (Σ)— of the firms' marginal cost curves above their respective minimum average variable costs.

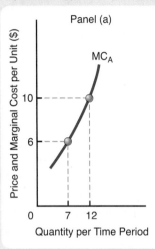

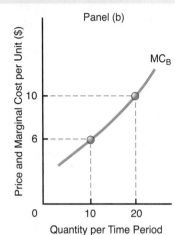

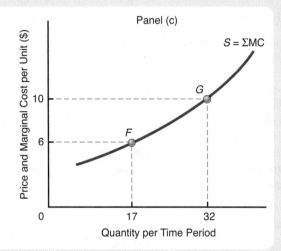

Industry supply curve

The locus of points showing the minimum prices at which given quantities will be forthcoming; also called the *market supply curve.*

and MC_B in panel (b). Those two marginal cost curves are drawn only for prices above the minimum average variable cost for each respective firm. In panel (a), for firm A, at a price of $6 per unit, the quantity supplied would be 7 units. At a price of $10 per unit, the quantity supplied would be 12 units. In panel (b), we see the two different quantities that would be supplied by firm B corresponding to those two prices. Now, at a price of $6, we add horizontally the quantities 7 and 10 to obtain 17 units. This gives us one point, *F*, for our short-run **industry supply curve,** *S*. We obtain the other point, *G*, by doing the same horizontal adding of quantities at a price of $10 per unit.

When we connect all points such as *F* and *G*, we obtain the industry supply curve *S*, which is also marked ΣMC (where the capital Greek sigma, Σ, is the symbol for summation), indicating that it is the horizontal summation of the marginal cost curves (at and above the respective minimum average variable cost of each firm). Because the law of diminishing marginal product makes marginal cost curves rise as output rises, the short-run supply curve of a perfectly competitive industry must be upward sloping.

How have increases in the market prices of a number of veterinary services affected the quantity of services provided?

EXAMPLE

Vets Respond to Higher Market Prices of Treatments for Fido

More than 16,000 U.S. veterinary clinics compete to provide health care services for household pets. Although slight quality differences surely exist across clinics, most offer relatively standard treatments and a wide array of basic pet health care services. The veterinary clinic industry, therefore, approximates a perfectly competitive industry.

During the past decade, the market demand for veterinary services has increased considerably, which has caused average pet health care prices to rise by more than 50 percent. Individual veterinary clinics have responded by moving upward along the portions of their marginal cost curves above their short-run shutdown points—that is, their individual supply curves. Consequently, there has been a substantial increase in the total quantity of pet care services provided by all clinics—an upward movement along the market supply curve.

FOR CRITICAL THINKING

Why do you suppose that a number of veterinary clinics have expanded their pet "clienteles" and hired more veterinarians to provide more hours of service?

Factors That Influence the Industry Supply Curve

As you have just seen, the industry supply curve is the horizontal summation of all of the individual firms' marginal cost curves at and above their respective minimum average variable cost points. This means that anything that affects the marginal cost curves of the firm will influence the industry supply curve. Therefore, the individual factors that will influence the supply schedule in a competitive industry can be summarized as the factors that cause the variable costs of production to change. These are factors that affect the individual marginal cost curves, such as changes in the individual firm's productivity, in factor prices (such as wages paid to labor and prices of raw materials), in per-unit taxes, and in anything else that would influence the individual firm's marginal cost curve.

All of these are *ceteris paribus* conditions of supply (see page 62 in Chapter 3). Because they affect the position of the marginal cost curve for the individual firm, they affect the position of the industry supply curve. A change in any of these will shift the firms' marginal cost curves and thus shift the industry supply curve.

QUICK QUIZ   See page 531 for the answers. Review concepts from this section in MyEconLab.

Short-run average profits or losses are determined by comparing _____ total costs with _____ at the **profit-maximizing rate of output.** In the short run, the perfectly competitive firm can make economic profits or economic losses.

The perfectly competitive firm's short-run _____-_____ price equals the firm's minimum average total cost, which is at the point at which the _____ cost curve intersects the average total cost curve.

The perfectly competitive firm's short-run _____ price equals the firm's minimum average variable cost, which is at the point at which the _____ cost curve intersects the average variable cost curve. Shutdown will occur if price falls below average variable cost.

The firm will continue production at a price that exceeds average variable costs because revenues exceed total _____ costs of producing.

At the short-run break-even price, the firm is making _____ economic profits, which means that it is just making a _____ rate of return for industries with similar risks.

The firm's short-run supply curve is the portion of its marginal cost curve at and above its minimum average _____ cost. The industry short-run supply curve is a horizontal _____ of the individual firms' marginal cost curves at and above their respective minimum average _____ costs.

Price Determination under Perfect Competition

How is the market, or "going," price established in a competitive market? This price is established by the interaction of all the suppliers (firms) and all the demanders (consumers).

The Market Clearing Price

The market demand schedule, *D*, in panel (a) of Figure 23-8 on the following page represents the demand schedule for the entire industry, and the supply schedule, *S*, represents the supply schedule for the entire industry. The market clearing price, P_e, is established by the forces of supply and demand at the intersection of *D* and the short-run industry supply curve, *S*. Even though each individual firm has no control or effect on the price of its product in a competitive industry, the interaction of *all* the producers and buyers determines the price at which the product will be sold.

We say that the price P_e and the quantity Q_e in panel (a) of Figure 23-8 on the next page constitute the competitive solution to the resource allocation problem in that particular industry. It is the equilibrium at which quantity demanded equals quantity supplied, and both suppliers and demanders are doing as well as they can. The resulting individual firm demand curve, *d*, is shown in panel (b) of Figure 23-8 at the price P_e.

FIGURE 23-8

Industry Demand and Supply Curves and the Individual Firm Demand Curve

The industry demand curve is represented by D in panel (a). The short-run industry supply curve is S and is equal to ΣMC. The intersection of the demand and supply curves at E determines the equilibrium or market clearing price at P_e. The demand curve faced by the individual firm in panel (b) is perfectly elastic at the market clearing price determined in panel (a). If the producer has a marginal cost curve MC, its profit-maximizing output level is at q_e. Consider average cost curves AC_3, AC_1, and AC_2 associated with successively higher levels of fixed costs. For AC_1, economic profits are zero. For AC_2, profits are negative. For AC_3, profits are positive.

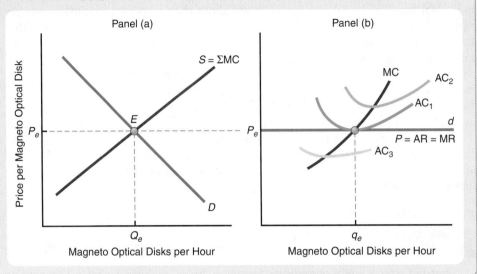

Market Equilibrium and the Individual Firm

In a purely competitive industry, the individual producer takes price as a given and chooses the output level that maximizes profits. (This is also the equilibrium level of output from the producer's standpoint.) We see in panel (b) of Figure 23-8 above that this is at q_e. If the producer's average costs are given by AC_1, the short-run break-even price arises at q_e (see Figure 23-5 on page 516). If its average costs are given by AC_2, then at q_e, AC exceeds price (average revenue), and the firm is incurring losses. Alternatively, if average costs are given by AC_3, the firm will be making economic profits at q_e. In the former case, we would expect, over time, that some firms will cease production (exit the industry), causing supply to shift inward. In the latter case, we would expect new firms to enter the industry to take advantage of the economic profits, thereby causing supply to shift outward. We now turn to these long-run considerations.

WHAT IF...   the government mandated that prices stay at long-run equilibrium levels?

Politicians often complain whenever the prices of commodities such as oil, gasoline, minerals, or foods show considerable variability, and they commonly call for the government to "do something" to limit price variations. If the government were to force firms to keep prices fixed at anticipated long-run equilibrium levels, however, prices would be unable to adjust in response to short-run changes in market demand or supply. For instance, if an industry's price were fixed at the expected long-run level and market demand were to rise, the quantity demanded would rise while quantity supplied would remain unchanged. A shortage would result. In contrast, if the market supply were to increase, the quantity supplied would rise while quantity demanded would remain unchanged. The result would be a surplus. Thus, well-intentioned efforts to keep prices near long-run equilibrium levels likely would produce numerous shortages and surpluses over time.

The Long-Run Industry Situation: Exit and Entry

In the long run in a competitive situation, firms will be making zero economic profits. (Actually, this is true only for identical firms. Throughout the remainder of the discussion, we assume firms have the same cost structures.) We surmise, therefore, that in the long run a perfectly competitive firm's price (marginal and average revenue) curve will just touch its average total cost curve. How does this occur? It comes about through an adjustment process that depends on economic profits and losses.

Exit and Entry of Firms

Look back at both Figure 23-3 on page 513 and Figure 23-4 on page 514. The existence of either profits or losses is a signal to owners of capital both inside and outside the industry. If an industry is characterized by firms showing economic profits as represented in Figure 23-3, these economic profits signal owners of capital elsewhere in the economy that they, too, should enter this industry. In contrast, if some firms in an industry are suffering economic losses as represented in Figure 23-4, these economic losses signal resource owners outside the industry to stay out. In addition, these economic losses signal resource owners within the industry not to reinvest and if possible to leave the industry. It is in this sense that we say that profits direct resources to their highest-valued use. In the long run, capital will flow into industries in which profitability is highest and will flow out of industries in which profitability is lowest.

ALLOCATION OF CAPITAL AND MARKET SIGNALS The price system therefore allocates capital according to the relative expected rates of return on alternative investments. Hence, entry restrictions (such as limits on the numbers of taxicabs and banks permitted to enter the taxi service and banking industries) will hinder economic efficiency by not allowing resources to flow to their highest-valued use. Similarly, exit restrictions (such as laws that require firms to give advance notice of closings) will act to trap resources (temporarily) in sectors in which their value is below that in alternative uses. Such laws will also inhibit the ability of firms to respond to changes in both the domestic and international marketplaces.

Not every industry presents an immediate source of opportunity for every firm. In a brief period of time, it may be impossible for a firm that produces tractors to switch to the production of digital devices, even if there are very large profits to be made. Over the long run, however, we would expect to see owners of some other resources switch to producing digital devices. In a market economy, investors supply firms in the more profitable industry with more investment funds, which they take from firms in less profitable industries. (Also, positive economic profits induce existing firms to use internal investment funds for expansion.) Consequently, resources useful in the production of more profitable goods, such as labor, will be bid away from lower-valued opportunities. Investors and other suppliers of resources respond to market **signals** about their highest-valued opportunities.

What consistent market signals have many hamburger sellers been receiving during the past few years?

Signals
Compact ways of conveying to economic decision makers information needed to make decisions. An effective signal not only conveys information but also provides the incentive to react appropriately. Economic profits and economic losses are such signals.

EXAMPLE

For Many Hamburger Sellers, the Exit Signal Is Flashing

During the 2000s, a number of firms entered the hamburger fast-food market as market demand increased in response to a rising U.S. population and higher incomes. In today's dampened economy, however, market demand is stagnant. Consequently, market prices of hamburgers—and, hence, sellers' revenues—have remained nearly unchanged for several years. During the same period, however, beef prices have increased by more than 25 percent, which has led to a rapid escalation in costs of producing hamburgers. As a result, a number of sellers have earned negative economic profits in recent years. These economic losses are signals that many firms have been acting upon by exiting the market.

FOR CRITICAL THINKING
If market demand for hamburgers were to increase once again, is it possible that some sellers might reconsider exiting the market even if beef prices continue to rise?

TENDENCY TOWARD EQUILIBRIUM Market adjustment to changes in demand will occur regardless of the wishes of the managers of firms in less profitable markets. They can either attempt to adjust their product line to respond to the new demands, be replaced by managers who are more responsive to new conditions, or see their firms go bankrupt as they find themselves unable to replace worn-out plant and equipment.

In addition, when we say that in a competitive long-run equilibrium situation firms will be making zero economic profits, we must realize that at a particular point in time it would be pure coincidence for a firm to be making *exactly* zero economic profits. Real-world information is not as precise as the curves we use to simplify our analysis. Things change all the time in a dynamic world, and firms, even in a very competitive situation, may for many reasons not be making exactly zero economic profits. We say that there is a *tendency* toward that equilibrium position, but firms are adjusting all the time to changes in their cost curves and in the market demand curves.

Long-Run Industry Supply Curves

In panel (a) of Figure 23-8 on page 520, we drew the summation of all of the portions of the individual firms' marginal cost curves at and above each firm's respective minimum average variable costs as the upward-sloping supply curve of the entire industry. We should be aware, however, that a relatively inelastic supply curve may be appropriate only in the short run. After all, one of the prerequisites of a competitive industry is freedom of entry.

Why has the number of firms offering "online daily deals" grown considerably in a very short time?

EXAMPLE

Economic Profits Attract Online-Daily-Deals Entrants in Droves

For a couple of years, companies such as Groupon and LivingSocial were among the only deals in town—at least in terms of daily deals sold on the Internet. These firms send e-mails to subscribers offering deep discounts on products and services provided by retailers. The firms and retailers split the revenues generated by these e-mails. Between late 2008 and early 2011, Groupon and LivingSocial were among only a handful of online firms competing in the daily-deals market. These few online competitors earned substantial economic profits from their operations.

Since the middle of 2011, though, a number of firms have responded to the observation of positive economic profits by entering the daily-deals market. Examples include nationwide online-daily-deal services now provided by Facebook, Google, TravelZoo, and Yipit. In addition, firms are now competing to offer online daily-deal services in local areas. Today, at least 500 daily-deal competitors are active, and several more enter the industry each month. Thus, positive economic profits have attracted a substantial number of entrants into this industry.

FOR CRITICAL THINKING
Why do you suppose that the entry of so many other competitors has resulted in declines in economic profits earned by firms such as Groupon and LivingSocial?

Long-run industry supply curve
A market supply curve showing the relationship between prices and quantities after firms have been allowed the time to enter into or exit from an industry, depending on whether there have been positive or negative economic profits.

Remember that our definition of the long run is a period of time in which all adjustments can be made. The **long-run industry supply curve** is a supply curve showing the relationship between quantities supplied by the entire industry at different prices after firms have been allowed to either enter or leave the industry, depending on whether there have been positive or negative economic profits. Also, the long-run industry supply curve is drawn under the assumption that firms are identical and that entry and exit have been completed. This means that along the long-run industry supply curve, firms in the industry earn zero economic profits.

The long-run industry supply curve can take one of three shapes, depending on whether input prices stay constant, increase, or decrease as the number of firms in the industry changes. In Chapter 22, we assumed that input prices remained constant to the *firm* regardless of the firm's rate of output. When we look at the entire *industry*, however, when all firms are expanding and new firms are entering, they may simultaneously bid up input prices.

CONSTANT-COST INDUSTRIES In principle, there are industries that use such a small percentage of the total supply of inputs required for industrywide production that firms can enter the industry without bidding up input prices. In such a situation, we are dealing with a **constant-cost industry.** Its long-run industry supply curve is therefore horizontal and is represented by S_L in panel (a) of Figure 23-9 below.

We can work through the case in which constant costs prevail. We start out in panel (a) with demand curve D_1 and supply curve S_1. The equilibrium price is P_1. Market demand shifts rightward to D_2. In the short run, the equilibrium price rises to P_2. This generates positive economic profits for existing firms in the industry. Such economic profits induce capital to flow into the industry. The existing firms expand or new firms enter (or both). The short-run supply curve shifts outward to S_2. The new intersection with the new demand curve is at E_3. The new equilibrium price is again P_1. The long-run supply curve, labeled S_L, is obtained by connecting the intersections of the corresponding pairs of demand and short-run supply curves, E_1 and E_3.

In a constant-cost industry, long-run supply is perfectly elastic. Any shift in demand is eventually met by just enough entry or exit of suppliers that the long-run price is constant at P_1. Retail trade is often given as an example of such an industry because output can be expanded or contracted without affecting input prices. Banking is another example.

INCREASING-COST INDUSTRIES In an **increasing-cost industry,** expansion by existing firms and the addition of new firms cause the price of inputs specialized to that industry to be bid up. As costs of production rise, the ATC curve and the firms' MC curves shift upward, causing short-run supply curves (each firm's marginal cost curve) to shift vertically upward. Hence, industry supply shifts out by less than in a constant-cost industry. The result is a long-run industry supply curve that slopes upward, as represented by S_L' in panel (b) of Figure 23-9. Examples are residential construction and coal mining—both use specialized inputs that cannot be obtained in ever-increasing quantities without causing their prices to rise.

DECREASING-COST INDUSTRIES An expansion in the number of firms in an industry can lead to a reduction in input costs and a downward shift in the ATC and MC curves. When this occurs, the long-run industry supply curve will slope downward. An example, S_L'', is given in panel (c) of Figure 23-9. This is a **decreasing-cost industry.**

Constant-cost industry
An industry whose total output can be increased without an increase in long-run per-unit costs. Its long-run supply curve is horizontal.

Increasing-cost industry
An industry in which an increase in industry output is accompanied by an increase in long-run per-unit costs, such that the long-run industry supply curve slopes upward.

Decreasing-cost industry
An industry in which an increase in output leads to a reduction in long-run per-unit costs, such that the long-run industry supply curve slopes downward.

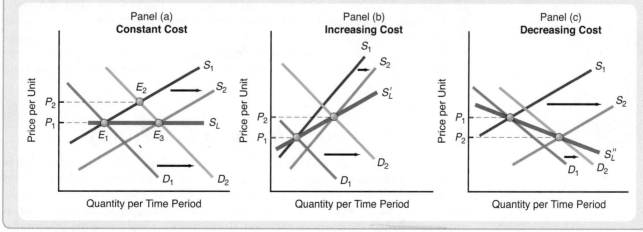

FIGURE 23-9

Constant-Cost, Increasing-Cost, and Decreasing-Cost Industries

In panel (a), we show a situation in which the demand curve shifts from D_1 to D_2. Price increases from P_1 to P_2. In time, the short-run supply curve shifts outward because entry occurs in response to positive profits, and the equilibrium changes from E_2 to E_3. The market clearing price is again P_1. If we connect points such as E_1 and E_3, we come up with the long-run supply curve S_L. This is a constant-cost industry. In panel (b), costs are increasing for the industry, and therefore the long-run supply curve, S_L', slopes upward and long-run prices rise from P_1 to P_2. In panel (c), costs are decreasing for the industry as it expands, and therefore the long-run supply curve, S_L'', slopes downward such that long-run prices decline from P_1 to P_2.

Panel (a)
Constant Cost

Panel (b)
Increasing Cost

Panel (c)
Decreasing Cost

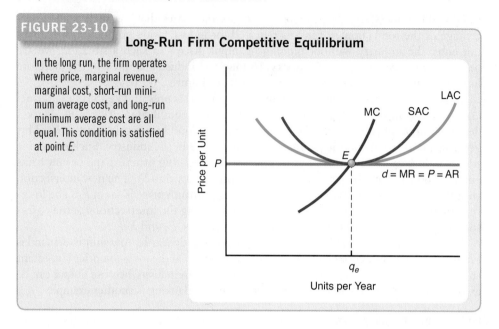

FIGURE 23-10

Long-Run Firm Competitive Equilibrium

In the long run, the firm operates where price, marginal revenue, marginal cost, short-run minimum average cost, and long-run minimum average cost are all equal. This condition is satisfied at point E.

Long-Run Equilibrium

In the long run, the firm can change the scale of its plant, adjusting its plant size in such a way that it has no further incentive to change. It will do so until profits are maximized.

The Firm's Long-Run Situation

Figure 23-10 above shows the long-run equilibrium of the perfectly competitive firm. Given a price of P and a marginal cost curve, MC, the firm produces at output q_e. Because economic profits must be zero in the long run, the firm's short-run average costs (SAC) must equal P at q_e, which occurs at minimum SAC. In addition, because we are in long-run equilibrium, any economies of scale must be exhausted, so we are on the minimum point of the long-run average cost curve (LAC). In other words, the long-run equilibrium position is where "everything is equal," which is at point E in Figure 23-10. There, *price* equals *marginal revenue* equals *marginal cost* equals *average cost* (minimum, short-run, and long-run).

Perfect Competition and Minimum Average Total Cost

Look again at Figure 23-10 above. In long-run equilibrium, the perfectly competitive firm finds itself producing at output rate q_e. At that rate of output, the price is just equal to the minimum long-run average cost as well as the minimum short-run average cost. In this sense, perfect competition results in the production of goods and services using the least costly combination of resources. This is an important attribute of a perfectly competitive long-run equilibrium, particularly when we wish to compare the market structure of perfect competition with other market structures that are less than perfectly competitive. We will examine these other market structures in later chapters.

Competitive Pricing: Marginal Cost Pricing

In a perfectly competitive industry, each firm produces where its marginal cost curve intersects its marginal revenue curve from below. Thus, perfectly competitive firms always sell their goods at a price that just equals marginal cost. This is said to be the optimal price of this good because the price that consumers pay reflects the opportunity cost to society of producing the good. Recall that marginal cost is the amount that a firm must spend to purchase the additional resources needed to expand output by one unit. Given competitive markets, the amount paid for a resource will be the same in all of its alternative uses. Thus, MC reflects relative resource input use. That is, if the MC of good 1 is twice the MC of good 2, one more unit of good 1 requires twice the resource input of one more unit of good 2.

Marginal Cost Pricing

The competitive firm produces up to the point at which the market price just equals the marginal cost. Herein lies the element of the optimal nature of a competitive solution. It is called **marginal cost pricing.** The competitive firm sells its product at a price that just equals the cost to society—the opportunity cost—for that is what the marginal cost curve represents. (But note here that it is the self-interest of firm owners that causes price to equal the marginal cost to society.) In other words, the marginal benefit to consumers, given by the price that they are willing to pay for the last unit of the good purchased, just equals the marginal cost to society of producing the last unit. (If the marginal benefit exceeds the marginal cost, that is, if $P > MC$, too little is being produced in that people value additional units more than the cost to society of producing them. If $P < MC$, the opposite is true.)

When an individual pays a price equal to the marginal cost of production, the cost to the user of that product is equal to the sacrifice or cost to society of producing that quantity of that good as opposed to more of some other good. (We are assuming that all marginal social costs are accounted for.) The competitive solution, then, is called *efficient*, in the economic sense of the word. Economic efficiency means that it is impossible to increase the output of any good without lowering the *value* of the total output produced in the economy. No juggling of resources, such as labor and capital, will result in an output that is higher in total value than the value of all of the goods and services already being produced. In an efficient equilibrium, it is impossible to make one person better off without making someone else worse off. All resources are used in the most advantageous way possible, and society therefore enjoys an efficient allocation of productive resources. All goods and services are sold at their opportunity cost, and marginal cost pricing prevails throughout.

Marginal cost pricing
A system of pricing in which the price charged is equal to the opportunity cost to society of producing one more unit of the good or service in question. The opportunity cost is the marginal cost to society.

Market Failure

Although perfect competition does offer many desirable results, situations arise when perfectly competitive markets cannot efficiently allocate resources. Either too many or too few resources are used in the production of a good or service. These situations are instances of **market failure.** Externalities arising from failures to fully assign property rights and public goods are examples. For reasons discussed in later chapters, perfectly competitive markets cannot efficiently allocate resources in these situations, and alternative allocation mechanisms are called for. In some cases, alternative market structures or government intervention *may* improve the economic outcome.

Market failure
A situation in which an unrestrained market operation leads to either too few or too many resources going to a specific economic activity.

QUICK QUIZ   See page 531 for the answers. Review concepts from this section in MyEconLab.

The perfectly competitive price is determined by the _____ of the market demand curve and the market supply curve. The market supply curve is equal to the horizontal summation of the portions of the individual marginal cost curves above their respective minimum average _____ costs.

In the long run, perfectly competitive firms make _____ economic profits because of entry and exit whenever there are industrywide economic profits or losses.

A constant-cost industry has a _____ long-run supply curve. An increasing-cost industry has an _____-sloping

long-run supply curve. A decreasing-cost industry has a _____-sloping long-run supply curve.

In the long run, a perfectly competitive firm produces to the point at which price, marginal revenue, marginal cost, short-run minimum average cost, and long-run minimum average cost are all _____.

Perfectly competitive pricing is essentially _____ _____ pricing. Therefore, the perfectly competitive solution is called efficient because _____ _____ represents the social opportunity cost of producing one more unit of the good.

YOU ARE THERE
Looking to Enter a Competitive Online Market? Rent a Desk!

Many people entering markets to provide online services such as business consulting, legal advising, or educational tutoring require little working space. In most cases, all they require is a desk and Internet access. Saeed Amidi, chief executive of Plug and Play Tech Centers, has established a business that assists entrepreneurs in attempting to enter such online service markets.

To ease the task of entering these competitive service markets, Amidi's company rents, at rates as low as $275 per month, shared workspaces consisting of desks and Internet access points. Plug and Play's centers typically contain approximately 20,000 square feet of space for rent to about 1,000 individuals. Thus, at one of the firm's Tech Centers, an entrepreneur seeking a low-cost means of entering an online service

market can rent a desk positioned within about 20 square feet of workspace. All that is required to start an online service business is an appropriate set of digital devices and apps. Exiting also is simple: The individual ends the workspace rental contract and removes all private belongings from the shared-workspace center.

Critical Thinking Questions

1. Why are many online service markets likely to be perfectly competitive?
2. Recently, competitors of Plug and Play have been opening their own shared-workspace centers. Does the market for shared workspace likely possess characteristics of a perfectly competitive market? Explain.

ISSUES & APPLICATIONS

A Decreasing-Cost, "White Gold" Industry

CONCEPTS APPLIED

▶ Perfect Competition

▶ Decreasing-Cost Industry

▶ Long-Run Industry Supply Curve

Lithium is a naturally occurring, superlight element often called "white gold." It is the key component of ion batteries that power mobile digital devices, so the market demand for lithium has increased substantially.

Changing Methods of Extracting Lithium Alter Input Prices

For many years, a number of U.S. companies were key providers of lithium. These firms mined the element from seams of a mineral called spodumene that is found in large quantities in North Carolina and a few other states.

During the past two decades, however, many South American companies have developed less expensive ways of extracting lithium using alternative inputs. These firms pump brine from ancient lakebeds into giant evaporation ponds and let the sun's rays extract the lithium. Then special equipment collects the element.

A Downward-Sloping Long-Run Lithium Supply Curve

Figure 23-11 on the facing page displays what has happened to the market price of lithium since 1952. As market demand has risen and the means of extracting lithium has switched from mining to brine pumping combined with evaporation, the prices of inputs used to produce the metal

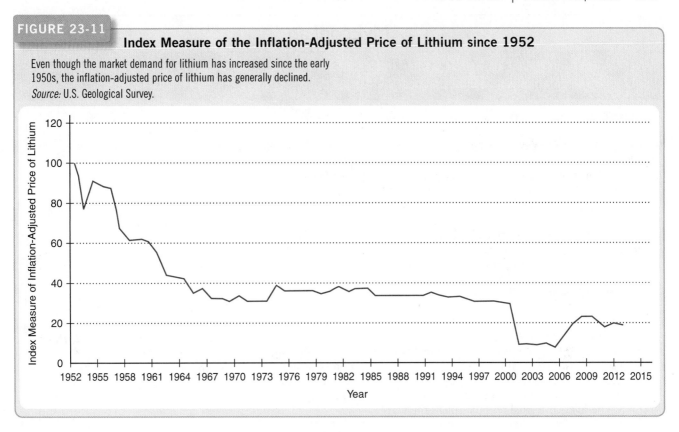

FIGURE 23-11

Index Measure of the Inflation-Adjusted Price of Lithium since 1952

Even though the market demand for lithium has increased since the early 1950s, the inflation-adjusted price of lithium has generally declined.
Source: U.S. Geological Survey.

have fallen. The consequence has been a general decrease in the price of the "white gold" element.

The decline in the price of lithium following the entry of more firms in response to increasing demand indicates that the long-run lithium supply curve slopes downward. Thus, the lithium industry is a decreasing-cost industry.

For Critical Thinking

1. If input prices had increased as firms entered the lithium industry in response to rising demand, what would have been the shape of the long-run supply curve?

2. If the market demand for lithium were to decrease during the 2020s, what would happen to the market clearing price of lithium in the long run?

Web Resources

1. To view a list that indicates the large number of firms producing lithium today, go to **www.econtoday.com/chap23**.

2. To learn why some observers worry that the lithium market may become less nearly perfectly competitive many years from now, go to **www.econtoday.com/chap23**.

MyEconLab

For more questions on this chapter's Issues & Applications, go to MyEconLab. In the Study Plan for this chapter, select Section N: News.

MyEconLab

Here is what you should know after reading this chapter. MyEconLab will help you identify what you know, and where to go when you need to practice.

WHAT YOU SHOULD KNOW		WHERE TO GO TO PRACTICE
The Characteristics of a Perfectly Competitive Market Structure A perfectly competitive industry has four key characteristics: (1) there are large numbers of buyers and sellers, (2) firms in the industry produce and sell a homogeneous product, (3) information is equally accessible to both buyers and sellers, and (4) there are insignificant barriers to industry entry or exit. These characteristics imply that each firm in a perfectly competitive industry is a price taker: The firm takes the market price as given and outside its control.	perfect competition, 508 perfectly competitive firm, 508 price taker, 508	• MyEconLab Study Plan 23.1
How a Perfectly Competitive Firm Decides How Much to Produce A perfectly competitive firm sells the amount that it wishes at the market price, so the additional revenue from selling an additional unit of output is the market price. Thus, the firm's marginal revenue equals the market price, and its marginal revenue curve is the firm's perfectly elastic demand curve. The firm maximizes economic profits when marginal cost equals marginal revenue, as long as the market price is not below the short-run shutdown price, where the marginal cost curve crosses the average variable cost curve.	total revenues, 510 profit-maximizing rate of production, 510 marginal revenue, 512 **Key Figures** Figure 23-1, 509 Figure 23-2, 511	• MyEconLab Study Plans 23.2, 23.3 • Animated Figures 23-1, 23-2
The Short-Run Supply Curve of a Perfectly Competitive Firm If the market price is below the short-run shutdown price, the firm's total revenues fail to cover its variable costs. The firm would be better off halting production and minimizing its economic loss in the short run. If the market price is above the short-run shutdown price, however, the firm produces the rate of output where marginal revenue, the market price, equals marginal cost. Thus, the range of the firm's marginal cost curve above the short-run shutdown price is the firm's short-run supply curve, which gives the firm's combinations of market prices and production choices.	short-run break-even price, 515 short-run shutdown price, 515 industry supply curve, 518 **Key Figures** Figure 23-3, 513 Figure 23-4, 514 Figure 23-5, 516 Figure 23-6, 517 Figure 23-7, 518	• MyEconLab Study Plans 23.4, 23.5, 23.6, 23.7 • Animated Figures 23-3, 23-4, 23-5, 23-6, 23-7
The Equilibrium Price in a Perfectly Competitive Market The short-run supply curve for a perfectly competitive industry is obtained by summing the quantities supplied by all firms at each price. At the equilibrium market price, the total amount of output supplied by all firms is equal to the total amount of output demanded by all buyers.	**Key Figure** Figure 23-8, 520	• MyEconLab Study Plan 23.8 • Animated Figure 23-8

MyEconLab *continued*

┌─ **WHAT YOU SHOULD KNOW** ──────────────────── **WHERE TO GO TO PRACTICE** ─┐

Incentives to Enter or Exit a Perfectly Competitive Industry In the short run, a perfectly competitive firm will continue to produce as long as the market price exceeds the short-run shutdown price. This is so even if the market price is below the short-run break-even point where the marginal cost curve crosses the firm's average total cost curve. Even though the firm earns an economic loss, it minimizes its loss by continuing to produce in the short run. In the long run, continued losses will induce exit from the industry.

signals, 521

- MyEconLab Study Plan 23.9

The Long-Run Industry Supply Curve and Constant-, Increasing-, and Decreasing-Cost Industries The long-run industry supply curve in a perfectly competitive industry shows the relationship between prices and quantities after firms have entered or left the industry in response to economic profits or losses. In a constant-cost industry, total output can increase without a rise in long-run per-unit costs, so the long-run industry supply curve is horizontal. In an increasing-cost industry, per-unit costs increase with a rise in industry output, so the long-run industry supply curve slopes upward. In a decreasing-cost industry per-unit costs decline as industry output increases, and the long-run industry supply curve slopes downward.

long-run industry supply curve, 522
constant-cost industry, 523
increasing-cost industry, 523
decreasing-cost industry, 523
marginal cost pricing, 525
market failure, 525

Key Figure
Figure 23-10, 524

- MyEconLab Study Plans 23.10, 23.11
- Animated Figure 23-10

Log in to MyEconLab, take a chapter test, and get a personalized Study Plan that tells you which concepts you understand and which ones you need to review. From there, MyEconLab will give you further practice, tutorials, animations, videos, and guided solutions. For more information, visit www.myeconlab.com

PROBLEMS

All problems are assignable in MyEconLab. Answers to odd-numbered problems appear at the back of the book.

23-1. Explain why each of the following examples is not a perfectly competitive industry. (See page 508.)

    a. One firm produces a large portion of the industry's total output, but there are many firms in the industry, and their products are indistinguishable. Firms can easily exit and enter the industry.

    b. There are many buyers and sellers in the industry. Consumers have equal information about the prices of firms' products, which differ moderately in quality from firm to firm.

    c. Many taxicabs compete in a city. The city's government requires all taxicabs to provide identical service. Taxicabs are nearly identical, and all drivers must wear a designated uniform. The government also enforces a binding limit on the number of taxicab companies that can operate within the city's boundaries.

23-2. Consider a market for online movie rentals. The market supply curve slopes upward, the market demand curve slopes downward, and the equilibrium rental price equals $3.50. Consider each of the following events, and discuss the effects they will have on the market clearing price and on the demand curve faced by the individual online rental firm. (See page 509.)

a. People's tastes change in favor of going to see more movies at cinemas with their friends and family members.

b. More online movie-rental firms enter the market.

c. There is a significant increase in the price to consumers of purchasing movies online.

23-3. Consider the diagram below, which applies to a perfectly competitive firm, which at present faces a market clearing price of $20 per unit and produces 10,000 units of output per week. (See pages 509–512.)

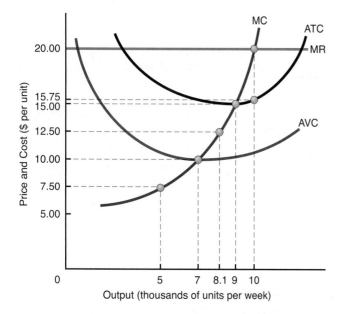

a. What is the firm's current average revenue per unit?

b. What are the present economic profits of this firm? Is the firm maximizing economic profits? Explain.

c. If the market clearing price drops to $12.50 per unit, should this firm continue to produce in the short run if it wishes to maximize its economic profits (or minimize its economic losses)? Explain.

d. If the market clearing price drops to $7.50 per unit, should this firm continue to produce in the short run if it wishes to maximize its economic profits (or minimize its economic losses)? Explain.

23-4. The table in the next column represents the hourly output and cost structure for a local pizza shop. The market is perfectly competitive, and the market price of a pizza in the area is $10. Total costs include all opportunity costs. (See pages 509–514.)

Total Hourly Output and Sales of Pizzas	Total Hourly Cost ($)
0	5
1	9
2	11
3	12
4	14
5	18
6	24
7	32
8	42
9	54
10	68

a. Calculate the total revenue and total economic profit for this pizza shop at each rate of output.

b. Assuming that the pizza shop always produces and sells at least one pizza per hour, does this appear to be a situation of short-run or long-run equilibrium?

c. Calculate the pizza shop's marginal cost and marginal revenue at each rate of output. Based on marginal analysis, what is the profit-maximizing rate of output for the pizza shop?

d. Draw a diagram depicting the short-run marginal revenue and marginal cost curves for this pizza shop, and illustrate the determination of its profit-maximizing output rate.

23-5. Consider the information provided in Problem 23-4. Suppose the market price drops to only $5 per pizza. In the short run, should this pizza shop continue to make pizzas, or will it maximize its economic profits (that is, minimize its economic loss) by shutting down? (See pages 514–515.)

23-6. Yesterday, a perfectly competitive producer of construction bricks manufactured and sold 10,000 bricks per week at a market price that was just equal to the minimum average variable cost of producing each brick. Today, all the firm's costs are the same, but the market price of bricks has declined. (See pages 514–515.)

a. Assuming that this firm has positive fixed costs, did the firm earn economic profits, economic losses, or zero economic profits yesterday?

b. To maximize economic profits today, how many bricks should this firm produce today?

23-7. Suppose that a firm in a perfectly competitive industry finds that at its current output rate, marginal revenue exceeds the minimum average total cost of producing any feasible rate of output. Furthermore, the firm is producing an output rate at which marginal cost is less than the average total cost at that rate of output. Is the firm maximizing its economic profits? Why or why not? (See pages 512–513.)

23-8. A perfectly competitive industry is initially in a short-run equilibrium in which all firms are earning zero economic profits but in which firms are operating below their minimum efficient scale. Explain the long-run adjustments that will take place for the industry to attain long-run equilibrium with firms operating at their minimum efficient scale. (See pages 520–521.)

23-9. Two years ago, a large number of firms entered a market in which existing firms had been earning positive economic profits. By the end of last year, the typical firm in this industry had begun earning negative economic profits. No other events occurred in this market during the past two years. (See pages 520–521.)

   a. Explain the adjustment process that occurred last year.

   b. Predict what adjustments will take place in this market beginning this year, other things being equal.

23-10. The minimum feasible long-run average cost for firms in a perfectly competitive industry is $40 per

unit. If every firm in the industry currently is producing an output consistent with a long-run equilibrium, what is the marginal cost incurred by each firm? What is the market price? (See page 524.)

23-11. In several markets for digital devices that can be viewed as perfectly competitive, steady increases in demand for the required minerals ultimately have generated long-run reductions in the market prices of these devices. Describe in words the types of adjustments that must have occurred in these markets to have brought about this outcome, and evaluate whether such digital-device industries are increasing-, constant-, or decreasing-cost industries. (See pages 522–524.)

23-12. In several perfectly competitive markets for minerals used as inputs in digital devices, persistent increases in demand eventually have generated long-run increases in the market prices of these devices. Describe in words the types of adjustments that must have occurred in these markets to have brought about this outcome, and evaluate whether such mineral-extraction industries are increasing-, constant-, or decreasing-cost industries. (See pages 522–524.)

ECONOMICS ON THE NET

The Cost Structure of the Movie Theater Business A key idea in this chapter is that competition among firms in an industry can influence the long-run cost structure within the industry. Here you get a chance to apply this concept to a multinational company that owns movie theaters.

Title: AMC International

Navigation: Follow the link at **www.econtoday.com/chap23** to visit American Multi-Cinema's home page.

Application Answer the following questions.

1. At the bottom of the home page, click on *Investor Relations*, and then click on *Fact Sheet*. What is the average number of screens in an AMC theater? How many theaters does AMC own and manage?

2. Based on the *Fact Sheet* information, which of AMC's theaters serves the largest volume of viewing customers?

3. Back up to the home page, and under "See a Movie," click on *Find a Theater*. Enter a few zip codes and make a list of the numbers of screens at the theaters that appear in each list. Based on the numbers of screens in this sample you have collected and your answers to questions 1 and 2 above, what can you conclude about the likely cost structure of this industry? Illustrate the long-run average cost curve for this industry.

For Group Discussion and Analysis A theater with a particularly large number of screens is called a multiplex. What do you suppose constrains the size of a multiplex theater in a typical locale? What factors do you think determine whether it is likely to be less costly for AMC to have fewer facilities that are larger in size or to have many smaller facilities?

ANSWERS TO QUICK QUIZZES

p. 513: (i) large . . . homogeneous . . . unrestrained; (ii) no . . . all; (iii) marginal . . . marginal; (iv) revenue . . . cost . . . price

p. 519: (i) average . . . price; (ii) break-even . . . marginal; (iii) shutdown . . . marginal; (iv) variable; (v) zero . . . normal; (vi) variable . . . summation . . . variable

p. 525: (i) intersection . . . variable; (ii) zero; (iii) horizontal . . . upward . . . downward; (iv) equal; (v) marginal cost . . . marginal cost

24

Monopoly

Have you ever wanted to be a kick boxer in the state of Ohio? If so, you must pay at least $100 to obtain a license before you can take the ring. Or perhaps you would like to be an interior designer. In some states, you can start to work immediately. In others, however, you must spend hundreds of hours in classes at tuition rates totaling thousands of dollars in order to qualify for a license to operate your own interior design business. A few states will even require a bachelor's degree in interior design from an accredited university program. What are the economic effects of these and other legal requirements that people must meet before they can engage in certain occupations? You will learn the answer by reading this chapter.

among U.S. companies receiving the highest rates of profits as percentages of revenues are private hospitals located in small- to medium-sized cities? Hospitals with profit rates exceeding 30 cents for every dollar of revenues are located in cities such as Northridge, California; Englewood, Colorado; Rochester, Minnesota; and El Paso, Texas. A hospital in Dothan, Alabama, takes in more than 50 cents in profits for each dollar of revenues it receives. A key characteristic shared by these hospitals is that they are all the only large, full-service hospitals located within regions surrounding the cities in which they are based. In this chapter, you will learn why a business that is the only seller—called a *monopoly*—often can earn substantial profits.

Definition of a Monopolist

The word *monopoly* probably brings to mind notions of a business that gouges the consumer and gets rich in the process. But if we are to succeed in analyzing and predicting the behavior of imperfectly competitive firms, we will have to be more objective in our definition. Although most monopolies in the United States are relatively large, our definition will be equally applicable to small businesses: A **monopolist** is the *single supplier* of a good or service for which there is no close substitute.

In a monopoly market structure, the firm (the monopolist) and the industry are one and the same. Occasionally, there may be a problem in identifying an industry and therefore determining if a monopoly exists. For example, should we think of aluminum and steel as separate industries, or should we define the industry in terms of basic metals? Our answer depends on the extent to which aluminum and steel can be substituted in the production of a wide range of products.

As we shall see in this chapter, a seller prefers to have a monopoly rather than to face competitors. In general, we think of monopoly prices as being higher than prices under perfect competition and of monopoly profits as typically being higher than profits under perfect competition (which are, in the long run, merely equivalent to a normal rate of return). How does a firm obtain a monopoly in an industry? Basically, there must be *barriers to entry* that enable firms to receive monopoly profits in the long run. Barriers to entry are restrictions on who can start a business or who can stay in a business.

Monopolist
The single supplier of a good or service for which there is no close substitute. The monopolist therefore constitutes its entire industry.

Barriers to Entry

For any amount of monopoly power to continue to exist in the long run, the market must be closed to entry in some way. Either legal means or certain aspects of the industry's technical or cost structure may prevent entry. We will discuss several of the barriers to entry that have allowed firms to reap monopoly profits in the long run (even if they are not pure monopolists in the technical sense).

Ownership of Resources without Close Substitutes

Preventing a newcomer from entering an industry is often difficult. Indeed, some economists contend that no monopoly acting without government support has been able to prevent entry into the industry unless that monopoly has had the control of some essential natural resource. Consider the possibility of one firm's owning the entire supply of a raw material input that is essential to the production of a particular commodity.

The exclusive ownership of such a vital resource serves as a barrier to entry until an alternative source of the raw material input is found or an alternative technology not requiring the raw material in question is developed. A good example of control over a vital input is the Aluminum Company of America (Alcoa), a firm that prior to World War II owned most world stocks of bauxite, the essential raw material in the production of aluminum. Such a situation is rare, though, and is ordinarily temporary.

Economies of Scale

Sometimes it is not profitable for more than one firm to exist in an industry. This is true if one firm would have to produce such a large quantity in order to realize lower unit costs that there would not be sufficient demand to warrant a second producer of the same product. Such a situation may arise because of a phenomenon we discussed in Chapter 22—economies of scale. When economies of scale exist, proportional increases in output yield proportionately smaller increases in total costs, and per-unit costs drop. When economies of scale exist, larger firms (with larger output) have an advantage in that they have lower costs that enable them to charge lower prices and thereby drive smaller firms out of business.

When economies of scale occur over a wide range of outputs, a **natural monopoly** may develop. A natural monopoly is the first firm to take advantage of persistent declining long-run average costs as scale increases. The natural monopolist is able to underprice its competitors and eventually force all of them out of the market.

Figure 24-1 below shows a downward-sloping long-run average cost curve (LAC). Recall that when average costs are falling, marginal costs are less than average costs. Thus, when the long-run average cost curve slopes downward, the long-run marginal cost curve (LMC) will be below the LAC.

In our example, long-run average costs are falling over such a large range of production rates that we would expect only one firm to survive as a natural monopolist. It would be the first one to take advantage of the decreasing average costs. That is, it would construct the large-scale facilities first. As its average costs fell, it would lower prices and get an ever-larger share of the market. Once that firm had driven all other firms out of the industry, it would raise its price to maximize profits.

Legal or Governmental Restrictions

Governments and legislatures can also erect barriers to entry. These include licenses, franchises, patents, tariffs, and specific regulations that tend to limit entry.

LICENSES, FRANCHISES, AND CERTIFICATES OF CONVENIENCE It is illegal to enter many industries without a government license, or a "certificate of convenience and public necessity." For example, in some states you cannot form an electrical utility to compete with the electrical utility already operating in your area. You would first have to obtain a certificate of convenience and public necessity from the appropriate authority, which is usually the state's public utility commission. Yet public utility

Natural monopoly
A monopoly that arises from the peculiar production characteristics in an industry. It usually arises when there are large economies of scale relative to the industry's demand such that one firm can produce at a lower average cost than can be achieved by multiple firms.

YOU ARE THERE

To contemplate why a city government might prefer that a firm have a monopoly, take a look at **Seeking Higher Rents from Souvenir Vendors in Atlanta** on page 548.

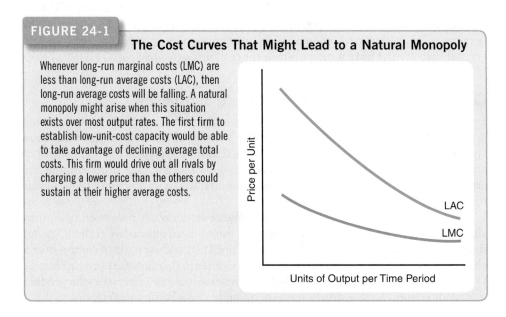

FIGURE 24-1

The Cost Curves That Might Lead to a Natural Monopoly

Whenever long-run marginal costs (LMC) are less than long-run average costs (LAC), then long-run average costs will be falling. A natural monopoly might arise when this situation exists over most output rates. The first firm to establish low-unit-cost capacity would be able to take advantage of declining average total costs. This firm would drive out all rivals by charging a lower price than the others could sustain at their higher average costs.

commissions in these states rarely, if ever, issue a certificate to a group of investors who want to compete directly in the same geographic area as an existing electrical utility. Hence, entry into the industry in a particular geographic area is prohibited, and long-run monopoly profits conceivably could be earned by the electrical utility already serving the area.

To enter interstate (and also many intrastate) markets for pipelines, television and radio broadcasting, and transmission of natural gas, to cite a few such industries, it is often necessary to obtain similar permits. Because these franchises or licenses are restricted, long-run monopoly profits might be earned by the firms already in the industry.

Why is it that some adults object to children operating lemonade stands?

POLICY EXAMPLE

Waging Economic War on Children's Lemonade Stands

The battles continue unabated across the land. The skirmishes begin when children as young as age 4 seek to learn about entrepreneurship—and to earn income to purchase toys or comic books—by opening lemonade stands and selling tall, cool drinks to their neighbors. Then, in towns and cities ranging from Cedar Rapids, Iowa, to Midway, Georgia, the police arrive to enforce laws requiring $50 permits or $200 licenses to sell cold drinks that compete with those offered by other sellers. Typically, the children respond by giving up on lemonade sales and instead begin to earn incomes by doing chores for neighbors—unless they run afoul of laws requiring "handyman licenses."

FOR CRITICAL THINKING

Who gains from laws requiring permits or licenses to sell cold drinks such as lemonade?

PATENTS A patent is issued to an inventor to provide protection from having the invention copied or stolen for a period of 20 years. Suppose that engineers working for Ford Motor Company discover a way to build an engine that requires half the parts of a regular engine and weighs only half as much. If Ford is successful in obtaining a patent on this discovery, it can (in principle) prevent others from copying it. The patent holder has a monopoly. It is the patent holder's responsibility to defend the patent, however. That means that Ford—like other patent owners—must expend resources to prevent others from imitating its invention. If the costs of enforcing a particular patent are greater than the benefits, though, the patent may not bestow any monopoly profits on its owner. The policing costs would be too high.

Go to www.econtoday.com/chap24 to learn more about patents and trademarks from the U.S. Patent and Trademark Office and to learn all about copyrights from the U.S. Copyright Office.

Tariffs
Taxes on imported goods.

TARIFFS **Tariffs** are special taxes that are imposed on certain imported goods. Tariffs make imports more expensive relative to their domestic counterparts, encouraging consumers to switch to the relatively cheaper domestically made products. If the tariffs are high enough, domestic producers may be able to act together like a single firm and gain monopoly advantage as the sole suppliers. Many countries have tried this protectionist strategy by using high tariffs to shut out foreign competitors.

REGULATIONS Throughout the twentieth century and to the present, government regulation of the U.S. economy has increased, especially along the dimensions of safety and quality. U.S. firms incur hundreds of billions of dollars in expenses each year to comply with federal, state, and local government regulations of business conduct relating to workplace conditions, environmental protection, product safety, and various other activities. Presumably, these large fixed costs of complying with regulations can be spread over a greater number of units of output by larger firms than by smaller firms, thereby putting the smaller firms at a competitive disadvantage. Entry will also be deterred to the extent that the scale of operation of a potential entrant must be sufficiently large to cover the average fixed costs of compliance. We examine regulation in more detail in Chapter 27.

A **monopolist** is the single seller of a product or good for which there is no _____ substitute.

To maintain a monopoly, there must be barriers to entry. Barriers to entry include _____ of resources without

close substitutes; economies of _____; legally required licenses, franchises, and certificates of convenience; patents; tariffs; and safety and quality regulations.

The Demand Curve a Monopolist Faces

A *pure monopolist* is the sole supplier of *one* product. A pure monopolist faces the demand curve for the entire market for that good or service.

The monopolist faces the industry demand curve because the monopolist is the entire industry.

Because the monopolist faces the industry demand curve, which is by definition downward sloping, its choice regarding how much to produce is not the same as for a perfect competitor. When a monopolist changes output, it does not automatically receive the same price per unit that it did before the change.

Profits to Be Made from Increasing Production

How do firms benefit from changing production rates? What happens to price in each case? Let's first review the situation among perfect competitors.

MARGINAL REVENUE FOR THE PERFECT COMPETITOR Recall that a firm in a perfectly competitive industry faces a perfectly elastic demand curve. That is because the perfectly competitive firm is such a small part of the market that it cannot influence the price of its product. It is a *price taker*. If the forces of supply and demand establish that the price per constant-quality pair of shoes is $50, the individual firm can sell all the pairs of shoes it wants to produce at $50 per pair. The per-unit price is $50, and the marginal revenue is also $50.

Let us again define marginal revenue:

Marginal revenue equals the change in total revenue due to a one-unit change in the quantity produced and sold.

In the case of a perfectly competitive industry, each time a single firm changes production by one unit, total revenue changes by the going price, and price is unchanged.

MARGINAL REVENUE FOR THE MONOPOLIST What about a monopoly firm? We begin by considering a situation in which a monopolist charges every buyer the same price for each unit of its product. Because a monopoly is the entire industry, the monopoly firm's demand curve is the market demand curve. The market demand curve slopes downward, just like the other demand curves that we have seen. Therefore, to induce consumers to buy more of a particular product, given the industry demand curve, the monopoly firm must lower the price. Thus, the monopoly firm moves *down* the demand curve. If all buyers are to be charged the same price, the monopoly must lower the price on *all* units sold in order to sell more. It cannot lower the price on just the *last* unit sold in any given time period in order to sell a larger quantity.

Put yourself in the shoes of a monopoly ferryboat owner. You have a government-bestowed franchise, and no one can compete with you. Your ferryboat goes between two islands. If you are charging $8 per crossing, a certain quantity of your services

FIGURE 24-2

Demand Curves for the Perfect Competitor and the Monopolist

The perfect competitor in panel (a) faces a perfectly elastic demand curve, *d*. The monopolist in panel (b) faces the entire industry demand curve, which slopes downward.

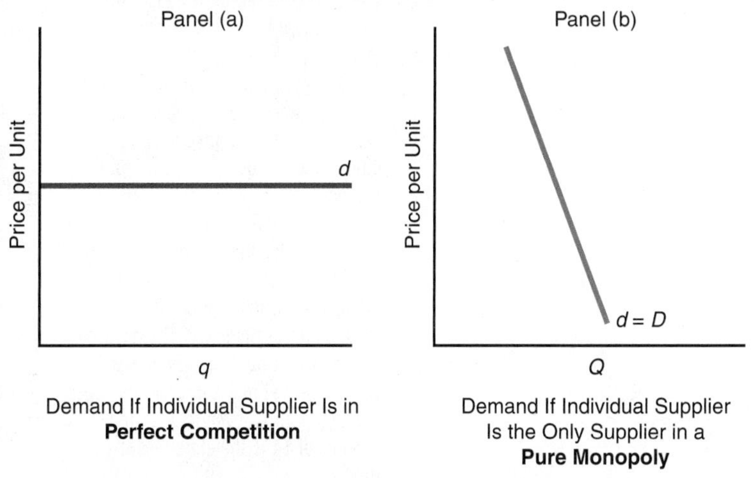

Panel (a)

Demand If Individual Supplier Is in
Perfect Competition

Panel (b)

Demand If Individual Supplier
Is the Only Supplier in a
Pure Monopoly

will be demanded. Let's say that you are ferrying 4 people per hour each way at that price. If you decide that you would like to ferry more individuals, you must lower your price to all individuals—you must move *down* the existing demand curve for ferrying services. To calculate the marginal revenue of your change in price, you must first calculate the total revenues you received at $8 per passenger per crossing and then calculate the total revenues you would receive at, say, $7 per passenger per crossing.

PERFECT COMPETITION VERSUS MONOPOLY It is sometimes useful to compare monopoly markets with perfectly competitive markets. The monopolist is constrained by the demand curve for its product, just as a perfectly competitive firm is constrained by its demand. The key difference is the nature of the demand curve each type of firm faces. We see this in Figure 24-2 above.

Here we see the fundamental difference between the monopolist and the perfect competitor. The perfect competitor doesn't have to worry about lowering price to sell more. In a perfectly competitive situation, the perfectly competitive firm accounts for such a small part of the market that it can sell its entire output, whatever that may be, at the same price. The monopolist cannot.

The more the monopolist wants to sell, the lower the price it has to charge on the last unit (and on *all* units put on the market for sale). To sell the last unit, the monopolist has to lower the price because it is facing a downward-sloping demand curve, and the only way to move down the demand curve is to lower the price. As long as this price must be the same for all units, the extra revenues the monopolist receives from selling one more unit are going to be smaller than the extra revenues received from selling the next-to-last unit.

The Monopolist's Marginal Revenue: Less Than Price

An essential point is that for the monopolist, marginal revenue is always less than price. To understand why, look at Figure 24-3 on the next page, which shows a unit increase in output sold due to a reduction from $8 to $7 in the price of ferry crossings provided by a monopolistic ferry company. The new $7 price is the price received for the last unit, so selling this unit contributes $7 to revenues. That is equal to the vertical column (area A). Area A is one unit wide by $7 high.

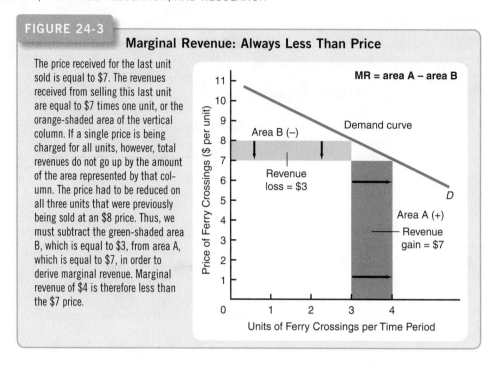

FIGURE 24-3

Marginal Revenue: Always Less Than Price

The price received for the last unit sold is equal to $7. The revenues received from selling this last unit are equal to $7 times one unit, or the orange-shaded area of the vertical column. If a single price is being charged for all units, however, total revenues do not go up by the amount of the area represented by that column. The price had to be reduced on all three units that were previously being sold at an $8 price. Thus, we must subtract the green-shaded area B, which is equal to $3, from area A, which is equal to $7, in order to derive marginal revenue. Marginal revenue of $4 is therefore less than the $7 price.

But price times the last unit sold is *not* the net addition to *total* revenues received from selling that last unit. Why? Because price had to be reduced on the three previous units sold in order to sell the larger quantity—four ferry crossings. The reduction in price is represented by the vertical distance from $8 to $7 on the vertical axis. We must therefore subtract area B from area A to come up with the *change* in total revenues due to a one-unit increase in sales. Clearly, the change in total revenues—that is, marginal revenue—must be less than price because marginal revenue is always the difference between areas A and B in Figure 24-3. Thus, at a price of $7, marginal revenue is $7 − $3 = $4 because there is a $1 per unit price reduction on three previous units. Hence, marginal revenue, $4, is less than price, $7.

Elasticity and Monopoly

The monopolist faces a downward-sloping market demand curve. That fact means that the monopolist cannot charge just *any* price with no changes in quantity (a common misconception) because, depending on the price charged, a different quantity will be demanded.

Earlier we defined a monopolist as the single seller of a well-defined good or service with no *close* substitute. This does not mean, however, that the demand curve for a monopoly is vertical or exhibits zero price elasticity of demand. After all, consumers have limited incomes and unlimited wants. The market demand curve, which the monopolist alone faces in this situation, slopes downward because individuals compare the marginal satisfaction they will receive to the cost of the commodity to be purchased. Take the example of a particular type of sports car. Even if miraculously there were absolutely no substitutes whatsoever for that sports car, the market demand curve would still slope downward. At lower prices, people will purchase more of those sports cars, perhaps buying cars for other family members.

Furthermore, the demand curve for the sports car slopes downward because there are at least several *imperfect* substitutes, such as other types of sports cars, used sports cars, sport utility vehicles, and other stylish vehicles. The more such substitutes there are, and the better these substitutes are, the more elastic will be the monopolist's demand curve, all other things held constant.

QUICK QUIZ See page 553 for the answers. Review concepts from this section in MyEconLab.

The monopolist estimates its marginal revenue curve, where marginal revenue is defined as the _____ in _____ revenues due to a one-unit change in quantity sold.

For the perfect competitor, price equals _____ revenue equals average revenue. For the monopolist,

_____ revenue is always less than price because price must be reduced on all units to sell more.

The price _____ of demand for the monopolist depends on the number and similarity of substitutes. The more numerous the imperfect substitutes, the greater the price _____ of the monopolist's demand curve.

Costs and Monopoly Profit Maximization

To find the rate of output at which the perfect competitor would maximize profits, we had to add cost data. We will do the same now for the monopolist. We assume that profit maximization is the goal of the pure monopolist, just as it is for the perfect competitor. The perfect competitor, however, has only to decide on the profit-maximizing rate of output because price is given. The perfect competitor is a price taker.

For the pure monopolist, we must seek a profit-maximizing *price-output combination* because the monopolist is a **price searcher.** We can determine this profit-maximizing price-output combination with either of two equivalent approaches—by looking at total revenues and total costs or by looking at marginal revenues and marginal costs. We shall examine both approaches.

Price searcher
A firm that must determine the price-output combination that maximizes profit because it faces a downward-sloping demand curve.

The Total Revenues–Total Costs Approach

Suppose that the government of a small town located in a remote desert area grants a single satellite television company the right to offer services within its jurisdiction. It enforces rules that prevent other firms from offering television services. We show demand (weekly rate of output and price per unit), revenues, costs, and other data in panel (a) of Figure 24-4 on the next page. In column 3, we see total revenues for this TV service monopolist, and in column 4, we see total costs. We can transfer these two columns to panel (b). The fundamental difference between the total revenue and total cost diagram in panel (b) and the one we showed for a perfect competitor in Chapter 23 is that the total revenue line is no longer straight. Rather, it curves. For any given demand curve, in order to sell more, the monopolist must lower the price. This reflects the fact that the basic difference between a monopolist and a perfect competitor has to do with the demand curve for the two types of firms. The monopolist faces a downward-sloping demand curve.

Profit maximization involves maximizing the positive difference between total revenues and total costs. This occurs at an output rate of between 9 and 10 units per week.

The Marginal Revenue–Marginal Cost Approach

Profit maximization will also occur where marginal revenue equals marginal cost. This is as true for a monopolist as it is for a perfect competitor (but the monopolist will charge a price in excess of marginal revenue). When we transfer marginal cost and marginal revenue information from columns 6 and 7 in panel (a) to panel (c) in Figure 24-4 on the next page, we see that marginal revenue equals marginal cost at a weekly quantity of satellite TV services of between 9 and 10 units. Profit maximization must occur at the same output as in panel (b).

WHY PRODUCE WHERE MARGINAL REVENUE EQUALS MARGINAL COST? If the monopolist produces past the point where marginal revenue equals marginal cost, marginal cost will exceed marginal revenue. That is, the incremental cost of producing any more units will exceed the incremental revenue. It would not be worthwhile, as was true also in perfect competition. Furthermore, just as in the case of perfect competition, if the monopolist produces less than that, it is not making maximum profits.

FIGURE 24-4

Monopoly Costs, Revenues, and Profits

In panel (a), we give demand (weekly satellite television services and price), revenues, costs, and other relevant data. As shown in panel (b), the satellite TV monopolist maximizes profits where the positive difference between TR and TC is greatest. This is at an output rate of between 9 and 10 units per week. Put another way, profit maximization occurs where marginal revenue equals marginal cost, as shown in panel (c). This is at the same weekly service rate of between 9 and 10 units. (The MC curve must cut the MR curve from below.)

Panel (a)

(1) Output (units)	(2) Price per Unit	(3) Total Revenues (TR) (3) = (2) x (1)	(4) Total Costs (TC)	(5) Total Profit (5) = (3) – (4)	(6) Marginal Cost (MC)	(7) Marginal Revenue (MR)
0	$8.00	$ .00	$10.00	–$10.00		
					$4.00	$7.80
1	7.80	7.80	14.00	–6.20		
					3.50	7.40
2	7.60	15.20	17.50	–2.30		
					3.25	7.00
3	7.40	22.20	20.75	1.45		
					3.05	6.60
4	7.20	28.80	23.80	5.00		
					2.90	6.20
5	7.00	35.00	26.70	8.30		
					2.80	5.80
6	6.80	40.80	29.50	11.30		
					2.75	5.40
7	6.60	46.20	32.25	13.95		
					2.85	5.00
8	6.40	51.20	35.10	16.10		
					3.20	4.60
9	6.20	55.80	38.30	17.50		
					4.40	4.20
10	6.00	60.00	42.70	17.30		
					6.00	3.80
11	5.80	63.80	48.70	15.10		
					9.00	3.40
12	5.60	67.20	57.70	9.50		

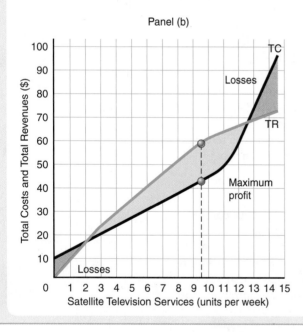

Panel (b)

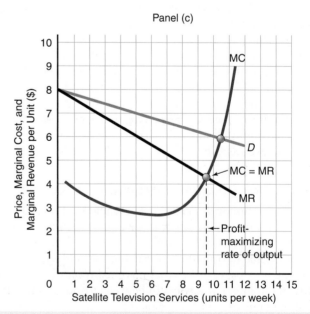

Panel (c)

Look at output rate Q_1 in Figure 24-5 on the facing page. Here the monopolist's marginal revenue is at *A*, but marginal cost is at *B*. Marginal revenue exceeds marginal cost on the last unit sold. The profit for that *particular* unit, Q_1, is equal to the vertical difference between *A* and *B*, or the difference between marginal revenue and marginal cost.

FIGURE 24-5

Maximizing Profits

The profit-maximizing production rate is Q_m, and the profit-maximizing price is P_m. The monopolist would be unwise to produce at the rate Q_1 because here marginal revenue would be Q_1A, and marginal cost would be Q_1B. Marginal revenue would exceed marginal cost. The firm will keep producing until the point Q_m, where marginal revenue just equals marginal cost. It would be foolish to produce at the rate Q_2, for here marginal cost exceeds marginal revenue. It would behoove the monopolist to cut production back to Q_m.

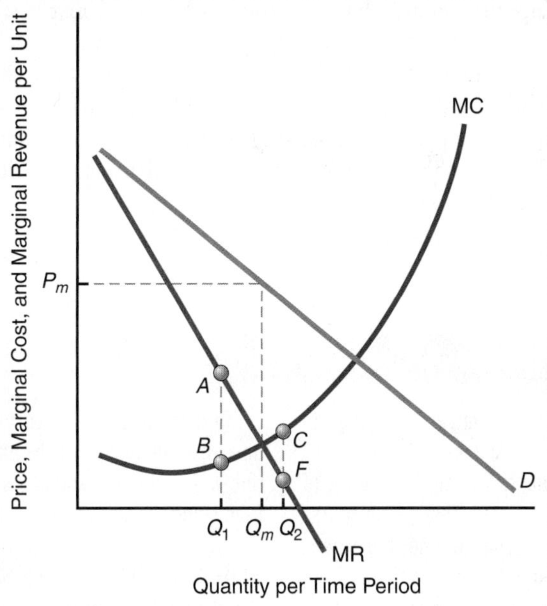

The monopolist would be foolish to stop at output rate Q_1 because if output is expanded, marginal revenue will still exceed marginal cost, and therefore total profits will be increased by selling more. In fact, the profit-maximizing monopolist will continue to expand output and sales until marginal revenue equals marginal cost, which is at output rate Q_m.

The monopolist won't produce at rate Q_2 because here, as we see, marginal costs are C and marginal revenues are F. The difference between C and F represents the *reduction* in total profits from producing that additional unit. Total profits will rise as the monopolist reduces its rate of output back toward Q_m.

What Price to Charge for Output?

How does the monopolist set prices? We know the quantity is set at the point at which marginal revenue equals marginal cost. The monopolist then finds out how much can be charged—how much the market will bear—for that particular quantity, Q_m, in Figure 24-5 above.

THE MONOPOLY PRICE We know that the demand curve shows the *maximum* price for which a given quantity can be sold. That means that our monopolist knows that to sell Q_m, it can charge only P_m because that is the price at which that specific quantity, Q_m, is demanded. This price is found by drawing a vertical line from the quantity, Q_m, to the market demand curve. Where that line hits the market demand curve, the price is determined. We find that price by drawing a horizontal line from the demand curve to the price axis. Doing that gives us the profit-maximizing price, P_m.

In our example, at a profit-maximizing quantity of satellite TV services of between 9 and 10 units in Figure 24-4 on the preceding page, the firm can charge a maximum price of just over $6 and still sell all the services it provides, all at the same price.

The basic procedure for finding the profit-maximizing price-quantity combination for the monopolist is first to determine the profit-maximizing rate of output, by either the total revenue–total cost method or the marginal revenue–marginal cost method. Then it is possible to determine by use of the demand curve, D, the maximum price that can be charged to sell that output.

REAL-WORLD INFORMATIONAL LIMITATIONS Don't get the impression that just because we are able to draw an exact demand curve in Figures 24-4 and 24-5, real-world monopolists have such perfect information. The process of price searching by a less-than-perfect competitor is just that—a process. A monopolist can only estimate the actual demand curve and therefore can make only an educated guess when it sets its profit-maximizing price. This is not a problem for the perfect competitor because price is given already by the intersection of market demand and market supply. The monopolist, in contrast, reaches the profit-maximizing output-price combination by trial and error.

In recent years, what services have airlines provided to passengers at prices passengers have proved willing to pay?

EXAMPLE

Trial and Error Yields Profits from Monopoly Time in the Air

For years, airline ticket prices covered flying passengers and bags to their destinations while providing drinks and snacks along the way. Since the late 2000s, airlines have been trying to take full advantage of their position as monopoly sellers during flights. First, they began charging for checked bags, snacks, and pillows. Now some airlines are experimenting with charging extra fees for more comfortable seats that provide a few more inches of leg room and for seats that recline more than standard seats. Other airlines offer "travel concierge" services that assist passengers with booking items such as restaurant reservations and theater tickets in their destination cities.

To determine the prices for these and other new services, airlines have been searching for the prices that passengers are willing to pay. In this way, airlines eventually settle on prices that maximize the profits from being the only available seller *during* passengers' flights.

FOR CRITICAL THINKING
Some airlines are aiming to be "virtual shopping malls" by offering to take orders for a variety of "buy-while-you-fly" items for delivery to passengers' homes. Why might this new line of business be less likely to yield monopoly profits for airlines?

Calculating Monopoly Profit

We have talked about the monopolist's profit. We have yet to indicate how much profit the monopolist makes, which we do in Figure 24-6 on the facing page.

The Graphical Depiction of Monopoly Profits

We have actually shown total profits in column 5 of panel (a) in Figure 24-4 on page 540. We can also find total profits by adding an average total cost curve to panel (c) of that figure, as shown in Figure 24-6. When we add the average total cost curve, we find that the profit a monopolist makes is equal to the green-shaded area—or total revenues ($P \times Q$) minus total costs (ATC $\times$ Q).

Given the demand curve and that all units sold at the same price, a monopolist cannot make greater profits than those shown by the green-shaded area. The monopolist is maximizing profits where marginal cost equals marginal revenue. If the monopolist produces less than that, it will forfeit some profits. If the monopolist produces more than that, it will also forfeit some profits.

No Guarantee of Profits

The term *monopoly* conjures up the notion of a greedy firm ripping off the public and making exorbitant profits. The mere existence of a monopoly, however, does not guarantee high profits. Numerous monopolies have gone bankrupt. Figure 24-7 on the next page shows the monopolist's demand curve as *D* and the resultant marginal revenue curve as MR. It does not matter at what rate of output this particular monopolist operates. Total costs cannot be covered.

Look at the position of the average total cost curve. It lies everywhere above *D* (the average revenue curve). Thus, there is no price-output combination that will allow the monopolist even to cover costs, much less earn profits. This monopolist will, in the short run, suffer economic losses as shown by the red-shaded area. The graph in

FIGURE 24-6

Monopoly Profit

We find monopoly profit by subtracting total costs from total revenues at a quantity of satellite TV services of between 9 and 10 units per week, labeled Q_m, which is the profit-maximizing rate of output for the satellite TV monopolist. The profit-maximizing price is therefore slightly more than $6 per week and is labeled P_m. Monopoly profit is given by the green-shaded area, which is equal to total revenues ($P \times Q$) minus total costs (ATC $\times$ Q). This diagram is similar to panel (c) of Figure 24-4 on page 540, with the short-run average total cost curve (ATC) added.

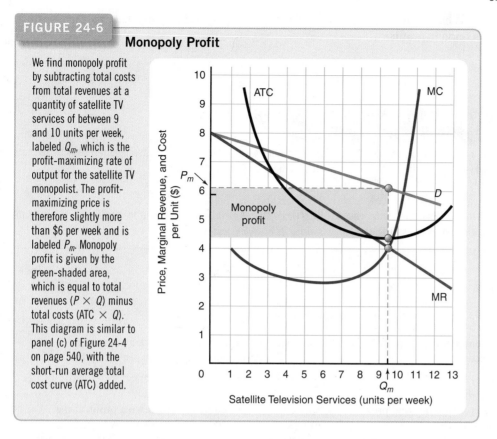

Figure 24-7, which applies to many inventions, depicts a situation of resulting monopoly. The owner of a patented invention or discovery has a pure legal monopoly, but the demand and cost curves are such that production is not profitable. Every year at inventors' conventions, one can see many inventions that have never been put into production because they were deemed "uneconomic" by potential producers and users.

FIGURE 24-7

Monopolies: Not Always Profitable

Some monopolists face the situation shown here. The average total cost curve, ATC, is everywhere above the average revenue, or demand, curve, D. In the short run, the monopolist will produce where MC = MR at point A. Output Q_m will be sold at price P_m, but average total cost per unit is C_1. Losses are the red-shaded rectangle. Eventually, the monopolist will go out of business.

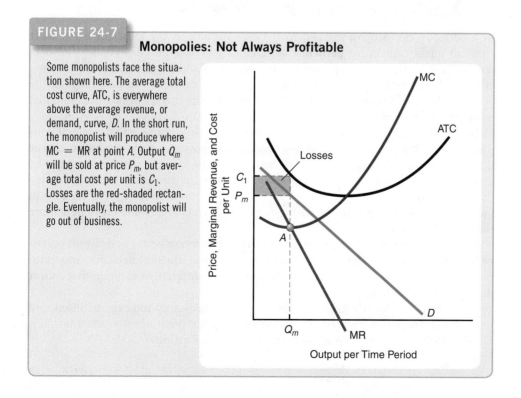

What government-sanctioned U.S. monopoly persistently fails to earn positive economic profits?

POLICY EXAMPLE

The U.S. Rail Monopoly That Subsists on Taxpayer Handouts

The passenger rail company Amtrak has a near-monopoly on U.S. intercity rail service. Nevertheless, year in and year out, this firm suffers economic losses. In recent years, these losses have exceeded $1 billion per year. To keep Amtrak's rail lines operating across the country, the federal government pays the company subsidies to cover its losses. Thus, while Amtrak undoubtedly charges loss-minimizing prices to passengers who use its rail lines, the revenues that its passenger rail services generate are less than its incurred total costs.

FOR CRITICAL THINKING

What would Amtrak eventually have to do if the government stopped subsidizing its economic losses?

QUICK QUIZ   See page 553 for the answers. Review concepts from this section in MyEconLab.

The basic difference between a monopolist and a perfect competitor is that a monopolist faces a _____-sloping demand curve, and therefore marginal revenue is _____ than price.

The monopolist must choose the profit-maximizing price-output combination—the output at which _____ revenue equals _____ cost and the highest price possible as given by the _____ curve for that particular output rate.

Monopoly profits are found by looking at average _____ costs compared to price per unit. This difference multiplied by the _____ sold at that price determines monopoly profit.

A monopolist does not necessarily earn a profit. If the average _____ cost curve lies entirely _____ the demand curve for a monopoly, no production rate will be profitable.

On Making Higher Profits: Price Discrimination

In a perfectly competitive market, each buyer is charged the same price for every constant-quality unit of the particular commodity (corrected for differential transportation charges). Because the product is homogeneous and we also assume full knowledge on the part of the buyers, a difference in price cannot exist. Any seller of the product who tried to charge a price higher than the going market price would find that no one would purchase it from that seller.

In this chapter, we have assumed until now that the monopolist charged all consumers the same price for all units. A monopolist, however, may be able to charge different people different prices or different unit prices for successive units sought by a given buyer. When there is no cost difference, such strategies are called **price discrimination.** A firm will engage in price discrimination whenever feasible to increase profits. A price-discriminating firm is able to charge some customers more than other customers.

It must be made clear at the outset that charging different prices to different people or for different units to reflect differences in costs of production does not amount to price discrimination. This is **price differentiation:** differences in price that reflect differences in marginal cost.

We can also say that a uniform price does not necessarily indicate an absence of price discrimination. Charging all customers the same price when production costs vary by customer is actually a situation of price discrimination.

Price discrimination
Selling a given product at more than one price, with the price difference being unrelated to differences in marginal cost.

Price differentiation
Establishing different prices for similar products to reflect differences in marginal cost in providing those commodities to different groups of buyers.

Necessary Conditions for Price Discrimination

Three conditions are necessary for price discrimination to exist:

1. The firm must face a downward-sloping demand curve.

2. The firm must be able to readily (and cheaply) identify buyers or groups of buyers with predictably different elasticities of demand.

3. The firm must be able to prevent resale of the product or service.

Has it ever occurred to you that most of the other students seated in your college classroom pay different overall tuition rates than you do because your college and others use financial aid packages to engage in price discrimination?

EXAMPLE

Why Students Pay Different Prices to Attend College

Out-of-pocket tuition rates for any two college students can differ by considerable amounts, even if the students happen to major in the same subjects and enroll in many of the same courses. The reason is that colleges offer students diverse financial aid packages depending on their "financial need."

To document their "need" for financial aid, students must provide detailed information about family income and wealth. This information, of course, helps the college determine the prices that different families are most likely to be willing and able to pay, so that it can engage in price discrimination. Figure 24-8 below, shows how this collegiate price-discrimination process works. The college charges the price P_7, which is the college's official posted "tuition rate," to students with families judged to be most willing and able to pay the highest price. Students whose families have the lowest levels of income and wealth are judged to be willing and able to pay a much lower price, such as P_1. To charge

these students this lower tuition rate, the college provides them with a financial aid package that reduces the price they pay by the difference between P_7, the full tuition price, and P_1. In this way, the actual price paid by these "neediest" students is only P_1.

Likewise, the college groups other, somewhat less "needy" students into a slightly higher income-and-wealth category and determines that they are likely to be willing to pay a somewhat higher price, P_2. Hence, it grants them a smaller financial aid package, equal to $P_7 - P_2$, so that the students actually pay the price P_2. The college continues this process for other groups, thereby engaging in price discrimination in its tuition charges.

FOR CRITICAL THINKING

Does the educational product supplied by colleges satisfy all three conditions necessary for price discrimination?

FIGURE 24-8

Toward Perfect Price Discrimination in College Tuition Rates

Students that a college determines to be "neediest" and least able to pay the full tuition price, P_7, receive a financial aid package equal to $P_7 - P_1$. These students effectively pay only the price P_1. The college groups the remaining students into categories on the basis of their willingness and ability to pay a higher price, and each group receives a progressively smaller financial aid package. Those students who are willing and able to pay the full price, P_7, receive no financial aid from the college.

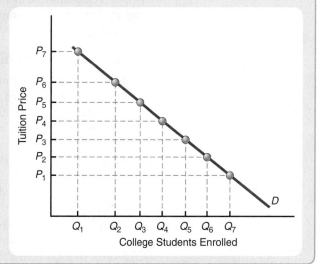

FIGURE 24-9

The Effects of Monopolizing an Industry

In panel (a), we show a perfectly competitive situation in which equilibrium is established at the intersection of D and S at point E. The equilibrium price is P_e and the equilibrium quantity is Q_e. Each individual perfectly competitive producer faces a demand curve that is perfectly elastic at the market clearing price, P_e. What happens if the industry is suddenly monopolized? We assume that the costs stay the same. The only thing that changes is that the monopolist now faces the entire downward-sloping demand curve. In panel (b), we draw the marginal revenue curve. Marginal cost is S because that is the horizontal summation of all the individual marginal cost curves. The monopolist therefore produces at Q_m and charges price P_m. This price P_m in panel (b) is higher than P_e in panel (a), and Q_m is less than Q_e.

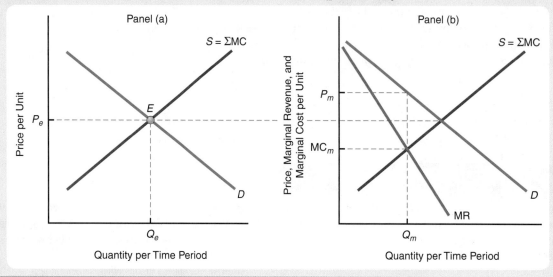

The Social Cost of Monopolies

Let's run a little experiment. We will start with a purely competitive industry with numerous firms, each one unable to affect the price of its product. The supply curve of the industry is equal to the horizontal sum of the marginal cost curves of the individual producers above their respective minimum average variable costs. In panel (a) of Figure 24-9 above, we show the market demand curve and the market supply curve in a perfectly competitive situation. The perfectly competitive price in equilibrium is equal to P_e, and the equilibrium quantity at that price is equal to Q_e. Each individual perfect competitor faces a demand curve (not shown) that is coincident with the price line P_e. No individual supplier faces the market demand curve, D.

Comparing Monopoly with Perfect Competition

Now let's assume that a monopolist comes in and buys up every single perfect competitor in the industry. In so doing, we'll assume that monopolization does not affect any of the marginal cost curves or demand. We can therefore redraw D and S in panel (b) of Figure 24-9 above, exactly the same as in panel (a).

How does this monopolist decide how much to charge and how much to produce? If the monopolist is profit maximizing, it is going to look at the marginal revenue curve and produce at the output where marginal revenue equals marginal cost. But what is the marginal cost curve in panel (b) of Figure 24-9? It is merely S, because we said that S was equal to the horizontal summation of the portions of the individual marginal cost curves above each firm's respective minimum average variable cost. The monopolist therefore produces quantity Q_m, and sells it at price P_m.

Notice that Q_m is less than Q_e and that P_m is greater than P_e. Hence, a monopolist produces a smaller quantity and sells it at a higher price. This is the reason usually given when economists criticize monopolists. Monopolists raise the price and restrict production, compared to a perfectly competitive situation. For a monopolist's product, consumers pay a price that exceeds the marginal cost of production. Resources are misallocated in such a situation—too few resources are being used in the monopolist's industry, and too many are used elsewhere. (See Appendix G on deadweight loss at the end of this chapter.)

WHAT IF... governments protect local retailers from "big-box" retailers such as Walmart and Target?

In some cities, such as Chicago and New York City, protesters have united in opposition to efforts to open new outlets on the part of national retailers such as Walmart and Target. When activist groups succeed in preventing entry by these so-called big-box retailers, the groups also succeed in protecting local retailers from competition.

In areas with very few local sellers, protected sellers are able to search for profit-maximizing prices higher than those that would have prevailed under perfect competition. In the absence of entry by big-box retailers, therefore, local retailers are able to maintain higher-than-competitive prices, resulting in misallocations of resources.

Implications of Higher Monopoly Prices

Notice from Figure 24-9 that by setting MR = MC, the monopolist produces at a rate of output where P is greater than MC (compare P_m to MC_m). The marginal cost of a commodity (MC) represents what society had to give up in order to obtain the last unit produced. Price, by contrast, represents what buyers are willing to pay to acquire that last unit. Thus, the price of a good represents society's valuation of the last unit produced. The monopoly outcome of P exceeding MC means that the value to society of the last unit produced is greater than its cost (MC). Hence, not enough of the good is being produced. As we have pointed out before, these differences between monopoly and perfect competition arise not because of differences in costs but rather because of differences in the demand curves the individual firms face. The monopolist faces a downward-sloping demand curve. The individual perfect competitor faces a perfectly elastic demand curve.

Before we leave the topic of the cost to society of monopolies, we must repeat that our analysis is based on a heroic assumption: The monopolization of the perfectly competitive industry does not change the cost structure. If monopolization results in higher marginal cost, the net cost of monopoly to society is even greater.

Conversely, if monopolization results in cost savings, the net cost of monopoly to society is less than we infer from our analysis. Indeed, we could have presented a hypothetical example in which monopolization led to such a dramatic reduction in cost that society actually benefited. Such a situation is a possibility in industries in which economies of scale exist for a very great range of outputs.

QUICK QUIZ   See page 553 for the answers. Review concepts from this section in MyEconLab.

Three conditions are necessary for price discrimination: (1) The firm must face a _____-sloping demand curve, (2) the firm must be able to identify buyers with predictably different price _____ of demand, and (3) _____ of the product or service must be preventable.

Price _____ should not be confused with price _____, which occurs when differences in price reflect differences in marginal cost.

Monopoly tends to result in a _____ quantity being sold, because the price is _____ than it would be in an ideal perfectly competitive industry in which the cost curves were essentially the same as the monopolist's.

YOU ARE THERE
Seeking Higher Rents from Souvenir Vendors in Atlanta

For more than 20 years, Stanley Hambrick and Larry Miller have operated a vending stand at Turner Field in Atlanta. Until recently, they paid a rental fee of $250 per year for the right to sell baseball souvenirs and T-shirts.

Now, however, the city of Atlanta has, in exchange for a share of profits, granted a Chicago-based management company called General Growth Properties a monopoly in renting vending spaces around Turner Field. The rental fees of General Growth Properties are considerably higher than what Hambrick and Miller used to pay. These new fees range from as low as $500 per *month* for out-of-the-way sites to $1,600 per *month* for sites along main paths. Hambrick and Miller quickly convert these rates to annual amounts and realize that General Growth Properties has utilized its

monopoly position to search for rental rates that will maximize profits it will share with the city of Atlanta. The two vendors now face annual rental rates ranging from 24 times to 77 times more than they used to pay.

Critical Thinking Questions

1. Is the number of vendor stands next to Turner Field likely to grow or to shrink under the management of General Growth Properties? Explain.

2. Why might General Growth Properties and the city of Atlanta prefer for Hambrick and Miller and some other vendors to close their souvenir and T-shirt stands?

ISSUES & APPLICATIONS

The U.S. Occupational License Explosion

CONCEPTS APPLIED

▶ License

▶ Barriers to Entry

▶ Monopoly

Are you looking for a job washing people's hair at a hair salon? If you live in Texas, you will require a license first. What if you would like to braid hair at a salon? If the salon is in Utah, a license is also necessary. In states across the land, licensing rules have expanded with each passing year.

A Sharp Increase in Occupations Requiring State Approval

Table 24-1 lists some of the occupations that require licenses in at least a few states. All told, 1,100 different jobs now require a license in at least one state—a number nearly 40 percent larger than three decades ago.

Indeed, more than 30 percent of U.S. residents are in occupations requiring licenses. By way of comparison, in 2000, fewer than 20 percent of U.S. residents were in licensed occupations, and in 1950, only about 5 percent required licenses.

Economic Effects of Occupational Barriers to Entry

To obtain occupational licenses, people typically must pay fees. Many must also engage in a period of study—perhaps through or even beyond an undergraduate degree. Such licensing requirements constitute barriers to entry.

For incumbents who already have positions in regulated occupations, licenses create monopoly profits. Consumers pay higher prices to obtain the services of people in licensed occupations. The total price tag to consumers exceeds $100 billion per year nationwide, or about 1 percent of total spending by U.S. consumers. Thus, people in licensed occupations earn higher incomes. After controlling for other determinants of incomes, economists have found that occupations in states with licensing requirements yield annual incomes 15 percent higher than do the same occupations in states without such requirements.

For Critical Thinking

1. Why do you suppose that employment growth is about 20 percent greater in unlicensed occupations than in licensed occupations?

2. What do you suppose a typical state government does with the millions of dollars of occupational license fees it receives each year?

TABLE 24-1

Selected Occupations Requiring Licenses in Some U.S. States

Acupuncturists	Glass installers	Nutritionists
Athletic trainers	Hearing-aid fitters	Secondhand booksellers
Ballroom-dancing teachers	Hunting guides	Shampoo specialists
Barbers	Librarians	Tattoo artists
Dieticians	Locksmiths	Tour guides
Electricians	Manicurists	Tree-trimmers
Frozen-dessert retailers	Massage therapists	Wig specialists
Funeral directors	Private detectives	Windshield repairers
Hair braiders	Respiratory therapists	Yoga instructors

Web Resources

1. Take a look at more information about the growth of occupational licensing in the United States at www.econtoday.com/chap24.

2. To learn more about the economic impacts of occupational licensing, go to www.econtoday.com/chap24.

> ### MyEconLab
> For more questions on this chapter's Issues & Applications, go to MyEconLab. In the Study Plan for this chapter, select Section N: News.

MyEconLab

Here is what you should know after reading this chapter. MyEconLab will help you identify what you know, and where to go when you need to practice.

WHAT YOU SHOULD KNOW		WHERE TO GO TO PRACTICE
Why Monopoly Can Occur Monopoly, a situation in which a single firm produces and sells a good or service, can occur when there are significant barriers to market entry. Examples of barriers to entry include (1) ownership of important resources for which there are no close substitutes, (2) economies of scale for ever-larger ranges of output, and (3) governmental restrictions.	monopolist, 533 natural monopoly, 534 tariffs, 535	• MyEconLab Study Plans 24.1, 24.2
Demand and Marginal Revenue Conditions a Monopolist Faces A monopolist faces the entire market demand curve. When it reduces the price of its product, it is able to sell more units at the new price, which boosts revenues, but it also sells other units at this lower price, which reduces revenues somewhat. Thus, the monopolist's marginal revenue at any given quantity is less than the price at which it sells that quantity. Its marginal revenue curve slopes downward and lies below the demand curve.	Key Figures Figure 24-2, 537 Figure 24-3, 538	• MyEconLab Study Plans 24.3, 24.4 • Animated Figures 24-2, 24-3

MyEconLab *continued*

WHAT YOU SHOULD KNOW		WHERE TO GO TO PRACTICE
How a Monopolist Determines How Much Output to Produce and What Price to Charge A monopolist is a price searcher that seeks to charge the price that maximizes its economic profits. It produces to the point at which marginal revenue equals marginal cost. The monopolist then charges the maximum price that consumers are willing to pay for that quantity.	price searcher, 539 Key Figures Figure 24-4, 540 Figure 24-5, 541	• MyEconLab Study Plan 24.5 • Animated Figures 24-4, 24-5
A Monopolist's Profits A monopolist's profits equal the difference between the price it charges and its average production cost times the quantity it sells. The monopolist's price is at the point on the demand curve corresponding to the profit-maximizing output rate, and its average total cost of producing this output rate is at the corresponding point on the average total cost curve.	Key Figures Figure 24-6, 543 Figure 24-7, 544	• MyEconLab Study Plan 24.6 • Animated Figures 24-6, 24-7
Price Discrimination A price-discriminating monopolist sells its product at more than one price, with the price difference being unrelated to differences in costs. To be able to price discriminate successfully, a monopolist must be able to sell some of its output at higher prices to consumers with less elastic demand.	price discrimination, 545 price differentiation, 545	• MyEconLab Study Plan 24.7
Social Cost of Monopolies A monopoly is able to charge the highest price that people are willing to pay. This price exceeds marginal cost. If the monopolist's marginal cost curve corresponds to the sum of the marginal cost curves for the number of firms that would exist if the industry were perfectly competitive instead, then the monopolist produces and sells less output than perfectly competitive firms would have produced and sold.	Key Figure Figure 24-9, 546	• MyEconLab Study Plan 24.8 • Animated Figure 24-9

Log in to MyEconLab, take a chapter test, and get a personalized Study Plan that tells you which concepts you understand and which ones you need to review. From there, MyEconLab will give you further practice, tutorials, animations, videos, and guided solutions. For more information, visit www.myeconlab.com

PROBLEMS

All problems are assignable in MyEconLab. Answers to odd-numbered problems appear at the back of the book.

24-1. The following table depicts the daily output, price, and costs of a monopoly dry cleaner located near the campus of a remote college town. (See page 540.)

Output (suits cleaned)	Price per Suit ($)	Total Costs ($)
0	8.00	3.00
1	7.50	6.00
2	7.00	8.50
3	6.50	10.50
4	6.00	11.50
5	5.50	13.50
6	5.00	16.00
7	4.50	19.00
8	4.00	24.00

   a. Compute revenues and profits at each output rate.

   b. What is the profit-maximizing rate of output?

   c. Calculate the dry cleaner's marginal revenue and marginal cost at each output level. What is the profit-maximizing level of output?

24-2. A manager of a monopoly firm notices that the firm is producing output at a rate at which average total cost is falling but is not at its minimum feasible point. The manager argues that surely the firm must not be maximizing its economic profits. Is this argument correct? (See pages 540–541.)

24-3. Use the following graph to answer the questions below. (See pages 541–544.)

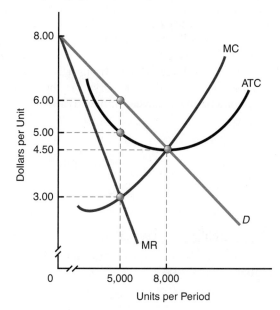

a. What is the monopolist's profit-maximizing output?

b. At the profit-maximizing output rate, what are average total cost and average revenue?

c. At the profit-maximizing output rate, what are the monopolist's total cost and total revenue?

d. What is the maximum profit?

e. Suppose that the marginal cost and average total cost curves in the diagram also illustrate the horizontal summation of the firms in a perfectly competitive industry in the long run. What would the equilibrium price and output be if the market were perfectly competitive? Explain the economic cost to society of allowing a monopoly to exist.

24-4. The marginal revenue curve of a monopoly crosses its marginal cost curve at $30 per unit and an output of 2 million units. The price that consumers are willing to pay for this output is $40 per unit. If it produces this output, the firm's average total cost is $43 per unit, and its average fixed cost is $8 per unit. What is the profit-maximizing (loss-minimizing) output? What are the firm's economic profits (or economic losses)? (See pages 541–544.)

24-5. A monopolist's maximized rate of economic profits is $500 per week. Its weekly output is 500 units, and at this output rate, the firm's marginal cost is $15 per unit. The price at which it sells each unit is $40 per unit. At these profit and output rates, what are the firm's average total cost and marginal revenue? (See pages 541–544.)

24-6. Currently, a monopolist's profit-maximizing output is 200 units per week. It sells its output at a price of $60 per unit and collects $30 per unit in revenues from the sale of the last unit produced each week. The firm's total costs each week are $9,000. Given this information, what are the firm's maximized weekly economic profits and its marginal cost? (See pages 541–544.)

24-7. Consider the revenue and cost conditions for a monopolist that are depicted in the figure at the top of the next page. (See pages 541–544.)

   a. What is this producer's profit-maximizing (or loss-minimizing) output?

   b. What are the firm's economic profits (or losses)?

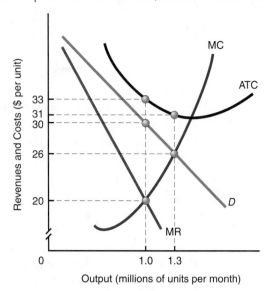

24-8. For each of the following examples, explain how and why a monopoly would try to price discriminate. (See pages 545–546.)

a. Air transport for businesspeople and tourists

b. Serving food on weekdays to businesspeople and retired people. (Hint: Which group has more flexibility during a weekday to adjust to a price change and, hence, a higher price elasticity of demand?)

c. A theater that shows the same movie to large families and to individuals and couples. (Hint: For which set of people will the overall expense of a movie be a larger part of their budget, so that demand is more elastic?)

24-9. A monopolist's revenues vary directly with price. Is it maximizing its economic profits? Why or why not? (Hint: Recall that the relationship between revenues and price depends on price elasticity of demand. See page 539.)

24-10. A new competitor enters the industry and competes with a second firm, which had been a monopolist. The second firm finds that although demand is not perfectly elastic, it is now more elastic. What will happen to the second firm's marginal revenue curve and to its profit-maximizing price? (See pages 539–541.)

24-11. A monopolist's marginal cost curve has shifted upward. What is likely to happen to the monopolist's price, output rate, and economic profits? (See pages 541–544.)

24-12. Demand has fallen. What is likely to happen to the monopolist's price, output rate, and economic profits? (See pages 541–544.)

ECONOMICS ON THE NET

Patents, Trademarks, and Intellectual Property This Internet application explores a firm's view on legal protections.

Title: Intellectual Property

Navigation: Follow the link at **www.econtoday.com/chap24** to the GlaxoSmithKline Web site. Select *Investors* and then *Reports and Publications*. View the PDF of Annual Report 2007. Scroll down to Intellectual Property (page 28).

Application Read the statement and table; then answer the following questions.

1. How do patents, trademarks, and registered designs and copyrights differ?

2. What are GlaxoSmithKline's intellectual property goals? Do patents or trademarks seem to be more important?

For Group Discussion and Analysis In 1969, GlaxoSmith-Kline developed Ventolin, a treatment for asthma symptoms. Though the patent and trademark have long expired, the company still retains over a third of the annual market sales of this treatment. Explain, in economic terms, the source of GlaxoSmithKline's strength in this area. Discuss whether patents and trademarks are beneficial for the development and discovery of new treatments.

ANSWERS TO QUICK QUIZZES

p. 536: (i) close; (ii) ownership . . . scale

p. 539: (i) change . . . total; (ii) marginal . . . marginal; (iii) elasticity . . . elasticity

p. 544: (i) downward . . . less; (ii) marginal . . . marginal . . . demand; (iii) total . . . quantity; (iv) total . . . above

p. 548: (i) downward . . . elasticities . . . resale; (ii) discrimination . . . differentiation; (iii) lower . . . higher

APPENDIX G

Consumer Surplus and the Deadweight Loss Resulting from Monopoly

You have learned that a monopolist produces fewer units than would otherwise be produced in a perfectly competitive market and that it sells these units at a higher price. It seems that consumers surely must be worse off under monopoly than they would be under perfect competition. This appendix shows that, indeed, consumers are harmed by the existence of a monopoly in a market that otherwise could be perfectly competitive.

Consumer Surplus in a Perfectly Competitive Market

Consider the determination of consumer surplus in a perfectly competitive market (for consumer surplus, see page 96 in Appendix B). Take a look at the market diagram depicted in Figure G-1 below. In the figure, we assume that all firms producing in this market incur no fixed costs. We also assume that each firm faces the same marginal cost, which does not vary with its output. These assumptions imply that the marginal cost curve is horizontal and that marginal cost is the same as average total cost at any level of output. Thus, if many perfectly competitive firms operate in this market, the horizontal summation of all firms' marginal cost curves, which is the market supply curve, is this same horizontal curve, labeled MC = ATC.

Under perfect competition, the point at which this market supply curve crosses the market demand curve, D, determines the equilibrium quantity, Q_{pc}, and the market clearing price, P_{pc}. Thus, in a perfectly competitive market, consumers obtain Q_{pc} units at the same per-unit price of P_{pc}. Consumers gain surplus values—vertical distances between the demand curve and the level of the market clearing price—for each unit consumed, up to the total of Q_{pc} units. This totals to the entire striped area under the demand curve above

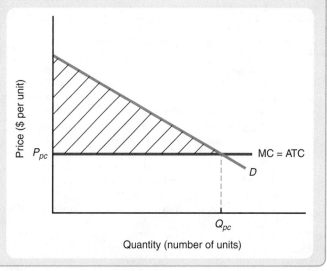

FIGURE G-1

Consumer Surplus in a Perfectly Competitive Market

If all firms in this market incur no fixed costs and face the same, constant marginal costs, then the marginal cost curve, MC, and the average total cost curve, ATC, are equivalent and horizontal. Under perfect competition, the horizontal summation of all firms' marginal cost curves is this same horizontal curve, which is the market supply curve, so the market clearing price is P_{pc}, and the equilibrium quantity is Q_{pc}. The total consumer surplus in a perfectly competitive market is the striped area.

the market clearing price. Consumer surplus is the difference between the total amount that consumers would have been willing to pay and the total amount that they actually pay, given the market clearing price that prevails in the perfectly competitive market.

How Society Loses from Monopoly

Now let's think about what happens if a monopoly situation arises in this market, perhaps because a government licenses the firms to conduct joint operations as a single producer. These producers respond by acting as a single monopoly firm, which searches for the profit-maximizing quantity and price.

In this altered situation, which is depicted in Figure G-2 below, the new monopolist (which we assume is unable to engage in price discrimination—see page 544) will produce to the point at which marginal revenue equals marginal cost. This rate of output is Q_m units. The demand curve indicates that consumers are willing to pay a price per unit equal to P_m for this quantity of output. Consequently, as you learned in this chapter, the monopolist will produce fewer units of output than the quantity, Q_{pc}, that firms would have produced in a perfectly competitive market. The monopolist also charges a higher price than the market clearing price, P_{pc}, that would have prevailed under perfect competition.

Recall that the monopolist's maximized economic profits equal its output times the difference between price and average total cost, or the yellow-shaded rectangular area equal to $Q_m \times (P_m - \text{ATC})$. By setting its price at P_m, therefore, the monopolist is able to transfer this portion of the competitive level of consumer surplus to itself in the form of monopoly profits. Consumers are still able to purchase Q_m units of output at a per-unit price, P_m, below the prices they would otherwise have been willing to pay. Hence, the blue-shaded triangular area above this monopoly-profit rectangle is consumer surplus that remains in the new monopoly situation.

Once the monopoly is formed, what happens to the light-green-shaded portion of the competitive consumer surplus? The answer is that this portion of consumer surplus is lost to society. The monopolist's failure to produce the additional $Q_{pc} - Q_m$ units of output that would have been forthcoming in a perfectly competitive market eliminates this portion of the original consumer surplus. This lost consumer surplus resulting from monopoly production and pricing is called a **deadweight loss** because it is a portion of the competitive level of consumer surplus that no one in society can obtain in a monopoly situation.

Thus, as a result of monopoly, consumers are worse off in two ways. First, the monopoly profits that result constitute a transfer of a portion of consumer surplus away from consumers to the monopolist. Second, the failure of the monopoly to produce as many units as would have been produced under perfect competition eliminates consumer surplus that otherwise would have been a benefit to consumers. No one in society, not even the monopoly, can obtain this deadweight loss.

Deadweight loss
The portion of consumer surplus that no one in society is able to obtain in a situation of monopoly.

FIGURE G-2

Losses Generated by Monopoly

If firms are able to act as a single monopoly, then the monopolist will produce only Q_m units at the point at which marginal revenue equals marginal cost and charge the price P_m. Economic profits, $Q_m \times (P_m - \text{ATC})$, equal the yellow-shaded rectangular area, which is a portion of the competitive level of consumer surplus (the original striped area) transferred to the monopolist. Consumers can now purchase Q_m units of output at a per-unit price, P_m, below the prices they otherwise would have been willing to pay, so the blue-shaded triangular area above this monopoly-profit rectangle is remaining consumer surplus. The green-shaded triangular area is lost consumer surplus that results from the monopoly producing Q_m units instead of the Q_{pc} units that would have been produced under perfect competition. This is called a *deadweight loss* because it is a portion of the competitive level of consumer surplus that no one in society can obtain under monopoly.

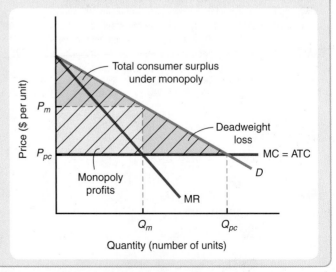

Monopolistic Competition

25

LEARNING OBJECTIVES

After reading this chapter, you should be able to:

▶ Discuss the key characteristics of a monopolistically competitive industry

▶ Contrast the output and pricing decisions of monopolistically competitive firms with those of perfectly competitive firms

▶ Explain why brand names and advertising are important features of monopolistically competitive industries

▶ Describe the fundamental properties of information products and evaluate how the prices of these products are determined under monopolistic competition

MyEconLab helps you master each objective and study more efficiently. See end of chapter for details.

ohn Locke is a Louisville, Kentucky, businessman who also happens to be a best-selling author of crime-adventure e-books priced at 99 cents on Amazon's Web site. Locke says, "When I saw that highly successful authors were charging $9.99 for an e-book, I thought that if I can make a profit at 99 cents, I no longer have to prove I'm as good as them—rather, they have to prove they are ten times better than me." E-books written by Locke and other crime-adventure authors share certain similarities but also exhibit differences in writing style, characterization, and plot. Hence, the market for crime-adventure e-books is one in which sellers' products are differentiated. Product differentiation, or heterogeneity, is a fundamental characteristic of *monopolistic competition*, the topic of this chapter. For book publishers, the growing importance of e-books is complicating the task of competing in selling *both* e-books *and* physical books. By the time you have completed the chapter, you will understand why this is so.

a company called J&D Foods offers bacon-flavored and turkey-and-gravy-flavored soft drinks? For individuals who prefer less fizz, a firm called Meatwater sells flavored water aimed to satisfy a number of different tastes. Its flavors include Buffalo wings, cheeseburger, chicken teriyaki, fish and chips, and fried oysters. Of course, as alternatives to J&D Foods' and Meatwater's meaty-flavored drinks, a large number of companies also sell soft drinks and bottled waters with a wide array of cola, non-cola, and fruity flavors. Many sellers of soft drinks and bottled water advertise their products in an effort to promote their distinctive flavors.

Product heterogeneity—variations in product characteristics—and advertising did not show up in our analysis of perfect competition. They play large roles, however, in industries that cannot be described as perfectly competitive but cannot be described as pure monopolies, either. A combination of consumers' preferences for variety and competition among producers has led to similar but *differentiated* products in the marketplace. This situation has been described as *monopolistic competition,* the subject of this chapter.

Monopolistic Competition

In the 1920s and 1930s, economists became increasingly aware that there were many industries to which both the perfectly competitive model and the pure monopoly model did not apply and did not seem to yield very accurate predictions. Theoretical and empirical research was instituted to develop some sort of middle ground. Two separately developed models of **monopolistic competition** resulted. At Harvard, Edward Chamberlin published *Theory of Monopolistic Competition* in 1933. The same year, Britain's Joan Robinson published *The Economics of Imperfect Competition*. In this chapter, we will outline the theory as presented by Chamberlin.

Monopolistic competition
A market situation in which a large number of firms produce similar but not identical products. Entry into the industry is relatively easy.

Chamberlin defined monopolistic competition as a market structure in which a relatively large number of producers offer similar but differentiated products. Monopolistic competition therefore has the following features:

1. Significant numbers of sellers in a highly competitive market

2. Differentiated products

3. Sales promotion and advertising

4. Easy entry of new firms in the long run

Even a cursory look at the U.S. economy leads to the conclusion that monopolistic competition is an important form of market structure in the United States. Indeed, that is true of all developed economies.

Number of Firms

In a perfectly competitive industry, there are an extremely large number of firms. In pure monopoly, there is only one. In monopolistic competition, there are a large number of firms, but not so many as in perfect competition. This fact has several important implications for a monopolistically competitive industry.

1. *Small share of market.* With so many firms, each firm has a relatively small share of the total market.

2. *Lack of collusion.* With so many firms, it is very difficult for all of them to get together to collude—to cooperate in setting a pure monopoly price (and output). Collusive pricing in a monopolistically competitive industry is nearly impossible. Also, barriers to entry are minor, and the flow of new firms into the industry makes collusive agreements less likely. The large number of firms makes the monitoring and detection of cheating very costly and extremely difficult. This difficulty is compounded by differentiated products and high rates of innovation. Collusive agreements are easier for a homogeneous product than for heterogeneous ones.

3. *Independence.* Because there are so many firms, each one acts independently of the others. No firm attempts to take into account the reaction of all of its rival firms—that would be impossible with so many rivals. Thus, an individual producer does not try to take into account possible reactions of rivals to its own output and price changes.

Follow the link at www.econtoday.com/chap25 to *Wall Street Journal* articles about real-world examples of monopolistic competition.

Product Differentiation

Perhaps the most important feature of the monopolistically competitive market is **product differentiation.** We can say that each individual manufacturer of a product has an absolute monopoly over its own product, which is slightly differentiated from other similar products. This means that the firm has some control over the price it charges. Unlike the perfectly competitive firm, it faces a downward-sloping demand curve.

Consider the abundance of brand names for toothpaste, soap, gasoline, vitamins, shampoo, and most other consumer goods and a great many services. We are not obliged to buy just one type of video game, just one type of jeans, or just one type of footwear. We can usually choose from a number of similar but differentiated products. The greater a firm's success at product differentiation, the greater the firm's pricing options.

Each separate differentiated product has numerous similar substitutes. This clearly has an impact on the price elasticity of demand for the individual firm. Recall that one determinant of price elasticity of demand is the availability of substitutes: The greater the number and closeness of substitutes available, other things being equal, the greater the price elasticity of demand. If the consumer has a vast array of alternatives that are just about as good as the product under study, a relatively small increase in the price of that product will lead many consumers to switch to one of the many close substitutes. Thus, the ability of a firm to raise the price above the price of *close* substitutes is very small. At a given price, the demand curve is highly elastic compared to a monopolist's demand curve. In the extreme case, with perfect competition, the substitutes are perfect because we are dealing with only one particular undifferentiated product. In that case, the individual firm has a perfectly elastic demand curve.

Product differentiation
The distinguishing of products by brand name, color, and other minor attributes. Product differentiation occurs in other than perfectly competitive markets in which products are, in theory, homogeneous, such as wheat or corn.

YOU ARE THERE

To contemplate how an automaker is using scents to differentiate its vehicles from those of its competitors, take a look at **Have You Smelled a Ford Lately?** on page 568.

Sales Promotion and Advertising

Monopolistic competition differs from perfect competition in that no individual firm in a perfectly competitive market will advertise. A perfectly competitive firm, by definition, can sell all that it wants to sell at the going market price anyway. Why, then, would it spend even one penny on advertising? Furthermore, by definition, the perfect competitor is selling a product that is identical to the product that all other firms in the industry are selling. Any advertisement that induces consumers to buy more of that product will, in effect, be helping all the competitors too. A perfect competitor therefore cannot be expected to incur any advertising costs (except when all firms in an industry collectively agree to advertise to urge the public to buy more beef or drink more milk, for example).

The monopolistic competitor, however, has at least *some* monopoly power. Because consumers regard the monopolistic competitor's product as distinguishable from the products of the other firms, the firm can search for the most profitable price that consumers are willing to pay for its differentiated product. Advertising, therefore, may result in increased profits. Advertising is used to increase demand and to differentiate one's product. How much advertising should be undertaken? It should be carried to the point at which the additional net revenue from one more dollar of advertising just equals that one dollar of additional cost.

How has one company used an unintended feature of its product to differentiate it further from similar products of competitors? See the following page.

EXAMPLE

A Biodegradable Chips Bag Is Crunchier Than the Chips

As is true of most consumer-products firms, Frito-Lay is always on the lookout for new ways of differentiating its snack brands from those of competing companies. Frito-Lay recently sought to make purchases of its Sun Chips snack more desirable to increasingly environmentally conscious consumers. Toward this end, the company's engineers developed a new biodegradable bag composed of materials that naturally break down in the environment.

The engineers' efforts had another result: perhaps the crunchiest snack bags on the planet. When squeezed, the bag produces a crunching sound at a level of 95 decibels—sufficiently loud that if the bag were squeezed continuously, it would exceed government noise standards.

Although the bag's loudness can be annoying, Frito-Lay decided to integrate the crunchiness of the bags containing crunchy chips into its marketing. Display ads on store shelves with Sun Chips read, "Yes, the bag is loud—that's what change sounds like." In this way, Frito-Lay took advantage of an unexpected characteristic of its product to differentiate it further from similar chips—and bags—sold by competitors.

FOR CRITICAL THINKING

If Frito-Lay's bag-differentiation plan accomplished its aims, what should have happened to the demand for its Sun Chips product?

Ease of Entry

For any current monopolistic competitor, potential competition is always lurking in the background. The easier—that is, the less costly—entry is, the more a current monopolistic competitor must worry about losing business.

A good example of a monopolistic competitive industry is the computer software industry. Many small firms provide different programs for many applications. The fixed capital costs required to enter this industry are small. All you need are skilled programmers. In addition, there are few legal restrictions. The firms in this industry also engage in extensive advertising in more than 150 computer publications.

QUICK QUIZ See page 572 for the answers. Review concepts from this section in MyEconLab.

In a **monopolistically competitive** industry, a relatively _____ number of firms interact in a _____ competitive market.

Because monopolistically competitive firms sell _____ products, sales promotion and advertising are common features of a monopolistically competitive industry.

There is _____ entry (or exit) of new firms in a monopolistically competitive industry.

Price and Output for the Monopolistic Competitor

Now that we are aware of the assumptions underlying the monopolistic competition model, we can analyze the price and output behavior of each firm in a monopolistically competitive industry. We assume in the analysis that follows that the desired product type and quality have been chosen. We further assume that the budget and the type of promotional activity have already been chosen and do not change.

The Individual Firm's Demand and Cost Curves

Because the individual firm is not a perfect competitor, its demand curve slopes downward, as in all three panels of Figure 25-1 on the facing page. Hence, it faces a marginal revenue curve that is also downward sloping and below the demand curve. To find the profit-maximizing rate of output and the profit-maximizing price, we go to the output where the marginal cost (MC) curve intersects the marginal revenue (MR) curve from below.

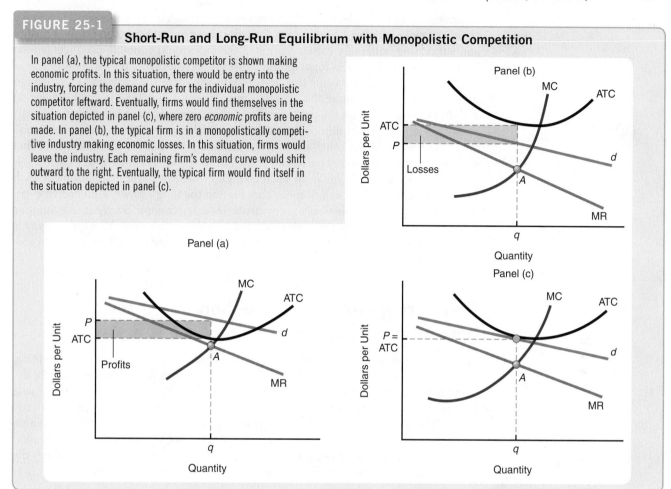

FIGURE 25-1

Short-Run and Long-Run Equilibrium with Monopolistic Competition

In panel (a), the typical monopolistic competitor is shown making economic profits. In this situation, there would be entry into the industry, forcing the demand curve for the individual monopolistic competitor leftward. Eventually, firms would find themselves in the situation depicted in panel (c), where zero *economic* profits are being made. In panel (b), the typical firm is in a monopolistically competitive industry making economic losses. In this situation, firms would leave the industry. Each remaining firm's demand curve would shift outward to the right. Eventually, the typical firm would find itself in the situation depicted in panel (c).

That gives us the profit-maximizing output rate. Then we draw a vertical line up to the demand curve. That gives us the price that can be charged to sell exactly that quantity produced. This is what we have done in Figure 25-1 above. In each panel, a marginal cost curve intersects the marginal revenue curve at *A*. The profit-maximizing rate of output is *q*, and the profit-maximizing price is *P*.

Short-Run Equilibrium

In the short run, it is possible for a monopolistic competitor to make economic profits—profits over and above the normal rate of return or beyond what is necessary to keep that firm in that industry. We show such a situation in panel (a) of Figure 25-1. The average total cost (ATC) curve is drawn below the demand curve, *d*, at the profit-maximizing rate of output, *q*. Economic profits are shown by the blue-shaded rectangle in that panel.

Losses in the short run are clearly also possible. They are presented in panel (b) of Figure 25-1. Here the average total cost curve lies everywhere above the individual firm's demand curve, *d*. The losses are indicated by the red-shaded rectangle.

Just as with any market structure or any firm, in the short run it is possible to observe either economic profits or economic losses. In either case, the price does not equal marginal cost but rather is above it.

The Long Run: Zero Economic Profits

The long run is where the similarity between perfect competition and monopolistic competition becomes more obvious. In the long run, because so many firms produce substitutes for the product in question, any economic profits will disappear with competition. They will be reduced to zero either through entry by new firms seeing a chance to make a higher rate of return than elsewhere or by changes in product quality and advertising outlays by existing firms in the industry. (Profitable products will be imitated by other firms.) As for economic losses in the short run, they will disappear in the long run because the firms that suffer them will leave the industry. They will go into another business where the expected rate of return is at least normal. Panels (a) and (b) of Figure 25-1 on the preceding page therefore represent only short-run situations for a monopolistically competitive firm. In the long run, the individual firm's demand curve *d* will just touch the average total cost curve at the particular price that is profit maximizing for that particular firm. This is shown in panel (c) of Figure 25-1.

A word of warning: This is an idealized, long-run equilibrium situation for each firm in the industry. It does not mean that even in the long run we will observe every single firm in a monopolistically competitive industry making *exactly* zero economic profits or *just* a normal rate of return. We live in a dynamic world. All we are saying is that if this model is correct, the rate of return will *tend toward* normal—economic profits will *tend toward* zero.

Comparing Perfect Competition with Monopolistic Competition

If both the monopolistic competitor and the perfect competitor make zero economic profits in the long run, how are they different? The answer lies in the fact that the demand curve for the individual perfect competitor is perfectly elastic. Such is not the case for the individual monopolistic competitor—its demand curve is less than perfectly elastic. This firm has some control over price. Price elasticity of demand is not infinite.

We see the two situations in Figure 25-2 below. Both panels show average total costs just touching the respective demand curves at the particular price at which the firm is selling the product. Notice, however, that the perfect competitor's average

---

FIGURE 25-2

Comparison of the Perfect Competitor with the Monopolistic Competitor

In panel (a), the perfectly competitive firm has zero economic profits in the long run. The price is set equal to marginal cost, and the price is P_1. The firm's demand curve is just tangent to the minimum point on its average total cost curve. With the monopolistically competitive firm in panel (b), there are also zero economic profits in the long run. The price is greater than marginal cost, though. The monopolistically competitive firm does not find itself at the minimum point on its average total cost curve. It is operating at a rate of output, q_2, to the left of the minimum point on the ATC curve.

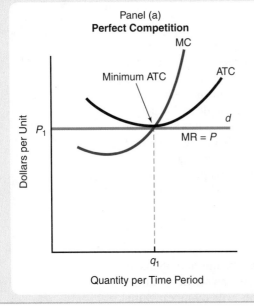

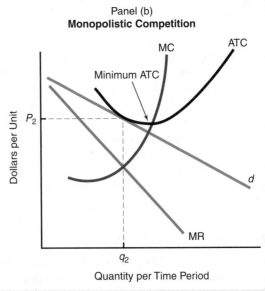

total costs are at a minimum. This is not the case with the monopolistic competitor. The equilibrium rate of output is to the left of the minimum point on the average total cost curve where price is greater than marginal cost. The monopolistic competitor cannot expand output to the point of minimum costs without lowering price, and then marginal cost would exceed marginal revenue. A monopolistic competitor at profit maximization charges a price that exceeds marginal cost. In this respect it is similar to the monopolist.

It has consequently been argued that monopolistic competition involves *waste* because minimum average total costs are not achieved and price exceeds marginal cost. There are too many firms, each with excess capacity, producing too little output. According to critics of monopolistic competition, society's resources are being wasted.

Chamberlin had an answer to this criticism. He contended that the difference between the average cost of production for a monopolistically competitive firm in an open market and the minimum average total cost represented what he called the cost of producing "differentness." Chamberlin did not consider this difference in cost between perfect competition and monopolistic competition a waste. In fact, he argued that it is rational for consumers to have a taste for differentiation. Consumers willingly accept the resultant increased production costs in return for more choice and variety of output.

QUICK QUIZ See page 572 for the answers. Review concepts from this section in MyEconLab.

In the _____ run, it is possible for monopolistically competitive firms to make economic profits or economic losses.

In the _____ run, monopolistically competitive firms will make _____ economic profits—that is, they will make a _____ rate of return.

Because the monopolistic competitor faces a downward-sloping demand curve, it does not produce at the minimum point on its average _____ cost curve.

Hence, we say that a monopolistic competitor has higher average _____ costs per unit than a perfect competitor would have.

Chamberlin argued that the difference between the _____ _____ cost of production for a monopolistically competitive firm and the _____ average total cost at which a perfectly competitive firm would produce is the cost of producing "differentness."

Brand Names and Advertising

Because "differentness" has value to consumers, monopolistically competitive firms regard their brand names as valuable. Firms use trademarks—words, symbols, and logos—to distinguish their product brands from goods or services sold by other firms. Consumers associate these trademarks with the firms' products. Thus, companies regard their brands as valuable private (intellectual) property, and they engage in advertising to maintain the differentiation of their products from those of other firms.

Brand Names and Trademarks

A firm's ongoing sales generate current profits and, as long as the firm is viable, the prospect of future profits. A company's value in the marketplace, depends largely on its current profitability and perceptions of its future profitability.

Table 25-1 on the following page gives the market values of the world's most valuable product brands. Each valuation is calculated as the market price of shares of stock in a company times the number of shares traded. Brand names, symbols, logos, and unique color schemes such as the color combinations trademarked by FedEx relate to consumers' perceptions of product differentiation and hence to the market values of firms. Companies protect their trademarks from misuse by registering them with the U.S. Patent and Trademark Office. Once its trademark application is approved, a

TABLE 25-1

Values of the Top Ten Brands

The market value of a company is equal to the number of shares of stock issued by the company times the market price of each share. To a large extent, the company's value reflects the value of its brand.

Brand	Estimates Value ($ billions)
Apple	183.0
International Business Machines (IBM)	156.0
Google	107.9
McDonald's	95.2
Microsoft	76.7
Coca cola	74.3
Marlboro	73.6
AT&T	68.9
Verizon	49.2
China Mobile	47.0

Source: Brand Z Most Valuable Brands Study, 2012.

company has the right to seek legal damages if someone makes unauthorized use of its brand name, spreads false rumors about the company, or engages in other devious activities that can reduce the value of its brand.

Advertising

To help ensure that consumers differentiate their product brands from those of other firms, monopolistically competitive firms commonly engage in advertising. Advertising comes in various forms, and the nature of advertising can depend considerably on the types of products that firms wish to distinguish from competing brands.

Direct marketing
Advertising targeted at specific consumers, typically in the form of postal mailings, telephone calls, or e-mail messages.

Mass marketing
Advertising intended to reach as many consumers as possible, typically through television, newspaper, radio, or magazine ads.

METHODS OF ADVERTISING Figure 25-3 below shows the current distribution of advertising expenses among the various advertising media. Today, as in the past, firms primarily rely on two approaches to advertising their products. One is **direct marketing,** in which firms engage in personalized advertising using postal mailings, phone calls, and e-mail messages (excluding so-called banner and pop-up ads on Web sites). The other is **mass marketing,** in which firms aim advertising messages at as many consumers as possible via media such as television, newspapers, radio, and magazines.

FIGURE 25-3

Distribution of U.S. Advertising Expenses

Direct marketing accounts for more than half of advertising expenses in the United States.

Sources: Advertising Today; Direct Marketing Today; and Internet Advertising Bureau.

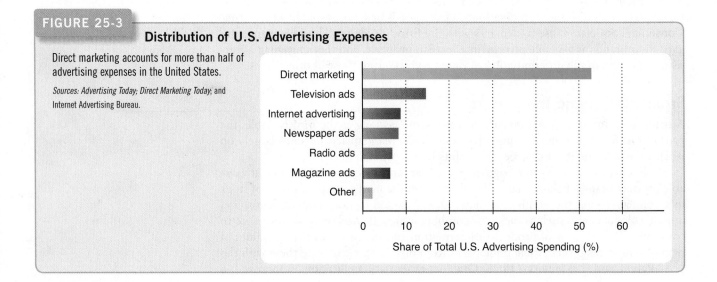

A third advertising method is called **interactive marketing.** This advertising approach allows a consumer to respond directly to an advertising message. Often the consumer is able to search for more detailed information and place an order as part of the response. Sales booths and some types of Internet advertising, such as banner ads with links to sellers' Web pages, are forms of interactive marketing.

Advertising that uses signs, billboards, and other public displays traditionally has been categorized as a form of mass marketing. Why is this classification now in doubt?

Interactive marketing
Advertising that permits a consumer to follow up directly by searching for more information and placing direct product orders.

INTERNATIONAL EXAMPLE

A Push to Make Electronic Billboards Interactive in Japan

In Japan, when a person glances at an electronic display advertising a product, the mechanism projecting the image often looks back at that individual. Such ad display mechanisms can identify the person's gender with an accuracy rate as high as 90 percent and can determine the individual's age within a 10-year range about 70 percent of the time. Hence, if the ad display is mounted above another mechanism that actually dispenses the product, such as a vending machine, the display can recommend a product based on the person's estimated age and gender.

The latest version of electronic ad display mechanisms can also interpret an individual's body language, including facial expressions such as smiling or frowning. The ad display responds by tailoring its message to try matching the indicated mood of the individual. Thus, recognition capabilities transform the display into an interactive-marketing device.

FOR CRITICAL THINKING
Why do you suppose that marketers are working on enabling ad-display mechanisms to recognize faces and to search the Web for information about a specific person who glances at the ad?

SEARCH, EXPERIENCE, AND CREDENCE GOODS The qualities and characteristics of a product determine how the firm should advertise that product. Some types of products, known as **search goods,** possess qualities that are relatively easy for consumers to assess in advance of their purchase. Clothing and music are common examples of items that have features that a consumer may assess, or perhaps even sample, before purchasing.

Other products, known as **experience goods,** are products that people must actually consume before they can determine their qualities. Soft drinks, restaurant meals, and haircutting services are examples of experience goods.

A third category of products, called **credence goods,** includes goods and services with qualities that might be difficult for consumers who lack specific expertise to evaluate without assistance. Products such as pharmaceuticals and services such as health care and legal advice are examples of credence goods.

INFORMATIONAL VERSUS PERSUASIVE ADVERTISING The forms of advertising that firms use vary considerably depending on whether the item being marketed is a search good or an experience good. If the item is a search good, a firm is more likely to use **informational advertising** that emphasizes the features of its product. A video trailer for the latest movie starring Emma Stone will include snippets of the film, which help potential buyers assess the quality of the movie.

In contrast, if the product is an experience good, a firm is more likely to engage in **persuasive advertising** intended to induce a consumer to try the product and, as a consequence, discover a previously unknown taste for it. For example, a soft-drink ad is likely to depict happy people drinking the clearly identified product during breaks from enjoyable outdoor activities on a hot day.

If a product is a credence good, producers commonly use a mix of informational and persuasive advertising. For instance, an ad for a pharmaceutical product commonly provides both detailed information about the product's curative properties and side effects and suggestions to consumers to ask physicians to help them assess the drug.

ADVERTISING AS SIGNALING BEHAVIOR Recall from Chapter 23 that *signals* are compact gestures or actions that convey information. For example, high profits in an industry

Search good
A product with characteristics that enable an individual to evaluate the product's quality in advance of a purchase.

Experience good
A product that an individual must consume before the product's quality can be established.

Credence good
A product with qualities that consumers lack the expertise to assess without assistance.

Informational advertising
Advertising that emphasizes transmitting knowledge about the features of a product.

Persuasive advertising
Advertising that is intended to induce a consumer to purchase a particular product and discover a previously unknown taste for the item.

are signals that resources should flow to that industry. Individual companies can explicitly engage in signaling behavior. A firm can do so by establishing brand names or trademarks and then promoting them heavily. This is a signal to prospective consumers that this is a company that plans to stay in business. Before the modern age of advertising, U.S. banks needed a way to signal their soundness. To do this, they constructed large, imposing bank buildings using marble and granite. Stone structures communicated permanence. The effect was to give bank customers confidence that they were not doing business with fly-by-night operations.

When Ford Motor Company advertises its brand name heavily, it incurs substantial costs. The only way it can recoup those costs is by selling many Ford vehicles over a long period of time. Heavy advertising in the company's brand name thereby signals to car buyers that Ford intends to stay in business a long time and wants to develop a loyal customer base—because loyal customers are repeat customers.

WHAT IF... the government were to limit or even ban "excessive" advertising?

Informational advertising is informative to buyers of search goods, and even a firm's spending on persuasive advertising indicates its intent to expand its customer base and hence to continue operations for the foreseeable future. Thus, both informational and persuasive forms of advertising arguably offer measurable informational benefits to consumers. Arbitrarily defining an "excessive" level of advertising in order to limit or ban it undoubtedly would reduce these benefits.

QUICK QUIZ   See page 572 for the answers. Review concepts from this section in MyEconLab.

_____ such as words, symbols, and logos distinguish firms' products from those of other firms. Firms seek to differentiate their brands through advertising, via _____ marketing, _____ marketing, or _____ marketing.

A firm is more likely to use _____ advertising that emphasizes the features of its product if the item is a **search good** with features that consumers can assess in advance.

A firm is more likely to use _____ advertising to affect consumers' tastes and preferences if it sells an **experience good.** This is an item that people must actually consume before they can determine its qualities.

A firm that sells a _____ good, which is an item possessing qualities that consumers lack the expertise to fully assess, typically uses a combination of informational and persuasive advertising.

Information Products and Monopolistic Competition

Information product
An item that is produced using information-intensive inputs at a relatively high fixed cost but distributed for sale at a relatively low marginal cost.

A number of industries sell **information products,** which entail relatively high fixed costs associated with the use of knowledge and other information-intensive inputs as key factors of production. Once the first unit has been produced, however, it is possible to produce additional units at a relatively low per-unit cost. Most information products can be put into digital form. Good examples are computer games, computer operating systems, digital music and videos, educational and training software, electronic books and encyclopedias, and office productivity software.

Special Cost Characteristics of Information Products

Creating the first copy of an information product often entails incurring a relatively sizable up-front cost. Once the first copy is created, however, making additional copies can be very inexpensive. For instance, a firm that sells a computer game can simply make properly formatted copies of the original digital file of the game available for consumers to download, at a price, via the Internet.

COSTS OF PRODUCING INFORMATION PRODUCTS To think about the cost conditions faced by the seller of an information product, consider the production and sale of a computer game. The company that creates a computer game must devote many hours of labor to developing and editing its content. Each hour of labor and each unit of other resources devoted to performing this task entail an opportunity cost. The sum of all these up-front costs constitutes a relatively sizable *fixed cost* that the company must incur to generate the first copy of the computer game.

Once the company has developed the computer game in a form that is readable by personal computers, the marginal cost of making and distributing additional copies is very low. In the case of a computer game, it is simply a matter of incurring a minuscule cost to place the required files on a data disk or on the company's Web site.

COST CURVES FOR AN INFORMATION PRODUCT Suppose that a manufacturer decides to produce and sell a computer game. Creating the first copy of the game requires incurring a total fixed cost equal to $250,000. The marginal cost that the company incurs to place the computer game on a data disk or in downloadable format is a constant amount equal to $2.50 per computer game.

Figure 25-4 below displays the firm's cost curves for this information product. By definition, average fixed cost is total fixed cost divided by the quantity produced and sold. Hence, the average fixed cost of the first computer game is $250,000. But if the company sells 5,000 copies, the average fixed cost drops to $50 per game. If the total quantity sold is 50,000, average fixed cost declines to $5 per game. The average fixed cost (AFC) curve slopes downward over the entire range of possible quantities of computer games.

Average variable cost equals total variable cost divided by the number of units of a product that a firm sells. If this company sells only one copy, then the total variable cost it incurs is the per-unit cost of $2.50, and this is also the average variable cost of producing one unit. Because the per-unit cost of producing the computer game is a constant $2.50, producing two games entails a total variable cost of $5.00, and the average variable cost of producing two games is $5.00 ÷ 2 = $2.50. Thus, as shown in Figure 25-4, the average variable cost of producing and selling this computer game is always equal to the constant marginal cost of $2.50 per game that the company incurs. The average variable cost (AVC) curve is the same as the marginal cost (MC) curve, which for this company is the horizontal line depicted in Figure 25-4.

FIGURE 25-4

Cost Curves for a Producer of an Information Product

The total fixed cost of producing a computer game is $250,000. If the producer sells 5,000 copies, average fixed cost falls to $50 per copy. If quantity sold rises to 50,000, average fixed cost decreases to $5 per copy. Thus, the producer's average fixed cost (AFC) curve slopes downward. If the per-unit cost of producing each copy of the game is $2.50, then both the marginal cost (MC) and average variable cost (AVC) curves are horizontal at $2.50 per copy. Adding the AFC and AVC curves yields the ATC curve. Because the ATC curve slopes downward, the producer of this information product experiences short-run economies of operation.

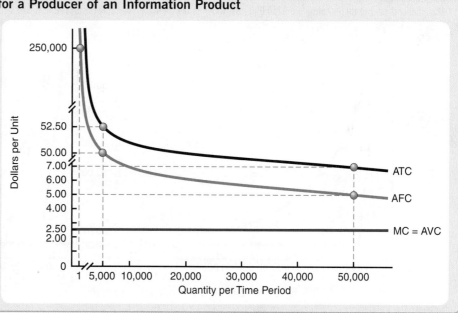

SHORT-RUN ECONOMIES OF OPERATION By definition, average total cost equals the sum of average fixed cost and average variable cost. The average total cost (ATC) curve for this computer game company slopes downward over its entire range.

Recall from Chapter 22 that along the downward-sloping range of an individual firm's *long-run* average cost curve, the firm experiences *economies of scale*. For the producer of an information product such as a computer game, the *short-run* average total cost curve slopes downward. Consequently, sellers of information products typically experience **short-run economies of operation.** The average total cost of producing and selling an information product declines as more units of the product are sold. Short-run economies of operation are a distinguishing characteristic of information products that sets them apart from most other goods and services.

Short-run economies of operation

A distinguishing characteristic of an information product arising from declining short-run average total cost as more units of the product are sold.

Monopolistic Competition and Information Products

In the example depicted in Figure 25-4 on the preceding page, the information product is a computer game. There are numerous computer games among which consumers can choose. Hence, there are many products that are close substitutes in the market for computer games. Yet no two computer games are exactly the same. This means that the particular computer game product sold by the company in our example is distinguishable from other competing products.

For the sake of argument, therefore, let's suppose that this company participates in a monopolistically competitive market for this computer game. Panels (a) and (b) of Figure 25-5 below display a possible demand curve for the computer game manufactured and sold by this particular company.

MARGINAL COST PRICING AND INFORMATION PRODUCTS What if the company making this particular computer game were to behave *as if* it were a perfectly competitive firm by

The Infeasibility of Marginal Cost Pricing of an Information Product

In panel (a), if the firm with the average total cost and marginal cost curves shown in Figure 25-4 on page 565 sets the price of the computer game equal to its constant marginal cost of $2.50 per copy, then consumers will purchase 20,000 copies. This yields $50,000 in revenues. The firm's average total cost of 20,000 games is $15 per copy, so its total cost of selling that number of copies is $15 × 20,000 = $300,000. Marginal cost pricing thereby entails a $250,000 loss, which is the total fixed cost of producing the computer game. Panel (b) illustrates how the

price of the game is ultimately determined under monopolistic competition. Setting a price of $27.50 per game induces consumers to buy 10,000 copies, and the average total cost of producing this number of copies is also $27.50. Consequently, total revenues equal $275,000, which just covers the sum of the $250,000 in total fixed costs and $25,000 (the 10,000 copies times the constant $2.50 average variable cost) in total variable costs. The firm earns zero economic profits.

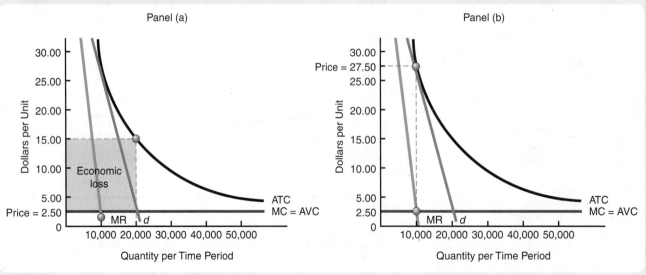

setting the price of its product equal to marginal cost? Panel (a) of Figure 25-5 on the facing page provides the answer to this question. If the company sets the price of the computer game equal to marginal cost, it will charge only $2.50 per game it sells. Naturally, a larger number of people desire to purchase computer games at this price, and given the demand curve in the figure, the company could sell 20,000 copies of this game.

The company would face a problem, however. At a price of $2.50 per computer game, it would earn $50,000 in revenues on sales of 20,000 copies. The average fixed cost of 20,000 copies equals $250,000/20,000, or $12.50 per computer game. Adding this to the constant $2.50 average variable cost implies an average total cost of selling 20,000 copies of $15 per game. Under marginal cost pricing, therefore, the company would earn an average loss of $12.50 (price − average total cost = $2.50 − $15.00 = −$12.50) per computer game for all 20,000 copies sold. The company's total economic loss from selling 20,000 computer games at a price equal to marginal cost would amount to $250,000. Hence, the company would fail to recoup the $250,000 total fixed cost of producing the computer game. If the company had planned to set its price equal to the computer game's marginal cost, it would never have developed the computer game in the first place!

The failure of marginal cost pricing to allow firms selling information products to cover the fixed costs of producing those products is intrinsic to the nature of such products. In the presence of short-run economies of operation in producing information products, marginal cost pricing is simply not feasible in the marketplace.

Recall that marginal cost pricing is associated with perfect competition. An important implication of this example is that markets for information products cannot function as perfectly competitive markets. Imperfect competition is the rule, not the exception, in the market for information products.

THE CASE IN WHICH PRICE EQUALS AVERAGE TOTAL COST Panel (b) of Figure 25-5 on the preceding page illustrates how the *price* of the computer game is ultimately determined in a monopolistically competitive market. After all entry or exit from the market has occurred, the price of the computer game will equal the producer's average cost of production, including all implicit opportunity costs. The price charged for the game generates total revenues sufficient to cover all explicit and implicit costs and therefore is consistent with earning a normal return on invested capital.

Given the demand curve depicted in Figure 25-5, at a price of $27.50 per computer game, consumers are willing to purchase 10,000 copies. The company's average total cost of offering 10,000 copies for sale is also equal to $27.50 per computer game. Consequently, the price of each copy equals the average total cost of producing the game.

At a price of $27.50 per computer game, the company's revenues from selling 10,000 copies equal $275,000. This amount of revenues is just sufficient to cover the company's total fixed cost (including the opportunity cost of capital) of $250,000 and the $25,000 total variable cost it incurs in producing 10,000 copies at an average variable cost of $2.50 per game. Thus, the company earns zero economic profits.

LONG-RUN EQUILIBRIUM FOR AN INFORMATION PRODUCT INDUSTRY When competition drives the price of an information product to equality with average total cost, sellers charge the minimum price required to cover their production costs, including the relatively high initial costs they must incur to develop their products in the first place. Consumers thereby pay the lowest price necessary to induce sellers to provide the item.

The situation illustrated in panel (b) of Figure 25-5 on the facing page corresponds to a long-run equilibrium for this particular firm in a monopolistically competitive market for computer games. If this and other companies face a situation such as the diagram depicts, there is no incentive for additional companies to enter or leave the computer game industry. Consequently, the product price naturally tends to adjust to equality with average total cost as a monopolistically competitive industry composed of sellers of information products moves toward long-run equilibrium.

QUICK QUIZ See page 572 for the answers. Review concepts from this section in MyEconLab.

Firms that sell **information products** experience relatively _____ fixed costs, but once they have produced the first unit, they can sell additional units at a relatively _____ per-unit cost. Consequently, the manufacturer of an information product experiences short-run _____ of _____.

If a firm sets the price of an information product equal to marginal cost, it earns only sufficient revenues to cover its

_____ costs. Engaging in marginal cost pricing, therefore, fails to cover the relatively high fixed costs of making an information product.

In a long-run equilibrium outcome under monopolistic competition, the price of an information product equals _____ _____ cost. The seller's total revenues exactly cover _____ costs, including the opportunity cost of capital.

YOU ARE THERE
Have You Smelled a Ford Lately?

Years ago, Ford Motor Company based a marketing campaign on the slogan "Have you driven a Ford lately?" Today, the company wants prospective buyers assessing a vehicle's handling characteristics during test drives to be captivated as well by the car's scent.

Linda Schmalz, a body interior materials engineer, has been charged with determining the appropriate scents to be emitted by a Ford vehicle's air bag covers, cup holders, floor mats, and seat fabrics. Her first discovery is that people's perceptions of odors differ by regions. Schmalz wonders, therefore, if perhaps Ford should offer customized scents. Allowing consumers to choose

among smells along with other vehicle features would, she concludes, differentiate Ford's products from those of all competitors in the auto market. The result, she argues, would be increased sales of Ford vehicles.

Critical Thinking Questions

1. What is the economic objective of differentiating the scents of vehicles?
2. Why do you suppose that Schmalz's boss has emphasized that he wants vehicle odors that "produce a sense of well-being inside a Ford"?

CONCEPTS APPLIED

▶ Monopolistic Competition

▶ Information Products

▶ Short-Run Economies of Operation

ISSUES & APPLICATIONS

Why E-Books Are Upending the Publishing Business

It is a typical day at Amazon.com, Inc. Of its top 50 digital-book best-sellers, about one-third are priced below $5, a fact of major consternation for book publishers.

The Economics of E-Books versus Traditional Physical Books

The book-publishing industry exhibits features of monopolistic competition:

1. Many competitive sellers, each of which produces a relatively small share of total output
2. Heterogeneous products
3. Considerable advertising
4. Easy entry and exit

Publishers have long sold information products—books that can be produced at relatively low and constant per-unit cost but at significant total fixed costs. Thus, average variable costs are constant, but average fixed costs decline as more books are produced, so publishers' short-run average total cost curves slope downward.

The advent of e-books—books in electronic formats for digital devices—has publishers rethinking how to compete. Most publishers wish to sell physical books alongside e-books, but plummeting e-book prices threaten this strategy.

How Much Are Physically Printed Words Worth in the Market?

The fixed costs incurred by a publisher in paying an author to write a book to be printed on paper or stored as a digital file are the same. Variable costs, however, are much lower for e-books. Hence, the prices at which books generate sufficient revenues to cover total costs are lower for e-books than for physical books.

Selling e-books cuts average costs and hence the prices at which zero economic profits can be maintained in the long run. Furthermore, the lower prices of e-books— sometimes as low as 99 cents—are inducing many consumers to substitute away from traditional physical books. For publishers continuing to produce physical books, these substitutions are resulting in decreases in demand.

Maintaining prices sufficiently high to cover average total costs and to earn at least zero economic profits is becoming an increasingly difficult proposition for book publishers. Thus, a number of publishers that currently specialize in producing physical books likely will have to respond to economic losses either by switching to e-books or by exiting the book-publishing market.

For Critical Thinking

1. Why do you suppose that some publishers are selling space for advertisements in their e-books—and sometimes even in physical books?

2. From an economic standpoint, how could we explain the willingness of someone to pay $19.99 for a physical book that is available as an e-book for $9.99?

Web Resources

1. To contemplate how e-books are changing the economics of publishing for both publishers and authors, go to **www.econtoday.com/chap25**.

2. To consider how an author's fixed costs of publishing e-books can be covered at a price of 99 cents per book, go to **www.econtoday.com/chap25**.

MyEconLab

For more questions on this chapter's Issues & Applications, go to MyEconLab. In the Study Plan for this chapter, select Section N: News.

MyEconLab

Here is what you should know after reading this chapter. MyEconLab will help you identify what you know, and where to go when you need to practice.

— WHAT YOU SHOULD KNOW —		— WHERE TO GO TO PRACTICE —
The Key Characteristics of a Monopolistically Competitive Industry A monopolistically competitive industry consists of a large number of firms that sell differentiated products that are close substitutes. Firms can easily enter or exit the industry. Monopolistically competitive firms can increase their profits if they can successfully distinguish their products from those of their rivals. Thus, they have an incentive to advertise.	monopolistic competition, 556 product differentiation, 557	• MyEconLab Study Plan 25.1
Contrasting the Output and Pricing Decisions of Monopolistically Competitive Firms with Those of Perfectly Competitive Firms In the short run, a monopolistically competitive firm produces to the point at which marginal revenue equals marginal cost. The price it charges can exceed both marginal cost and average total cost in the short run. The resulting economic profits induce new firms to enter the industry. In the long run, therefore, monopolistically competitive firms earn zero economic profits, but price exceeds marginal cost.	Key Figures Figure 25-1, 559 Figure 25-2, 560	• MyEconLab Study Plans 25.2, 25.3 • Animated Figures 25-1, 25-2

MyEconLab *continued*

Why Brand Names and Advertising Are Important Features of Monopolistically Competitive Industries Monopolistically competitive firms engage in advertising. If the product is a search good with features that consumers can evaluate prior to purchase, the seller is more likely to use advertising to transmit information about product features. If the firm sells an experience good, with features that are apparent only when consumed, it is more likely to use persuasive advertising to induce consumers to discover unknown tastes. If the product is a credence good with characteristics that consumers cannot readily assess unaided, then the firm often uses a mix of informational and persuasive advertising.

direct marketing, 562
mass marketing, 562
interactive marketing, 563
search good, 563
experience good, 563
credence good, 563
informational advertising, 563
persuasive advertising, 563

• MyEconLab Study Plan 25.4

Properties of Information Products and Determining Their Prices Providing an information product entails high fixed costs but a relatively low per-unit cost. Hence, the average total cost curve for a firm that sells an information product slopes downward, meaning that the firm experiences short-run economies of operation. In a long-run equilibrium, price adjusts to equality with average total cost.

information product, 564
short-run economies of operation, 566

Key Figures
Figure 25-4, 565
Figure 25-5, 566

• MyEconLab Study Plan 25.5
• Animated Figures 25-4, 25-5

Log in to MyEconLab, take a chapter test, and get a personalized Study Plan that tells you which concepts you understand and which ones you need to review. From there, MyEconLab will give you further practice, tutorials, animations, videos, and guided solutions. For more information, visit www.myeconlab.com

PROBLEMS

All problems are assignable in MyEconLab. Answers to odd-numbered problems appear at the back of the book.

25-1. Explain why the following are examples of monopolistic competition. (See page 556.)

    a. There are a number of fast-food restaurants in town, and they compete fiercely. Some restaurants cook their hamburgers over open flames. Others fry their hamburgers. In addition, some serve broiled fish sandwiches, while others serve fried fish sandwiches. A few serve ice cream cones for dessert, while others offer frozen ice cream pies.

    b. There are a vast number of colleges and universities across the country. Each competes for top students. All offer similar courses and programs, but some have better programs in business, while others have stronger programs in the arts and humanities. Still others are academically stronger in the sciences.

25-2. Consider the diagram on the facing page depicting the demand and cost conditions faced by a monopolistically competitive firm. (See page 559.)

    a. What are the total revenues, total costs, and economic profits experienced by this firm?

    b. Is this firm more likely in short- or long-run equilibrium? Explain.

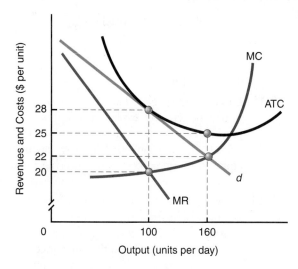

25-3. In a perfectly competitive market, price equals marginal cost, but this condition is not satisfied for the firm with the revenue and cost conditions depicted in Problem 25-2. In the long run, what would happen if the government decided to require the firm in Problem 25-2 to charge a price equal to marginal cost at the firm's long-run output rate? (See page 560.)

25-4. Based on your answer to Problem 25-3, is the firm with the revenue and cost conditions depicted in Problem 25-2 behaving "anticompetitively" in the sense of intentionally "taking advantage" of consumers by charging them a price greater than marginal cost? Explain your reasoning. (See page 561.)

25-5. The table below depicts the prices and total costs a local used-book store faces. The bookstore competes with a number of similar stores, but it capitalizes on its location and the word-of-mouth reputation of the coffee it serves to its customers. Calculate the store's total revenue, total profit, marginal revenue, and marginal cost at each level of output, beginning with the first unit. Based on marginal analysis, what is the approximate profit-maximizing level of output for this business? (See page 560.)

Output	Price per Book ($)	Total Costs ($)
0	6.00	2.00
1	5.75	5.25
2	5.50	7.50
3	5.25	9.60
4	5.00	12.10
5	4.75	15.80
6	4.50	20.00
7	4.00	24.75

25-6. Calculate total average costs for the bookstore in Problem 25-5. Illustrate the store's short-run equilibrium by plotting demand, marginal revenue, average total costs, and marginal costs. What is its total profit? (See page 560.)

25-7. Suppose that after long-run adjustments take place in the used-book market, the business in Problem 25-5 ends up producing 4 units of output. What are the market price and economic profits of this monopolistic competitor in the long run? (See page 560.)

25-8. It is a typical Christmas electronics shopping season, and makers of flat-panel TVs are marketing the latest available models through their own Web sites as well as via retailers such as Best Buy and Walmart. Each manufacturer offers its own unique versions of flat-panel TVs in differing arrays of shapes and sizes. As usual, each is hoping to maintain a stream of economic profits earned since it first introduced these most recent models late last year or perhaps just a few months before Christmas. Nevertheless, as sales figures arrive at the headquarters of companies such as Dell, Samsung, Sharp, and Sony, it is clear that most of the companies will end up earning only a normal rate of return this year. (See page 560.)

a. How can makers of flat-panel TVs earn economic profits during the first few months after the introduction of new models?

b. What economic forces result in the dissipation of economic profits earned by manufacturers of flat-panel TVs?

25-9. Classify each of the following as an example of direct, interactive, and/or mass marketing. (See page 562.)

a. The sales force of a pharmaceutical company visits physicians' offices to promote new medications and to answer physicians' questions about treatment options and possible side effects.

b. A mortgage company targets a list of specific low-risk borrowers for a barrage of e-mail messages touting its low interest rates and fees.

c. An online bookseller pays fees to an Internet search engine to post banner ads relating to each search topic chosen by someone conducting a search. In part, this helps promote the bookseller's brand, but clicking on the banner ad also directs the person to a Web page displaying books on the topic that are available for purchase.

d. A national rental car chain runs advertisements on all of the nation's major television networks.

25-10. Classify each of the following as an example of direct, interactive, and/or mass marketing. (See page 562.)

a. A cosmetics firm pays for full-page display ads in a number of top women's magazines.

b. A magazine distributor mails a fold-out flyer advertising its products to the addresses of all individuals it has identified as possibly interested in magazine subscriptions.

c. An online gambling operation arranges for pop-up ads to appear on the computer screen every time a person uses a media player to listen to digital music or play video files, and clicking on the ads directs an individual to its Web gambling site.

d. A car dealership places advertisements in newspapers throughout the region where potential customers reside.

25-11. Categorize each of the following as an experience good, a search good, or a credence good or service, and justify your answer. (See page 563.)

   a. A heavy-duty filing cabinet

   b. A restaurant meal

   c. A wool overcoat

   d. Psychotherapy

25-12. Categorize each of the following as an experience good, a search good, or a credence good or service, and justify your answer. (See page 563.)

   a. Services of a carpet cleaning company

   b. A new cancer treatment

   c. Athletic socks

   d. A silk necktie

25-13. In what ways do credence goods share certain characteristics of both experience goods and search goods? How do credence goods differ from both experience goods and search goods? Why does advertising of credence goods commonly contain both informational and persuasive elements? Explain your answers. (See page 563.)

25-14. Is each of the following items more likely to be the subject of an informational or a persuasive advertisement? Why? (See page 563.)

   a. An office copying machine

   b. An automobile loan

   c. A deodorant

   d. A soft drink

25-15. Discuss the special characteristics of an information product, and explain the implications for a producer's short-run average and marginal cost curves. In addition, explain why having a price equal to marginal cost is not feasible for the producer of an information product. (See page 565.)

25-16. A firm that sells e-books—books in digital form downloadable from the Internet—sells all e-books relating to do-it-yourself topics (home plumbing, gardening, and the like) at the same price. At present, the company can earn a maximum annual profit of $25,000 when it sells 10,000 copies within a year's time. The firm incurs a 50-cent expense each time a consumer downloads a copy, but the company must spend $100,000 per year developing new editions of the e-books. The company has determined that it would earn zero economic profits if price were equal to average total cost, and in this case it could sell 20,000 copies. Under marginal cost pricing, it could sell 100,000 copies. (See page 565.)

   a. In the short run, what is the profit-maximizing price of e-books relating to do-it-yourself topics?

   b. At the profit-maximizing quantity, what is the average total cost of producing e-books?

ECONOMICS ON THE NET

Legal Services on the Internet A number of legal firms now offer services on the Internet, and in this application you contemplate features of the market for Web-based legal services.

Title: Nolo.com—Law for All

Navigation: Link to the Nolo.com site via **www.econtoday.com/chap25**.

Application Answer the following questions.

1. In what respects does the market for legal services, such as those provided online by Nolo.com, have the characteristics of a monopolistically competitive industry?

2. How can providers of legal services differentiate their products? How does Nolo.com attempt to do this?

For Group Discussion and Analysis Assign groups to search the Web for at least three additional online legal firms and compare the services these firms offer. Reconvene the entire class and discuss whether it is reasonable to classify the market for online legal services as monopolistically competitive.

ANSWERS TO QUICK QUIZZES

p. 558: (i) large . . . highly; (ii) differentiated; (iii) easy

p. 561: (i) short; (ii) long . . . zero . . . normal; (iii) total . . . total; (iv) average total . . . minimum

p. 564: (i) Trademarks . . . direct . . . mass . . . interactive; (ii) informational; (iii) persuasive; (iv) credence

p. 568: (i) high . . . low . . . economies . . . operation; (ii) variable; (iii) average total . . . total

Oligopoly and Strategic Behavior

26

The United States is home to several textbook publishers, so the textbook-publishing industry is not a monopoly. Nevertheless, three textbook publishers together account for more than four-fifths of all U.S. textbook sales. The production and pricing decisions of any one of the top three publishers influence the production and pricing decisions of its competitors. Consequently, the U.S. textbook industry is neither perfectly competitive nor monopolistically competitive. Instead, this industry is an *oligopoly*, a type of market structure in which only a handful of competitors exist. This particular market structure is the subject of the present chapter.

since 2009, the percentage of daily minutes devoted to Facebook's Web site by the average U.S. resident who surfs the Internet has increased from less than 3 percent to more than 15 percent? During the same period, the percentages of minutes spent on AOL, eBay, MySpace, Yahoo, and other sites that were among the most common Web destinations a decade ago have steadily declined. Even the percentage of online time spent on Google's site has leveled off at about 10 percent.

What accounts for the substantial increase in time that people devote to Facebook? Most economists agree that a fundamental key to Facebook's growth has been that the benefit a person perceives from spending an additional minute at Facebook's site is influenced by how many other people use Facebook. In this chapter, you will learn about how firms in industries with just a few competitors can benefit—or lose out—when a consumer's willingness to purchase their products is influenced by other consumers' decisions about whether to buy them.

Oligopoly

An important market structure that we have yet to discuss involves a situation in which a few large firms constitute essentially an entire industry. They are not perfectly competitive in the sense that we have used the term. They are not even monopolistically competitive. And because there are several of them, a pure monopoly does not exist. We call such a situation an **oligopoly,** which consists of a small number of *interdependent* sellers. Each firm in the industry knows that other firms will react to its changes in prices, quantities, and qualities. An oligopoly market structure can exist for either a homogeneous or a differentiated product.

Characteristics of Oligopoly

Oligopoly is characterized by a small number of interdependent firms that constitute the entire market.

SMALL NUMBER OF FIRMS How many is "a small number of firms"? More than two but less than a hundred? The question is not easy to answer. Basically, though, oligopoly exists when the top few firms in the industry account for an overwhelming percentage of total industry output.

Oligopolies often involve three to five big companies that produce the bulk of industry output. Between World War II and the 1970s, three firms—General Motors, Chrysler, and Ford—produced and sold nearly all the output of the U.S. automobile industry. Among manufacturers of chewing gum and cigarettes, four large firms produce and sell almost the entire output of each industry.

INTERDEPENDENCE All markets and all firms are, in a sense, interdependent. But only when a few large firms produce most of the output in an industry does the question of **strategic dependence** of one on the others' actions arise. In this situation, when any one firm changes its output, its product price, or the quality of its product, other firms notice the effects of its decisions. The firms must recognize that they are interdependent and that any action by one firm with respect to output, price, quality, or product differentiation will cause a reaction by other firms. A model of such mutual interdependence is difficult to build, but examples of such behavior are not hard to find in the real world. Oligopolists in the cigarette industry, for example, are constantly reacting to each other.

Recall that in the model of perfect competition, each firm ignores the behavior of other firms because each firm is able to sell all that it wants at the going market price. At the other extreme, the pure monopolist does not have to worry about the reaction of current rivals because there are none. In an oligopolistic market structure, the managers of firms are like generals in a war: *They must attempt to predict the reaction of rival firms.* It is a strategic game.

Oligopoly
A market structure in which there are very few sellers. Each seller knows that the other sellers will react to its changes in prices, quantities, and qualities.

Strategic dependence
A situation in which one firm's actions with respect to price, quality, advertising, and related changes may be strategically countered by the reactions of one or more other firms in the industry. Such dependence can exist only when there are a limited number of major firms in an industry.

Why Oligopoly Occurs

Follow the link at www.econtoday.com /chap26 to *Wall Street Journal* articles about real-world examples involving oligopoly.

Why are some industries composed chiefly of a few large firms? What causes an industry that might otherwise be competitive to tend toward oligopoly? We can provide some partial answers here.

ECONOMIES OF SCALE Perhaps the most common reason that has been offered for the existence of oligopoly is economies of scale. Recall that economies of scale exist when a doubling of output results in less than a doubling of total costs. When economies of scale exist, the firm's long-run average total cost curve will slope downward as the firm produces more and more output. Average total cost can be reduced by continuing to expand the scale of operation to the *minimum efficient scale*, or the output rate at which long-run average cost is minimized. (See page 500 in Chapter 22.) Smaller firms in a situation in which the minimum efficient scale is relatively large will have average total costs greater than those incurred by large firms. Little by little, they will go out of business or be absorbed into larger firms.

BARRIERS TO ENTRY It is possible that certain barriers to entry have prevented more competition in oligopolistic industries. They include legal barriers, such as patents, and control and ownership of critical supplies. Indeed, we can find periods in the past when firms were able not only to erect a barrier to entry but also to keep it in place year after year. In principle, the chemical, electronics, and aluminum industries have been at one time or another either monopolistic or oligopolistic because of the ownership of patents and the control of strategic inputs by specific firms.

OLIGOPOLY BY MERGER Another reason that oligopolistic market structures may sometimes develop is that firms merge. A merger is the joining of two or more firms under single ownership or control. The merged firm naturally becomes larger, enjoys greater economies of scale as output increases, and may ultimately have a greater ability to influence the market price for the industry's output.

There are two key types of mergers, vertical and horizontal. A **vertical merger** occurs when one firm merges with either a firm from which it purchases an input or a firm to which it sells its output. Vertical mergers occur, for example, when a coal-using electrical utility purchases a coal-mining firm or when a shoe manufacturer purchases retail shoe outlets.

Obviously, vertical mergers cannot *create* oligopoly as we have defined it. But that can indeed occur via a **horizontal merger,** which involves firms selling a similar product. If two shoe manufacturing firms merge, that is a horizontal merger. If a group of firms, all producing steel, merge into one, that is also a horizontal merger.

So far we have been talking about oligopoly in a theoretical manner. Now it is time to look at the actual oligopolies in the United States.

Vertical merger
The joining of a firm with another to which it sells an output or from which it buys an input.

Horizontal merger
The joining of firms that are producing or selling a similar product.

YOU ARE THERE

To think about why firms sometimes engage in vertical mergers, take a look at **Hyundai Goes Vertical** on page 588.

WHAT IF... **the government promoted competition among more firms by prohibiting horizontal mergers?**

Sometimes media observers suggest that the government could increase market competition by making it illegal for firms within the same industry to engage in horizontal mergers. Recall from Chapter 22 (page 500), however, that firms operate at lowest long-run average cost when they are able to attain their minimum efficient scale—the minimum point on the long-run average cost curve. If the government were to prohibit firms from merging horizontally within the same industry, many firms' scales of operations would be held artificially below the minimum efficient scale. This would cause long-run average costs to be higher than the minimum feasible level, which would result in higher prices for consumers.

TABLE 26-1

TABLE 26-1

Computing the Four-Firm Concentration Ratio

Firm	Annual Sales ($ millions)	
1	150	
2	100	= 400 Total number of firms in industry = 25
3	80	
4	70	
5 through 25	50	
Total	450	

Four-firm concentration ratio = 400/450 = 88.9%

Measuring Industry Concentration

As we have stated, oligopoly is a market structure in which a few interdependent firms produce a large part of total output in an industry. This situation is often called one of high *industry concentration*. Before we show the concentration statistics in the United States, let's determine how industry concentration can be measured.

CONCENTRATION RATIO The most common way to compute industry concentration is to determine the percentage of total sales or production accounted for by the top four or top eight firms in an industry. This gives the four- or eight-firm **concentration ratio,** also known as the *industry concentration ratio*. An example of an industry with 25 firms is given in Table 26-1 above. We can see in that table that the four largest firms account for almost 90 percent of total output in the hypothetical industry. This is an example of an oligopoly because a few firms will recognize the interdependence of their output, pricing, and quality decisions.

Concentration ratio

The percentage of all sales contributed by the leading four or leading eight firms in an industry; sometimes called the *industry concentration ratio*.

U.S. CONCENTRATION RATIOS Table 26-2 below shows the four-firm *domestic* concentration ratios for various industries. Is there any way that we can show or determine which industries to classify as oligopolistic? There is no definite answer. If we arbitrarily picked a four-firm concentration ratio of 75 percent, we could infer that cigarettes and breakfast cereals were oligopolistic. But we would always be dealing with an arbitrary definition.

What is the four-firm concentration ratio in the U.S. auto industry?

TABLE 26-2

Four-Firm Domestic Concentration Ratios for Selected U.S. Industries

Industry	Share of Total Sales Accounted for by the Top Four Firms (%)
Cigarettes	95
Breakfast cereals	78
Household vacuum cleaners	62
Primary aluminum	51
Computers	50
Soft drinks	48
Printing and publishing	38
Commercial banking	29.5

Source: U.S. Bureau of the Census.

EXAMPLE

The Four-Firm Concentration Ratio in the U.S. Auto Industry

In a recent year, seven companies accounted for the bulk of U.S. auto sales. Percentage sales shares for these firms were as follows: General Motors, 19.1 percent; Ford, 16.5 percent; Toyota, 15.3 percent; Honda, 10.6 percent; Chrysler, 9.3 percent; Nissan, 7.9 percent; and Hyundai, 7.7 percent. A few other smaller firms accounted for the remaining 13.6 percent of total auto sales. Consequently, the four-firm concentration ratio

for the U.S. auto industry was 19.1 percent + 16.5 percent + 15.3 percent + 10.6 percent, or 61.5 percent.

FOR CRITICAL THINKING

What was the seven-firm concentration ratio in the U.S. auto industry?

The Herfindahl-Hirschman Index

A problem with using concentration ratios is that these measures of industry concentration can fail to reflect differences in the relative sizes of firms within an industry. To understand why this is so, consider Table 26-3 below, which applies to two fictitious industries, called Industry A and Industry B.

Table 26-3 indicates that in Industry A, the four-firm concentration ratio is the sum of the percentage sales shares of the only four firms in the industry, which equals 81.25% + 6.25% + 6.25% + 6.25% = 100%. If we compute the four-firm concentration for Industry B, we obtain 25% + 25% + 25% + 25% = 100%. Thus, even though the top firm in Industry A has far more than half of all sales in that industry, whereas the top firm in Industry B has 25 percent of all sales, the four-firm concentration ratios are the same for the two industries. Thus, this example shows that using concentration ratios can potentially fail to reflect considerable variations in the distribution of firm sizes within industries.

To account for variations in sizes of firms when measuring industry concentration, economists use the **Herfindahl-Hirschman Index (HHI),** which is equal to the sum of the squared percentage sales shares of all firms in an industry. For a monopoly, in which only one firm has 100 percent of all industry sales, the value of the HHI equals $100^2 = 10{,}000$. Consequently, 10,000 is the maximum feasible level of the HHI for any industry.

Herfindahl-Hirschman Index (HHI)
The sum of the squared percentage sales shares of all firms in an industry.

Table 26-3 uses the sales shares for the firms in Industries A and B to calculate the HHI values for each industry. For Industry A, the sum of the squared values of all firms' percentage sales shares yields an HHI level of approximately 6,718.9. For Industry B, performing the same calculation gives an HHI value of 2,500. Thus, the HHI value for Industry B is less than half as large as the HHI level for Industry A. This substantial difference in HHI levels reflects the fact that the distribution of firm sizes

TABLE 26-3

Dollar Sales and Percentage Sales Shares for Two Industries

	Industry A				Industry B		
Firm	Annual Sales ($ millions)	Sales Share (%)	Squared Sales Share	Firm	Annual Sales ($ millions)	Sales Share (%)	Squared Sales Share
1	65	81.25	6,601.6	1	20	25.00	625.0
2	5	6.25	39.1	2	20	25.00	625.0
3	5	6.25	39.1	3	20	25.00	625.0
4	5	6.25	39.1	4	20	25.00	625.0
	Total sales = 80	Total percentage = 100.00	HHI = 6,718.9		Total sales = 80	Total percentage = 100.00	HHI = 2,500.0

is more even in Industry B than in Industry A, despite the identical values of the industries' four-firm concentration ratios.

What is the value of the Herfindahl-Hirschman Index for the world's Internet browser industry?

INTERNATIONAL EXAMPLE

The HHI for the Global Internet Browser Industry

Recently, the worldwide percentage shares of sales for the five firms offering Internet browsers were as follows: Microsoft's Internet Explorer, 60 percent; Google's Chrome, 25 percent; Mozilla's Firefox, 7 percent; Apple's Safari, 5 percent; and Opera Software's Opera, 3 percent. The HHI for the global Internet browser industry is equal to the sum of the squared percentage industry sales shares for these firm's browsers, or $HHI = 60^2 + 25^2 + 7^2 + 5^2 + 3^2 = 3,600 + 625 + 49 + 25 + 9 = 4,308$.

The HHI level for the global Internet browser industry is below the maximum feasible monopoly value of 10,000. Nevertheless, it is more than twice as large as the HHI level of 2,000 that we would have observed if the five

sellers of Internet browsers instead had equal industry sales shares of 20 percent. (Note that $20^2 + 20^2 + 20^2 + 20^2 + 20^2 = 400 + 400 + 400 + 400 + 400 = 2,000$.) Therefore, the global Internet browser industry is a concentrated industry.

FOR CRITICAL THINKING
What would be the revised HHI value if Mozilla and Opera Software decided to conduct a horizontal merger and offer a single "Firefox Opera" Internet browser?

Oligopoly, Efficiency, and Resource Allocation

Although oligopoly is not the dominant form of market structure in the United States, oligopolistic industries do exist. To the extent that oligopolists have *market power*—the ability to *individually* affect the *market* price for the industry's output—they lead to resource misallocations, just as monopolies do. Oligopolists charge prices that exceed marginal cost. But what about oligopolies that occur because of economies of scale? Consumers might actually end up paying lower prices than if the industry were composed of numerous smaller firms.

All in all, there is no definite evidence of serious resource misallocation in the United States because of oligopolies. In any event, *the more U.S. firms face competition from the rest of the world, the less any current oligopoly will be able to exercise market power.*

QUICK QUIZ See page 593 for the answers. Review concepts from this section in MyEconLab.

An **oligopoly** is a market situation with a _____ number of _____ sellers.

Oligopoly may result from _____ of scale, barriers to entry, and _____.

_____ mergers involve the merging of one firm with either the supplier of an input or the purchaser of its output.

_____ mergers involve the joining of firms selling a similar product.

Industry concentration can be measured by the combined _____ of total _____ accounted for by the top four firms in the industry.

Strategic Behavior and Game Theory

Reaction function
The manner in which one oligopolist reacts to a change in price, output, or quality made by another oligopolist in the industry.

At this point, we would like to be able to show oligopoly price and output determination in the way we did for perfect competition, pure monopoly, and monopolistic competition, but we cannot. Whenever there are relatively few firms competing in an industry, each can and does react to the price, quantity, quality, and product innovations that the others undertake. In other words, each oligopolist has a **reaction function.** Oligopolistic competitors are interdependent. Consequently, the decision makers in such firms must employ strategies. And we must be able to model their strategic behavior if we wish to predict how prices and outputs are determined in oligopolistic market structures.

In general, we can think of reactions of other firms to one firm's actions as part of a *game* that is played by all firms in the industry. Economists have developed **game theory** models to describe firms' rational interactions. Game theory is the analytical framework in which two or more individuals, companies, or nations compete for certain payoffs that depend on the strategy that the others employ. Poker is such a game situation because it involves a strategy of reacting to the actions of others.

Some Basic Notions about Game Theory

Games can be either cooperative or noncooperative. If firms work together to obtain a jointly shared objective, such as maximizing profits for the industry as a whole, then they participate in a **cooperative game.** Whenever it is too costly for firms to coordinate their actions to obtain cooperative outcomes, they are in a **noncooperative game** situation. Most strategic behavior in the marketplace is best described as a noncooperative game.

Games can be classified by whether the payoffs are zero, negative, or positive. In a **zero-sum game,** one player's losses are offset by another player's gains. If two retailers have an absolutely fixed total number of customers, for example, the customers that one retailer wins over are exactly equal to the customers that the other retailer loses. In a **negative-sum game,** players as a group lose during the process of the game (although one perhaps by more than the other, and it's possible for one or more players to win). In a **positive-sum game,** players as a group end up better off. Some economists describe all voluntary exchanges as positive-sum games. After an exchange, both the buyer and the seller are better off than they were prior to the exchange.

STRATEGIES IN NONCOOPERATIVE GAMES Players, such as decision makers in oligopolistic firms, have to devise a **strategy,** which is defined as a rule used to make a choice. The goal of the decision maker is to devise a strategy that is more successful than alternative strategies. Whenever a firm's decision makers can come up with certain strategies that are generally successful no matter what actions competitors take, these are called **dominant strategies.** The dominant strategy always yields the unique best action for the decision maker no matter what action the other "players" undertake. Relatively few business decision makers over a long period of time have successfully devised dominant strategies. We know this by observation: Few firms in oligopolistic industries consistently have maintained relatively high profits over time.

How can a real-world situation faced by two captured bank robbers help to illustrate basic principles of game theory?

Game theory
A way of describing the various possible outcomes in any situation involving two or more interacting individuals when those individuals are aware of the interactive nature of their situation and plan accordingly. The plans made by these individuals are known as *game strategies.*

Cooperative game
A game in which the players explicitly cooperate to make themselves jointly better off. As applied to firms, it involves companies colluding in order to make higher than perfectly competitive rates of return.

Noncooperative game
A game in which the players neither negotiate nor cooperate in any way. As applied to firms in an industry, this is the common situation in which there are relatively few firms and each has some ability to change price.

Zero-sum game
A game in which any gains within the group are exactly offset by equal losses by the end of the game.

Negative-sum game
A game in which players as a group lose during the process of the game.

Positive-sum game
A game in which players as a group are better off at the end of the game.

Strategy
Any rule that is used to make a choice, such as "Always pick heads."

Dominant strategies
Strategies that always yield the highest benefit. Regardless of what other players do, a dominant strategy will yield the most benefit for the player using it.

EXAMPLE

The Prisoners' Dilemma

An example of game theory occurs when two people involved in a bank robbery are caught. What should they do when questioned by police? Their situation has been called the **prisoners' dilemma.** The two suspects, Sam and Carol, are interrogated separately (they cannot communicate with each other) and are given various alternatives. The interrogator indicates separately to Sam and Carol the following:

1. If both confess to the bank robbery, they will both go to prison for 5 years.
2. If neither confesses, they will each be given a sentence of 2 years on a lesser charge.
3. If one prisoner turns state's evidence and confesses, that prisoner goes free and the other one, who did not confess, will serve 10 years for bank robbery.

You can see the prisoners' alternatives in the **payoff matrix** in Figure 26-1 on the following page. The two possibilities for each prisoner are "confess" and "don't confess." There are four possibilities:

1. Both confess.
2. Neither confesses.
3. Sam confesses (turns state's evidence) but Carol doesn't.
4. Carol confesses (turns state's evidence) but Sam doesn't.

In Figure 26-1, all of Sam's possible outcomes are shown on the upper half of each rectangle, and all of Carol's possible outcomes are shown on the lower half.

By looking at the payoff matrix, you can see that if Carol confesses, Sam's best strategy is to confess also—he'll get only 5 years

Continued

instead of 10. Conversely, if Sam confesses, Carol's best strategy is also to confess—she'll get 5 years instead of 10. Now let's say that Sam is being interrogated and Carol doesn't confess. Sam's best strategy is still to confess, because then he goes free instead of serving 2 years. Conversely, if Carol is being interrogated, her best strategy is still to confess even if Sam hasn't. She'll go free instead of serving 2 years. To confess is a dominant strategy for Sam. To confess is also a dominant strategy for Carol. The situation is exactly symmetrical. So this is the prisoners' dilemma. The prisoners know that both of them will be better off if neither confesses. Yet it is in each individual prisoner's interest to confess, even though the *collective* outcome of each prisoner's pursuit of his or her own interest is inferior for both.

FOR CRITICAL THINKING

Can you apply the prisoners' dilemma to the firms in a two-firm industry that agree to share market sales equally? (Hint: Think about the payoff to cheating on the market-sharing agreement.)

Prisoners' dilemma

A famous strategic game in which two prisoners have a choice between confessing and not confessing to a crime. If neither confesses, they serve a minimum sentence. If both confess, they serve a longer sentence. If one confesses and the other doesn't, the one who confesses goes free. The dominant strategy is always to confess.

Payoff matrix

A matrix of outcomes, or consequences, of the strategies available to the players in a game.

FIGURE 26-1

The Prisoners' Dilemma Payoff Matrix

Regardless of what the other prisoner does, each prisoner is better off if he or she confesses. So confessing is the dominant strategy, and each ends up behind bars for 5 years.

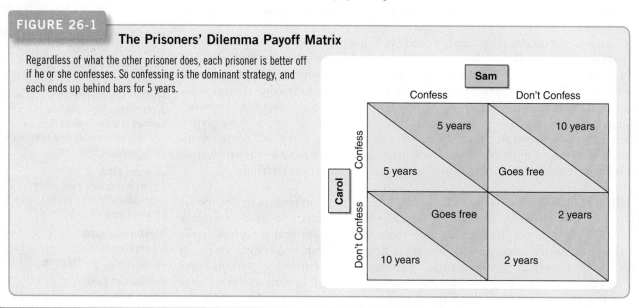

Applying Game Theory to Pricing Strategies

We can apply game strategy to two firms—oligopolists—that have to decide on their pricing strategy. Each can choose either a high or a low price. Their payoff matrix is shown in Figure 26-2 on the facing page. If they both choose a high price, each will make $6 million, but if they both choose a low price, each will make only $4 million. If one sets a high price and the other a low one, the low-priced firm will make $8 million, but the high-priced firm will make only $2 million. As in the prisoners' dilemma, in the absence of collusion, they will end up choosing low prices.

Opportunistic Behavior

Opportunistic behavior

Actions that focus solely on short-run gains because long-run benefits of cooperation are perceived to be smaller.

In the prisoners' dilemma, it is clear that cooperative behavior—both parties standing firm without admitting to anything—leads to the best outcome for both players. But each prisoner (player) stands to gain by cheating. Such action is called **opportunistic behavior.** Our daily economic activities involve the potential for the prisoners' dilemma all the time. We could engage in opportunistic behavior. You could write a check for a purchase knowing that it is going to bounce because you have just closed that bank account. When you agree to perform a specific task for pay, you could perform your work in a substandard way. When you go to buy a product, the seller might be able to cheat you by selling you a defective item.

In short, if all of us—sellers and buyers—engaged in opportunistic behavior all of the time, we would constantly be acting in a world of noncooperative behavior. That is not the world in which most of us live, however. Why not? Because most of us engage in

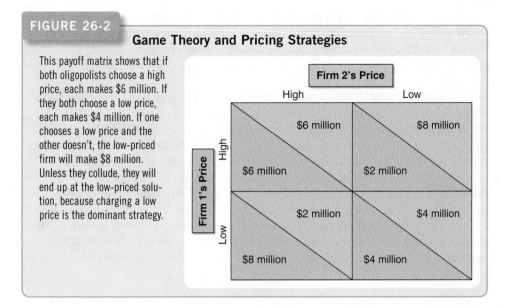

FIGURE 26-2

Game Theory and Pricing Strategies

This payoff matrix shows that if both oligopolists choose a high price, each makes $6 million. If they both choose a low price, each makes $4 million. If one chooses a low price and the other doesn't, the low-priced firm will make $8 million. Unless they collude, they will end up at the low-priced solution, because charging a low price is the dominant strategy.

repeat transactions. Manufacturers would like us to keep purchasing their products. Sellers would like us to keep coming back to their stores. As sellers of labor services, we all would like to keep our jobs, get promotions, or be hired away by another firm at a higher wage rate. Therefore, we engage in **tit-for-tat strategic behavior.** A consumer using a tit-for-tat strategy may, for instance, continue to purchase items from a firm each period as long as the firm provides products of the same quality and abides by any guarantees. If the firm fails in any period to provide high-quality products and honor its product guarantees, the consumer purchases items elsewhere.

Tit-for-tat strategic behavior
In game theory, cooperation that continues as long as the other players continue to cooperate.

QUICK QUIZ See page 593 for the answers. Review concepts from this section in MyEconLab.

Each oligopolist has a _____ function because oligopolistic competitors are interdependent. They must therefore engage in _____ behavior. One way to model this behavior is to use **game theory.**

Games can be either **cooperative** or **noncooperative.** In a _____-sum game, one player's losses are exactly offset by another player's gains. In a _____-sum

game, all players collectively lose, perhaps one player more than the others. In a _____-sum game, the players as a group end up better off.

Decision makers in oligopolistic firms must devise a strategy. A _____ strategy is one that is generally successful no matter what actions competitors take.

The Cooperative Game: A Collusive Cartel

According to Adam Smith (1723–1790), "People of the same trade seldom meet together, even for merriment and diversion, but the conversation ends in a conspiracy against the public, or in some contrivance to raise prices." Why can firms profit from engaging in a "conspiracy against the public"? How can firms work together to create a "contrivance to raise prices"? Why does accomplishing this task turn out to be a feat only occasionally achieved by certain industries? Let's consider each of these questions in turn.

The Rationale for a Cartel and the Seeds of Its Undoing

If all the firms in an industry can find a way to cooperatively determine how much to produce to maximize their combined profits, then they can form a **cartel** and jointly act as a single producer. This means that they *collude.* They act together to attain the same outcome that a monopoly firm would aim to achieve: producing to the point at which

Cartel
An association of producers in an industry that agree to set common prices and output quotas to prevent competition.

marginal revenue derived from the *market* demand curve is equal to marginal cost. To do so, they must set common prices and output quotas for their members. If the firms are able to accomplish this task, they can all charge the same profit-maximizing price that a monopoly would have charged. Then they can share in the maximized monopoly profits.

CUTTING BACK ON PRODUCTION Although the prospect of monopoly profits provides a strong incentive to collude, a fledgling cartel faces two fundamental problems. First, recall that a monopoly producer maximizes economic profits by restraining its production to a rate below the competitive output rate. Thus, the first problem for the members of the cartel is to determine how much each producer will restrain its output.

Once the first problem is solved, another immediately appears. As soon as all producers in the cartel begin restraining production and charging a higher price, each individual member could increase its revenues and profits by charging a slightly lower price, raising production, and selling more units. Hence, if all other cartel members honor their agreement to reduce production, one member could boost its economic profits by reneging on its promise to the rest of the cartel and increasing its production.

Enforcing a Cartel Agreement

Go to www.econtoday.com/chap26 to find out from WTRG Economics how effective the Organization of Petroleum Exporting Countries has been in acting as an oil market cartel.

There are four conditions that make it more likely that firms will be able to coordinate their efforts to restrain output and detect cheating, thereby reducing the temptation for participating firms to cheat:

1. *A small number of firms in the industry.* If an industry consists of only a few firms, it is easier to assess how much each firm should restrain production to yield the monopoly output and hence maximum industry profits. In addition, it is easier for each cartel member to monitor other firms' output rates for signs of cheating. For instance, when a cartel has only a few members, they might agree to keep their sales a certain percentage below pre-cartel levels. Failure to do so could be regarded as evidence of cheating.

2. *Relatively undifferentiated products.* If cartel members sell nearly homogeneous products, it is easier for them to agree on how much each firm should reduce its production. In contrast, if each firm sells a highly differentiated product, then some members can reasonably claim that the prices of their products should differ from the prices of other firms' products to reflect differences in costs of production. Thus, a firm with a differentiated product can reasonably claim that it is selling at a lower price for its differentiated good because its good is less valued by consumers—when in fact the firm may simply be using this claim as an excuse to cheat on the cartel agreement.

3. *Easily observable prices.* Naturally, one way to make sure that a producer is abiding by a cartel agreement is to look at the prices at which it actually sells its output. If the terms of industry transactions are publicly available, cartel members can more readily spot a firm's efforts to cheat.

4. *Little variation in prices.* If the industry's market is susceptible to frequent shifts in demand for firms' products or in prices of key inputs, the firms' prices will tend to fluctuate. Establishing a cartel agreement and monitoring cheating consequently will be more difficult. Hence, stable demand and cost conditions help a cartel form and continue to operate effectively.

Sometimes cartels prevent cheating on prices by using mechanisms that masquerade as contracts that are favorable to buyers. For example, all members of a cartel might agree to offer buyers contracts that permit a buyer to switch to another seller if that seller offers the product at a lower price. Naturally, if a customer can provide evidence that a lower price is available from another firm claiming to participate in the cartel, this fact would constitute evidence that the other firm is cheating. In this way, cartel members use their customers to police other cartel participants!

Why Cartel Agreements Usually Break Down

Studies have shown that it is very rare for cartel agreements to last more than 10 years. In many cases, cartel agreements break down more quickly than that. Even industries that usually satisfy the four conditions listed above have difficulty keeping cartels together over time.

One reason that cartels tend to break down is that the economic profits that existing firms obtain from holding prices above competitive levels provide an incentive for new firms to enter the market. Effectively, market entrants can earn profits by acting as a cheating cartel firm would behave. Their entry then provides incentives to cartel members to reduce their own prices and boost their production, and ultimately the cartel unravels.

Variations in overall economic activity also tend to make cartels unsustainable. During general business downturns, market demands tend to decline across all industries as consumers' incomes fall. So do profits of firms participating in a cartel. This increases the incentive for individual firms to cheat on a cartel agreement.

QUICK QUIZ   See page 593 for the answers. Review concepts from this section in MyEconLab.

A _____ is a group of firms in an industry that agree to set common prices and output quotas to restrict competition.

Characteristics of an industry that make it more likely that firms can coordinate efforts to restrain output and earn economic profits are a _____ number of firms,

relatively _____ products, easily _____ prices, and little _____ in prices.

Factors that contribute to the breakdown of a cartel are the _____ of firms seeking the economic profits earned by the cartel members and _____ in economic activity.

Network Effects

A feature sometimes present in oligopolistic industries is **network effects,** or situations in which a consumer's willingness to use an item depends on how many others use it. Commonplace examples are telephones and fax machines. Ownership of a phone or fax machine is not particularly useful if no one else has one, but once a number of people own a phone or fax machine, the benefits that others gain from consuming these devices increases.

In like manner, people who commonly work on joint projects within a network of fellow employees, consultants, or clients naturally find it useful to share computer files. Trading digital files is an easier process if all use common spreadsheet programs and office productivity software. The benefit that each person receives from using spreadsheet programs and office productivity software increases when others use the same software.

Network effect
A situation in which a consumer's willingness to purchase a good or service is influenced by how many others also buy or have bought the item.

Network Effects and Market Feedback

Industries in which firms produce goods or services subject to network effects can experience sudden surges in growth, but the fortunes of such industries can also undergo significant and sometimes sudden reversals.

POSITIVE MARKET FEEDBACK When network effects are an important characteristic of an industry's product, an industry can experience **positive market feedback.** This is the potential for a network effect to arise when an industry's product catches on with consumers. Increased use of the product by some consumers then induces other consumers to purchase the product.

Positive market feedback can affect the prospects of an entire industry. The market for Internet service provider (ISP) servers is an example. The growth of this industry has roughly paralleled the rapid growth of Internet servers worldwide. Undoubtedly, positive market feedback resulting from network effects associated with Internet communications and interactions resulted in additional people desiring to obtain access to the Internet.

Positive market feedback
A tendency for a good or service to come into favor with additional consumers because other consumers have chosen to buy the item.

NEGATIVE MARKET FEEDBACK Network effects can also result in **negative market feedback,** in which a speedy downward spiral of product sales occurs for a product subject to

Negative market feedback
A tendency for a good or service to fall out of favor with more consumers because other consumers have stopped purchasing the item.

network effects. If a sufficient number of consumers cut back on their use of the product, others are induced to reduce their consumption as well, and the product can rapidly become a "has-been."

An example of an industry that has experienced negative market feedback of late is the telecommunications industry. Traditional telecommunications firms such as AT&T, WorldCom, and Sprint experienced positive market feedback during the late 1980s and early 1990s as cell phones and fax machines proliferated and individuals and firms began making long-distance phone calls from cell phones or via fax machines. Since the mid-1990s, as more people have acquired Internet access via cable and satellite Internet service providers, e-mail communications and e-mail document attachments have supplanted large volumes of phone and fax communications. For the telecommunications industry, the greater use of e-mail and e-mail attachments by some individuals induced others to follow suit. This resulted in negative market feedback that reduced the overall demand for traditional long-distance phone services.

Network Effects and Industry Concentration

In some industries, a few firms can potentially reap most of the benefits of positive market feedback. Suppose that firms in an industry sell differentiated products that are subject to network effects. If the products of two or three firms catch on, these firms will capture the bulk of the sales due to industry network effects.

A good example is the market for online auction services. An individual is more likely to use the services of an auction site if there is a significant likelihood that many other potential buyers or sellers also trade items at that site. Hence, there is a network effect present in the online auction industry, in which eBay and Overstock account for more than 80 percent of total sales. eBay in particular has experienced positive market feedback, and its share of sales of online auction services has increased to more than 50 percent.

Consequently, in an industry that produces and sells products subject to network effects, a small number of firms may be able to secure the bulk of the payoffs resulting from positive market feedback. In such an industry, oligopoly is likely to emerge as the prevailing market structure.

QUICK QUIZ   See page 593 for the answers. Review concepts from this section in MyEconLab.

_____ effects exist when a consumer's demand for an item depends in part on how many other consumers also use the product.

_____ market feedback arises if consumption of a product by a sufficient number of individuals induces others to purchase it. _____ market feedback can take

place if a falloff in usage of a product by some consumers causes others to stop purchasing the item.

In an industry with differentiated products subject to **network effects,** an oligopoly may arise if a few firms can reap most of the sales _____ resulting from _____ market feedback.

Two-Sided Markets, Network Effects, and Oligopoly

Two-sided Market
A market in which an intermediary firm provides services that link groups of producers and consumers.

Network effects are especially important to firms operating in **two-sided markets.** In such markets, an intermediary firm provides services that link other groups of producers and consumers. When you watch TV programming, for instance, your TV service provider links you and others among the TV audience to advertisers. The TV industry, therefore, is one of many examples of an industry operating in a two-sided market.

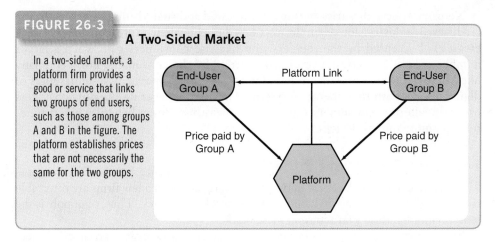

FIGURE 26-3

A Two-Sided Market

In a two-sided market, a platform firm provides a good or service that links two groups of end users, such as those among groups A and B in the figure. The platform establishes prices that are not necessarily the same for the two groups.

Types of Two-Sided Markets

Figure 26-3 above depicts the basic structure of a two-sided market, in which economists typically call the intermediary firm a *platform* and the groups of producers and consumers that it links—groups A and B in the figure—*end users*. Thus, in the TV industry, a TV service provider is a platform, and the two groups of end users are the advertisers and the audience.

Two-sided markets are of four types:

1. *Audience-seeking markets.* TV, radio, newspaper, and various Internet-portal industries fall into this group of two-sided markets, in which media platforms link advertisers to audiences.

2. *Matchmaking markets.* Operating in these two-sided markets are platform firms such as real estate agents, companies providing Web auction services, and online dating firms.

3. *Transaction-based markets.* Banks, credit- and debit-card companies, and other firms that finalize transactions between groups such as retailers and cardholders function as platforms within these two-sided markets.

4. *Shared-input markets.* In shared-input markets, groups of end users utilize a key input obtained from a platform firm in order to interact with one another. For instance, Microsoft has traditionally served as a platform that provides an operating system as a key input for digital devices sold to consumer end users by firms such as Hewlett-Packard and Dell. In addition, broadband-Internet-access firms are platforms that provide a key interactive-communications input for use by online firms and Web-surfing consumers.

Network Effects in Two-Sided Markets

Network effects are a common feature of two-sided markets. In an audience-seeking market, the perceived benefit received by each advertiser increases as the audience size grows. At the same time, even audience members who pay no attention to ads benefit from an expansion of a TV service provider's content made possible by a rise in the number of advertisers.

In a matchmaking market, a platform's task of matching an end user in one group to an end user in another is simplified when both groups are larger, which causes each end user to experience a greater benefit when group sizes increase. For instance, a person using an online dating site to try to find a date this Friday evening perceives a greater benefit if the dating site can search among a larger group for someone with desired characteristics.

Network effects also arise in transaction-based and shared-input markets. In the credit-card industry, for example, retailers benefit when more consumers use a credit card accepted by the retailers, and likewise consumers gain when a larger number of retailers accept a credit card carried by the consumers. For a company like Microsoft, which provides a shared input such as an operating system, sellers of digital devices with that operating system gain when a larger number of consumers use it. In addition, consumers who use the operating system benefit when it functions on more digital devices.

Two-Sided Oligopolistic Pricing

The presence of network effects in two-sided markets means a few firms are often able to capture most of the payoffs associated with market feedback. Thus, oligopoly is the most common industry structure in these markets.

Platform firms setting prices in a two-sided market must consider group differences in network effects. In a transaction-based market for debit cards, for example, banks may find that network effects are greater for retailers than for consumers. Suppose that the willingness of retailers to accept debit cards responds more strongly to greater consumer use than consumers' willingness to use the cards responds to retailers' acceptance. Also suppose that both groups are equally responsive to changes in card fees. Banks' profits would be higher if they charge lower card-usage fees to consumers than to retailers. Then more consumers will use the cards, which will give retailers a greater incentive to accept them even at a higher fee.

In a number of two-sided markets, platform firms maximize profits by charging an explicit price of zero to one group of end users. Many online media sites, for instance, charge fees to advertisers but post news articles and videos for consumer audiences at no explicit charge. In a few cases, platform firms may even establish *negative* prices, or *subsidies*, for one of the end-user groups. For instance, Microsoft commonly pays subsidies to developers of software applications that function with the company's Windows operating system. Microsoft is willing to do this because it has determined that the availability of more Windows applications increases consumers' willingness to purchase the Windows operating system.

Of course, platform firms in two-sided markets must also take into account strategic interactions. Thus, when a news media firm such as CNN decides how much to charge advertisers for news articles it makes available to readers online at no charge, it must consider as well the advertising fees that Fox News will establish. Likewise, when choosing subsidies to pay Windows application developers and the prices to charge Windows consumers, Microsoft must consider how Apple will set developer subsidies and consumer prices for its operating system.

How did the online matchmaker PlentyOfFish break into the top ranks of the online dating industry by borrowing an idea from audience-making markets?

EXAMPLE

Fishing for Date Seekers with Ads Boosts PlentyOfFish

During the first several years that the online dating industry existed, the few competing firms charged fees to people on both sides of a match. In the mid-2000s, though, the online matchmaking firm PlentyOfFish eliminated most fees for date seekers, which induced more people to look for dates at its site. This increase in customers in turn generated network effects as people responded to the upswing in registered users by searching the site for matches. PlentyOfFish convinced advertisers that all of its customers could be regarded as a large audience in an audience-seeking two-sided market. The firm restructured its Internet site so that

people looking for matches viewed advertisements on every Web page, and it earned nearly all of its revenues from fees paid by advertisers. As Figure 26-4 on the facing page indicates, after PlentyOfFish adopted this pricing strategy, it became one of the top online dating firms.

FOR CRITICAL THINKING
Why do you suppose that some competitors of PlentyOfFish have maintained the strategy of charging fees to date seekers rather than placing ads on their sites?

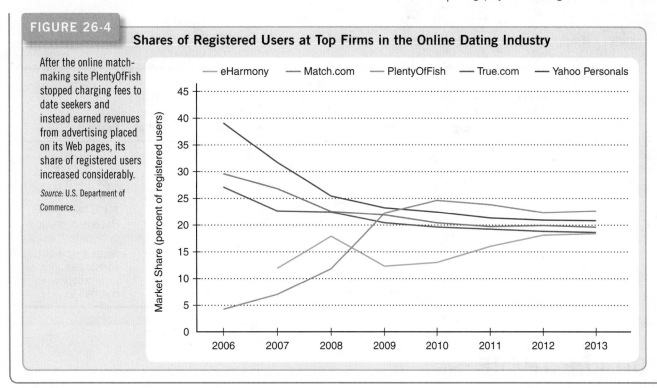

FIGURE 26-4

Shares of Registered Users at Top Firms in the Online Dating Industry

After the online match-making site PlentyOfFish stopped charging fees to date seekers and instead earned revenues from advertising placed on its Web pages, its share of registered users increased considerably.

Source: U.S. Department of Commerce.

QUICK QUIZ   See page 593 for the answers. Review concepts from this section in MyEconLab.

In **two-sided markets,** an intermediary firm called a _____ provides services that link other groups of producers and consumers that are known as _____.

The four types of **two-sided markets** are _____-_____ markets, _____ markets, _____-_____ markets, and _____-_____ markets.

Differences in network effects across different groups of end users can induce platforms to establish positive prices to one group but to establish _____ prices or even _____ prices, or subsidies, for another group.

The Old and New of Two-Sided Markets

Newspapers have existed since 59 B.C., so two-sided markets are not new. Now, however, Barnes & Noble and Amazon compete to link publishers to readers via digital devices. Apple and Google vie to link app designers to consumers via smartphones. Facebook and LinkedIn compete to link people via social media sites. Today, two-sided markets are everywhere.

Comparing Market Structures

Now that we have looked at perfect competition, pure monopoly, monopolistic competition, and oligopoly, we are in a position to compare the attributes of these four different market structures. We do this in summary form in Table 26-4 on the next page, in which we compare the number of sellers, their ability to set price, and the degree of product differentiation and also give some examples of each of the four market structures.

TABLE 26-4

Comparing Market Structures

Market Structure	Number of Sellers	Unrestricted Entry and Exit	Ability to Set Price	Long-Run Economic Profits Possible	Product Differentiation	Nonprice Competition	Examples
Perfect competition	Numerous	Yes	None	No	None	None	Agriculture, roofing nails
Monopolistic competition	Many	Yes	Some	No	Considerable	Yes	Toothpaste, toilet paper, soap, retail trade
Oligopoly	Few	Partial	Some	Yes	Frequent	Yes	Recorded music, college textbooks
Pure monopoly	One	No (for entry)	Considerable	Yes	None (product is unique)	Yes	Some electric companies, some local telephone companies

YOU ARE THERE
Hyundai Goes Vertical

"I think Henry Ford had it right at the start," says John Krafcik, CEO of Hyundai Motor America, about the founder of Ford Motor Company, "when he said 'The more you control production, the more you control what you sell the car for, too.'" Following up on Ford's original idea, Krafcik has led Hyundai through a series of vertical mergers that have created a subsidiary that makes 12 million tons of steel per year.

Krafcik offers two rationales for the vertical mergers. One is that manufacturing steel inputs for its vehicles instead of buying steel from other suppliers allows Hyundai to coordinate its vehicle production process at lower short-run costs. The other rationale is that Hyundai can now directly influence the development of lightweight steel used in constructing automotive products. In this way, Hyundai hopes to reduce its long-run costs as well.

Critical Thinking Questions

1. Did Hyundai's vertical mergers directly affect the automotive industry's four-firm concentration ratio or Herfindahl-Hirschman Index? Explain your reasoning.

2. If vertical mergers throughout the auto industry raised the minimum efficient scale for the industry, could industry concentration eventually increase? Explain.

CONCEPTS APPLIED

▶ Horizontal Mergers

▶ Concentration Ratio

▶ Herfindahl-Hirschman Index

ISSUES & APPLICATIONS

Concentration in the Textbook-Publishing Industry

Over the past two decades, textbook-publishing firms have undergone a series of horizontal mergers—that is, combinations of previously competing publishers. These mergers have created a concentrated textbook-publishing industry.

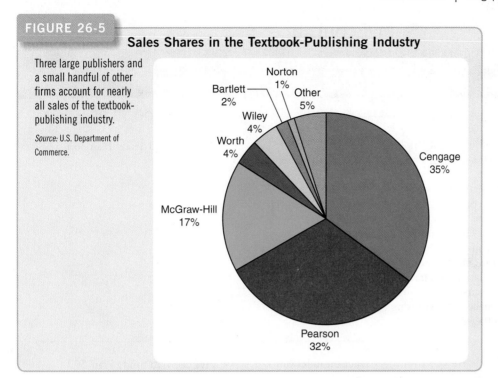

FIGURE 26-5

Sales Shares in the Textbook-Publishing Industry

Three large publishers and a small handful of other firms account for nearly all sales of the textbook-publishing industry.

Source: U.S. Department of Commerce.

Norton 1%
Bartlett 2%
Other 5%
Wiley 4%
Worth 4%
Cengage 35%
McGraw-Hill 17%
Pearson 32%

Overall Concentration in the Textbook-Publishing Industry

Figure 26-5 above displays recent shares of textbook sales by U.S. textbook publishers. The four-firm concentration ratio for this industry—the sum of the shares of sales going to Cengage, Pearson, McGraw-Hill, and Worth—is 88 percent.

Squaring the market-share percentages of all firms listed in Figure 26-5 and summing the results yields 2,600 as the approximate value of the Herfindahl-Hirschman Index (HHI). This HHI level is well below the maximum feasible HHI value of 10,000 for a monopoly. It is more than twice as large, however, as the value of about 1,250 that we would have observed if publishers had equal shares of industry sales. Taken together, therefore, the four-firm concentration ratio and HHI value suggest a very concentrated textbook-publishing industry.

Oligopolistic Interdependence in the Textbook Market

A key implication of Figure 26-5 is apparent without computing either the four-firm concentration ratio or the industry HHI. The figure shows that the top three publishers account for most of the sales—84 percent—in the industry.

In light of the substantial concentration among only three textbook publishers, economists view the industry as an oligopoly. When one of the top three firms decides how many textbooks to publish and what prices to charge, that publisher must take into account choices of quantities and prices made by the other two publishers among the top three. Thus, the textbook-publishing industry exhibits oligopolistic interdependence.

For Critical Thinking

1. If the industry sales shares of the top four publishers in Figure 26-5 remained unchanged, but the remaining firms merged to form a single company, would the four-firm concentration ratio change? Would the HHI change? Explain.

2. How would the prices that you pay for textbooks likely change if the textbook publishers in Figure 26-5 switched from behaving noncooperatively to determining production and prices collusively? Explain your reasoning.

Web Resources

1. To view a slideshow about the textbook-publishing industry, go to www.econtoday.com/chap26.

2. To contemplate why the textbook-publishing industry may become less concentrated in the future, go to www.econtoday.com/chap26.

> ### MyEconLab
> For more questions on this chapter's Issues & Applications, go to MyEconLab. In the Study Plan for this chapter, select Section N: News.

MyEconLab

Here is what you should know after reading this chapter. MyEconLab will help you identify what you know, and where to go when you need to practice.

WHAT YOU SHOULD KNOW		WHERE TO GO TO PRACTICE

The Fundamental Characteristics of Oligopoly
Oligopoly is a situation in which a few firms produce most of an industry's output. To measure the extent to which a few firms account for an industry's production and sales, economists use concentration ratios, which are the top few firms' percentages of total sales, and the Herfindahl-Hirschman Index, which is the sum of the squared percentage sales shares of all firms in an industry. An important characteristic of oligopoly is strategic dependence, meaning that one firm's decisions about its production, price, product quality, or advertising can bring about responses by other firms.

oligopoly, 574
strategic dependence, 574
vertical merger, 575
horizontal merger, 575
concentration ratio, 576
Herfindahl-Hirschman Index (HHI), 577

• MyEconLab Study Plan 26.1

Applying Game Theory to Evaluate the Pricing Strategies of Oligopolistic Firms Game theory is the analytical framework used to evaluate how two or more firms compete for payoffs that depend on the strategies that others employ. When firms work together for a common objective such as maximizing industry profits, they participate in cooperative games, but when they cannot work together, they engage in noncooperative games. One important type of game is the prisoners' dilemma, in which the inability to cooperate in determining prices of their products can cause firms to choose lower prices than they otherwise would prefer.

reaction function, 578
game theory, 579
cooperative game, 579
noncooperative game, 579
zero-sum game, 579
negative-sum game, 579
positive-sum game, 579
strategy, 579
dominant strategies, 579
prisoners' dilemma, 580
payoff matrix, 580
opportunistic behavior, 580
tit-for-tat strategic behavior, 581

Key Figures
Figure 26-1, 580
Figure 26-2, 581

• MyEconLab Study Plan 26.2
• Animated Figures 26-1, Figure 26-2

Industry Features That Contribute to or Detract from Efforts to Form a Cartel A cartel is an organization of firms in an industry that collude to earn economic profits by producing a combined output consistent with monopoly profit maximization. Four conditions make a collusive cartel agreement easier to create and enforce: (1) a small number of firms in the industry, (2) relatively undifferentiated products, (3) easily observable prices, and (4) little variation in prices.

cartel, 581

• MyEconLab Study Plan 26.3

WHAT YOU SHOULD KNOW ────────────── WHERE TO GO TO PRACTICE ──

Why Network Effects and Market Feedback Encourage Oligopoly Network effects arise when a consumer's demand for an item is affected by how many other consumers also use it. There is positive market feedback when enough people consume a product to induce others to do so. Negative market feedback occurs when decreased purchases of an item by some consumers give others an incentive to stop buying it.

network effect, 583
positive market feedback, 583
negative market feedback, 583

• MyEconLab Study Plan 26.4

Two-Sided Markets In a two-sided market, an intermediary firm known as a platform links groups called end users. When the extent of network effects differs for the groups of end users, the platform typically establishes contrasting prices for the different groups. When one group is particularly susceptible to network effects, the platform may choose to charge an explicit price of zero to that group and generate revenues solely by charging a positive price to the other group. In certain situations, the platform may even establish negative prices for (that is, pay subsidies to) one group while setting a positive price for the other group.

two-sided market, 584

Key Table
Table 26-4, 588

• MyEconLab Study Plans 26.5, 26.6
• Animated Table 26-4

Log in to MyEconLab, take a chapter test, and get a personalized Study Plan that tells you which concepts you understand and which ones you need to review. From there, MyEconLab will give you further practice, tutorials, animations, videos, and guided solutions. For more information, visit www.myeconlab.com

PROBLEMS

All problems are assignable in MyEconLab. Answers to odd–numbered problems appear at the back of the book.

26-1. Suppose that the distribution of sales within an industry is as shown in the table. (See page 576.)

Firm	Share of Total Market Sales
A	15%
B	14
C	12
D	11
E	10
F	10
G	8
H	7
All others	13
Total	100%

a. What is the four-firm concentration ratio for this industry?

b. What is the eight-firm concentration ratio for this industry?

26-2. The table below shows recent worldwide market shares of producers of inkjet printers. (See page 576.)

Firm	Share of Worldwide Market Sales
Brother	3%
Canon	17
Dell	6
Epson	18
Hewlett-Packard	41
Lexmark	13
Samsung	1
Other	1

a. In this year, what was the four-firm concentration ratio in the inkjet-printer industry?

b. In this year, what was the seven-firm concentration ratio in the inkjet-printer industry?

26-3. If there are 13 "All others" in the industry in Problem 26-1, each of which has a share of sales equal to 1 percent, what is the value of the Herfindahl-Hirschman Index for this industry? (See page 577.)

26-4. What is the value of the Herfindahl-Hirschman Index for the industry in Problem 26-2? (See page 577.)

26-5. Characterize each of the following as a positive-sum game, a zero-sum game, or a negative-sum game. (See page 579.)

a. Office workers contribute $10 each to a pool of funds, and whoever best predicts the winners in a professional sports playoff wins the entire sum.

b. After three years of fighting with large losses of human lives and materiél, neither nation involved in a war is any closer to its objective than it was before the war began.

c. Two collectors who previously owned incomplete and nearly worthless sets of trading cards exchange several cards, and as a result both end up with completed sets with significant market value.

26-6. Characterize each of the following as a positive-sum game, a zero-sum game, or a negative-sum game. (See page 579.)

a. You play a card game in your dorm room with three other students. Each player brings $5 to the game to bet on the outcome, winner take all.

b. Two nations exchange goods in a mutually beneficial transaction.

c. A thousand people buy $1 lottery tickets with a single payoff of $800.

26-7. Last weekend, Bob attended the university football game. At the opening kickoff, the crowd stood up. Bob therefore realized that he would have to stand up as well to see the game. For the crowd (not the football team), explain the outcomes of a cooperative game and a noncooperative game. Explain what Bob's "tit-for-tat strategic behavior" would be if he wished to see the game. (See page 581.)

26-8. Consider two strategically dependent firms in an oligopolistic industry, Firm A and Firm B. Firm A knows that if it offers extended warranties on its products but Firm B does not, it will earn $6 million in profits, and Firm B will earn $2 million. Likewise, Firm B knows that if it offers extended warranties but Firm A does not, it will earn $6 million in profits, and Firm A will earn $2 million. The two firms know that if they both offer extended warranties on their products, each will earn $3 million

in profits. Finally, the two firms know that if neither offers extended warranties, each will earn $5 million in profits. (See page 581.)

a. Set up a payoff matrix that fits the situation faced by these two firms.

b. What is the dominant strategy for each firm in this situation? Explain.

26-9. Take a look back at the data regarding the inkjet-printer industry in Problem 26-2, and answer the following questions. (See pages 581–583.)

a. Suppose that consumer demands for inkjet printers, the prices of which are readily observable in office supply outlets and at Internet sites, are growing at a stable pace. Discuss whether circumstances are favorable to an effort by firms in this industry to form a cartel.

b. If the firms successfully establish a cartel, why will there naturally be pressures for the cartel to break down, either from within or from outside?

26-10. Explain why network effects can cause the demand for a product *either* to expand *or* to contract relative to what it would be if there were no network effects. (See pages 583–584.)

26-11. List three products that you think are subject to network effects. For each product, indicate whether, in your view, all or just a few firms within the industry that produces each product experience market feedback effects. In your view, are any market feedback effects in these industries currently positive or negative? (See pages 583–584.)

26-12. Consider the following list, and classify each item according to the appropriate type of two-sided market—audience-making, matchmaking, shared-input, or transaction-based—and write a one-sentence answer justifying your classification. (See page 585. Hint: In some cases, you may wish to check out the firms' Web sites to assist in answering this question.)

a. Realtor.com

b. NYTimes.com

c. Linux.com

d. Paypal.com

26-13. Consider the following list, and classify each item according to the appropriate type of two-sided market—audience-making, matchmaking, shared-input, or transaction-based—and write a one-sentence answer justifying your classification. (See page 585. Hint: In some cases, you may wish to check out the firms' Web sites to assist in answering this question.)

a. Mastercard.com

b. FreeBSD.com

c. Plentyofish.com

d. WSJ.com

ECONOMICS ON THE NET

Current Concentration Ratios in U.S. Manufacturing Industries As you learned in this chapter, economists sometimes use concentration ratios to evaluate whether industries are oligopolies. In this application, you will make your own determination using the most recent data available.

Title: Concentration Ratios in Manufacturing

Navigation: Follow the link at **www.econtoday.com /chap26** to get to the U.S. Census Bureau's report on Concentration Ratios in Manufacturing.

Application Answer the following questions.

1. Select the report for the most recent year. Find the four-firm concentration ratios for the following industries: fluid milk (311511), women's and girls' cut & sew dresses (315233), envelopes (322232), electronic computers (334111).

2. Which industries are characterized by a high level of competition? Which industries are characterized by a low level of competition? Which industries qualify as oligopolies?

3. Name some of the firms that operate in the industries that qualify as oligopolies.

For Group Study and Analysis Discuss whether the four-firm concentration ratio is a good measure of competition. Consider some of the firms you named in item 3. Do you consider these firms to be "competitive" in their pricing and output decisions? Consider the four-firm concentration ratio for ready-mix concrete (327320). Do you think that on a local basis, this industry is competitive? Why or why not?

ANSWERS TO QUICK QUIZZES

p. 578: (i) small . . . interdependent; (ii) economies . . . mergers; (iii) Vertical; (iv) Horizontal; (v) percentage . . . sales

p. 581: (i) reaction . . . strategic; (ii) zero . . . negative . . . positive; (iii) dominant

p. 583: (i) cartel; (ii) small . . . undifferentiated . . . observable . . . variation; (iii) entry . . . variations

p. 584: (i) Network; (ii) Positive . . . Negative; (iii) gains . . . positive

p. 587: (i) platform . . . end users; (ii) audience-making . . . matchmaking . . . transaction-based . . . shared-input; (iii) zero . . . negative

27

Regulation and Antitrust Policy in a Globalized Economy

Since 2008, millions of U.S. residents have lost their jobs and struggled to find new positions in our dampened economy. Positions first disappeared in the private sector. Then jobs with state governments became harder to find as lower household incomes translated into lower state tax revenues. By the early 2010s, even the federal government was cutting back on overall hiring. Nevertheless, positions in one area of the federal government have continued to expand dramatically. U.S. government regulation of business has become a "growth industry," and federal hiring of people to supervise enforcement of laws overseeing business activities has increased even as employment in all other areas has stagnated. Thus, individuals with expertise in regulating businesses have benefited from an upswing in federal regulatory activities. As you will learn in this chapter, it is more difficult to assess other benefits of government regulation.

? **DID YOU KNOW THAT...** California recently adopted a regulation requiring farmers to raise egg-laying hens in conditions that allow them to fully extend their limbs, lie down, and turn in a circle? The legislation has posed practical difficulties, however. First, a typical hen requires 138 square inches to stretch her wings fully, but the largest cages provide only 116 square inches of space. Second, if California farmers respond to the law by allowing chickens to roam freely, the birds react by clustering together, thereby preventing satisfaction of the law's requirement. Furthermore, uncaged hens often slap and trample one another, which has long been a key rationale for farmers to place the birds in cages. Third, the law did not explain how the state would apply the new rules to eggs shipped to California by farmers in other states. Fourth, the legislation failed to specify how the space requirement for egg-laying hens would be enforced. California legislators left all of these details of the law to be sorted out by state regulatory agencies, courts, and perhaps future legislatures.

The only certainty associated with California's space regulation for egg-laying hens was that it likely would lead to higher costs of producing eggs sold within the state. How regulations such as California's "hen law" and other forms of government oversight *should act* to promote greater economic efficiency and how they *actually act* are important topics for understanding how every economy works. Nevertheless, before you can begin your study of the economic effects of regulation, it is important to understand the various ways in which the government oversees the activities of U.S. businesses.

Forms of Industry Regulation

The U.S. government began regulating social and economic activity early in the nation's history. The amount of government regulation began increasing in the twentieth century and has grown considerably since 1970. Figure 27-1 below displays two common measures of regulation in the United States. Panel (a) shows that regulatory spending by federal agencies (in 2005 dollars) has generally trended upward since 1970 and has risen considerably since 2000. New national security regulations following the 2001 terrorist attacks in New York City and Washington, D.C., have fueled a significant

FIGURE 27-1

Regulation on the Rise

Panel (a) shows that federal government regulatory spending is now more than $50 billion per year. State and local spending is not shown. As panel (b) shows, the number of pages in the *Federal Register* per year rose sharply in the 1970s, dropped off somewhat in the 1980s, and then began to rise once more.

Sources: Institute for University Studies; *Federal Register*, various issues.

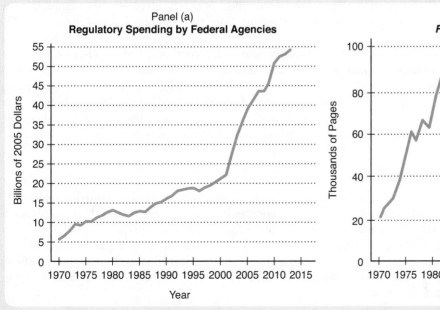

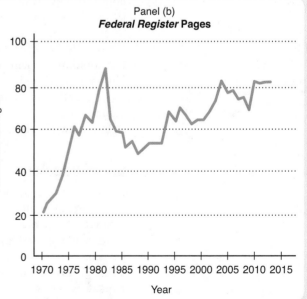

portion of this growth. The remainder of the increase in spending is related to a general upswing in regulatory enforcement by the federal government during this period. Panel (b) of Figure 27-1 on the previous page depicts the number of pages in the *Federal Register*, a government publication that lists all new regulatory rules. According to this measure, the scope of new federal regulations increased sharply during the 1970s, dropped off in the 1980s, and has generally increased since then.

There are two basic types of government regulation. One is *economic regulation* of natural monopolies and of specific nonmonopolistic industries. For instance, some state commissions regulate the prices and quality of services provided by electric power companies, which are considered natural monopolies (See page 534 in Chapter 24) that experience lower long-run average costs as their output increases. Financial services industries and interstate transportation industries are examples of nonmonopolistic industries that are subjected to considerable government regulation. The other form of government regulation is *social regulation*, which covers all industries. Examples include various occupational, health, and safety rules that federal and state governments impose on most businesses.

Economic Regulation

Initially, most economic regulation in the United States was aimed at controlling prices in industries considered to be natural monopolies. Over time, federal and state governments have also sought to influence the characteristics of products or processes of firms in a variety of industries without inherently monopolistic features.

REGULATION OF NATURAL MONOPOLIES The regulation of natural monopolies has tended to emphasize restrictions on product prices. Various public utility commissions throughout the United States regulate the rates (prices) of electrical utility companies and some telephone operating companies. This *rate regulation*, as it is usually called, officially has been aimed at preventing such industries from earning monopoly profits.

REGULATION OF NONMONOPOLISTIC INDUSTRIES The prices charged by firms in many other industries that do not have steadily declining long-run average costs, such as financial services industries, have also been subjected to regulations. Every state in the United States, for instance, has a government agency devoted to regulating the prices that insurance companies charge.

More broadly, government regulations establish rules pertaining to production, product (or service) features, and entry and exit within a number of specific nonmonopolistic industries. The federal government is heavily involved, for instance, in regulating the securities, banking, transportation, and communications industries. The Securities and Exchange Commission regulates securities markets. The Federal Reserve, Office of the Comptroller of the Currency, and Federal Deposit Insurance Corporation regulate commercial banks and savings banks. The National Credit Union Administration supervises credit unions. The Federal Aviation Administration supervises the airline industry, and the Federal Motor Carrier Safety Administration regulates the trucking industry. The Federal Communications Commission has oversight powers relating to broadcasting and telephone and communications services.

Social Regulation

In contrast to economic regulation, which covers only particular industries, social regulation applies to all firms in the economy. In principle, the aim of social regulation is a better quality of life through improved products, a less polluted environment, and better working conditions. Since the 1970s, an increasing array of government resources has been directed toward regulating product safety, advertising, and environmental effects. Table 27-1 on the facing page lists some major federal agencies involved in these broad regulatory activities.

TABLE 27-1

Federal Agencies Engaged in Social Regulation

Agency	Jurisdiction	Date Formed	Major Regulatory Functions
Federal Trade Commission (FTC)	Product markets	1914	Responsible for preventing businesses from engaging in misleading advertising, unfair trade practices, and monopolistic actions, as well as for protecting consumer rights.
Food and Drug Administration (FDA)	Food and pharmaceuticals	1938	Regulates the quality and safety of foods, health and medical products, pharmaceuticals, cosmetics, and animal feed.
Equal Employment Opportunity Commission (EEOC)	Labor markets	1964	Investigates complaints of discrimination based on race, religion, gender, or age in hiring, promotion, firing, wages, testing, and all other conditions of employment.
Environmental Protection Agency (EPA)	Environment	1970	Develops and enforces environmental standards for air, water, waste, and noise.
Occupational Safety and Health Administration (OSHA)	Health and safety	1970	Regulates workplace safety and health conditions.
Consumer Product Safety Commission (CPSC)	Consumer product safety	1972	Responsible for protecting consumers from products posing fire, electrical, chemical, or mechanical hazards or dangers to children.
Mining Enforcement and Safety Administration	Mining and oil drilling safety	1973	Establishes and enforces operational safety rules for mines and oil rigs.

The *possible* benefits of social regulations are many. For example, the water supply in some cities is known to be contaminated with potentially hazardous chemicals, and air pollution contributes to many illnesses. Society might well benefit from cleaning up these pollutants. As we shall discuss, however, broad social regulations also entail costs that we all pay, and not just as taxpayers who fund the regulatory activities of agencies such as those listed in Table 27-1 above.

QUICK QUIZ See page 617 for the answers. Review concepts from this section in MyEconLab.

_____ regulation applies to specific industries, whereas _____ regulation applies to businesses throughout the economy.

Governments commonly regulate the prices and quality of services provided by electric, gas, and other utilities, which traditionally have been considered _____ monopolies.

Governments also single out various nonmonopolistic industries, such as the financial and transportation industries, for special forms of _____ regulation.

Among the common forms of _____ regulation covering all industries are the occupational, health, and safety rules that federal and state governments impose on producers.

Regulating Natural Monopolies

At one time, much government regulation of business purportedly aimed to solve the so-called monopoly problem. Of particular concern was implementing appropriate regulations for natural monopolies.

The Theory of Natural Monopoly Regulation

Recall from Chapter 24 that a natural monopoly arises whenever a single firm can produce all of an industry's output at a lower per-unit cost than other firms attempting to produce less than total industry output. In a natural monopoly, therefore, economies of large-scale production exist, leading to a single-firm industry.

THE UNREGULATED NATURAL MONOPOLY Like any other firm, an unregulated natural monopolist will produce to the point at which marginal revenue equals marginal cost. Panel (a) of Figure 27-2 below depicts a situation in which a monopolist faces the market demand curve, D, and the marginal revenue curve, MR. The monopolist searches along the demand curve for the profit-maximizing price and quantity. The profit-maximizing quantity is at point A, at which the marginal revenue curve crosses the long-run marginal cost curve, LMC, and the unregulated monopolist maximizes profits by producing the quantity Q_m. Consumers are willing and able to pay the price

FIGURE 27-2

Profit Maximization and Regulation through Marginal Cost Pricing

The profit-maximizing natural monopolist produces at the point in panel (a) at which marginal costs equal marginal revenue. This is point A, which gives the quantity of production Q_m. The per-unit price is P_m at point F. If a regulatory commission attempted to require equating price with long-run marginal cost, production would have to be at the point where the long-run marginal cost (LMC) curve intersects the demand schedule. This is shown in panel (b). The quantity produced would be Q_1, and the per-unit price would be P_1. Average costs would be AC_1, however, so losses would equal the shaded area.

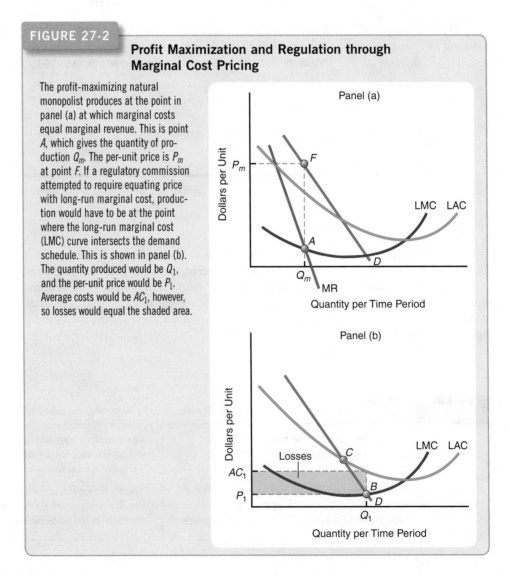

per unit P_m for this quantity at point F. This price is above marginal cost, so it leads to a socially inefficient allocation of resources by restricting production to a rate below that at which price equals marginal cost.

THE IMPRACTICALITY OF MARGINAL COST PRICING What would happen if the government were to require the monopolist in Figure 27-2 on the facing page to produce to the point at which price equals marginal cost, which is point B in panel (b)? Then it would produce a larger output rate, Q_1. Consumers, however, would pay only the price per unit P_1 for this quantity, which would be less than the average cost of producing this output rate, AC_1. Consequently, requiring the monopolist to engage in marginal cost pricing would yield a loss for the firm equal to the shaded rectangular area in panel (b). The profit-maximizing monopolist would go out of business rather than face such regulation.

AVERAGE COST PRICING Regulators cannot practically force a natural monopolist to engage in marginal cost pricing. Thus, regulation of natural monopolies has often taken the form of allowing the firm to set price at the point at which the long-run average cost (LAC) curve intersects the demand curve. In panel (b) of Figure 27-2, this is point C. In this situation, the regulator forces the firm to engage in *average cost pricing*, with average cost including what the regulators deem a "fair" rate of return on investment. For instance, a regulator might impose **cost-of-service regulation,** which requires a natural monopoly to charge only prices that reflect the actual average cost of providing products to consumers. Alternatively, although in a similar vein, a regulator might use **rate-of-return regulation,** which allows firms to set prices that ensure a normal return on investment.

> **Cost-of-service regulation**
> Regulation that allows prices to reflect only the actual average cost of production and no monopoly profits.
>
> **Rate-of-return regulation**
> Regulation that seeks to keep the rate of return in an industry at a competitive level by not allowing prices that would produce economic profits.

Natural Monopolies No More?

Traditionally, a feature common to the electricity, natural gas, and telecommunications industries has been that they utilize large networks of wires or pipelines to transmit their products to consumers. Governments concluded that the average costs of providing electricity, natural gas, and telecommunications declined as output rates of firms in these industries increased. Consequently, governments treated these industries as natural monopolies and established regulatory commissions to subject the industries to forms of cost-of-service and rate-of-return regulation.

ELECTRICITY AND NATURAL GAS: SEPARATING PRODUCTION FROM DELIVERY Today, numerous producers of natural gas vie to market their product in a number of cities across the country. In nearly half of the U.S. states, there is active competition in the production of electricity and natural gas.

What circumstances led to this transformation? The answer is that regulators of electricity and natural gas companies figured out that the function of *producing* electricity or natural gas did not necessarily have to be combined with the *delivery* of the product. Since the mid-1980s, various regulators have gradually implemented policies that have separated production of electricity and natural gas from the distribution of these items to consumers. Thus, in a growing number of U.S. locales, multiple producers now pay to use wire and pipeline networks to get their products to buyers.

TELECOMMUNICATIONS SERVICES MEET THE INTERNET As the production and sale of electricity and natural gas began to become more competitive undertakings, regulators started to apply the same principles to telecommunications services. At the same time, other forces reshaped the cost structure of the telecommunications industry. First, significant technological advances drastically reduced the costs of providing wireless telecommunications. Second, Internet phone service became more widely available. Most cable television companies that provide Internet access now offer Web-based telephone services as well. Many other companies also offer Web phone services for purchase by anyone who already has access to the Internet.

Go to www.econtoday.com/chap27 to learn about the latest broadband regulations proposed by the Federal Communications Commission.

ARE NATURAL MONOPOLIES RELICS OF THE PAST? Clearly, the scope of the government's role as regulator of natural monopolies has decreased with the unraveling of conditions that previously created this particular market structure. In many U.S. electricity and natural gas markets, government agencies now apply traditional cost-of-service or rate-of-return regulations primarily to wire and pipeline owners. Otherwise, the government's main role in many regional markets is to serve as a "traffic cop," enforcing property rights and rules governing the regulated networks that serve competing electricity and natural gas producers.

In telecommunications, there are competing views on natural monopoly and the role of regulation. According to one perspective, any natural monopoly rationale for a governmental regulatory role is dissipating rapidly as more and more households and businesses substitute cellular and Web-based phone services for wired phone services. Under the alternative view, network effects (see Chapter 26, page 583) contribute to the potential for a natural monopoly problem that regulators must continue to address.

Why is it that governments around the world are seeking to regulate broadband-Internet-access providers?

INTERNATIONAL EXAMPLE

A Perceived Monopoly Threat Motivates Net Neutrality Rules

According to U.S. Federal Communications Commission (FCC) chair Julius Genachowski, "Once a consumer chooses a broadband provider, then that provider has monopoly power over access to that consumer for any application or content provider that wants to reach that consumer." Telecommunications regulators across the globe, such as those in Australia, Japan, and the European Union, have reached the same conclusion. They have responded by proposing or adopting *net neutrality regulations* aimed at preventing broadband-Internet-access providers from limiting interaction among consumers and Web content and application firms.

Critics of net neutrality rules point out that if broadband providers cannot limit access to any content, then it is difficult for them to charge higher prices to consumers who use much larger amounts of signal bandwidth than others.

The critics also point out that a growing number of households now obtain broadband access *both* through traditional cable or direct-service-line providers *and* via wireless service providers. As a consequence, many consumers already can choose among different broadband providers, none of which possess any natural monopoly status, in spite of what the chair of the FCC says. Thus, for an expanding set of consumers, there is no "monopoly power" for broadband providers to misuse.

FOR CRITICAL THINKING

How might the development of an expanding array of wired and wireless Internet-ready digital devices lead to increased competition among broadband providers?

QUICK QUIZ   See page 617 for the answers. Review concepts from this section in MyEconLab.

A **natural monopoly** arises when one firm can produce all of an industry's output at a _____ per-unit cost than other firms. A profit-maximizing natural monopolist produces to the point at which marginal _____ equals long-run marginal _____ and charges the price that people are willing to pay for the quantity produced.

Because a natural monopolist that is required to set price equal to long-run marginal cost will sustain long-run losses and shut down, regulators typically allow natural monopolists to charge prices that just cover _____ costs. Normally, regulators have done this

through **cost-of-service regulation**, in which prices are based on actual production costs, or **rate-of-return regulation**, in which prices are set to yield a rate of return consistent with _____ economic profits.

Technological and regulatory innovations have made the concept of natural monopoly less relevant. In the electricity, natural gas, and telecommunications industries, production increasingly is accomplished by numerous competing firms that _____ their products through regulated _____.

Regulating Nonmonopolistic Industries

Traditionally, one of the fundamental purposes of governments has been to provide a co-ordinated system of safeguarding the interests of their citizens. Not surprisingly, protecting consumer interests is the main rationale offered for governmental regulatory functions.

Rationales for Consumer Protection in Nonmonopolistic Industries

The Latin phrase *caveat emptor*, or "let the buyer beware," was once the operative principle in most consumer dealings with businesses. The phrase embodies the idea that the buyer alone is ultimately responsible for assessing a producer and the quality of the items it sells before agreeing to purchase the firm's product. Today, in contrast, various federal agencies require companies to meet specific minimal standards in their dealings with consumers. For instance, a few years ago, the U.S. Federal Trade Commission assessed monetary penalties on Toys "Я" Us and KB Toys because they failed to ship goods sold on their Web sites in time for a pre-Christmas delivery. Such a government action would have been unheard of a few decades ago.

In some industries, federal agencies dictate the rules of the game for firms' interactions with consumers. The Federal Aviation Administration (FAA), for example, oversees almost every aspect of the delivery of services by airline companies. The FAA regulates the process by which tickets for flights are sold and distributed, oversees all flight operations, and even establishes rules governing the procedures for returning luggage after flights are concluded.

Go to www.econtoday.com/chap27 to view a full list of the regulations put into place by the Federal Aviation Administration.

REASONS FOR GOVERNMENT-ORCHESTRATED CONSUMER PROTECTION Two rationales are commonly advanced for heavy government involvement in overseeing and supervising nonmonopolistic industries. One, which you encountered in Chapter 5, is the possibility of *market failures*. For example, the presence of negative externalities such as pollution may induce governments to regulate industries that create such externalities.

The second common rationale is *asymmetric information*. In the context of many producer-consumer interactions, this term refers to situations in which a producer has information about a product that the consumer lacks. For instance, administrators of your college or university may know that another school in your vicinity offers better-quality degree programs in certain fields. If so, it would not be in your college or university's interest to transmit this information to applicants who are interested in pursuing degrees in those fields.

For certain products, asymmetric information problems can pose special difficulties for consumers trying to assess product quality in advance of purchase. In unregulated financial markets, for example, individuals contemplating buying a company's stock, a municipality's bond, or a bank's certificate of deposit might struggle to assess the associated risks of financial loss. If the air transportation industry were unregulated, a person might have trouble determining if one airline's planes were less safe than those of competing airlines. In an unregulated market for pharmaceuticals, parents might worry about whether one company's childhood-asthma medication could have more dangerous side effects than medications sold by other firms.

ASYMMETRIC INFORMATION AND PRODUCT QUALITY In extreme cases, asymmetric information can create situations in which most of the available products are of low quality. A commonly cited example is the market for used automobiles. Current owners of cars that *appear* to be in good condition know the autos' service records. Some owners know that their cars have been well maintained and really do run great. Others, however, have not kept their autos in good repair and thus are aware that they will be susceptible to greater-than-normal mechanical or electrical problems.

Suppose that in your local used-car market, half of all used cars offered for sale are high-quality autos. The other half are low-quality cars, commonly called "lemons," that are likely to break down within a few months or perhaps even weeks. In addition, suppose that a consumer is willing to pay $20,000 for a particular car model if it is in excellent condition but is willing to pay only $10,000 if it is a lemon. Finally, suppose that people who own truly high-quality used cars are only willing to sell at a price of at least $20,000, but people who own lemons are willing to sell at any price at or above $10,000.

Because there is a 50–50 chance that a given car up for sale is of either quality, the average amount that a prospective buyer is willing to pay equals $\left(\frac{1}{2} \times \$20,000\right) + \left(\frac{1}{2} \times \$10,000\right) = \$15,000$. Owners of low-quality used cars are willing to sell them at this price, but owners of high-quality used cars are not. In this example, only lemons will be traded, at the "lemon" price of $10,000, because owners of cars in excellent condition will not sell their cars at a price that prospective buyers are willing to pay.

Lemons problem

The potential for asymmetric information to bring about a general decline in product quality in an industry.

THE LEMONS PROBLEM Economists refer to the possibility that asymmetric information can lead to a general reduction in product quality in an industry as the **lemons problem.** This problem does not apply only to the used-car industry. In principle, any product with qualities that are difficult for consumers to fully assess is susceptible to the same problem. *Credence goods*, which as you learned in Chapter 25 on page 563 are items such as pharmaceuticals, health care, and professional services, also may be particularly vulnerable to the lemons problem.

MARKET SOLUTIONS TO THE LEMONS PROBLEM Firms offering truly high-quality products for sale can address the lemons problem in a variety of ways. They can offer product guarantees and warranties. In addition, to help consumers separate high quality producers from incompetent or unscrupulous competitors, the high-quality producers may work together to establish industry standards.

In some cases, firms in an industry may even seek external product certification. They may, for example, solicit scientific reports supporting proposed industry standards and bearing witness that products of certain firms in the industry meet those standards. To legitimize a product-certification process, firms may hire outside companies or groups to issue such reports.

Implementing Consumer Protection Regulation

Governments offering asymmetric information and lemons problems as rationales for regulation presumably have concluded that private market solutions such as warranties, industry standards, and product certification are insufficient. To address asymmetric information problems, governments may offer legal remedies to consumers or enforce licensing requirements in an effort to provide minimum product standards. In some cases, governments go well beyond simple licensing requirements by establishing a regulatory apparatus for overseeing all aspects of an industry's operations.

Go to www.econtoday.com/chap27 to see how the Federal Trade Commission imposes regulations intended to protect consumers.

LIABILITY LAWS AND GOVERNMENT LICENSING Sometimes liability laws, which specify penalties for product failures, provide consumers with protections similar to guarantees and warranties. When the Federal Trade Commission (FTC) charged Toys "Я" Us and KB Toys with failing to meet pre-Christmas delivery dates for Internet toy orders, it operated under a mail-order statute Congress passed in the early 1970s. The mail-order law effectively made the toy companies' delivery guarantees legally enforceable. Although the FTC applied the law in this particular case, any consumer could have filed suit for damages under the terms of the statute.

Federal and state governments also get involved in consumer protection by issuing licenses granting only "qualifying" firms the legal right to produce and sell certain products. For instance, governments of nearly half of the states give the right to sell caskets only to people who have a mortuary or funeral director's license, allegedly to ensure that bodies of deceased individuals are handled with care and dignity.

Although government licensing may successfully limit the sale of low-quality goods, licensing requirements also often limit the number of providers. As you learned in Chapter 24, such requirements can ease efforts by established firms to act as monopolists. In addition, if governments rely on the expertise of established firms for assistance in drafting licensing requirements, these firms certainly have strong incentives to recommend low standards for themselves but high standards for prospective entrants.

DIRECT ECONOMIC AND SOCIAL REGULATION In some instances, governments determine that liability laws and licensing requirements are insufficient to protect the interests of consumers. A government may decide that asymmetric-information problems in banking are so severe that without an extensive banking regulatory apparatus, consumers will lose confidence in banks, and banking crises may ensue. It may rely on similar rationales to establish economic regulation of other financial services industries. Eventually, it may apply consumer protection rationales to justify the economic regulation of additional industries such as trucking or air transportation.

The government may establish an oversight authority to make certain that consumers are protected from incompetent producers of foods and pharmaceuticals. Eventually, the government may determine that a host of other products should meet government consumer protection standards. It may also decide that the people who produce the products also require government agencies to ensure workplace safety. In this way, widespread social regulation emerges, as it has in the United States and almost all developed nations.

QUICK QUIZ   See page 617 for the answers. Review concepts from this section in MyEconLab.

Governments tend to regulate industries in which they think market _____ and _____ information problems are most severe.

A common justification for government regulation is to protect consumers from adverse effects of _____ information.

To address the _____ problem, or the potential for _____-quality products to predominate when asymmetric information is widespread, governments often supplement private firms' guarantees, warranties, and certification standards with liability laws and licensing requirements.

Incentives and Costs of Regulation

Abiding by government regulations is a costly undertaking for firms. Consequently, businesses engage in a number of activities intended to avoid the true intent of regulations or to bring about changes in the regulations that government agencies establish.

Creative Response and Feedback Effects: Results of Regulation

Sometimes individuals and firms respond to a regulation in a way that conforms to the letter of the law but undermines its spirit. When they do so, they engage in **creative response** to regulations.

One type of creative response has been labeled a *feedback effect*. Individuals' behaviors may change after a regulation has been put into effect. If a regulation requires fluoridated water, then parents know that their children's teeth have significant protection against tooth decay. Consequently, the feedback effect is that parents become less concerned about how many sweets their children eat.

How has a new law regulating information provided to college students about textbook prices created an unanticipated feedback effect?

Creative response
Behavior on the part of a firm that allows it to comply with the letter of the law but violate the spirit, significantly lessening the law's effects.

EXAMPLE

Learn the Price and Buy from the College Bookstore in One Step

Recently, Congress passed a law called the Higher Education Opportunity Act. A key provision of the legislation mandates that U.S. colleges and universities disclose information about course textbooks on their Web sites. The schools must provide for each course both the International Standard Book Numbers (ISBNs) and the prices of required and recommended texts and other supplemental materials.

A number of colleges and universities responded to this requirement in an unexpected way. They combined the required information with direct Internet links to Web pages on which students could place immediate orders at prices charged by the schools' own bookstores. In most cases, of course, text prices

charged by colleges and universities are higher than the prices at other competing outlets, such as discount textbook Web sites. By meeting the letter of the law, these colleges and universities found a way to encourage students to place orders with their own retail outlets instead of shopping for lower-priced copies at competing bookstores and Web sites. In this way, the schools engaged in a creative response to the regulation imposed by the new law.

FOR CRITICAL THINKING
What feedback effects might occur if publishers were required to sell textbooks at prices below a regulatory maximum price?

Explaining Regulators' Behavior

Those charged with enforcing government regulations operate outside the market, so their decisions are determined by nonmarket processes. A number of theories have emerged to describe the behavior of regulators. These theories explain how regulation can harm consumers by generating higher prices and fewer product choices while benefiting producers by reducing competitive forces and allowing higher profits. Two of the best-known theories of regulatory behavior are the *capture hypothesis* and the *share-the-gains, share-the-pains theory*.

THE CAPTURE HYPOTHESIS Regulators often end up becoming champions of the firms they are charged with regulating. According to the **capture hypothesis,** regardless of why a regulatory agency was originally established, eventually special interests of the industry it regulates will capture it. After all, the people who know the most about a regulated industry are the people already in the industry. Thus, people who have been in the industry and have allegiances and friendships with others in the industry will most likely be asked to regulate the industry.

> **Capture hypothesis**
> A theory of regulatory behavior that predicts that regulators will eventually be captured by special interests of the industry being regulated.

According to the capture hypothesis, individual consumers of a regulated industry's products and individual taxpayers who finance a regulatory agency have interests too diverse to be greatly concerned with the industry's actions. In contrast, special interests of the industry are well organized and well defined. These interests also have more to offer political entrepreneurs within a regulatory agency, such as future employment with one of the regulated firms. Therefore, regulators have a strong incentive to support the position of a well-organized special-interest group within the regulated industry.

How did the Food and Drug Administration (FDA) recently pursue a policy action that raised suspicions it might be a captured regulator?

POLICY EXAMPLE

New Nicotine Market Entry? Not If the FDA Can Help It!

When Congress authorized the FDA to regulate tobacco products containing the drug called nicotine, critics noted that tobacco companies had sought FDA oversight. Protecting incumbent tobacco firms from competition could become a key FDA objective, some critics suggested, if the FDA was prone to regulatory capture.

Indeed, one of the FDA's initial acts as tobacco regulator was an attempt to prohibit the sale of battery-powered devices that transform nicotine-laced liquid into a vapor mist. For many smokers, these so-called e-cigarettes offer a way to satisfy their nicotine habits without generating the tar-laden smoke that accompanies traditional cigarettes. The FDA's stance was that e-cigarettes legally constituted a new "drug or medical device" that required the FDA's approval before being marketed to consumers—approval that the FDA refused to provide. Ultimately, however, courts overruled the FDA's legal position. Judges ruled that the FDA had authority only to *regulate* e-cigarettes. The FDA could *not*, the judges concluded, ban firms from competing with incumbent sellers of nicotine-laced tobacco by offering an alternative means of dispensing the long-legal drug nicotine.

FOR CRITICAL THINKING
Who do you think had the most to gain if the FDA had successfully banned the sale of e-cigarettes that generate sales exceeding $100 million per year?

> **Share-the-gains, share-the-pains theory**
> A theory of regulatory behavior that holds that regulators must take account of the demands of three groups: legislators, who established and oversee the regulatory agency; firms in the regulated industry; and consumers of the regulated industry's products.

"SHARE THE GAINS, SHARE THE PAINS" The **share-the-gains, share-the-pains theory** offers a somewhat different view of regulators' behavior. This theory focuses on the specific aims of regulators. It proposes that a regulator's main objective is simply to keep his or her job as a regulator. To do so, the regulator must obtain the approval of both the legislators who originally established and continue to oversee the regulatory agency and the regulated industry. The regulator must also take into account the views of the industry's customers.

In contrast to the capture hypothesis, which holds that regulators must take into account only industry special interests, the share-the-gains, share-the-pains theory contends that regulators must worry about legislators and consumers as well. After all, if industry customers who are hurt by improper regulation complain to legislators, the regulators might lose their jobs. Whereas the capture theory predicts that regulators will quickly allow electric utilities to raise their rates in the face of higher fuel costs, the share-the-gains, share-the-pains theory predicts a slower, more measured regulatory response. Ultimately, regulators will permit an increase in utility rates, but the allowed adjustment will not be as speedy or complete as predicted by the capture hypothesis. The regulatory agency is not completely captured by the industry. It also has to consider the views of consumers and legislators.

The Benefits and Costs of Regulation

As noted earlier, regulation offers many *potential* benefits. *Actual* benefits, however, are difficult to measure. Putting a dollar value on safer products, a cleaner environment, and better working conditions is a difficult proposition. Furthermore, the benefits of most regulations accrue to society over a long time.

THE DIRECT COSTS OF REGULATION TO TAXPAYERS Measuring the costs of regulation is also a challenging undertaking. After all, about 5,000 new federal and state regulations are issued each year. One cost, though, is certain: U.S. federal taxpayers pay nearly $55 billion per year to staff regulatory agencies with more than 300,000 employees and to fund their various activities. Figure 27-3 below displays the distribution of total federal government outlays for economic and social regulation of various areas of the economy.

The *total* cost of regulation is much higher than just the explicit government outlays to fund the administration of various regulations, however. After all, businesses must expend resources complying with regulations, developing creative responses to regulations, and funding special-interest lobbying efforts directed at legislators and regulatory officials. Sometimes companies find that it is impossible to comply with one regulation without violating another, and determining how to avoid the resulting legal entanglements can entail significant expenditures.

THE TOTAL SOCIAL COST OF REGULATION According to the Office of Management and Budget, annual expenditures that U.S. businesses must make solely to comply with regulations issued by various federal agencies amount to more than $700 billion per year. Nevertheless, this estimate encompasses only the *explicit* costs of satisfying regulatory demands placed on businesses. It ignores relevant opportunity costs. After all, owners, managers, and employees of companies could be doing other things with their time and resources than complying with regulations. Economists estimate that the additional opportunity costs of complying with federal regulations may be as high as $300 billion per year. A portion of this amount is passed on to consumers in the form of higher prices.

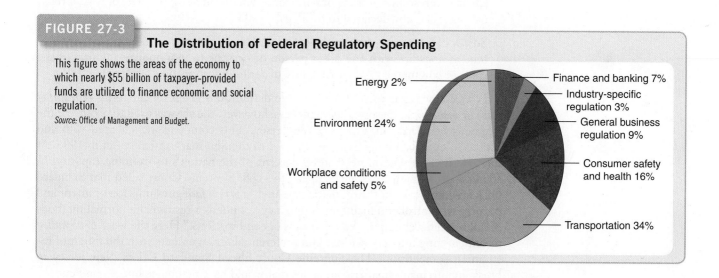

FIGURE 27-3

The Distribution of Federal Regulatory Spending

This figure shows the areas of the economy to which nearly $55 billion of taxpayer-provided funds are utilized to finance economic and social regulation.
Source: Office of Management and Budget.

Energy 2%
Environment 24%
Workplace conditions and safety 5%
Finance and banking 7%
Industry-specific regulation 3%
General business regulation 9%
Consumer safety and health 16%
Transportation 34%

YOU ARE THERE

To contemplate why the costs of regulation can total to large dollar amounts when summed across many affected firms, take a look at **No Longer in a State of Sticker Shock in Michigan** on page 612.

All told, therefore, the total social cost associated with satisfying federal regulations in the United States probably exceeds $1 trillion per year. This figure, of course, applies only to federal regulations. It does not include the explicit and implicit opportunity costs associated with regulations issued by 50 different state governments and tens of thousands of municipalities. Undoubtedly, the annual cost of regulation throughout the United States exceeds $1.75 trillion per year.

QUICK QUIZ See page 617 for the answers. Review concepts from this section in MyEconLab.

The **capture hypothesis** holds that regulatory agencies will eventually be captured by industry special interests because _____ individually are not greatly influenced by regulation, whereas regulated _____ are directly affected.

According to the **share-the-gains, share-the-pains theory** of regulation, regulators must take into account the interests of three groups: the _____, _____, and _____.

Regulation has benefits that are difficult to quantify in dollars. The costs of regulation include direct _____ expenditures on regulatory agencies and _____ explicit and implicit opportunity costs of complying.

Antitrust Policy

An expressed aim of the U.S. government is to foster competition. To this end, Congress has made numerous attempts to legislate against business practices that Congress has perceived to be anticompetitive. This is the general idea behind antitrust legislation. If the courts can prevent collusion among sellers of a product, there will be no restriction of output, and monopoly prices will not result. Instead, prices of goods and services will be close to their marginal social opportunity costs.

Antitrust Policy in the United States

Congress has enacted four key antitrust laws, which are summarized in Table 27-2 on the facing page. The most important of these is the original U.S. antitrust law, called the Sherman Act.

THE SHERMAN ANTITRUST ACT OF 1890 The Sherman Antitrust Act, which was passed in 1890, was the first attempt by the federal government to control the growth of monopoly in the United States. The most important provisions of that act are as follows:

Section 1: Every contract, combination in the form of a trust or otherwise, or conspiracy, in restraint of trade or commerce among the several states, or with foreign nations, is hereby declared to be illegal.

Section 2: Every person who shall monopolize, or attempt to monopolize, or combine or conspire with any other person or persons to monopolize any part of the trade or commerce . . . shall be guilty of a misdemeanor [now a felony].

Notice how vague this act really is. No definition is given for the terms *restraint of trade* or *monopolize*. Despite this vagueness, however, the act was used to prosecute the infamous Standard Oil Trust of New Jersey. This company was charged with and convicted of violations of Sections 1 and 2 of the Sherman Antitrust Act in 1906. At the time it controlled more than 80 percent of the nation's oil-refining capacity. In addressing the company's legal appeal, the U.S. Supreme Court ruled that Standard Oil's predominance in the oil market created "a *prima facie* presumption of intent and purpose to control and maintain dominancy . . . not as a result from normal methods of industrial development, but by means of combinations." Here the word *combination* meant entering into associations and preferential arrangements with the intent of restraining competition. The Supreme Court forced Standard Oil of New Jersey to break up into many smaller companies that would have no choice but to compete.

TABLE 27-2		
Key U.S. Antitrust Laws	Sherman Antitrust Act of 1890	Forbids any contract, combination, or conspiracy to restrain trade or commerce within the United States or across U.S. borders. Holds any person who attempts to monopolize trade or commerce criminally liable.
	Clayton Act of 1914	Prohibits specific business practices deemed to restrain trade or commerce. Bans discrimination in prices charged to various purchasers when price differences are not due to actual differences in selling or transportation costs. Also forbids a company from selling goods on the condition that the purchaser must deal exclusively with that company. Finally, it prevents corporations from holding stock in other companies when this may lessen competition.
	Federal Trade Commission Act of 1914 (and 1938 Amendment)	Outlaws business practices that reduce the extent of competition, such as alleged cutthroat pricing intended to drive rivals from the marketplace. Also established the Federal Trade Commission and empowered it to issue cease and desist orders in situations in which it determines "unfair methods of competition in commerce" exist. The 1938 amendment added deceptive business practices to the list of illegal acts.
	Robinson-Patman Act of 1936	Bans selected discriminatory price cuts by chain stores that allegedly drive smaller competitors from the marketplace. In addition, forbids price discrimination through special concessions in the form of price or quantity discounts, free advertising, or promotional allowances granted to one buyer but not to others, if these actions substantially reduce competition.

The Sherman Act applies today just as it did more than a century ago. Recently, Samsung and other producers of DRAM computer chips admitted that they had violated the Sherman Act by conspiring to fix the price of DRAM chips by holding down production. Samsung paid a $300 million fine for this Sherman Act violation.

Why did the Federal Trade Commission block a proposed merger between two video-rental chains?

POLICY EXAMPLE

The FTC Blocks a Merger in Advance of the Firms' Bankruptcy

In 2005, the video-rental firm Blockbuster sought a merger with a major competitor, Hollywood Videos. The Federal Trade Commission blocked the merger, however, in an effort to protect independent stores that rented DVDs and Blu-ray disks from alleged monopolization by a combination of Blockbuster and Hollywood Videos.

Even as the FTC was blocking this merger on antitrust grounds, Netflix, Amazon, and a host of other Internet firms were entering the market for video rentals. These companies' services allow people to pay fees to view streaming videos online instead of troubling themselves to rent physical DVDs or Blu-ray disks. Thus, the demand for the services of video-rental chains withered. By the early 2010s, Hollywood Videos no longer existed, and Blockbuster was struggling to reorganize. Instead of forming a monopoly in the video-rental market, these two firms had gone bankrupt. Nearly all of the independent video-rental stores had also exited the market.

FOR CRITICAL THINKING

Why is correctly assessing all actual and likely competition crucial to determining whether a firm or firms may be committing actions that run afoul of antitrust laws?

OTHER IMPORTANT ANTITRUST LEGISLATION Table 27-2 above lists three other antitrust laws. In 1914, Congress passed the Clayton Act to clarify some of the vague provisions of the Sherman Act by identifying specific business practices that were to be legally prohibited.

Congress also passed the Federal Trade Commission Act in 1914. In addition to establishing the Federal Trade Commission to investigate unfair trade practices, this law enumerated certain business practices that, according to Congress, involved overly aggressive competition. A 1938 amendment to this law expressly prohibited "unfair or deceptive acts or practices in commerce" and empowered the FTC to regulate advertising and marketing practices by U.S. firms.

The Robinson-Patman Act of 1936 amended the Clayton Act by singling out specific business practices, such as selected price cuts, aimed at driving smaller competitors out of business. The act is often referred to as the "Chain Store Act" because it was intended to protect *independent* retailers and wholesalers from "unfair competition" by chain stores.

EXEMPTIONS FROM ANTITRUST LAWS Numerous laws exempt the following industries and business practices from antitrust legislation:

- Labor unions

- Public utilities—electric, gas, and telephone companies

- Professional baseball

- Cooperative activities among U.S. exporters

- Hospitals

- Public transit and water systems

- Suppliers of military equipment

- Joint publishing arrangements in a single city by two or more newspapers

Thus, not all U.S. businesses are subject to antitrust laws.

WHAT IF... all U.S. business organizations *were* subject to antitrust laws?

If U.S. antitrust laws provided for no exemptions, hundreds of organizations would be subject to investigation and prosecution for illegally forming monopolies. Labor unions with monopoly positions in numerous industries would have to open themselves to competition from other unions. Public utilities and hospitals in many communities across the nation would no longer be legally protected monopolies. It would also be illegal for the American League and National League teams of Major League Baseball to operate effectively as a single monopoly firm providing sports entertainment businesses. Thus, more than one baseball World Series might compete for sports enthusiasts' attention.

International Discord in Antitrust Policy

What, if anything, should U.S. antitrust authorities do if AT&T decides that it wishes to merge with British Telecommunications or if Germany's Deutsche Telecom wants to acquire Sprint Nextel? What, if anything, should they do if Time Warner, the largest U.S. entertainment company, attempts to merge with London-based EMI, one of the world's largest recorded-music companies? These are not just rhetorical questions, as U.S. and European antitrust authorities learned in the 2000s when these issues actually surfaced. Growing international linkages among markets for many goods and services have increasingly made antitrust policy a global undertaking.

Go to www.econtoday.com/chap27 to take a look at the guidelines the U.S. Department of Justice uses to decide whether to challenge proposed mergers under antitrust laws.

The international dimensions of antitrust pose a problem for U.S. antitrust authorities in the Department of Justice and the Federal Trade Commission. In the United States, the overriding goal of antitrust policies has traditionally been protecting the interests of consumers. This is also a formal objective of European Union (EU) antitrust authorities. In the EU, however, policymakers are also required to reject any business combination that "creates or strengthens a dominant position as a result of which effective competition would be significantly impeded."

This additional clause has sometimes created tension between U.S. and EU policy-making. In the United States, increasing dominance of a market by a single firm arouses the concern of antitrust authorities. Nevertheless, U.S. authorities typically will remain passive if they determine that the increased market dominance arises from factors such as exceptional management and greater cost efficiencies that ultimately benefit consumers by reducing prices. In contrast, under EU rules antitrust authorities are obliged to block *any* business combination that increases the dominance of any producer. They must do so regardless of what factors might have caused the business's preeminence in the marketplace or whether the antitrust action might have adverse implications for consumers.

QUICK QUIZ See page 617 for the answers. Review concepts from this section in MyEconLab.

The first national antitrust law was the _____ Antitrust Act of 1890, which made illegal every contract and combination in restraint of trade. It remains the single most important antitrust law in the United States.

The _____ Act of 1914 made illegal various specific business practices, such as price discrimination.

The _____ _____ _____ Act of 1914 and its 1938 amendment established the Federal Trade Commission and prohibited "unfair or deceptive acts or practices in commerce."

The _____-_____ Act of 1936 aimed to prevent large producers from driving out small competitors by means of selective discriminatory price cuts.

Antitrust Enforcement

How are antitrust laws enforced? In the United States, most enforcement continues to be based on the Sherman Act. The Supreme Court has defined the offense of **monopolization** as involving the following elements: "(1) the possession of monopoly power in the relevant market and (2) the willful acquisition or maintenance of that power, as distinguished from growth or development as a consequence of a superior product, business acumen, or historical accident."

The Relevant Market

The Sherman Act does not define monopoly. To assess whether a monopolistic capability might exist, antitrust authorities seek to define a market and then to measure the degree of concentration in that market. They begin by determining the **relevant market** within which firms' products are in competition.

The relevant market consists of two elements. One is the relevant *product* market, which involves products that are closely substitutable for one another. The second element is the relevant *geographic* market, which involves a particular set of firms whose substitutable products actually are available to consumers in a particular area, ranging from a limited region to the entire nation. Combining the two elements yields the market in which firms in an industry compete.

Measuring Concentration in the Relevant Market to Assess Mergers

Once the relevant market has been determined, antitrust enforcement focuses on the degree of competition within that market. The two federal enforcement agencies, the Antitrust Division of the U.S. Department of Justice and the Federal Trade Commission (FTC), utilize the Herfindahl-Hirschman Index, or HHI, for this purpose. As you learned in Chapter 26 (see page 577), the HHI is equal to the sum of the squared shares of total sales or output by all firms in an industry. Thus, once the relevant market has been determined, antitrust enforcers compute the HHI for all firms within the industry defined by the scope of that market.

Monopolization
The possession of monopoly power in the relevant market and the willful acquisition or maintenance of that power, as distinguished from growth or development as a consequence of a superior product, business acumen, or historical accident.

Relevant market
A group of firms' products that are closely substitutable and available to consumers within a particular geographic area.

When assessing whether a proposed horizontal merger among two or more firms competing in a relevant market might create a monopoly pricing capability, enforcers consider *both* the resulting change in the HHI *and* the level of the postmerger HHI. Under current U.S. antitrust enforcement guidelines, *either* a combined HHI *change* greater than 100 and postmerger HHI in excess of 1,000 *or* a combined HHI *change* exceeding 50 and a postmerger HHI above 1,800 raise antitrust concerns. The Justice Department's Antitrust Division or the FTC can follow up on such concerns by trying to determine the predicted effects of the merger on overall industry output and on the equilibrium price in the relevant market.

If the antitrust enforcement authority's position is that the proposed merger would lead to a substantial output reduction and price increase, then the authority files a lawsuit seeking to block the merger. The firms proposing the merger can respond either by dropping their merger plan or by defending the plan in court. Then it is up to a court to determine whether the merger legally can proceed, whether the merger must be abandoned, or, in some cases, whether the merger might be allowed under certain conditions. Sometimes, for instance, a merger is permitted on the condition that merging firms sell parts of their operations to other firms in the same industry.

Why did AT&T have to give up on a proposed merger with T-Mobile?

POLICY EXAMPLE

A Proposed Wireless Merger Experiences a Dropped Connection

Recently, AT&T and T-Mobile sought to merge their wireless operations into a single firm providing cellular phone and broadband Internet services. The proposed merger would have increased the HHI value for the nationwide wireless market—which the Justice Department's Antitrust Division determined to be the relevant market—by nearly 600. The postmerger level of the HHI would have exceeded 2,800. These amounts were well above thresholds sufficient to raise U.S. antitrust authorities' concerns about potential monopoly capability generated by a horizontal merger. Thus, the Antitrust Division filed a lawsuit seeking to block the merger, based on a claim that if the merger occurred, consumers ultimately would face much higher prices for wireless services. A few weeks later, AT&T and T-Mobile abandoned their merger plans rather than combat the lawsuit in court.

FOR CRITICAL THINKING
By definition, any horizontal merger increases industry concentration. Why might some mergers lead to lower prices for consumers? (Hint: Recall that mergers might enable firms to experience economies of scale that reduce long-run average cost.)

Product Packaging and Antitrust Enforcement

A particular problem in U.S. antitrust enforcement is determining whether a firm has engaged in "willful acquisition or maintenance" of market power. Actions that appear to some observers to be good business look like antitrust violations to others. To illustrate why quandaries can arise in antitrust enforcement, let's consider two examples: *versioning* and *bundling*.

Versioning
Selling a product in slightly altered forms to different groups of consumers.

PRODUCT VERSIONING A firm engages in product **versioning** when it sells an item in slightly altered forms to different groups of consumers. A typical method of versioning is to remove certain features from an item and offer what remains as a somewhat stripped-down version of the product at a different price.

Consider an office-productivity software program, such as Adobe Acrobat or Microsoft Word. Firms selling such programs typically offer both a "professional" version containing a full range of features and a "standard" version providing only basic functions. One perspective on this practice regards it as a form of price discrimination, or selling essentially the same product at different prices to different consumers. People who desire to use the full range of features in Adobe Acrobat or Microsoft Word are likely to be computing professionals. Compared to most other consumers, their demand for the full-featured version of an office-productivity software program is likely to be less elastic. In principle, therefore, Adobe and Microsoft can earn higher profits by offering "professional" versions at higher prices and selling a "standard" version at a lower price.

Price discrimination—charging varying prices to different consumers when the price differences are not a result of different production or transportation costs—is illegal under the Clayton Act of 1914. Are Adobe, Microsoft, and other companies engaging in illegal price discrimination? Another perspective on versioning indicates that they are not. According to this point of view, consumers regard "professional" and "standard" versions of software packages as imperfect substitutes. Consequently, each version is a distinctive product sold in a unique market. If so, versioning increases overall consumer satisfaction because consumers who are not computing professionals are able to utilize certain features of software products at a lower price. So far, antitrust authorities in the United States and elsewhere have been inclined toward this view of the economic effects of versioning, rather than perceiving it as a form of price discrimination.

PRODUCT BUNDLING Antitrust authorities have been less tolerant of another form of product packaging, known as **bundling,** which involves the joint sale of two or more products as a set. Antitrust authorities usually are not concerned if a firm allows consumers to purchase the products either individually or as a set. They are more likely to investigate a firm's business practices, however, when it allows consumers to purchase one product only when it is bundled with another. Antitrust officials often view this form of bundling as a method of price discrimination known as **tie-in sales,** in which a firm requires consumers who wish to buy one of its products to purchase another item the firm sells as well.

To understand their reasoning, consider a situation in which one group of consumers is willing to pay $200 for a computer operating system but only $100 for an Internet-browsing program. A second group of consumers is willing to pay only $100 for the same operating system but is willing to pay $200 for the same Internet-browsing program. If the same company that sells both types of software offers the operating system at a price above $100, then only consumers in the first group will buy this software. Likewise, if it sells the Internet-browsing program at a price above $100, then only the second group of consumers will purchase that program.

But if the firm sells both products as a bundled set, it can charge $300 and generate sales of both products to both groups. One interpretation is that the first group pays $200 for the operating system, but for the second group, the operating system's price is $100. At the same time, the first group has paid $100 for the Internet-browsing program, while the second group perceives the price of the program to be $200. Effectively, bundling enables the software company to engage in price discrimination by charging different prices to different groups.

Antitrust enforcers in the Justice Department applied this interpretation in their prosecution of Microsoft, which for years had bundled its Internet-browsing program, Internet Explorer, together with its Windows operating system. Enforcement officials added another twist by contending that Microsoft also had monopoly power in the market for computer operating systems. By bundling the two products, they argued, Microsoft had sought both to price-discriminate and to extend its monopoly power to the market for Internet-browsing software. The remedy that the courts imposed was for Microsoft to alter some of its business practices. As part of this legal remedy, Microsoft was required to unbundle its Windows and Internet Explorer products.

Bundling
Offering two or more products for sale as a set.

Tie-in sales
Purchases of one product that are permitted by the seller only if the consumer buys another good or service from the same firm.

QUICK QUIZ See page 617 for the answers. Review concepts from this section in MyEconLab.

As part of the enforcement of antitrust laws, officials at the U.S. Department of Justice and the Federal Trade Commission typically define a _____ market and compute the change in and new level of the _____-_____ _____ to assess whether to legally challenge a proposed merger.

Antitrust enforcers must decide whether producers seek to monopolize the relevant market, which involves determining both the relevant _____ market and the relevant _____ market.

Antitrust authorities generally have not considered product _____, or offering different versions of essentially the same product for sale at different prices, to be illegal price discrimination. U.S. authorities have, however, raised antitrust concerns about product _____, which they view as a method of engaging in **tie-in sales** that require consumers to purchase one product in order to obtain another.

YOU ARE THERE
No Longer in a State of Sticker Shock in Michigan

In the early 1980s, the Michigan legislature established the Item Pricing Law. This legislation required all retailers selling physical items within the state to affix a price sticker displaying a printed dollar price on every individual item. For David Hansen at the Hansen Foods market in the town of Hart, Michigan, the years since have been "a real pain." Price stickers do not remain attached to most refrigerated and frozen items for very long. Hence, each day over the years, Hansen's employees have had to get down on their hands and knees to remove from drains the dozens of stickers that have come off during the preceding 24 hours. Then they have had to attach new stickers, which in due time fell into the drains as well. Hansen estimates that his store could have saved 80 hours per week in labor costs—about $40,000 per year—in the absence of the rule.

Thus, Hansen recently joined with many Michigan retailers in celebrating a price-tag-freedom day when the Michigan legislature and governor agreed to rescind the Item Pricing Law. Estimates indicate that during the years the law was in force, it added a total of at least $2 billion to Michigan retailers' costs.

Critical Thinking Questions

1. Was Michigan's Item Pricing Law an example of economic or social regulation?

2. How do you think that the Item Pricing Law was intended to protect consumers? (Hint: Recall the asymmetric information rationale for regulation.)

ISSUES & APPLICATIONS

More Regulations Breed More Federal Regulatory Jobs

CONCEPTS APPLIED

▶ Economic Regulation

▶ Social Regulation

▶ Rate-of-Return Regulation

How has the upswing in government regulations affected the prospects for landing a job with a federal agency charged with implementing economic or social regulation or supervising rate-of-return regulation? The answer is that the availability of such positions has risen by more than two-thirds during the past decade.

Government Workers Apply Government Regulations

According to an old joke, the answer to the question "How many government regulators does it take to screw in a light bulb?" is "45—one to screw in the light bulb and 44 to do the paperwork." In recent years, the federal government has employed many people to regulate *types* of light bulbs. To reach the decision to ban interstate trade of incandescent light bulbs and to enforce this ban, for instance, the federal government has utilized labor from several agencies. Among these agencies are the Environmental Protection Agency, the Federal Trade Commission, and the Department of Energy. Workers at these agencies also supervise enforcement of laws regulating the production and sale of legal fluorescent light bulbs.

Of course, there is a vast array of products beyond light bulbs, and there is a rapidly expanding volume of government rules regulating production and sale of all of these products. Consequently, the number of people employed by the government to perform regulatory tasks is increasing at a rapid pace.

How Many Federal Workers Regulate Tasks of Other Workers?

Figure 27-4 on the facing page provides an indication of how many federal workers the U.S. government has employed to regulate the activities of other workers. The figure displays the number of federal regulatory workers for every 1,000 workers employed elsewhere in the U.S. economy since 1980. Since the early 2000s, the number of federal positions allocated to regulatory agencies for every 1,000 employed workers in the U.S. economy has risen from 1.3 to 2.2, an increase of 69 percent.

FIGURE 27-4

Federal Regulatory Workers per Thousand U.S. Employees

In the early 2000s, the federal government allocated only about 1.3 positions to regulatory duties per 1,000 employed people in the United States. Now that figure is close to 2.2 federal regulatory positions per 1,000 U.S. workers.

Source: U.S. Government Office of Information and Regulatory Affairs.

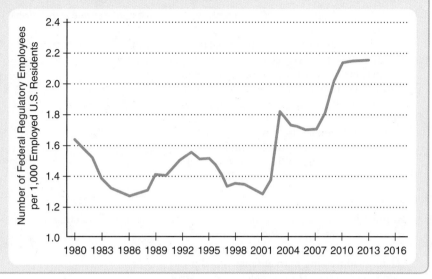

In 2001, about 190,000 federal workers regulated U.S. businesses. Today, more than 300,000 federal employees perform these functions. At the current pace of federal regulatory employment growth, a decade from now more than 500,000 people will regulate the way businesses operate. If so, the federal regulatory "industry" will become the nation's third-largest employer, behind the U.S. Postal Service and Walmart.

For Critical Thinking

1. Why might regulatory agencies utilize labor more intensively than private firms?

2. What will happen to the regulatory share of employment if the rate of growth of regulatory employment stays five times higher than overall employment growth?

Web Resources

1. Learn about sources of the growth of federal government employment at **www.econtoday.com/chap27**.

2. For a list of federal and state regulators, go to **www.econtoday.com/chap27**.

MyEconLab

For more questions on this chapter's Issues & Applications, go to MyEconLab. In the Study Plan for this chapter, select Section N: News.

MyEconLab

Here is what you should know after reading this chapter. MyEconLab will help you identify what you know, and where to go when you need to practice.

— WHAT YOU SHOULD KNOW —

Government Regulation of Business There are two basic forms of government regulation of business: economic regulation and social regulation. Economic regulation applies to specific industries. Social regulations affect nearly all businesses and encompass a broad range of objectives concerning such issues as product safety, environmental quality, and working conditions.

Key Figure
Figure 27-1, 595

— WHERE TO GO TO PRACTICE —

• MyEconLab Study Plan 27.1
• Animated Figure 27-1

MyEconLab *continued*

WHAT YOU SHOULD KNOW ────────────────────────────── WHERE TO GO TO PRACTICE ──

Practical Difficulties in Regulating the Prices Charged by Natural Monopolies A natural monopoly's long-run marginal cost is less than long-run average total cost, so requiring marginal cost pricing causes an economic loss. Hence, regulators normally aim for a natural monopoly's price to equal average total cost, so it earns zero economic profits. In recent years, uncoupling production of electricity, natural gas, and telecommunications from their distribution has enabled regulators to promote competition in these industries.

cost-of-service regulation, 599
rate-of-return regulation, 599

Key Figure
Figure 27-2, 598

- MyEconLab Study Plan 27.2
- Animated Figure 27-2

Rationales for Regulating Nonmonopolistic Industries The two most common rationales for regulation of nonmonopolistic industries relate to addressing market failures and protecting consumers from problems arising from information asymmetries. Asymmetric information can also create a lemons problem, which occurs when uncertainty about product quality leads to markets containing mostly low-quality items.

lemons problem, 602

- MyEconLab Study Plan 27.3

Regulators' Incentives and the Costs of Regulation The capture theory of regulator behavior predicts that regulators will eventually find themselves supporting the positions of the firms that they regulate. The share-the-gains, share-the-pains theory predicts that a regulator will try to satisfy all constituencies, at least in part. The costs of regulation, which include both the direct costs to taxpayers of funding regulatory agencies and the explicit and implicit opportunity costs that businesses must incur to comply, are easier to quantify in dollar terms than the benefits.

creative response, 603
capture hypothesis, 604
share-the-gains, share-the-pains theory, 604

Key Figure
Figure 27-3, 605

- MyEconLab Study Plan 27.4
- Animated Figure 27-3

Foundations of Antitrust There are four key antitrust laws. The Sherman Act of 1890 forbids attempts to monopolize an industry. The Clayton Act of 1914 clarified antitrust law by prohibiting specific types of business practices. The Federal Trade Commission Act of 1914, as amended in 1938, seeks to prohibit deceptive business practices and to prevent "cutthroat pricing." The Robinson-Patman Act of 1936 outlawed price cuts deemed to be discriminatory and predatory.

- MyEconLabStudy Plan 27.5

---- WHAT YOU SHOULD KNOW ----   ---- WHERE TO GO TO PRACTICE ----

Issues in Enforcing Antitrust Laws The Supreme Court has defined monopolization as possessing or seeking monopoly pricing power in the "relevant market." Authorities charged with enforcing antitrust laws evaluate concentration of production or sales within a defined relevant market as compared with regulatory threshold concentration levels. In recent years, antitrust officials have raised questions about whether product packaging, either in the form of different versions or as bundled sets, is a type of price discrimination involving tie-in sales.

monopolization, 609
relevant market, 609
versioning, 610
bundling, 611
tie-in sales, 611

• MyEconLab Study Plan 27.6

Log in to MyEconLab, take a chapter test, and get a personalized Study Plan that tells you which concepts you understand and which ones you need to review. From there, MyEconLab will give you further practice, tutorials, animations, videos, and guided solutions. For more information, visit www.myeconlab.com

PROBLEMS

All problems are assignable in MyEconLab. Answers to odd-numbered problems appear at the back of the book.

27-1. Local cable television companies are sometimes granted monopoly rights to service a particular territory of a metropolitan area. The companies typically pay special taxes and licensing fees to local municipalities. Why might a municipality give monopoly rights to a cable company? (See pages 604–605.)

27-2. A local cable company, the sole provider of cable television service, is regulated by the municipal government. The owner of the company claims that she is normally opposed to regulation by government, but asserts that regulation is necessary because local residents would not want a large number of different cables crisscrossing the city. Why do you think the owner is defending regulation by the city? (See pages 604–605.)

27-3. The table below depicts the cost and demand structure a natural monopoly faces. (See page 598.)

Quantity	Price ($)	Long-Run Total Cost ($)
0	100	0
1	95	92
2	90	177
3	85	255
4	80	331
5	75	406
6	70	480

a. Calculate total revenues, marginal revenue, and marginal cost at each output level. If this firm is allowed to operate as a monopolist, what will be the quantity produced and the price charged by the firm? What will be the amount of monopoly profit? [Hint: Recall that marginal revenue equals the change in total revenues ($P \times Q$) from each additional unit and that marginal cost equals the change in total costs from each additional unit.]

b. If regulators require the firm to practice marginal cost pricing, what quantity will it produce, and what price will it charge? What is the firm's profit under this regulatory framework? [Hint: Recall that average total cost equals total cost divided by quantity and that profits equal $(P - \text{ATC}) \times Q$.]

c. If regulators require the firm to practice average cost pricing, what quantity will it produce, and what price will it charge? What is the firm's profit under this regulatory framework?

27-4. As noted in the chapter, separating the *production* of electricity from its *delivery* has led to considerable deregulation of producers. (See page 599.)

a. Briefly explain which of these two aspects of the sale of electricity remains susceptible to natural monopoly problems.

b. Suppose that the potential natural monopoly problem you identified in part (a) actually arises. Why is marginal cost pricing not a feasible solution? What makes average cost pricing a feasible solution?

c. Discuss two approaches that a regulator could use to try to implement an average-cost-pricing solution to the problem identified in part (a).

27-5. Are lemons problems likely to be more common in some industries and less common in others? Based on your answer to this question, should government regulatory activities designed to reduce the scope of lemons problems take the form of economic regulation or social regulation? Take a stand, and support your reasoning. (See page 602.)

27-6. Research into genetically modified crops has led to significant productivity gains for countries such as the United States that employ these techniques. Countries such as the European Union's member nations, however, have imposed controls on the import of these products, citing concern for public health. Is the European Union's regulation of genetically modified crops social regulation or economic regulation? (See page 596.)

27-7. Do you think that the regulation described in Problem 27-6 is more likely an example of the capture hypothesis or the share-the-gains, share-the-pains theory? Why? (See page 604.)

27-8. Prices of tickets for seats on commercial passenger planes are typically in the hundreds of dollars, whereas trips can be made by automobile at much lower cost. Accident rates per person per trip in the airline industry are considerably lower than auto accident rates per person per trip. Based on these facts, discuss how regulatory costs and benefits may help to explain why government regulations require children to be placed in safety seats in automobiles but not on commercial passenger planes. (See page 605.)

27-9. A few years ago, the U.S. government created a "Do Not Call Registry" and forbade marketing firms from calling people who placed their names on this list. Today, an increasing number of companies are sending mail solicitations to individuals inviting them to send back an enclosed postcard for more information about the firms' products. What these solicitations fail to mention is that they are worded in such a way that someone who returns the postcard gives up protection from telephone solicitations, even if they are on the government's "Do Not Call Registry." In what type of behavior are these companies engaging? Explain your answer. (See page 603. Hint: Are these firms meeting the letter of the law but violating its spirit?)

27-10. Suppose that a business has developed a very high-quality product and operates more efficiently in producing that product than any other potential competitor. As a consequence, at present it is the only seller of this product, for which there are few close substitutes. Is this firm in violation of U.S. antitrust laws? Explain. (See pages 606–607.)

27-11. Consider the following fictitious sales data (in thousands of dollars) for both e-books and physical books. Firms have numbers instead of names, and Firm 1 generates only e-book sales. Suppose that antitrust authorities' initial evaluation of whether a single firm may possess "monopoly power" is whether its share of sales in the relevant market exceeds 70 percent. (See page 609.)

E-Book Sales		Physical Book Sales		Combined Book Sales	
Firm	Sales	Firm	Sales	Firm	Sales
1	$ 750	2	$4,200	2	$ 4,250
2	50	3	2,000	3	2,050
3	50	4	1,950	4	2,000
4	50	5	450	1	750
5	50	6	400	5	500
6	50			6	450
Total	$1,000		$9,000		$10,000

a. Suppose that the antitrust authorities determine that selling physical books and e-bookselling are individually separate relevant markets. Does an initial evaluation suggest that any single firm has monopoly power, as defined by the antitrust authorities?

b. Suppose that in fact there is really only a single book industry, in which firms compete in selling both physical books and e-books. According to the antitrust authorities' initial test of the potential for monopoly power, is there actually cause for concern?

27-12. Consider the data from Problem 27-11. Suppose that antitrust authorities have determined that there are separate relevant markets for e-books and physical books. In addition, these authorities perceive that a monopoly situation exists that can be challenged on legal grounds if the value of the Herfindahl-Hirschman Index exceeds 5,000. On the basis of this criterion, do the antitrust authorities conclude that there are grounds for a legal challenge in either market? Explain. (See page 610.)

27-13. Consider the data from Problem 27-11. Suppose that antitrust authorities have determined that the relevant market includes both e-books and physical books. These authorities perceive that a monopoly situation exists that can be challenged on legal grounds if the value of the Herfindahl-Hirschman Index exceeds 5,000. On the basis of this criterion, do the antitrust authorities conclude that there are grounds for a legal challenge? Explain. (See page 610.)

27-14. A package delivery company provides both overnight and second-day delivery services. It charges almost twice as much to deliver an overnight package to any world location as it does to deliver the same package to the same location in two days. Often, second-day packages arrive at company warehouses in destination cities by the next day, but drivers intentionally do not deliver these packages until the following day. What is this business practice called? Briefly summarize alternative perspectives concerning whether this activity should or should not be viewed as a form of price discrimination. (See pages 610–611.)

27-15. A firm that sells both Internet-security software and computer antivirus software will sell the antivirus software as a stand-alone product. It will only sell the Internet-security software to consumers in a combined package that also includes the antivirus software. What is this business practice called? Briefly explain why an antitrust authority might

view this practice as a form of price discrimination. (See page 611.)

27-16. Recently, a food retailer called Whole Foods sought to purchase Wild Oats, a competitor in the market for organic foods. When the Federal Trade Commission (FTC) sought to block this merger on antitrust grounds, FTC officials argued that such a merger would dramatically increase concentration in the market for "premium organic foods." Whole Foods' counterargument was that it considered itself to be part of the broadly defined supermarket industry that includes retailers such as Albertson's, Kroger, and Safeway. What key issue of antitrust regulation was involved in this dispute? Explain. (See page 609.)

ECONOMICS ON THE NET

Guidelines for U.S. Antitrust Merger Enforcement How does the U.S. government apply antitrust laws to mergers? This application gives you the opportunity to learn about the standards applied by the Antitrust Division of the U.S. Department of Justice when it evaluates a proposed merger.

Title: U.S. Department of Justice Antitrust Merger Enforcement Guidelines

Navigation: Go to www.econtoday.com/chap27 to access the home page of the Antitrust Division of the U.S. Department of Justice.

Application Answer the following questions.

1. Click on *Horizontal Merger Guidelines*. In section 1, click on *Overview*, and read this section. What factors do U.S. antitrust authorities consider when evaluating

the potential for a horizontal merger to "enhance market power"—that is, to place the combination in a monopoly situation?

2. Read the *Horizontal Merger Guidelines*. In what situations will the antitrust authorities most likely question a horizontal merger?

For Group Study and Analysis Have three groups of students from the class examine sections 1, 2, and 3 of the *Horizontal Merger Guidelines* discussed in item 1. After each group reports on all the factors that the antitrust authorities consider when evaluating a horizontal merger, discuss why large teams of lawyers and many economic consultants are typically involved when the Antitrust Division of the Department of Justice alleges that a proposed merger would be "anticompetitive."

ANSWERS TO QUICK QUIZZES

p. 597: (i) Economic . . . social; (ii) natural . . . economic; (iii) social

p. 600: (i) lower . . . revenue . . . cost; (ii) average . . . zero; (iii) deliver . . . networks

p. 603: (i) failures . . . asymmetric; (ii) asymmetric; (iii) lemons . . . low

p. 606: (i) consumers . . . firms; (ii) industry . . . legislators . . . consumers; (iii) government . . . firms'

p. 609: (i) Sherman; (ii) Clayton; (iii) Federal Trade Commission; (iv) Robinson-Patman

p. 611: (i) relevant . . . Herfindahl-Hirschman Index; (ii) product . . . geographic; (iii) versioning . . . bundling

28

The Labor Market: Demand, Supply, and Outsourcing

Nearly a century ago, during World War I, the British military developed the first pilotless powered aircraft. Today, pilotless flight using "autopilots" is commonplace. Indeed, in principle, digital systems could replace human pilots, even for plane takeoffs and landings. Robots can also drive vehicles on highways, as was proved by Mercedes-Benz's first "autonomous van" in the1980s, and more recently on busy city streets, as robot cars developed by Google have demonstrated in thousands of miles of road tests. Could robots replace human airline pilots, bus drivers, and taxi drivers—or perhaps even human physicians, dentists, or teachers? From a technological standpoint, the answer is definitely yes. As you will learn in this chapter, though, whether robots actually *will* replace humans in performing particular tasks is an *economic* issue.

LEARNING OBJECTIVES

After reading this chapter, you should be able to:

▶ Understand why a firm's marginal revenue product curve is its labor demand curve

▶ Explain in what sense the demand for labor is a "derived" demand

▶ Identify the key factors influencing the elasticity of demand for inputs

▶ Describe how equilibrium wage rates are determined for perfectly competitive firms

▶ Explain what labor outsourcing is and how it is ultimately likely to affect U.S. workers' earnings and employment prospects

▶ Contrast the demand for labor and wage determination by a product market monopolist with outcomes that would arise under perfect competition

MyEconLab helps you master each objective and study more efficiently. See end of chapter for details.

data from the National Association of Colleges and Employers indicate that only about 75 percent of employers associated with the organization now conduct campus interviews, down from nearly 90 percent in 2007? In addition, a nationwide study of a recent class of college students found that a full year after their graduation, employers had hired just over half of the students, compared with 90 percent in 2007. Furthermore, only about half of those who were hired within a year after completing their degrees obtained jobs for which employers actually required a college degree. Clearly, the overall demand for the college graduates' labor by businesses is restrained in today's dampened economy.

The demand for labor provided by college graduates or for all types of inputs by businesses can be studied in much the same manner as we studied the demand for output. Our analysis will always end with the same conclusion: A firm will hire employees up to the point beyond which it isn't profitable to hire any more. It will hire employees to the point at which the marginal benefit of hiring a worker will just equal the marginal cost. Indeed, in every profit-maximizing situation, it is most profitable to carry out an activity up to the point at which the marginal benefit equals the marginal cost. Remembering that guideline will help you in analyzing decision making at the firm level, which is where we will begin our discussion of the demand for labor.

Labor Demand for a Perfectly Competitive Firm

We will start our analysis under the assumption that the market for input factors is perfectly competitive. We will further assume that the output market is perfectly competitive. This provides a benchmark against which to compare other situations in which labor markets or product markets are not perfectly competitive.

Competition in the Product Market

Let's take as our example a firm that sells magneto optical (MO) disks and is in competition with many companies selling the same kind of product. Assume that the laborers hired by this manufacturing firm do not need any special skills. This firm sells MO disks in a perfectly competitive market. It also buys labor (its variable input) in a perfectly competitive market. A firm that hires labor under perfectly competitive conditions hires only a minuscule proportion of all the workers who are potentially available to the firm. By "potentially available," we mean all the workers in a geographic area who possess the skills demanded by our perfect competitor.

In such a market, it is always possible for the individual firm to hire extra workers without having to offer a higher wage. Thus, the supply of labor to the firm is perfectly elastic at the going wage rate established by the forces of supply and demand in the entire labor market. The firm is a *price taker* in the labor market.

Marginal Physical Product

Look at panel (a) of Figure 28-1 on the following page. In column 1, we show the number of workers per week that the firm can employ. In column 2, we show total physical product (TPP) per week, the total *physical* production of MO disks that different quantities of the labor input (in combination with a fixed amount of other inputs) will generate in a week's time. In column 3, we show the additional output gained when the company adds workers to its existing manufacturing facility.

This column, the **marginal physical product (MPP) of labor,** represents the extra (additional) output attributed to employing additional units of the variable input factor. If this firm employs seven workers rather than six, the MPP is 118. The law of diminishing marginal product predicts that additional units of a variable factor will, after some point, cause the MPP to decline, other things held constant.

We are assuming that all other nonlabor factors of production are held constant. So, if our manufacturing firm wants to add one more worker to its production line, it has to crowd all the existing workers a little closer together because it does not increase its

Marginal physical product (MPP) of labor
The change in output resulting from the addition of one more worker. The MPP of the worker equals the change in total output accounted for by hiring the worker, holding all other factors of production constant.

FIGURE 28-1

Marginal Revenue Product

In panel (a), column 4 shows marginal revenue product (MRP), which is the additional revenue the firm receives for the sale of that additional output. Marginal revenue product is simply the revenue the additional worker brings in—the combination of that worker's contribution to production and the revenue that that production will bring to the firm.

For this perfectly competitive firm, marginal revenue is equal to the price of the product, which we will assume in this example to be $10 per unit. At a weekly wage of $830, the profit-maximizing employer will pay for only 12 workers because then the marginal revenue product is just equal to the wage rate or weekly salary.

Panel (a)

(1) Labor Input (workers per week)	(2) Total Physical Product (TPP) (magneto optical disks per week)	(3) Marginal Physical Product (MPP) (magneto optical disks per week)	(4) Marginal Revenue (MR = P = $10) x MPP = Marginal Revenue Product (MRP) ($ per additional worker)	(5) Wage Rate ($ per week) = Marginal Factor Cost (MFC) = Change in Total Costs ÷ Change in Labor
6	882			
		118	$1,180	$830
7	1,000			
		111	1,110	830
8	1,111			
		104	1,040	830
9	1,215			
		97	970	830
10	1,312			
		90	900	830
11	1,402			
		83	830	830
12	1,485			
		76	760	830
13	1,561			

In panel (b), we find the number of workers the firm will want to hire by observing the wage rate that is established by the forces of supply and demand in the entire labor market. We show that this employer is hiring labor in a perfectly competitive labor market and therefore faces a perfectly elastic supply curve represented by *s* at a constant marginal factor cost (MFC) of $830 per week. As in other situations, we have a supply and demand model. In this firm-level example, the demand curve is represented by MRP, and the supply curve is *s*. Profit maximization occurs at their intersection, which is the point at which MRP = MFC.

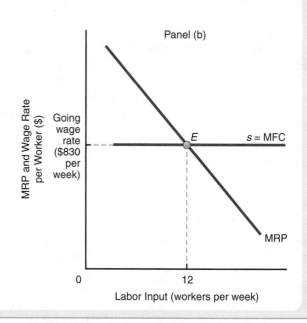

capital stock (the production equipment). Therefore, as we add more workers, each one has a smaller and smaller fraction of the available capital stock with which to work. If one worker uses one machine, adding another worker usually won't double the output because the machine can run only so fast and for so many hours per day. In other words, MPP declines because of the law of diminishing marginal product (see Chapter 22).

Marginal Revenue Product

We now need to translate into a dollar value the physical product that results from hiring an additional worker. This is done by multiplying the marginal physical product by the marginal revenue of the firm. Because this firm sells MO disks in a perfectly competitive market, marginal revenue is equal to the price of the product. If employing seven workers rather than six yields an MPP of 118 and the marginal revenue is assumed to be $10 per MO disk, the **marginal revenue product (MRP)** is $1,180 (118 × $10). The MRP is shown in column 4 of panel (a) of Figure 28-1 on the facing page. *The marginal revenue product represents the incremental worker's contribution to the firm's total revenues.*

When a firm operates in a perfectly competitive product market, the marginal physical product times the product price is also referred to as the *value of marginal product (VMP)*. Because price and marginal revenue are the same for a perfectly competitive firm, the VMP is also the MRP for such a firm.

In column 5 of panel (a) of Figure 28-1, we show the wage rate, or *marginal factor cost*, of each worker. The marginal cost of workers is the extra cost incurred in employing an additional unit of that factor of production. We call that cost the **marginal factor cost (MFC)**. Otherwise stated,

$$\text{Marginal factor cost} = \frac{\text{change in total cost}}{\text{change in amount of resource used}}$$

Because each worker is paid the same competitively determined wage of $830 per week, the MFC is the same for all workers. And because the firm is buying labor in a perfectly competitive labor market, the wage rate of $830 per week really represents the supply curve of labor to the firm. That supply curve is perfectly elastic because the firm can purchase all labor at the same wage rate, considering that it is a minuscule part of the entire labor-purchasing market. (Recall the definition of perfect competition.) We show this perfectly elastic supply curve as *s* in panel (b) of Figure 28-1.

GENERAL RULE FOR HIRING Nearly every optimizing rule in economics involves comparing marginal benefits with marginal cost. Because the benefit from added workers is extra output and consequently more revenues, the general rule for the hiring decision of a firm is this:

> *The firm hires workers up to the point at which the additional cost associated with hiring the last worker is equal to the additional revenue generated by hiring that worker.*

In a perfectly competitive market, this is the point at which the wage rate just equals the marginal revenue product. If the firm were to hire more workers, the additional wages would not be covered by additional increases in total revenue. If the firm were to hire fewer workers, it would be forfeiting the contributions that those workers otherwise could make to total profits.

Therefore, referring to columns 4 and 5 in panel (a) of Figure 28-1 on the facing page, we see that this firm would certainly employ at least seven workers because the MRP is $1,180 while the MFC is only $830. The firm would continue to add workers up to the point at which MFC = MRP because as workers are added, those additional workers contribute more to revenue than to cost.

THE MRP CURVE: DEMAND FOR LABOR We can also use panel (b) of Figure 28-1 to find how many workers our firm should hire. First, we draw a line at the going wage rate, which is determined by demand and supply in the labor market. The line is labeled *s* to indicate that it is the supply curve of labor for the *individual* firm purchasing labor in a perfectly competitive labor market. That firm can purchase all the labor it wants of equal quality at $830 per worker. This perfectly elastic supply curve, *s*, intersects the marginal revenue product curve at 12 workers per week. At the intersection, *E*, in

Marginal revenue product (MRP)
The marginal physical product (MPP) times marginal revenue (MR). The MRP gives the additional revenue obtained from a one-unit change in labor input.

Marginal factor cost (MFC)
The cost of using an additional unit of an input. For example, if a firm can hire all the workers it wants at the going wage rate, the marginal factor cost of labor is that wage rate.

panel (b) in Figure 28-1 on page 620, the wage rate is equal to the marginal revenue product. The firm maximizes profits where its demand curve for labor, which turns out to be its MRP curve, intersects the firm's supply curve for labor, shown as *s*. The firm in our example would not hire 13 workers, because using 13 rather than 12 would add only $760 to revenue but $830 to cost. If the price of labor should fall to, say, $760 per worker per week, the firm would hire an additional worker. Thus, the quantity of labor demanded increases as the wage decreases.

Derived Demand for Labor

We have identified an individual firm's demand for labor curve, which shows the quantity of labor that the firm will wish to hire at each wage rate, as its MRP curve. Under conditions of perfect competition in both product and labor markets, MRP is determined by multiplying MPP times the product's price. This suggests that the demand for labor is a **derived demand.** Factors of production are rented or purchased not because they give any intrinsic satisfaction to the firms' owners but because they can be used to manufacture output that is expected to be sold at a profit.

We know that an increase in the market demand for a given product raises the product's price (all other things held constant), which in turn increases the marginal revenue product, or demand for the resource. Figure 28-2 below illustrates the effective role played by changes in product demand in a perfectly competitive product market. The MRP curve shifts whenever there is a change in the price of the final product that the workers are producing.

Suppose, for example, that the market price of MO disks declines. In that case, the MRP curve will shift to the left from MRP_0 to MRP_1. We know that MRP $\equiv$ MPP $\times$ MR. If marginal revenue (here the output price) falls, so does the demand for labor. At the initial equilibrium, therefore, the price of labor (here the MFC) becomes greater than MRP. At the same going wage rate, the firm will hire fewer workers. This is because at various levels of labor use, the marginal revenue product of labor is now lower. Thus, the firm would reduce the number of workers hired. Conversely, if marginal revenue (the output price) rises, the demand for labor will also rise, and the firm will want to hire more workers at each and every possible wage rate.

Derived demand
Input factor demand derived from demand for the final product being produced.

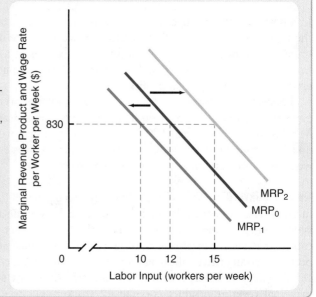

FIGURE 28-2

Demand for Labor, a Derived Demand

The demand for labor is derived from the demand for the final product being produced. Therefore, the marginal revenue product curve will shift whenever the price of the product changes. If we start with the marginal revenue product curve MRP_0 at the going wage rate of $830 per week, 12 workers will be hired. If the price of magneto optical disks goes down, the marginal revenue product curve will shift to MRP_1, and the number of workers hired will fall, in this case to 10. If the price of MO disks goes up, the marginal revenue product curve will shift to MRP_2, and the number of workers hired will increase, in this case to 15.

We just pointed out that MRP ≡ MPP × MR. Clearly, then, a change in marginal productivity, or in the marginal physical product of labor, will shift the MRP curve. If the marginal productivity of labor decreases, the MRP curve, or demand curve, for labor will shift inward to the left. Again, this is because at every quantity of labor used, the MRP will be lower. A lower amount of labor will be demanded at every possible wage rate.

Why has book publishers' demand for the labor of authors declined in recent years?

EXAMPLE

E-Books' Popularity Is Reducing the Demand for Authors' Labor

Publishers are finding that e-book sales are booming, as consumers substitute away from purchases of physical books to buying books in electronic formats viewable on digital devices. For authors, this is bad news. The prices that publishers receive for selling e-books are considerably lower than the prices of physical books. Hence, publishers' marginal-revenue-product-of-labor curves for authors have shifted leftward and downward. The consequence has been a reduction in the market demand for authors' labor. Thus, at any given wage rate, publishers desire to buy less labor from authors. Equivalently, at any given amount of labor demanded, publishers offer lower wages.

FOR CRITICAL THINKING

What do you suppose has happened to publishers' demand for the labor of editors as a result of consumers' substitution of e-books for physical books?

QUICK QUIZ   See page 641 for the answers. Review concepts from this section in MyEconLab.

The change in total _____ due to a one-unit change in one variable _____, holding all other _____ constant, is called the **marginal physical product (MPP)**. When we multiply marginal physical product times _____ _____, we obtain the **marginal revenue product (MRP)**.

A firm will hire workers up to the point at which the additional cost of hiring one more worker is equal to the additional revenue generated. For the individual firm, therefore, its MRP of labor curve is also its _____ _____ labor curve.

The demand for labor is a _____ demand, _____ from the demand for final output. Therefore, a change in the price of the final output will cause a _____ in the MRP curve (which is also the firm's demand for labor curve).

The Market Demand for Labor

The downward-sloping portion of each individual firm's marginal revenue product curve is also its demand curve for the one variable factor of production—in our example, labor. When we go to the entire market for a particular type of labor in a particular industry, we will also find that the quantity of labor demanded will vary inversely as the wage rate changes.

Constructing the Market Labor Demand Curve

Given that the market demand curve for labor is made up of the individual firms' downward-sloping demand curves for labor, we can safely infer that the market demand curve for labor will look like *D* in panel (b) of Figure 28-3 on the following page: It will slope downward. That market demand curve for labor in the magneto optical disk industry shows the quantities of labor demanded by all of the firms in the industry at various wage rates.

Nevertheless, the market demand curve for labor is *not* a simple horizontal summation of the labor demand curves of all individual firms. Remember that the demand for labor is a derived demand. Even if we hold labor productivity constant, the demand for labor still depends on both the wage rate and the price of the final output.

FIGURE 28-3

Derivation of the Market Demand Curve for Labor

The market demand curve for labor is not simply the horizontal summation of each individual firm's demand curve for labor. If wage rates fall from $20 to $10, all 200 firms will increase employment and therefore output, causing the price of the product to fall. This causes the marginal

revenue product curve of each firm to shift inward, from d_0 to d_1 in panel (a). The resulting market demand curve, D, in panel (b) is therefore less elastic around prices from $10 to $20 than it would be if the output price remained constant.

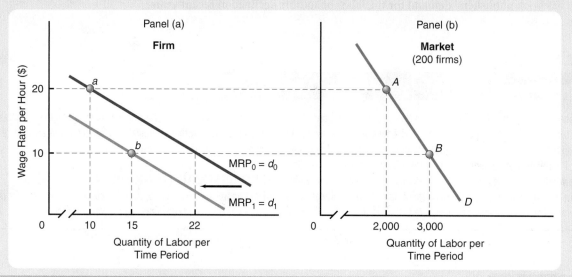

For instance, suppose that we start at a wage rate of $20 per hour and employment level 10 in panel (a) of Figure 28-3 above. If we sum all such employment levels—point *a* in panel (a)—across 200 firms, we get a market quantity demanded of 2,000, or point *A* in panel (b), at the wage rate of $20. A decrease in the wage rate to $10 per hour would induce individual firms' employment levels to increase toward a quantity demanded of 22 *if the product price did not change.*

As all 200 firms simultaneously increase employment, total industry output also increases at the present price. Indeed, this would occur at *any* price, meaning that the industry product supply curve will shift rightward, and the market clearing price of the product must fall. The fall in the output price in turn causes a downward shift of each firm's MRP curve (d_0) to MRP_1 (d_1) in panel (a). Thus, each firm's employment of labor increases to 15 rather than to 22 at the wage rate of $10 per hour. A summation of all such 200 employment levels gives us 3,000—point *B*—in panel (b).

Determinants of Demand Elasticity for Inputs

Just as we were able to discuss the price elasticity of demand for different commodities in Chapter 19, we can discuss the price elasticity of demand for inputs. The price elasticity of demand for labor is defined in a manner similar to the price elasticity of demand for goods: the percentage change in the quantity of labor demanded divided by the percentage change in the price of labor. When the *numerical* (or absolute) value of this ratio is less than 1, demand is inelastic. When it is 1, demand is unit-elastic. When it is greater than 1, demand is elastic.

There are four principal determinants of the price elasticity of demand for an input. The price elasticity of demand for a variable input will be greater:

1. The greater the price elasticity of demand for the final product

2. The easier it is to employ substitute inputs in production

3. The larger the proportion of total costs accounted for by the particular variable input

4. The longer the time period available for adjustment

FINAL PRODUCT PRICE ELASTICITY An individual radish farmer faces an extremely elastic demand for radishes, given the existence of many competing radish growers. If the farmer's laborers tried to obtain a significant wage increase, the farmer couldn't pass on the resultant higher costs to radish buyers. So any wage increase would lead to a large reduction in the quantity of labor demanded by the individual radish farmer.

EASE OF SUBSTITUTION Clearly, the easier it is for producers to switch to using another factor of production, the more responsive those producers will be to an increase in an input's price. If plastic can easily substitute for chrome plating in the production of, say, car bumpers, then a rise in the price of chrome plating will cause automakers to greatly reduce the quantity of chrome plating they demand.

PORTION OF TOTAL COST When a particular input's costs account for a very large share of total costs, any increase in that input's price will affect total costs relatively more. If labor costs are 80 percent of total costs, companies will cut back on employment more aggressively than if labor costs are only 8 percent of total costs, for any given wage increase.

ADJUSTMENT PERIOD Finally, over longer periods, firms have more time to figure out ways to economize on the use of inputs whose prices have gone up. Furthermore, over time, technological change will allow for easier substitution in favor of relatively cheaper inputs and against inputs whose prices went up. At first, a pay raise obtained by a strong telephone industry union may not result in many layoffs, but over time, the telephone companies will use new technology to replace many of the now more expensive workers.

QUICK QUIZ See page 641 for the answers. Review concepts from this section in MyEconLab.

Because the demand for labor is a derived demand that depends on both the _____ rate and the _____ of final output, the market demand curve for labor is not a simple horizontal summation of the labor demand curves of all individual firms. The market demand curve for labor does slope _____, however.

Input price elasticity of demand depends on the final product's _____ of demand, the ease of substituting other _____, the relative importance of the input's cost in total _____, and the time available for _____.

Wage Determination in a Perfectly Competitive Labor Market

Having developed the demand curve for labor (and all other variable inputs) in a particular industry, let's turn to the labor supply curve. By adding supply to the analysis, we can determine the equilibrium wage rate that workers earn in an industry. We can think in terms of a supply curve for labor that slopes upward in a particular industry.

At higher wage rates, more workers will want to enter that particular industry. The individual firm, however, does not face the entire *market* supply curve. Rather, in a perfectly competitive case, the individual firm is such a small part of the market that it can hire all the workers that it wants at the going wage rate. We say, therefore, that the industry faces an upward-sloping supply curve but that the individual *firm* faces a perfectly elastic supply curve for labor.

Labor Market Equilibrium

The demand curve for labor in the MO disk industry is D in Figure 28-4 on the following page, and the supply curve of labor is S. The equilibrium wage rate of $830 a week is established at the intersection of the two curves. The quantity of workers both supplied and demanded at that rate is Q_1. If for some reason the wage rate fell to $800

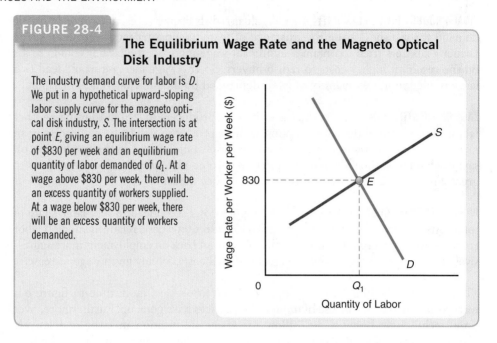

FIGURE 28-4

The Equilibrium Wage Rate and the Magneto Optical Disk Industry

The industry demand curve for labor is D. We put in a hypothetical upward-sloping labor supply curve for the magneto optical disk industry, S. The intersection is at point E, giving an equilibrium wage rate of $830 per week and an equilibrium quantity of labor demanded of Q_1. At a wage above $830 per week, there will be an excess quantity of workers supplied. At a wage below $830 per week, there will be an excess quantity of workers demanded.

a week, in our hypothetical example, there would be an excess number of workers demanded at that wage rate. Conversely, if the wage rate rose to $900 a week, there would be an excess quantity of workers supplied at that wage rate. In either case, competition would quickly force the wage back to the equilibrium level.

We have just found the equilibrium wage rate for the entire MO disk industry. The individual firm must take that equilibrium wage rate as given in the perfectly competitive model used here because the individual firm is a very small part of the total demand for labor. Thus, each firm purchasing labor in a perfectly competitive market can purchase all of the input it wants at the going market price.

Shifts in the Market Demand for and the Supply of Labor

Just as we discussed shifts in the supply curve and the demand curve for various products in Chapter 3, we can discuss the effects of shifts in supply and demand in labor markets.

REASONS FOR LABOR DEMAND CURVE SHIFTS Many factors can cause the demand curve for labor to shift. We have already discussed a number of them. Clearly, because the demand for labor or any other variable input is a derived demand, the labor demand curve will shift if there is a shift in the demand for the final product. There are two other important determinants of the position of the demand curve for labor: changes in labor's productivity and changes in the price of related factors of production (substitute inputs and complementary inputs).

1. *Changes in the demand for the final product.* The demand for labor or any other variable input is derived from the demand for the final product. The marginal revenue product is equal to marginal physical product times marginal revenue. Therefore, any change in the demand for the final product will change its price and hence the MRP of the input. The rule of thumb is as follows:

   A change in the demand for the final product that labor (or any other variable input) is producing will shift the market demand curve for labor in the same direction.

2. *Changes in labor productivity.* The second part of the MRP equation is MPP, which relates to labor productivity. We can surmise, then, that, other things being equal:

A change in labor productivity will shift the market labor demand curve in the same direction.

Labor productivity can increase because labor has more capital or land to work with, because of technological improvements, or because labor's quality has improved. Such considerations explain why the real standard of living of workers in the United States is higher than in most other countries. U.S. workers generally work with a larger capital stock, have more natural resources, are in better physical condition, and are better trained than workers in many countries. Hence the demand for labor in the United States is, other things held constant, greater.

3. *Change in the price of related factors.* Labor is not the only resource that firms use. Some resources are substitutes and some are complements in the production process. If we hold output constant, we have the following general rule:

A change in the price of a substitute input will cause the demand for labor (or any other input) to change in the same direction.

Thus, if the price of an input for which labor can substitute as a factor of production decreases, the demand for labor falls. For instance, if the price of mechanized ditch-digging equipment decreases, the demand for workers who, in contrast, can use only shovels to dig ditches decreases.

Suppose that a particular type of capital equipment and labor are complementary. In general, we predict the following:

A change in the price of a complementary input will cause the demand for labor to change in the opposite direction.

If the price of machines goes up but they must be used with labor, fewer machines will be purchased and therefore fewer workers will be used.

DETERMINANTS OF THE SUPPLY OF LABOR Labor supply curves may shift in a particular industry for a number of reasons. For example, if wage rates for factory workers in the smartphone industry remain constant while wages for factory workers in the computer industry go up dramatically, the supply curve of factory workers in the smartphone industry will shift inward to the left as these workers move to the computer industry.

Changes in working conditions in an industry can also affect its labor supply curve. If employers in the smartphone industry discover a new production technique that makes working conditions much more pleasant, the supply curve of labor to the digital camera industry will shift outward to the right.

Job flexibility also determines the position of the labor supply curve. For example, when an industry allows workers more flexibility, such as the ability to work at home via computer, the workers are likely to provide more hours of labor. That is to say, their supply curve will shift outward to the right. Some industries in which firms offer *job sharing*, particularly to people raising families, have found that the supply curve of labor has shifted outward to the right.

How have recent changes in both the demand for and supply of the labor of attorneys specializing in contract law affected the equilibrium wages earned by these lawyers?

EXAMPLE

Why Contract Attorneys' Wages Have Plummeted

As in previous years, people who become attorneys often spend in excess of $100,000 on law school tuition and devote many hours to studying for grueling bar exams. In contrast to years past, however, many who become contract attorneys—lawyers who specialize in analyzing disputed contracts—are earning much lower wages.

(continued)

One reason for the drop in the equilibrium wage rate earned by contract attorneys is that the derived market demand for their skills has dropped. Law firms are earning lower prices for handling contract litigation, so the value of the marginal product of contract attorneys has fallen. Another reason is an increase in the supply of lawyers who specialize in analyzing contracts. The resulting drop in the average wage rate earned by new contract attorneys has been steep—from nearly $30 per hour to less than $20 per hour.

FOR CRITICAL THINKING

How might the decline in contract attorney's current wage rate relative to wages in other occupations affect the future supply of labor of contract attorneys? Explain.

QUICK QUIZ   See page 641 for the answers. Review concepts from this section in MyEconLab.

The individual perfectly competitive firm faces a perfectly _____ labor supply curve—it can hire all the labor it wants at the going market wage rate. The industry supply curve of labor slopes _____.

By plotting an industrywide supply curve for labor and an industrywide demand curve for labor on the same

graph, we obtain the _____ wage rate in the industry.

The labor demand curve can shift because the _____ for the final product shifts, labor _____ changes, or the price of a related (_____ or _____) factor of production changes.

Labor Outsourcing, Wages, and Employment

In addition to making it easier for people to work at home, computer technology has made it possible for them to provide labor services to companies located in another country. Some companies based in Canada regularly transmit financial records—often via the Internet—to U.S. accountants so that they can process payrolls and compile income statements. Meanwhile, some U.S. manufacturers of personal computers and peripheral devices arrange for customers' calls for assistance to be directed to call centers in India, where English-speaking technical-support specialists help the customers with their problems.

Outsourcing
A firm's employment of labor outside the country in which the firm is located.

A firm that employs labor located outside the country in which it is based engages in labor **outsourcing.** Canadian companies that hire U.S. accountants outsource accounting services to the United States. U.S. computer manufacturers that employ Indian call-center staff outsource technical-support services to India. How does outsourcing affect employment and wages in the United States? Who loses and who gains from outsourcing? Let's consider each of these questions in turn.

Wage and Employment Effects of Outsourcing

Equilibrium wages and levels of employment in U.S. labor markets are determined by the demands for and supplies of labor in those markets. As you have learned, one of the determinants of the market demand for labor is the price of a substitute input. Availability of a lower-priced substitute, you also learned, causes the demand for labor to fall. Thus, the *immediate* economic effects of labor outsourcing are straightforward.

When a home industry's firms can obtain *foreign* labor services that are a close substitute for *home* labor services, the demand for labor services provided by home workers will decrease. What this economic reasoning ultimately implies for U.S. labor markets, however, depends on whether we view the United States as the "home" country or the "foreign" country.

U.S. LABOR MARKET EFFECTS OF OUTSOURCING BY U.S. FIRMS   To begin, let's view the United States as the home country. Suppose that initially all U.S. firms employ only U.S. workers. Then developments in computer, communications, and transportation technologies enable an increasing number of U.S. firms to regard the labor of foreign workers as a close substitute for labor provided by U.S. workers. Take a look at Figure 28-5 on the facing page. Panel (a) depicts demand and supply curves in the U.S. market

FIGURE 28-5

Outsourcing of U.S. Computer Technical-Support Services

Initially, the market wage for U.S. workers providing technical support for customers of U.S. computer manufacturers is $19 per hour at point E_1 in panel (a), while the market wage for Indian workers who provide similar services is $8 per hour in panel (b). Then, improvements in communications technologies enable U.S. firms to substitute away from U.S. workers in favor of Indian workers. The market demand for U.S. labor decreases in panel (a), generating a new equilibrium at point E_2 at a lower U.S. market wage and employment level. The market demand for Indian labor increases in panel (b), bringing about higher wages and employment at point E_2.

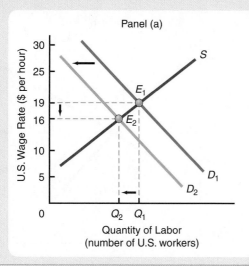
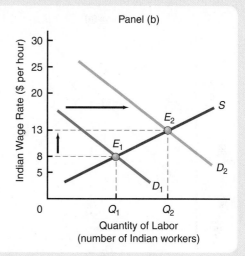

for workers who handle calls for technical support for U.S. manufacturers of personal computers. Suppose that before technological change makes foreign labor substitutable for U.S. labor, point E_1 is the initial equilibrium. At this point, the market wage rate in this U.S. labor market is $19 per hour.

Now suppose that improvements in communications technologies enable U.S. personal computer manufacturers to consider foreign labor as a substitute input for U.S. labor. Panel (b) displays demand and supply curves in a market for substitutable labor services in India. At the initial equilibrium point E_1, the wage rate denominated in U.S. dollars is $8 per hour. Firms in this U.S. industry will respond to the lower price of substitute labor in India by increasing their demand for labor services in that country and reducing their demand for U.S. labor. Thus, in panel (b), the market demand for the substitute labor services available in India rises. The market wage in India rises to $13 per hour, at point E_2, and Indian employment increases. In panel (a), the market demand for U.S. labor services decreases. At the new equilibrium point E_2, the U.S. market wage has fallen to $16 per hour, and equilibrium employment has decreased.

Consequently, when U.S. firms are the home firms engaging in labor outsourcing, the effects are lower wages and decreased employment in the relevant U.S. labor markets. In those nations where workers providing the outsourced labor reside, the effects are higher wages and increased employment.

U.S. LABOR MARKET EFFECTS OF OUTSOURCING BY FOREIGN FIRMS U.S. firms are not the only companies that engage in outsourcing. Consider the Canadian companies that hire U.S. accountants to calculate their payrolls and maintain their financial records. Figure 28-6 on the following page shows the effects in the Canadian and U.S. markets for labor services provided by accountants before and after *Canadian* outsourcing of accountants' labor. At point E_1 in panel (a), before any outsourcing takes place, the initial market wage for qualified accountants in Canada is $29 per hour. In panel (b), the market wage for similarly qualified U.S. accountants is $21 per hour.

FIGURE 28-6

Outsourcing of Accounting Services by Canadian Firms

Suppose that the market wage for accounting services in Canada is initially $29 per hour, at point E_1 in panel (a), but in the United States accountants earn just $21 per hour at point E_1 in panel (b). Then, Internet access enables Canadian firms to substitute labor services provided by U.S. accountants for the services of Canadian accountants. The market demand for the services of Canadian accountants decreases in panel (a), and at point E_2 fewer Canadian accountants are employed at a lower market wage. The market demand for U.S. accounting services increases in panel (b). This generates higher wages and employment for U.S. accountants at point E_2.

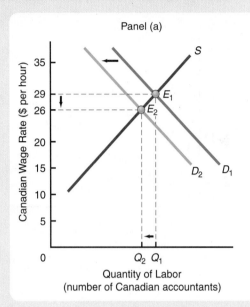

Panel (a)

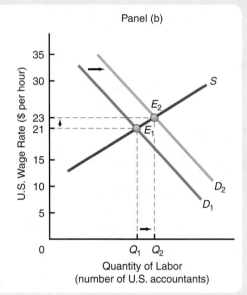

Panel (b)

After Internet access allows companies in Canada to transfer financial data electronically, the services of U.S. accountants become available as a less expensive substitute for those provided by Canadian accountants. When Canadian firms respond by seeking to outsource to U.S. accountants, the demand for U.S. accountants' labor services rises in panel (b). This causes the market wage earned by U.S. accountants to increase to $23 per hour. Canadian firms substitute away from the services of Canadian accountants, so in panel (a) the demand for the labor of accountants in Canada declines. Canadian accountants' wages decline to $26 per hour.

In contrast to the situation in which U.S. firms are the home firms engaging in labor outsourcing, when foreign firms outsource by hiring workers in the United States, wages and employment levels rise in the affected U.S. markets. In the nations where the firms engaging in outsourcing are located, the effects are lower wages and decreased employment.

Why are fewer nations' firms outsourcing labor to China?

INTERNATIONAL EXAMPLE

China's Declining Status as an Outsourcing Destination

For years, many firms based outside China, including companies in the United States and Europe, have engaged in international outsourcing to that nation. The incentive to outsource to China has diminished in recent years, however.

On the one hand, so many foreign firms have engaged in labor outsourcing in China that the market demand for labor in that nation has increased considerably. On the other hand, China's population is aging, and fewer young workers are entering the labor force to provide the necessary hours of labor for tasks desired by many foreign firms. Thus, the market supply of labor in China has decreased somewhat. Together, these changes in market demand for and supply of labor have raised the equilibrium wage rate earned by a typical Chinese worker. Chinese wages are now close to wages earned by workers in other outsourcing nations. This is why fewer foreign firms have been choosing China as an outsourcing destination in recent years.

FOR CRITICAL THINKING

How has recent wage stagnation in the United States likely affected the incentive for U.S. firms to engage in labor outsourcing in China?

Gauging the Net Effects of Outsourcing on the U.S. Economy

In the example depicted in Figure 28-5 on page 629, the market wage and employment level for U.S. technical-support workers declined as a result of outsourcing by U.S. firms. In contrast, in the example shown in Figure 28-6 on the facing page, U.S. accountants earned higher wages and experienced increased employment as a result of outsourcing by Canadian firms. Together, these examples illustrate a fundamental conclusion concerning the short-run effects of global labor outsourcing in U.S. labor markets:

To read a Heritage Foundation lecture about the net effects of outsourcing on U.S. jobs, use the link at www.econtoday.com/chap28.

> *Labor outsourcing by U.S. firms tends to reduce U.S. wages and employment. Whenever foreign firms engage in labor outsourcing in the United States, however, U.S. wages and employment tend to increase.*

Consequently, the immediate effects of increased worldwide labor outsourcing are lower wages and employment in some U.S. labor markets and higher wages and employment in others. In this narrow sense, some U.S. workers "lose" from outsourcing while others "gain," just as some Canadian workers "lose" while some Indian workers "gain."

SUMMING UP THE ECONOMIC IMPLICATIONS OF OUTSOURCING Even in the best of times, workers in labor markets experience short-run ups and downs in wages and jobs. During normal times in the United States, after all, about 4 million jobs typically come and go every month.

Certainly, various groups of U.S. workers earn lower pay or experience reduced employment opportunities, at least for a time, as a result of labor outsourcing. Nevertheless, outsourcing is a two-way street. Labor outsourcing does not just involve U.S. firms purchasing the labor services of residents located abroad. This phenomenon also entails the purchase of labor services from U.S. workers who provide outsourcing services to companies located in other nations.

Indeed, outsourcing really amounts to another way for residents of different nations to conduct trade with one another. As you learned in Chapter 2, trade allows nations' residents to specialize according to their *comparative advantages* and thereby obtain gains from exchanging items across country boundaries. To be sure, not all workers gain equally from the trade of outsourced labor services, and some people temporarily lose, in the form of either lower wages or reduced employment opportunities. Nevertheless, specialization and trade of labor services through outsourcing generate overall gains from trade for participating nations, such as India, Canada, and the United States.

YOU ARE THERE

To learn how some unemployed U.S. workers are now outsourcing their efforts to find new employment, take a look at **Combating U.S. Unemployment via Job-Search Outsourcing**, on page 636.

WHAT IF... the government required U.S. firms to hire only workers who reside in the United States?

Prohibiting the hiring of foreign labor would put an end to international labor outsourcing. Thus, either U.S. firms would pay higher wages for U.S. workers they had not hired previously, which would push up their costs and generate lower production, or U.S. firms would not replace the outsourced labor and would produce less.

In any event, firms would reduce the amounts of goods and services offered for sale in the United States at any given prices, and the resulting decreases in supply would lead to higher equilibrium product prices. Thus, the effect of a ban on international labor outsourcing would generate higher prices for U.S. consumers.

QUICK QUIZ See page 641 for the answers. Review concepts from this section in MyEconLab.

Advances in telecommunications and computer networking are making foreign labor more easily _____ for home labor. Home firms' _____ of foreign labor for home labor is known as labor **outsourcing.**

In the short run, outsourcing by U.S. firms _____ the demand for labor, market wages, and equilibrium employment in U.S. labor markets. Outsourcing by

foreign firms that hire U.S. labor _____ the demand for labor, market wages, and equilibrium employment in U.S. labor markets. The net short-run effects on U.S. wages and employment are mixed.

In the long run, outsourcing enables U.S. firms to operate more efficiently and this activity generates overall _____ _____ _____ for U.S. residents.

Monopoly in the Product Market

So far we've considered only perfectly competitive markets, both in selling the final product and in buying factors of production. We will continue our assumption that the firm purchases its factors of production in a perfectly competitive factor market. Now, however, we will assume that the firm sells its product in an *imperfectly* competitive output market. In other words, we are considering the output market structures of monopoly, oligopoly, and monopolistic competition. In all such cases, the firm, be it a monopolist, an oligopolist, or a monopolistic competitor, faces a downward-sloping demand curve for its product.

Throughout the rest of this chapter, we will simply refer to a monopoly situation for ease of analysis. The analysis holds for all industry structures that are less than perfectly competitive. In any event, the fact that our firm now faces a downward-sloping demand curve for its product means that if it wants to sell more of its product (at a uniform price), it has to lower the price, *not just on the last unit, but on all preceding units.* The *marginal revenue* received from selling an additional unit is continuously falling (and is less than price) as the firm attempts to sell more and more. This relationship between marginal revenue and output is certainly different from our earlier discussions in this chapter in which the firm could sell all it wanted at a constant price. Why? Because the firm we discussed until now was a perfect competitor.

Constructing the Monopolist's Input Demand Curve

In reconstructing our demand schedule for an input, we must account for the facts that (1) the marginal *physical* product falls because of the law of diminishing marginal product as more workers are added and (2) the price (and marginal revenue) received for the product sold also falls as more is produced and sold. That is, for the monopolist, we have to account for both the diminishing marginal physical product and the diminishing marginal revenue. Marginal revenue is always less than price for the monopolist. The marginal revenue curve always lies below the downward-sloping product demand curve.

MARGINAL REVENUE PRODUCT FOR A PERFECTLY COMPETITIVE FIRM Marginal revenue for the perfect competitor is equal to the price of the product because all units can be sold at the going market price. In our example involving the production of magneto optical disks on page 620, we assumed that the perfect competitor could sell all it wanted at $10 per unit. A one-unit change in sales always led to a $10 change in total revenues. Hence, marginal revenue was always equal to $10 for that perfect competitor. Multiplying this unchanging marginal revenue by the marginal physical product of labor then yielded the perfectly competitive firm's marginal revenue product.

MARGINAL REVENUE PRODUCT FOR A MONOPOLY FIRM The monopolist, however, cannot simply calculate marginal revenue by looking at the price of the product. To sell the additional output from an additional unit of input, the monopolist has to cut prices on all previous units of output. As output is increasing, then, marginal revenue is falling.

The underlying concept is, of course, the same for both the perfect competitor and the monopolist. We are asking exactly the same question in both cases: When an additional worker is hired, what is the benefit? In either case, the benefit is obviously the change in total revenues due to the one-unit change in the variable input, labor. In our discussion of the perfect competitor, we were able simply to multiply the marginal physical product by the *constant* per-unit price of the product because the price of the product never changed (for the perfect competitor, $P \equiv \text{MR}$).

LABOR DEMAND FOR A MONOPOLIST A single monopolist ends up hiring fewer workers than would all of the perfectly competitive firms added together. To see this, we must consider the marginal revenue product for the monopolist, which varies with each one-unit change in the monopolist's labor input. This is what we do in panel (a) of Figure 28-7 on the facing page, where column 5, "Marginal Revenue Product," gives the monopolist a quantitative notion of how additional workers and additional production generate additional revenues. The marginal revenue product curve for this monopolist has been plotted in panel (b) of the figure. To emphasize the lower elasticity of the monopolist's MRP curve (MRP_m) around the wage rate $830, the labor demand curve for a perfectly competitive industry (labeled D) has been plotted on the same graph in Figure 28-7 below.

Recall that this curve is not simply the sum of the marginal revenue product curves of all perfectly competitive firms, because when competitive firms together increase employment, their output expands and the product price declines. Nevertheless, at any given wage rate, the quantity of labor demanded by the monopoly is still less than the quantity of labor demanded by a perfectly competitive industry.

Why does MRP_m represent the monopolist's input demand curve? As always, our profit-maximizing monopolist will continue to hire labor as long as additional profits result. Profits are made as long as the additional cost of more workers is outweighed by the additional revenues made from selling the output of those workers. When the wage rate equals these additional revenues, the monopolist stops hiring. That is, the

---

FIGURE 28-7

A Monopolist's Marginal Revenue Product

Panel (a)

(1) Labor Input (workers per week)	(2) Marginal Physical Product (MPP) (magneto optical disks per week)	(3) Price of Product (P)	(4) Marginal Revenue (MR)	(5) Marginal Revenue Product (MRP_m) = (2) x (4)	(6) Wage Rate
8	111	$11.60	$9.40	$1,043.40	$830.00
9	104	11.40	9.00	936.00	830.00
10	97	11.20	8.60	834.20	830.00
11	90	11.00	8.20	738.00	830.00
12	83	10.80	7.80	647.40	830.00
13	76	10.60	7.40	562.40	830.00

The monopolist hires just enough workers to make marginal revenue product equal to the going wage rate. If the going wage rate is $830 per week, as shown by the labor supply curve, s, in panel (b), the monopolist would want to hire approximately 10 workers per week. That is the profit-maximizing amount of labor. The labor demand curve for a perfectly competitive industry from Figure 28-4 on page 626 is also plotted (D). The monopolist's MRP curve will always be less elastic around the going wage rate than it would be if marginal revenue were constant.

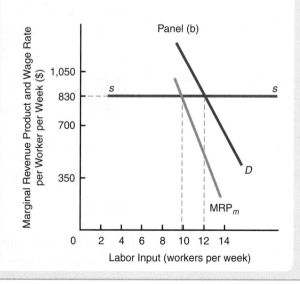

firm stops hiring when the wage rate is equal to the marginal revenue product because additional workers would add more to cost than to revenue.

Why the Monopolist Hires Fewer Workers

Because we have used the same numbers as in Figure 28-1 on page 620, we can see that the monopolist hires fewer workers per week than firms in a perfect competitive market would. That is to say, if we could magically change the magneto optical disk industry in our example from one in which there is perfect competition in the output market to one in which there is monopoly in the output market, the amount of employment would fall. Why? Because the monopolist must take account of the declining product price that must be charged in order to sell a larger number of MO disks. Remember that every firm hires up to the point at which marginal benefit equals marginal cost. The marginal benefit to the monopolist of hiring an additional worker is not simply the additional output times the price of the product. Rather, the monopolist faces a reduction in the price charged on *all* units sold in order to be able to sell more.

So the monopolist ends up hiring fewer workers than all of the perfect competitors taken together, assuming that all else remains the same for the two hypothetical examples. But this should not come as a surprise. In considering product markets, by implication we saw that a monopolized magneto optical disk industry would produce less output than a competitive one. Therefore, the monopolized industry would hire fewer workers.

The Utilization of Other Factors of Production

The analysis in this chapter has been given in terms of the demand for the variable input labor. The same analysis holds for any other variable factor input. We could have talked about the demand for fertilizer or the demand for the services of tractors by a farmer instead of the demand for labor and reached the same conclusions. The entrepreneur will hire or buy any variable input up to the point at which its price equals the marginal revenue product.

A further question remains: How much of each variable factor should the firm utilize when all the variable factors are combined to produce the product? We can answer this question by looking at either the cost-minimizing side of the question or the profit-maximizing side.

Cost Minimization and Factor Utilization

From the cost minimization point of view, how can the firm minimize its total costs for a given output? Assume that you are an entrepreneur attempting to minimize costs. Consider a hypothetical situation in which if you spend $1 more on labor, you would get 20 more units of output, but if you spend $1 more on machines, you would get only 10 more units of output. What would you want to do in such a situation? You would wish to hire more workers or sell off some of your machines, for you are not getting as much output per *last* dollar spent on machines as you are per *last* dollar spent on labor. You would want to employ factors of production so that the marginal products per last dollar spent on each are equal. Thus, the least-cost, or cost minimization, rule will be as follows:

> *To minimize total costs for a particular rate of production, the firm will hire factors of production up to the point at which the marginal physical product per last dollar spent on each factor of production is equalized.*

That is,

$$\frac{\text{MPP of labor}}{\text{price of labor (wage rate)}} = \frac{\text{MPP of capital}}{\text{price of capital (cost per unit of service)}} = \frac{\text{MPP of land}}{\text{price of land (rental rate per unit)}}$$

All we are saying here is that the cost-minimizing firm will always utilize *all* resources in such combinations that cost will be minimized for any given output rate. This is commonly called the *least-cost combination of resources.*

How has a ruling by the Internal Revenue Service contributed to lower equilibrium employment in the United States?

POLICY EXAMPLE

A "Reclassification Regulation" Cuts Overall Labor Employment

Many firms employ independent contractors to perform labor tasks alongside regular employees. Recently, the Internal Revenue Service ruled that a number of U.S. companies had improperly classified some workers as independent contractors and hence failed to withhold Social Security and Medicare taxes.

This IRS ruling changed the cost minimization calculation for thousands of affected companies. When confronted with paying a higher wage rate to people who previously had been classified as independent contractors, these firms experienced an increase in the denominator of the ratio of these workers' MPP to their wage rate. This ratio thereby declined in relation

to the ratio for regular employees. Although a portion of affected firms responded by converting some of their former independent contractors into regular employees, a number of firms ended their employment of the labor services of independent contractors. The IRS ruling therefore contributed to a net decline in employment.

FOR CRITICAL THINKING
Why were firms most likely to reclassify as regular employees the prior independent contractors who exhibited the highest marginal physical product of labor?

Profit Maximization Revisited

If a firm wants to maximize profits, how much of each factor should be hired (or bought)? As you have learned, the firm will never utilize a factor of production unless the marginal benefit from hiring that factor is at least equal to the marginal cost. What is the marginal benefit? As we have pointed out several times, the marginal benefit is the change in total revenues due to a one-unit change in utilization of the variable input. What is the marginal cost? In the case of a firm buying in a perfectly competitive market, it is the price of the variable factor—the wage rate if we are referring to labor.

The profit-maximizing combination of resources for the firm will be where, in a perfectly competitive market structure,

MRP of labor = price of labor (wage rate)

MRP of capital = price of capital (cost per unit of service)

MRP of land = price of land (rental rate per unit)

To attain maximum profits, the marginal revenue product of each of a firm's resources must be exactly equal to its price. If the MRP of labor is $20 and its price is only $15, the firm will expand its employment of labor.

There is an exact match between the profit-maximizing combination of resources and the least-cost combination of resources discussed above. In other words, either rule can be used to yield the same cost-minimizing rate of utilization of each variable resource.

QUICK QUIZ   See page 641 for the answers. Review concepts from this section in MyEconLab.

When a firm sells its output in a monopoly market, marginal revenue is _____ than price.

Just as the MRP is the perfectly competitive firm's input demand curve, the MRP is also the _____ input demand curve.

The profit-maximizing combination of factors will occur when each factor is used up to the point at which its MRP is equal to its unit _____.

To minimize total costs for a given output, the profit-maximizing firm will hire each factor of production up to the point at which the marginal _____ product per last dollar spent on each factor is equal to the marginal _____ product per last dollar spent on each of the other factors of production.

To maximize profits, the marginal _____ product of each resource must equal the resource's _____.

YOU ARE THERE

Combating U.S. Unemployment via Job-Search Outsourcing

Recently, U.S. resident Frankie Balint had been out of work for some time and was concerned about finding a job. Balint turned to an Indian outsourcing company to help him find a position in the United States.

At a price of $98, the online firm JobSerf.com collected information about Balint's qualifications. JobSerf.com's employees who performed these tasks are based in Visakhapatnam, India, but they scanned the Web for available U.S. positions for which Balint appeared to be qualified and submitted online job applications on his behalf. Ultimately, one of the applications that JobSerf.com submitted for Balint succeeded in helping him to obtain a position, thereby boosting equilibrium U.S. employment by one worker.

Critical Thinking Questions

1. How is employment at U.S. employment agencies affected by the existence of Indian-based job-search firms such as JobSerf.com?

2. If JobSerf.com were to hire some employees who live in the United States to find positions for other U.S. residents, would this be an example of labor outsourcing? Explain.

ISSUES & APPLICATIONS

Will You Be Replaced by an App?

CONCEPTS APPLIED

▶ Derived Demand

▶ Marginal Revenue Product

▶ Cost-Minimizing Factor Utilization

The derived demand for an input depends on the marginal revenue product of that input. This is true for any input, whether it is the labor provided by a human being or a robotic device guided by digital apps of varying degrees of sophistication.

App-Guided Devices as Replacements for Human Labor

Apps such as ForeFlight Mobile HD can perform airline navigation, and digital technologies can pilot planes on runways or through the skies and can drive automobiles along city streets. Advanced robotic systems can perform an increasing array of tasks, ranging from laying sealant on vehicle windshields in auto plants to performing surgeries in hospitals. Online apps can provide teaching instruction to any child or adult with a digital device capable of accessing the Internet.

Nevertheless, just because it is technologically feasible for app-guided digital technology to replace human labor in performing many tasks does not mean that significant substitutions of robotic inputs for human labor will necessarily take place. Decisions about how many units of human labor versus robotic inputs to employ are economic choices made with an aim to minimize costs.

Determining If Humans Are in the Cost-Minimizing Input Mix

Applying cost minimization to human and robotic inputs—digital devices guided by apps—indicates that the two factors will be employed up to the point at which the marginal physical product per last dollar spent on each input is equalized. That is, the cost minimization rule is

$$\frac{\text{MPP of human labor}}{\text{price of human labor}} = \frac{\text{MPP of robotic input}}{\text{price of robotic input}}$$

Today, most firms that employ robotic inputs also employ human beings to perform many tasks. Why don't these firms replace human beings almost entirely? The answer is implied by the cost minimization rule. Humans are part of these firms' mixes of inputs both because the MPP of human labor is sufficiently high in relation to the MPP of a robotic input and because the price of human labor is sufficiently low relative to the price of that robotic input.

This perspective suggests that as technical improvements raise the marginal physical product of many app-guided digital devices and reduce the prices of utilizing these devices, firms will substitute some robotic inputs for human labor. Nevertheless, it is unlikely that firms will substantially replace human labor with robotic inputs as long as humans remain *both* relatively productive *and* relatively inexpensive, compared with robotic inputs. Thus, the demand for human labor will never disappear.

For Critical Thinking

1. Under the cost minimization rule, when will a firm employ *only* human labor?

2. Why does the cost minimization rule suggest that it is unlikely a firm actually would replace human labor *entirely* with robotic inputs?

Web Resources

1. Find out about advances in robotic surgery at **www.econtoday.com/chap28**.

2. Learn how schools are applying teaching apps for "teacherless" educational instruction at **www.econtoday.com/chap28**.

MyEconLab

For more questions on this chapter's Issues & Applications, go to **MyEconLab**. In the Study Plan for this chapter, select Section N: News.

MyEconLab

Here is what you should know after reading this chapter. MyEconLab will help you identify what you know, and where to go when you need to practice.

— WHAT YOU SHOULD KNOW —		— WHERE TO GO TO PRACTICE —
Why a Firm's Marginal Revenue Product Curve Is Its Labor Demand Curve The marginal revenue product of labor equals marginal revenue times the marginal physical product of labor. Because of the law of diminishing marginal product, the marginal revenue product curve slopes downward. To maximize profits, a firm hires labor to the point at which the marginal factor cost of labor—the addition to total input costs resulting from employing an additional unit of labor—equals the marginal revenue product.	marginal physical product (MPP) of labor, 619 marginal revenue product (MRP), 621 marginal factor cost (MFC), 621 **Key Figure** Figure 28-1, 620	• MyEconLab Study Plan 28.1 • Animated Figure 28-1
The Demand for Labor as a Derived Demand For perfectly competitive firms, marginal revenue equals the market price of their output, so the marginal revenue product of labor equals the product price times the marginal physical product of labor. As product market conditions vary and cause the market price to change, marginal revenue product curves shift. Hence, the demand for labor is derived from the demand for final products.	derived demand, 622 **Key Figure** Figure 28-2, 622	• MyEconLab Study Plan 28.2 • Animated Figure 28-2

MyEconLab *continued*

WHAT YOU SHOULD KNOW		WHERE TO GO TO PRACTICE
Key Factors Affecting the Elasticity of Demand for Inputs The price elasticity of demand for an input equals the percentage change in the quantity of the input demanded divided by the percentage change in the input's price. An input's price elasticity of demand is relatively high when any one of the following is true: (1) the price elasticity of demand for the final product is relatively high, (2) it is relatively easy to substitute other inputs in production, (3) the proportion of total costs accounted for by the input is relatively large, or (4) the firm has a longer time period to adjust to the change in the input's price.	Key Figure Figure 28-3, 624	• MyEconLab Study Plan 28.2 • Animated Figure 28-3
How Equilibrium Wage Rates at Perfectly Competitive Firms Are Determined In a competitive labor market, at the equilibrium wage rate, the quantity of labor demanded by all firms is equal to the quantity of labor supplied by all workers. At this wage rate, each firm looks to its own labor demand curve to determine how much labor to employ.	Key Figure Figure 28-4, 626	• MyEconLab Study Plan 28.3 • Animated Figure 28-4
U.S. Wage and Employment Effects of Labor Outsourcing The immediate, short-run effects of labor outsourcing on wages and employment in U.S. labor markets are mixed. Outsourcing by U.S. firms reduces the demand for labor in affected U.S. labor markets and thereby pushes down wages and employment. Outsourcing by foreign firms that hire U.S. labor, however, raises the demand for labor in related U.S. labor markets, which boosts U.S. wages and employment.	outsourcing, 628 Key Figures Figure 28-5, 629 Figure 28-6, 630	• MyEconLab Study Plan 28.4 • Animated Figures 28-5, 28-6
Contrasting the Demand for Labor and Wage Determination under Monopoly with Outcomes under Perfect Competition If a product market monopolist competes for labor in a competitive labor market, it takes the market wage rate as given. Its labor demand curve, however, lies to the left of the labor demand curve that would have arisen in a competitive industry. Thus, at the competitively determined wage rate, a monopolized industry employs fewer workers than the industry otherwise would if it were perfectly competitive.	Key Figure Figure 28-7, 633	• MyEconLab Study Plans 28.5, 28.6 • Animated Figure 28-7

Log in to MyEconLab, take a chapter test, and get a personalized Study Plan that tells you which concepts you understand and which ones you need to review. From there, MyEconLab will give you further practice, tutorials, animations, videos, and guided solutions. For more information, visit www.myeconlab.com

PROBLEMS

All problems are assignable in MyEconLab. *Answers to the odd-numbered problems appear at the back of the book.*

28-1. The following table depicts the output of a firm that manufactures computer printers. The printers sell for $100 each.

Labor Input (workers per week)	Total Physical Output (printers per week)
10	200
11	218
12	234
13	248
14	260
15	270
16	278

Calculate the marginal physical product and marginal revenue product at each input level above 10 units. (See page 620.)

28-2. Refer back to your answers to Problem 28-1 in answering the following questions. (See pages 620–622.)

a. What is the maximum wage the firm will be willing to pay if it hires 15 workers?

b. The weekly wage paid by computer printer manufacturers in a perfectly competitive market is $1,200. How many workers will the profit-maximizing employer hire?

c. Suppose that there is an increase in the demand for printed digital photos. Explain the likely effects on marginal revenue product, marginal factor cost, and the number of workers hired by the firm.

28-3. Explain what happens to the elasticity of demand for labor in a given industry after each of the following events. (See pages 624–625.)

a. A new manufacturing technique makes capital easier to substitute for labor.

b. There is an increase in the number of substitutes for the final product that labor produces.

c. After a drop in the prices of capital inputs, labor accounts for a larger portion of a firm's factor costs.

28-4. Explain how the following events would affect the demand for labor. (See pages 621–622.)

a. A new education program administered by the company increases labor's marginal product.

b. The firm completes a new plant with a larger workspace and new machinery.

28-5. The following table depicts the product market and labor market a digital device manufacturer faces. (See page 620.)

Labor Input (workers per day)	Total Physical Product	Product Price ($)
10	100	50
11	109	49
12	116	48
13	121	47
14	124	46
15	125	45

a. Calculate the firm's marginal physical product, total revenue, and marginal revenue product at each input level above 10 units.

b. The firm competes in a perfectly competitive labor market, and the market wage it faces is $100 per worker per day. How many workers will the profit-maximizing employer hire?

28-6. Recently, there has been an increase in the market demand for products of firms in manufacturing industries. The production of many of these products requires the skills of welders. Because welding is a dirty and dangerous job compared with other occupations, in recent years fewer people have sought employment as welders. Draw a diagram of the market for the labor of welders. Use this diagram to explain the likely implications of these recent trends for the market clearing wage earned by welders and the equilibrium quantity of welding services hired. (See pages 626–627.)

28-7. Since the early 2000s, there has been a significant increase in the price of corn-based ethanol. (See pages 626–627.)

a. A key input in the production of corn-based ethanol is corn. Use an appropriate diagram to explain what has likely occurred in the market for corn.

b. In light of your answer to part (a), explain why many hog farmers, who in the past used corn as the main feed input in hog production, have switched to cookies, licorice, cheese curls, candy bars, and other human snack foods instead of corn as food for their hogs.

28-8. A firm hires labor in a perfectly competitive labor market. Its current profit-maximizing hourly output is 100 units, which the firm sells at a price of $5 per unit. The marginal physical product of the last unit of labor employed is 5 units per hour. The firm pays each worker an hourly wage of $15. (See pages 626 and 633.)

a. What marginal revenue does the firm earn from sale of the output produced by the last worker employed?

b. Does this firm sell its output in a perfectly competitive market?

28-9. Suppose that until recently, U.S. firms that produce digital apps had been utilizing only the labor of qualified U.S. workers at a wage rate of $35 per hour. Now, however, these firms have begun engaging in labor outsourcing to Russia, where qualified workers are available at a dollar wage rate of $15 per hour. Evaluate the effects of this new U.S. app-labor outsourcing initiative on U.S. and Russian employment levels and wages. (See pages 628–630.)

28-10. Recently, Swedish companies have outsourced manufacturing labor previously performed by Swedish workers at $20 per hour to U.S. workers who receive a wage rate of $10 per hour. Evaluate the effects of Swedish manufacturing-labor outsourcing on Swedish and U.S. employment levels and wages. (See pages 628–630.)

28-11. Explain why the short-term effects of outsourcing on U.S. wages and employment tend to be more ambiguous than the long-term effects. (See page 631.)

28-12. A profit-maximizing monopolist hires workers in a perfectly competitive labor market. Employing the last worker increased the firm's total weekly output from 110 units to 111 units and caused the firm's weekly revenues to rise from $25,000 to $25,750. What is the current prevailing weekly wage rate in the labor market? (See page 621.)

28-13. A monopoly firm hires workers in a perfectly competitive labor market in which the market wage rate is $20 per day. If the firm maximizes profit, and if the marginal revenue from the last unit of output produced by the last worker hired equals $10, what is the marginal physical product of that worker? (See page 633.)

28-14. The current market wage rate is $10, the rental rate of land is $1,000 per unit, and the rental rate of capital is $500. Production managers at a firm find that under their current allocation of factors of production, the marginal physical product of labor is 100, the marginal physical product of land is 10,000, and the marginal physical product of capital is 4,000. Is the firm minimizing costs? Why or why not? (See page 634.)

28-15. The current wage rate is $10, and the rental rate of capital is $500. A firm's marginal physical product of labor is 200, and its marginal physical product of capital is 20,000. Is the firm maximizing profits for the given cost outlay? Why or why not? (See page 635.)

ECONOMICS ON THE NET

Current Trends in U.S. Labor Markets The Federal Reserve's "Beige Book," which summarizes regional economic conditions around the United States, provides a wealth of information about the current status of U.S. labor markets. This Internet application helps you assess developments in employment and wages in the United States.

Title: The Beige Book—Summary

Navigation: Go to www.econtoday.com/chap28 to access the home page of the Federal Reserve's Board of Governors. Click on *A–Z Index*, and then click on *Beige Book*. Then select the report for the most recent period.

Application Read the section titled "Prices and Wages," and answer the following questions.

1. Has overall employment been rising or falling during the most recent year? Based on what you learned in this chapter, what factors might account for this pattern? Does the Beige Book summary bear out any of these explanations for changes in U.S. employment?

2. Have U.S. workers' wages been rising or falling during the most recent year?

For Group Study and Analysis The left-hand margin of the Beige Book site lists the reports of the 12 Federal Reserve districts. Divide the class into two groups, and have each group develop brief summaries of the main conclusions of one district's report concerning employment and wages within that district. Reconvene and compare the reports. Are there pronounced regional differences?

ANSWERS TO QUICK QUIZZES

p. 623: (i) output . . . input . . . inputs . . . marginal revenue; (ii) demand for; (iii) derived . . . derived . . . shift

p. 625: (i) wage . . . price . . . downward; (ii) elasticity . . . inputs . . . costs . . . adjustment

p. 628: (i) elastic . . . upward; (ii) equilibrium; (iii) demand . . . productivity . . . substitute . . . complementary

p. 631: (i) substitutable . . . substitution; (ii) reduces . . . increases; (iii) gains from trade

p. 635: (i) less; (ii) monopolist's; (iii) price; (iv) physical . . . physical; (v) revenue . . . price

29

Unions and Labor Market Monopoly Power

O n an average day, many thousands of people around the world who otherwise might have been gainfully employed have chosen not to work. Instead, these individuals are taking part in labor-union-coordinated work stoppages. Most of these work stoppages are legal strikes. A few of the stoppages, though, might be illegal strikes or other means of shutting down employing firms' operations, such as having key workers call in "sick." What is the economic purpose of union-directed work stoppages? More generally, what are the economic benefits and costs of the activities of labor unions? In this chapter, you will learn the answers to these questions.

14.6 million U.S. workers belong to **labor unions**—organizations that seek to secure economic improvements for their members? Private firms employ 7 million of these workers, or just over 7 percent of the private-sector labor force. Federal, state, and local government agencies employ the remaining 7.6 million union members, or about 38 percent of the public-sector labor force.

Traditionally, a key rationale for forming a union has been for members to be able to earn more than they would in a competitive labor market by obtaining a type of monopoly power. Because the entire supply of a particular group of workers is controlled by a single source when a union bargains as a single entity with management, a certain monopoly element enters into the determination of employment and wages. In such situations, we can no longer talk about a perfectly competitive supply of labor. Later in the chapter, we will examine the converse—a single employer who is the sole employer of a particular group of workers.

Labor unions
Worker organizations that seek to secure economic improvements for their members. They also seek to improve the safety, health, and other benefits (such as job security) of their members.

Industrialization and Labor Unions

In most parts of the world, labor movements began with local **craft unions.** These were groups of workers in individual trades, such as shoemaking, printing, or baking. Beginning around the middle of the eighteenth century, new technologies permitted reductions in unit production costs through the formation of larger-scale enterprises that hired dozens or more workers. By the late 1790s, workers in some British craft unions began trying to convince employers to engage in **collective bargaining,** in which business management negotiates with representatives of all union members about wages and hours of work.

In 1799 and 1800, the British Parliament passed laws called the Combination Acts aimed at prohibiting the formation of unions. In 1825, Parliament enacted a replacement Combination Act allowing unions to exist and to engage in limited collective bargaining. Unions on the European continent managed to convince most governments throughout Europe to enact similar laws during the first half of the nineteenth century.

Craft unions
Labor unions composed of workers who engage in a particular trade or skill, such as baking, carpentry, or plumbing.

Collective bargaining
Negotiation between the management of a company or and the management of a union for the purpose of reaching a mutually agreeable contract that sets wages, fringe benefits, and working conditions for all employees in all the unions involved.

Unions in the United States

The development of unions in the United States lagged several decades behind events in Europe. In the years between the Civil War and World War I (1861–1914), the Knights of Labor, an organized group of both skilled and unskilled workers, pushed for an eight-hour workday and equal pay for women and men. In 1886, a dissident group split from the Knights of Labor to form the American Federation of Labor (AFL) under the leadership of Samuel Gompers. During World War I, union membership increased to more than 5 million. But after the war, the government de-emphasized protecting labor's right to organize. Membership began to fall.

THE FORMATION OF INDUSTRIAL UNIONS The Great Depression was a landmark event in U.S. labor history. Franklin Roosevelt's National Industrial Recovery Act of 1933 gave labor the federal right to bargain collectively, but that act was declared unconstitutional. The 1935 National Labor Relations Act (NLRA), otherwise known as the Wagner Act, took its place. The NLRA guaranteed workers the right to form unions, to engage in collective bargaining, and to be members of any union.

In 1938, the Congress of Industrial Organizations (CIO) was formed by John L. Lewis, the president of the United Mine Workers. Prior to the formation of the CIO, most labor organizations were craft unions. The CIO was composed of **industrial unions,** which drew their membership from an entire industry such as steel or automobiles. In 1955, the CIO and the AFL merged because the leaders of both associations thought a merger would help organized labor grow faster.

Industrial unions
Labor unions that consist of workers from a particular industry, such as automobile manufacturing or steel manufacturing.

CONGRESSIONAL CONTROL OVER LABOR UNIONS Since the Great Depression, Congress has occasionally altered the relationship between labor and management through significant legislation. One of the most important pieces of legislation was the Taft-Hartley

Go to www.econtoday.com/chap29 to link to the Legal Information Institute's review of all the key U.S. labor laws.

Right-to-work laws
Laws that make it illegal to require union membership as a condition of continuing employment in a particular firm.

Closed shop
A business enterprise in which employees must belong to the union before they can be hired and must remain in the union after they are hired.

Union shop
A business enterprise that may hire nonunion members, conditional on their joining the union by some specified date after employment begins.

Jurisdictional dispute
A disagreement involving two or more unions over which should have control of a particular jurisdiction, such as a particular craft or skill or a particular firm or industry.

Sympathy strike
A work stoppage by a union in sympathy with another union's strike or cause.

Secondary boycott
A refusal to deal with companies or purchase products sold by companies that are dealing with a company being struck.

Act of 1947 (the Labor Management Relations Act). In general, the Taft-Hartley Act outlawed certain labor practices of unions, such as imposing make-work rules and forcing unwilling workers to join a particular union. Among other things, it allowed individual states to pass their own **right-to-work laws.** A right-to-work law makes it illegal for union membership to be a requirement for continued employment in any establishment.

The Taft-Hartley Act also made a **closed shop** illegal. A closed shop requires union membership before employment can be obtained. A **union shop,** however, is legal. A union shop does not require membership as a prerequisite for employment, but it can, and usually does, require that workers join the union after a specified amount of time on the job. (Even a union shop is illegal in states with right-to-work laws.)

Jurisdictional disputes, sympathy strikes, and secondary boycotts were also made illegal by the Taft-Hartley Act. In a **jurisdictional dispute,** two or more unions fight (and strike) over which should have control in a particular jurisdiction. For example, should carpenters working for a steel manufacturer be members of the steelworkers' union or the carpenters' union? A **sympathy strike** occurs when one union strikes in sympathy with another union's cause or strike. For example, if the retail clerks' union in a city is striking grocery stores, Teamsters union members may refuse to deliver products to those stores in sympathy with the retail clerks' demands for higher wages or better working conditions. A **secondary boycott** is a boycott of a company that deals with a struck company. For example, if union workers strike a baking company, a boycott of grocery stores that continue to sell that company's products is a secondary boycott. A secondary boycott brings pressure on third parties to force them to stop dealing with an employer who is being struck.

Perhaps the most famous provision of the Taft-Hartley Act allows the president to obtain a court injunction that will stop a strike for an 80-day cooling-off period if the strike is expected to imperil the nation's safety or health.

The Current Status of U.S. Labor Unions

As shown in Figure 29-1 below, union membership has been declining in the United States since the 1960s. At present, slightly less than 12 percent of U.S. workers are union members. Less than 8 percent of workers in the private sector belong to unions.

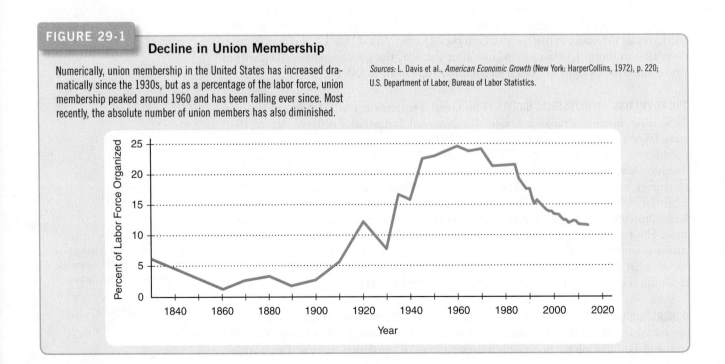

FIGURE 29-1

Decline in Union Membership

Numerically, union membership in the United States has increased dramatically since the 1930s, but as a percentage of the labor force, union membership peaked around 1960 and has been falling ever since. Most recently, the absolute number of union members has also diminished.

Sources: L. Davis et al., *American Economic Growth* (New York: HarperCollins, 1972), p. 220; U.S. Department of Labor, Bureau of Labor Statistics.

TABLE 29-1

	Union	Industry	Members
The Ten Largest Unions in the United States Half of the top ten U.S. unions have members who work in service and government occupations.	National Education Association	Education	2,731,000
	Service Employees International Union	Health care, public, and janitorial services	1,505,000
	American Federation of State, County, and Municipal Employees	Government services	1,460,000
	International Brotherhood of Teamsters	Trucking, delivery	1,396,000
	United Food and Commercial Workers International Union	Food and grocery services	1,312,000
	American Federation of Teachers	Education	829,000
	United Steelworkers of America	Steel	755,000
	International Brotherhood of Electrical Workers	Electrical	705,000
	Laborers' International Union of North America	Construction, utilities	670,000
	International Association of Machinists and Aerospace Workers	Machine and aerospace	654,000

Source: U.S. Department of Labor.

A DECLINE IN MANUFACTURING EMPLOYMENT A large part of the explanation for the decline in union membership has to do with the shift away from manufacturing. In 1948, workers in manufacturing industries, transportation, and utilities, which traditionally have been among the most heavily unionized industries, constituted more than half of private nonagricultural employment. Today, that fraction is less than one-fifth.

The relative decline in manufacturing employment helps explain why most of the largest U.S. unions now draw their members primarily from workers in service industries and governments. As you can see in Table 29-1 above, five of the ten largest unions now represent workers in these areas. The remaining five largest unions do still represent the manufacturing industries, transportation, and utilities that once dominated the U.S. union movement.

DEREGULATION AND IMMIGRATION The trend away from manufacturing is the main reason for the decline in unionism. Nevertheless, the deregulation of certain industries, such as airlines and trucking, has also contributed, as has increased global competition. In addition, immigration has weakened the power of unions. Much of the unskilled and typically nonunionized work in the United States is done by foreign-born workers, and immigrant workers who are undocumented cannot legally join a union.

CHANGES IN THE STRUCTURE OF THE U.S. UNION MOVEMENT After its founding in 1955, the AFL-CIO remained the predominant labor union organization for 50 years. In 2005, however, seven unions with more than 45 percent of total AFL-CIO membership broke off to form a separate union organization called Change to Win. More recently, two construction industry unions also left the AFL-CIO and joined with ironworkers and bricklayers unions to form the National Construction Alliance.

Unions in these new umbrella groups, which represent mainly workers in growing service industries, had become frustrated because they felt that the AFL-CIO was not working hard enough to expand union membership. In addition, some of these unions were more interested than the AFL-CIO in pursuing boycotts against companies viewed as anti-union, such as Walmart. These unions also sought strikes against industries trying to slow the growth of union membership, such as the hotel industry.

QUICK QUIZ See page 662 for the answers. Review concepts from this section in MyEconLab.

The _____ _____ of _____, composed of **craft unions,** was formed in 1886 under the leadership of Samuel Gompers. Membership increased until after World War I, when the government temporarily stopped protecting labor's right to organize.

During the Great Depression, legislation was passed that allowed for **collective bargaining.** The _____ _____ _____ Act of 1935 guaranteed workers

the right to form unions. The Congress of Industrial Organizations (CIO), composed of _____ unions, was formed during the Great Depression. The AFL and the CIO merged in 1955.

In the United States, union membership as a percentage of the labor force peaked at nearly _____ percent in 1960 and has declined since then to less than _____ percent.

Union Goals and Strategies

Through collective bargaining, unions establish the wages below which no individual worker may legally offer his or her services. Each year, union representatives and management negotiate collective bargaining contracts covering wages as well as working conditions and fringe benefits for about 5 million workers. If approved by the members, a union labor contract sets wage rates, maximum workdays, working conditions, fringe benefits, and other matters, usually for the next two or three years.

Strike: The Ultimate Bargaining Tool

Whenever union-management negotiations break down, union negotiators may turn to their ultimate bargaining tool, the threat or the reality of a strike. Strikes make headlines, but a strike occurs in less than 2 percent of all labor-management disputes before the contract is signed. In the other 98 percent, contracts are signed without much public fanfare.

The purpose of a strike is to impose costs on stubborn management to force it to accept the union's proposed contract terms. Strikes disrupt production and interfere with a company's or an industry's ability to sell goods and services. The strike works both ways, though, because workers receive no wages while on strike (though they may be partly compensated out of union strike funds). Striking union workers may also be eligible to draw state unemployment benefits.

The impact of a strike is closely related to the ability of striking unions to prevent nonstriking (and perhaps nonunion) employees from continuing to work for the targeted company or industry. Therefore, steps are usually taken to prevent others from working for the employer. **Strikebreakers** can effectively destroy whatever bargaining power rests behind a strike. Numerous methods have been used to prevent strikebreakers from breaking strikes. Violence has been known to erupt, almost always in connection with union attempts to prevent strikebreaking.

In recent years, companies have had less incentive to hire strikebreakers because work stoppages have become much less common. From 1945 until 1990, on average more than 200 union strikes took place in the United States each year. Since 1990, however, the average has been closer to 25 strikes per year.

Why might a union perceive that a strike is successful even if it results in a pay cut for the union's membership?

Strikebreakers
Temporary or permanent workers hired by a company to replace union members who are striking.

EXAMPLE

Symphony Musicians "Win" a Lengthy Strike

Since 1887, the Detroit Symphony has been among the nation's highest-regarded orchestras. Recently, however, the symphony experienced a very protracted labor dispute: a six-month-long strike by violinists, violists,

cellists, bassists, percussionists, and players of woodwind and brass wind instruments.

Following the strike, the new three-year contract's minimum threshold for a musician's annual pay was $79,000, a reduction from $104,650 specified in the previous contract. In addition, the number of musicians playing in the orchestra was reduced from 96 to 81. Nevertheless, the symphony's union declared victory. The strike had achieved a net gain, union leaders proclaimed, over management's opening offer of a pay cut in excess of 40 percent. The leaders concluded that achieving a pay cut of only 25 percent—plus preserving existing health care and pension benefits for the union's members—constituted a substantial achievement.

FOR CRITICAL THINKING

Taking all outcomes into account, including the fact that Detroit Symphony musicians earned no wages during the six-month period of the strike, do you think the union's "victory" was as substantial as claimed?

Union Goals with Direct Wage Setting

We have already pointed out that one of the goals of unions is to set minimum wages. The effects of setting a wage rate higher than a competitive market clearing wage rate can be seen in Figure 29-2 below. The market for labor initially is perfectly competitive. The market demand curve is D, and the market supply curve is S. The market clearing wage rate is W_e. The equilibrium quantity of labor is Q_e. If a union is formed and establishes by collective bargaining a minimum wage rate that exceeds W_e, an excess quantity of labor will be supplied (assuming no change in the labor demand schedule). If the minimum wage established by union collective bargaining is W_U, the quantity supplied will be Q_S. The quantity demanded will be Q_D. The difference is the excess quantity supplied, or surplus. Hence, the following point becomes clear:

> *One of the major roles of a union that establishes a wage rate above the market clearing wage rate is to ration available jobs among the excess number of workers who wish to work in the unionized industry.*

Note also that the surplus of labor is equivalent to a shortage of jobs at wage rates above equilibrium.

To ration jobs, the union may use a seniority system, lengthen the apprenticeship period to discourage potential members from joining, or institute other rationing methods. This has the effect of shifting the supply of labor curve to the left in order to support the higher wage, W_U.

There is a trade-off here that any union's leadership must face: Higher wages inevitably mean a reduction in total union employment—fewer union positions. When facing higher wages, management may replace part of the workforce with machinery or may even seek to hire nonunion workers.

FIGURE 29-2

Unions Must Ration Jobs

The market clearing wage rate is W_e, at point E, at which the equilibrium quantity of labor is Q_e. If the union succeeds in obtaining wage rate W_U, the quantity of labor demanded will be Q_D, at point A on the labor demand curve, but the quantity of labor supplied will be Q_S, at point B on the labor supply curve. The union must ration a limited number of jobs among a greater number of workers. The surplus of labor is equivalent to a shortage of jobs at that wage rate.

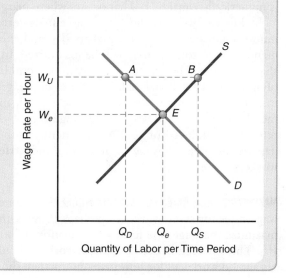

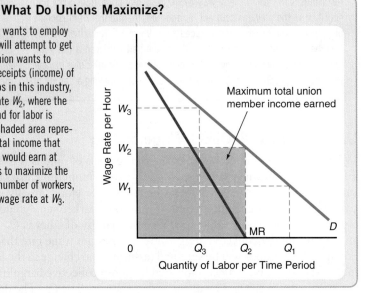

FIGURE 29-3

What Do Unions Maximize?

Assume that the union wants to employ all its Q_1 members. It will attempt to get wage rate W_1. If the union wants to maximize total wage receipts (income) of members who have jobs in this industry, it will do so at wage rate W_2, where the elasticity of the demand for labor is equal to 1. (The blue-shaded area represents the maximum total income that the union membership would earn at W_2.) If the union wants to maximize the wage rate for a given number of workers, say, Q_3, it will set the wage rate at W_3.

Three Possible Union Goals

If we view unions as monopoly sellers of a service, we can identify three different goals that they may pursue: ensuring employment for all members of the union, maximizing aggregate income of workers, and maximizing wage rates for some workers.

EMPLOYING ALL MEMBERS IN THE UNION Assume that the union has Q_1 workers. If it faces a labor demand curve such as D in Figure 29-3 above, the only way it can "sell" all of those workers' services is to accept a wage rate of W_1. As in any market, the demand curve tells the maximum price that can be charged to sell any particular quantity of a good or service. Here the service happens to be labor.

MAXIMIZING MEMBER INCOME If the union is interested in maximizing the gross income of its members, it will normally want a smaller membership than Q_1—namely, Q_2 workers, all employed and paid a wage rate of W_2. The aggregate income to all members of the union is represented by the wages of only the ones who work. Total income earned by union members is maximized where the price elasticity of demand is numerically equal to 1. That occurs where marginal revenue equals zero.

In Figure 29-3, marginal revenue equals zero at a quantity of labor Q_2. If the union obtains a wage rate equal to W_2, and therefore Q_2 union workers are demanded, their total income will be maximized. In other words, $Q_2 \times W_2$ (the blue-shaded area) will be greater than any other combination of wage rates and quantities of union workers demanded. It is, for example, greater than $Q_1 \times W_1$. Note that in this situation, if the union started out with Q_1 members, there would be $Q_1 - Q_2$ members out of *union* work at the wage rate W_2. (Those out of union work either remain unemployed or seek employment in other industries. Such actions have a depressing effect on wages in nonunion industries due to the increase in supply of workers there.)

MAXIMIZING WAGE RATES FOR CERTAIN WORKERS Assume that the union wants to maximize wage rates for some workers—perhaps those with the most seniority. If it wants to maximize the wage rate for a given quantity of workers, Q_3, it will seek a wage rate W_3. This will require deciding which workers should be unemployed and which workers should work and for how many hours they should be employed.

Union Strategies to Raise Wages Indirectly

One way or another, unions seek above-market wages for some or all of their members. Sometimes unions try to achieve this goal without making wage increases direct features of contract negotiations.

LIMITING ENTRY OVER TIME One way to raise wage rates without specifically setting wages is for a union to limit the size of its membership to the size of its employed workforce at the time the union was first organized. No workers are put out of work when the union is formed. Over time, as the demand for labor in the industry increases, the union prevents any net increase in membership, so larger wage increases are obtained than would otherwise be the case. We see this in Figure 29-4 below. In this example, union members freeze entry into their union, thereby obtaining a wage rate of $24 per hour instead of allowing a wage rate of only $22 per hour with no restriction on labor supply.

ALTERING THE DEMAND FOR UNION LABOR Another way that unions can increase wages is to shift the demand curve for labor outward to the right. This approach has the advantage of increasing both wage rates and the employment level. The demand for union labor can be increased by increasing worker productivity, increasing the demand for union-made goods, and decreasing the demand for non-union-made goods.

1. *Increasing worker productivity.* Supporters of unions have argued that unions provide a good system of industrial jurisprudence. The presence of unions may induce workers to feel that they are working in fair and just circumstances. If so, they work harder, increasing labor productivity. Productivity is also increased when unions

YOU ARE THERE

To consider what a recent hiring decision by a Washington, D.C., carpenters' union revealed about its strategies and objectives, read **A Union Hires a Nonunion Picketer to Protest Nonunion Hiring** on page 656.

FIGURE 29-4

Restricting Supply over Time

When the union was formed, it didn't affect wage rates or employment, which remained at $20 and Q_1 (the equilibrium wage rate and quantity at point E_1). As demand increased—that is, as the demand schedule shifted outward from D_1 to D_2—the union restricted membership to its original level of Q_1, however. The new supply curve is S_1S_2, which intersects D_2 at E_2, or at a wage rate of $24. Without the union, equilibrium would be at E_3, with a wage rate of $22 and employment of Q_2.

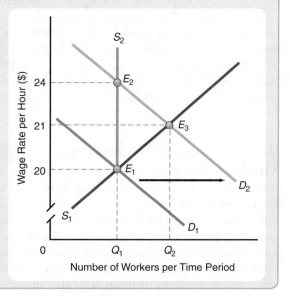

resolve differences and reduce conflicts between workers and management, thereby providing a more peaceful administrative environment.

2. *Increasing demand for union-made goods.* Because the demand for labor is a derived demand, a rise in the demand for products produced by union labor will increase the demand for union labor itself. One way that unions attempt to increase the demand for goods produced by union labor is by advertising "Look for the union label."

3. *Decreasing the demand for non-union-made goods.* When the demand for goods that are competing with (or are substitutes for) union-made goods is reduced, consumers shift to union-made goods, increasing the demand. The campaigns of various unions against buying foreign imports are a good example. The result is greater demand for goods "made in the USA," which in turn presumably increases the demand for U.S. union (and nonunion) labor.

Economic Effects of Labor Unions

Today, the most heavily unionized occupations are government service, transportation and material moving, and construction. Do union members in these and other occupations earn higher wages? Are they more or less productive than nonunionized workers in their industries? What are the broader economic effects of unionization? Let's consider each of these questions in turn.

Unions and Wages

You have learned that unions are able to raise the wages of their members if they can successfully limit the supply of labor in a particular industry. Unions are also able to raise wages if they can induce increases in the demand for union labor.

Economists have extensively studied the differences between union wages and nonunion wages. They have found that the average *hourly* wage (not including benefits) earned by a typical private-sector union worker is about $2.25 higher than the hourly wage earned by a typical worker who is not a union member. Adjusted for inflation, this union-nonunion hourly wage differential is only about half as large as it was two decades ago, however.

Comparisons of the *annual* earnings of union and nonunion workers indicate that in recent years, unions have *not* succeeded in raising the annual incomes of their members. In 1985, workers who belonged to unions earned nearly 7 percent more per year than nonunion workers, even though union workers worked fewer hours per week. Today, a typical nonunion employee still works slightly longer each week, but the average nonunion worker also has a higher annual income than the average union worker.

Even the $2.25 hourly wage differential already mentioned is somewhat misleading because it is an average across *all* U.S. workers. In the private sector, union workers earn only about 4 percent more than nonunion workers, or a little less than 60 cents per hour. The hourly wage gain for government workers is more than six times higher at about $3.55 per hour. A state government employee who belongs to a union currently earns an hourly wage more than 20 percent higher than a state government worker who is not a union member.

Unions and Labor Productivity

A traditional view of union behavior is that unions decrease productivity by artificially shifting the demand curve for union labor outward through excessive staffing and make-work requirements. For example, some economists have traditionally argued that unions tend to bargain for excessive use of workers, as when an airline union requires an engineer on all flights. This is called **featherbedding.** Many painters' unions, for example, resisted the use of paint sprayers and required that their members use only brushes. They even specified the maximum width of the brush. Moreover, whenever a union strikes, productivity drops, and this reduction in productivity in one sector of the economy can spill over into other sectors.

Featherbedding
Any practice that forces employers to use more labor than they would otherwise or to use existing labor in an inefficient manner.

Economic Benefits and Costs of Labor Unions

As should be clear by now, there are two opposing views of unions. One sees them as monopolies whose main effect is to raise the wage rate of high-seniority members at the expense of low-seniority members (and nonunion workers). The other contends that unions can increase labor productivity by promoting safer working conditions and generally better work environments. According to this view, unions contribute to workforce stability by providing arbitration and grievance procedures.

Critics point out that the positive view of unionism overlooks the fact that many of the benefits that unions provide do not require that unions engage in restrictive labor practices, such as the closed shop (see page 644). Unions could still provide benefits for their members without restricting the labor market.

Consequently, a key issue that economists seek to assess when judging the social costs of unions is the extent to which their existence has a negative effect on employment growth. Most evidence indicates that while unions do significantly reduce employment in some of the most heavily unionized occupations, the overall effects on U.S. employment are modest. On the whole, therefore, the social costs of unions in the U.S. *private* sector are probably relatively low.

Why is the overall compensation of unionized government workers much higher than the total compensation of private employees?

INTERNATIONAL EXAMPLE

The Global Public-Union Benefits Explosion

Many people are surprised that nearly 40 percent of U.S. government workers are unionized, but in many nations the union share of public employees is even higher. In the United Kingdom, 56 percent of government workers belong to unions, and in Canada and Ireland, about 70 percent of government employees do. In Scandinavian countries, public-sector unionization shares exceed 80 percent.

Benefits provided to unionized public workforces also have expanded. In the United Kingdom, government workers log an average of 23 percent *fewer* hours than private workers, mainly because government workers have lower retirement ages. In Brazil, police officers can retire with pensions after 15 years, and female public school teachers can receive retirement pensions following 25 years of service. In addition, easy eligibility for "disability retirements" boosts retirement income for many public workers, including 90 percent of workers for government-owned Long Island Rail Road in New York and 82 percent of California state troopers. When benefits are included in tabulating workers' overall compensation packages, unionized public workers earn at least 70 percent more than private employees.

FOR CRITICAL THINKING
Who pays for the benefits of government workers around the world?

QUICK QUIZ　See page 662 for the answers. Review concepts from this section in MyEconLab.

When unions set wage rates _____ market clearing prices, they face the problem of _____ a restricted number of jobs to workers who desire to earn the higher wages.

Unions may pursue any one of three goals: (1) to employ _____ union members, (2) to maximize total _____ of the union's members, or (3) to _____ wages for certain, usually high-seniority, workers.

Unions can increase the wage rate of members by engaging in practices that shift the union labor supply curve _____ or shift the demand curve for union labor _____ (or both).

Some economists believe that unions can increase _____ by promoting safer working conditions and generally better work environments.

Monopsony: A Buyer's Monopoly

Let's assume that a firm is a perfect competitor in the product market. The firm cannot alter the price of the product it sells, and it faces a perfectly elastic demand curve for its product. We also assume that the firm is the only buyer of a particular input. Although this situation may not occur often, it is useful to consider. Let's think in terms of a factory town, like those that used to be dominated by textile mills or those

Monopsonist
The only buyer in a market.

in the mining industry. One company not only hires the workers but also owns the businesses in the community, owns the apartments that workers live in, and hires the clerks, waiters, and all other personnel. This buyer of labor is called a **monopsonist**, the only buyer in the market.

What does this situation mean to a monopsonist in terms of the costs of hiring extra workers? It means that if the monopsonist wants to hire more workers, it has to offer higher wages. Our monopsonist firm cannot hire all the labor it wants at the going wage rate. Instead, it faces an upward-sloping supply curve. If it wants to hire more workers, it has to raise wage rates, including the wages of all its current workers (assuming a non-wage-discriminating monopsonist). It therefore has to take account of these increased costs when deciding how many more workers to hire.

Marginal Factor Cost

The monopsonist faces an upward-sloping supply curve of the input in question because as the only buyer, it faces the entire market supply curve. Each time the monopsonist buyer of labor, for example, wishes to hire more workers, it must raise wage rates. Thus, the marginal cost of another unit of labor is rising. In fact, the marginal cost of increasing its workforce will always be greater than the wage rate. This is because the monopsonist must pay the same wage rate to everyone in order to obtain another unit of labor. Consequently, the higher wage rate has to be offered not only to the last worker but also to *all* its other workers. We call the additional cost to the monopsonist of hiring one more worker the marginal factor cost (MFC).

The marginal factor cost of hiring the last worker is therefore that worker's wages plus the increase in the wages of all other existing workers. As we pointed out in Chapter 28, marginal factor cost is equal to the change in total variable costs due to a one-unit change in the one variable factor of production—in this case, labor. In Chapter 28, marginal factor cost was simply the competitive wage rate because the employer could hire all workers at the same wage rate.

Derivation of a Marginal Factor Cost Curve

Panel (a) of Figure 29-5 on the facing page shows the quantity of labor purchased, the wage rate per hour, the total cost of the quantity of labor supplied per hour, and the marginal factor cost per hour for the additional labor bought.

We translate the columns from panel (a) to the graph in panel (b) of the figure. We show the supply curve as S, which is taken from columns 1 and 2. The marginal factor cost curve (MFC) is taken from columns 1 and 4. The MFC curve must be above the supply curve whenever the supply curve is upward sloping. If the supply curve is upward sloping, the firm must pay a higher wage rate in order to attract a larger amount of labor. This higher wage rate must be paid to all workers. Thus, the increase in total costs due to an increase in the labor input will exceed the wage rate. (Recall from Chapter 28 that in a perfectly competitive input market, in contrast, the supply curve facing the firm is perfectly elastic and the marginal factor cost curve is identical to the supply curve.)

Employment and Wages under Monopsony

To determine the number of workers that a monopsonist desires to hire, we compare the marginal benefit to the marginal cost of each hiring decision. The marginal cost is the marginal factor cost (MFC) curve, and the marginal benefit is the marginal revenue product (MRP) curve. In Figure 29-6 on page 654, we assume competition in the output market and monopsony in the input market. A monopsonist finds its profit-maximizing quantity of labor demanded at A, where the marginal revenue product is just equal to the marginal factor cost. The monopsonist will therefore desire to hire exactly Q_m workers.

FIGURE 29-5

Derivation of a Marginal Factor Cost Curve

The supply curve, *S*, in panel (b) is taken from columns 1 and 2 of panel (a). The marginal factor cost curve (MFC) is taken from columns 1 and 4. It is the increase in the total wage bill resulting from a one-unit increase in labor input.

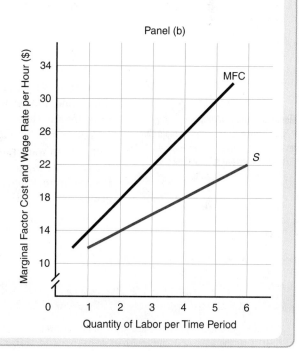

Panel (a)

(1) Quantity of Labor Supplied to Management	(2) Required Hourly Wage Rate	(3) Total Wage Bill (3) = (1) x (2)	(4) Marginal Factor Cost (MFC) = $\dfrac{\text{Change in (3)}}{\text{Change in (1)}}$
0	—	—	
			$12
1	$12	$12	
			16
2	14	28	
			20
3	16	48	
			24
4	18	72	
			28
5	20	100	
			32
6	22	132	

Panel (b)

THE INPUT PRICE PAID BY A MONOPSONY How much is the firm going to pay these workers? The monopsonist sets the wage rate so that it will get exactly the quantity, Q_m, supplied to it by its "captive" labor force. We find that wage rate is W_m. There is no reason to pay the workers any more than W_m because at that wage rate, the firm can get exactly the quantity it wants. The actual quantity used is determined by the intersection of the marginal factor cost curve and the marginal revenue product curve for labor—that is, at the point at which the marginal revenue from expanding employment just equals the marginal cost of doing so (point *A* in Figure 29-6 on the following page).

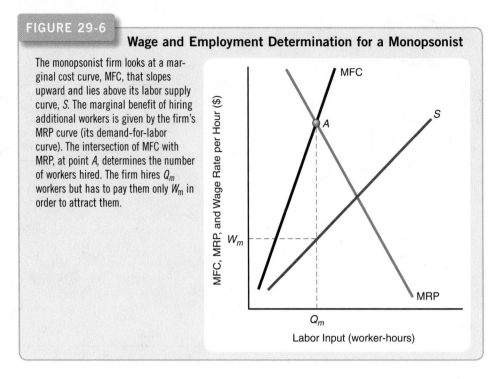

FIGURE 29-6

Wage and Employment Determination for a Monopsonist

The monopsonist firm looks at a marginal cost curve, MFC, that slopes upward and lies above its labor supply curve, S. The marginal benefit of hiring additional workers is given by the firm's MRP curve (its demand-for-labor curve). The intersection of MFC with MRP, at point A, determines the number of workers hired. The firm hires Q_m workers but has to pay them only W_m in order to attract them.

Notice that the profit-maximizing wage rate paid to workers (W_m) is lower than the marginal revenue product. That is to say, workers are paid a wage that is less than their contribution to the monopsonist's revenues. This is sometimes referred to as **monopsonistic exploitation** of labor.

You learned in Chapter 4 that in a perfectly competitive labor market, establishing a minimum wage rate above the market clearing wage rate causes employers to reduce the quantity of labor demanded, resulting in a decline in employment. What happens if a minimum wage rate is established above the wage rate that a *monopsony* would otherwise pay its workers?

Monopsonistic exploitation

Paying a price for the variable input that is less than its marginal revenue product; the difference between marginal revenue product and the wage rate.

POLICY EXAMPLE

Can Minimum Wage Laws Ever Boost Employment?

How does a monopsony respond to a minimum wage law that sets a wage floor above the wage rate it otherwise would pay its workers? Figure 29-7 on the facing page provides the answer to this question. In the figure, the entire upward-sloping curve labeled S is the labor supply curve in the absence of a minimum wage. Given the associated MFC curve and the firm's MRP curve, Q_m is the quantity of labor hired by a monopsony in the absence of a minimum wage law. The profit-maximizing wage rate is W_m.

If the government establishes a minimum wage equal to W_{min}, however, then the supply of labor to the firm becomes horizontal at the minimum wage and includes only the upward-sloping portion of the curve S above this legal minimum. In addition, the wage rate W_{min} becomes the monopsonist's marginal factor cost along the horizontal portion of this new labor supply curve, because when the firm hires one more unit of labor, it must pay each unit of labor the same wage rate, W_{min}.

To maximize its economic profits under the minimum wage, the monopsony equalizes the minimum wage rate with marginal revenue product and hires Q_{min} units of labor. This quantity exceeds the amount of labor, Q_m, that the monopsony would have hired in the absence of the minimum wage law. Thus, establishing a minimum wage can generate a rise in employment at a monopsony firm.

FOR CRITICAL THINKING

If a government establishes a minimum wage law covering all firms within its jurisdiction, including firms operating in both perfectly competitive and monopsonistic labor markets, will overall employment necessarily increase?

FIGURE 29-7

A Monopsony's Response to a Minimum Wage

In the absence of a minimum wage law, a monopsony faces the upward-sloping labor supply curve, S, and the marginal factor cost curve, MFC. To maximize its profits, the monopsony hires Q_m units of labor, at which MFC is equal to MRP, and it pays the wage rate W_m. Once the minimum wage rate, W_{min}, is established, the supply of labor becomes horizontal at the minimum wage and includes only the upward-sloping portion of the labor supply curve above this legal minimum. The monopsony must pay the same wage rate W_{min} for each unit of labor along this horizontal portion of the new labor supply curve, so its marginal factor cost is also equal to the minimum wage rate, W_{min}. Thus, the monopsony hires Q_{min} units of labor. Employment at the monopsony firm increases.

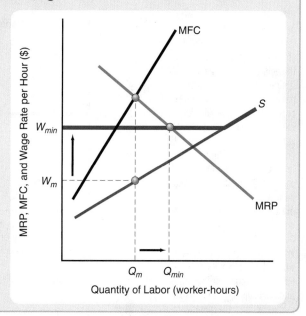

BILATERAL MONOPOLY We have studied the pricing of labor in various situations, including perfect competition in both the output and input markets and monopoly in both the output and input markets. Figure 29-8 on the following page shows four possible situations graphically.

The organization of workers into a union normally creates a monopoly supplier of labor, which gives the union some power to bargain for higher wages. What happens when a monopsonist meets a monopolist? This situation is called **bilateral monopoly,** defined as a market structure in which a single buyer faces a single seller. An example of bilateral monopoly is a county education employer facing a single teachers' union in that labor market. Another example is a players' union facing an organized group of team owners, as has occurred in professional baseball and football. To analyze bilateral monopoly, we would have to look at the interaction of both sides, buyer and seller. The wage outcome turns out to be indeterminate.

Bilateral monopoly

A market structure consisting of a monopolist and a monopsonist.

QUICK QUIZ

See page 662 for the answers. Review concepts from this section in MyEconLab.

A **monopsonist** is the _____ _____ in a market. The monopsonist faces an _____-sloping supply curve of labor.

Because the monopsonist faces an _____-sloping supply curve of labor, the marginal factor cost of increasing the labor input by one unit is _____ than the wage rate. Thus, the marginal factor cost curve always lies _____ the supply curve.

A monopsonist will hire workers up to the point at which marginal _____ cost equals marginal _____ product. Then the monopsonist will find the lowest necessary wage to attract that number of workers, as indicated by the supply curve.

Pricing and Employment under Various Market Conditions

In panel (a), the firm operates in perfect competition in both the input and output markets. It purchases labor up to the point where the going rate W_e is equal to MRP_c. It hires quantity Q_e of labor. In panel (b), the firm is a perfect competitor in the input market but has a monopoly in the output market. It purchases labor up to the point where W_e is equal to MRP_m. In panel (c), the firm is a monopsonist in the input market and a perfect competitor in the output market. It hires labor up to the point where $MFC = MRP_c$. It will hire quantity Q_1 and pay wage rate W_c. Panel (d) shows a situation in which the firm is both a monopolist in the market for its output and a monopsonist in its labor market. It hires the quantity of labor Q_2 at which $MFC = MRP_m$ and pays the wage rate W_m.

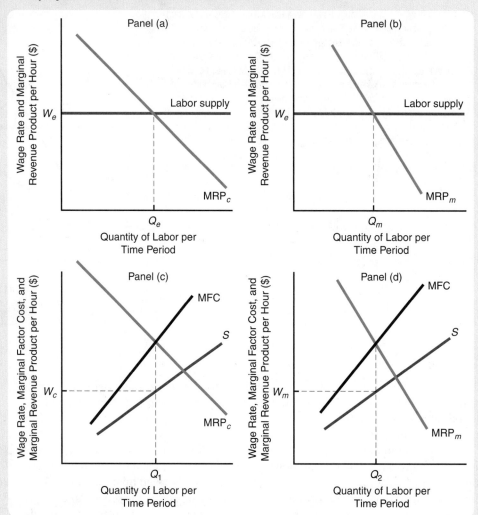

YOU ARE THERE

A Union Hires a Nonunion Picketer to Protest Nonunion Hiring

After months of not working, Billy Raye, a 51-year-old unemployed bicycle courier, has finally found a short-term position. His new job is with the Mid-Atlantic Regional Council of Carpenters (MARCC), a union that is paying him to march and chant in a picket line outside an office complex in Washington, D.C. The union's hired picketers are protesting a building contractor's decision to employ nonunionized workers to work on the buildings. Regarding his picketing job, Raye says, "I could care less. I am being paid to march around and sound off."

By hiring Raye and numerous other picketers at the minimum wage of $8.25 per hour, the MARCC has revealed both a strategy and an objective. The strategy is to try to raise wages for its members by increasing the demand for union members by contractors. The objective is to maximize the net incomes of all its members by hiring low-paid, non-union picketers instead of its own higher-wage union members.

Critical Thinking Questions

1. Why is hiring nonunion picketers at the minimum wage rate likely more consistent with maximizing net incomes of MARCC members than is hiring members of some other union to serve as picketers?

2. Why do you suppose that many unions hire nonunionized staff employees who earn market wages less than those typically available to unionized staff people?

ISSUES & APPLICATIONS

Gauging Labor Lost to Union Disputes Each Year

CONCEPTS APPLIED

▶ Labor Unions

▶ Collective Bargaining

▶ Strikes

Labor unions rely on their relatively large numbers of members in relation to employers' overall employment levels. Strikes and other union-directed work stoppages are crucial weapons that unions can use in their efforts to induce employers to engage in collective bargaining that benefits union members.

Millions of Hours of Work Lost to Union Disputes Globally

On a worldwide basis, more than 10 million days of labor are lost to union disputes each year. This number of lost days is equivalent to idling about 40,000 workers for a full year.

Figure 29-9 below displays how the days of work lost to labor disputes are distributed across various nations. The figure shows that in Canada, South Africa, France, and Spain, union-directed work stoppages cost employers more than 1 million days of labor.

FIGURE 29-9

U.S. firms lose a total of about 300,000 days of work to disputes with labor unions, which is several times smaller than the losses of working days in Canada, South Africa, France, and Spain.

Source: International Labor Organization.

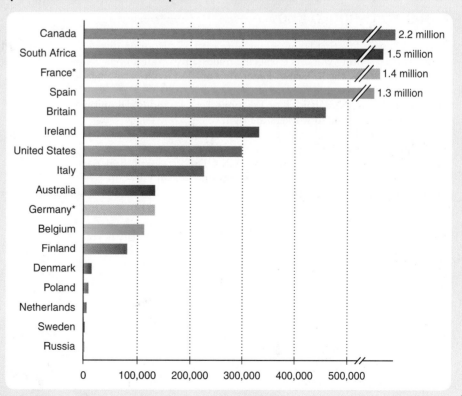

Working Days per Year Lost to Union Disputes in Selected Nations

"Only" 300,000 Lost U.S. Labor Days

Figure 29-9 on the previous page also indicates that union disputes reduce labor time at U.S. firms by about 300,000 days annually. Thus, losses of labor time caused by union work stoppages are smaller in the United States than in several other nations.

Nevertheless, at the 2013 average hourly wage rate of $24, these hours of lost labor otherwise would have generated more than $58 million of labor income. At current rates of household spending, this amount of income could provide sufficient food to sustain nearly 10,000 U.S. households every year. Consequently, the opportunity cost of labor lost each year to U.S. union disputes is far from inconsequential.

For Critical Thinking

1. How could union members' current *annual* incomes decline on net even if a long-lived strike induces a firm's management to increase the *hourly* wage rate?

2. Sometimes union memberships coordinate work stoppages when all workers call in sick. From an economic standpoint, is there any difference between coordinated sick-day work stoppages and strikes? Explain.

Web Resources

1. To see that the annual amount of labor lost to disputes in Canada are actually lower than in years past, go to www.econtoday.com/chap29.

2. For the latest statistics on union work stoppages in the United States, go to www.econtoday.com/chap29.

MyEconLab

For more questions on this chapter's
Issues & Applications, go to MyEconLab.
In the Study Plan for this chapter,
select Section N: News.

MyEconLab

Here is what you should know after reading this chapter. MyEconLab will help you identify what you know, and where to go when you need to practice.

WHAT YOU SHOULD KNOW

Labor Unions The first labor unions were craft unions, representing workers in specific trades. In the United States, the American Federation of Labor (AFL) emerged in the late nineteenth century. In 1935, the National Labor Relations Act (or Wagner Act) granted workers the right to form unions and bargain collectively. In 1955, the AFL merged with the Congress of Industrial Organizations (CIO) to form the AFL-CIO. The Taft-Hartley Act of 1947 placed limitations on unions' rights to organize, strike, and boycott.

labor unions, 643
craft unions, 643
collective bargaining, 643
industrial unions, 643
right-to-work laws, 644
closed shop, 644
union shop, 644
jurisdictional dispute, 644
sympathy strike, 644
secondary boycott, 644

WHERE TO GO TO PRACTICE

• MyEconLab Study Plan 29.1

MyEconLab *continued*

WHAT YOU SHOULD KNOW   WHERE TO GO TO PRACTICE

The Current Status of Labor Unions A key reason for an ongoing decline in U.S. union membership rates is the relative decline in manufacturing jobs as a share of total employment. Greater domestic and global competition has also had a part in bringing about a decline in unions.

- MyEconLab Study Plan 29.1

Basic Goals and Strategies of Labor Unions A key goal of most unions is to achieve higher wages. Often this entails bargaining for wages above competitive levels, which produces surplus labor. Thus, a major task of many unions is to ration available jobs. Unions often address this trade-off between wages and the number of jobs by maximizing the total income of members. Strategies to raise wages indirectly include placing limits on the entry of new workers, increasing worker productivity, and lobbying consumers to increase their demands for union-produced goods.

strikebreakers, 646

Key Figures
Figure 29-2, 647
Figure 29-3, 648
Figure 29-4, 649

- MyEconLab Study Plan 29.2
- Animated Figures 29-2, 29-3, 29-4

Effects of Labor Unions on Wages and Productivity On average, union hourly wages are higher than wages of nonunionized workers. Unionized employees typically work fewer hours per year, however, so their average annual earnings are lower than those of nonunionized employees. Some collective bargaining rules specifying how jobs are performed appear to reduce productivity, but unionization promotes generally better work environments, which may enhance productivity.

featherbedding, 650

- MyEconLab Study Plan 29.3

How a Monopsonist Determines How Much Labor to Employ and What Wage Rate to Pay For a monopsonist, which is the only buyer of an input such as labor, paying a higher wage to attract an additional unit of labor increases total factor costs for all other labor employed. The monopsonist employs labor to the point at which the marginal factor cost of labor equals the marginal revenue product of labor. It then pays workers the wage at which they are willing to work, as determined by the labor supply curve, which is less than marginal factor cost and marginal revenue product.

monopsonist, 652
monopsonistic exploitation, 654
bilateral monopoly, 655

Key Figures
Figure 29-5, 653
Figure 29-6, 654
Figure 29-7, 655

- MyEconLab Study Plan 29.4
- Animated Figures 29-5, 29-6, 29-7

── WHAT YOU SHOULD KNOW ──────────────────────   ── WHERE TO GO TO PRACTICE ──

Comparing a Monopsonist's Wage and Employment Decisions with Choices by Firms in Industries with Other Market Structures Perfectly competitive firms take the wage rate as market determined. A product market monopolist tends to employ fewer workers, but the product market monopolist nonetheless cannot affect the market wage rate. In contrast, a monopsonist is the only employer of labor, so it searches for the wage rate that maximizes its profit. This wage rate is less than the marginal revenue product of labor. If a firm is both a product market monopolist and a labor market monopsonist, its demand for labor is also lower than it would be if the firm's product market were competitive, so the firm hires fewer workers as well.

Key Figure
Figure 29-8, 656

- MyEconLab Study Plan 29.4
- Animated Figure 29-8

Log in to MyEconLab, take a chapter test, and get a personalized Study Plan that tells you which concepts you understand and which ones you need to review. From there, MyEconLab will give you further practice, tutorials, animations, videos, and guided solutions. For more information, visit www.myeconlab.com

PROBLEMS

All problems are assignable in MyEconLab. Answers to the odd-numbered problems appear at the back of the book.

29-1. Discuss three aspects of collective bargaining that society might deem desirable. (See pages 650–651.)

29-2. Give three reasons why a government might seek to limit the power of a union. (See pages 650–651.)

29-3. The Writers Guild of America (WGA), which represents TV and film screenwriters, called for a strike, and most screenwriters stopped working. Nevertheless, writers for certain TV soap operas, such as *The Young and the Restless*—which have had shrinking audiences for years, draw small numbers of viewers for repeat shows, and rarely sell on Blu-ray discs—opted to drop their WGA memberships and tried to continue working during the strike. Why do you suppose that the WGA posted on its Web site a phone number for union members to report "strike-breaking activities and 'scab writing'" to the union's 12-person Strike Rules Compliance Committee? What effect do strikebreakers have on the collective bargaining power of a union? (See page 646.)

29-4. Suppose that the objective of a union is to maximize the total dues paid to the union by its membership.

Explain the union's strategy, in terms of the wage level and employment level, under the following two scenarios. (See page 648.)

a. Union dues are a percentage of total earnings of the union membership.

b. Union dues are paid as a flat amount per union member employed.

29-5. Explain why, in economic terms, the total income of union membership is maximized when marginal revenue is zero. (See page 648. Hint: How much more revenue is forthcoming when marginal revenue is equal to zero?)

29-6. Explain the impact of each of the following events on the market for union labor. (See pages 649–450.)

a. Union-produced TV and radio commercials convince consumers to buy domestically manufactured clothing instead of imported clothing.

b. The union sponsors periodic training programs that instruct union laborers about the most efficient use of machinery and tools.

29-7. Why are unions in industries in which inputs such as machines are poor substitutes for labor more likely to be able to bargain for wages higher than market levels? (See pages 649–650.)

29-8. How is it possible for the average annual earnings of nonunionized workers to exceed those of unionized workers even though unionized workers' hourly wages are more than $2 higher? (See page 650.)

29-9. In the short run, a tool manufacturer has a fixed amount of capital. Labor is a variable input. The cost and output structure that the firm faces is depicted in the following table:

Labor Supplied	Total Physical Product	Hourly Wage Rate ($)
10	100	5
11	109	6
12	116	7
13	121	8
14	124	9
15	125	10

Derive the firm's total wage costs and marginal factor cost at each level of labor supplied. (See pages 652–653.)

29-10. Suppose that for the firm in Problem 29-9, the goods market is perfectly competitive. The market price of the product the firm produces is $4 at each quantity supplied by the firm. What is the amount of labor that this profit-maximizing firm will hire, and what wage rate will it pay? (See page 653.)

29-11. The price and wage structure that a firm faces is depicted in the following table.

Labor Supplied	Total Physical Product	Hourly Wage Rate ($)	Product Price ($)
10	100	5	3.11
11	109	6	3.00
12	116	7	2.95
13	121	8	2.92
14	124	9	2.90
15	125	10	2.89

The firm finds that the price of its product changes with the rate of output. In addition, the wage it pays its workers varies with the amount of labor it employs. This firm maximizes profits. How many units of labor will it hire? What wage will it pay? (See pages 652–653.)

29-12. What is the amount of monopsonistic exploitation that takes place at the firm examined in Problem 29-11? (See page 654.)

29-13. A profit-maximizing clothing producer in a remote area is the only employer of people in that area. It sells its clothing in a perfectly competitive market. The firm pays each worker the same weekly wage rate. The last worker hired raised the firm's total weekly wage expenses from $105,600 to $106,480. What is the marginal revenue product of the last worker hired by this firm if it is maximizing profits? (See pages 652–653.)

29-14. Why does marginal factor cost increase as a monopsonistic firm utilizes more labor but remain unchanged as a perfectly competitive firm employs additional labor? (See pages 652–653.)

29-15. Why does a monopsonistic firm pay the last unit of labor that it employs a wage that is less than that unit's marginal revenue product? (See page 654.)

29-16. A single firm is the only employer in a labor market. The marginal revenue product, labor supply, and marginal factor cost curves that it faces are displayed in the diagram below. Use this information to answer the following questions. (See pages 652–653.)

a. How many units of labor will this firm employ in order to maximize its economic profits?

b. What hourly wage rate will this firm pay its workers?

c. What is the total amount of wage payments that this firm will make to its workers each hour?

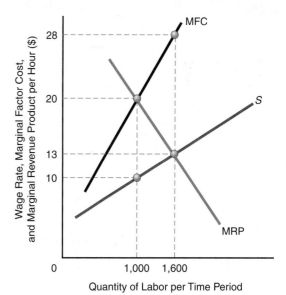

ECONOMICS ON THE NET

ANSWERS TO QUICK QUIZZES

p. 646: (i) American Federation . . . Labor; (ii) National Labor Relations . . . industrial; (iii) 25 . . . 12

p. 651: (i) above . . . rationing; (ii) all . . . income . . . maximize; (iii) inward . . . outward; (iv) productivity

p. 655: (i) only buyer . . . upward; (ii) upward . . . greater . . . above; (iii) factor . . . revenue

Income, Poverty, and Health Care

30

LEARNING OBJECTIVES

After reading this chapter, you should be able to:

▶ Describe how to use a Lorenz curve to represent a nation's income distribution

▶ Identify the key determinants of income differences across individuals

▶ Discuss theories of desired income distribution

▶ Distinguish among alternative approaches to measuring and addressing poverty

▶ Recognize the role played by third-party payments in rising health care costs

▶ Explain the key elements of the new U.S. national health insurance program and evaluate its potential economic effects

MyEconLab helps you master each objective and study more efficiently. See end of chapter for details.

Three decades ago, a typical female worker in the United States earned an annual rate of income equivalent to 63 percent of the income received by an average male worker. In contrast, today the average woman's annual earnings are almost 83 percent of those of a typical man's. How has an upswing in educational attainment by women helped to account for the movement toward income equality between the two genders? Why do some economists suggest that if women continue to earn a majority of college and university degrees, average annual earnings of female workers may eventually surpass those of male workers? By the time you have completed this chapter, you will understand the answers to these questions.

today, only 51 percent of adult U.S. residents are married, compared with 72 percent in 1960? A number of economic elements have contributed to the decrease in the number of married adults. For instance, the U.S. income tax code includes a "marriage penalty" under which the overall tax rate imposed on two married people is higher than they would face separately if unmarried. In addition, the national health care plan that went into place in 2013 also discourages marriage by lower-income individuals. For example, single people earning $43,000 per year each are eligible for government-subsidized health care under the new program, but married people earning a combined $86,000 annual income are not.

Among the most important economic elements leading to a lower number of married adults is that so many more young people now perceive a college education to be crucial for improving their future income prospects. Today, many individuals between the ages of 18 and 24 put off marriage to pursue education at colleges and technical schools. This fact helps explain why only 9 percent of people in this age group marry, compared with 45 percent in 1960.

Economists have found that the number of people marrying and the ages at which they do so have substantial effects on the **distribution of income**—the way that income is allocated among the population. Economists have devised various theories to explain income distribution. We will present some of these theories in this chapter. We will also present some of the more obvious institutional reasons why income is not distributed equally in the United States. In addition, we will examine the health care problems confronting individuals in all income groups and how the federal government's new health care program proposes to solve these problems.

Distribution of income
The way income is allocated among the population based on groupings of residents.

Income

Income provides each of us with the means of consuming and saving. Income can be the result of a payment for labor services or a payment for ownership of one of the other factors of production besides labor—land, physical capital, or entrepreneurship. In addition, individuals obtain spendable income from gifts and government transfers. (Some individuals also obtain income by stealing, but we will not treat this matter here.) Right now, let's examine how money income is distributed across classes of income earners within the United States.

Measuring Income Distribution: The Lorenz Curve

We can represent the distribution of money income graphically with what is known as the **Lorenz curve**, named after a U.S.-born statistician, Max Otto Lorenz, who proposed it in 1905. The Lorenz curve shows what share of total money income is accounted for by different proportions of the nation's households. Look at Figure 30-1 on the facing page. On the horizontal axis, we measure the *cumulative* percentage of households, lowest-income households first. Starting at the left corner, there are zero households. At the right corner, we have 100 percent of households. In the middle, we have 50 percent of households. The vertical axis represents the cumulative percentage of money income. The 45-degree line represents complete equality: 50 percent of the households obtain 50 percent of total income, 60 percent of the households obtain 60 percent of total income, and so on. Of course, in no real-world situation is there such complete equality of income. No actual Lorenz curve would be a straight line.

Rather, it would be some curved line, like the one labeled "Actual money income distribution" in Figure 30-1. For example, the bottom 50 percent of households in the United States receive about 22 percent of total money income.

In Figure 30-2 on the facing page, we again show the actual money income distribution Lorenz curve for the United States, and we also compare it to the distribution of money income in 1929. Since that year, the Lorenz curve has generally become less bowed. That is, it has moved closer to the line of complete equality.

Lorenz curve
A geometric representation of the distribution of income. A Lorenz curve that is perfectly straight represents complete income equality. The more bowed a Lorenz curve, the more unequally income is distributed.

CRITICISMS OF THE LORENZ CURVE In recent years, economists have placed less and less emphasis on the shape of the Lorenz curve as an indication of the degree of income inequality in a country. There are five basic reasons why the Lorenz curve has been criticized:

1. The Lorenz curve is typically presented in terms of the distribution of *money* income only. It does not include **income in kind,** such as government-provided food

Income in kind
Income received in the form of goods and services, such as housing or medical care. Income in kind differs from money income, which is simply income in dollars, or general purchasing power, that can be used to buy *any* goods and services.

FIGURE 30-1

The Lorenz Curve

The horizontal axis measures the cumulative percentage of house-holds, with lowest-income house-holds first, from 0 to 100 percent. The vertical axis measures the cumulative percentage of money income from 0 to 100. A straight line at a 45-degree angle cuts the box in half and represents a line of complete income equality, along which 25 percent of the families get 25 percent of the money income, 50 percent get 50 percent, and so on. The observed Lorenz curve, showing the actual U.S. money income dis-tribution, is not a straight line but rather a curved line as shown. The difference between complete money income equality and the Lorenz curve is the inequality gap.

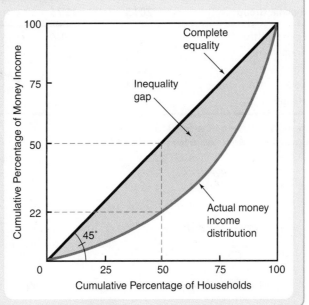

stamps, education, medical care, or housing aid, and goods or services produced and consumed in the home or on the farm.

2. The Lorenz curve does not account for differences in the size of households or the number of wage earners they contain.

3. It does not account for age differences. Even if all families in the United States had exactly the same *lifetime* incomes, chances are that young families would have modest incomes, middle-aged families would have relatively high incomes,

FIGURE 30-2

Lorenz Curves of Income Distribution, 1929 and 2013

Since 1929, the Lorenz curve has moved inward toward the straight line of perfect income equality.

Source: U.S. Department of Commerce.

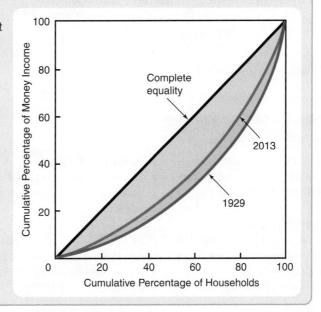

TABLE 30-1

Percentage Share of
Money Income for
Households before
Direct Taxes

Income Group	2013	1975	1960	1947
Lowest fifth	3.3	4.4	4.8	5.1
Second fifth	8.5	10.5	12.2	11.8
Third fifth	14.6	17.1	17.8	16.7
Fourth fifth	23.4	24.8	24.0	23.2
Highest fifth	50.2	43.2	41.3	43.3

Note: Figures may not sum to 100 percent due to rounding.
Sources: U.S. Bureau of the Census; author's estimates.

and retired families would have lower incomes. Because the Lorenz curve is drawn at a moment in time, it can never tell us anything about the inequality of *lifetime* income.

4. The Lorenz curve ordinarily reflects money income *before* taxes.

5. It does not measure unreported income from the underground economy, a substantial source of income for some individuals.

Income Distribution in the United States

Go to www.econtoday/chap30 to view the U.S. Census Bureau's most recent data on the U.S. income distribution. Click on the most recent year next to "Money Income in the United States."

In Table 30-1 above, we see the percentage share of income for households before direct taxes. The table groups households according to whether they are in the lowest 20 percent of the income distribution, the second lowest 20 percent, and so on. We see that in 2013, the lowest 20 percent had an estimated combined money income of 3.3 percent of the total money income of the entire population. This is less than the lowest 20 percent had at the end of World War II.

Accordingly, some have concluded that the distribution of money income has become slightly more unequal. *Money* income, however, understates *total* income for individuals who receive in-kind transfers from the government in the form of food stamps, public housing, education, and the like. In particular, since World War II, the share of *total* income—money income plus in-kind benefits—going to the bottom 20 percent of households has more than doubled.

To what extent do shares of income shift among different groups of U.S. residents over the course of a decade?

EXAMPLE

U.S. Residents Move among Income Groups over Time

Gerald Auten and Geoffrey Gee of the U.S. Department of the Treasury recently examined the mobility of people across the distribution of income during the 1987–1996 and 1996–2005 decades. The Treasury economists found that within a given 10-year period, about 57 percent of people initially receiving money incomes placing them in the lowest 20 percent moved into the group with the next-highest 20 percent of incomes. Furthermore, the average money incomes of people who began with incomes among the top 20 percent declined within each decade. Indeed, people initially within the group receiving the highest 1 percent

of incomes were most likely, of all U.S. residents, to drop into a lower-income group. Thus, there is evidence of considerable mobility of individuals within the U.S. income distribution over periods of a decade or longer.

FOR CRITICAL THINKING
How might well-intentioned policies that reduce incentives for lower-income people to make human capital investments reduce upward mobility within the income distribution?

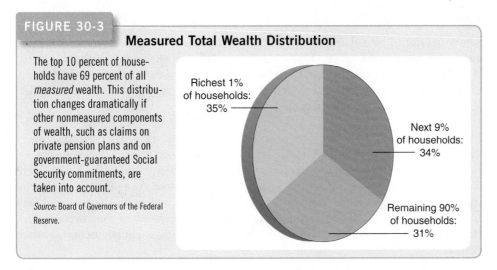

FIGURE 30-3

Measured Total Wealth Distribution

The top 10 percent of households have 69 percent of all *measured* wealth. This distribution changes dramatically if other nonmeasured components of wealth, such as claims on private pension plans and on government-guaranteed Social Security commitments, are taken into account.

Source: Board of Governors of the Federal Reserve.

Richest 1% of households: 35%

Next 9% of households: 34%

Remaining 90% of households: 31%

The Distribution of Wealth

When referring to the distribution of income, we must realize that income—a flow—can be viewed as a return on wealth (both human and nonhuman)—a stock. A discussion of the distribution of income is not necessarily the same thing as a discussion of the distribution of wealth, however. A complete concept of wealth would include not only tangible objects, such as buildings, machinery, land, cars, and houses—nonhuman wealth—but also people who have skills, knowledge, initiative, talents, and the like—human wealth. The total of human and nonhuman wealth in the United States makes up our nation's capital stock.

Figure 30-3 above shows that the richest 10 percent of U.S. households hold more than two-thirds of all *measured* wealth. The problem with those data gathered by the Federal Reserve System, however, is that they do not include many important assets. One of these assets is workers' claims on private pension plans, which equal at least $4 trillion. If you add the value of these pensions, household wealth increases by almost 25 percent and reveals that many more U.S. households are middle-wealth households (popularly known as the *middle class*). Another asset excluded from the data is anticipated claims on the Social Security system, which tend to comprise a larger share of the wealth of lower-income individuals.

QUICK QUIZ See page 687 for the answers. Review concepts from this section in MyEconLab.

The **Lorenz curve** graphically represents the distribution of _____. If it is a straight line, there is complete _____ of income. The more it is bowed, the more _____ income is distributed.

The distribution of wealth is not the same as the distribution of income. Wealth includes _____ such as

houses, stocks, and bonds. Although the apparent distribution of wealth seems to be _____ concentrated at the top than income, the data used are not very accurate, and most summary statistics fail to take account of workers' claims on private and public pensions, which are substantial.

Determinants of Income Differences

We know that there are income differences—that is not in dispute. A more important question is why these differences in income occur. We will look at four determinants of income differences: age, productivity, inheritance, and discrimination.

Age

Age turns out to be a determinant of income because with age come, usually, more education, more training, and more experience. It is not surprising that within every class of income earners, there seem to be regular cycles of earning behavior. Most individuals earn more when they are middle-aged than when they are younger or older. We call this the **age-earnings cycle**.

THE AGE-EARNINGS CYCLE Every occupation has its own age-earnings cycle, and every individual will probably experience some variation from the average. Nonetheless, we can characterize the typical age-earnings cycle graphically in Figure 30-4 below. Here we see that at age 18, earnings from wages are relatively low. As a person's productivity increases through more training and experience, earnings gradually rise until they peak at about age 50. Then earnings fall until retirement, when they become zero (that is, currently earned wages become zero, although retirement payments may then commence).

Note that general increases in overall productivity for the entire workforce will result in an upward shift in the typical age-earnings profile depicted in Figure 30-4. Thus, even at the end of the age-earnings cycle, when just about to retire, the worker would receive a relatively high wage compared with the starting wage 45 years earlier. The wage would be higher due to factors that contribute to rising real wages for everyone, regardless of the stage in the age-earnings cycle.

Now we have some idea why specific individuals earn different incomes at different times in their lives, but we have yet to explain why different people are paid different amounts for their labor. One way to explain this is to recall the marginal productivity theory developed in Chapter 28.

Marginal Productivity

When trying to determine how many workers a firm would hire, we had to construct a marginal revenue product curve. We found that as more workers were hired, the marginal revenue product fell due to diminishing marginal product. If the forces of demand and supply established a certain wage rate, workers would be hired until their marginal physical product times marginal revenue (which equals the market price under perfect competition) was equal to the going wage rate. Then the hiring would stop. This analysis suggests what workers can expect to be paid in the labor market: As long as there are low-cost information flows and the labor and product markets are competitive, each worker can expect to be paid his or her marginal revenue product.

Age-earnings cycle
The regular earnings profile of an individual throughout his or her lifetime. The age-earnings cycle usually starts with a low income, builds gradually to a peak at around age 50, and then gradually curves down until it approaches zero at retirement.

FIGURE 30-4

Typical Age-Earnings Profile

Within every class of income earners, there is usually an age-earnings profile. Earnings from wages are lowest when starting work at age 18, reach their peak at around age 50, and then taper off until retirement around age 65, when they become zero for most people. The rise in earnings up to age 50 is usually due to increased experience, longer working hours, and better training and schooling. (We abstract from economywide productivity changes that would shift the entire curve upward.)

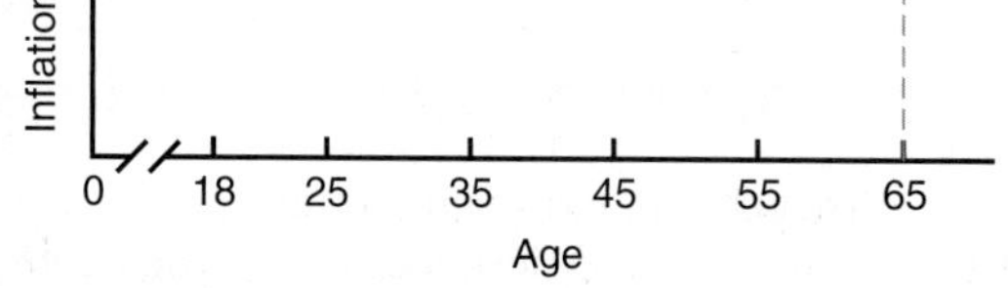

DETERMINANTS OF MARGINAL PRODUCTIVITY According to marginal revenue product theory, if people can increase their marginal physical product, they can expect to earn higher incomes. Key determinants of marginal physical product are talent, experience, and training.

Talent Talent is the easiest factor to explain, but it is difficult to acquire if you don't have it. Innate abilities and attributes can be very strong, if not overwhelming, determinants of a person's potential productivity. Strength, coordination, and mental alertness are facets of nonacquired human capital and thus have some bearing on the ability to earn income. Someone who is tall and agile has a better chance of being a basketball player than someone who is short and unathletic. A person born with a superior talent for abstract thinking has a better chance of earning a relatively high income as a mathematician or a physicist than someone who is not born with that capability.

Experience Additional experience at particular tasks is another way to increase productivity. Experience can be linked to the well-known *learning curve* that applies when the same task is done over and over. The worker repeating a task becomes more efficient: The worker can do the same task in less time or in the same amount of time but better. Take an example of a person going to work on an automobile assembly line. At first she is able to fasten only three bolts every two minutes. Then the worker becomes more adept and can fasten four bolts in the same time plus insert a rubber guard on the bumper. After a few more weeks, another task can be added. Experience allows this individual to improve her productivity. The more effectively people learn to do something, the more productive they are.

Training Training is similar to experience but is more formal. Much of a person's increased productivity is due to on-the-job training. Many companies have training programs for new workers.

INVESTMENT IN HUMAN CAPITAL Investment in human capital is just like investment in anything else. If you invest in yourself by going to college, rather than going to work after high school and earning more current income, you will presumably be rewarded in the future with a higher income or a more interesting job (or both). This is exactly the motivation that underlies the decision of many college-bound students to obtain formal higher education.

As with other investments, we can determine the rate of return on an investment in a college education. To do so, we first have to figure out the marginal cost of going to school. The cost is not simply what you have to pay for books, fees, and tuition but also includes the income you forgo. *A key cost of education is the income forgone—the opportunity cost of not working.* In addition, the direct expenses of college must be paid for. Certainly, not all students forgo all income during their college years. Many work part time. Taking account of those who work part time and those who are supported by tuition grants and other scholarships, the average rate of return on going to college ranges between 6 and 8 percent per year. The gain in lifetime income has a present value ranging from $200,000 to more than $500,000.

YOU ARE THERE

To contemplate the income earnings that a person can forgo by failing to invest in human capital, take a look at **A Portuguese Woman Rethinks Her Human Capital Investment** on page 681.

Inheritance

It is not unusual to inherit cash, jewelry, stocks, bonds, homes, or other real estate. Yet only about 10 percent of income inequality in the United States can be traced to differences in inherited wealth. If for some reason the government confiscated all property that had been inherited, the immediate result would be only a modest change in the distribution of income in the United States. In any event, at both federal and state levels substantial inheritance taxes generally are levied on the estates of relatively wealthy deceased Americans (although there are some legally valid ways to avoid certain estate taxes).

Discrimination

Economic discrimination occurs whenever workers with the same marginal revenue product receive unequal pay due to some noneconomic factor such as their race, gender, or age. It is possible—and indeed quite obvious—that discrimination affects the distribution of income. Certain groups in our society are not paid wages at rates comparable to those received by other groups, even when we correct for productivity. Differences in income remain between whites and nonwhites and between men and women. For example, the median income of black families is about 65 percent that of white families. The average wage rate of women is about 83 percent that of men. Some people argue that all of these differences are due to discrimination against nonwhites and against women.

We cannot simply assume that *any* differences in income are due to discrimination, though. What we need to do is discover why differences in income between groups exist and then determine if factors other than discrimination in the labor market can explain them. The unexplained part of income differences can rightfully be considered the result of discrimination.

Theories of Desired Income Distribution

We have talked about the factors affecting the distribution of income, but we have not yet mentioned the normative issue of how income *ought* to be distributed. This, of course, requires a value judgment. We are talking about the problem of economic justice. We can never completely resolve this problem because there are always going to be conflicting values. It is impossible to give all people what each thinks is just. Nonetheless, two particular normative standards for the distribution of income have been popular with economists. These are income distribution based on productivity and income distribution based on equality.

Productivity

The *productivity standard* for the distribution of income can be stated simply as "To each according to what he or she produces." This is also called the *contributive standard* because it is based on the principle of rewarding according to the contribution to society's total output. It is also sometimes referred to as the *merit standard* and is one of the oldest concepts of justice. People are rewarded according to merit, and merit is judged by one's ability to produce what is considered useful by society.

We measure a person's productive contribution in a capitalist system by the market value of that person's output. We have already referred to this as the marginal revenue product theory of wage determination.

Equality

The *egalitarian principle* of income distribution is simply "To each exactly the same." Everyone would have exactly the same amount of income. This criterion of income distribution has been debated as far back as biblical times. This system of income distribution has been considered equitable, meaning that presumably everybody is dealt with fairly and equally. There are problems, however, with an income distribution that is completely equal.

Some jobs are more unpleasant or more dangerous than others. Should the people undertaking these jobs be paid exactly the same as everyone else? Indeed, under an equal distribution of income, what incentive would there be for individuals to take risky, hazardous, or unpleasant jobs at all? What about overtime? Who would be willing to work overtime without additional pay? There is yet another problem: If everyone earned the same income, what incentive would there be for individuals to invest in their own human capital—a costly and time-consuming process?

Just consider the incentive structure within a corporation. Within corporations, much of the differential between, say, the pay of the CEO and the pay of all of the vice presidents is meant to create competition among the vice presidents for the CEO's job.

The result is higher productivity. If all incomes were the same, much of this competition would disappear, and productivity would fall.

There is some evidence that differences in income lead to higher rates of economic growth. Future generations are therefore made better off. Elimination of income differences may reduce the rate of economic growth and cause future generations to be poorer than they otherwise might have been.

QUICK QUIZ   See page 687 for the answers. Review concepts from this section in MyEconLab.

Most people follow an _____-_____ cycle in which they earn relatively small incomes when they first start working, increase their incomes until about age 50, and then slowly experience a decrease in their real incomes as they approach retirement.

According to the marginal _____ theory of wages, workers can expect to be paid their marginal _____ product.

Marginal physical productivity depends on _____, _____, and _____.

Going to school and receiving on-the-job training can be considered an investment in _____ capital. A key cost of education is the _____ cost of not working.

Two normative standards for income distribution are income distribution based on _____ and income distribution based on _____.

Poverty and Attempts to Eliminate It

Throughout the history of the world, mass poverty has been accepted as inevitable. This nation and others, particularly in the Western world, however, have sustained enough economic growth in the past several hundred years so that *mass* poverty can no longer be said to be a problem for these fortunate countries. As a matter of fact, the residual of poverty in the United States strikes us as bizarre, an anomaly. How can there still be so much poverty in a nation of such abundance? Having talked about the determinants of the distribution of income, we now have at least some ideas of why some people are destined to remain low-income earners throughout their lives.

Income can be transferred from the relatively well-to-do to the relatively poor by various methods, and as a nation we have been using them for a long time. Today, we have a vast array of welfare programs set up for the purpose of redistributing income. As we know, however, these programs have not been entirely successful. Are there alternatives to our current welfare system? Is there a better method of helping the poor? Before we answer these questions, take a look at Figure 30-5 on the following page, which displays the percentage of the U.S. population determined to be in a state of poverty by the U.S. government. This percentage, called the *poverty rate*, has varied between roughly 11 percent and 16 percent since 1965.

Defining Poverty

The threshold income level, which is used to determine who falls into the poverty category, was originally based on the cost of a nutritionally adequate food plan designed by the U.S. Department of Agriculture. The threshold was determined by multiplying the food plan cost by 3 on the assumption that food expenses comprise approximately one-third of a poor family's income. Annual revisions of the threshold level were based only on price changes in the food budget.

In 1969, a federal interagency committee looked at the calculations of the threshold and decided to set new standards, with adjustments made on the basis of changes in the Consumer Price Index. For example, in 2013, the official poverty level for an urban family of four was around $23,000. It typically goes up each year to reflect whatever inflation has occurred.

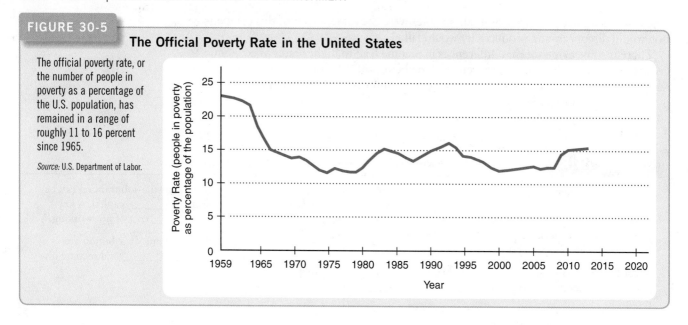

FIGURE 30-5

The Official Poverty Rate in the United States

The official poverty rate, or the number of people in poverty as a percentage of the U.S. population, has remained in a range of roughly 11 to 16 percent since 1965.

Source: U.S. Department of Labor.

Absolute Poverty

Go to www.econtoday.com/chap30 to learn about the World Bank's programs intended to combat global poverty.

Because the low-income threshold is an absolute measure, we know that if it never changes in real terms, we will reduce poverty even if we do nothing. How can that be? The reasoning is straightforward. Real incomes in the United States have been growing at a compounded annual rate of almost 2 percent per capita for at least the past century and at about 2.5 percent since World War II. If we define the poverty line at a specific real income level, more and more individuals will make incomes that exceed that poverty line. Thus, in absolute terms, we will eliminate poverty (assuming continued per capita growth and no change in income distribution).

Relative Poverty

Be careful with this analysis, however. Poverty can also be defined in relative terms, that is, in terms of the income levels of individuals or families relative to the rest of the population. As long as the distribution of income is not perfectly equal, there will always be some people who make less income than others, even if their relatively low income is high by historical standards. Thus, in a relative sense, the problem of poverty will always exist.

Attacks on Poverty: Major Income Maintenance Programs

There are a variety of income maintenance programs designed to help the poor. We examine a few of them here.

SOCIAL SECURITY For the retired, the unemployed, and the disabled, social insurance programs provide income payments in prescribed situations. The best known is Social Security, which includes what has been called old-age, survivors', and disability insurance (OASDI). As discussed in Chapter 6, this was originally supposed to be a program of compulsory saving financed from payroll taxes levied on both employers and employees. Workers pay for Social Security while working and receive the benefits after retirement. The benefit payments are usually made to people who have reached retirement age. When the insured worker dies, benefits accrue to the survivors, including widows and children. Special benefits provide for disabled workers.

More than 90 percent of all employed persons in the United States are covered by OASDI. Today, Social Security is an intergenerational income transfer that is only vaguely related to past earnings. It transfers income from U.S. residents who work (the young through the middle-aged) to those who do not work—older retired persons.

In 2013, more than 55 million people were receiving OASDI checks averaging about $1,200 a month. Benefit payments from OASDI redistribute income to some degree. Benefit payments, however, are not based on recipient need. Participants' contributions give them the right to benefits even if they would be financially secure without the benefits. Social Security is not really an insurance program because people are not guaranteed that the benefits they receive will be in line with the "contributions" they have made. It is not a personal savings account. The benefits are legislated by Congress. In the future, Congress may not be as sympathetic toward older people as it is today. It could (and probably will have to) legislate for lower real levels of benefits instead of higher ones.

SUPPLEMENTAL SECURITY INCOME AND TEMPORARY ASSISTANCE TO NEEDY FAMILIES Many people who are poor but do not qualify for Social Security benefits are assisted through other programs. The federally financed and administered Supplemental Security Income (SSI) program was instituted in 1974. The purpose of SSI is to establish a nationwide minimum income for the aged, the blind, and the disabled. SSI has become one of the fastest-growing transfer programs in the United States. Whereas in 1974 less than $8 billion was spent, the prediction for 2014 is in excess of $60 billion. U.S. residents currently eligible for SSI include children and individuals with mental disabilities, including drug addicts and alcoholics.

Temporary Assistance to Needy Families (TANF) is a state-administered program, financed in part by federal grants. The program provides aid to families in need. TANF payments are intended to be temporary. Projected expenditures for TANF in 2013 are $35 billion.

SUPPLEMENTAL NUTRITION ASSISTANCE PROGRAM The Supplemental Nutrition Assistance Program (SNAP, commonly known as "food stamps") provides government-issued, electronic debit cards that can be used to purchase food. In 1964, some 367,000 Americans were receiving SNAP benefits. For 2013, the estimate is more than 47 million recipients. The annual cost has jumped from $860,000 to more than $80 billion. In 2013, almost one in every seven citizens (including children) was receiving SNAP benefits.

THE EARNED INCOME TAX CREDIT PROGRAM In 1975, the Earned Income Tax Credit (EITC) Program was created to provide rebates of Social Security taxes to low-income workers. More than one-fifth of all tax returns claim an earned income tax credit. Each year the federal government grants more than $46 billion in these credits. In some states, such as Mississippi, nearly half of all families are eligible for an EITC. The program works as follows: Single-income households with two children that report income of about $42,000 (exclusive of welfare payments) receive EITC benefits up to about $5,000.

There is a catch, though. Those with earnings up to a threshold of about $13,000 receive higher benefits as their incomes rise. But families earning more than this threshold income are penalized about 18 cents for every dollar they earn above the income threshold. Thus, on net the EITC discourages work by low- or moderate-income earners more than it rewards work. In particular, it discourages low-income earners from taking on second jobs. The Government Accountability Office estimates that hours worked by working wives in EITC-beneficiary households have consequently decreased by 15 percent. The average EITC recipient works 1,700 hours a year compared to a normal work year of about 2,000 hours.

No Apparent Reduction in Poverty Rates

In spite of the numerous programs in existence and the trillions of dollars transferred to the poor, the officially defined rate of poverty in the United States has shown no long-run tendency to decline. From 1945 until the 1970s, the percentage of U.S. residents in poverty fell steadily every year. As Figure 30-5 on the facing page shows, it reached a low of around 11 percent in 1974, shot back up beyond 15 percent in 1983, fell to nearly 12 percent by 2007, and has since risen above 15 percent once more. Why this pattern has emerged is a puzzle. Since the War on Poverty was launched under President Lyndon B. Johnson in 1965, more than $15 trillion has been transferred to the poor, and yet more U.S. residents are poor today than ever before. This fact created the political will to pass the Welfare Reform Act of 1996, putting limits on people's use of welfare. The law's goal has been to get people off public assistance and into jobs.

QUICK QUIZ See page 687 for the answers. Review concepts from this section in MyEconLab.

If poverty is defined in _____ terms, economic growth eventually decreases the number of officially defined poor. If poverty is defined in _____ terms, however, we will never eliminate it.

The percentage of people officially in poverty exhibits _____ apparent change over time because the official U.S. poverty measure is _____.

Major attacks on poverty have been made through social insurance programs, including _____ Security, _____ Security Income (SSI), Temporary Assistance to Needy Families, the _____ _____ tax credit, and the Supplemental _____ Assistance Program.

Health Care

It may seem strange to be reading about health care in a chapter on the distribution of income and poverty. Yet health care is intimately related to those two topics. For example, sometimes people become poor because they do not have adequate health insurance (or have none at all), fall ill, and deplete all of their wealth in obtaining medical care. Moreover, some individuals remain in certain jobs simply because their employer's health care package seems so good that they are afraid to change jobs and risk not being covered by health insurance in the process.

As you will see, much of the cause of the increased health care spending in the United States can be attributed to a change in the incentives that U.S. residents face. Finally, we will examine the economic impact of the new national health care program.

The U.S. Health Care Situation

Spending for health care is estimated to account for about 17 percent of U.S. real GDP. You can see from Figure 30-6 on the facing page that in 1965, about 6 percent of annual income was spent on health care, but that percentage has been increasing ever since.

WHY HAVE HEALTH CARE COSTS RISEN SO MUCH? There are numerous explanations for why health care costs have risen so much. At least one has to do with changing demographics: The U.S. population is getting older.

The Age–Health Care Expenditure Equation The top 5 percent of health care users incur more than 50 percent of all health costs. The bottom 70 percent of health care users account for only 10 percent of health care expenditures. Not surprisingly, the elderly make up most of the top users of health care services. Nursing home expenditures are made primarily by people older than 70. The use of hospitals is also dominated by the aged.

The U.S. population is aging steadily. More than 13 percent of the 315 million U.S. residents are over 65. It is estimated that by the year 2035, senior citizens will comprise about 22 percent of our population. This aging population stimulates the demand for health care. The elderly consume more than four times as much per capita health care services as the rest of the population. In short, whatever the demand for health care services is today, it is likely to be considerably higher in the future as the U.S. population ages.

FIGURE 30-6

Percentage of Total National Income Spent on Health Care in the United States

The portion of total national income spent on health care has risen steadily since 1965.

Sources: U.S. Department of Commerce; U.S. Department of Health and Human Services; Deloitte and Touche LLP; VHA, Inc.

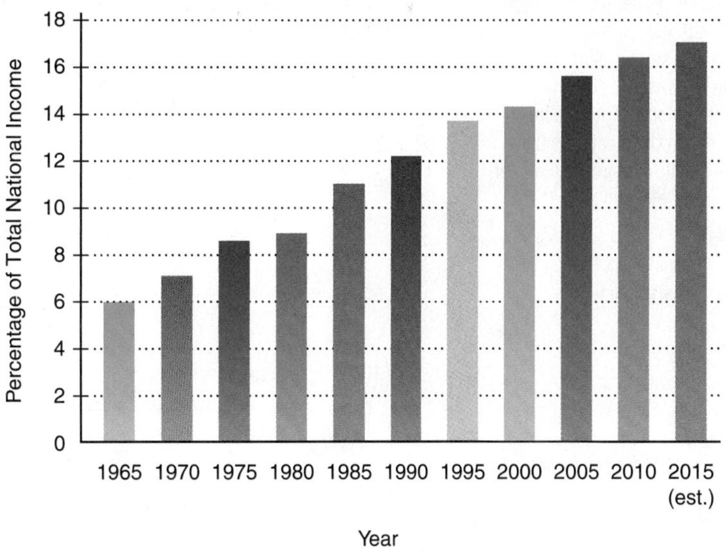

New Technologies Another reason that health care costs have risen so dramatically is advancing technology. Each CT (computerized tomography) scanner costs at least $100,000. An MRI (magnetic resonance imaging) scanner can cost over $2 million. A PET (positron emission tomography) scanner costs around $4 million. All of these machines have become increasingly available in recent decades and are desired throughout the country. Typical fees for procedures using them range from $300 to $400 for a CT scan to as high as $2,000 for a PET scan. The development of new technologies that help physicians and hospitals prolong human life is an ongoing process in an ever-advancing industry. New procedures at even higher prices can be expected in the future.

WHAT IF... the government forced lower spending on health care by placing legal limits on prices?

Legal ceilings on prices of health care services would reduce the quantities of services offered by physicians and hospitals, which would indeed generate a decrease in total annual expenditures on health care. By definition, of course, the resulting reductions in health care services would be associated with the inability of many people to obtain, at legally limited prices, care for painful and potentially deadly illnesses or injuries.

Third-Party Financing Currently, government spending on health care constitutes more than 40 percent of total health care spending (of which *federal* taxpayers fund about 70 percent). Private insurance funded by consumers' premium payments accounts for a little over 35 percent of payments for health care. The remainder—less than 20 percent—is paid out of pocket by individuals. Figure 30-7 on the following page shows the change in the payment scheme for medical care in the United States since 1930. Medicare and Medicaid are the main sources of hospital and other medical benefits for more than 40 million U.S. residents, most of whom are over 65. Medicaid—the joint state-federal program—provides long-term health care, particularly for people living in nursing homes.

FIGURE 30-7

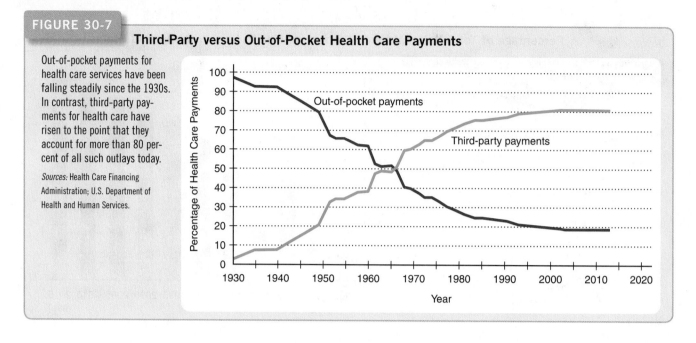

FIGURE 30-7

Third-Party versus Out-of-Pocket Health Care Payments

Out-of-pocket payments for health care services have been falling steadily since the 1930s. In contrast, third-party payments for health care have risen to the point that they account for more than 80 percent of all such outlays today.

Sources: Health Care Financing Administration; U.S. Department of Health and Human Services.

Third parties
Parties who are not directly involved in a given activity or transaction. For example, in the relationship between caregivers and patients, fees may be paid by third parties (insurance companies, government).

Medicare, Medicaid, and private insurance companies are considered **third parties** in the medical care equation. Caregivers and patients are the two primary parties. When third parties step in to pay for medical care, the quantity demanded of those services increases. For example, within four years after Medicare went into effect in 1966, the volume of federal government–reimbursed medical services increased to a level 65 percent higher than anticipated when the program was enacted.

PRICE, QUANTITY DEMANDED, AND THE QUESTION OF MORAL HAZARD Although some people may think that the demand for health care is insensitive to price changes, significant increases in quantities of medical services demanded follow reductions in people's out-of-pocket costs. Look at Figure 30-8 below. There you see a hypothetical demand curve for health care services. To the extent that third parties—whether government or private insurance—pay for health care, the out-of-pocket cost, or net price, to the individual decreases. If all medical expenses were paid for by third parties, dropping the price to zero in Figure 30-8, the quantity demanded would increase.

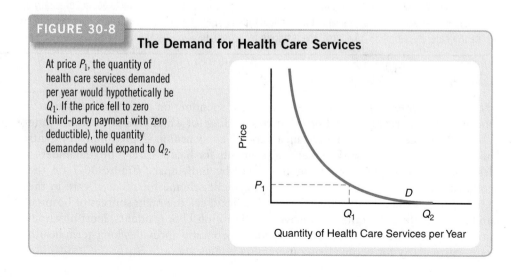

FIGURE 30-8

The Demand for Health Care Services

At price P_1, the quantity of health care services demanded per year would hypothetically be Q_1. If the price fell to zero (third-party payment with zero deductible), the quantity demanded would expand to Q_2.

One of the issues here has to do with the problem of *moral hazard*. Consider two individuals with two different health insurance policies. The first policy pays for all medical expenses, but under the second, the individual has to pay the first $1,000 a year (this amount is known as the *deductible*). Will the behavior of the two individuals be different? Generally, the answer is yes.

The individual with no deductible is more likely to seek treatment for health problems after they develop rather than try to avoid them and will generally seek medical attention on a more regular basis. In contrast, the individual who faces the first $1,000 of medical expenses each year will tend to engage in more wellness activities and will be less inclined to seek medical care for minor problems. The moral hazard here is that the individual with the zero deductible for medical care expenses will tend to engage in a less healthful lifestyle than will the individual with the $1,000 deductible.

MORAL HAZARD AS IT AFFECTS PHYSICIANS AND HOSPITALS The issue of moral hazard also has a direct effect on the behavior of physicians and hospital administrators. Due to third-party payments, patients rarely have to worry about the expense of operations and other medical procedures. As a consequence, both physicians and hospitals order more procedures. Physicians are typically reimbursed on the basis of medical procedures. Thus, they have no financial interest in trying to keep hospital costs down. Indeed, many have an incentive to increase costs.

Such actions are most evident with terminally ill patients. A physician may order a CT scan and other costly procedures for a terminally ill patient. The physician knows that Medicare or some other type of insurance will pay. Then the physician can charge a fee for analyzing the CT scan. Fully 30 percent of Medicare expenditures are for U.S. residents who are in the last six months of their lives.

Rising Medicare expenditures are one of the most serious problems facing the federal government today. The number of beneficiaries has increased from 19.1 million in 1966 (first year of operation) to more than 40 million in 2013. Figure 30-9 below shows that federal spending on Medicare has been growing at an average of about 10 percent per year, adjusted for inflation. The rate of growth in Medicare spending has further increased as a result of the Medicare prescription drug benefit that was implemented in 2006.

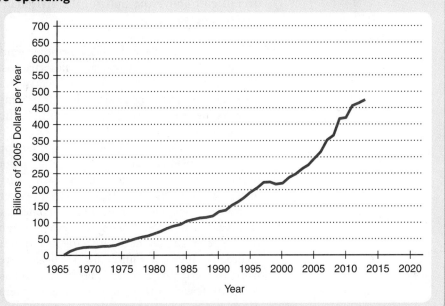

FIGURE 30-9

Federal Medicare Spending

Federal spending on Medicare has increased about 10 percent per year, *after adjusting for inflation*, since its inception in 1966. (All figures expressed in constant 2005 dollars per year.)

Sources: *Economic Report of the President*; U.S. Bureau of Labor Statistics.

How are people who receive "dual coverage" from both Medicare and Medicaid pushing up the federal government's overall health care expenses?

POLICY EXAMPLE

Dual Coverage Drives Up Federal Health Care Spending

At present, 61 million elderly and disabled people are enrolled in Medicare, and 65 million low-income people are covered by Medicaid. Both groups of people include about 10 million individuals who qualify for "dual coverage," meaning that their health care expenses are eligible for coverage by *both* federal programs simultaneously. Poor administrative coordination between Medicare and Medicaid gives a health care provider an incentive to send a bill for each service provided to a dual-coverage patient to whichever program reimburses the service at a higher rate. This fact helps explain why dual-coverage patients generate one-third of the federal government's total combined spending on Medicare and Medicaid.

FOR CRITICAL THINKING

Why do you suppose that most health care economists agree that tens of billions of dollars per year could be slashed from federal spending if the Medicare and Medicaid programs offered identical reimbursements to health care providers?

The Nationalization of U.S. Health Care Spending

In March 2010, President Barack Obama signed a roughly 2,000-page law that will govern the future operation of U.S. health care markets. Before we contemplate the law's likely effect on the economics of health care, let's review its key features.

GOVERNMENT HEALTH INSURANCE MANDATES Table 30-2 on the facing page summarizes the fundamental components of the federal government's new national health care program, which is to be phased in through the mid-2010s. The first two elements of the program are restraints on choices of individuals and families and on decisions of employers. People must either purchase health insurance or pay a fine to the federal government. Thus, a young person in good health who otherwise might have opted not to purchase health insurance must buy insurance or pay a penalty (tax).

In addition, firms with more than 50 employees must either provide health insurance or pay fines when uninsured employees receive tax subsidies to purchase insurance. A firm that otherwise would have hired another worker but determines that the additional cost imposed by the health care program pushes the overall cost above the individual's marginal revenue product will choose not to hire that person.

GOVERNMENT HEALTH CARE SUBSIDIES Another fundamental feature is federal health care subsidies. The government's subsidies vary based on individual and family incomes. The national health care program directs more relatively low-income people into the Medicaid program by raising the maximum-income threshold for government-provided health care to 133 percent of the official poverty level. As a result, millions of people may now qualify for the Medicaid program's coverage of health care with very few out-of-pocket payments (depending on their state).

Other individuals and families earning incomes as high as four times the official poverty income level receive *tax subsidies*. These are reductions in federal tax payments intended to assist these people in covering required expenditures on health insurance. Thus, some families with incomes exceeding $100,000 per year will receive tax breaks of about $2,400—some of their own income that the government will allow them to keep and direct to satisfying its requirement to buy health insurance. Lower-income families not eligible for Medicaid coverage receive larger tax subsidies. Finally, the program also offers tax credits to businesses that provide health insurance to 25 or fewer workers who receive an average salary of no more than $50,000 per year.

TABLE 30-2

Key Components of the Federal Government's National Health Care Program

Individual mandate	Nearly all U.S. residents must either purchase health insurance coverage or pay a fine (tax) of up to $750 per year for an individual (up to $2,250 per year for a family).
Employer mandate	Firms with more than 50 employees must offer health insurance coverage or pay an annual fine of up to $750 per employee who obtains federal subsidies for coverage.
Health care insurance subsidies	1. Families with incomes up to 133% of the federal poverty level may be eligible for federal Medicaid coverage. 2. Families with incomes up to 400% of the federal poverty level are eligible for thousands of dollars in tax subsidies per year (amounts vary with family incomes). 3. Tax credits are available to businesses providing health insurance to 25 or fewer workers and paying annual salaries averaging no more than $50,000.
National health insurance exchanges	Government-directed exchanges will assist in matching individuals and small businesses with health insurance policies that satisfy government requirements.
Health insurance regulations	1. All private health insurance plans must satisfy a number of federal rules and regulations. 2. Health insurers must cover all who apply, including people who already have health problems. 3. Ceilings are placed on health insurance premium increases for elderly people.
Higher tax rates to help fund the program	A special tax rate of 3.8% is applied to certain income earnings above $200,000 for individuals or $250,000 for married couples.

GOVERNMENT HEALTH INSURANCE EXCHANGES Under the new program, the federal government will coordinate the establishment of **health insurance exchanges.** These are government agencies tasked with helping individuals and families—especially the roughly 30 million additional people who will obtain health insurance—find policies to buy. The exchanges, which state governments are charged with operating, also will assist small businesses in finding health insurance they can purchase for employees.

REGULATIONS AND TAXES The national health care program also imposes new federal regulations on health care insurers and assesses special tax rates on higher-income families to help finance the tax subsidies extended to lower-income families. All health insurance policies now must satisfy a variety of requirements. For example, insurers cannot deny anyone health insurance, and a ceiling is imposed on the rate of increase in health insurance prices charged to elderly people.

Finally, the national health care plan imposes a special health care tax. A tax rate of 3.8 percent will be assessed on certain earnings above $200,000 per year for individuals and above $250,000 per year for married couples.

Health insurance exchanges
Government agencies to which the national health care program assigns the task of assisting individuals, families, and small businesses in identifying health insurance policies to purchase.

Economic Effects of the National Health Care Program

Naturally, the new U.S. health care program will have significant effects on health care markets. In addition, the program will also have effects on labor markets, product markets, and government budgets.

HIGHER HEALTH CARE SPENDING AND A WORSENED MORAL HAZARD PROBLEM The government's national health care program enlarges the scope of third-party payments for health care services. As we noted earlier, health care expenditures already consume about 17 percent of national income. The program promises to boost that spending and to expand the size of the moral hazard problem in U.S. health care markets.

Once the national health care program goes into effect during the mid-2010s, tens of millions of people will pay fewer of their health care expenses out of their own pockets than they did previously. This change will have three primary consequences. First, because the price people actually pay out of their own pockets to consume health care services will decline, the quantity of health care services demanded will increase. Second, because health insurers will be required to cover this expanded quantity demanded of services, total expenditures on health care will increase. Third, there will be an increased moral hazard problem. Because people will pay a smaller portion of the actual cost of treating health problems, more individuals will have reduced incentives to make decisions that promote better health. As people have more health problems as a consequence of this rise in moral hazard, the demand for health care will increase.

What types of costs are many Greek hospital patients incurring to obtain government-funded health care?

INTERNATIONAL POLICY EXAMPLE

In Greece, "Free" Care Now Includes Substantial Implicit Costs

Any Greek resident is entitled to health care provided by a plan called IKA National Insurance. IKA instructs holders of an IKA health care card to make an appointment with a physician or dentist, fill out a form, and arrive on time to receive care at no explicit cost. IKA also covers all forms of hospital care.

All Greek hospitals are financed directly by the nation's government, which recently has had difficulties borrowing sufficient funds to cover its high budget deficits. As a consequence, hospitals are often short of funds to pay their bills, including bills for medications obtained from pharmaceuticals companies. When Greek hospitals failed to pay for more than 60 percent of the market value of medications they received, Roche and other drug firms halted additional hospital medication deliveries. After hospitals exhaust their inventories of drugs, patients must sign out of their hospital rooms and go to private pharmacies, which usually have the drugs in stock because they acquire the drugs in advance. After the patients use their IKA cards to obtain the required medications, the hospitals readmit them, and their physicians begin administering the drugs. Thus, the pharmaceuticals are explicitly "free," but patients incur significant implicit costs.

FOR CRITICAL THINKING
If patients experience extremely long waits to obtain dental care through IKA, is the care really "free"?

IMPACTS ON THE REST OF THE U.S. ECONOMY Implementation of the new national health care program will have effects on labor markets, markets for goods and services, and budgets of federal and state governments:

1. *Labor market impacts.* In labor markets, the requirement for many firms to provide health insurance will raise the effective wage rate that they must pay for each unit of labor. Recall from Chapter 28 that firms employ labor to the point at which the marginal revenue product of labor—marginal revenue times the marginal physical product—equals the wage rate. The increase in the effective wage rate will induce firms to move upward along their downward-sloping marginal-revenue-product-of-labor curves. Thus, the quantity of labor demanded by firms will decline. Other things being equal, U.S. employment will be lower than it otherwise would have been.

2. *Markets for goods and services.* In markets for goods and services, the increase in labor costs firms incur in hiring each unit of labor will raise their marginal costs. Because

each firm maximizes profits by producing to the point at which marginal revenue equals marginal cost, the increase in marginal costs will induce firms to decrease their output at all prices. Other things being equal, this will place pressure on equilibrium prices to rise in a number of markets. Consequently, consumers will pay higher inflation-adjusted prices for many goods and services.

3. *Effects on government budgets.* The new tax rate applied to higher-income individuals went into effect in 2013, so tax revenues began flowing into the new program at that time. Federal government expenditures on the program are being phased in more gradually, so the program initially is being financed by the revenues collected in advance. Most observers agree, however, that the new tax revenues will be insufficient to cover the increases in government health care spending that surely will occur in future years. Hence, the federal government ultimately will have to search for ways to reduce its health care expenditures or to raise more tax revenues to fund the program. The federal program does not include revenues for states to cover the higher expenses of the additional people that may be admitted to the Medicaid program, which state governments administer. Thus, state governments will also face pressures to boost tax revenues.

QUICK QUIZ   See page 687 for the answers. Review concepts from this section in MyEconLab.

The U.S. national health care program adopted in 2010 expands the scope of health care coverage across millions of additional people by covering more lower-income people under the existing _____ program and by subsidizing health care expenses for people with incomes up to _____ percent of the poverty income level.

Key elements of the national health care program include _____ for individuals to buy health insurance and for firms employing more than 50 workers to provide insurance access or pay fines; establishment of government-operated

_____ to assist individuals and small businesses in finding health insurance plans; a requirement for health insurers to accept _____ applicants; and imposition of a new _____ on high-income earners.

Economic analysis suggests that likely effects of the adoption of the national health care program include _____ employment in U.S. labor markets, _____ prices of goods and services for consumers, and a _____ shortfall of federal and state tax revenues in relation to government expenses.

YOU ARE THERE

A Portuguese Woman Rethinks Her Human Capital Investment

Isabel Fernandes is a 22-year-old Portuguese woman who stopped attending school after the eighth grade. Hence, she is among the 72 percent of residents of Portugal between the ages of 25 and 64 who did not complete high school. She has been finding it difficult to obtain a job because employers "are asking for higher education."

To improve her employment prospects, Fernandes has become a part-time student at a private, nonprofit school. Friends have told her that completing high school might give her sufficient background to wait tables at restaurants. Fernandes has also learned that obtaining a college degree in Portugal would enable her to find a higher-paying occupation—offering perhaps twice the wages she could earn as a high school graduate serving

customers at restaurants. Nevertheless, her current dream job is waiting tables. Her immediate job search centers on finding a position as a cleaning woman, which she hopes might yield sufficient income to get by while she works to complete the ninth grade.

Critical Thinking Questions

1. Why do you suppose that average incomes in Portugal lag far behind average incomes in most other European nations?

2. How would completing high school likely affect Fernandes's age-earnings profile?

ISSUES & APPLICATIONS

Why Is the Female Income Gap Shrinking?

CONCEPTS APPLIED

▶ Distribution of Income

▶ Investment in Human Capital

▶ Age-Earnings Cycle

For many years, the U.S. income distribution favored male wage earners, because women experienced a pay gap in comparison with men. Over time, though, the distribution of income between the genders has been evening out.

The Female Income Gap

As Figure 30-10 below shows, women earn lower average incomes than men. It also reveals, however, that the gap between the average female income and the average male income has dropped from 37 percent in 1980 to about 17 percent today.

What accounts for the shrinkage of the female income gap? Most economists agree that the key explanation is a substantial increase in female investment in human capital. For a number of years, more females than males have graduated from U.S. high schools. Since 1996, more women than men have held bachelor's degrees. Today, 20 million women have bachelor's degrees, compared with 18.7 million men. Furthermore, 100,000 more women than men have obtained master's and doctoral degrees each year

since 2010. Thus, women are now better trained for many higher-income jobs.

Could the Income Gap between Men and Women Disappear?

Overall, women currently are earning 57 percent of the degrees issued each year by U.S. colleges and universities. This fact means that the flow of women into higher-income positions that require educational training is likely to more than keep pace with the flow of men into such jobs.

At the same time, female workers of prior generations who did not receive as much education and hence earned less than their male counterparts will begin departing the

---

FIGURE 30-10

The Shrinking Female Income Gap

The percentage differential between the average income earned by female workers and male workers has decreased to less than half of its 1980 level.

Sources: U.S. Department of Labor; author's estimate.

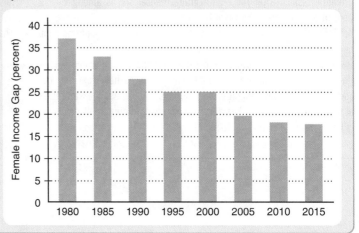

workforce during the coming years. As age-earnings cycles readjust for the two genders, the average income earned by female workers undoubtedly will continue to climb in relation to the average income of male workers. Thus, the female wage gap should dissipate over time and in principle really could disappear at some point in the future.

For Critical Thinking

1. How is the fact that more low-income families are sending daughters, rather than sons, to college likely to affect the female income gap in the future?

2. Why do you think economists argue that the female wage gap will not entirely disappear unless women earn more degrees in sciences and business?

Web Resources

1. To learn about one country in which young women are already earning a higher average income than young men, go to **www.econtoday.com/chap30**.

2. For a view suggesting that young U.S. women have already closed the income gap with men, go to **www.econtoday.com/chap30**.

MyEconLab

For more questions on this chapter's Issues & Applications, go to MyEconLab. In the Study Plan for this chapter, select Section N: News.

MyEconLab

Here is what you should know after reading this chapter. MyEconLab will help you identify what you know, and where to go when you need to practice.

WHAT YOU SHOULD KNOW		WHERE TO GO TO PRACTICE
Using a Lorenz Curve to Represent a Nation's Income Distribution A Lorenz curve depicts the distribution of income geometrically by measuring the percentage of households in relation to the cumulative percentage of income earnings. A perfectly straight Lorenz curve depicts perfect income equality because at each percentage of households measured along a straight-line Lorenz curve, those households earn exactly the same percentage of income. The more bowed a Lorenz curve is, the more unequally income is distributed.	distribution of income, 664 Lorenz curve, 664 income in kind, 664 **Key Figures** Figure 30-1, 665 Figure 30-2, 665	• MyEconLab Study Plan 30.1 • Animated Figures 30-1, 30-2
Key Determinants of Income Differences across Individuals Because of the age-earnings cycle, in which people typically earn relatively low incomes when young, age is an important factor influencing income differences. So are marginal productivity differences, which arise from variations in talent, experience, and training due to different investments in human capital.	age-earnings cycle, 668 **Key Figure** Figure 30-4, 668	• MyEconLab Study Plan 30.2 • Animated Figure 30-4

MyEconLab *continued*

Theories of Desired Income Distribution
One theory of desired income distribution is the productivity standard (also called the contributive or merit standard), according to which each person receives income based on the value of what he or she produces. The other is the egalitarian principle of income distribution, which proposes that each person should receive exactly the same income.

- MyEconLab Study Plan 30.3

Alternative Approaches to Measuring and Addressing Poverty One approach to measuring poverty is to define an absolute poverty standard. Another approach defines poverty in terms of income levels *relative* to the rest of the population. Currently, the U.S. government seeks to address poverty via income maintenance programs such as Social Security, Supplemental Security Income, Temporary Assistance to Needy Families, Supplemental Nutrition Assistance Program benefits, and the Earned Income Tax Credit Program.

Key Figure
Figure 30-5, 672

- MyEconLab Study Plan 30.4
- Animated Figure 30-5

Rising Health Care Costs and Third-Party Payments Spending on health care has been rising as a percentage of total U.S. national income. Third-party financing of health care expenditures by private and government insurance programs provides an incentive to buy more health care than if all expenses were paid out of pocket.

third parties, 676

Key Figures
Figure 30-6, 675
Figure 30-7, 676
Figure 30-8, 676

- MyEconLab Study Plan 30.5
- Animated Figures 30-6, 30-7, 30-8

Key Provisions of the New U.S. National Health Insurance Program The national health care program adopted in March 2010 requires all individuals to purchase health insurance and mandates that firms with more than 50 employees either provide health insurance or pay penalties. The program places more lower-income people in the Medicaid program and subsidizes health insurance for families with incomes up to 400 percent of the official poverty level. To help finance the program, people earning incomes above relatively high thresholds will face a special 3.8 percent tax rate applied to certain sources of income above those thresholds.

health insurance exchanges, 679

- MyEconLab Study Plan 30.5

Log in to MyEconLab, take a chapter test, and get a personalized Study Plan that tells you which concepts you understand and which ones you need to review. From there, MyEconLab will give you further practice, tutorials, animations, videos, and guided solutions. For more information, visit www.myeconlab.com

PROBLEMS

All problems are assignable in MyEconLab. *Answers to the odd-numbered problems appear at the back of the book.*

30-1. Consider the graph below, which depicts Lorenz curves for countries X, Y, and Z. (See page 665.)

   a. Which country has the least income inequality?

   b. Which country has the most income inequality?

   c. Countries Y and Z are identical in all but one respect: population distribution. The share of the population made up of children below working age is much higher in country Z. Recently, however, birthrates have declined in country Z and risen in country Y. Assuming that the countries remain identical in all other respects, would you expect that in 20 years the Lorenz curves for the two countries will be closer together or farther apart? (Hint: According to the age-earnings cycle, what typically happens to income as an individual begins working and ages?)

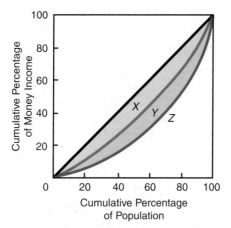

30-2. Consider the following estimates from the early 2010s of shares of income to each group. Use graph paper or a hand-drawn diagram to draw rough Lorenz curves for each country. Which has the most nearly equal distribution, based on your diagram? (See page 666.)

Country	Poorest 40%	Next 30%	Next 20%	Richest 10%
Bolivia	13	21	26	40
Chile	13	20	26	41
Uruguay	22	26	26	26

30-3. Suppose that the 20 percent of people with the highest incomes decide to increase their annual giving to charities, which pass nearly all the funds on to the 20 percent of people with the lowest incomes. What is the effect on the shape of the Lorenz curve? (See pages 665–666.)

30-4. Suppose that a nation has implemented a system for applying a tax rate of 2 percent to the incomes earned by the 10 percent of its residents with the highest incomes. All funds collected are then transferred directly to the 10 percent of the nation's residents with the lowest incomes. (See pages 665–666.)

   a. What is the general effect on the shape of a Lorenz curve based on incomes prior to collection and redistribution of the tax?

   b. What is the general effect on the shape of a Lorenz curve based on incomes after collection and redistribution of the tax?

30-5. Estimates indicate that during the early 2010s, the poorest 40 percent of the population earned about 15 percent of total income in Argentina. In Brazil, the poorest 40 percent earned about 10 percent of total income. The next-highest 30 percent of income earners in Argentina received roughly 25 percent of total income. In Brazil, the next-highest 30 percent of income earners received approximately 20 percent of total income. Can you determine, without drawing a diagram (though you can if you wish), which country's Lorenz curve was bowed out farther to the right? (See pages 665–666.)

30-6. Explain why the productivity standard for the distribution of income entails rewarding people based on their contribution to society's total output. Why does the productivity standard typically fail to yield an equal distribution of income? (See page 670.)

30-7. Identify whether each of the following proposed poverty measures is an absolute or relative measure of poverty, and discuss whether poverty could ever be eliminated if that measure were utilized. (See page 672.)

   a. An inflation-adjusted annual income of $25,000 for an urban family of four

   b. Individuals with annual incomes among the lowest 15 percent

   c. An inflation-adjusted annual income of $10,000 per person

30-8. Some economists have argued that if the government wishes to subsidize health care, it should instead provide predetermined amounts of payments (based on the type of health care problems experienced) directly to patients, who then would be free to choose their health care providers. Whether or not you agree, can you give an economic rationale for this approach to governmental health care funding? (See page 676.)

30-9. Suppose that a government agency guarantees to pay all of an individual's future health care expenses after the end of this year, so that the effective price of health care for the individual will be zero from that date onward. In what ways might this well-intended policy induce the individual to consume "excessive" health care services in future years? (See pages 675–676.)

30-10. Suppose that a group of physicians establishes a joint practice in a remote area. This group provides the only health care available to people in the local community, and its objective is to maximize total economic profits for the group's members. Draw a diagram illustrating how the price and quantity of health care will be determined in this community. (See page 676. Hint: How does a single producer of any service determine its output and price?)

30-11. A government agency determines that the entire community discussed in Problem 30-12 qualifies for a special program in which the government will pay for a number of health care services that most residents previously had not consumed. Many residents immediately make appointments with the community physicians' group. Given the information in Problem 30-12, what is the likely effect on the profit-maximizing price and the equilibrium quantity of health care services provided by the physicians' group in this community? (See page 676.)

30-12. A government agency notifies the physicians' group in Problem 30-12 that to continue providing services in the community, the group must document its activities. The resulting paperwork expenses raise the cost of each unit of health care services that the group provides. What is the likely effect on the profit-maximizing price and the equilibrium quantity of health care services provided by the physicians' group in this community? (See page 676.)

ECONOMICS ON THE NET

Measuring Poverty In this application, you will learn why poverty can be difficult to measure.

Title: World Bank PovertyNet: Understanding Poverty

Navigation: Go to **www.econtoday.com/chap30** to visit the World Bank's home page. Click on *Topics* and then *Poverty Analysis*. Then click on *Measuring Poverty*.

Application Perform the indicated operations, and answer the following questions.

1. Click on "Defining welfare measures." Why does this discussion suggest that measures of consumption are more useful in measuring poverty than income measures? Does the U.S. government's use of income thresholds for its official definition of poverty accord with this discussion?

2. Click on "Choose and estimate a poverty line." What alternative absolute poverty definitions are discussed? If the U.S. government were to adopt any of these absolute measures for its official poverty definition, what would happen to the U.S. poverty rate as real incomes and living standards rise over time?

For Group Study and Analysis Click on "Choose and estimate poverty indicators." What are the advantages and disadvantages of the poverty indicators that are discussed? Which indicator does the U.S. government utilize?

ANSWERS TO QUICK QUIZZES

p. 667: (i) income . . . equality . . . unequally; (ii) assets . . . more

p. 671: (i) age-earnings; (ii) productivity . . . revenue; (iii) talent . . . experience . . . training; (iv) human . . . opportunity; (v) productivity . . . equality

p. 674: (i) absolute . . . relative; (ii) little . . . relative; (iii) Social . . . Supplemental . . . earned income . . . Nutrition

p. 681: (i) Medicaid . . . 400; (ii) mandates . . . exchanges . . . all . . . tax; (iii) lower . . . higher . . . larger

Environmental Economics

31

LEARNING OBJECTIVES

After reading this chapter, you should be able to:

▶ Distinguish between private costs and social costs

▶ Understand market externalities and possible ways to correct externalities

▶ Explain how economists can conceptually determine the optimal quantity of pollution

▶ Contrast the roles of private and common property rights in alternative approaches to addressing the problem of pollution

▶ Describe how many of the world's governments are seeking to reduce pollution by capping and controlling the use of pollution-generating resources

▶ Discuss how the assignment of property rights may influence the fates of endangered species

MyEconLab helps you master each objective and study more efficiently. See end of chapter for details.

"Cap and trade" is an approach to air pollution control under which governments place a limit on allowed emissions, create rights to emit polluting substances, and permit firms to trade those rights in a free market. One example is a U.S. cap-and-trade program narrowly focused on limiting sulfur dioxide emissions. This program, which focused on electrical power plants in midwestern states, has been credited with reducing such emissions by about one-half. Governments in Europe and California recently implemented cap-and-trade programs aimed more broadly at controlling release of all emissions into the atmosphere. These governments indicated their wish to emulate the successes of the U.S. sulfur dioxide cap-and-trade program. This U.S. program recently collapsed, however. What can administrators of similar programs learn from this program's breakdown? What are alternative approaches to limiting pollution? This chapter provides the answers.

the Environmental Protection Agency (EPA) is requiring that by 2025, all U.S. passenger vehicles will have to operate at an average of 54.5 miles per gallon, more than twice the current average of 27 miles per gallon? The EPA's projections indicate that attaining this gas-mileage limit will substantially reduce the release of air pollutants and "greenhouse gases"—such as carbon dioxide—into the air. In addition, though, other government estimates indicate that complying with the regulations will raise automakers' costs sufficiently to yield at least a 10 percent increase in the average price of a vehicle. Consumers, of course, will have to pay these higher prices.

The economic way of thinking about policies intended to reduce air pollutants and greenhouse gases requires that the costs of such policies be considered. Likewise, the economic way of thinking about nonrenewable resources or endangered species requires that we take into account the costs of resource conservation and protection of wildlife. How much of your weekly wages are you willing to sacrifice to be used to reduce aggregate emissions of carbon dioxide, a gas that you exhale every time you breathe? To some people, framing questions in terms of the dollars-and-cents costs of environmental improvement sounds anti-ecological. But this is not so. Economists want to help citizens and policymakers opt for informed policies that have the maximum possible *net* benefits (benefits minus costs). As you will see, every decision made in favor of "the environment" involves a trade-off.

Private versus Social Costs

Human actions often give rise to unwanted side effects—the destruction of our environment is one. Human actions generate pollutants that go into the air and the water. The question often asked is, Why do individuals and businesses continue to create pollution without necessarily paying directly for the negative consequences?

Private Costs

Private costs
Costs borne solely by the individuals who incur them. Also called *internal costs*.

Until now, we've been dealing with settings in which the costs of an individual's actions are borne directly by the individual. When a business has to pay wages to workers, it knows exactly what its labor costs are. When it has to buy materials or build a plant, it knows quite well what these will cost. An individual who has to pay for car repairs or a theater ticket knows exactly what the cost will be. These costs are what we term *private costs*. **Private costs** are borne solely by the individuals who incur them. They are *internal* in the sense that the firm or household must explicitly take account of them.

Social Costs

Social costs
The full costs borne by society whenever a resource use occurs. Social costs can be measured by adding external costs to private, or internal, costs.

Now consider the actions of a business that dumps the waste products from its production process into a nearby river or an individual who litters a public park or beach. Obviously, these actions involve a cost. When the firm pollutes the water, people downstream suffer the consequences. They may not want to swim in or drink the polluted water. They may catch fewer fish than before because of the pollution. In the case of littering, the people who come along after the litterer has cluttered the park or the beach are the ones who bear the costs.

The cost of these actions is borne by people other than those who commit the actions. The creator of the cost is not the sole bearer. The costs are not internalized by the individual or firm—they are external.

When we add *external* costs to *internal*, or private, costs, we obtain **social costs.** Pollution problems—indeed, all problems pertaining to the environment—may be viewed as situations in which social costs exceed private costs. Because some economic participants pay only the smaller private costs of their actions, not the full social costs, their actions ultimately contribute to higher external costs on the rest of society. Therefore, in such situations in which social and private costs diverge, we see "too much" steel production, automobile driving, or beach littering, to name only a few of the many possible examples.

The Costs of Polluted Air

Why is the air in cities so polluted with automobile exhaust fumes? When automobile drivers step into their cars, they bear only the private costs of driving. That is, they must pay for the gas, maintenance, depreciation, and insurance on their automobiles. But they cause an additional cost—air pollution—which they are not forced to take into account when they make the decision to drive.

Air pollution is a cost because it causes harm to individuals—burning eyes, respiratory ailments, and dirtier clothes, cars, and buildings—and adds to accumulations of various gases that may contribute to global warming. The air pollution created by automobile exhausts is a cost that individual operators of automobiles do not yet bear directly. The social cost of driving includes all the private costs plus at least the cost of air pollution, which society bears. Decisions made only on the basis of private costs lead to too much automobile driving. Clean air is a scarce resource used by automobile drivers free of charge. They use more of it than they would if they had to pay the full social costs.

Externalities

When a private cost differs from a social cost, we say that there is an **externality** because individual decision makers are not paying (internalizing) all the costs. (We briefly covered this topic in Chapter 5.) Some of these costs remain external to the decision-making process. Remember that the full cost of using a scarce resource is borne one way or another by all who live in the society. That is, members of society must pay the full opportunity cost of any activity that uses scarce resources. The individual decision maker is the firm or the customer, and external costs and benefits will not enter into that individual's or firm's decision-making processes.

We might want to view the problem as it is presented in Figure 31-1 below. Here we have the market demand curve, D, for product X and the supply curve, S_1, for product X. The supply curve, S_1, includes only internal, or private, costs. The intersection of the demand and supply curves as drawn will be at price P_1 and quantity Q_1 (at E_1). We now assume that the production of good X involves externalities that the private firms did not take into account. Those externalities could be air pollution, water pollution, scenery destruction, or anything of that nature.

Externality

A consequence of a diversion of a private cost (or benefit) from a social cost (or benefit). A situation in which the costs (or benefits) of an action are not fully borne (or gained) by the decision makers engaged in an activity that uses scarce resources.

FIGURE 31-1

Reckoning with Full Social Costs

The supply curve, S_1, is equal to the horizontal summation (represented by the capital Greek letter sigma, Σ) of the individual marginal cost curves above the respective minimum average variable costs of all the firms producing good X. These individual marginal cost curves include only internal, or private, costs.

If the external costs were included and added to the private costs, we would have social costs. The supply curve would shift upward to S_2. In the uncorrected situation, the equilibrium price is P_1, and the equilibrium quantity is Q_1.

In the corrected situation, the equilibrium price would rise to P_2, and the equilibrium quantity would fall to Q_2.

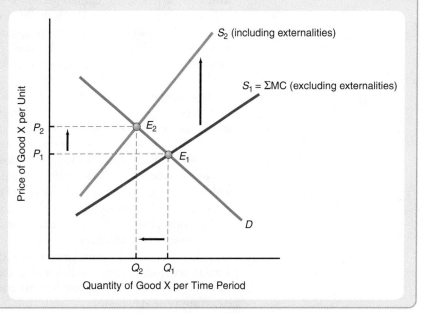

We know that the social costs of producing product X exceed the private costs. We show this by drawing curve S_2. It is above the original supply curve S_1 because it includes the full social costs of producing the product. If firms could be made to bear these costs, their willingness to supply the good would be reduced, so the price would be P_2 and the quantity Q_2 (at E_2). The inclusion of external costs in the decision-making process would lead to a higher-priced product and a decline in quantity produced. Thus, we see that when social costs are not fully borne by the creators of those costs, the quantity produced is "excessive" because the price to consumers is too low.

Correcting for Externalities

We can see here a method for reducing pollution and environmental degradation. Somehow the signals in the economy must be changed so that decision makers will take into account *all* the costs of their actions. In the case of automobile pollution, we might want to devise some method of taxing motorists according to the amount of pollution they cause. In the case of a firm, we might want to devise a system of taxing businesses according to the amount of pollution for which they are responsible. They might then have an incentive to install pollution abatement equipment.

The Polluters' Choice

Facing an additional private cost for polluting, firms will be induced to (1) install pollution abatement equipment or otherwise change production techniques so as to reduce the amount of pollution, (2) reduce pollution-causing activity, or (3) simply pay a government-mandated cost for the right to pollute. The relative costs and benefits of each option for each polluter will determine which one or combination will be chosen.

Allowing the choice is the efficient way to decide who pollutes and who doesn't. In principle, just as with the use of all other scarce resources, each polluter faces the full social cost of its actions and makes a production decision accordingly. No matter what each firm decides, the firm is forced to take into account the additional cost. Hence, the cost of pollution-causing activity is now higher, so pollution will be reduced.

Is a Uniform Tax Appropriate?

It may not be appropriate to levy a *uniform* tax according to physical quantities of pollution. After all, we're talking about external costs. Such costs are not necessarily the same everywhere in the United States for the same action.

Essentially, we must establish the amount of the *economic damages* rather than the amount of the physical pollution. A polluting electrical plant in New York City will cause much more damage than the same plant in Montana. There are already innumerable demands on the air in New York City, so the pollution from smokestacks will not be cleansed away naturally. Millions of people will breathe the polluted air and thereby incur the costs of sore throats, sickness, emphysema, and even early death. Buildings will become dirtier faster because of the pollution, as will cars and clothes. A given quantity of pollution will cause more harm in concentrated urban environments than it will in less dense rural environments.

If we were to establish some form of taxation to align private costs with social costs and to force people to internalize externalities, we would somehow have to come up with a measure of *economic* costs instead of *physical* quantities. But the tax, in any event, would fall on the private sector and modify individuals' and firms' behavior.

Therefore, because the economic cost for the same physical quantity of pollution would be different in different locations, depending on population density, natural formations of mountains and rivers, and the like, so-called optimal taxes on pollution would vary from location to location. (Nonetheless, a uniform tax might make sense when administrative costs, particularly the cost of ascertaining the actual economic costs, are relatively high.)

_____ costs are costs that are borne directly by consumers and producers when they engage in any resource-using activity.

Social costs are _____ costs plus any other costs that are external to the decision maker. For example, the

social costs of driving include all the _____ costs plus, at a minimum, any pollution caused.

When _____ costs differ from social costs, _____ exist because individual decision makers are not internalizing all the costs that society is bearing.

Pollution

The term *pollution* is used quite loosely and can refer to a variety of by-products of any activity. Industrial pollution involves mainly air and water but can also include noise and even aesthetic pollution, as when a landscape is altered in a negative way. For the most part, we will be analyzing the most common forms—air and water pollution.

Assessing the Appropriate Amount of Pollution

When asked how much pollution there should be in the economy, many people will respond, "None." But if we ask those same people how much starvation or deprivation of consumer products should exist in the economy, many will again say, "None." Growing and distributing food or producing consumer products creates pollution, however. There is no correct answer to how much pollution should be in an economy because when we ask how much pollution there *should* be, we are entering the realm of normative economics. We are asking people to express values. There is no way to disprove somebody's value system scientifically.

One way we can approach a discussion of the "correct" amount of pollution is to set up the same type of marginal analysis we used in our discussion of a firm's employment and output decisions. That is, we can consider pursuing measures to reduce pollution only up to the point at which the marginal benefit from pollution reduction equals the marginal cost of pollution reduction.

THE MARGINAL BENEFIT OF A LESS POLLUTED ENVIRONMENT Look at Figure 31-2 on the following page. On the horizontal axis, we show the degree of air cleanliness. A vertical line is drawn at 100 percent cleanliness—the air cannot become any cleaner. Consider the benefits of obtaining a greater degree of air cleanliness. The benefits of obtaining cleaner air are represented by the marginal benefit curve, which slopes downward.

When the air is very dirty, the marginal benefit from air that is a little cleaner appears to be relatively high, as shown on the vertical axis. As the air becomes cleaner, however, the marginal benefit of a little bit more air cleanliness falls.

THE MARGINAL COST OF POLLUTION ABATEMENT Consider the marginal cost of pollution abatement—that is, the marginal cost of obtaining cleaner air. In the 1960s, automobiles had no pollution abatement devices. Eliminating only 20 percent of the pollutants emitted by internal-combustion engines entailed a relatively small cost per unit of pollution removed. The per-unit cost of eliminating the next 20 percent increased, though. Finally, as we now get to the upper limits of removal of pollutants from the emissions of internal-combustion engines, we find that the elimination of one more percentage point of the amount of pollutants becomes astronomically expensive.

In the short run, moving from 97 percent cleanliness to 98 percent cleanliness involves a marginal cost that is many times greater than the marginal cost of going from 10 percent cleanliness to 11 percent cleanliness.

FIGURE 31-2

The Optimal Quantity of Air Pollution

As we attempt to achieve a greater degree of air cleanliness, the marginal cost rises until trying to increase air cleanliness even slightly leads to a very high marginal cost, as can be seen at the upper right of the graph. Conversely, the marginal benefit curve slopes downward: The more pure air we have, the less we value an additional unit of pure air. Marginal cost and marginal benefit intersect at point E. The optimal degree of air cleanliness is something less than 100 percent at Q_0. The price that we should pay for the last unit of air cleanup is no greater than P_0, for that is where marginal cost equals marginal benefit.

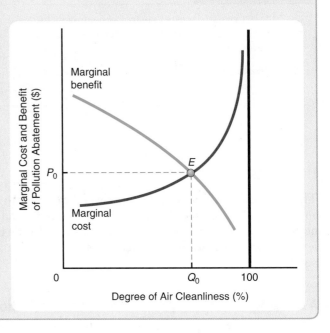

It is realistic, therefore, to draw the marginal cost of pollution abatement as an upward-sloping curve, as shown in Figure 31-2 above. (The marginal cost curve slopes up because of the law of diminishing marginal product.)

The Optimal Quantity of Pollution

Optimal quantity of pollution
The level of pollution for which the marginal benefit of one additional unit of pollution abatement just equals the marginal cost of that additional unit of pollution abatement.

The **optimal quantity of pollution** is the level of pollution at which the marginal benefit equals the marginal cost of pollution abatement. This occurs at the intersection of the marginal benefit curve and the marginal cost curve in Figure 31-2, at point E. This solution is analytically exactly the same as for every other economic activity. If we increased pollution control by one unit beyond Q_0, the marginal cost of that small increase in the degree of air cleanliness would be greater than the marginal benefit to society.

As is usually the case in economic analysis, the optimal quantity occurs when marginal cost equals marginal benefit. That is, the optimal quantity of pollution occurs at the point at which the marginal cost of reducing (or abating) pollution is just equal to the marginal benefit of doing so. The marginal cost of pollution abatement rises as more and more abatement is achieved (as the environment becomes cleaner and cleaner, the *extra* cost of cleansing rises). Early units of pollution abatement are easily achieved (at low cost), but attaining higher and higher levels of environmental quality becomes progressively more difficult (as the extra cost rises to prohibitive levels).

At the same time, the marginal benefits of an increasingly cleaner environment fall. The marginal benefit of pollution abatement declines as our notion of a cleaner environment moves from the preservation of human life to recreation to beauty to a perfectly pure environment. The point at which the increasing marginal cost of pollution abatement equals the decreasing marginal benefit of pollution abatement defines the optimal quantity of pollution.

Go to www.econtoday.com/chap31 to learn from the National Center for Policy Analysis about alternative programs for reducing pollution related to global warming.

Recognizing that the optimal quantity of pollution is not zero becomes easier when we realize that it takes scarce resources to reduce pollution. A trade-off exists between producing a cleaner environment and producing other goods and services. In that sense, environmental cleanliness is a good that can be analyzed like any other good, and a cleaner environment must take its place with other human wants.

Why is the marginal cost of pollution abatement increasing in the electrical power industry?

POLICY EXAMPLE

Increasing the Marginal Cost of U.S. Air Pollution Abatement

Coal-fired plants generate nearly half of all electricity produced in the United States each year. In an effort to increase the degree of air cleanliness, the Environmental Protection Agency has issued 1,117 pages of rules that require electrical power companies to begin shutting down or retrofitting nearly 20 percent of these plants in 2015. Companies likely will replace retired coal-fired plants with electricity-generating facilities powered by natural gas. Retrofitted coal-fired plants will be equipped with special "scrubbers" that remove air pollutants and certain greenhouse gases from the plants' emissions.

Estimates indicate that the additional cost to the electrical power industry and its customers of complying with this requirement will be about $30 billion per year through the end of the 2010s. Thus, attaining a hoped-for higher degree of air cleanliness will entail a higher marginal cost of pollution abatement for society.

FOR CRITICAL THINKING

For the EPA's new pollution abatement requirement to move society toward the optimal degree of air cleanliness, would the initial degree of cleanliness have to have been below, at, or above a level such as Q_0 in Figure 31-2 on the facing page?

QUICK QUIZ   See page 703 for the answers. Review concepts from this section in MyEconLab.

The marginal cost of cleaning up the environment _____ as we get closer to 100 percent cleanliness. Indeed, it _____ at an _____ rate.

The marginal benefit of environmental cleanliness _____ as we have more of it.

The **optimal quantity of pollution** is the quantity at which the _____ _____ of cleanup equals the _____ _____ of cleanup.

Pollution abatement is a trade-off. We trade off _____ and _____ for cleaner air and water, and vice versa.

Common Property

In most cases, you do not have **private property rights,** or exclusive ownership rights, to the air surrounding you, nor does anyone else. Air is a **common property,** or a nonexclusive resource. Therein lies the crux of the problem. When no one owns a particular resource, no one has any incentive (conscience aside) to consider externality spillovers associated with that resource. If one person decides not to add to externality spillovers and avoids polluting the air, normally there will not be any significant effect on the total level of pollution. If one person decides not to pollute the ocean, there will still be approximately the same amount of ocean pollution—provided, of course, that the individual was previously responsible for only a small part of the total amount of ocean pollution.

Basically, pollution and other activities that create spillovers occur when we have open access and poorly defined private property rights, as in air and common bodies of water. We do not, for example, have a visual pollution problem in people's attics. That is their own property, which they keep as clean as they want, depending on their preferences for cleanliness weighed against the costs of keeping the attic neat and tidy.

When private property rights exist, individuals have legal recourse for any damages sustained through the use of their property. When private property rights are well defined, the use of property—that is, the use of resources—will generally involve contracts between the owners of those resources. If you own land, you might contract with another person who wants to access your land for raising cattle. The contract would most likely take the form of a written lease agreement.

Private property rights
Exclusive rights of ownership that allow the use, transfer, and exchange of property.

Common property
Property that is owned by everyone and therefore by no one. Air and water are examples of common property resources.

Voluntary Agreements and Transaction Costs

Is it possible for externalities to be internalized via voluntary agreement? Take a simple example. You live in a house with a nice view of a lake. The family living below you plants a tree. The tree grows so tall that it eventually starts to cut off your view. In most cities, no one has property rights to views, so you usually cannot go to court to obtain relief. You do have the option of contracting with your neighbors, however.

VOLUNTARY AGREEMENTS: CONTRACTING You have the option of paying your neighbors (contracting) to trim the tree. You could start out by offering a small amount and keep going up until your neighbors agree or until you reach your limit. Your limit will equal the value you place on having an unobstructed view of the lake. Your neighbors will be willing if the payment is at least equal to the reduction in their intrinsic property value due to a stunted tree. Your offer of the payment makes your neighbors aware of the social cost of their actions. The social cost here is equal to the care of the tree plus the cost suffered by you from an impeded view of the lake.

In essence, then, your offer of money income to your neighbors indicates to them that there is an opportunity cost to their actions. If they don't comply, they forfeit the payments that you are offering them. The point here is that *opportunity cost always exists, no matter who has property rights*. Therefore, we would expect that under some circumstances voluntary contracting will occur to internalize externalities. The question is, When will voluntary agreements occur?

TRANSACTION COSTS One major condition for the outcome just outlined is that the **transaction costs**—all costs associated with making and enforcing agreements—must be low relative to the expected benefits of reaching an agreement. (We already looked at this topic briefly in Chapter 4.) If we expand our example to a much larger one such as air pollution, the transaction costs of numerous homeowners trying to reach agreements with the individuals and companies that create the pollution are relatively high. Consequently, people may not always engage in voluntary contracting, even though it can be an effective way to internalize the externality of air pollution.

Changing Property Rights

We can approach the issue of property rights by assuming that initially in a society, many property rights to resources are not defined. But this situation does not cause a problem so long as no one wants to use the resources for which there are no property rights or resources are available in desired quantities at a zero price. Only if and when a use is found for a resource at a zero price does a problem develop. Unless some decision then is made about property rights, the resource will be wasted and possibly even destroyed. Property rights can be assigned to individuals who will then assert control. Alternatively, the rights may be assigned to government, which can maintain and preserve the resource, charge for its use, or implement some other rationing device.

Another way of viewing the problem of pollution spillovers is to argue that it cannot continue if a way can be found to assign and enforce private property rights for all resources. We can then say that each individual does not have the right to act on anything that is not his or her property. Hence, no individual has the right to create pollution spillovers on property that the individual does not specifically own.

Clearly, we must fill the gap between private costs and social costs in situations in which property rights are not well defined or assigned. There are three ways to fill this gap: taxation, subsidization, and regulation. Government is involved in all three. Unfortunately, government does not have perfect information and may not pick the appropriate tax, subsidy, or type of regulation. Furthermore, in some situations, it may be difficult to enforce taxes or direct subsidies to "worthy" recipients. In such cases, outright prohibition of the polluting activity may be the optimal solution to a particular pollution spillover. For example, if it is difficult to monitor the level of a particular type of pollution that even in small quantities can cause severe environmental damage, outright prohibition of activities that cause such pollution may be the best alternative.

Transaction costs
All costs associated with making, reaching, and enforcing agreements.

YOU ARE THERE

To contemplate the transaction costs associated with the most basic form of environmental cleanup—regular removal of city residents' trash—consider **A Mayor Faces the Grimy Economics of Trash Removal** on page 698.

QUICK QUIZ See page 703 for the answers. Review concepts from this section in MyEconLab.

A **common property** resource is one that _____ _____ owns—or, otherwise stated, that _____ owns. Common property exists when property rights are indefinite or nonexistent.	economic incentive to care for the common property in question, be it air, water, or scenery.
When no _____ _____ rights exist, pollution occurs because no one individual or firm has a sufficient	Private costs will equal _____ costs for common property only if a few individuals or companies are involved and they are able to voluntarily _____ among themselves.

Reducing Humanity's Carbon Footprint: Restraining Pollution-Causing Activities

In light of the costs arising from spillovers that polluting activities create, one solution might seem to be for governments to try to stop them from taking place. Why don't more governments simply *require* businesses and households to cut back on pollution-causing activities?

Mixing Government Controls and Market Processes: Cap and Trade

In fact, many governments are implementing schemes aimed at capping and controlling the use of pollution-generating resources. In recent years, certain scientific research has suggested that emissions of carbon dioxide and various other so-called *greenhouse gases* might be contributing to atmospheric warming. The result, some scientists fear, might be global climate changes harmful to people inhabiting various regions of the planet.

In response, the governments of more than three dozen nations agreed to participate in the *Kyoto Protocol* of a broader set of international treaties called the Framework Convention on Climate Change. Under this 1997 agreement, the governments of participating nations agreed to reduce their overall emissions of greenhouse gases by 2020 to as much as 20 percent below 1990 levels.

EMISSIONS CAPS AND PERMITS TRADING European Union (EU) nations are participants in the Kyoto Protocol, which expired in 2012 but to which EU nations are adhering. In January 2005, the EU established a set of rules called the *Emissions Trading Scheme*. Under this so-called cap-and-trade program, each EU nation seeks to cap its total greenhouse gas emissions. After setting its cap, each EU nation established an *allowance* of metric tons of gas, such as carbon dioxide, that each firm legally can release. If the firm's emissions exceed its allowance—that is, if its "carbon footprint" is too large—then the firm must buy more allowances through a trading system. These allowances can be obtained, at the market clearing price, from companies that are releasing fewer emissions than their permitted amounts and therefore have unused allowances.

The United States is not a Kyoto Protocol participant. Nevertheless, in 2013 California began implementing its own cap-and-trade program. That state also placed a limit on emissions of greenhouse gases within its borders. Under the California program, the overall limitation on emissions will decline over seven years. Electrical power companies, oil refiners, and other firms—more than 600 companies in all—that generate greenhouse gases will have to reduce their emissions or buy allowances to continue releasing the emissions. Ultimately, California's objective is to reduce the state's total carbon emissions by 30 percent by 2020.

Why has California tried to enlist other western states to join its cap-and-trade program? See the following page.

POLICY EXAMPLE

California Dreaming: A Western Cap-and-Trade Pact?

During the period preceding implementation of California's cap-and-trade program, state officials tried to persuade governments of other western states to enter into a "regional cap-and-trade pact." Every state that California officials approached said no, however, as it became clear that the induced reduction in the energy supply required to decrease emissions would bring about considerably higher energy prices.

Although the exact annual costs of California's energy program to the state's households may not be tabulated until early 2014, most estimates indicate the costs will amount to hundreds of dollars per household per year. Businesses will face significant cost increases as well, which most economists anticipate will lead to dampened employment

prospects in the state. Some observers are predicting that a number of California firms will respond to higher energy costs by moving their operations to other western states. Indeed, state officials admitted that one incentive for a regional pact was to ensure that neighboring states' energy costs also would rise, thereby reducing the motivation for California firms to relocate to those states.

FOR CRITICAL THINKING
Why do you suppose that some economists argue that if the United States were to incur the costs of capping emissions, while other nations did not, a number of U.S. firms might relocate to those other countries?

IN EUROPE, THEORY CONFRONTS POLICY AND MARKET REALITIES The European cap-and-trade program has yielded mixed results to date. In theory, if EU governments had set the national emissions caps low enough to force companies to reduce greenhouse gases, the market clearing price of emissions allowances should have reflected this constraint. In addition, as governments voluntarily continue to tighten the caps to meet limits that require greenhouse gas emissions to be reduced to 20 percent below 1990 levels by 2020, more firms should respond by purchasing allowances.

Then the market clearing price of allowances would rise. Rather than paying a higher price for emissions allowances, many firms would instead opt to develop methods of reducing their emissions. In this way, this market-based mechanism established by the Emissions Trading Scheme would induce firms to reduce their emissions, and the EU nations would achieve the emissions targets.

In fact, in the spring of 2006, the market clearing price of EU emissions allowances dropped by more than 60 percent. The reason that prices dropped, many economists agree, is that most EU governments issued more allowances than were consistent with capping emissions. Indeed, the price drop was consistent with an initial surplus of more than 200 million allowances.

Most observers suspect that the Emissions Trading Scheme's fundamental weakness was that each nation's government was permitted to establish the emissions target and allowances for its own country. Each government feared making its own nation's firms less cost-competitive than those in other nations, so every government inflated its estimate of its mid-2000s emissions of greenhouse gases. Doing so allowed each government to set its overall emissions cap at a level that actually failed to constrain emissions. One result was the big drop in prices of emissions allowances, which have remained substantially lower than when the Emissions Trading Scheme was first established. Another outcome is that instead of declining, greenhouse gas emissions by companies based in the EU actually *increased* during the late 2000s and early 2010s.

Why is a separately administered EU cap-and-trade program for airline emissions driving up prices of flying to European airports?

INTERNATIONAL EXAMPLE

Passengers Help Pay for Emissions on EU Airline Routes

In 2012, the European Union implemented a new, independently administered cap-and-trade program aimed at reducing carbon emissions created by airplane engines. This program applies to all airlines operating flights into and out of all EU member nations' airports. The EU allocated total pollution allowances to airlines to emit exhaust gases from airplanes

slightly below the airlines' past average level of emissions for the full durations of all flights, even if they originated on other continents. To exceed its limit, an airline can purchase allowances from another airline that has total emissions below its allowances.

Imposing this separate cap-and-trade program has raised airlines' per-passenger costs of providing air travel services, which has reduced the market supply of these services. The result has been predictable: The equilibrium price of a ticket into or out of an airport located in an EU nation has risen by about $10.

FOR CRITICAL THINKING

Flights that either originate or end at EU airports carry at least 800 million passengers each year. What is the approximate aggregate annual cost imposed on airline passengers by the new EU airline cap-and-trade program?

Are There Alternatives to Pollution-Causing Resource Use?

Some people cannot understand why, if pollution is bad, we still use pollution-causing resources such as coal and oil to generate electricity. Why don't we forgo the use of such polluting resources and opt for one that apparently is pollution-free, such as solar energy? The plain fact is that the cost of generating solar power in many circumstances is much higher than generating that same power through conventional means. We do not yet have the technology that allows us the luxury of driving solar-powered cars. Moreover, with current technology, the solar panels necessary to generate the electricity for the average town would cover massive sections of the countryside, and the manufacturing of those solar panels would itself generate pollution.

Wild Species, Common Property, and Trade-Offs

One common property problem that receives considerable media attention involves endangered species, usually in the wild. Few are concerned about not having enough dogs, cats, cattle, sheep, and horses. The reason is that those species are almost always private property. People have economic incentives—satisfaction from pet ownership or desire for food products—to protect members of these species. In contrast, spotted owls, bighorn mountain sheep, condors, and the like are typically openly accessible common property. Therefore, no one has a vested interest in making sure that they perpetuate in good health.

Go to www.econtoday.com/chap31 to contemplate the issue of endangered species via a link to the National Center for Policy Analysis.

In 1973, the federal government passed the Endangered Species Act in an attempt to prevent species from dying out. Initially, few individuals were affected by the rulings of the Interior Department regarding which species were listed as endangered. Eventually, however, as more and more species were put on the endangered list, a trade-off became apparent. Nationwide, the trade-off was brought to the public's attention when the snail darter was declared an endangered species in the Tennessee valley. Ultimately, thousands of construction jobs were lost when the courts halted completion of a dam in the snail darter's habitat. Then two endangered small birds, the spotted owl and marbled murrelet, were found in the Pacific Northwest, inducing lumber companies to cut back their logging practices. In 1995, the U.S. Supreme Court ruled that the federal government has the right to regulate activities on private land in order to save endangered species.

The issues are not straightforward. Today, the earth has only 0.02 percent of all of the species that have ever lived, and nearly all the 99.98 percent of extinct species became extinct before humans appeared. Every year, 1,000 to 3,000 new species are discovered and classified. Estimates of how many species are actually dying out range from a high of 50,000 a year (based on the assumption that undiscovered insect species are dying off before being discovered) to a low of one every four years.

WHAT IF... governments allowed people to own endangered animals as private property?

If all animals of endangered species could be marked and cataloged as private property, some people undoubtedly would mishandle the animals they owned, just as they misuse other resources in their possession. Nevertheless, by definition, animals of endangered species are scarce resources that would have positive values—and sometimes relatively high dollar values—in private markets. This fact would give most self-interested people the incentive to preserve such animal life. Indeed, the most successful programs for preventing "too much" fishing, seal hunting, rhino poaching, and so on have been those that assign property rights. These programs motivate the rights holders to rein in such injurious activities and to preserve endangered species.

QUICK QUIZ See page 703 for the answers. Review concepts from this section in MyEconLab.

The more than three dozen countries that participated in the 1997 Kyoto Protocol of the Framework Convention on Climate Change agreed to reduce their emissions of greenhouse gases by the year _____ to at least _____ percent below the levels that prevailed in the year _____.

Under a program called the Emissions Trading Scheme, the governments of European Union member nations established overall targets for greenhouse gas emissions and issued _____, or permits, authorizing companies to emit certain amounts. In theory, an increase in the market clearing price of _____ should induce firms to develop methods of _____ their emissions of greenhouse gases.

In contrast to domesticated animals that are _____ property, most endangered species are _____ property. Consequently, there is a problem in perpetuating these species that the federal government has sought to address through legislation governing use of lands where such species reside.

YOU ARE THERE

A Mayor Faces the Grimy Economics of Trash Removal

The task of keeping the physical environment clean begins with figuring out how to handle trash. For Chicago mayor Rahm Emanuel, how to go about moving trash for disposal or recycling has become a substantial economic issue.

Chicago does not have one trash removal system to serve its 600,000 households. Instead, it has a different system for each of its 50 political wards. In addition, during a typical garbage laborer's workday, only 5½ hours are devoted to moving trash. Facts such as these, Emanuel realizes, help to explain why the $231 cost per ton of moving trash in Chicago is higher than for any other large U.S. city.

Emanuel examines a study that proposes a reorganization of the city's trash removal procedures. The study suggests that switching to a more efficient citywide system for trash disposal and recycling could accomplish the same task each year with 25 percent fewer workers and at an annual cost savings of $40 million. Emanuel decides that with an annual city budget deficit in excess of $600 million, cutting the expense of trash removal will have to become a top priority.

Critical Thinking Questions

1. Why do you suppose that governments of towns and cities rarely seek to keep streets 100 percent free of trash?

2. Once city workers collect trash from a house or apartment building, it becomes common property. How can this fact pose problems for deciding how best to handle disposal and recycling of the trash?

ISSUES & APPLICATIONS

The New Sulfur Dioxide "Cap and Fade" Program

CONCEPTS APPLIED

▶ Externality

▶ Private versus Social Costs

▶ Optimal Quantity of Pollution

The U.S. government successfully operated a narrowly focused cap-and-trade program for more than a decade. Nonetheless, recent policy actions caused this program, which some observers now call "cap and fade," to collapse.

Caps and Allowances to Contain an Acid Rain Externality

For years, coal-fired electrical-power-generating plants in midwestern states emitted smoke containing sulfur dioxide. In other states, these emissions have contributed to a phenomenon known as "acid rain"—rainfalls contaminated by acids formed when the sulfur dioxide combined with other elements in the atmosphere. Thus, a mismatch has occurred between the private costs incurred by electricity producers in some states and the people in other states adversely affected by acid rain. That is, a negative externality has arisen.

In 1995, the U.S. government placed a cap on emissions of sulfur dioxide by electricity providers in the midwestern states. The government handed out a fixed number of emission allowances to the companies. Plant operators surrendered one allowance for each ton of sulfur dioxide they emitted. If firms reduced emissions by switching to low-sulfur coals or by adding emission-control equipment, they could sell unused allowances to other electrical power producers.

Success Followed by a Policy-Induced Market Fadeout

From 1995 through 2007, the U.S. sulfur dioxide cap-and-trade program was regarded as one of the most successful such programs in the world. By 2005, the equilibrium price of a sulfur-dioxide-emission allowance had reached $1,600. This price was sufficiently high to induce many firms to reduce their emissions. In fact, during the first 13 years the program was in operation, total emissions of sulfur dioxide in the United States declined by 50 percent, toward a level more consistent with the government's view of the optimal quantity of pollution.

In 2008, however, the EPA began ordering plant operators to cut back directly on their emissions. The EPA also decided not to allow firms to purchase allowances to avoid the new emissions restrictions. Since then, the equilibrium price of a sulfur-dioxide-emission allowance has "faded away" to zero—hence the new "cap and fade" term used to describe the program.

For Critical Thinking

1. There is currently a surplus of allowances at the price of zero. What must be true of the relative positions of the market demand and supply curves? Explain.

2. If the EPA were to allow firms to use allowances to emit sulfur dioxide as they did in the past, what would happen to the equilibrium allowance price? Why?

Web Resources

1. Consider how the pre-"fade" version of the cap-and-trade program for sulfur dioxide has been held up as a model for other cap-and-trade programs at www.econtoday.com/chap31.

2. Learn about the substantial decline in the price of sulfur-dioxide-emission allowances at www.econtoday.com/chap31.

MyEconLab
For more questions on this chapter's Issues & Applications, go to MyEconLab. In the Study Plan for this chapter, select Section N: News.

MyEconLab

Here is what you should know after reading this chapter. MyEconLab will help you identify what you know, and where to go when you need to practice.

— WHAT YOU SHOULD KNOW — WHERE TO GO TO PRACTICE —

Private Costs versus Social Costs Private, or internal, costs are borne solely by individuals who use resources. Social costs are the full costs that society bears whenever resources are used. Problems related to the environment arise when individuals take into account only private costs instead of the broader social costs arising from their use of resources.

private costs, 688
social costs, 688

• MyEconLab Study Plan 31.1

Market Externalities and Ways to Correct Them A market externality arises if a private cost (or benefit) differs from the social cost (or benefit) associated with a market transaction between two parties or from the use of a scarce resource. An externality can be corrected by requiring individuals to account for all the social costs (or benefits).

externality, 689

Key Figure
Figure 31-1, 689

• MyEconLab Study Plan 31.2
• Animated Figure 31-1

MyEconLab *continued*

Determining the Optimal Amount of Pollution The marginal benefit of pollution abatement declines and the marginal cost of pollution abatement increases as more and more resources are devoted to achieving an improved environment. The optimal quantity of pollution is the amount of pollution for which the marginal benefit of pollution abatement just equals the marginal cost of pollution abatement.

optimal quantity of pollution, 692

Key Figure
Figure 31-2, 692

• **MyEconLab** Study Plan 31.3
• Animated Figure 31-2

Private and Common Property Rights and the Pollution Problem Private property rights permit the use and exchange of a resource. Common property is owned by everyone and hence by no single person. A pollution problem often arises because air and many water resources are common property, and private property rights are not well defined. This is a common rationale for using taxes, subsidies, or regulations to address the pollution problem.

private property rights, 693
common property, 693
transaction costs, 694

• **MyEconLab** Study Plan 31.4

Restraining Pollution-Causing Activities through Caps and Allowances Under the European Union's (EU's) Emissions Trading Scheme, each EU nation's government established an overall target level of greenhouse gas emissions and distributed allowances, or permits, granting firms the right to emit a certain amount of gases. If a firm's greenhouse gas emissions exceed its allowances, it must purchase a sufficient number of allowances from firms emitting less than the allowances they possess. In theory, the market clearing price of allowances will increase, giving firms incentives to develop methods of restraining their emissions of greenhouse gases.

• **MyEconLab** Study Plan 31.5

Endangered Species and the Assignment of Property Rights Many members of such species as dogs, pigs, and horses are the private property of human beings. Thus, people have economic incentives to protect members of these species. In contrast, most members of species such as spotted owls, condors, or tigers are common property, so no specific individuals have incentives to keep these species in good health. A possible way to address the endangered species problem is government involvement via regulations.

• **MyEconLab** Study Plan 31.6

Log in to MyEconLab, take a chapter test, and get a personalized Study Plan that tells you which concepts you understand and which ones you need to review. From there, MyEconLab will give you further practice, tutorials, animations, videos, and guided solutions. For more information, visit www.myeconlab.com

PROBLEMS

All problems are assignable in MyEconLab. Answers to the odd-numbered problems appear at the back of the book.

31-1. The market price of insecticide is initially $10 per unit. To address a negative externality in this market, the government decides to charge producers of insecticide for the privilege of polluting during the production process. A fee that fully takes into account the social costs of pollution is determined, and once it is put into effect, the market supply curve for insecticide shifts upward by $4 per unit. The market price of insecticide also increases, to $12 per unit. What fee is the government charging insecticide manufacturers? (See page 689.)

31-2. One possible method for reducing emissions of greenhouse gases such as carbon dioxide is to inject the gases into deep saltwater-laden rock formations where they would be trapped for thousands of years. Suppose that the federal government provides a fixed per-unit subsidy to firms that utilize this technology in West Virginia and other locales where such rock formations are known to exist. (See page 692.)

    a. Use an appropriate diagram to examine the effects of the government subsidy on the production and sale of equipment that injects greenhouse gases into underground rock formations. What happens to the market clearing price of such pollution abatement equipment?

    b. Who pays to achieve the results discussed in part (a)?

31-3. Examine the following marginal costs and marginal benefits associated with water cleanliness in a given locale (see page 692):

Quantity of Clean Water (%)	Marginal Cost ($)	Marginal Benefit ($)
0	3,000	200,000
20	15,000	120,000
40	50,000	90,000
60	85,000	85,000
80	100,000	40,000
100	Infinite	0

    a. What is the optimal degree of water cleanliness?

    b. What is the optimal degree of water pollution?

    c. Suppose that a company creates a food additive that offsets most of the harmful effects of drinking polluted water. As a result, the marginal benefit of water cleanliness declines by $40,000 at each degree of water cleanliness at or less than 80 percent. What is the optimal degree of water cleanliness after this change?

31-4. Consider the diagram below, which displays the marginal cost and marginal benefit of water pollution abatement in a particular city, and answer the following questions. (See page 692.)

    a. What is the optimal percentage degree of water cleanliness?

    b. When the optimal percentage degree of water cleanliness has been attained, what cost will be incurred for the last unit of water cleanup?

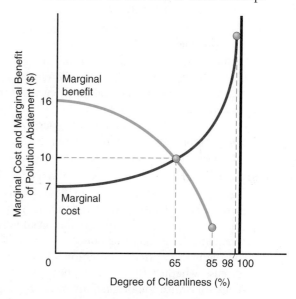

31-5. Consider the diagram in Problem 31-4, and answer the following questions. (See page 692.)

    a. Suppose that a new technology for reducing water pollution generates a reduction in the marginal cost of pollution abatement at every degree of water cleanliness. After this event occurs, will the optimal percentage degree of water cleanliness rise or fall? Will the cost incurred for the last unit of water cleanup increase or decrease? Provide a diagram to assist in your explanation.

    b. Suppose that the event discussed in part (a) occurs and that, in addition, medical studies determine that the marginal benefit from water pollution abatement is higher at every degree of water cleanliness. Following *both* events, will the optimal percentage degree of water cleanliness increase or decrease? In comparison with the *initial* optimum, can you determine whether the cost incurred for the last unit of water cleanup will increase or decrease? Use a new diagram to assist in explaining your answers.

31-6. Under an agreement with U.S. regulators, American Electric Power Company of Columbus, Ohio, has agreed to offset part of its 145 million metric tons of carbon dioxide emissions by paying another company to lay plastic tarps. These tarps cover farm lagoons holding rotting livestock wastes that emit methane gas 21 times more damaging to the atmosphere than carbon dioxide. The annual methane produced by a typical 1,330-pound cow translates into about 5 metric tons of carbon dioxide emissions per year. (See pages 691–693.)

a. How many cows' worth of manure would have to be covered to offset the carbon dioxide emissions of this single electric utility?

b. Given that there are about 9 million cows in the United States in a typical year, what percentage of its carbon dioxide emissions could this firm offset if it paid for all cow manure in the entire nation to be covered with tarps?

31-7. A government agency caps aggregate emissions of an air pollutant within its borders, establishes initial pollution allowances across all firms, and grants the firms the right to trade these allowances among themselves. The demand and supply curves for these pollution allowances have normal shapes and intersect at a positive price. Explain in your own words the government's intent in establishing this private market for pollution allowances. (See page 695.)

31-8. Suppose that a new chief of the government agency discussed in Problem 31-7 decides to restrict considerably the extent to which firms in this nation can legally utilize pollution allowances. Evaluate the effects this policy change will have on the market price of pollution allowances, and discuss whether the policy appears to be fully consistent with the original intent of creating the market for these allowances. (See page 696.)

31-9. The following table displays hypothetical annual total costs and total benefits of conserving wild tigers at several possible worldwide tiger population levels. (See page 697.)

Population of Wild Tigers	Total Cost ($ millions)	Total Benefit ($ millions)
0	0	40
2,000	25	90
4,000	35	130
6,000	50	160
8,000	75	185
10,000	110	205
12,000	165	215

a. Calculate the marginal costs and benefits.

b. Given the data, what is the socially optimal world population of wild tigers?

c. Suppose that tiger farming is legalized and that this has the effect of reducing the marginal cost of tiger conservation by $15 million for each 2,000-tiger population increment in the table. What is the new socially optimal population of wild tigers?

31-10. The following table gives hypothetical annual total costs and total benefits of maintaining alternative populations of Asian elephants. (See page 697.)

Population of Asian Elephants	Total Cost ($ millions)	Total Benefit ($ millions)
0	0	0
7,500	20	100
15,000	45	185
22,500	90	260
30,000	155	325
37,500	235	375
45,000	330	410

a. Calculate the marginal costs and benefits, and draw marginal benefit and cost schedules.

b. Given the data, what is the socially optimal world population of Asian elephants?

c. Suppose that two events occur simultaneously. Technological development allows machines to do more efficiently much of the work that elephants once did, which reduces by $10 million the marginal benefit of maintaining the elephant population for each 7,500 increment in the elephant population. In addition, new techniques for breeding, feeding, and protecting elephants reduce the marginal cost by $40 million for each 7,500 increment in the elephant population. What is the new socially optimal population of Asian elephants?

ECONOMICS ON THE NET

Economic Analysis at the Environmental Protection Agency
In this chapter, you learned how to use economic analysis to think about environmental problems. Does the U.S. government use economic analysis? This application helps you learn the extent to which the government uses economics in its environmental policymaking.

Title: National Center for Environmental Economics (NCEE)

Navigation: Go to **www.econtoday.com/chap31** to view the NCEE's link to "Environmental Protection: Is It Bad for the Economy? A Non-Technical Summary of the Literature." Download the article and read the section entitled "What Do We Spend on Environmental Protection?"

Application Read this section of the article. Then answer the following questions.

1. According to the article, what are the key objectives of the Environmental Protection Agency (EPA)? What role does cost-benefit analysis appear to play in the EPA's efforts? Does the EPA appear to take other issues into account in its policymaking?

2. Read the next section, titled "Regardless of the Cost of Environmental Protection, Is It Still Money Well Spent?" In what ways does this discussion help clarify your answers in Question 1?

For Group Study and Analysis Have a class discussion of the following question: Should the EPA apply economic analysis in all aspects of its policymaking? If not, why not? If so, in what manner should economic analysis be applied?

ANSWERS TO QUICK QUIZZES

p. 691: (i) Private; (ii) private . . . private; (iii) private . . . externalities

p. 693: (i) rises . . . rises . . . increasing; (ii) falls; (iii) marginal cost . . . marginal benefit; (iv) goods . . . services

p. 695: (i) no one . . . everyone; (ii) private property; (iii) social . . . contract

p. 698: (i) 2020 . . . 20 . . . 1990; (ii) allowances . . . allowances . . . reducing; (iii) private . . . common

32

Comparative Advantage and the Open Economy

In 2001, the U.S. government slashed *tariffs*—taxes on imported items—that it imposed on goods and services imported into the United States from countries located along the Andes mountain range in South America. From that year through the early 2010s, the dollar value of U.S. imports of cut flowers from the Andean nation of Colombia grew by about 400 percent, while Californian production and sale of cut flowers declined considerably. California flower growers responded by successfully lobbying Congress to increase tariff rates on Andean products to previous levels, and Colombian cut-flower imports promptly plummeted. To understand how tariffs affect volumes of imports and, ultimately, prices in markets in which imported goods and services are traded, you must learn about the economics of international trade, which is the subject of this chapter.

since 2011, more oil-based fuels have been exported each year from the United States than have been imported? Thus, recent years represent the first time since 1949 that international trade statistics have classified the United States as a "net exporter" of fossil fuels. Current projections indicate that it likely will remain a net fuel exporter for many years to come. In this chapter, you will learn about the fundamental economic determinants of whether a nation's residents become net exporters or importers of particular goods and services.

The Worldwide Importance of International Trade

Look at panel (a) of Figure 32-1 below. Since the end of World War II, world output of goods and services (world real gross domestic product, or world real GDP) has increased almost every year. It is now about 10 times what it was then. Look at the top line in panel (a) of Figure 32-1. Even taking into account its recent dip, world trade has increased to about 26 times its level in 1950.

FIGURE 32-1

The Growth of World Trade

In panel (a), you can see the growth in world trade in relative terms because we use an index of 100 to represent real world trade in 1950. By the early 2010s, that index had exceeded 2,500. At the same time, the index of world real GDP (annual world real income) had gone up only about 1,000. Thus, generally world trade has been on the rise. In the United States, both imports and exports, expressed as a percentage of annual national income (GDP) in panel (b), generally rose after 1950 and recovered following the 2008–2009 recession.

Sources: Steven Husted and Michael Melvin, *International Economics*, 3rd ed. (New York: HarperCollins, 1995), p. 11, used with permission; World Trade Organization; Federal Reserve System; U.S. Department of Commerce.

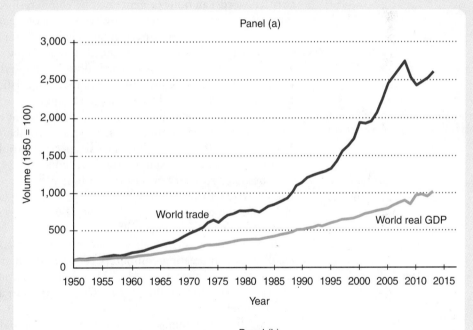

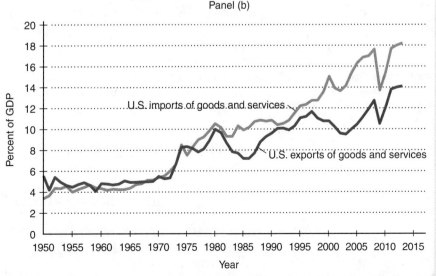

Go to www.econtoday.com/chap32 for the World Trade Organization's most recent data on world trade.

The United States has figured prominently in this expansion of world trade. In panel (b) of Figure 32-1 on page 705, you see imports and exports expressed as a percentage of total annual yearly income (GDP). Whereas imports amounted to barely 4 percent of annual U.S. GDP in 1950, today they account for more than 18 percent. International trade has become more important to the U.S. economy, and it may become even more so as other countries loosen their trade restrictions.

Why We Trade: Comparative Advantage and Mutual Gains from Exchange

You have already been introduced to the concept of specialization and mutual gains from trade in Chapter 2. These concepts are worth repeating because they are essential to understanding why the world is better off because of more international trade. The best way to understand the gains from trade among nations is first to understand the output gains from specialization between individuals.

The Output Gains from Specialization

Suppose that a creative advertising specialist can come up with two pages of ad copy (written words) an hour or generate one computerized art rendering per hour. At the same time, a computer art specialist can write one page of ad copy per hour or complete one computerized art rendering per hour. Here the ad specialist can come up with more pages of ad copy per hour than the computer specialist and seemingly is just as good as the computer specialist at doing computerized art renderings. Is there any reason for the ad specialist and the computer specialist to "trade"? The answer is yes because such trading will lead to higher output.

Go to www.econtoday.com/chap32 for data on U.S. trade with all other nations of the world.

Consider the scenario of no trading. Assume that during each eight-hour day, the ad specialist and the computer whiz devote half of their day to writing ad copy and half to computerized art rendering. The ad specialist would create eight pages of ad copy (4 hours × 2) and four computerized art renderings (4 × 1). During that same period, the computer specialist would create four pages of ad copy (4 hours × 1) and four computerized art renderings (4 × 1). Each day, the combined output for the ad specialist and the computer specialist would be 12 pages of ad copy and eight computerized art renderings.

If the ad specialist specialized only in writing ad copy and the computer whiz specialized only in creating computerized art renderings, their combined output would rise to 16 pages of ad copy (8 × 2) and eight computerized art renderings (8 × 1). Overall, production would increase by four pages of ad copy per day with no decline in art renderings.

Note that this example implies that to create one additional computerized art rendering during a day, the ad specialist has to sacrifice the creation of two pages of ad copy. The computer specialist, in contrast, has to give up the creation of only one page of ad copy to generate one more computerized art rendering. Thus, the ad specialist has a comparative advantage in writing ad copy, and the computer specialist has a comparative advantage in doing computerized art renderings. **Comparative advantage** is simply the ability to produce something at a lower *opportunity cost* than other producers, as we pointed out in Chapter 2.

Comparative advantage
The ability to produce a good or service at a lower opportunity cost than other producers.

Specialization among Nations

To demonstrate the concept of comparative advantage for nations, let's consider a simple two-country, two-good world. As a hypothetical example, let's suppose that the nations in this world are India and the United States.

PRODUCTION AND CONSUMPTION CAPABILITIES IN A TWO-COUNTRY, TWO-GOOD WORLD In Table 32-1 on the facing page, we show maximum feasible quantities of high-performance

TABLE 32-1

Maximum Feasible Hourly Production Rates of Either Digital Apps or Tablet Devices Using All Available Resources

This table indicates maximum feasible rates of production of digital apps and tablet devices if all available resources are allocated to producing either one item or the other. If U.S. residents allocate all resources to producing a single good, they can produce either 90 digital apps per hour or 225 tablets per hour. If residents of India allocate all resources to manufacturing one good, they can produce either 100 apps per hour or 50 tablets per hour.

Product	United States	India
Digital apps	90	100
Tablet devices	225	50

commercial digital apps (apps) and tablet devices (tablets) that may be produced during an hour using all resources—labor, capital, land, and entrepreneurship—available in the United States and in India. As you can see from the table, U.S. residents can utilize all their resources to produce either 90 apps per hour or 225 tablets per hour. If residents of India utilize all their resources, they can produce either 100 apps per hour or 50 tablets per hour.

COMPARATIVE ADVANTAGE Suppose that in each country, there are constant opportunity costs of producing apps and tablets. Table 32-1 above implies that to allocate all available resources to production of 50 tablets, residents of India would have to sacrifice the production of 100 apps. Thus, the opportunity cost in India of producing 1 tablet is equal to 2 apps. At the same time, the opportunity cost of producing 1 app in India is 0.5 tablet.

In the United States, to allocate all available resources to production of 225 tablets, U.S. residents would have to give up producing 90 apps. This means that the opportunity cost in the United States of producing 1 tablet is equal to 0.4 app. Alternatively, we can say that the opportunity cost to U.S. residents of producing 1 app is 2.5 tablets ($225 \div 90 = 2.5$).

The opportunity cost of producing a tablet is lower in the United States than in India. At the same time, the opportunity cost of producing apps is lower in India than in the United States. Consequently, the United States has a comparative advantage in manufacturing tablets, and India has a comparative advantage in producing apps.

PRODUCTION WITHOUT TRADE Table 32-2 on the following page tabulates two possible production choices in a situation in which U.S. and Indian residents choose not to engage in international trade. Let's suppose that in the United States, residents choose to produce and consume 30 digital apps. To produce this number of apps requires that 75 fewer tablets (30 apps times 2.5 tablets per app) be produced than the maximum feasible tablet production of 225 tablets, or 150 tablets. Thus, in the absence of trade, 30 apps and 150 tablets are produced and consumed in the United States.

Table 32-2 indicates that during an hour's time in India, residents choose to produce and consume 37.5 tablets. Obtaining this number of tablets entails the production of 75 fewer apps (37.5 tablets times 2 apps per tablet) than the maximum of 100 apps, or 25 apps. Hence, in the absence of trade, 37.5 tablets and 25 apps are produced and consumed in India.

Finally, Table 32-2 displays production of apps and tablets for this two-country world, given the nations' production (and, implicitly, consumption) choices in the absence of trade. In an hour's time, U.S. app production is 30 units, and Indian app production is 25 units, so the total apps produced and available for consumption worldwide

TABLE 32-2

U.S. and Indian Production and Consumption without Trade

This table indicates two possible hourly combinations of production and consumption of digital apps and tablet devices in the absence of trade in a "world" encompassing the United States and India. U.S. residents produce 30 apps, and residents of India produce 25 apps, so the total apps that can be consumed worldwide is 55. In addition, U.S. residents produce 150 tablets, and Indian residents produce 37.5 tablets, so worldwide production and consumption of tablets amount to 187.5 tablets per hour.

Product	United States	India	Actual World Output
Digital apps (per hour)	30	25	55
Tablet devices (per hour)	150	37.5	187.5

is 55. Hourly U.S. tablet production is 150 tablets, and Indian tablet production is 37.5 tablets, so a total of 187.5 tablets per hour is produced and available for consumption in this two-country world.

SPECIALIZATION IN PRODUCTION More realistically, residents of the United States will choose to specialize in the activity for which they experience a lower opportunity cost. In other words, U.S. residents will specialize in the activity in which they have a comparative advantage, which is the production of tablet devices, which they can offer in trade to residents of India. Likewise, Indian residents will specialize in the manufacturing industry in which they have a comparative advantage, which is the production of digital apps, which they can offer in trade to U.S. residents.

By specializing, the two countries can gain from engaging in international trade. To see why, suppose that U.S. residents allocate all available resources to producing 225 tablets, the good in which they have a comparative advantage. In addition, residents of India utilize all resources they have on hand to produce 100 apps, the good in which they have a comparative advantage.

CONSUMPTION WITH SPECIALIZATION AND TRADE U.S. residents will be willing to buy an Indian digital app as long as they must provide in exchange no more than 2.5 tablet devices, which is the opportunity cost of producing 1 app at home. At the same time, residents of India will be willing to buy a U.S. tablet as long as they must provide in exchange no more than 2 apps, which is their opportunity cost of producing a tablet.

Suppose that residents of both countries agree to trade at a rate of exchange of 1 tablet for 1 app and that they agree to trade 75 U.S. tablets for 75 Indian apps. Table 32-3 on the facing page displays the outcomes that result in both countries. By specializing in tablet production and engaging in trade, U.S. residents can continue to consume 150 tablets. In addition, U.S. residents are also able to import and consume 75 apps produced in India. At the same time, specialization and exchange allow residents of India to continue to consume 25 apps. Producing 75 more apps for export to the United States allows India to import 75 tablets.

GAINS FROM TRADE Table 32-4 on the facing page summarizes the rates of consumption of U.S. and Indian residents with and without trade. Column 1 displays U.S. and Indian app and tablet consumption rates with specialization and trade from Table 32-3, and it sums these to determine total consumption rates in this two-country world. Column 2 shows U.S., Indian, and worldwide consumption rates without international trade from Table 32-2 above. Column 3 gives the differences between the two columns.

TABLE 32-3

U.S. and Indian Production and Consumption with Specialization and Trade

In this table, U.S. residents produce 225 tablet devices, and no digital apps and Indian residents produce 100 digital apps and no tablets. Residents of the two nations then agree to a rate of exchange of 1 tablet for 1 app and proceed to trade 75 U.S. tablets for 75 Indian apps. Specialization and trade allow U.S. residents to consume 75 apps imported from India and to consume 150 tablets produced at home. By specializing and engaging in trade, Indian residents consume 25 apps produced at home and import 75 tablets from the United States.

Product	U.S. Production and Consumption with Trade		Indian Production and Consumption with Trade	
Digital apps (per hour)	U.S. production	0	Indian production	100
	+Imports from India	75	−Exports to U.S.	75
	Total U.S. consumption	75	Total Indian consumption	25
Tablet devices (per hour)	U.S. production	225	Indian production	0
	−Exports to India	75	+Imports from U.S.	75
	Total U.S. consumption	150	Total Indian consumption	75

Table 32-4 below indicates that by producing 75 additional tablets for export to India in exchange for 75 apps, U.S. residents are able to expand their app consumption from 30 to 75. Thus, the U.S. gain from specialization and trade is 45 apps. This is a net gain in app consumption for the two-country world as a whole, because neither country had to give up consuming any tablets for U.S. residents to realize this gain from trade.

In addition, without trade residents of India could have used all resources to produce and consume only 37.5 tablets and 25 apps. By using all resources to specialize in producing 100 apps and engaging in trade, residents of India can consume 37.5 *more* tablets than they could have produced and consumed alone without reducing their app consumption. Thus, the Indian gain from trade is 37.5 tablets. This represents a worldwide gain in tablet consumption, because neither country had to give up consuming any tablets for Indian residents to realize this gain from trade.

TABLE 32-4

National and Worldwide Gains from Specialization and Trade

This table summarizes the consumption gains experienced by the United States, India, and the two-country world. U.S. and Indian app and tablet consumption rates with specialization and trade from Table 32-3 above are listed in column 1, which sums the national consumption rates to determine total worldwide consumption with trade. Column 2 shows U.S., Indian, and worldwide consumption rates without international trade, as reported in Table 32-2 on the facing page. Column 3 gives the differences between the two columns, which are the resulting national and worldwide gains from international trade.

Product	(1) National and World Consumption with Trade		(2) National and World Consumption without Trade		(3) Worldwide Consumption Gains from Trade	
Digital apps (per hour)	U.S. consumption	75	U.S. consumption	30	Change in U.S. consumption	+45
	+Indian consumption	25	+Indian consumption	25	Change in Indian consumption	+0
	World consumption	100	World consumption	55	**Change in world consumption**	**+45**
Tablet devices (per hour)	U.S. consumption	150	U.S. consumption	150	Change in U.S. consumption	+0
	+Indian consumption	75	+Indian consumption	37.5	Change in Indian consumption	+37.5
	World consumption	225	World consumption	187.5	**Change in world consumption**	**+37.5**

SPECIALIZATION IS THE KEY This example shows that when nations specialize in producing goods for which they have a comparative advantage and engage in international trade, considerable consumption gains are possible for those nations and hence for the world. Why is this so? The answer is that specialization and trade enable Indian residents to obtain each tablet device at an opportunity cost of 1 digital app instead of 2 apps and permit U.S. residents to obtain each app at an opportunity cost of 1 tablet instead of 2.5 tablets.

Indian residents effectively experience a gain from trade of 1 app for each tablet purchased from the United States, and U.S. residents experience a gain from trade of 1.5 tablets for each app purchased from India. Thus, specializing in producing goods for which the two nations have a comparative advantage allows both nations to produce more efficiently. As a consequence, worldwide production capabilities increase. This makes greater worldwide consumption possible through international trade.

Of course, not everybody in our example is better off when free trade occurs. In our example, the U.S. app industry and Indian tablet industry have disappeared. Thus, U.S. app makers and Indian tablet manufacturers are worse off.

Some people worry that the United States (or any country, for that matter) might someday "run out of exports" because of overaggressive foreign competition. The analysis of comparative advantage tells us the contrary. No matter how much other countries compete for our business, the United States (or any other country) will always have a comparative advantage in something that it can export. In 10 or 20 years, that something may not be what we export today, but it will be exportable nonetheless because we will have a comparative advantage in producing it. Consequently, the significant flows of world trade shown in Figure 32-2 below will continue because the United States and other nations will retain comparative advantages in producing various goods and services.

FIGURE 32-2

World Trade Flows

International merchandise trade amounts to nearly $20 trillion worldwide. The percentage figures show the proportion of trade flowing in the various directions throughout the globe.

Sources: World Trade Organization and author's estimates (data are for 2013).

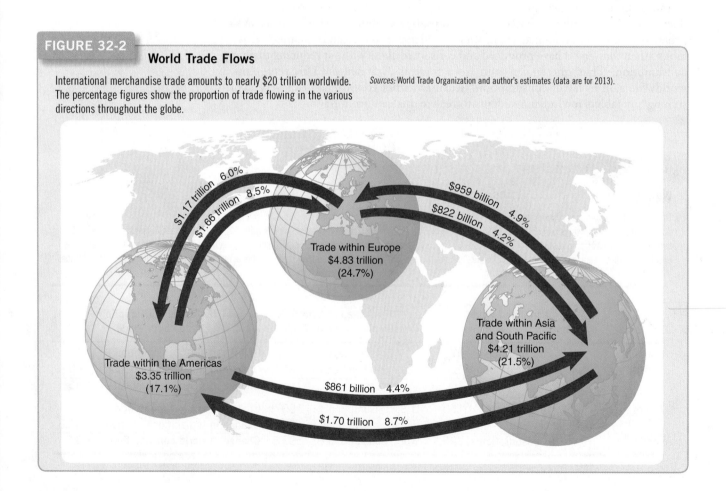

$1.17 trillion 6.0%
$1.66 trillion 8.5%
$959 billion 4.9%
$822 billion 4.2%

Trade within Europe
$4.83 trillion
(24.7%)

Trade within Asia
and South Pacific
$4.21 trillion
(21.5%)

Trade within the Americas
$3.35 trillion
(17.1%)

$861 billion 4.4%
$1.70 trillion 8.7%

What accounts for the fact that the bulk of the world's linen fabrics are produced within a very small area on the earth's surface?

INTERNATIONAL EXAMPLE

Comparative Advantage and Specialization in European Linens

The production of linen requires twice as much land and labor as the production of an equivalent amount of cotton. Nevertheless, linen is a staple material utilized in designer clothing, such as women's blazers and dresses with prices exceeding $2,000, men's trench coats that sell for more than $1,500, and wedding gowns priced above $5,500.

Two-thirds of the world's linen is derived from a fiber called flax that is harvested within a narrow belt of farmland stretching from northern France into the Netherlands. The European coastal climate provides alternating sunshine and rain that contribute to development of a fungus that grows on the flax stems. The fungus breaks down the stems so that the linen fibers can be more readily separated from the plants. Thus, farmers residing this area are able to produce flax at a lower opportunity cost, in terms of forgone production of other goods, than almost anywhere else on the planet. This fact explains why this region of Europe has a comparative advantage in growing flax and specializes in the production of linen.

FOR CRITICAL THINKING

Why do you think that linen production generates gains from trade for European producers of flax and linen, even though cotton-based fabrics can be produced at lower absolute cost in many other parts of the world?

Other Benefits from International Trade: The Transmission of Ideas

Beyond the fact that comparative advantage results in an overall increase in the output of goods produced and consumed, there is another benefit to international trade. International trade also aids in the transmission of ideas. According to economic historians, international trade has been the principal means by which new goods, services, and processes have spread around the world. For example, coffee was initially grown in Arabia near the Red Sea. Around AD 675, it began to be roasted and consumed as a beverage. Eventually, it was exported to other parts of the world, and the Dutch started cultivating it in their colonies during the seventeenth century and the French in the eighteenth century. The lowly potato is native to the Peruvian Andes. In the sixteenth century, it was brought to Europe by Spanish explorers. Thereafter, its cultivation and consumption spread rapidly. Finally, it became part of the North American agricultural scene in the early eighteenth century.

New processes have also been transmitted through international trade. An example is the Japanese manufacturing innovation that emphasized redesigning the system rather than running the existing system in the best possible way. Inventories were reduced to just-in-time levels by reengineering machine setup methods.

In addition, international trade has enabled *intellectual property* to spread throughout the world. New music, such as rock and roll in the 1950s and 1960s and hip-hop in the 1990s and 2000s, has been transmitted in this way, as have the digital devices applications and application tools that are common for online and wireless users everywhere.

The Relationship between Imports and Exports

The basic proposition in understanding all of international trade is this:

> *In the long run, imports are paid for by exports.*

The reason that imports are ultimately paid for by exports is that foreign residents want something in exchange for the goods that are shipped to the United States. For the most part, they want U.S.-made goods. From this truism comes a remarkable corollary:

> *Any restriction of imports ultimately reduces exports.*

This is a shocking revelation to many people who want to restrict foreign competition to protect domestic jobs. Although it is possible to "protect" certain U.S. jobs by restricting foreign competition, it is impossible to make *everyone* better off by imposing import restrictions. Why? The reason is that ultimately such restrictions lead to a reduction in employment and output—and hence incomes—in the export industries of the nation.

WHAT IF... the government saved U.S. jobs from foreign competition by prohibiting all imports?

In the long run, U.S. imports are paid for by U.S. exports. Shutting out all imports of goods and services from abroad certainly would protect U.S. firms from competition and hence would protect many U.S. workers' jobs with those firms. A prohibition on all imports additionally would lead to an eventual halt in all purchases of U.S. firms' exports by residents of other nations, however. The consequence would be a reduction in production and sales by U.S. exporting firms, which would respond by eliminating positions for U.S. workers. Ultimately, therefore, a prohibition on U.S. imports would not really "save" jobs for U.S. workers.

International Competitiveness

"The United States is falling behind." "We need to stay competitive internationally." Statements such as these are often heard when the subject of international trade comes up. There are two problems with such talk. The first has to do with a simple definition. What does "global competitiveness" really mean? When one company competes against another, it is in competition. Is the United States like one big corporation, in competition with other countries? Certainly not. The standard of living in each country is almost solely a function of how well the economy functions *within that country*, not relative to other countries.

Another point relates to real-world observations. According to the Institute for Management Development in Lausanne, Switzerland, the United States is among the top ten nations in overall productive efficiency. According to the report, the relatively high ranking of the United States over the years has been due to widespread entrepreneurship, economic restructuring, and information-technology investments. Other factors include the open U.S. financial system and large investments in scientific research.

QUICK QUIZ   See page 724 for the answers. Review concepts from this section in MyEconLab.

A nation has a **comparative advantage** when its residents are able to produce a good or service at a _____ opportunity cost than residents of another nation.

Specializing in production of goods and services for which residents of a nation have a _____ _____ allows the nation's residents to _____ more of all goods and services.

_____ from trade arise for all nations in the world that engage in international trade because specialization and trade allow countries' residents to _____ more goods and services without necessarily giving up consumption of other goods and services.

Arguments against Free Trade

Numerous arguments are raised against free trade. These arguments focus mainly on the costs of trade. They do not consider the benefits or the possible alternatives for reducing the costs of free trade while still reaping benefits.

The Infant Industry Argument

A nation may feel that if a particular industry is allowed to develop domestically, it will eventually become efficient enough to compete effectively in the world market. Therefore, the nation may impose some restrictions on imports in order to give domestic producers the time they need to develop their efficiency to the point where they can compete in the domestic market without any restrictions on imports. In graphic terminology, we would expect that if the protected industry truly does experience improvements in production techniques or technological breakthroughs toward greater efficiency in the future, the supply curve will shift outward to the right so that the domestic industry can produce larger quantities at each and every price. National policymakers often assert that this **infant industry argument** has some merit in the short run. They have used it to protect a number of industries in their infancy around the world.

Such a policy can be abused, however. Often the protective import-restricting arrangements remain even after the infant has matured. If other countries can still produce more cheaply, the people who benefit from this type of situation are obviously the stockholders (and specialized factors of production that will earn economic rents—see pages 463–465 in Chapter 21) in the industry that is still being protected from world competition. The people who lose out are the consumers, who must pay a price higher than the world price for the product in question. In any event, because it is very difficult to know beforehand which industries will eventually survive, it is possible, perhaps even likely, that policymakers will choose to protect industries that have no reasonable chance of competing on their own in world markets. Note that when we speculate about which industries "should" be protected, we are in the realm of *normative economics*. We are making a value judgment, a subjective statement of what *ought to be*.

Infant industry argument
The contention that tariffs should be imposed to protect from import competition an industry that is trying to get started. Presumably, after the industry becomes technologically efficient, the tariff can be lifted.

Countering Foreign Subsidies and Dumping

Another common argument against unrestricted foreign trade is that a nation must counter other nations' subsidies to their own producers. When a foreign government subsidizes its producers, our producers claim that they cannot compete fairly with these subsidized foreign producers. To the extent that such subsidies fluctuate, it can be argued that unrestricted free trade will seriously disrupt domestic producers. They will not know when foreign governments are going to subsidize their producers and when they are not. Our competing industries will be expanding and contracting too frequently.

How do government credit subsidies promote international trade by some U.S. industries while assisting foreign competitors of another industry?

POLICY EXAMPLE

A U.S. Agency Subsidizes U.S. Exports—and Also Foreign Firms

The U.S. Export-Import (Ex-Im) Bank regularly extends about $100 billion in subsidized loans to foreign buyers of U.S.-manufactured products, including aircraft, hair-care products, and construction equipment. The Ex-Im Bank's extensions of taxpayer-subsidized credit to companies in other nations gives these foreign firms incentives to buy U.S. exports.

Airlines based in the United States are not enthused about aircraft-loan subsidies to competitors based in other nations, however. The U.S. airlines argue that the Ex-Im Bank's low-interest loans to foreign carriers provide a

cost advantage that enables the foreign airlines to compete at lower expense in the international air transportation market. Thus, from the U.S. airlines' point of view, U.S. taxpayers are subsidizing their foreign competitors.

FOR CRITICAL THINKING
Why do you suppose that some U.S. makers of hair-care products and certain U.S. construction contractors that bid for work in other nations have lodged complaints similar to those of the U.S. airlines?

The phenomenon called *dumping* is also used as an argument against unrestricted trade. **Dumping** is said to occur when a producer sells its products abroad below the price that is charged in the home market or at a price below its cost of production. Often, when a foreign producer is accused of dumping, further investigation reveals that the

Dumping
Selling a good or a service abroad below the price charged in the home market or at a price below its cost of production.

foreign nation is in the throes of a recession. The foreign producer does not want to slow down its production at home. Because it anticipates an end to the recession and doesn't want to hold large inventories, it dumps its products abroad at prices below home prices. U.S. competitors may also allege that the foreign producer sells its output at prices below its full costs to be assured of covering variable costs of production.

Protecting Domestic Jobs

Perhaps the argument used most often against free trade is that unrestrained competition from other countries will eliminate jobs in the United States because other countries have lower-cost labor than we do. (Less restrictive environmental standards in other countries might also lower their private costs relative to ours.) This is a compelling argument, particularly for politicians from areas that might be threatened by foreign competition. For example, a representative from an area with shoe factories would certainly be upset about the possibility of constituents' losing their jobs because of competition from lower-priced shoe manufacturers in Brazil and Italy. But, of course, this argument against free trade is equally applicable to trade between the states within the United States.

Economists David Gould, G. L. Woodbridge, and Roy Ruffin examined the data on the relationship between increases in imports and the unemployment rate. They concluded that there is no causal link between the two. Indeed, in half the cases they studied, when imports increased, the unemployment rate fell.

Another issue involves the cost of protecting U.S. jobs by restricting international trade. The Institute for International Economics examined the restrictions on foreign textiles and apparel goods. The study found that U.S. consumers pay $9 billion a year more than they would otherwise pay for those goods to protect jobs in those industries. That comes out to $50,000 *a year* for each job saved in an industry in which the average job pays only $20,000 a year. Similar studies have yielded similar results: Restrictions on imports of Japanese cars have cost $160,000 *per year* for every job saved in the auto industry. Every job preserved in the glass industry has cost $200,000 each and every year. Every job preserved in the U.S. steel industry has cost an astounding $750,000 per year.

Emerging Arguments against Free Trade

In recent years, two new antitrade arguments have been advanced. One of these focuses on environmental and safety concerns. For instance, many critics of free trade have suggested that genetic engineering of plants and animals could lead to accidental production of new diseases and that people, livestock, and pets could be harmed by tainted foods imported for human and animal consumption. These worries have induced the European Union to restrain trade in such products.

Another argument against free trade arises from national defense concerns. Major espionage successes by China in the late 1990s and 2000s led some U.S. strategic experts to propose sweeping restrictions on exports of new technology.

Free trade proponents counter that at best these are arguments for the judicious regulation of trade. They continue to argue that, by and large, broad trade restrictions mainly harm the interests of the nations that impose them.

QUICK QUIZ See page 724 for the answers. Review concepts from this section in MyEconLab.

The _____ industry argument against free trade contends that new industries should be _____ against world competition so that they can become technologically efficient in the long run.

Unrestricted foreign trade may allow foreign governments to subsidize exports or foreign producers to engage in

_____, or selling products in other countries below their cost of production. Critics claim that to the extent that foreign export subsidies and _____ create more instability in domestic production, they may impair our well-being.

Ways to Restrict Foreign Trade

International trade can be stopped or at least stifled in many ways. These include quotas and taxes (the latter are usually called *tariffs* when applied to internationally traded items). Let's talk first about quotas.

Quotas

Under a **quota system,** individual countries or groups of foreign producers are restricted to a certain amount of trade. An import quota specifies the maximum amount of a commodity that may be imported during a specified period of time. For example, the government might allow no more than 200 million barrels of foreign crude oil to enter the United States in a particular month.

Consider the example of quotas on textiles. Figure 32-3 below presents the demand and supply curves for imported textiles. In an unrestricted import market, the equilibrium quantity imported is 900 million yards at a price of $1 per yard (expressed in constant-quality units). When an import quota is imposed, the supply curve is no longer *S*. Instead, the supply curve becomes vertical at some amount less than the equilibrium quantity—here, 800 million yards per year. The price to the U.S. consumer increases from $1.00 to $1.50.

Clearly, the output restriction generated by a quota on foreign imports of a particular item has the effect of raising the domestic price of the imported item. Two groups benefit. One group is importers that are able to obtain the rights to sell imported items domestically at the higher price, which raises their revenues and boosts their profits. The other group is domestic producers. Naturally, a rise in the price of an imported item induces an increase in the demand for domestic substitutes. Thus, the domestic prices of close substitutes for the item subject to the import restriction also increase, which generates higher revenues and profits for domestic producers.

Quota system
A government-imposed restriction on the quantity of a specific good that another country is allowed to sell in the United States. In other words, quotas are restrictions on imports. These restrictions are usually applied to one or several specific countries.

YOU ARE THERE

To consider why domestic producers often desire protection from competing foreign products, read **A French Family Bookshop Seeks Protection from U.S. E-Books** on page 720.

FIGURE 32-3

The Effect of Quotas on Textile Imports

Without restrictions, at point E_1, 900 million yards of textiles would be imported each year into the United States at the world price of $1.00 per yard. If the federal government imposes a quota of only 800 million yards, the effective supply curve becomes vertical at that quantity. It intersects the demand curve at point E_2, so the new equilibrium price is $1.50 per yard.

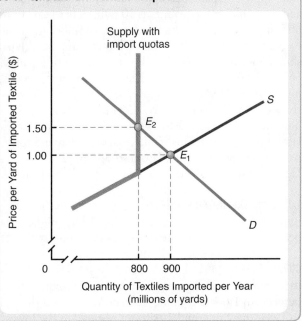

Why did U.S. government agents recently conduct a raid on a U.S. guitar manufacturer?

Gibson Guitars Confronts a Very Particular Import Quota

One of the most famous U.S. guitar makers is Gibson Guitars, which places a "Made in the U.S.A." label on each instrument it sells. Recently, federal agents raided the company's corporate offices and its two guitar factories. The agents seized 24 pallets of rosewood and ebony imported from India, which Gibson had planned to use in making fingerboards for its guitars.

The company, the U.S. government alleged, had run afoul of an international trade quota on unfinished rosewood and ebony products. Finished rosewood or ebony, though, had no U.S. trade quota. Hence, if Indian workers

had finished the rosewood and ebony prior to shipment, instead of Gibson's U.S. workers finishing the materials following shipment. Gibson would not have violated any U.S. trade quotas.

FOR CRITICAL THINKING
Gibson presumably violated an environmental protection law. Why does this trade quota have the same economic effects as laws designed to protect domestic firms from foreign competition?

Voluntary restraint agreement (VRA)
An official agreement with another country that "voluntarily" restricts the quantity of its exports to the United States.

Voluntary import expansion (VIE)
An official agreement with another country in which it agrees to import more from the United States.

VOLUNTARY QUOTAS Quotas do not have to be explicit and defined by law. They can be "voluntary." Such a quota is called a **voluntary restraint agreement (VRA)**. In the early 1980s, Japanese automakers voluntarily restrained exports to the United States. These restraints stayed in place into the 1990s. Today, there are VRAs on machine tools and textiles.

The opposite of a VRA is a **voluntary import expansion (VIE)**. Under a VIE, a foreign government agrees to have its companies import more foreign goods from another country. The United States almost started a major international trade war with Japan in 1995 over just such an issue. The U.S. government wanted Japanese automobile manufacturers to voluntarily increase their imports of U.S.-made automobile parts. Ultimately, Japanese companies did make a token increase in their imports of U.S. auto parts.

Tariffs

Go to www.econtoday.com/chap32 to take a look at the U.S. State Department's reports on economic policy and trade practices.

We can analyze tariffs by using standard supply and demand diagrams. Let's use as our commodity laptop computers, some of which are made in Japan and some of which are made domestically. In panel (a) of Figure 32-4 on the facing page, you see the demand for and supply of Japanese laptops. The equilibrium price is $500 per constant-quality unit, and the equilibrium quantity is 10 million per year. In panel (b), you see the same equilibrium price of $500, and the *domestic* equilibrium quantity is 5 million units per year.

Now a tariff of $250 is imposed on all imported Japanese laptops. The supply curve shifts upward by $250 to S_2. For purchasers of Japanese laptops, the price increases to $625. The quantity demanded falls to 8 million per year. In panel (b), you see that at the higher price of imported Japanese laptops, the demand curve for U.S.-made laptops shifts outward to the right to D_2. The equilibrium price increases to $625, and the equilibrium quantity increases to 6.5 million units per year. So the tariff benefits domestic laptop producers because it increases the demand for their products due to the higher price of a close substitute, Japanese laptops. This causes a redistribution of income from Japanese producers and U.S. consumers of laptops to U.S. producers of laptops.

TARIFFS IN THE UNITED STATES In Figure 32-5 on the facing page, we see that tariffs on all imported goods have varied widely. The highest rates in the twentieth century occurred with the passage of the Smoot-Hawley Tariff in 1930.

CURRENT TARIFF LAWS The Trade Expansion Act of 1962 gave the president the authority to reduce tariffs by up to 50 percent. Subsequently, tariffs were reduced by about 35 percent. In 1974, the Trade Reform Act allowed the president to reduce tariffs further. In 1984, the Trade and Tariff Act resulted in the lowest tariff rates ever. All such trade agreement obligations of the United States were carried out under the auspices of the

FIGURE 32-4

The Effect of a Tariff on Japanese-Made Laptop Computers

Without a tariff, the United States buys 10 million Japanese laptops per year at an average price of $500, at point E_1 in panel (a). U.S. producers sell 5 million domestically made laptops, also at $500 each, at point E_1 in panel (b). A $250 tariff per laptop will shift the Japanese import supply curve to S_2 in panel (a), so that the new equilibrium is at E_2 with price increased to $625 and quantity sold reduced to 8 million per year. The demand curve for U.S.-made laptops (for which there is no tariff) shifts to D_2, in panel (b). Domestic sales increase to 6.5 million per year, at point E_2.

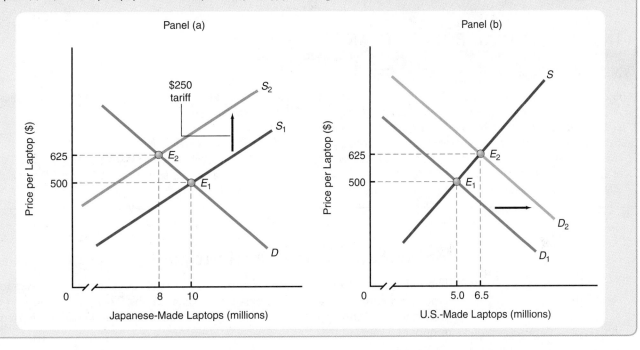

FIGURE 32-5

Tariff Rates in the United States Since 1820

Tariff rates in the United States have bounced around like a football. Indeed, in Congress, tariffs are a political football. Import-competing industries prefer high tariffs. In the twentieth century, the highest tariff was the Smoot-Hawley Tariff of 1930, which was about as high as the "tariff of abominations" in 1828.

Source: U.S. Department of Commerce.

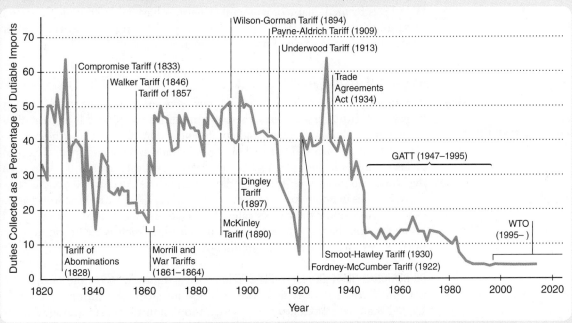

General Agreement on Tariffs and Trade (GATT)

An international agreement established in 1947 to further world trade by reducing barriers and tariffs. The GATT was replaced by the World Trade Organization in 1995.

General Agreement on Tariffs and Trade (GATT), which was signed in 1947. Member nations of the GATT account for more than 85 percent of world trade. As you can see in Figure 32-5 on the previous page, U.S. tariff rates have declined since the early 1960s, when several rounds of negotiations under the GATT were initiated.

How have recently reduced barriers to trade with the United States affected nations in Africa?

INTERNATIONAL POLICY EXAMPLE

African Nations Benefit from Lower U.S. Trade Barriers

In 2000, the U.S. Congress passed the African Growth and Opportunity Act, which reduced substantially the tariffs faced by African companies seeking to export goods and services to the United States. African-U.S. trade has risen considerably since. Earnings that African companies derive from exports are now 500 percent higher than in 2001. Furthermore, estimates indicate that export industries in African nations now employ 300,000 additional workers as a consequence of the increased volume of trade. Thus, slashing trade barriers has generated welfare gains for African residents.

FOR CRITICAL THINKING
How might U.S. residents have benefited from the fact that African countries granted reciprocal reductions in tariffs on imports into their nations from the United States?

International Trade Organizations

The widespread effort to reduce tariffs around the world has generated interest among nations in joining various international trade organizations. These organizations promote trade by granting preferences in the form of reduced or eliminated tariffs, duties, or quotas.

The World Trade Organization (WTO)

World Trade Organization (WTO)

The successor organization to the GATT that handles trade disputes among its member nations.

The most important international trade organization with the largest membership is the **World Trade Organization (WTO),** which was ratified by the final round of negotiations of the General Agreement on Tariffs and Trade at the end of 1993. The WTO, which as of 2012 had 157 member nations and included 30 observer governments, began operations on January 1, 1995. The WTO has fostered important and far-reaching global trade agreements. There is considerable evidence that since the WTO was formed, many of its member nations have adopted policies promoting international trade. The WTO also adjudicates trade disputes between nations in an effort to reduce the scope of protectionism around the globe.

Regional Trade Agreements

Regional trade bloc

A group of nations that grants members special trade privileges.

Numerous other international trade organizations exist alongside the WTO. Sometimes known as **regional trade blocs,** these organizations are created by special deals among groups of countries that grant trade preferences only to countries within their groups. Currently, more than 475 bilateral or regional trade agreements are in effect around the globe. Examples include groups of industrial powerhouses, such as the European Union, the North American Free Trade Agreement, and the Association of Southeast Asian Nations. Nations in South America with per capita real GDP nearer the world average have also formed regional trade blocs called Mercosur and the Andean Community. Less developed nations have also formed regional trade blocs, such as the Economic Community of West African States and the Community of East and Southern Africa.

DO REGIONAL TRADE BLOCS SIMPLY DIVERT TRADE? Figure 32-6 on the facing page shows that the formation of regional trade blocs, in which the European Union and the United States are often key participants, is on an upswing. An average African nation participates in four separate regional trading agreements. A typical Latin American country belongs to eight different regional trade blocs.

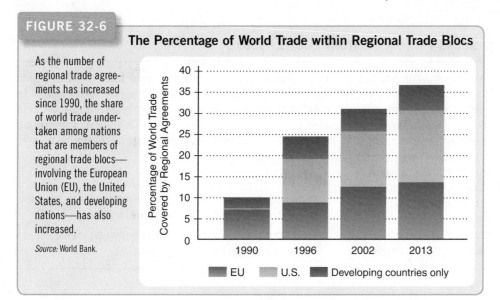

FIGURE 32-6

The Percentage of World Trade within Regional Trade Blocs

As the number of regional trade agreements has increased since 1990, the share of world trade undertaken among nations that are members of regional trade blocs—involving the European Union (EU), the United States, and developing nations—has also increased.

Source: World Bank.

EU   U.S.   Developing countries only

In the past, economists worried that the formation of regional trade blocs could mainly result in **trade diversion,** or the shifting of trade from countries outside a regional trade bloc to nations within a bloc. Indeed, a study by Jeffrey Frankel of Harvard University found evidence that some trade diversion does take place. Nevertheless, Frankel and other economists have concluded that the net effect of regional trade agreements has been to boost overall international trade, in some cases considerably.

THE TRADE DEFLECTION ISSUE Today, the primary issue associated with regional trade blocs is **trade deflection.** This occurs when a company located in a nation outside a regional trade bloc moves goods that are not quite fully assembled into a member country, completes assembly of the goods there, and then exports them to other nations in the bloc. To try to reduce incentives for trade deflection, regional trade agreements often include **rules of origin,** which are regulations carefully defining categories of products that are eligible for trading preferences under the agreements. Some rules of origin, for instance, require any products trading freely among members of a bloc to be composed mainly of materials produced within a member nation.

Proponents of free trade worry, however, about the potential for parties to regional trade agreements to use rules of origin to create barriers to trade. Sufficiently complex rules of origin, they suggest, can provide disincentives for countries to utilize the trade-promoting preferences that regional trade agreements ought to provide. Indeed, some free trade proponents applaud successful trade deflection. They contend that it helps to circumvent trade restrictions and thus allows nations within regional trade blocs to experience additional gains from trade.

Trade diversion
Shifting existing international trade from countries outside a regional trade bloc to nations within the bloc.

Trade deflection
Moving partially assembled products into a member nation of a regional trade bloc, completing assembly, and then exporting them to other nations within the bloc, so as to benefit from preferences granted by the trade bloc.

Rules of origin
Regulations that nations in regional trade blocs establish to delineate product categories eligible for trading preferences.

QUICK QUIZ   See page 724 for the answers. Review concepts from this section in MyEconLab.

One means of restricting foreign trade is an import quota, which specifies a _____ amount of a good that may be imported during a certain period. The resulting increase in import prices benefits domestic _____ that receive higher prices resulting from substitution to domestic goods.

Another means of restricting imports is a **tariff,** which is a _____ on imports only. An import tariff _____ import-competing industries and harms consumers by raising prices.

The main international institution created to improve trade among nations was the General Agreement on Tariffs and Trade (GATT). The last round of trade talks under the GATT led to the creation of the _____ _____ _____.

_____ _____ agreements among numerous nations of the world have established more than 475 bilateral and _____ _____ blocs, which grant special trade privileges such as reduced tariff barriers and quota exemptions to member nations.

YOU ARE THERE
A French Family Bookshop Seeks Protection from U.S. E-Books

For more than three decades, Thierry Meaudre's family bookshop in Paris has been protected from competition with large foreign booksellers by a French law restricting the distribution of imported "printed volumes." The legislation effectively constrains the number of physical books imported into the country and thereby restrains the nationwide market supply of books, which raises book prices. This enables Meaudre's store and the other 3,000 independent bookstores operating in France, a nation of 65 million people, to earn sufficient profits to remain in business. By way of comparison, fewer than 2,000 independent bookstores operate in the United States, a country with over 300 million residents.

The advent of low-priced U.S. e-book imports fills Meaudre with dread, because the existing law's limits of "printed volumes" do not include e-books.

"I have been having nightmares about digital books for years," admits Meaudre. If French consumers are allowed to purchase e-book imports, he thinks that his store might be able to remain open "perhaps at most another 10 years." In the face of the e-book threat, Meaudre is supporting a proposed law that would boost e-book prices and help keep Meaudre's bookshop in business.

Critical Thinking Questions

1. Why might imports of e-books be more difficult for the French government to limit than imports of "physical volumes"?

2. If the proposed French law succeeds in limiting e-book imports into France, who will pay higher e-book prices?

ISSUES & APPLICATIONS

U.S. Flower Growers Induce Congress to Snip Foreign Imports

CONCEPTS APPLIED
▶ Regional Trade Bloc
▶ Tariffs
▶ Subsidies

When the U.S. Congress passed the 1991 Andean Trade Promotion Act, it established a regional trade bloc encompassing the United States and several South American nations located along the Andes mountain range. This law slashed tariff rates on goods imported into the United States from Andean nations.

Budding Colombian Imports of Cut Flowers Ultimately Blossom

Among the imported items for which the 1991 legislation sharply reduced U.S. tariff rates were Colombian cut flowers. The Colombian climate is superior to that of the western United States for growing most flowers, and Colombian farm labor costs are much lower. Thus, within a few years after the reduction in tariffs, Colombian flower growers had established a network for selling cut flowers in California. Furthermore, in 2010, the Colombian firms opened a large distribution center in Los Angeles to increase the flow of cut-flower imports into the United States.

As Figure 32-7 on the facing page indicates, Colombian flower growers' efforts led to a substantial increase in

U.S. flower imports from that nation during the 2000s. By 2010, U.S. imports of Colombian cut flowers were nearly 400 percent greater than the 2002 level.

California Flower Growers Lobby for Protection

As Colombian flower imports into California bloomed, the sales of cut flowers by California growers shriveled. When Congress passed the Andean Trade Promotion Act, there were 450 Californian flower farms. By 2010, there were 250.

In response to the upsurge in competition from Colombia, the California Cut Flower Commission, a trade association, successfully lobbied to delay congressional approval of a renewal of the Andean regional trade pact. The consequence

FIGURE 32-7

U.S. Imports of Cut Flowers from Colombia since 2002

The dollar value of cut flowers imported from Colombia increased substantially during the 2000s but plummeted after California flower growers succeeded in delaying renewal of the Andean Trade Promotion Act.

Sources: U.S. International Trade Commission; author's estimates.

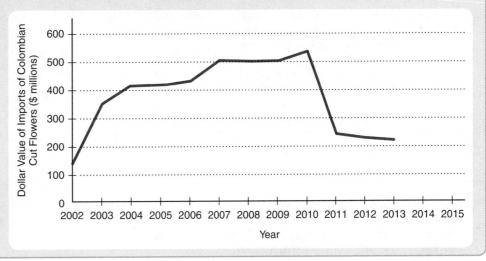

was a reimposition in 2011 of tariffs on Colombian flower growers, whose tariff payments increased sharply. As shown in Figure 32-7 above, this significant tariff increase resulted in a considerable reduction in cut-flower imports from Colombia. As a consequence, the foreign supply of cut flowers in California decreased, and the demand for Californian cut flowers increased, which pushed up U.S. prices of cut flowers. Even as California flower growers' earnings flourished, they began lobbying for U.S. government subsidies to enable them to establish their own cut-flower distribution center to compete with Colombia's.

For Critical Thinking

1. Which region appears to have a comparative advantage in producing cut flowers: Colombia or California? Explain.

2. How have U.S. consumers of cut flowers been affected by the cutback in Colombian imports?

Web Resources

1. Find out more about the Andean Trade Promotion Act at **www.econtoday.com/chap32**.

2. Learn about the Colombian flower industry at **www.econtoday .com/chap32**.

MyEconLab

For more questions on this chapter's Issues & Applications, go to MyEconLab. In the Study Plan for this chapter, select Section N: News.

MyEconLab

Here is what you should know after reading this chapter. MyEconLab will help you identify what you know, and where to go when you need to practice.

— WHAT YOU SHOULD KNOW —

The Worldwide Importance of International Trade Total trade among nations has been growing faster than total world GDP. The growth of U.S. exports and imports relative to U.S. GDP parallels this global trend. Today, exports constitute more than 14 percent of total national production. In some countries, trade accounts for a much higher share of total economic activity.

Key Figure
Figure 32-1, 705

— WHERE TO GO TO PRACTICE —

• MyEconLab Study Plan 32.1
• Animated Figure 32-1

MyEconLab *continued*

Why Nations Can Gain from Specializing in Production and Engaging in Trade A country has a comparative advantage in producing a good if it can produce that good at a lower opportunity cost, in terms of forgone production of a second good, than another nation. Both nations can gain by specializing in producing the goods in which they have a comparative advantage and engaging in trade. Together, they can consume more than they would have in the absence of specialization and trade.

comparative advantage, 706

Key Figure
Figure 32-2, 710

- MyEconLab Study Plan 32.2
- Animated Figure 32-2

Arguments against Free Trade One argument against free trade is that temporary import restrictions might permit an "infant industry" to develop. Another argument concerns dumping, in which foreign firms allegedly sell some of their output in domestic markets at prices below the prices in their home markets or even below their costs of production. In addition, some environmentalists support restrictions on foreign trade to protect their nations from exposure to environmental hazards. Finally, some contend that countries should limit exports of technologies that could pose a threat to their national defense.

infant industry argument, 713
dumping, 713

- MyEconLab Study Plans 32.3, 32.4, 32.5

Ways That Nations Restrict Foreign Trade One way to restrain trade is to impose a quota, or a limit on imports of a good. This action restricts the supply of the good in the domestic market, thereby pushing up the equilibrium price of the good. Another way to reduce trade is to place a tariff on imported goods. This reduces the supply of foreign-made goods and increases the demand for domestically produced goods, thereby bringing about a rise in the price of the good.

quota system, 715
voluntary restraint agreement (VRA), 716
voluntary import expansion (VIE), 716
General Agreement on Tariffs and Trade (GATT), 718

Key Figures
Figure 32-3, 715
Figure 32-4, 717

- MyEconLab Study Plan 32.6
- Animated Figures 32-3, 32-4

Key International Trade Agreements and Organizations From 1947 to 1995, nations agreed to abide by the General Agreement on Tariffs and Trade (GATT), which laid an international legal foundation for relaxing quotas and reducing tariffs. Since 1995, the World Trade Organization (WTO) has adjudicated trade disputes that arise between or among nations. Now there are also more than 475 bilateral and regional trade blocs, including the North American Free Trade Agreement and the European Union, that provide special trade preferences to member nations.

World Trade Organization, 718
regional trade bloc, 718
trade diversion, 719
trade deflection, 719
rules of origin, 719

Key Figure
Figure 32-5, 717

- MyEconLab Study Plan 32.7
- Animated Figure 32-5

Log in to MyEconLab, take a chapter test, and get a personalized Study Plan that tells you which concepts you understand and which ones you need to review. From there, MyEconLab will give you further practice, tutorials, animations, videos, and guided solutions. For more information, visit www.myeconlab.com

PROBLEMS

All problems are assignable in MyEconLab. Answers to the odd-numbered problems appear at the back of the book.

32-1. To answer the questions below, consider the following table for the neighboring nations of Northland and West Coast. The table lists maximum feasible hourly rates of production of pastries if no sandwiches are produced and maximum feasible hourly rates of production of sandwiches if no pastries are produced. Assume that the opportunity costs of producing these goods are constant in both nations. (See page 707.)

Product	Northland	West Coast
Pastries (per hour)	50,000	100,000
Sandwiches (per hour)	25,000	200,000

  a. What is the opportunity cost of producing pastries in Northland? Of producing sandwiches in Northland?

  b. What is the opportunity cost of producing pastries in West Coast? Of producing sandwiches in West Coast?

32-2. Based on your answers to Problem 32-1, which nation has a comparative advantage in producing pastries? Which nation has a comparative advantage in producing sandwiches? (See page 707.)

32-3. Suppose that the two nations in Problems 32-1 and 32-2 choose to specialize in producing the goods for which they have a comparative advantage. They agree to trade at a rate of exchange of 1 pastry for 1 sandwich. At this rate of exchange, what are the maximum possible numbers of pastries and sandwiches that they could agree to trade? (See page 708.)

32-4. Residents of the nation of Border Kingdom can forgo production of digital televisions and utilize all available resources to produce 300 bottles of high-quality wine per hour. Alternatively, they can forgo producing wine and instead produce 60 digital TVs per hour. In the neighboring country of Coastal Realm, residents can forgo production of digital TVs and use all resources to produce 150 bottles of high-quality wine per hour, or they can forgo wine production and produce 50 digital TVs per hour. In both nations, the opportunity costs of producing the two goods are constant. (See pages 707–708.)

  a. What is the opportunity cost of producing digital TVs in Border Kingdom? Of producing bottles of wine in Border Kingdom?

  b. What is the opportunity cost of producing digital TVs in Coastal Realm? Of producing bottles of wine in Coastal Realm?

32-5. Based on your answers to Problem 32-4, which nation has a comparative advantage in producing digital TVs? Which nation has a comparative advantage in producing bottles of wine? (See page 708.)

32-6. Suppose that the two nations in Problem 32-4 decide to specialize in producing the good for which they have a comparative advantage and to engage in trade. Would residents of both nations find a rate of exchange of 4 bottles of wine for 1 digital TV potentially agreeable? Why or why not? (See pages 708–709.)

To answer Problems 32-7 and 32-8, refer to the following table, which shows possible combinations of hourly outputs of modems and flash memory drives in South Shore and neighboring East Isle, in which opportunity costs of producing both products are constant.

South Shore		East Isle	
Modems	Flash Drives	Modems	Flash Drives
75	0	100	0
60	30	80	10
45	60	60	20
30	90	40	30
15	120	20	40
0	150	0	50

32-7. Consider the above table and answer the questions that follow. (See pages 707–709.)

  a. What is the opportunity cost of producing modems in South Shore? Of producing flash memory drives in South Shore?

  b. What is the opportunity cost of producing modems in East Isle? Of producing flash memory drives in East Isle?

  c. Which nation has a comparative advantage in producing modems? Which nation has a comparative advantage in producing flash memory drives?

32-8. Refer to your answers to Problem 32-7 when answering the following questions. (See page 709.)

  a. Which *one* of the following rates of exchange of modems for flash memory drives will be acceptable to *both* nations: (i) 3 modems for 1 flash drive; (ii) 1 modem for 1 flash drive; or (iii) 1 flash drive for 2.5 modems? Explain.

  b. Suppose that each nation decides to use all available resources to produce only the good for which it has a comparative advantage and to engage in trade at the single feasible rate of exchange you identified in part (a). Prior to specialization and trade, residents of South Shore chose to produce and consume 30 modems per hour and 90 flash drives per hour, and residents of East Isle chose to produce and consume 40 modems per hour and 30 flash drives per hour. Now, residents of South Shore agree to export to East Isle the same quantity of South Shore's specialty good that East Isle residents were consuming prior to engaging in international trade. How many units of East Isle's specialty good does South Shore import from East Isle?

c. What is South Shore's hourly consumption of modems and flash drives after the nation specializes and trades with East Isle? What is East Isle's hourly consumption of modems and flash drives after the nation specializes and trades with South Shore?

d. What consumption gains from trade are experienced by South Shore and East Isle?

32-9. Critics of the North American Free Trade Agreement (NAFTA) suggest that much of the increase in exports from Mexico to the United States now involves goods that Mexico otherwise would have exported to other nations. Mexican firms choose to export the goods to the United States, the critics argue, solely because the items receive preferential treatment under NAFTA tariff rules. What term describes what these critics are claiming is occurring with regard to U.S.-Mexican trade as a result of NAFTA? Explain your reasoning. (See pages 718–719.)

32-10. Some critics of the North American Free Trade Agreement (NAFTA) suggest that firms outside NAFTA nations sometimes shift unassembled inputs to Mexico, assemble the inputs into final goods there, and then export the final product to the United States in order to take advantage of Mexican trade preferences. What term describes what these critics are claiming is occurring with regard to U.S.-Mexican trade as a result of NAFTA? Explain your reasoning. (See page 719.)

32-11. How could multilateral trade agreements established for all nations through the World Trade Organization help to prevent both trade diversion and trade deflection that can occur under regional trade agreements, thereby promoting more overall international trade? (See page 719.)

ECONOMICS ON THE NET

How the World Trade Organization Settles Trade Disputes
A key function of the WTO is to adjudicate trade disagreements that arise among nations. This application helps you learn about the process that the WTO follows when considering international trade disputes.

Title: The World Trade Organization: Settling Trade Disputes

Navigation: Go to www.econtoday.com/chap32 to access the WTO's Web page titled *Dispute Settlement*. Under "Introduction to dispute settlement in the WTO," click on *How does the WTO settle disputes?*

Application Read the article. Then answer the following questions.

1. As the article discusses, settling trade disputes often takes at least a year. What aspects of the WTO's dispute settlement process take the longest time?

2. Does the WTO actually "punish" a country it finds has broken international trading agreements? If not, who does impose sanctions?

For Group Study and Analysis Go to the WTO's main site at www.econtoday.com/chap32, and click on *The WTO*. Divide the class into groups, and have the groups explore this information on areas of WTO involvement. Have a class discussion of the pros and cons of WTO involvement in these areas. Which are most important for promoting world trade? Which are least important?

ANSWERS TO QUICK QUIZZES

p. 712: (i) lower; (ii) comparative advantage . . . consume; (iii) Gains . . . consume

p. 714: (i) infant . . . protected; (ii) dumping . . . dumping

p. 719: (i) maximum . . . producers; (ii) tax . . . benefits; (iii) World Trade Organization; (iv) Regional trade . . . regional trade

Exchange Rates and the Balance of Payments

33

LEARNING OBJECTIVES

After reading this chapter, you should be able to:

▶ Distinguish between the balance of trade and the balance of payments

▶ Identify the key accounts within the balance of payments

▶ Outline how exchange rates are determined in the markets for foreign exchange

▶ Discuss factors that can induce changes in equilibrium exchange rates

▶ Understand how policymakers can go about attempting to fix exchange rates

MyEconLab helps you master each objective and study more efficiently. See end of chapter for details.

Every few months, a U.S. media story reports on the substantial gap between U.S. imports of physical goods from China and U.S. exports of goods to China. Typically, media commentators follow up with complaints that U.S. residents are thoughtlessly paying prices for Chinese imports that effectively transfer a portion of U.S. residents' incomes to people in China. Does every dollar that you pay for a Chinese-manufactured item translate into an income transfer from the United States to China? Before you can answer this question, you must learn how economists use an accounting system called the *balance of payments* to track flows of spending on goods and services exported from and imported into the United States.

the annual dollar value of trading in *foreign exchange markets*—markets in which people buy and sell national currencies, such as the U.S. dollar, European euro, Japanese yen, or Chinese yuan—exceeds $4 trillion? Thus, the total value of exchanges of the world's currencies during a given year amounts to more than one-fourth of the value of exchanges for all goods and services produced per year in the United States. By the time you have completed this chapter, you will understand why people desire to obtain so many currencies of other nations in foreign exchange markets scattered around the globe. First, however, you must learn how we keep track of flows of payments across a country's borders.

The Balance of Payments and International Capital Movements

Governments typically keep track of each year's economic activities by calculating the gross domestic product—the total of expenditures on all newly domestic-produced final goods and services—and its components. A summary information system has also been developed for international trade. It covers the balance of trade and the balance of payments. The **balance of trade** refers specifically to exports and imports of physical goods, or merchandise, as discussed in Chapter 32. When international trade is in balance, the value of exports equals the value of imports. When the value of imports exceeds the value of exports, we are running a deficit in the balance of trade. When the value of exports exceeds the value of imports, we are running a surplus.

The **balance of payments** is a more general concept that expresses the total of all economic transactions between a nation and the rest of the world, usually for a period of one year. Each country's balance of payments summarizes information about that country's exports and imports of services as well as physical goods, earnings by domestic residents on assets located abroad, earnings on domestic assets owned by residents of foreign nations, international capital movements, and official transactions by central banks and governments. In essence, then, the balance of payments is a record of all the transactions between households, firms, and the government of one country and the rest of the world. Any transaction that leads to a *payment* by a country's residents (or government) is a deficit item, identified by a negative sign (−) when the actual numbers are given for the items listed in the second column of Table 33-1 on the facing page. Any transaction that leads to a *receipt* by a country's residents (or government) is a surplus item and is identified by a plus sign (+) when actual numbers are considered. Table 33-1 provides a list of the surplus and deficit items on international accounts.

Accounting Identities

Accounting identities—definitions of equivalent values—exist for financial institutions and other businesses. We begin with simple accounting identities that must hold for families and then go on to describe international accounting identities.

If a family unit is spending more than its current income, the family unit must necessarily be doing one of the following:

1. Reducing its money holdings or selling stocks, bonds, or other assets

2. Borrowing

3. Receiving gifts from friends or relatives

4. Receiving public transfers from a government, which obtained the funds by taxing others (a transfer is a payment, in money or in goods or services, made without receiving goods or services in return)

We can use this information to derive an identity: If a family unit is currently spending more than it is earning, it must draw on previously acquired wealth, borrow, or receive either private or public aid. Similarly, an identity exists for a family unit that is

---

Balance of trade
The difference between exports and imports of physical goods.

Balance of payments
A system of accounts that measures transactions of goods, services, income, and financial assets between domestic households, businesses, and governments and residents of the rest of the world during a specific time period.

Accounting identities
Values that are equivalent by definition.

TABLE 33-1

Surplus (+) and Deficit (−) Items on the International Accounts

Surplus Items (+)	Deficit Items (−)
Exports of merchandise	Imports of merchandise
Private and governmental gifts from foreign residents	Private and governmental gifts to foreign residents
Foreign use of domestically operated travel and transportation services	Use of foreign-operated travel and transportation services
Foreign tourists' expenditures in this country	U.S. tourists' expenditures abroad
Foreign military spending in this country	Military spending abroad
Interest and dividend receipts from foreign entities	Interest and dividends paid to foreign individuals and businesses
Sales of domestic assets to foreign residents	Purchases of foreign assets
Funds deposited in this country by foreign residents	Funds placed in foreign depository institutions
Sales of gold to foreign residents	Purchases of gold from foreign residents
Sales of domestic currency to foreign residents	Purchases of foreign currency

currently spending less than it is earning: It must be increasing its money holdings or be lending and acquiring other financial assets, or it must pay taxes or bestow gifts on others. When we consider businesses and governments, each unit in each group faces its own accounting identities or constraints. Ultimately, *net* lending by households must equal *net* borrowing by businesses and governments.

DISEQUILIBRIUM Even though our individual family unit's accounts must balance, in the sense that the identity discussed previously must hold, sometimes the item that brings about the balance cannot continue indefinitely. *If family expenditures exceed family income and this situation is financed by borrowing, the household may be considered to be in disequilibrium because such a situation cannot continue indefinitely.* If such a deficit is financed by drawing on previously accumulated assets, the family may also be in disequilibrium because it cannot continue indefinitely to draw on its wealth.

Eventually, the family will find it impossible to continue that lifestyle. (Of course, if the family members are retired, they may well be in equilibrium by drawing on previously acquired assets to finance current deficits. This example illustrates that it is necessary to understand all circumstances fully before pronouncing an economic unit in disequilibrium.)

EQUILIBRIUM Individual households, businesses, and governments, as well as the entire group of all households, businesses, and governments, must eventually reach equilibrium. Certain economic adjustment mechanisms have evolved to ensure equilibrium. Deficit households must eventually increase their income or decrease their expenditures. They will find that they have to pay higher interest rates if they wish to borrow to finance their deficits. Eventually, their credit sources will dry up, and they will be forced into equilibrium. Businesses, on occasion, must lower costs or prices—or go bankrupt—to reach equilibrium.

AN ACCOUNTING IDENTITY AMONG NATIONS When people from different nations trade or interact, certain identities or constraints must also hold. People buy goods from people in other nations. They also lend to and present gifts to people in other nations. If residents of a nation interact with residents of other nations, an accounting identity ensures a balance (but not necessarily an equilibrium, as will soon become clear). Let's look at the three categories of balance of payments transactions: current account transactions, capital account transactions, and official reserve account transactions.

Current Account Transactions

Current account
A category of balance of payments transactions that measures the exchange of merchandise, the exchange of services, and unilateral transfers.

During any designated period, all payments and gifts that are related to the purchase or sale of both goods and services constitute the **current account** in international trade. Major types of current account transactions include the exchange of merchandise, the exchange of services, and unilateral transfers.

MERCHANDISE TRADE EXPORTS AND IMPORTS The largest portion of any nation's balance of payments current account is typically the importing and exporting of merchandise. During 2013, for example, as shown in lines 1 and 2 of Table 33-2 below, the United States exported an estimated $1,609.7 billion of merchandise and imported $2,404.5 billion. The balance of merchandise trade is defined as the difference between the value of merchandise exports and the value of merchandise imports. For 2013, the United States had a balance of merchandise trade deficit because the value of its merchandise imports exceeded the value of its merchandise exports. This deficit was about $794.8 billion (line 3).

SERVICE EXPORTS AND IMPORTS The balance of (merchandise) trade involves tangible items—things you can feel, touch, and see. Service exports and imports involve invisible or intangible items that are bought and sold, such as shipping, insurance, tourist expenditures, and banking services. Also, income earned by foreign residents on U.S. investments and income earned by U.S. residents on foreign investments are part of service imports and exports. As shown in lines 4 and 5 of Table 33-2, in 2013, estimated service exports were $564.6 billion, and service imports were $416.8 billion. Thus, the balance of services was about $147.8 billion in 2013 (line 6). Exports constitute receipts or inflows into the United States and are positive. Imports constitute payments abroad or outflows of money and are negative.

When we combine the balance of merchandise trade with the balance of services, we obtain a balance on goods and services equal to −$647.0 billion in 2013 (line 7).

TABLE 33-2

U.S. Balance of Payments Account, Estimated for 2013 (in billions of dollars)

Current Account

(1) Exports of merchandise goods	+1,609.7	
(2) Imports of merchandise goods	−2,404.5	
(3) Balance of merchandise trade		−794.8
(4) Exports of services	+564.6	
(5) Imports of services	−416.8	
(6) Balance of services		+147.8
(7) Balance on goods and services [(3) + (6)]		−647.0
(8) Net unilateral transfers	−159.3	
(9) Balance on current account		−806.3

Capital Account

(10) U.S. private capital going abroad	−299.2	
(11) Foreign private capital coming into the United States	+665.3*	
(12) Balance on capital account [(10) + (11)]		+366.1
(13) Balance on current account plus balance on capital account [(9) + (12)]		−440.2

Official Reserve Transactions Account

(14) Official transactions balance		+440.2
(15) Total (balance)		0

Sources: U.S. Department of Commerce, Bureau of Economic Analysis; author's estimates.

*Includes an approximately $28 billion statistical discrepancy, probably uncounted capital inflows, many of which relate to the illegal drug trade.

UNILATERAL TRANSFERS U.S. residents give gifts to relatives and others abroad, the federal government makes grants to foreign nations, foreign residents give gifts to U.S. residents, and in the past some foreign governments have granted funds to the U.S. government. In the current account, we see that net unilateral transfers—the total amount of gifts given by U.S. residents and the government minus the total amount received from abroad by U.S. residents and the government—came to an estimated −$159.3 billion in 2013 (line 8). The minus sign before the number for unilateral transfers means that U.S. residents and the U.S. government gave more to foreign residents than foreign residents gave to U.S. residents.

BALANCING THE CURRENT ACCOUNT The balance on current account tracks the value of a country's exports of goods and services (including income on investments abroad) and transfer payments (private and government) relative to the value of that country's imports of goods and services and transfer payments (private and government). In 2013, it was estimated to be −$806.3 billion (line 9).

If the sum of net exports of goods and services plus net unilateral transfers plus net investment income exceeds zero, a **current account surplus** *is said to exist. If this sum is negative, a* **current account deficit** *is said to exist. A current account deficit means that we are importing more goods and services than we are exporting. Such a deficit must be paid for by the export of financial assets.*

Go to www.econtoday.com/chap33 for the latest U.S. balance of payments data from the Bureau of Economic Analysis.

WHAT IF... all governments attempted to require their nations to have current account surpluses?

By definition, a current account surplus arises in a nation when its residents export more goods and services than they import. The only way for some nations to have current account surpluses, though, is for others to operate with current account deficits. That is, residents of some countries must import more goods and services than they export in order for other nations to be able to export more goods and services than they import. Thus, if all governments were to require that their countries have current account surpluses, their efforts would be doomed to failure.

Capital Account Transactions

In world markets, it is possible to buy and sell not only goods and services but also financial assets. These international transactions are measured in the **capital account.** Capital account transactions occur because of foreign investments—either by foreign residents investing in the United States or by U.S. residents investing in other countries. The purchase of shares of stock in British firms on the London stock market by a U.S. resident causes an outflow of funds from the United States to Britain. The construction of a Japanese automobile factory in the United States causes an inflow of funds from Japan to the United States. Any time foreign residents buy U.S. government securities, there is an inflow of funds from other countries to the United States. Any time U.S. residents buy foreign government securities, there is an outflow of funds from the United States to other countries. Loans to and from foreign residents cause outflows and inflows.

Line 10 of Table 33-2 on the facing page indicates that in 2013, the value of private capital going out of the United States was an estimated −$299.2 billion, and line 11 shows that the value of private capital coming into the United States (including a statistical discrepancy) was $665.3 billion. U.S. capital going abroad constitutes payments or outflows and is therefore negative. Foreign capital coming into the United States constitutes receipts or inflows and is therefore positive. Thus, there was a positive net capital movement of $366.1 billion into the United States (line 12). This net private flow of capital is also called the balance on capital account.

There is a relationship between the current account balance and the capital account balance, assuming no interventions by the finance ministries or central banks of nations.

Capital account
A category of balance of payments transactions that measures flows of financial assets.

In the absence of interventions by finance ministries or central banks, the current account balance and the capital account balance must sum to zero. Stated differently, the current account deficit must equal the capital account surplus when governments or central banks do not engage in foreign exchange interventions. In this situation, any nation experiencing a current account deficit, such as the United States, must also be running a capital account surplus.

This basic relationship is apparent in the United States, as you can see in Figure 33-1 below. As the figure shows, U.S. current account deficits experienced since the early 1980s have been balanced by private capital inflows and *official reserve transactions,* to which we now turn our attention.

Official Reserve Account Transactions

The third type of balance of payments transaction concerns official reserve assets, which consist of the following:

1. Foreign currencies

2. Gold

3. **Special drawing rights (SDRs)**, which are reserve assets that the **International Monetary Fund** created to be used by countries to settle international payment obligations

4. The reserve position in the International Monetary Fund

5. Financial assets held by an official agency, such as the U.S. Treasury Department

To consider how official reserve account transactions occur, look again at Table 33-2 on page 728. The surplus in the U.S. capital account was $366.1 billion. But the deficit in the U.S. current account was −$806.3 billion, so the United States had a net deficit

Special drawing rights (SDRs)
Reserve assets created by the International Monetary Fund for countries to use in settling international payment obligations.

International Monetary Fund
An agency founded to administer an international foreign exchange system and to lend to member countries that had balance of payments problems. The IMF now functions as a lender of last resort for national governments.

FIGURE 33-1   MyEconLab Real-time data

The Relationship between the Current Account and the Capital Account

The current account balance is the mirror image of the sum of the capital account balance and the official transactions balance. We can see this in years since 1970. When the current account balance was in surplus, the sum of the capital account balance and the official transactions balance was negative. When the current account balance was in deficit, the sum of the current account balance and the official transactions balance was positive.

Sources: International Monetary Fund; *Economic Indicators.*

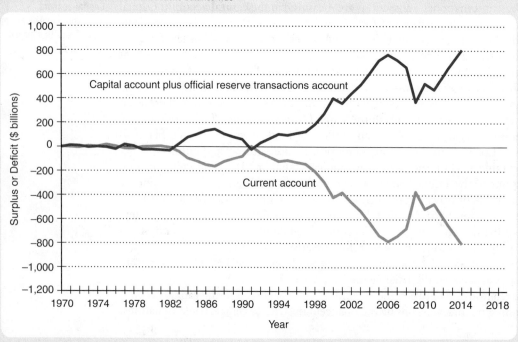

on the combined accounts (line 13) of −$440.2 billion. In other words, the United States obtained less in foreign funds in all its international transactions than it used. How is this deficiency made up? By foreign central banks and governments adding to their U.S. funds, shown by the +$440.2 billion in official transactions on line 14 in Table 33-2 on page 728. There is a plus sign on line 14 because this represents an *inflow* of foreign exchange in our international transactions.

The U.S. balance of payments deficit is measured by the official transactions figure on line 14. The balance (line 15) in Table 33-2 is zero, as it must be with double-entry bookkeeping. Hence, as shown in Figure 33-1 on the facing page, the current account balance is a mirror image of the sum of the capital account balance and the official reserve transactions account.

What Affects the Distribution of Account Balances within the Balance of Payments?

A major factor affecting the distribution of account balances within any nation's balance of payments is its rate of inflation relative to that of its trading partners. Assume that the rates of inflation in the United States and in the European Monetary Union (EMU)—the nations that use the euro as their currency—are equal. Now suppose that all of a sudden, the U.S. inflation rate increases. EMU residents will find that U.S. products are becoming more expensive, and U.S. firms will export fewer of them to EMU nations. At the current dollar-euro exchange rate, U.S. residents will find EMU products relatively cheaper, and they will import more. Other things being equal, the reverse will occur if the U.S. inflation rate suddenly falls relative to that of the EMU. All other things held constant, whenever the U.S. rate of inflation exceeds that of its trading partners, we expect to see a larger deficit in the U.S. balance of merchandise trade and in the U.S. current account balance. Conversely, when the U.S. rate of inflation is less than that of its trading partners, other things being constant, we expect to see a smaller deficit in the U.S. balance of merchandise trade and in the U.S. current account balance.

Another important factor that sometimes influences account balances within a nation's balance of payments is its relative political stability. Political instability causes *capital flight*. Owners of capital in countries anticipating or experiencing political instability will often move assets to countries that are politically stable, such as the United States. Hence, the U.S. capital account balance is likely to increase whenever political instability looms in other nations in the world.

QUICK QUIZ See page 746 for the answers. Review concepts from this section in MyEconLab.

The _____ of _____ reflects the value of all transactions in international trade, including goods, services, financial assets, and gifts.

The merchandise trade balance gives us the difference between exports and imports of _____ items.

Included in the _____ account along with merchandise trade are service exports and imports relating to commerce in intangible items, such as shipping, insurance, and tourist expenditures. The _____ account also includes income earned by foreign residents on U.S. investments and income earned by U.S. residents on foreign investments.

_____ _____ involve international private gifts and federal government grants or gifts to foreign nations.

When we add the balance of merchandise trade and the balance of services and take account of net unilateral transfers and net investment income, we come up with the balance on the _____ account, a summary statistic.

There are also _____ account transactions that relate to the buying and selling of financial assets. Foreign capital is always entering the United States, and U.S. capital is always flowing abroad. The difference is called the balance on the _____ account.

Another type of balance of payments transaction concerns the _____ _____ assets of individual countries, or what is often simply called official transactions. By standard accounting convention, official transactions are exactly equal to but opposite in sign from the sum of the current account balance and the capital account balance.

Account balances within a nation's balance of payments can be affected by its relative rate of _____ and by its _____ stability relative to other nations.

Determining Foreign Exchange Rates

When you buy foreign products, such as European pharmaceuticals, you have dollars with which to pay the European manufacturer. The European manufacturer, however, cannot pay workers in dollars. The workers are European, they live in Europe, and they must have euros to buy goods and services in nations that are members of the European Monetary Union (EMU) and use the euro as their currency. There must therefore be a way to exchange dollars for euros that the pharmaceuticals manufacturer will accept. That exchange occurs in a **foreign exchange market,** which in this case involves the exchange of euros and dollars.

The particular **exchange rate** between euros and dollars that prevails—the dollar price of the euro—depends on the current demand for and supply of euros and dollars. In a sense, then, our analysis of the exchange rate between dollars and euros will be familiar, for we have used supply and demand throughout this book. If it costs you $1.20 to buy 1 euro, that is the foreign exchange rate determined by the current demand for and supply of euros in the foreign exchange market. The European person going to the foreign exchange market would need about 0.83 euro to buy 1 dollar.

Now let's consider what determines the demand for and supply of foreign currency in the foreign exchange market. We will continue to assume that the only two regions in the world are Europe and the United States.

Demand for and Supply of Foreign Currency

You wish to purchase European-produced pharmaceuticals directly from a manufacturer located in Europe. To do so, you must have euros. You go to the foreign exchange market (or your U.S. bank). Your desire to buy the pharmaceuticals causes you to offer (supply) dollars to the foreign exchange market. Your demand for euros is equivalent to your supply of dollars to the foreign exchange market.

> *Every U.S. transaction involving the importation of foreign goods constitutes a supply of dollars and a demand for some foreign currency, and the opposite is true for export transactions.*

In this case, the import transaction constitutes a demand for euros.

In our example, we will assume that only two goods are being traded, European pharmaceuticals and U.S. tablet devices. The U.S. demand for European pharmaceuticals creates a supply of dollars and a demand for euros in the foreign exchange market. Similarly, the European demand for U.S. tablet devices creates a supply of euros and a demand for dollars in the foreign exchange market. Under a system of **flexible exchange rates,** the supply of and demand for dollars and euros in the foreign exchange market will determine the equilibrium foreign exchange rate. The equilibrium exchange rate will tell us how many euros a dollar can be exchanged for—that is, the euro price of dollars—or how many dollars a euro can be exchanged for—the dollar price of euros.

The Equilibrium Foreign Exchange Rate

To determine the equilibrium foreign exchange rate, we have to find out what determines the demand for and supply of foreign exchange. We will ignore for the moment any speculative aspect of buying foreign exchange. That is, we assume that there are no individuals who wish to buy euros simply because they think that their price will go up in the future.

The idea of an exchange rate is no different from the idea of paying a certain price for something you want to buy. Suppose that you have to pay about $1.50 for a cup of coffee. If the price goes up to $2.50, you will probably buy fewer cups. If the price goes down to 50 cents, you will likely buy more. In other words, the demand curve for cups of coffee, expressed in terms of dollars, slopes downward following the law of demand. The demand curve for euros slopes downward also, and we will see why.

Foreign exchange market
A market in which households, firms, and governments buy and sell national currencies.

Exchange rate
The price of one nation's currency in terms of the currency of another country.

Flexible exchange rates
Exchange rates that are allowed to fluctuate in the open market in response to changes in supply and demand. Sometimes called *floating exchange rates.*

Go to www.econtoday.com/chap33 for recent data from the Federal Reserve Bank of St. Louis on the exchange value of the U.S. dollar relative to the major currencies of the world.

Let's think more closely about the demand schedule for euros. If it costs you $1.10 to purchase 1 euro, that is the exchange rate between dollars and euros. If tomorrow you have to pay $1.25 for the same euro, the exchange rate would have changed. Looking at such a change, we would say that there has been an **appreciation** in the value of the euro in the foreign exchange market. But another way to view this increase in the value of the euro is to say that there has been a **depreciation** in the value of the dollar in the foreign exchange market. The dollar used to buy almost 0.91 euro, but tomorrow the dollar will be able to buy only 0.80 euro at a price of $1.25 per euro.

If the dollar price of euros rises, you will probably demand fewer euros. Why? The answer lies in the reason you and others demand euros in the first place.

APPRECIATION AND DEPRECIATION OF EUROS Recall that in our example, you and others demand euros to buy European pharmaceuticals. The demand curve for European pharmaceuticals follows the law of demand and therefore slopes downward. If it costs more U.S. dollars to buy the same quantity of European pharmaceuticals, presumably you and other U.S. residents will not buy the same quantity. Your quantity demanded will be less. We say that your demand for euros is *derived from* your demand for European pharmaceuticals. In panel (a) of Figure 33-2 on the following page, we present the hypothetical demand schedule for packages of European pharmaceuticals by a representative set of U.S. consumers during a typical week. In panel (b) of Figure 33-2, we show graphically the U.S. demand curve for European pharmaceuticals in terms of U.S. dollars taken from panel (a).

AN EXAMPLE OF DERIVED DEMAND Let us assume that the price of a package of European pharmaceuticals in Europe is 100 euros. Given that price, we can find the number of euros required to purchase 500 packages of European pharmaceuticals. That information is given in panel (c) of Figure 33-2. If purchasing one package of European pharmaceuticals requires 100 euros, 500 packages require 50,000 euros. Now we have enough information to determine the derived demand curve for euros. If 1 euro costs $1.20, a package of pharmaceuticals would cost $120 (100 euros per package × $1.20 per euro = $120 per package). At $120 per package, the representative group of U.S. consumers would, we see from panel (a) of Figure 33-2, demand 500 packages of pharmaceuticals.

From panel (c), we see that 50,000 euros would be demanded to buy the 500 packages of pharmaceuticals. We show this quantity demanded in panel (d). In panel (e), we draw the derived demand curve for euros. Now consider what happens if the price of euros goes up to $1.25. A package of European pharmaceuticals priced at 100 euros in Europe would now cost $125. From panel (a), we see that at $125 per package, 300 packages of pharmaceuticals will be imported from Europe into the United States by our representative group of U.S. consumers. From panel (c), we see that 300 packages of pharmaceuticals would require 30,000 euros to be purchased. Thus, in panels (d) and (e), we see that at a price of $1.25 per euro, the quantity demanded will be 30,000 euros.

We continue similar calculations all the way up to a price of $1.30 per euro. At that price, a package of European pharmaceuticals with a price of 100 euros in Europe would have a U.S. dollar price of $130, and our representative U.S. consumers would import only 100 packages of pharmaceuticals.

DOWNWARD-SLOPING DERIVED DEMAND As can be expected, as the price of the euro rises, the quantity demanded will fall. The only difference here from the standard demand analysis developed in Chapter 3 and used throughout this text is that the demand for euros is derived from the demand for a final product—European pharmaceuticals in our example.

SUPPLY OF EUROS Assume that European pharmaceutical manufacturers buy U.S. tablet devices. The supply of euros is a derived supply in that it is derived from the European demand for U.S. tablet devices. We could go through an example similar to the one for pharmaceuticals to come up with a supply schedule of euros in Europe. It slopes upward.

Appreciation

An increase in the exchange value of one nation's currency in terms of the currency of another nation.

Depreciation

A decrease in the exchange value of one nation's currency in terms of the currency of another nation.

YOU ARE THERE

To consider how an appreciation of Brazil's currency has affected Brazilian spending on U.S. goods and services, take a look at **An Exchange-Rate-Induced U.S. Shopping *Bagunça* for Brazilians** on page 742.

Panel (a)
Demand Schedule for Packages of European Pharmaceuticals in the United States per Week

Price per Package	Quantity Demanded
$130	100
125	300
120	500
115	700

Panel (b)
U.S. Demand Curve for European Pharmaceuticals

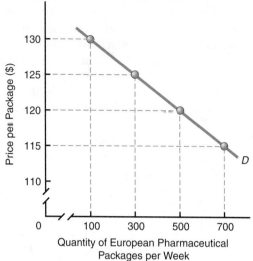

Panel (c)
Euros Required to Purchase Quantity Demanded (at *P* = 100 euros per package of pharmaceuticals)

Quantity Demanded	Euros Required
100	10,000
300	30,000
500	50,000
700	70,000

Panel (d)
Derived Demand Schedule for Euros in the United States with Which to Pay for Imports of Pharmaceuticals

Dollar Price of One Euro	Dollar Price of Pharmaceuticals	Quantity of Pharmaceuticals Demanded	Quantity of Euros Demanded per Week
$1.30	$130	100	10,000
1.25	125	300	30,000
1.20	120	500	50,000
1.15	115	700	70,000

FIGURE 33-2

Deriving the Demand for Euros

In panel (a), we show the demand schedule for European pharmaceuticals in the United States, expressed in terms of dollars per package of pharmaceuticals. In panel (b), we show the demand curve, *D*, which slopes downward. In panel (c), we show the number of euros required to purchase up to 700 packages of pharmaceuticals. If the price per package of pharmaceuticals is 100 euros, we can now find the quantity of euros needed to pay for the various quantities demanded. In panel (d), we see the derived demand for euros in the United States in order to purchase the various quantities of pharmaceuticals given in panel (a). The resultant demand curve, D_1, is shown in panel (e). This is the U.S. derived demand for euros.

Panel (e)
U.S. Derived Demand for Euros

Obviously, Europeans want dollars to purchase U.S. goods. European residents will be willing to supply more euros when the dollar price of euros goes up, because they can then buy more U.S. goods with the same quantity of euros. That is, the euro would be worth more in exchange for U.S. goods than when the dollar price for euros was lower.

FIGURE 33-3

The Supply of Euros

If the market price of a U.S.-produced tablet device is $200, then at an exchange rate of $1.20 per euro, the price of the tablet to a European consumer is 167.67 euros. If the exchange rate rises to $1.25 per euro, the European price of the tablet falls to 160 euros. This induces an increase in the quantity of tablets demanded by European consumers and consequently an increase in the quantity of euros supplied in exchange for dollars in the foreign exchange market. In contrast, if the exchange rate falls to $1.15 per euro, the European price of the tablet rises to 173.91 euros. This causes a decrease in the quantity of tablets demanded by European consumers. As a result, there is a decline in the quantity of euros supplied in exchange for dollars in the foreign exchange market. Hence, the euro supply curve slopes up.

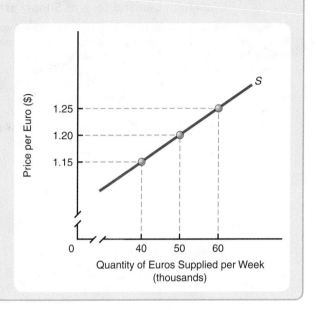

AN EXAMPLE Let's take an example. Suppose a U.S.-produced tablet device costs $200. If the exchange rate is $1.20 per euro, a European resident will have to come up with 166.67 euros ($200 ÷ $1.20 per euro = 166.67 euros) to buy one tablet. If, however, the exchange rate goes up to $1.25 per euro, a European resident must come up with only 160 euros ($200 ÷ $1.25 per euro = 160 euros) to buy a U.S. tablet. At this lower price (in euros) of U.S. tablets, Europeans will demand a larger quantity.

In other words, as the price of euros goes up in terms of dollars, the quantity of U.S. tablets demanded will go up, and hence the quantity of euros supplied will go up. Therefore, the supply schedule of euros, which is derived from the European demand for U.S. goods, will slope upward, as seen in Figure 33-3 above.

TOTAL DEMAND FOR AND SUPPLY OF EUROS Let us now look at the total demand for and supply of euros. We take all U.S. consumers of European pharmaceuticals and all European consumers of U.S. tablet devices and put their demands for and supplies of euros together into one diagram. Thus, we are showing the total demand for and total supply of euros. The horizontal axis in Figure 33-4 on the following page represents the quantity of foreign exchange—the number of euros per year. The vertical axis represents the exchange rate—the price of foreign currency (euros) expressed in dollars (per euro). The foreign currency price of $1.25 per euro means it will cost you $1.25 to buy 1 euro. At the foreign currency price of $1.20 per euro, you know that it will cost you $1.20 to buy 1 euro. The equilibrium, *E*, is again established at $1.20 for 1 euro.

In our hypothetical example, assuming that there are only representative groups of pharmaceutical consumers in the United States and tablet consumers in Europe, the equilibrium exchange rate will be set at $1.20 per euro.

This equilibrium is not established because U.S. residents like to buy euros or because Europeans like to buy dollars. Rather, the equilibrium exchange rate depends on how many tablet devices Europeans want and how many European pharmaceuticals U.S. residents want (given their respective incomes, their tastes, and, in our example, the relative prices of pharmaceuticals and tablet devices).

A SHIFT IN DEMAND Assume that a successful advertising campaign by U.S. pharmaceutical importers causes U.S. demand for European pharmaceuticals to rise. U.S. residents demand more pharmaceuticals at all prices. Their demand curve for European pharmaceuticals shifts outward to the right.

FIGURE 33-4

Total Demand for and Supply of Euros

The market supply curve for euros results from the total European demand for U.S. tablet devices. The demand curve, D, slopes downward like most demand curves, and the supply curve, S, slopes upward. The foreign exchange price, or the U.S. dollar price of euros, is given on the vertical axis. The number of euros is represented on the horizontal axis. If the foreign exchange rate is $1.25—that is, if it takes $1.25 to buy 1 euro—U.S. residents will demand 20 billion euros.

The equilibrium exchange rate is at the intersection of D and S, or point E. The equilibrium exchange rate is $1.20 per euro. At this point, 30 billion euros are both demanded and supplied each year.

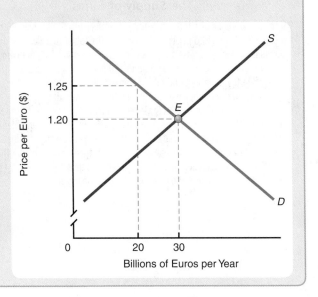

The increased demand for European pharmaceuticals can be translated into an increased demand for euros. All U.S. residents clamoring for European pharmaceuticals will supply more dollars to the foreign exchange market while demanding more euros to pay for the pharmaceuticals. Figure 33-5 below presents a new demand schedule, D_2, for euros. This demand schedule is to the right of the original demand schedule. If Europeans do not change their desire for U.S. tablet devices, the supply schedule for euros will remain stable.

A new equilibrium will be established at a higher exchange rate. In our particular example, the new equilibrium is established at an exchange rate of $1.25 per euro. It now takes $1.25 to buy 1 euro, whereas formerly it took $1.20. This will be translated into an increase in the price of European pharmaceuticals to U.S. residents and into a decrease in the price of U.S. tablet devices to Europeans. For example, a package of European pharmaceuticals priced at 100 euros that sold for $120 in the United States will now be priced at $125. Conversely, a U.S. tablet priced at $200 that previously sold for 166.67 euros will now sell for 160 euros.

FIGURE 33-5

A Shift in the Demand Schedule

The demand schedule for European pharmaceuticals shifts to the right, causing the derived demand schedule for euros to shift to the right also. We have shown this as a shift from D_1 to D_2. We have assumed that the supply schedule for euros has remained stable—that is, European demand for U.S. tablet devices has remained constant. The old equilibrium foreign exchange rate was $1.20 per euro.

The new equilibrium exchange rate will be E_2. It will now cost $1.25 to buy 1 euro. The higher price of euros will be translated into a higher U.S. dollar price for European pharmaceuticals and a lower euro price for U.S. tablet devices.

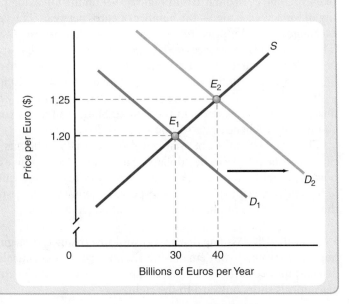

FIGURE 33-6

A Shift in the Supply of Euros

There has been a shift in the supply curve for euros. The new equilibrium will occur at E_1, meaning that $1.15, rather than $1.20, will now buy 1 euro. After the exchange rate adjustment, the annual amount of euros demanded and supplied will increase from 30 billion to 60 billion.

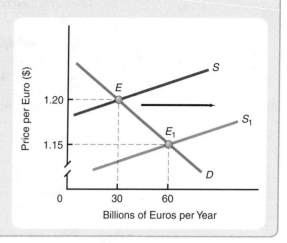

A SHIFT IN SUPPLY We just assumed that the U.S. demand for European pharmaceuticals shifted due to a successful ad campaign. The demand for euros is derived from the demand by U.S. residents for pharmaceuticals. This change in pharmaceuticals demand is translated into a shift in the demand curve for euros. As an alternative exercise, we might assume that the supply curve of euros shifts outward to the right. Such a supply shift could occur for many reasons, one of which is a relative rise in the European price level. For example, if the prices of all European-manufactured tablets went up 20 percent in euros, U.S. tablets would become relatively cheaper. That would mean that European residents would want to buy more U.S. tablets. But remember that when they want to buy more U.S. tablets, they supply more euros to the foreign exchange market.

Thus, we see in Figure 33-6 above that the supply curve of euros moves from S to S_1. In the absence of restrictions—that is, in a system of flexible exchange rates— the new equilibrium exchange rate will be $1.15 equals 1 euro. The quantity of euros demanded and supplied will increase from 30 billion per year to 60 billion per year. We say, then, that in a flexible international exchange rate system, shifts in the demand for and supply of foreign currencies will cause changes in the equilibrium foreign exchange rates. Those rates will remain in effect until world supply or demand shifts.

Which national currencies are most actively traded in global foreign exchange markets?

INTERNATIONAL EXAMPLE

The Most Traded Currencies in Foreign Exchange Markets

On a given day, the U.S. dollar is involved in more than 80 percent of trades of one currency for another in the world's foreign exchange markets. Thus, the dollar is utilized more than twice as often in exchange for other currencies as the second most commonly traded currency, the European euro. The dollar is involved in currency exchanges more than four times as often as either the Japanese yen or the British pound, the third and fourth most commonly exchanged currencies.

FOR CRITICAL THINKING
In light of the fact that the dollar valuation of all currency trades during a given year is $4 trillion, about how many U.S. dollars circulate within foreign exchange markets within a given year?

Market Determinants of Exchange Rates

The foreign exchange market is affected by many other variables in addition to changes in relative price levels, including the following:

- *Changes in real interest rates.* Suppose that the U.S. interest rate, corrected for people's expectations of inflation, increases relative to the rest of the world. Then international investors elsewhere seeking the higher returns now available in the United States will increase their demand for dollar-denominated assets, thereby increasing the demand for dollars in foreign exchange markets. An increased demand for dollars in foreign exchange markets, other things held constant, will cause the dollar to appreciate and other currencies to depreciate.

- *Changes in consumer preferences.* If Germany's citizens, for example, suddenly develop a taste for U.S.-made automobiles, this will increase the derived demand for U.S. dollars in foreign exchange markets.

- *Perceptions of economic stability.* As already mentioned, if the United States looks economically and politically more stable relative to other countries, more foreign residents will want to put their savings into U.S. assets rather than in their own domestic assets. This will increase the demand for dollars.

QUICK QUIZ See page 746 for the answers. Review concepts from this section in MyEconLab.

The foreign _____ _____ is the rate at which one country's currency can be exchanged for another's.

The _____ for foreign exchange is a derived _____, which is derived from the demand for foreign goods and services (and financial assets). The _____ of foreign exchange is derived from foreign residents' demands for U.S. goods and services.

The demand curve of foreign exchange slopes _____, and the supply curve of foreign exchange slopes

_____. The equilibrium foreign exchange rate occurs at the intersection of the demand and supply curves for a currency.

A _____ in the demand for foreign goods will result in a shift in the _____ for foreign exchange, thereby changing the equilibrium foreign exchange rate. A shift in the supply of foreign currency will also cause a change in the equilibrium exchange rate.

The Gold Standard and the International Monetary Fund

The current system of more or less freely floating exchange rates is a relatively recent development. In the past, we have had periods of a gold standard, fixed exchange rates under the International Monetary Fund, and variants of the two.

The Gold Standard

Until the 1930s, many nations were on a gold standard. The value of their domestic currency was fixed, or *pegged*, in units of gold. Nations operating under this gold standard agreed to redeem their currencies for a fixed amount of gold at the request of any holder of that currency. Although gold was not necessarily the means of exchange for world trade, it was the unit to which all currencies under the gold standard were pegged. And because all currencies in the system were pegged to gold, exchange rates between those currencies were fixed.

Two problems plagued the gold standard, however. One was that by fixing the value of its currency in relation to the amount of gold, a nation gave up control of its domestic monetary policy. Another was that the world's commerce was at the mercy of gold discoveries. Throughout history, each time new veins of gold were found, desired domestic expenditures on goods and services increased. If production of goods and services failed to increase proportionately, inflation resulted.

Bretton Woods and the International Monetary Fund

On December 27, 1945, the world's capitalist countries, which in 1944 had sent representatives to meetings in Bretton Woods, New Hampshire, created a new permanent institution, the International Monetary Fund (IMF). The IMF's task was to lend to member countries for which the sum of the current account balance and the capital account balance was negative, thereby helping them maintain an offsetting surplus in their official reserve transactions accounts. Governments that joined the Bretton Woods system agreed to maintain the value of their currencies within 1 percent of the declared **par value**—the officially determined value. The United States, which owned most of the world's gold stock, was similarly obligated to maintain gold prices within a 1 percent margin of the official rate of $35 an ounce. Except for a transitional arrangement permitting a one-time adjustment of up to 10 percent in par value, members could alter exchange rates thereafter only with the approval of the IMF.

Par value
The officially determined value of a currency.

On August 15, 1971, President Richard Nixon suspended the convertibility of the dollar into gold. On December 18, 1971, the United States officially devalued the dollar—that is, lowered its official value—relative to the currencies of 14 major industrial nations. Finally, on March 16, 1973, the finance ministers of the European Economic Community (now the European Union) announced that they would let their currencies float against the dollar, something Japan had already begun doing with its yen. Since 1973, the United States and most other trading countries have had either freely floating exchange rates or managed ("dirty") floating exchange rates, in which their governments or central banks intervene from time to time to try to influence world market exchange rates.

Fixed versus Floating Exchange Rates

The United States went off the Bretton Woods system of fixed exchange rates in 1973. As Figure 33-7 below indicates, many other nations of the world have been less willing to permit the values of their currencies to vary in the foreign exchange markets.

Fixing the Exchange Rate

How did nations fix their exchange rates in years past? How do many countries accomplish this today? Figure 33-8 on the following page shows the market for dinars, the currency of Bahrain. At the initial equilibrium point E_1, U.S. residents had to give up $2.66 to obtain 1 dinar. Suppose now that there is an increase in the supply of dinars for dollars, perhaps because Bahraini residents wish to buy more U.S. goods.

FIGURE 33-7

Current Foreign Exchange Rate Arrangements

Today, 21 percent of the member nations of the International Monetary Fund have an independent float, and 24 percent have a managed float exchange rate arrangement. Another 12 percent of all nations use the currencies of other nations instead of issuing their own currencies. The remaining 43 percent of countries have fixed exchange rates.

Source: International Monetary Fund.

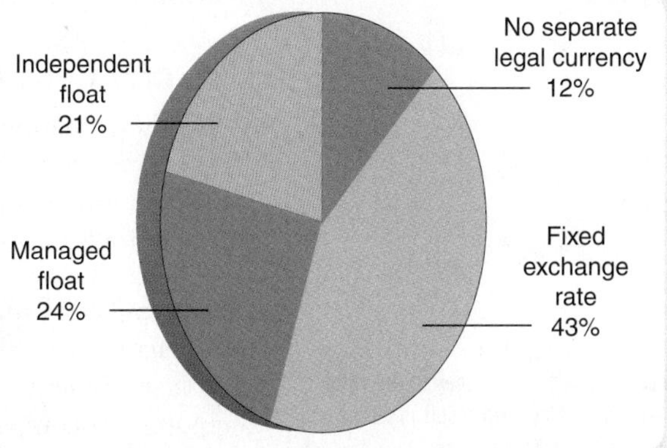

FIGURE 33-8

A Fixed Exchange Rate

This figure illustrates how the Central Bank of Bahrain could fix the dollar-dinar exchange rate in the face of an increase in the supply of dinars caused by a rise in the demand for U.S. goods by Bahraini residents. In the absence of any action by the Central Bank of Bahrain, the result would be a movement from point E_1 to point E_2. The dollar value of the dinar would fall from \$2.66 to \$2.00. The Central Bank of Bahrain can prevent this exchange rate change by purchasing dinars with dollars in the foreign exchange market, thereby increasing the demand for dinars. At the new equilibrium point, E_3, the dinar's value remains at \$2.66.

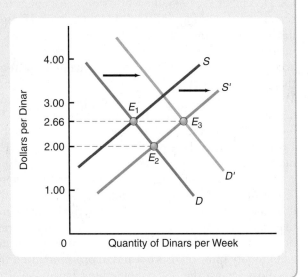

Other things being equal, the result would be a movement to point E_2 in Figure 33-8 above. The dollar value of the dinar would fall to \$2.00.

To prevent a dinar depreciation from occurring, however, the Central Bank of Bahrain could increase the demand for dinars in the foreign exchange market by purchasing dinars with dollars. The Central Bank of Bahrain can do this using dollars that it has on hand as part of its *foreign exchange reserves*. All central banks hold reserves of foreign currencies. Because the U.S. dollar is a key international currency, the Central Bank of Bahrain and other central banks typically hold billions of dollars in reserve so that they can make transactions such as the one in this example.

Note that a sufficiently large purchase of dinars could, as shown in Figure 33-8, cause the demand curve to shift rightward to achieve the new equilibrium point E_3, at which the dinar's value remains at \$2.66. Provided that it has enough dollar reserves on hand, the Central Bank of Bahrain could maintain—effectively fix—the exchange rate in the face of the rise in the supply of dinars.

The Central Bank of Bahrain has maintained the dollar-dinar exchange rate in this manner since 2001. This basic approach—varying the amount of the national currency demanded at any given exchange rate in foreign exchange markets when necessary—is also the way that *any* central bank seeks to keep its nation's currency value unchanged in light of changing market forces.

> *Central banks can keep exchange rates fixed as long as they have enough foreign exchange reserves to deal with potentially long-lasting changes in the demand for or supply of their nation's currency.*

Pros and Cons of a Fixed Exchange Rate

Why might a nation such as Bahrain wish to keep the value of its currency from fluctuating? One reason is that changes in the exchange rate can affect the market values of assets that are denominated in foreign currencies. This can increase the financial risks that a nation's residents face, thereby forcing them to incur costs to avoid these risks.

FOREIGN EXCHANGE RISK The possibility that variations in the market value of assets can take place due to changes in the value of a nation's currency is the **foreign exchange risk** that residents of a country face because their nation's currency value can vary. Suppose that companies in Bahrain have many loans denominated in dollars but earn nearly all their revenues in dinars from sales within Bahrain. A decline in the dollar

Foreign exchange risk
The possibility that changes in the value of a nation's currency will result in variations in the market value of assets.

value of the dinar would mean that Bahraini companies would have to allocate a larger portion of their earnings to make the same *dollar* loan payments as before. Thus, a fall in the dinar's value would increase the operating costs of these companies, thereby reducing their profitability and raising the likelihood of eventual bankruptcy.

Limiting foreign exchange risk is a classic rationale for adopting a fixed exchange rate. Nevertheless, a country's residents are not defenseless against foreign exchange risk. In what is known as a **hedge,** they can adopt strategies intended to offset the risk arising from exchange rate variations. For example, a company in Bahrain that has significant euro earnings from sales in Germany but sizable loans from U.S. investors could arrange to convert its euro earnings into dollars via special types of foreign exchange contracts called *currency swaps*. The Bahraini company could likewise avoid holdings of dinars and shield itself—*hedge*—against variations in the dinar's value.

Hedge
A financial strategy that reduces the chance of suffering losses arising from foreign exchange risk.

THE EXCHANGE RATE AS A SHOCK ABSORBER If fixing the exchange rate limits foreign exchange risk, why do so many nations allow the exchange rates to float? The answer must be that there are potential drawbacks associated with fixing exchange rates. One is that exchange rate variations can actually perform a valuable service for a nation's economy. Consider a situation in which residents of a nation speak only their own nation's language. As a result, the country's residents are very *immobile*: They cannot trade their labor skills outside their own nation's borders.

Now think about what happens if this nation chooses to fix its exchange rate. Imagine a situation in which other countries begin to sell products that are close substitutes for the products its people specialize in producing, causing a sizable drop in worldwide demand for that nation's goods. If wages and prices do not instantly and completely adjust downward, the result will be a sharp decline in production of goods and services, a falloff in national income, and higher unemployment. Contrast this situation with one which the exchange rate floats. In this case, a sizable decline in outside demand for the nation's products will cause it to experience a trade deficit, which will lead to a significant drop in the demand for that nation's currency. As a result, the nation's currency will experience a sizable depreciation, making the goods that the nation offers to sell abroad much less expensive in other countries. People abroad who continue to consume the nation's products will increase their purchases, and the nation's exports will increase. Its production will begin to recover somewhat, as will its residents' incomes. Unemployment will begin to fall.

This example illustrates how exchange rate variations can be beneficial, especially if a nation's residents are relatively immobile. It can be difficult, for example, for a Polish resident who has never studied Portuguese to move to Lisbon, even if she is highly qualified for available jobs there. If many residents of Poland face similar linguistic or cultural barriers, Poland could be better off with a floating exchange rate even if its residents must incur significant costs hedging against foreign exchange risk as a result.

How did having a separate currency and a floating exchange rate actually end up helping Poland in the early 2010s?

INTERNATIONAL POLICY EXAMPLE

Poland's Floating Exchange Rate Protects It from Euro Ills

During the 2000s, Estonia, Slovakia, and Slovenia rushed to adopt the euro as their currency, and other nations of Eastern Europe fixed their exchange rates in relation to the euro. In contrast, Poland retained its *zloty* currency and allowed its value to float in the foreign exchange market.

A European-wide economic slowdown that began during the early 2010s triggered downturns in Estonia, Slovakia, Slovenia, and other countries in Eastern Europe. When the Polish *zloty* depreciated sharply relative to the euro, Polish goods and services became cheaper for most Europeans. As a consequence, European spending on Polish merchandise exports rose sharply, and the Polish tourism industry boomed as

more Europeans selected Poland as a less expensive vacation destination. By maintaining its own currency and a floating exchange rate, Poland thereby helped to insulate its economy from problems afflicting the rest of Europe. Thus, Poland was the only European Union nation to experience uninterrupted economic growth during the early 2010s.

FOR CRITICAL THINKING
Why do you suppose that the Polish unemployment rate remained stable during the early 2010s while unemployment rates elsewhere in Eastern Europe rose?

The International Monetary Fund was developed after World War II as an institution to maintain _____ exchange rates in the world. Since 1973, however, _____ exchange rates have disappeared in most major trading countries. For these nations, exchange rates are largely determined by the forces of demand and supply in global foreign exchange markets.

Central banks can fix exchange rates by buying or selling foreign _____ and thereby adding to or subtracting from their foreign exchange _____.

Although fixing the exchange rate helps protect a nation's residents from foreign exchange _____, this policy makes less mobile residents susceptible to greater volatility in income and employment.

YOU ARE THERE
An Exchange-Rate-Induced U.S. Shopping *Bagunça* for *Brazilians*

Ana Ligia Paladino has traveled 5,000 miles from her home in the southernmost part of Brazil to engage in a 10-day-long shopping spree in New York City. When Paladino emerges from her first morning of shopping at Macy's, the only words she can think of to describe her experience are, "It was a *bagunça*!"—that is, a combination of "mess" and "mayhem." During the year of her visit, Paladino is among 700,000 Brazilians to visit New York City, where Brazilians have spent more than $1.6 billion. Within the same year, Brazilians also have spent more than $2 billion in Florida. In both U.S. locations, Brazilians have outspent visitors from any other country in the world.

What has induced Paladino and so many other Brazilians to engage in spending in the United States is that the Brazilian currency, the *real*, can now buy a great deal more U.S. goods and services than was true previously. Indeed, during the two years prior to Paladino's visit, the *real* appreciated relative to the U.S. dollar by 25 percent. Thus, during her New York shopping *bagunça*, Paladino was able to buy about 25 percent more items in the United States than she could have bought 24 months earlier.

Critical Thinking Questions

1. What happened to the U.S. dollar's value in relation to the Brazilian *real* during the preceding two years?

2. Why do you suppose that more Brazilian students are now studying at U.S. colleges and universities than was true several years ago?

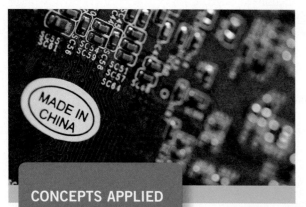

ISSUES & APPLICATIONS

CONCEPTS APPLIED

▶ Balance of Payments

▶ Merchandise Trade Deficit

▶ Balance on Goods and Services

Items "Made in China" Generate Income Elsewhere

In a typical year, the value of U.S. imports from China amounts to one-sixth of total U.S. import spending recorded in the nation's balance of payments. Expenditures on merchandise imported from China make up more than 70 percent of both the U.S. merchandise trade deficit and the U.S. balance on goods and services. These facts do not imply, however, that every dollar you spend as a consumer on an item "made in China" finds its way to people in China. In fact, less than half of each dollar you spend on Chinese merchandise actually reaches someone in China.

Only Part of the Price of a Chinese Import Is Chinese Income

Consider a toy action figure manufactured in China that has a price of $15 in the United States. A substantial portion of the U.S. retail price pays for transportation of the toy within the United States, rent for the U.S. retail outlet that sells the action figure, profits for the retailer's owners, and expenses incurred in marketing the toy. The latter expenses include the wages paid to managers and employees of the U.S. firms that marketed the action figure in the United States.

Alternatively, consider the iPhone, which earns substantial profits for U.S.-based Apple. iPhones are assembled in China from components that are made by and that generate revenues for firms located outside both the United States and China. Yet when an assembled iPhone is shipped from China for a U.S. consumer to purchase, that device is classified as a Chinese export and a U.S. import.

The U.S. Content of "Made in China"

Galina Hale and Bart Hoblin of the Federal Reserve Bank of San Francisco have calculated shares of spending on U.S. imports from China that flow to Chinese producers and to U.S. firms and their workers. They find that only 45 cents of each dollar U.S. consumers pay toward the price of a typical Chinese-imported good actually makes its way to China as income.

Thus, your spending on merchandise imported from China contributes dollar-for-dollar to the U.S. merchandise trade deficit, but fewer than half of the dollars that you spend on items "made in China" ultimately flow to that nation as income. The income that your spending generates is split among people who live in China, the United States, and sometimes—as in the case of iPhones—other nations.

For Critical Thinking

1. The United States is a net exporter of services to China. What does this imply about the magnitude of the deficit in the U.S. balance on goods and services with China compared with the size of the U.S. merchandise trade deficit with China?

2. Why does a portion of Chinese residents' expenditures on goods and services exported from the United States to China likely add to the earnings of Chinese firms and those firms' managers and workers?

Web Resources

1. To view key trade balance statistics for China, go to www .econtoday.com/chap33.

2. For a look at U.S. balance of payments data, go to www .econtoday.com/chap33.

> ### MyEconLab
> For more questions on this chapter's Issues & Applications, go to MyEconLab. In the Study Plan for this chapter, select Section N: News.

MyEconLab

Here is what you should know after reading this chapter. MyEconLab will help you identify what you know, and where to go when you need to practice.

— WHAT YOU SHOULD KNOW —

The Balance of Trade versus the Balance of Payments The balance of trade is the difference between exports and imports of physical goods, or merchandise, during a given period. The balance of payments is a system of accounts for all transactions between a nation's residents and the residents of other countries of the world.

balance of trade, 726
balance of payments, 726
accounting identities, 726

— WHERE TO GO TO PRACTICE —

• MyEconLab Study Plan 33.1

MyEconLab *continued*

The Key Accounts within the Balance of Payments There are three accounts within the balance of payments. The current account measures net exchanges of goods and services, transfers, and income flows across a nation's borders. The capital account measures net flows of financial assets. The official reserve transactions account tabulates exchanges of financial assets involving the home nation's and foreign nations' governments and central banks. Because each international exchange generates both an inflow and an outflow, the sum of the balances on all three accounts must equal zero.

current account, 728
capital account, 729
special drawing rights
(SDRs), 730
International Monetary
Fund, 730

Key Figure
Figure 33-1, 730

• MyEconLab Study Plan 33.1
• Animated Figure 33-1

Exchange Rate Determination in the Market for Foreign Exchange From the perspective of the United States, the demand for a nation's currency by U.S. residents is derived largely from the demand for imports from that nation. Likewise, the supply of a nation's currency is derived mainly from the supply of U.S. exports to that country. The equilibrium exchange rate is the rate of exchange between the dollar and the other nation's currency at which the quantity of the currency demanded is equal to the quantity supplied.

foreign exchange market,
732
exchange rate, 732
flexible exchange rates, 732
appreciation, 733
depreciation, 733

Key Figures
Figure 33-2, 734
Figure 33-3, 735
Figure 33-4, 736
Figure 33-5, 736

• MyEconLab Study Plan 33.2
• Animated Figures 33-2, 33-3,
33-4, 33-5

Factors That Can Induce Changes in Equilibrium Exchange Rates The equilibrium exchange rate changes in response to changes in the demand for or supply of another nation's currency. Changes in desired flows of exports or imports, real interest rates, tastes and preferences of consumers, and perceptions of economic stability affect the positions of the demand and supply curves in foreign exchange markets and induce variations in equilibrium exchange rates.

Key Figure
Figure 33-6, 737

• MyEconLab Study Plan 33.2
• Animated Figure 33-6

How Policymakers Can Attempt to Keep Exchange Rates Fixed If the current price of the home currency in terms of another nation's currency starts to fall below the level where the home country wants it to remain, the home country's central bank can use reserves of the other nation's currency to purchase the home currency in foreign exchange markets. This raises the demand for the home currency and thereby pushes up the currency's value in terms of the other nation's currency.

par value, 739
foreign exchange risk, 740
hedge, 741

Key Figure
Figure 33-8, 740

• MyEconLab Study Plans 33.3,
33.4
• Animated Figure 33-8

Log in to MyEconLab, take a chapter test, and get a personalized Study Plan that tells you which concepts you understand and which ones you need to review. From there, MyEconLab will give you further practice, tutorials, animations, videos, and guided solutions. For more information, visit www.myeconlab.com

PROBLEMS

All problems are assignable in MyEconLab; exercises that update with real-time data are marked with ⓦ. Answers to the odd-numbered problems appear at the back of the book.

33-1. Suppose that during a recent year for the United States, merchandise imports were $2 trillion, unilateral transfers were a net outflow of $0.2 trillion, service exports were $0.2 trillion, service imports were $0.1 trillion, and merchandise exports were $1.4 trillion. (See pages 728–729.)

  a. What was the merchandise trade deficit?

  b. What was the balance on goods and services?

  c. What was the current account balance?

33-2. Suppose that during a recent year for the United States, the current account balance was −0.2 trillion, the flow of U.S. private holdings of assets abroad was −$0.1 trillion, and the flow of foreign private assets held in the United States was +0.2 trillion. (See pages 729–730.)

  a. What was the balance on the capital account during the year?

  b. What was the change in official reserves during the year?

33-3. Over the course of a year, a nation tracked its foreign transactions and arrived at the following amounts:

Merchandise exports	500
Service exports	75
Net unilateral transfers	10
Domestic assets abroad (capital outflows)	−200
Foreign assets at home (capital inflows)	300
Changes in official reserves	−35
Merchandise imports	600
Service imports	50

What are this nation's balance of trade, current account balance, and capital account balance? (See pages 728–730.)

33-4. Identify whether each of the following items creates a surplus item or a deficit item in the current account of the U.S. balance of payments. (See page 726.)

  a. A Central European company sells products to a U.S. hobby-store chain.

  b. Japanese residents pay a U.S. travel company to arrange hotel stays, ground transportation, and tours of various U.S. cities, including New York, Chicago, and Orlando.

  c. A Mexican company pays a U.S. accounting firm to audit its income statements.

  d. U.S. churches and mosques send relief aid to Pakistan following a major earthquake in that nation.

  e. A U.S. microprocessor manufacturer purchases raw materials from a Canadian firm.

33-5. Explain how the following events would affect the market for the Mexican peso, assuming a floating exchange rate. (See pages 735–737.)

  a. Improvements in Mexican production technology yield superior guitars, and many musicians around the world buy these guitars.

  b. Perceptions of political instability surrounding regular elections in Mexico make international investors nervous about future business prospects in Mexico.

33-6. Explain how the following events would affect the market for South Africa's currency, the rand, assuming a floating exchange rate. (See page 736.)

  a. A rise in U.S. inflation causes many U.S. residents to seek to buy gold, which is a major South African export good, as a hedge against inflation.

  b. Major discoveries of the highest-quality diamonds ever found occur in Russia and Central Asia, causing a significant decline in purchases of South African diamonds.

33-7. Suppose that the following two events take place in the market for China's currency, the yuan: U.S. parents are more willing than before to buy action figures and other Chinese toy exports, and China's government tightens restrictions on the amount of U.S. dollar–denominated financial assets that Chinese residents may legally purchase. What happens to the dollar price of the yuan? Does the yuan appreciate or depreciate relative to the dollar? (See pages 735–737.)

33-8. On Wednesday, the exchange rate between the Japanese yen and the U.S. dollar was $0.010 per yen. On Thursday, it was $0.009. Did the dollar appreciate or depreciate against the yen? By how much, expressed as a percentage change? (See page 730.)

33-9. On Wednesday, the exchange rate between the euro and the U.S. dollar was $1.20 per euro, and the exchange rate between the Canadian dollar and the U.S. dollar was U.S. $1.05 per Canadian dollar. What is the exchange rate between the Canadian dollar and the euro? (See page 730.)

33-10. Suppose that signs of an improvement in the Japanese economy lead international investors to resume lending to the Japanese government and businesses. How would this event affect the market for the yen? How should the central bank, the Bank of Japan, respond to this event if it wants to keep the value of the yen unchanged? (See pages 739–740.)

33-11. Briefly explain the differences between a flexible exchange rate system and a fixed exchange rate system. (See pages 738–739.)

33-12. Suppose that under a gold standard, the U.S. dollar is pegged to gold at a rate of $35 per ounce and the pound sterling is pegged to gold at a rate of £17.50 per ounce. Explain how the gold standard constitutes an exchange rate arrangement between the dollar and the pound. What is the exchange rate between the U.S. dollar and the pound sterling? (See pages 738–739.)

33-13. Suppose that under the Bretton Woods system, the dollar is pegged to gold at a rate of $35 per ounce and the pound sterling is pegged to the dollar at a rate of $2 = £1. If the dollar is devalued against gold and the pegged rate is changed to

$40 per ounce, what does this imply for the exchange value of the pound in terms of dollars? (See page 739.)

33-14. Suppose that the People's Bank of China wishes to peg the rate of exchange of its currency, the yuan, in terms of the U.S. dollar. In each of the following situations, should it add to or subtract from its dollar foreign exchange reserves? Why? (See pages 739–740.)

  a. U.S. parents worrying about safety begin buying fewer Chinese-made toys for their children.

  b. U.S. interest rates rise relative to interest rates in China, so Chinese residents seek to purchase additional U.S. financial assets.

  c. Chinese furniture manufacturers produce high-quality early American furniture and successfully export large quantities of the furniture to the United States.

ECONOMICS ON THE NET

Daily Exchange Rates It is easy to keep up with daily changes in exchange rates by using the Web site of Oanda.com. In this application, you will learn how hard it is to predict exchange rate movements, and you will get some practice thinking about what factors can cause exchange rates to change.

Title: Oanda Currency Converter

Navigation: Go to **www.econtoday.com/chap33** to visit the Oanda.com's currency converter home page. Click on *Foreign Exchange 12 PM Rates.*

Application Answer the following questions.

  1. Choose a currency from the many available in the drop-down menu. How many dollars does it take to purchase a unit of the currency in the spot foreign exchange market?

  2. For currency you chose in Question 1, keep track of its value relative to the dollar over the course of several days. Based on your tabulations, try to predict the value of the currency at the end of the week *following* your data collections. Use any information you may have, or just do your best without any additional information. How far off did your prediction turn out to be?

For Group Study and Analysis Divide the class into groups, and assign a currency to each group. Ask the group to track the currency's value over the course of two days and to determine whether the currency's value appreciated or depreciated relative to the dollar from one day to the next. In addition, ask each group to discuss what kinds of demand or supply shifts could have caused the change that occurred during this interval.

ANSWERS TO QUICK QUIZZES

p. 731: (i) balance . . . payments; (ii) physical; (iii) current . . . current; (iv) Unilateral transfers; (v) current; (vi) capital . . . capital; (vii) official reserve; (viii) inflation . . . political

p. 738: (i) exchange rate; (ii) demand . . . demand . . . supply; (iii) downward . . . upward; (iv) shift . . . demand

p. 742: (i) fixed . . . fixed; (ii) currencies . . . reserves; (iii) risk

Answers to Odd-Numbered Problems

CHAPTER 1

1-1. Economics is the study of how individuals allocate limited resources to satisfy unlimited wants.

  a. Among the factors that a rational, self-interested student will take into account are her income, the price of the textbook, her anticipation of how much she is likely to study the textbook, and how much studying the book is likely to affect her grade.

  b. A rational, self-interested government official will, for example, recognize that higher taxes will raise more funds for mass transit while making more voters, who have limited resources, willing to elect other officials.

  c. A municipality's rational, self-interested government will, for instance, take into account that higher hotel taxes will produce more funds if as many visitors continue staying at hotels, but that the higher taxes will also discourage some visitors from spending nights at hotels.

1-3. Because wants are unlimited, the phrase applies to very high-income households as well as low- and middle-income households. Consider, for instance, a household with a low income and unlimited wants at the beginning of the year. The household's wants will still remain unlimited if it becomes a high-income household later in the year.

1-5. Sally is displaying rational behavior if all of these activities are in her self-interest. For example, Sally likely derives intrinsic benefit from volunteer and extracurricular activities and may believe that these activities, along with good grades, improve her prospects of finding a job after she completes her studies. Hence, these activities are in her self-interest even though they reduce some available study time.

1-7. The rationality assumption states that people do not intentionally make choices that leave them worse off. The bounded rationality hypothesis suggests that people are *almost*, but not completely, rational.

1-9. Suppose that a person faces a change in the environment, and the person adjusts to this change as predicted by the rationality assumption. If the new environment becomes predictable, then the individual who actually behaves as predicted by the traditional rationality assumption may settle into behavior that *appears* to involve repetitive applications of a rule of thumb.

1-11. a. Rationality assumption

  b. Bounded rationality

  c. Bounded rationality

1-13. a. The model using prices from the Iowa Electronic Market is more firmly based on the rationality assumption, because people who trade assets on this exchange that are based on poor forecasts actually experience losses. This gives them a strong incentive to make the best possible forecasts. Unpaid respondents to opinion polls have less incentive to give truthful answers about whether and how they will vote.

  b. An economist would develop a means of evaluating whether prices in the Iowa Electronic Market or results of opinion polls did a better job of matching actual electoral outcomes.

1-15. a. Positive

  b. Normative

  c. Normative

  d. Positive

APPENDIX A

  A-1. a. Independent: price of a notebook; Dependent: quantity of notebooks

  b. Independent: work-study hours; Dependent: credit hours

  c. Independent: hours of study; Dependent: economics grade

  A-3. a. Above x axis; to left of y axis

  b. Below x axis, to right of y axis

  c. On x axis; to right of y axis

A-5.

y	x
−20	−4
−10	−2
0	0
10	2
20	4

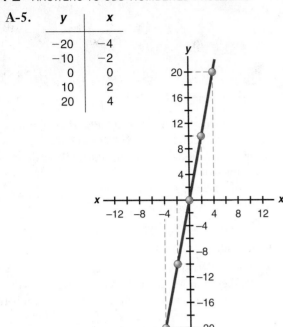

A-7. Each one-unit increase in *x* yields a 5-unit increase in *y*, so the slope given by the change in *y* corresponding to the change in *x* is equal to 5.

CHAPTER 2

2-1. The opportunity cost of attending a class at 11:00 a.m. is the next-best use of that hour of the day. Likewise, the opportunity cost of attending an 8:00 a.m. class is the next-best use of that particular hour of the day. If you are an early riser, it is arguable that the opportunity cost of the 8:00 a.m. hour is lower, because you will already be up at that time but have fewer choices compared with the 11:00 a.m. hour when shops, recreation centers, and the like are open. If you are a late riser, it may be that the opportunity cost of the 8:00 a.m. hour is higher, because you place a relatively high value on an additional hour of sleep in the morning.

2-3. The opportunity cost is the cost of the single, next-best forgone alternative to the $100 spent on the concert ticket, which for your friend was a restaurant meal she otherwise could have purchased and which for you was movie downloads that you otherwise could have bought.

2-5. The bank apparently determined that the net gain anticipated from trying to sell the house to someone else, taking into account the opportunity cost of resources that the bank would have had to devote to renovating the house, was less than $10.

2-7. If the student allocates additional study time to economics in order to increase her score from 90 to 100, her biology score declines from 50 to 40, so

the opportunity cost of earning 10 additional points in economics is 10 fewer points in biology.

2-9.

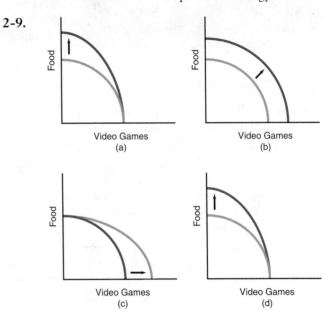

2-11. D

2-13. a. If the nation's residents increase production of consumption goods from 0 units to 10 units, the opportunity cost is 3 units of human capital forgone. If the nation's residents increase production of consumption goods from 0 units to 60 units, the opportunity cost is 100 units of human capital.

b. Yes, because successive 10-unit increases in production of consumption goods generate larger sacrifices of human capital, equal to 3, 7, 15, 20, 25, and 30.

2-15. Because it takes you less time to do laundry, you have an absolute advantage in laundry. Neither you nor your roommate has an absolute advantage in meal preparation. You require 2 hours to fold a basket of laundry, so your opportunity cost of folding a basket of laundry is 2 meals. Your roommate's opportunity cost of folding a basket of laundry is 3 meals. Hence, you have a comparative advantage in laundry, and your roommate has a comparative advantage in meal preparation.

2-17. It may be that the professor is very proficient at doing yard work relative to teaching and research activities, so in fact the professor may have a comparative advantage in doing yard work.

CHAPTER 3

3-1. The equilibrium price is $410 per tablet device, and the equilibrium quantity is 80 million tablet devices. At a price of $400 per tablet device, the quantity of tablet devices demanded is 90 million, and the quantity of tablet devices supplied is 60 million.

Hence, there is a shortage of 30 million tablet devices at a price of $400 per tablet device.

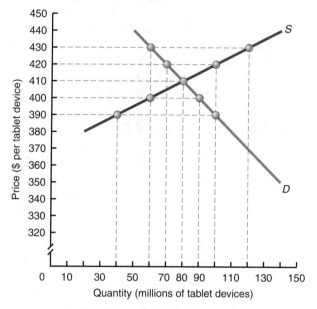

3-3. **a.** Wireless and cable Internet access services are substitutes, so a reduction in the price of wireless Internet access services causes a decrease in the demand for cable-based Internet access services.

   b. A decrease in the price of cable-based Internet access services generates an increase in the quantity of these services demanded.

   c. Cable-based Internet access services are a normal good, so a fall in the incomes of consumers reduces the demand for these services.

   d. If consumers' tastes shift away from wireless Internet access services in favor of cable-based Internet services, then the demand for the latter services increases.

3-5. **a.** Complement: eggs; Substitute: sausage

   b. Complement: tennis balls; Substitute: racquet-ball racquets

   c. Complement: cream; Substitute: tea

   d. Complement: gasoline; Substitute: city bus

3-7. b and d

3-9. **a.** At the $1,000 rental rate, the quantity of one-bed-room apartments supplied is 3,500 per month, but the quantity demanded is only 2,000 per month. Thus, the excess quantity of one-bedroom apartments supplied equals 1,500 apartments per month.

   b. To induce consumers to lease unrented one-bedroom apartments, some landlords will reduce their rental rates. As they do so, the quantity demanded will increase. In addition, some landlords will choose not to offer apartments for rent at lower rates, and the quantity supplied will decrease. At the equilibrium rental rate of $800 per month, no excess quantity will be supplied.

   c. At the $600 rental rate, the quantity of one-bedroom apartments demanded is 3,000 per month, but the quantity supplied is only 1,500 per month. Thus, the excess quantity of one-bedroom apartments demanded equals 1,500 apartments per month.

   d. To induce landlords to make more one-bedroom apartments available for rent, some consumers will offer to pay higher rental rates. As they do so, the quantity supplied will increase. In addition, some consumers will choose not to try to rent apartments at higher rates, and the quantity demanded will decrease. At the equilibrium rental rate of $800 per month, no excess quantity will be demanded.

3-11 **a.** Because touchscreens are an input in the production of smartphones, a decrease in the price of touchscreens causes an increase in the supply of smartphones. The market supply curve shifts to the right, which causes the market price of smartphones to fall and the equilibrium quantity of smartphones to increase.

   b. Machinery used to produce smartphones is an input in the production of these devices, so an increase in the price of machinery generates a decrease in the supply of smartphones. The market supply curve shifts to the left, which causes the market price of smartphones to rise and the equilibrium quantity of smartphones to decrease.

   c. An increase in the number of manufacturers of smartphones causes an increase in the supply of smartphones. The market supply curve shifts rightward. The market price of smartphones declines, and the equilibrium quantity of smartphones increases.

   d. The demand curve for smartphones shifts to the left along the same supply curve, so the quantity supplied decreases. The market price falls, and the equilibrium quantity declines.

3-13. Aluminum is an input in the production of canned soft drinks, so an increase in the price of aluminum reduces the supply of canned soft drinks (option c). The resulting rise in the market price of canned soft drinks brings about a decrease in the quantity of canned soft drinks demanded (option b). In equilibrium, the quantity of soft drinks supplied decreases (option d) to an amount equal to the quantity demanded. The demand curve does not shift, however, so option b does not apply.

CHAPTER 4

4-1. The ability to produce basic cell phones at lower cost and the entry of additional producers shift the supply curve rightward, from S_1 to S_2. At the same time, reduced prices of substitute smartphones result in a leftward shift in the demand for basic cell phones, from D_1 to D_2. Consequently, the equilibrium price of basic cell phones declines, from P_1 to P_2. The equilibrium quantity may rise, fall, or, as shown in the diagram, remain unchanged.

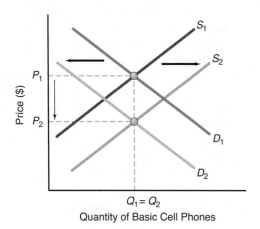

Quantity of Basic Cell Phones

4-3. An increase in demand for GPS devices and an accompanying reduction in supply of GPS devices could result in an unambiguous increase in the market clearing price but with no change in the equilibrium quantity.

4-5. The market rental rate is $700 per apartment, and the equilibrium quantity of apartments rented to tenants is 2,000. At a ceiling price of $650 per month, the number of apartments students desire to rent increases to 2,500 apartments. At the ceiling price, the number of apartments that owners are willing to supply decreases to 1,800 apartments. Thus, there is a shortage of 700 apartments at the ceiling price, and only 1,800 are rented at the ceiling price.

4-7. The market price is $400, and the equilibrium quantity of seats is 1,600. If airlines cannot sell tickets to more than 1,200 passengers, then passengers are willing to pay $600 per seat. Normally, airlines would be willing to sell each ticket for $200, but they will be able to charge a price as high as $600 for each of the 1,200 tickets they sell. Hence, the quantity of tickets sold declines from 1,600, and the price of a ticket rises from $400 to as high as $600.

4-9. a. Consumers buy 10 billion kilograms at the support price of $0.20 per kilogram and hence spend $2 billion on wheat.

b. The amount of surplus wheat at the support price is 8 billion kilograms, so at the $0.20-per-kilogram support price, the government must spend $1.6 billion to purchase this surplus wheat.

c. Pakistani wheat farmers receive a total of $3.6 billion for the wheat they produce at the support price.

4-11. a. At the present minimum wage of $11 per hour, the quantity of labor supplied is 102,000 workers, and the quantity of labor demanded by firms is 98,000. There is an excess quantity supplied of 4,000 workers, which is the number of people who are unemployed.

b. At a minimum wage of $9 per hour, nothing would prevent market forces from pushing the wage rate to the market clearing level of $10 per hour. This $10-per-hour wage rate would exceed the legal minimum and hence would prevail. There would be no unemployed workers.

c. At a $12-per-hour minimum wage, the quantity of labor supplied would increase to 104,000 workers, and the quantity of labor demanded would decline to 96,000. There would be an excess quantity of labor supplied equal to 8,000 workers, which would then be the number of people unemployed.

4-13. a. The rise in the number of wheat producers causes the market supply curve to shift rightward, so more wheat is supplied at the support price.

b. The quantity of wheat demanded at the same support price is unchanged.

c. Because quantity demanded is unchanged while quantity supplied has increased, the amount of surplus wheat that the government must purchase has risen.

CHAPTER 5

5-1. In the absence of laws forbidding cigar smoking in public places, people who are bothered by the odor of cigar smoke will experience costs not borne by cigar producers. Because the supply of cigars will not reflect these costs, from society's perspective, the market cigar supply curve will be in a position too far to the right. The market price of cigars will be too low, and too many cigars will be produced and consumed.

5-3. Imposing the tax on pesticides causes an increase in the price of pesticides, which are an input in the production of oranges. Hence, the supply curve in the orange market shifts leftward. The market price of oranges increases, and the equilibrium quantity of oranges declines. Thus, orange consumers indirectly help to pay for dealing with the spillover costs of pesticide production by paying more for oranges.

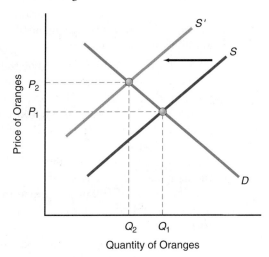

Quantity of Oranges

5-5. a. As shown in the figure below, if the social benefits associated with bus ridership were taken into account, the demand schedule would be D' instead of D, and the market price would be higher. The equilibrium quantity of bus rides would be higher.

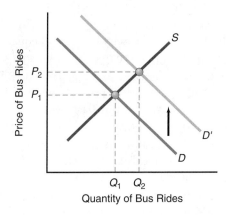

Quantity of Bus Rides

b. The government could pay commuters a subsidy to ride the bus, thereby shifting the demand curve outward and to the right. This would increase the market price and equilibrium number of bus rides.

5-7. If this nation's government does not provide people with property rights for a number of items and fails to enforce the property rights that it does assign for remaining items, externalities would be more common than in a country such as the United States. Any two parties undertaking transactions would experience no incentives to reduce or eliminate their transactions' spillover effects, resulting in widespread externalities.

5-9. At present, the equilibrium quantity of residences with Internet access is 2 million. To take into account the external benefit of Internet access and boost the quantity of residences with access to 3 million, the demand curve would have to shift upward by $20 per month at any given quantity, to D_2 from the current position D_1. Thus, the government would have to offer a $20-per-month subsidy to raise the quantity of residences with Internet access to 3 million.

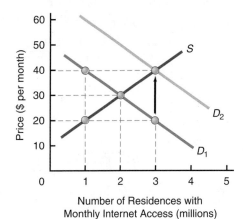

Number of Residences with Monthly Internet Access (millions)

5-11. No, the outcome will be different. If the government had simply provided grants to attend private schools at the current market tuition rate, parents and students receiving the grants would have paid a price equal to the market valuation of the last unit of educational services provided. Granting a subsidy to private schools allows the private schools to charge parents and students a price less than the market price. Private schools thereby will receive a higher-than-market price for the last unit of educational services they provide. Consequently, they will provide a quantity of educational services in excess of the market equilibrium quantity. At this quantity, parents and students place a lower value on the services than the price received by the private schools.

5-13. a. $40 million

b. The effective price of a tablet device to consumers will be lower after the government pays the subsidy, so people will purchase a larger quantity.

c. $60 million

d. $90 million

5-15. a. $60 − $50 = $10

b. Expenditures after the program expansion are $2.4 million. Before the program expansion, expenditures were $1 million. Hence, the increase in expenditures is $1.4 million.

c. At a per-unit subsidy of $50, the share of the per-unit $60 price paid by the government is 5/6, or 83.3 percent. Hence, this is the government's share of total expenditures on the 40,000 devices that consumers purchase.

CHAPTER 6

6-1. a. The average tax rate is the total tax of $40 divided by the $200 in income: $40/$200 = 0.2, or 20 percent.

b. The marginal tax rate for the last hour of work is the change in taxes, $3, divided by the change in income, $8: $3/$8 = 0.375, or 37.5 percent.

6-3. a. Christino's marginal tax rate is

$$\frac{\$300 - \$200}{\$2,000 - \$1,000} = \frac{\$400 - \$300}{\$3,000 - \$2,000}$$

$$= \frac{\$100}{\$1,000} = 0.1, \text{ or } 10 \text{ percent.}$$

b. Jarius's marginal tax rate is

$$\frac{\$400 - \$200}{\$2,000 - \$1,000} = \frac{\$600 - \$400}{\$3,000 - \$2,000}$$

$$= \frac{\$200}{\$1,000} = 0.2, \text{ or } 20 \text{ percent.}$$

c. Meg's marginal tax rate is

$$\frac{\$500 - \$200}{\$2,000 - \$1,000} = \frac{\$800 - \$500}{\$3,000 - \$2,000}$$

$$= \frac{\$300}{\$1,000} = 0.3, \text{ or } 30 \text{ percent.}$$

6-5. 2005: $300 million; 2007: $350 million; 2009: $400 million; 2011: $400 million; 2013: $420 million

6-7. a. The supply of tickets for flights into and out of London shifts upward by $154. The equilibrium quantity of flights into and out of London declines. The market clearing price of London airline tickets rises by an amount less than the tax.

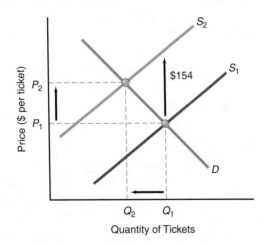

b. Tickets for flights into or out of London are substitutes for tickets for flights into and out of nearby cities. Thus, the demand for tickets for flights into and out of these cities will increase. This will cause an increase in the equilibrium

quantities of these tickets and an increase in the market clearing prices.

6-9. a. The initial market price is $7 per unit, at which the equilibrium quantity demanded equals the equilibrium quantity supplied at 125 units.

b. The supply curve shifts upward by the amount of the tax, so in the table, the quantity supplied at a price of $6 is 50 units; at a price of $7, 75 units; at a price of $8, 100 units; at a price of $9, 125 units; at a price of $10, 150 units; and at a price of $11, 175 units. The demand relationship is unchanged. Hence, the new market price is $8, at which the quantity demanded of 100 units is equal to the new quantity supplied at this price that is also equal to 100 units.

c. The market price rises from $7 to $8, and this $1 price increase is half of the $2 tax. Consequently, consumers pay half of the tax, and producers pay the other half.

CHAPTER 19

19-1. $-[(200 - 150)/(350/2)]/[(\$19 - \$20)/(\$39/2)]$, which is approximately equal to -5.6. Thus, the absolute price elasticity of demand equals 5.6.

19-3. a. $-[(90 - 80)/(85)]/[(\$0.20 - \$0.40)/(\$0.30)]$, which is approximately equal to -0.18. Consequently, the absolute price elasticity of demand is 0.18, so demand is inelastic over this range.

b. $-[(60 - 40)/(50)]/[(\$0.80 - \$1.20)/(\$1.00)] = -1.00$. The absolute price elasticity of demand, therefore, equals 1.00, which implies that demand is unit-elastic over this range.

c. $-[(20 - 10)/(15)]/[(\$1.60 - \$1.80)/(\$1.70)]$, which is approximately equal to -5.67. Thus, the absolute price elasticity of demand is 5.67, so demand is elastic over this range.

19-5. $-[(800 - 1,200)/(2,000/2)]/[(\$62.50 - \$57.50)/(\$120.00/2)] = -4.8$. Hence, the absolute price elasticity of demand equals 4.8. Demand is elastic over this range.

19-7. Because price and total revenue move in the same direction, then over this range of demand, the demand for hand-made guitars is inelastic.

19-9. a. More inelastic, because it represents a smaller portion of the budget

b. More elastic, because there are many close substitutes

c. More elastic, because there are a number of substitutes

d. More inelastic, because there are few close substitutes

e. More inelastic, because it represents a small portion of the budget

19-11. Let X denote the percentage change in the quantity of bacon. Then $X/10$ percent $= -0.5$. X, therefore, is -5 percent.

19-13. The income elasticity of demand is equal to $[(6 - 4)/(10/2)]/[(\$84,000 - \$80,000)/(\$164,000/2)] = +8.2$, so downloadable movies are a normal good.

19-15. $[(125,000 - 75,000)/(200,000/2)]/[(\$35,000 - \$25,000)/(\$60,000/2)] = 1.5$. Supply is elastic.

CHAPTER 20

20-1. The campus pizzeria indicates by its pricing policy that it recognizes the principle of diminishing marginal utility. As shown in Figure 20-1 on page 437, a customer's marginal utility for the second pizza is typically lower than for the first. Thus, the customer is likely to value the second pizza less and, therefore, only be willing to pay less for it.

20-3. The total utility of the third, fourth, and fifth cheeseburgers is 48, 56, and 60, respectively. The marginal utility of the first and second cheeseburgers is 20 and 16, respectively. The total utility of the first, second, and third bags of french fries is 10, 18, and 20, respectively. The marginal utility of the fourth and fifth bags of french fries is 1 and 0, respectively.

20-5. The new utility-maximizing combination is four cheeseburgers and two orders of french fries, at which the marginal utility per dollar spent is 2 units per dollar and the entire $6 is spent.

20-7. Other things being equal, when the price of soft drinks rises, the substitution effect comes into play, and the individual tends to consume less of the more expensive item, soft drinks, and more of the item with the unchanged price, tacos. Hence, the marginal utility of soft drinks rises, and the marginal utility of tacos falls.

20-9. a. Of all the possible one-unit increases in consumption displayed, the movement from point *A* to point *B* generates the highest marginal utility. Total utility rises by 5 units between these points, so the marginal utility of the first unit consumed is 5 units.

b. Between points *E* and *F*, a one-unit increase in the quantity consumed leaves total utility unchanged at 11 units, so marginal utility is equal to zero.

c. Between points *F* and *G*, a one-unit increase in the quantity consumed causes total utility to decline from 11 units to 10 units, so marginal utility is negative and equal to −1 unit.

20-11. For this consumer, at these prices the marginal utility per dollar spent on 2 fudge bars is 500 units of utility per dollar, and the marginal utility per dollar spent on 5 popsicles is also 500 units of utility per dollar. In addition, the entire budget of $9 is spent at this combination, which is the consumer optimum.

20-13. The marginal utility per dollar spent is equalized at 2.50 if 5 hot dogs and 3 baseball games are consumed, and this consumption combination just exhausts the now-available $190 in income.

20-15. The marginal utility of good Y is three times the marginal utility of good X, or 3×3 utils $= 9$ utils.

20-17. Because the price of good Y is three times greater than the price of good X, the marginal utility of good Y must be three times greater than the price of good X.

APPENDIX F

F-1. The indifference curve is convex to the origin because of a diminishing marginal rate of substitution. As an individual consumes more and more of an item, the individual becomes less willing to forgo the other item. The diminishing marginal rate of substitution is due to diminishing marginal utility.

F-3. Sue's marginal rate of substitution is calculated below:

Combination of Bottled Water and Soft Drinks	Bottled Water per Month	Soft Drinks per Month	MRS
A	5	11	
B	10	7	5:4
C	15	4	5:3
D	20	2	5:2
E	25	1	5:1

The diminishing marginal rate of substitution of soft drinks for water shows Sue's diminishing marginal utility of bottled water. She is willing to forgo fewer and fewer soft drinks to get an additional five bottles of water.

F-5. Given that water is measured along the horizontal axis and soft drinks are measured along the vertical axis, the slope of Sue's budget constraint is the price of water divided by the price of soft drinks, or $P_W/P_S = \frac{1}{2}$. The only combination of bottled water and soft drinks that is on Sue's indifference curve and budget constraint is combination *C*. For this combination, total expenditures on water and soft drinks equal $(15 \times \$1) + (4 \times \$2) = \$15 + \$8 = \$23$.

F-7. With the quantity of bottled water measured along the horizontal axis and the quantity of soft drinks measured along the vertical axis, the slope of Sue's budget constraint is the price of water divided by the price of soft drinks. This ratio equals ½. The only combination of bottled water and soft drinks that is on Sue's indifference curve and budget constraint is combination *C*, where expenditures on water and soft drinks total $23.

F-9. Yes, Sue's revealed preferences indicate that her demand for soft drinks obeys the law of demand. When the price of soft drinks declines from $2 to $1, her quantity demanded rises from 4 to 8.

CHAPTER 21

21-1. a. Bob earns a high economic rent. Because he has a specialized skill that is in great demand, his income is likely to be high, and his opportunity cost relatively low.

b. Sally earns a high economic rent. Because she is a supermodel, her income is likely to be relatively high, and, without any education, her opportunity cost is likely to be relatively low.

c. If Tim were to leave teaching, not a relatively high-paying occupation, he could sell insurance full time. Hence, his opportunity cost is high relative to his income, and his economic rent is low.

21-3. The answer is c only, because this is the only case in which the supply of the factor is very inelastic.

21-5. A sole proprietorship is a business entity owned by a single individual, whereas a partnership is a business entity jointly owned by more than one individual. A corporation, in contrast, is a legal entity that is owned by shareholders, who own shares of the profits of the entity. Sole proprietorships and partnerships do not face double taxation, but corporations do. The owners of corporations, however, enjoy limited liability, whereas the sole proprietor or partner does not.

21-7. Accounting profit is total revenue, $77,250, minus explicit costs, $37,000, for a total of $40,250. Economic profit is total revenue, $77,250, less explicit costs, $37,000, and implicit costs, $40,250, for a total equal to zero.

21-9. a. Physical capital

b. Financial capital

c. Financial capital

d. Physical capital

21-11. a. The owner of WebCity faces both tax rates if the firm is a corporation, but if it is a proprietorship, the owner faces only the 30 percent personal income tax rate. Thus, it should choose to be a proprietorship.

b. If WebCity is a corporation, the $100,000 in corporate earnings is taxed at a 20 percent rate, so that after-tax dividends are $80,000, and these are taxed at the personal income tax rate of 30 percent, leaving $56,000 in after-tax income for the owner. Hence, the firm should be organized as a proprietorship, with after-tax earnings of $70,000, or an advantage of $14,000.

c. Yes. In this case, incorporation raises earnings to $150,000, which are taxed at a rate of 20 percent, yielding after-tax dividends of $120,000 that are taxed at the personal rate of 30 percent. This leaves an after-tax income for the owner of $84,000, which is higher than the after-tax earnings of $70,000 if WebCity is a proprietorship that earns lower pre-tax income taxed at the personal rate.

d. After-tax profits rise from $56,000 to $84,000, or by $28,000.

e. This policy change would only increase the incentive to incorporate.

f. A corporate structure provides limited liability for owners, which can be a major advantage. Furthermore, owners may believe that the corporate structure will yield higher pre-tax earnings, as in the above example.

21-13. The real rate of interest in Japan is $2\% - 0.5\% = 1.5\%$. The real rate of interest in the United States is $4\% - 3\% = 1\%$. Japan, therefore, has the higher *real* rate of interest.

21-15. Ownership of common stock provides voting rights within the firm but also entails immediate loss if assets fall below the value of the firm's liabilities. Preferred stockholders are repaid prior to owners of common stock, but preferred stockholders do not have voting rights.

21-17. You should point out to your classmate that stock prices tend to drift upward following a random walk. That is, yesterday's price plus any upward drift is the best guide to today's price. Therefore, there are no predictable trends that can be used to "beat" the market.

CHAPTER 22

22-1. The short run is a time period during which the professor cannot enter the job market and find employment elsewhere. This is the nine-month period from August 15 through May 15. The professor can find employment elsewhere after the contract has been fulfilled, so the short run is nine months and the long run is greater than nine months.

22-3. Total variable costs are equal to total costs, $5 million, less total fixed costs, $2 million, which equals $3 million. Average variable costs are equal to total variable costs divided by the number of units produced. Average variable costs, therefore, equal $3 million divided by 10,000, or $300.

22-5. Marginal cost was equal to the change in total cost when the last pencil was produced, which was $12,500 − $12,425 = $75.

22-7. a. Total fixed costs equal average fixed costs, $10 per LCD screen, times the quantity produced per day, 100 LCD screens, which equals $1,000 per day.

 b. The total variable costs of producing 100 LCD screens equal average variable costs, $10 per unit, times the quantity produced per day, 100 LCD screens, which equals $1,000 per day.

 c. The total costs of producing 100 LCD screens equal total fixed costs plus the total variable costs of producing 100 LCD screens, or $1,000 per day plus $1,000 per day, which equals $2,000 per day.

 d. The average total costs of producing 99 LCD screens equal the average fixed costs of $10.101 plus the average variable costs of $10.070, or $20.171 per LCD screen. Thus, the total cost of producing 99 LCD screens equals $20.171 times 99, or $1,996.929. The marginal cost of producing the hundredth LCD screen equals the change in total costs from increasing production from 99 to 100, or $2,000 − $1,996.929, or $3.071 per LCD screen.

22-9. a. Average total costs are $20 per unit plus $30 per unit, or $50 per unit, and total costs divided by average total costs equal output, which therefore is $2,500/$50 per unit, or 50 units.

 b. TVC = AVC × Q = $20 per unit × 50 units = $1,000

 c. TFC = AFC × Q = $30 per unit × 50 units = $1,500; or TFC = TC − TVC = $2,500 − $1,000 = $1,500

22-11. a. The expense incurred in cutting back trees on a regular basis would be unrelated to the quantity of rail services provided on the tracks and hence would represent a fixed cost.

 b. The expense of dumping sand on the slippery tracks in advance of trains would vary with the number of trains that run on the tracks and hence would constitute a variable cost.

22-13. Hiring 1 more unit of labor at a wage rate of $20 to increase output by 1 unit causes total costs to rise by $20, so the marginal cost of the 251st unit is $20.

22-15. a. AVC = $2 million/1 million units = $2 per unit

 b. APP = 1 million units/1,000 units of labor = 1,000 units of output per unit of labor

 c. Wage rate = $2 million/1,000 units of labor = $2,000 per unit of labor

22-17. a. Plant size E, because this is the minimum output scale at which LRATC is at a minimum level

 b. Leftward movement, because the functioning plant size for the firm would decrease

CHAPTER 23

23-1. a. The single firm producing much of the industry's output can affect price. Therefore, this is currently not a perfectly competitive industry.

 b. The output of each firm is not homogeneous, so this is not a perfectly competitive industry.

 c. Firms must obtain government permission to enter the industry and hence cannot easily enter, so this is not a perfectly competitive industry.

23-3. a. For a perfectly competitive firm, marginal revenue and average revenue are equal to the market clearing price. Hence, average revenue equals $20 per unit at each possible output rate.

 b. At the present output of 10,000 units per week, the firm's total revenues equal price times output, or $20 per unit times 10,000 units per week, which equals $200,000 per week. The firm's total costs equal ATC times output, or $15.75 per unit times 10,000 units per week, which equals $157,500 per week. Weekly economic profits equal total revenues minus total costs, or $200,000 − $157,500 = $42,500. The firm is maximizing economic profits, because it is producing the output rate at which marginal revenue equals marginal cost.

 c. If the market clearing price were to fall to $12.50 per unit, the marginal revenue curve would shift down to this level. Average total costs would exceed the price at this output rate, but in the short run the firm would minimize its short-run economic losses by producing 8,100 units per week.

 d. If the market clearing price were to fall to $7.50 per unit, the marginal revenue curve would shift down to this level. Average variable costs at an output rate of 5,000 units per week would exceed the market clearing price, so total variable costs of producing 5,000 units per week would exceed total revenues. The firm should cease production if this event takes place.

23-5. Even though the price of pizzas, and hence marginal revenue, falls to only $5, this covers average variable costs. Thus, the shop should stay open.

23-7. In the described situation, the firm is producing an output rate at a point on the marginal cost curve below the average total cost curve. Marginal revenue is above the minimum point of the average total cost curve, however. Hence, marginal cost at the current rate of production is less than marginal revenue. The firm is not maximizing profit, and it should increase its rate of production.

23-9. a. There was a significant increase in market supply as more firms entered the industry. A consequence for the typical firm was that the market price fell below the minimum average total cost, resulting in negative economic profits.

b. Firms will consider leaving the industry, and some firms probably *will* leave the industry.

23-11. Increases in demand have initially led to higher economic profits for incumbent firms, which has generated entry by other firms into digital-device industries and caused market supply curves to shift outward. As more firms have entered and increased production of digital devices, input prices have declined, so firms' costs have decreased. On net, therefore, long-run equilibrium market prices have declined, implying that these digital-device industries are decreasing-cost industries.

CHAPTER 24

24-1. a. The total revenue and total profits of the dry cleaner are as follows.

Output (suits cleaned)	Price ($ per unit)	Total Costs ($)	Total Revenue ($)	Total Profit ($)
0	8.00	3.00	0	−3.00
1	7.50	6.00	7.50	1.50
2	7.00	8.50	14.00	5.50
3	6.50	10.50	19.50	9.00
4	6.00	11.50	24.00	12.50
5	5.50	13.50	27.50	14.00
6	5.00	16.00	30.00	14.00
7	4.50	19.00	31.50	12.50
8	4.00	24.00	32.00	8.00

b. The profit-maximizing rate of output is between 5 and 6 units.

c. The marginal cost and marginal revenue of the dry cleaner are as follows. The profit-maximizing rate of output is 6 units.

Output (suits cleaned)	Price ($ per unit)	Total Costs ($)	Total Revenue ($)	Total Profit ($)	Marginal Cost ($ per unit)	Marginal Revenue ($ per unit)
0	8.00	3.00	0	−3.00	—	—
1	7.50	6.00	7.50	1.50	3.00	7.50
2	7.00	8.50	14.00	5.50	2.50	6.50
3	6.50	10.50	19.50	9.00	2.00	5.50
4	6.00	11.50	24.00	12.50	1.00	4.50
5	5.50	13.50	27.50	14.00	2.00	3.50
6	5.00	16.00	30.00	14.00	2.50	2.50
7	4.50	19.00	31.50	12.50	3.00	1.50
8	4.00	24.00	32.00	8.00	4.00	0.50

24-3. a. The profit-maximizing output rate is 5,000 units.

b. Average total cost is $5 per unit. Average revenue is $6 per unit.

c. Total costs equal $5 per unit × 5,000 units = $25,000. Total revenue equals $6 per unit × 5,000 units = $30,000.

d. ($6 per unit − $5 per unit) × 5,000 units = $5,000

e. In a perfectly competitive market, price would equal marginal cost at $4.50 per unit, at which the quantity is 8,000 units. Because the monopolist produces less and charges a higher price than under perfect competition, price exceeds marginal cost at the profit-maximizing level of output. The difference between the price and marginal cost is the per-unit cost to society of a monopolized industry.

24-5. The monopolist's total revenues equal 500 units per week × $40 per unit = $2,000 per week. Thus, its total costs equal total revenues − economic profits = $2,000 per week − $500 per week = $1,500 per week. Average total cost equals the ratio of total costs to the output rate, or $1,500/500 units = $30 per unit. The firm has maximized profits by producing to the point at which marginal cost, which is $15 per unit, equals marginal revenue, so marginal revenue is $15 per unit.

24-7. a. The monopoly maximizes economic profits or minimizes economic losses by producing to the point at which marginal revenue is equal to marginal cost, which is 1 million units of output per month.

b. The profit-maximizing or loss-minimizing price of 1 million units per month is $30 per unit, so total revenues equal $30 million per month. The average total cost of producing 1 million units per month is $33 per unit, so total costs equal $33 million per month. Hence, in the short run, producing 1 million units per month minimizes the monopoly's loss at $3 million per month.

24-9. If price varies positively with total revenue, then the monopolist is operating on the inelastic portion of the demand curve. This corresponds to the range in which marginal revenue is negative. The monopolist cannot, therefore, be at the point at which its profits are maximized. In other words, the monopolist is not producing the output at which marginal cost equals marginal revenue.

24-11. Because marginal cost has risen, the monopolist will be operating at a lower rate of output and charging a higher price. Economic profits are likely to decline because even though the price is higher, its output will be more than proportionately lower.

CHAPTER 25

25-1. a. There are many fast-food restaurants producing and selling differentiated products. Both features of this industry are consistent with the theory of monopolistic competition.

b. There are numerous colleges and universities, but each specializes in different academic areas and hence produces heterogeneous products, as in the theory of monopolistic competition.

c. Although it is possible that this is a short-run equilibrium situation, it is more likely, given that economic profits are zero, that this is a long-run equilibrium in which price equals average total costs and there is no incentive for firms to enter or leave the industry.

25-3. If the firm had to reduce its price from the long-run equilibrium level of $28 per unit to marginal cost at $20 per unit, its revenues would drop from $2,800 per day for the long-run output rate of 100 units to $2,000 per day. Thus, it would experience a daily economic loss of $800 per unit and eventually choose to exit the industry rather than continue producing at a loss.

25-5. The values for marginal cost and marginal revenue appear below. Marginal revenue equals marginal cost at approximately the fifth unit of output, so marginal analysis indicates that 5 units is the profit-maximizing production level.

Output	Price ($ per unit)	Total Costs ($)	Total Revenue ($)	Marginal Cost ($ per unit)	Marginal Revenue ($ per unit)	Total Profit ($)
0	6.00	2.00	0	—	—	−2.00
1	5.75	5.25	5.75	3.25	5.75	0.00
2	5.50	7.50	11.00	2.25	5.25	3.50
3	5.25	9.60	15.75	2.10	4.75	6.15
4	5.00	12.10	20.00	2.50	4.25	7.90
5	4.75	15.80	23.75	3.70	3.75	7.95
6	4.50	20.00	27.00	4.20	3.25	7.00
7	4.00	24.75	28.00	4.75	1.00	3.25

26-7. After these long-run adjustments have occurred, the demand curve will have shifted to tangency, with the average total cost curve at 4 units of output. At this production level, average total cost is $3.03, so this will be the long-run equilibrium price. Because price and average total cost will be equal, the firm will earn zero economic profits.

25-9. a. Interactive

b. Direct

c. Mass and interactive

d. Mass

25-11. a. Search good. Given the knowledge that it is a heavy-duty filing cabinet, a photo and description providing features such as dimensions are sufficient to evaluate the characteristics of a filing cabinet.

b. Experience good. A meal must be eaten for its characteristics to be determined.

c. Search good. Given the knowledge that the coat is made of wool, a photo and description providing size information are sufficient to evaluate the characteristics of the coat.

d. Credence good. Psychotherapy services have characteristics that are likely to be difficult for consumers lacking expertise to assess without assistance from another health care provider, such as a general practitioner who guides someone experiencing depression to seek psychotherapy treatment from a psychiatrist.

25-13. Consumers may be able to assess certain features of a credence good in advance of purchase, so in this sense a credence good is similar to a search good. Consumers lack expertise to evaluate the full qualities of a credence good until after they have purchased it, which is somewhat analogous to the characteristics of an experience good. Nevertheless, the fact that consumers cannot fully evaluate a credence good's qualities in advance of purchase makes it different from a search good. Likewise, the inability to be certain, without assistance, of the qualities of a credence good following purchase of the good also distinguishes a credence good from an experience good. The fact that consumers can evaluate certain aspects of a credence good in advance of purchase, as in the case of a search good, explains why ads for credence goods, such as pharmaceuticals, often have informational elements. At the same time, however, the fact that consumers cannot truly evaluate credence goods until after purchase, and even then only with assistance, explains why ads for credence goods also commonly include persuasive elements.

25-15. Typically, the fixed costs of producing an information product are relatively high, while average variable cost is equal to a very small per-unit amount. As a consequence, the average total cost curve slopes downward with increased output, and average variable cost equals marginal cost at a low, constant amount irrespective of the quantity produced. For an information product, marginal cost is always below average total cost. Consequently, if price were equal to marginal cost, it would always be less than average total cost, so the producer would always earn short-run economic losses.

CHAPTER 26

26-1. a. 15 percent + 14 percent + 12 percent + 11 percent = 52 percent

    b. 52 percent + 10 percent + 10 percent + 8 percent + 7 percent = 87 percent; or 100 percent − 13 percent = 87 percent

26-3. $15^2 + 14^2 + 12^2 + 11^2 + 10^2 + 10^2 + 8^2 + 7^2 + 13 = 225 + 196 + 144 + 121 + 100 + 100 + 64 + 49 + 13 = 1,012$

26-5. a. Zero-sum game

    b. Negative-sum game

    c. Positive-sum game

26-7. Bob is currently a participant in a noncooperative game, in which some people stand and block his view of the football game. His tit-for-tat strategy is to stand up as well. If he stands, however, he will block the view of another spectator. In a cooperative game, all would sit or stand up simultaneously, so that no individual's view is blocked.

26-9. a. The fact that prices are growing at a stable rate and readily observable favors enforcing a cartel agreement So does the fact that only seven firms of significant size exist in the inkjet-printer industry, which is a relatively small number. Therefore, much depends on the degree of heterogeneity of inkjet printers; if these products are relatively homogeneous, then, taken together, these characteristics of the industry would generally support an effort to form a cartel.

    b. Once the cartel is formed, any one of the firms that produce inkjet printers could enlarge its profits by expanding production at the higher cartel price, so an incentive to cheat is always present. In addition, the presence of positive economic profits in the industry could induce firms outside the industry cartel to begin manufacturing and selling inkjet printers.

26-11. Possible examples include office productivity software, online auction services, telecommunications services, and Internet payment services. In each case, more people are likely to choose to consume the item when others do, because the inherent usefulness of consuming the item for each person increases as the number of consumers rises.

26-13. a. Mastercard.com is a platform for linking people making payments with credit cards to banks that clear the payments in a transaction-based market.

    b. FreeBSD.com is an open-source operating system utilized within a shared-input market.

    c. Plentyoffish.com is a platform that links people seeking romantic matches in a matchmaking market.

    d. WSJ.com provides business news reporting to attract an audience to advertisers within an audience-making market.

CHAPTER 27

27-1. If cable service is an industry that experiences diminishing long-run average total costs, then the city may determine that it is more efficient to have a single, large firm that produces at a lower long-run average cost. The city could then regulate the activity of the firm.

27-3. a. As the table indicates, long-run average cost and long-run marginal cost decline with greater output. If the firm were allowed to operate as a monopolist, it would produce to the point at which marginal cost equals marginal revenue, which is 2 units of output. The price that consumers are willing to pay for this quantity is $90 per unit, and maximum economic profits are $180 − $175 = $5.

Quantity	Price ($ per unit)	Long-Run Total Cost ($)	LRAC ($ per unit)	LRMC ($ per unit)	MR ($ per unit)
0	100	0	—	—	
1	95	92	92.00	92	95
2	90	177	88.50	85	85
3	85	255	85.00	78	75
4	80	331	82.75	76	65
5	75	406	81.20	75	55
6	70	480	80.00	74	45

    b. Long-run marginal cost and price both equal $75 per unit at 5 units of output. At a price of $75 per unit, the firm experiences economic losses equal to $375 − $406 = −$31.

    c. Long-run average cost and price both equal $85 per unit at 3 units of output. At a price of $85 per unit, the firm's economic profits equal $255 − $255 = $0.

27-5. Lemons problems are likely to be more common in industries in which evaluating the characteristics of goods or services by simple inspection is difficult, as is true of the credence goods discussed in Chapter 25. Unaddressed lemons problems tend to depress the prices that sellers of high-quality items can obtain, which induces them to refrain from selling their high-quality items, resulting in sales of only lower-quality items. The main concern of economic regulation is to balance the trade-off between service and price, with economic regulation aiming to keep price lower than the price a profit-maximizing monopolist would charge. Social regulation seeks to improve working conditions and minimize adverse spillovers of production. The adverse incentives resulting from lemons problems are a form of market spillover, so it is arguable that social regulation is most appropriate for addressing lemons problems.

27-7. If European regulation is designed to protect domestic industries, then this is an example of the capture hypothesis. If, on the other hand, legitimate health concerns exist, then this is an example of the share-the-pain, share-the-gain hypothesis.

27-9. This is a creative response to the do-not-call legislation, in which firms are legally satisfying the terms of the regulation but evading the regulation's intent.

27-11. a. In the e-book market, percentage sales shares are as follows: 75.0 percent for Firm 1 and 5.0 percent each for Firms 2, 3, 4, 5, and 6. In the physical book market, sales shares are as follows: 46.7 percent for Firm 2, 22.2 percent for Firm 3, 21.7 percent for Firm 4, 5.0 percent for Firm 5, and 4.4 percent for Firm 6. According to the antitrust authority's initial evaluation, a monopoly situation may exist in the e-book market, but not in the market for physical books.

b. In the combined market, percentage market shares are as follows: 42.5 percent for Firm 2, 20.5 percent for Firm 3, 20.0 percent for Firm 4, 7.5 percent for Firm 1, 5 percent for Firm 5, and 4.5 percent for Firm 6. Under this alternative definition, the antitrust authority's initial evaluation would suggest that there is no cause for concern about monopoly.

27-13. The HHI for the combined market equals $42.5^2 + 20.5^2 + 20^2 + 7.5^2 + 5^2 + 4.5^2$, which, rounding to nearest whole numbers, is approximately equal to $1,806 + 420 + 400 + 56 + 25 + 20 = 2,272$. This value is less than the 5,000 threshold, so the authorities would conclude that a legal challenge is unwarranted.

27-15. This is an example of bundling. Because consumers who purchase the bundled product perceive that they have effectively paid different prices for the bundled products based on their willingness to pay, an antitrust authority might view this practice as charging consumers different prices for the same products, or price discrimination.

CHAPTER 28

28-1.

Labor Input (workers per week)	Total Physical Output (printers per day)	Marginal Physical Product	Marginal Revenue Product ($)
10	200	—	—
11	218	18	1,800
12	234	16	1,600
13	248	14	1,400
14	260	12	1,200
15	270	10	1,000
16	278	8	800

28-3. a. The greater the substitutability of capital, the more elastic is the demand for labor.

b. Because the demand for labor is a derived demand, the greater the elasticity of demand for the final product, the greater is the elasticity of demand for labor.

c. The larger the portion of factor costs accounted for by labor, the larger is the price elasticity of demand for labor.

28-5. a.

Labor Input (workers per week)	Total Physical Product	Product Price ($ per unit)	Marginal Physical Product	Total Revenue ($)	Marginal Revenue Product ($)
10	100	50	—	5,000	—
11	109	49	9	5,341	341
12	116	48	7	5,568	227
13	121	47	5	5,687	119
14	124	46	3	5,704	17
15	125	45	1	5,625	−79

b. The profit-maximizing firm would hire 13 workers, which is the quantity of labor beyond which the marginal revenue product of labor falls below the marginal factor cost.

28-7. a. The rise in the price of ethanol results in an increase in the marginal revenue product of corn, the key input in production of ethanol. Thus, each ethanol producer's marginal revenue product curve shifts rightward, which ultimately translates into an increase in the demand for corn, from D_1 to D_2. The market clearing price of corn increases, from P_1 to P_2, and the equilibrium quantity of corn rises, from Q_1 to Q_2.

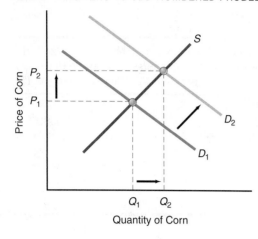

the marginal physical product of capital per dollar spent on capital, which is 20,000/$500, or 40 units of output per dollar spent on capital. Thus, the firm should increase the additional output per dollar spent on labor by reducing the number of labor units it hires, and it should reduce the additional output per dollar spent on capital by increasing its use of capital, to the point at which these amounts are equalized.

CHAPTER 29

29-1. Individual workers can air grievances to the collective voice, who then takes the issue to the employer. The individual does not run the risk of being singled out by an employer. The individual employee does not waste work time trying to convince the employer that changes are needed in the workplace.

29-3. The reporting system probably was intended to provide information to union officials charged with seeking to impede strikebreaking activities by nonunion workers such as the soap opera writers. Strikebreakers can replace union employees, so they diminish the collective bargaining power of a union.

29-5. When marginal revenue is zero, demand for labor is unit-elastic, and total revenue is neither rising nor falling. No additional revenues can be earned by altering the quantity of labor, so the union's total wage revenues are maximized.

29-7. When unions in these industries attempt to bargain for higher-than-market levels of wages, the firms that employ members of these unions will not be able to readily substitute to alternative inputs. Hence, these unions are more likely to be able to achieve their wage objectives.

b. Human snack foods are a substitute input in the production of hogs, so the increase in the price of corn induced farmers to substitute in favor of snack foods.

28-9. The demand for the labor of U.S. workers who develop digital apps will decline, which will reduce equilibrium employment in this U.S. labor market and generate a decrease in the wage rate for these workers to less than $35 per hour. The demand for labor of Russian workers who develop digital apps will increase, which will raise equilibrium employment in this Russian labor market and bring about an increase in the wage rate for these workers to above $15 per hour.

28-11. Labor outsourcing by U.S. firms tends to push down market wages and employment in affected U.S. labor markets, but labor outsourcing by foreign firms that hire U.S. workers tends to push up market wages and employment in affected U.S. labor markets. Consequently, the overall wage and employment effects are ambiguous in the short run. In the long run, however, outsourcing enables U.S. and foreign firms to specialize in producing and trading the goods and services that they can produce most efficiently. The resulting resource saving ultimately expands the ability of U.S. residents to consume more goods and services than they could have otherwise.

28-13. The wage rate, $20 per unit of labor, equals marginal revenue product, so the marginal physical product of labor is $20 per unit of labor divided by the marginal revenue, $10 per unit of output, or 2 units of output per unit of labor.

28-15. To maximize profits, the firm should hire inputs up to the point at which the marginal physical product per dollar spent on the input is equalized across all inputs. This is not the case in this example. The marginal physical product of labor per dollar spent on wages is 200/$10 = 20 units of output per dollar spent on labor, which is less than

29-9.

Quantity of Labor Supplied	Total Physical Product	Required Hourly Wage Rate ($ per unit of labor)	Total Wage Bill ($)	Marginal Factor Cost ($ per unit of labor)
10	100	5	50	—
11	109	6	66	16
12	116	7	84	18
13	121	8	104	20
14	124	9	126	22
15	125	10	150	24

29-11. At 11 units of labor, the marginal revenue product of labor equals $16. This is equal to the marginal factor cost at this level of employment. The firm, therefore, will hire 11 units of labor and pay a wage of $6 an hour.

Quantity of Labor Supplied	Required Hourly Wage Rate ($ per unit of labor)	Total Factor Cost ($)	Marginal Factor Cost ($ per unit of labor)	Total Physical Product	Product Price ($ per unit)	Total Revenue ($)	Marginal Revenue Product ($ per unit of labor)
10	5	50	—	100	3.11	311.00	—
11	6	66	16.00	109	3.00	327.00	16.00
12	7	84	18.00	116	2.95	342.20	15.20
13	8	104	20.00	121	2.92	353.32	11.12
14	9	126	22.00	124	2.90	359.60	6.28
15	10	150	24.00	125	2.89	361.25	1.65

29-13. The marginal factor cost of the last worker hired was $106,480 − $105,600 = $880, so this is the marginal product of this worker if the firm is maximizing its profits.

29-15. The marginal factor cost curve lies above the labor supply curve, so marginal factor cost exceeds the wage rate at any given quantity of labor employed. Thus, a monopsonist that utilizes the profit-maximizing quantity of labor at which marginal revenue product equals marginal factor cost must pay a wage that is less than that marginal revenue product.

CHAPTER 30

30-1. a. X, because for this country the Lorenz curve implies complete income equality.

  b. Z, because this country's Lorenz curve is bowed farthest away from the case of complete income equality.

  c. Closer, because if all other things, including aggregate income, remain unchanged, when more people in country Y are children below working age, the share of income to people this age will decline, while the reverse will occur in country Z as more of its people reach working age and begin to earn incomes.

30-3. If the Lorenz curve is based on incomes including transfer payments, then the Lorenz curve will become less bowed. But if the Lorenz curve does not account for transfer payments, its shape will remain unaffected.

30-5. Brazil

30-7. a. Absolute. If economic growth ultimately led to inflation-adjusted annual incomes for all urban families of four rising above $25,000 per year, then by this definition poverty would be ended.

  b. Relative. By this definition, the lowest 15 percent of income earners will always be classified as being in a state of poverty.

  c. Absolute. If economic growth eventually raised inflation-adjusted annual incomes of all individuals above $10,000, then by this definition poverty would cease to exist.

30-9. First, a moral hazard problem will exist, because government action would reduce the individual's incentive to continue a healthful lifestyle, thereby increasing the likelihood of greater health problems that will require future treatment. Second, an individual who currently has health problems will have an incentive to substitute future care that will be available at a zero price for current care that the individual must purchase at a positive price. Finally, in future years the patient will no longer have an incentive to contain health care expenses, and health care providers will have no incentive to minimize their costs.

30-11. The demand for health care will increase, and the marginal revenue curve will shift rightward. Hence, the profit-maximizing price and equilibrium quantity of health care services will increase.

CHAPTER 31

31-1. $4 per unit, which exactly accounts for the per-unit social cost of pollution.

31-3. a. 60 percent

  b. 40 percent

  c. 40 percent

31-5. a. There is a downward shift in the position of the marginal cost curve. The optimal degree of water cleanliness will rise above 65 percent, to a level such as 70 percent, and the cost incurred for the last unit of water clean-up will decrease to less than $10, such as a per-unit cost of $7.

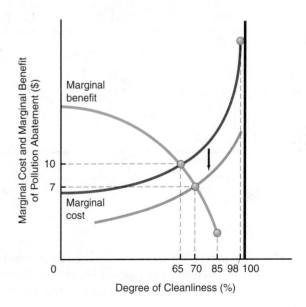

b. The second event induces an upward shift in the marginal benefit curve. Taken together, as shown in the diagram below, the two events unambiguously indicate that the optimal degree of water cleanliness increases above 65 percent, such as a level of 85 percent. The cost incurred for the last unit of water clean-up may rise or fall, however, and could end up at the initial level, which is the situation illustrated in the diagram.

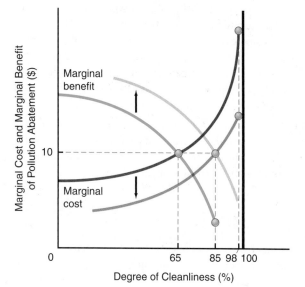

31-7. The positive market price of allowances is equivalent to a price that a firm must pay in order to release an additional unit of a pollutant. The idea behind establishing the market for pollution allowances, therefore, is to give firms an incentive to limit the quantity of pollutants released into the atmosphere.

31-9. a. The marginal costs and benefits are tabulated below:

Population of Wild Tigers	Marginal Cost ($)	Marginal Benefit ($)
0	—	—
2,000	25	50
4,000	10	40
6,000	15	30
8,000	25	25
10,000	35	20
12,000	50	10

b. 8,000

c. 10,000

CHAPTER 32

32-1. a. The opportunity cost of pastries in Northland is 0.5 sandwich per pastry. The opportunity cost of sandwiches in Northland is 2 pastries per sandwich.

b. The opportunity cost of pastries in West Coast is 2 sandwiches per pastry. The opportunity cost of sandwiches in West Coast is 0.5 pastry per sandwich.

32-3. If Northland specializes in producing pastries, the maximum number of pastries it can produce and trade to West Coast is 50,000 pastries. Hence, the maximum number of units of each good that the two countries can trade at a rate of exchange of 1 pastry for 1 sandwich is 50,000.

32-5. Coastal Realm has a comparative advantage in producing digital TVs, and Border Kingdom has a comparative advantage in wine production.

32-7. a. The opportunity cost of modems in South Shore is 2 flash drives per modem. The opportunity cost of flash drives in South Shore is 0.5 modem per flash drive.

b. The opportunity cost of modems in East Isle is 0.5 flash drive per modem. The opportunity cost of flash drives in East Isle is 2 modems per flash drive.

c. Residents of South Shore have a comparative advantage in producing flash drives, and residents of East Isle have a comparative advantage in producing modems.

32-9. The critics are suggesting that Mexican exporters are shifting exports that would have gone to other nations to the United States, a nation within NAFTA, which would constitute trade diversion.

32-11. Diversion and deflection occur when nations within or outside a particular regional trade bloc try to benefit from preferences that exist only within the bloc. As long as the WTO agreements involve all nations equally, no diversion or deflection could occur.

CHAPTER 33

33-1 a. −$0.6 trillion

b. −$0.5 trillion

c. −$0.7 trillion

33-3. The trade balance is merchandise exports minus merchandise imports, which equals 500 − 600 = −100, or a deficit of 100. Adding service exports of 75 and subtracting net unilateral transfers of 10 and service imports of 50 yields −100 + 75 − 10 − 50 = −85, or a current account balance of −85. The capital account balance equals the difference between capital inflows and capital outflows, or 300 − 200 = +100, or a capital account surplus of 100.

33-5. a. The increase in demand for Mexican-made guitars increases the demand for Mexican pesos, and the peso appreciates.

b. International investors will remove some of their financial capital from Mexico. The increase in the supply of pesos in the foreign exchange market will cause the peso to depreciate.

33-7. The demand for Chinese yuan increases, and the supply of yuan decreases. The dollar-yuan exchange rate rises, so the yuan appreciates.

33-9. The Canadian dollar–euro exchange rate is found by dividing the U.S. dollar–euro exchange rate by the U.S. dollar–Canadian dollar exchange rate, or (1.45 $U.S./euro)/(0.94 $U.S./$C) = 1.54 $C/euro, or 1.54 Canadian dollars per euro.

33-11. A flexible exchange rate system allows the exchange value of a currency to be determined freely in the foreign exchange market with no intervention by the government. A fixed exchange rate pegs the value of the currency, and the authorities responsible for the value of the currency intervene in foreign exchange markets to maintain this value.

33-13. When the dollar is pegged to gold at a rate of $35 and the pound is pegged to the dollar at $2 = £1, an implicit value between gold and the pound is established at £17.50 = 1 ounce of gold. If the dollar falls in value relative to gold, yet the pound is still valued to the dollar at $2 = £1, the pound become undervalued relative to gold. The exchange rate between the dollar and the pound will have to be adjusted to 2.29 $/£.

Glossary

A

Absolute advantage The ability to produce more units of a good or service using a given quantity of labor or resource inputs. Equivalently, the ability to produce the same quantity of a good or service using fewer units of labor or resource inputs.

Accounting identities Values that are equivalent by definition.

Accounting profit Total revenues minus total explicit costs.

Action time lag The time between recognizing an economic problem and implementing policy to solve it. The action time lag is quite long for fiscal policy, which requires congressional approval.

Active (discretionary) policymaking All actions on the part of monetary and fiscal policymakers that are undertaken in response to or in anticipation of some change in the overall economy.

Ad valorem **taxation** Assessing taxes by charging a tax rate equal to a fraction of the market price of each unit purchased.

Adverse selection The tendency for high-risk projects and clients to be over-represented among borrowers.

Age-earnings cycle The regular earnings profile of an individual throughout his or her lifetime. The age-earnings cycle usually starts with a low income, builds gradually to a peak at around age 50, and then gradually curves down until it approaches zero at retirement.

Aggregate demand The total of all planned expenditures in the entire economy.

Aggregate demand curve A curve showing planned purchase rates for all final goods and services in the economy at various price levels, all other things held constant.

Aggregate demand shock Any event that causes the aggregate demand curve to shift inward or outward.

Aggregate supply The total of all planned production for the economy.

Aggregate supply shock Any event that causes the aggregate supply curve to shift inward or outward.

Aggregates Total amounts or quantities. Aggregate demand, for example, is total planned expenditures throughout a nation.

Anticipated inflation The inflation rate that we believe will occur. When it

does occur, we are in a situation of fully anticipated inflation.

Antitrust legislation Laws that restrict the formation of monopolies and regulate certain anticompetitive business practices.

Appreciation An increase in the exchange value of one nation's currency in terms of the currency of another nation.

Asset demand Holding money as a store of value instead of other assets such as corporate bonds and stocks.

Assets Amounts owned; all items to which a business or household holds legal claim.

Asymmetric information Information possessed by one party in a financial transaction but not by the other party.

Automatic, or built-in, stabilizers Special provisions of certain federal programs that cause changes in desired aggregate expenditures without the action of Congress and the president. Examples are the federal progressive tax system and unemployment compensation.

Autonomous consumption The part of consumption that is independent of (does not depend on) the level of disposable income. Changes in autonomous consumption shift the consumption function.

Average fixed costs Total fixed costs divided by the number of units produced.

Average physical product Total product divided by the variable input.

Average propensity to consume (APC) Real consumption divided by real disposable income. For any given level of real income, the proportion of total real disposable income that is consumed.

Average propensity to save (APS) Real saving divided by real disposable income. For any given level of real income, the proportion of total real disposable income that is saved.

Average tax rate The total tax payment divided by total income. It is the proportion of total income paid in taxes.

Average total costs Total costs divided by the number of units produced; sometimes called *average per-unit total costs*.

Average variable costs Total variable costs divided by the number of units produced.

B

Balance of payments A system of accounts that measures transactions of goods, services, income, and financial assets between domestic households, businesses, and governments and residents of the rest of the world during a specific time period.

Balance of trade The difference between exports and imports of physical goods.

Balance sheet A statement of the assets and liabilities of any business entity, including financial institutions and the Federal Reserve System. Assets are what is owned; liabilities are what is owed.

Balanced budget A situation in which the government's spending is exactly equal to the total taxes and other revenues it collects during a given period of time.

Bank run Attempt by many of a bank's depositors to convert transactions and time deposits into currency out of fear that the bank's liabilities may exceed its assets.

Barter The direct exchange of goods and services for other goods and services without the use of money.

Base year The year that is chosen as the point of reference for comparison of prices in other years.

Base-year dollars The value of a current sum expressed in terms of prices in a base year.

Behavioral economics An approach to the study of consumer behavior that emphasizes psychological limitations and complications that potentially interfere with rational decision making.

Bilateral monopoly A market structure consisting of a monopolist and a monopsonist.

Black market A market in which goods are traded at prices above their legal maximum prices or in which illegal goods are sold.

Bond A legal claim against a firm, usually entitling the owner of the bond to receive a fixed annual coupon payment, plus a lump-sum payment at the bond's maturity date. Bonds are issued in return for funds lent to the firm.

Bounded rationality The hypothesis that people are *nearly*, but not fully, rational, so that they cannot examine every possible choice available to them but instead use simple rules of thumb to sort among the alternatives that happen to occur to them.

Budget constraint All of the possible combinations of goods that can be purchased (at fixed prices) with a specific budget.

Bundling Offering two or more products for sale as a set.

Business fluctuations The ups and downs in business activity throughout the economy.

C

Capital account A category of balance of payments transactions that measures flows of financial assets.

Capital consumption allowance Another name for depreciation, the amount that businesses would have to put aside in order to take care of deteriorating machines and other equipment.

Capital gain A positive difference between the purchase price and the sale price of an asset. If a share of stock is bought for $5 and then sold for $15, the capital gain is $10.

Capital goods Producer durables; nonconsumable goods that firms use to make other goods.

Capital loss A negative difference between the purchase price and the sale price of an asset.

Capture hypothesis A theory of regulatory behavior that predicts that regulators will eventually be captured by special interests of the industry being regulated.

Cartel An association of producers in an industry that agree to set common prices and output quotas to prevent competition.

Central bank A banker's bank, usually an official institution that also serves as a bank for a nation's government treasury. Central banks normally regulate commercial banks.

Ceteris paribus **[KAY-ter-us PEAR-uh-bus] assumption** The assumption that nothing changes except the factor or factors being studied.

Ceteris paribus **conditions** Determinants of the relationship between price and quantity that are unchanged along a curve. Changes in these factors cause the curve to shift.

Closed shop A business enterprise in which employees must belong to the union before they can be hired and must remain in the union after they are hired.

Collective bargaining Negotiation between the management of a company and the management of a union for the purpose of reaching a mutually agreeable contract that sets wages, fringe benefits, and working conditions for all employees in all the unions involved.

Collective decision making How voters, politicians, and other interested parties act and how these actions influence nonmarket decisions.

Common property Property that is owned by everyone and therefore by no one. Air and water are examples of common property resources.

Comparative advantage The ability to produce a good or service at a lower opportunity cost than other producers.

Complements Two goods are complements when a change in the price of one causes an opposite shift in the demand for the other.

Concentration ratio The percentage of all sales contributed by the leading four or leading eight firms in an industry; sometimes called the *industry concentration ratio*.

Constant dollars Dollars expressed in terms of real purchasing power, using a particular year as the base or standard of comparison, in contrast to current dollars.

Constant returns to scale No change in long-run average costs when output increases.

Constant-cost industry An industry whose total output can be increased without an increase in long-run per-unit costs. Its long-run supply curve is horizontal.

Consumer optimum A choice of a set of goods and services that maximizes the level of satisfaction for each consumer, subject to limited income.

Consumer Price Index (CPI) A statistical measure of a weighted average of prices of a specified set of goods and services purchased by typical consumers in urban areas.

Consumer surplus The difference between the total amount that consumers would have been willing to pay for an item and the total amount that they actually pay.

Consumption Spending on new goods and services to be used up out of a household's current income. Whatever is not consumed is saved. Consumption includes such things as buying food and going to a concert.

Consumption function The relationship between amount consumed and disposable income. A consumption function tells us how much people plan to consume at various levels of disposable income.

Consumption goods Goods bought by households to use up, such as food and movies.

Contraction A business fluctuation during which the pace of national economic activity is slowing down.

Cooperative game A game in which the players explicitly cooperate to make themselves jointly better off. As applied to firms, it involves companies colluding in order to make higher than perfectly competitive rates of return.

Corporation A legal entity that may conduct business in its own name just as an individual does. The owners of a corporation, called shareholders, own shares of the firm's profits and have the protection of limited liability.

Cost-of-living adjustments (COLAs) Clauses in contracts that allow for increases in specified nominal values to take account of changes in the cost of living.

Cost-of-service regulation Regulation that allows prices to reflect only the actual average cost of production and no monopoly profits.

Cost-push inflation Inflation caused by decreases in short-run aggregate supply.

Craft unions Labor unions composed of workers who engage in a particular trade or skill, such as baking, carpentry, or plumbing.

Creative response Behavior on the part of a firm that allows it to comply with the letter of the law but violate the spirit, significantly lessening the law's effects.

Credence good A product with qualities that consumers lack the expertise to assess without assistance.

Credit policy Federal Reserve policymaking involving direct lending to financial and nonfinancial firms.

Cross price elasticity of demand (E_{xy}) The percentage change in the amount of an item demanded (holding its price constant) divided by the percentage change in the price of a related good.

Crowding-out effect The tendency of expansionary fiscal policy to cause a decrease in planned investment or planned consumption in the private sector. This decrease normally results from the rise in interest rates.

Current account A category of balance of payments transactions that measures the exchange of merchandise, the exchange of services, and unilateral transfers.

Cyclical unemployment Unemployment resulting from business recessions that occur when aggregate (total) demand is insufficient to create full employment.

D

Dead capital Any capital resource that lacks clear title of ownership.

Deadweight loss The portion of consumer surplus that no one in society is able to obtain in a situation of monopoly.

Decreasing-cost industry An industry in which an increase in output leads to a reduction in long-run per-unit costs, such that the long-run industry supply curve slopes downward.

Deflation A sustained decrease in the average of all prices of goods and services in an economy.

Demand A schedule showing how much of a good or service people will purchase at any price during a specified time period, other things being constant.

Demand curve A graphical representation of the demand schedule. It is a negatively sloped line showing the inverse relationship between the price and the quantity demanded (other things being equal).

Demand-pull inflation Inflation caused by increases in aggregate demand not matched by increases in aggregate supply.

Dependent variable A variable whose value changes according to changes in the value of one or more independent variables.

Depository institutions Financial institutions that accept deposits from savers and lend funds from those deposits out at interest.

Depreciation A decrease in the exchange value of one nation's currency in terms of the currency of another nation.

Depression An extremely severe recession.

Derived demand Input factor demand derived from demand for the final product being produced.

Development economics The study of factors that contribute to the economic growth of a country.

Diminishing marginal utility The principle that as more of any good or service is consumed, its *extra* benefit declines. Otherwise stated, increases in total utility from the consumption of a good or service become smaller and smaller as more is consumed during a given time period.

Direct expenditure offsets Actions on the part of the private sector in spending income that offset government fiscal policy actions. Any increase in government spending in an area that competes with the private sector will have some direct expenditure offset.

Direct marketing Advertising targeted at specific consumers, typically in the form of postal mailings, telephone calls, or e-mail messages.

Direct relationship A relationship between two variables that is positive, meaning that an increase in one variable is associated with an increase in the other and a decrease in one variable is associated with a decrease in the other.

Discount rate The interest rate that the Federal Reserve charges for reserves that it lends to depository institutions.

It is sometimes referred to as the *rediscount rate* or, in Canada and England, as the *bank rate*.

Discounting The method by which the present value of a future sum or a future stream of sums is obtained.

Discouraged workers Individuals who have stopped looking for a job because they are convinced that they will not find a suitable one.

Diseconomies of scale Increases in long-run average costs that occur as output increases.

Disposable personal income (DPI) Personal income after personal income taxes have been paid.

Dissaving Negative saving; a situation in which spending exceeds income. Dissaving can occur when a household is able to borrow or use up existing assets.

Distribution of income The way income is allocated among the population based on groupings of residents.

Dividends Portion of a corporation's profits paid to its owners (shareholders).

Division of labor The segregation of resources into different specific tasks. For instance, one automobile worker puts on bumpers, another doors, and so on.

Dominant strategies Strategies that always yield the highest benefit. Regardless of what other players do, a dominant strategy will yield the most benefit for the player using it.

Dumping Selling a good or a service abroad below the price charged in the home market or at a price below its cost of production.

Durable consumer goods Consumer goods that have a life span of more than three years.

Dynamic tax analysis Economic evaluation of tax rate changes that recognizes that the tax base eventually declines with ever-higher tax rates, so that tax revenues may eventually decline if the tax rate is raised sufficiently.

E

Economic freedom The rights to own private property and to exchange goods, services, and financial assets with minimal government interference.

Economic goods Goods that are scarce, for which the quantity demanded exceeds the quantity supplied at a zero price.

Economic growth Increases in per capita real GDP measured by its rate of change per year.

Economic profits Total revenues minus total opportunity costs of all inputs used, or the total of all implicit and explicit costs.

Economic rent A payment for the use of any resource over and above its opportunity cost.

Economic system A society's institutional mechanism for determining the way in which scarce resources are used to satisfy human desires.

Economics The study of how people allocate their limited resources to satisfy their unlimited wants.

Economies of scale Decreases in long-run average costs resulting from increases in output.

Effect time lag The time that elapses between the implementation of a policy and the results of that policy.

Efficiency The case in which a given level of inputs is used to produce the maximum output possible. Alternatively, the situation in which a given output is produced at minimum cost.

Effluent fee A charge to a polluter that gives the right to discharge into the air or water a certain amount of pollution; also called a *pollution tax*.

Elastic demand A demand relationship in which a given percentage change in price will result in a larger percentage change in quantity demanded.

Empirical Relying on real-world data in evaluating the usefulness of a model.

Endowments The various resources in an economy, including both physical resources and such human resources as ingenuity and management skills.

Entitlements Guaranteed benefits under a government program such as Social Security, Medicare, or Medicaid.

Entrepreneurship The component of human resources that performs the functions of raising capital; organizing, managing, and assembling other factors of production; making basic business policy decisions; and taking risks.

Equation of exchange The formula indicating that the number of monetary units (M_s) times the number of times each unit is spent on final goods and services (V) is identical to the price level (P) times real GDP (Y).

Equilibrium The situation when quantity supplied equals quantity demanded at a particular price.

Exchange rate The price of one nation's currency in terms of the currency of another country.

Excise tax A tax levied on purchases of a particular good or service.

Expansion A business fluctuation in which the pace of national economic activity is speeding up.

Expenditure approach Computing GDP by adding up the dollar value at current market prices of all final goods and services.

Experience good A product that an individual must consume before the product's quality can be established.

Explicit costs Costs that business managers must take account of because they must be paid. Examples are wages, taxes, and rent.

Externality A consequence of a diversion of a private cost (or benefit) from a social cost (or benefit). A situation in which the costs (or benefits) of an action are not fully borne (or gained) by the decision makers engaged in an activity that uses scarce resources.

F

Featherbedding Any practice that forces employers to use more labor than they would otherwise or to use existing labor in an inefficient manner.

Federal Deposit Insurance Corporation (FDIC) A government agency that insures the deposits held in banks and most other depository institutions. All U.S. banks are insured this way.

Federal funds market A private market (made up mostly of banks) in which banks can borrow reserves from other banks that want to lend them. Federal funds are usually lent for overnight use.

Federal funds rate The interest rate that depository institutions pay to borrow reserves in the interbank federal funds market.

Fiduciary monetary system A system in which money is issued by the government and its value is based uniquely on the public's faith that the currency represents command over goods and services and will be accepted in payment for debts.

Final goods and services Goods and services that are at their final stage of production and will not be transformed into yet other goods or services. For example, wheat ordinarily is not considered a final good because it is usually used to make a final good, bread.

Financial capital Funds used to purchase physical capital goods, such as buildings and equipment, and patents and trademarks.

Financial intermediaries Institutions that transfer funds between ultimate lenders (savers) and ultimate borrowers.

Financial intermediation The process by which financial institutions accept savings from businesses, households, and governments and lend the savings to other businesses, households, and governments.

Firm A business organization that employs resources to produce goods or services for profit. A firm normally owns and operates at least one "plant" or facility in order to produce.

Fiscal policy The discretionary changing of government expenditures or taxes to achieve national economic goals, such as high employment with price stability.

Fixed costs Costs that do not vary with output. Fixed costs typically include such expenses as rent on a building. These costs are fixed for a certain period of time (in the long run, though, they are variable).

Fixed investment Purchases by businesses of newly produced producer durables, or capital goods, such as production machinery and office equipment.

Flexible exchange rates Exchange rates that are allowed to fluctuate in the open market in response to changes in supply and demand. Sometimes called *floating exchange rates*.

Flow A quantity measured per unit of time; something that occurs over time, such as the income you make per week or per year or the number of individuals who are fired every month.

FOMC Directive A document that summarizes the Federal Open Market Committee's general policy strategy, establishes near-term objectives for the federal funds rate, and specifies target ranges for money supply growth.

Foreign direct investment The acquisition of more than 10 percent of the shares of ownership in a company in another nation.

Foreign exchange market A market in which households, firms, and governments buy and sell national currencies.

Foreign exchange rate The price of one currency in terms of another.

Foreign exchange risk The possibility that changes in the value of a nation's currency will result in variations in the market value of assets.

45-degree reference line The line along which planned real expenditures equal real GDP per year.

Fractional reserve banking A system in which depository institutions hold reserves that are less than the amount of total deposits.

Free-rider problem A problem that arises when individuals presume that others will pay for public goods so that, individually, they can escape paying for their portion without causing a reduction in production.

Frictional unemployment Unemployment due to the fact that workers must search for appropriate job offers. This activity takes time, and so they remain temporarily unemployed.

Full employment An arbitrary level of unemployment that corresponds to "normal" friction in the labor market. In 1986, a 6.5 percent rate of unemployment was considered full employment. Today it is somewhat higher.

G

Gains from trade The sum of consumer surplus and producer surplus.

Game theory A way of describing the various possible outcomes in any situation involving two or more interacting individuals when those individuals are aware of the interactive nature of their situation and plan accordingly. The plans made by these individuals are known as *game strategies*.

GDP deflator A price index measuring the changes in prices of all new goods and services produced in the economy.

General Agreement on Tariffs and Trade (GATT) An international agreement established in 1947 to further world trade by reducing barriers and tariffs. The GATT was replaced by the World Trade Organization in 1995.

Goods All things from which individuals derive satisfaction or happiness.

Government budget constraint The limit on government spending and transfers imposed by the fact that every dollar the government spends, transfers, or uses to repay borrowed funds must ultimately be provided by the user charges and taxes it collects.

Government budget deficit An excess of government spending over government revenues during a given period of time.

Government budget surplus An excess of government revenues over government spending during a given period of time.

Government, or political, goods Goods (and services) provided by the public sector; they can be either private or public goods.

Government-inhibited good A good that has been deemed socially undesirable through the political process. Heroin is an example.

Government-sponsored good A good that has been deemed socially desirable through the political process. Museums are an example.

Gross domestic income (GDI) The sum of all income—wages, interest, rent, and profits—paid to the four factors of production.

Gross domestic product (GDP) The total market value of all final goods and services produced during a year by factors of production located within a nation's borders.

Gross private domestic investment The creation of capital goods, such as factories and machines, that can yield production and hence consumption in the future. Also included in this definition are changes in business inventories and repairs made to machines or buildings.

Gross public debt All federal government debt irrespective of who owns it.

H

Health insurance exchanges Government agencies to which the national health care program assigns the task of assisting individuals, families, and small businesses in identifying health insurance policies to purchase.

Hedge A financial strategy that reduces the chance of suffering losses arising from foreign exchange risk.

Herfindahl-Hirschman Index (HHI) The sum of the squared percentage sales shares of all firms in an industry.

Horizontal merger The joining of firms that are producing or selling a similar product.

Human capital The accumulated training and education of workers.

I

Implicit costs Expenses that managers do not have to pay out of pocket and hence normally do not explicitly calculate, such as the opportunity cost of factors of production that are owned. Examples are owner-provided capital and owner-provided labor.

Import quota A physical supply restriction on imports of a particular good, such as sugar. Foreign exporters are unable to sell in the United States more than the quantity specified in the import quota.

Incentive structure The system of rewards and punishments individuals face with respect to their own actions.

Incentives Rewards or penalties for engaging in a particular activity.

Income approach Measuring GDP by adding up all components of national income, including wages, interest, rent, and profits.

Income elasticity of demand (E_i) The percentage change in the amount of a good demanded, holding its price constant, divided by the percentage change in income. The responsiveness of the amount of a good demanded to a change in income, holding the good's relative price constant.

Income in kind Income received in the form of goods and services, such as housing or medical care. Income in kind differs from money income, which is simply income in dollars, or general purchasing power, that can be used to buy *any* goods and services.

Income velocity of money (V) The number of times per year a dollar is spent on final goods and services; identically equal to nominal GDP divided by the money supply.

Increasing-cost industry An industry in which an increase in industry output is accompanied by an increase in long-run per-unit costs, such that the long-run industry supply curve slopes upward.

Independent variable A variable whose value is determined independently of, or outside, the equation under study.

Indifference curve A curve composed of a set of consumption alternatives, each of which yields the same total amount of satisfaction.

Indirect business taxes All business taxes except the tax on corporate profits. Indirect business taxes include sales and business property taxes.

Industrial unions Labor unions that consist of workers from a particular industry, such as automobile manufacturing or steel manufacturing.

Industry supply curve The locus of points showing the minimum prices at which given quantities will be forthcoming; also called the *market supply curve*.

Inefficient point Any point below the production possibilities curve, at which the use of resources is not generating the maximum possible output.

Inelastic demand A demand relationship in which a given percentage change in price will result in a less-than-proportionate percentage change in the quantity demanded.

Infant industry argument The contention that tariffs should be imposed to protect from import competition an industry that is trying to get started. Presumably, after the industry becomes technologically efficient, the tariff can be lifted.

Inferior goods Goods for which demand falls as income rises.

Inflation A sustained increase in the average of all prices of goods and services in an economy.

Inflationary gap The gap that exists whenever equilibrium real GDP per year is greater than full-employment real GDP as shown by the position of the long-run aggregate supply curve.

Information product An item that is produced using information-intensive inputs at a relatively high fixed cost but distributed for sale at a relatively low marginal cost.

Informational advertising Advertising that emphasizes transmitting knowledge about the features of a product.

Innovation Transforming an invention into something that is useful to humans.

Inside information Information that is not available to the general public about what is happening in a corporation.

Interactive marketing Advertising that permits a consumer to follow up directly by searching for more information and placing direct product orders.

Interest The payment for current rather than future command over resources; the cost of obtaining credit.

Interest rate effect One of the reasons that the aggregate demand curve slopes downward: Higher price levels increase the interest rate, which in turn causes businesses and consumers to reduce desired spending due to the higher cost of borrowing.

Intermediate goods Goods used up entirely in the production of final goods.

International financial crisis The rapid withdrawal of foreign investments and loans from a nation.

International Monetary Fund An agency founded to administer an international foreign exchange system and to lend to member countries that had balance of payments problems. The IMF now functions as a lender of last resort for national governments.

Inventory investment Changes in the stocks of finished goods and goods in process, as well as changes in the raw materials that businesses keep on hand. Whenever inventories are decreasing, inventory investment is negative. Whenever they are increasing, inventory investment is positive.

Inverse relationship A relationship between two variables that is negative, meaning that an increase in one variable is associated with a decrease in the other and a decrease in one variable is associated with an increase in the other.

Investment Spending on items such as machines and buildings, which can be used to produce goods and services in the future. (It also includes changes in business inventories.) The investment part of real GDP is the portion that will be used in the process of producing goods *in the future*.

J

Job leaver An individual in the labor force who quits voluntarily.

Job loser An individual in the labor force whose employment was involuntarily terminated.

Jurisdictional dispute A disagreement involving two or more unions over which should have control of a particular jurisdiction, such as a particular craft or skill or a particular firm or industry.

K

Keynesian short-run aggregate supply curve The horizontal portion of the aggregate supply curve in which there is excessive unemployment and unused capacity in the economy.

L

Labor Productive contributions of humans who work.

Labor force Individuals aged 16 years or older who either have jobs or who are looking and available for jobs; the number of employed plus the number of unemployed.

Labor force participation rate The percentage of noninstitutionalized working-age individuals who are employed or seeking employment.

Labor productivity Total real domestic output (real GDP) divided by the number of workers (output per worker).

Labor unions Worker organizations that seek to secure economic improvements for their members. They also seek to improve the safety, health, and other benefits (such as job security) of their members.

Land The natural resources that are available from nature. Land as a resource includes location, original fertility and mineral deposits, topography, climate, water, and vegetation.

Law of demand The observation that there is a negative, or inverse, relationship between the price of any good or service and the quantity demanded, holding other factors constant.

Law of diminishing marginal product The observation that after some point, successive equal-sized increases in a variable factor of production, such as labor, added to fixed factors of production will result in smaller increases in output.

Law of increasing additional cost The fact that the opportunity cost of additional units of a good generally increases as people attempt to produce more of that good. This accounts for the bowed-out shape of the production possibilities curve.

Law of supply The observation that the higher the price of a good, the more of that good sellers will make available over a specified time period, other things being equal.

Leading indicators Events that have been found to occur before changes in business activity.

Lemons problem The potential for asymmetric information to bring about a general decline in product quality in an industry.

Lender of last resort The Federal Reserve's role as an institution that is willing and able to lend to a temporarily illiquid bank that is otherwise in good financial condition to prevent the bank's illiquid position from leading to a general loss of confidence in that bank or in others.

Liabilities Amounts owed; the legal claims against a business or household by nonowners.

Life-cycle theory of consumption A theory in which a person bases decisions about current consumption and saving on both current income and anticipated future income.

Limited liability A legal concept in which the responsibility, or liability, of the owners of a corporation is limited to the value of the shares in the firm that they own.

Liquidity The degree to which an asset can be acquired or disposed of without much danger of any intervening loss in *nominal* value and with small transaction costs. Money is the most liquid asset.

Liquidity approach A method of measuring the money supply by looking at money as a temporary store of value.

Long run The time period during which all factors of production can be varied.

Long-run aggregate supply curve A vertical line representing the real output of goods and services after full adjustment has occurred. It can also be viewed as representing the real GDP of the economy under conditions of full employment—the full-employment level of real GDP.

Long-run average cost curve The locus of points representing the minimum unit cost of producing any given rate of output, given current technology and resource prices.

Long-run industry supply curve A market supply curve showing the relationship between prices and quantities after firms have been allowed the time to enter into or exit from an industry, depending on whether there have been positive or negative economic profits.

Lorenz curve A geometric representation of the distribution of income. A Lorenz curve that is perfectly straight represents complete income equality. The more bowed a Lorenz curve, the more unequally income is distributed.

Lump-sum tax A tax that does not depend on income. An example is a $1,000 tax that every household must pay, irrespective of its economic situation.

M

M1 The money supply, measured as the total value of currency plus transactions deposits plus traveler's checks not issued by banks.

M2 M1 plus (1) savings deposits at all depository institutions, (2) small-denomination time deposits, and (3) balances in retail money market mutual funds.

Macroeconomics The study of the behavior of the economy as a whole, including such economywide phenomena as changes in unemployment, the general price level, and national income.

Majority rule A collective decision-making system in which group decisions are made on the basis of more than 50 percent of the vote. In other words, whatever more than half of the electorate votes for, the entire electorate has to accept.

Marginal cost pricing A system of pricing in which the price charged is equal to the opportunity cost to society of producing one more unit of the good or service in question. The opportunity cost is the marginal cost to society.

Marginal costs The change in total costs due to a one-unit change in production rate.

Marginal factor cost (MFC) The cost of using an additional unit of an input. For example, if a firm can hire all the workers it wants at the going wage rate, the marginal factor cost of labor is that wage rate.

Marginal physical product The physical output that is due to the addition of one more unit of a variable factor of production. The change in total product occurring when a variable input is increased and all other inputs are held constant. It is also called *marginal product*.

Marginal physical product (MPP) of labor The change in output resulting from the addition of one more worker. The MPP of the worker equals the change in total output accounted for by hiring the worker, holding all other factors of production constant.

Marginal propensity to consume (MPC) The ratio of the change in consumption to the change in disposable income. A marginal propensity to consume of 0.8 tells us that an additional $100 in take-home pay will lead to an additional $80 consumed.

Marginal propensity to save (MPS) The ratio of the change in saving to the change in disposable income. A marginal propensity to save of 0.2 indicates that out of an additional $100 in take-home pay, $20 will be saved. Whatever is not saved is consumed. The marginal propensity to save plus the marginal propensity to consume must always equal 1, by definition.

Marginal revenue The change in total revenues resulting from a one-unit change in output (and sale) of the product in question.

Marginal revenue product (MRP) The marginal physical product (MPP) times marginal revenue (MR). The MRP gives the additional revenue obtained from a one-unit change in labor input.

Marginal tax rate The change in the tax payment divided by the change in income, or the percentage of *additional* dollars that must be paid in taxes. The marginal tax rate is applied to the highest tax bracket of taxable income reached.

Marginal utility The change in total utility due to a one-unit change in the quantity of a good or service consumed.

Market All of the arrangements that individuals have for exchanging with one another. Thus, for example, we can speak of the labor market, the automobile market, and the credit market.

Market clearing, or equilibrium, price The price that clears the market, at which quantity demanded equals quantity supplied; the price where the demand curve intersects the supply curve.

Market demand The demand of all consumers in the marketplace for a particular good or service. The summation at each price of the quantity demanded by each individual.

Market failure A situation in which an unrestrained market operation leads to either too few or too many resources going to a specific economic activity.

Mass marketing Advertising intended to reach as many consumers as possible, typically through television, newspaper, radio, or magazine ads.

Medium of exchange Any item that sellers will accept as payment.

Microeconomics The study of decision making undertaken by individuals (or households) and by firms.

Minimum efficient scale (MES) The lowest rate of output per unit time at which long-run average costs for a particular firm are at a minimum.

Minimum wage A wage floor, legislated by government, setting the lowest hourly rate that firms may legally pay workers.

Models, or theories Simplified representations of the real world used as the basis for predictions or explanations.

Money Any medium that is universally accepted in an economy both by sellers of goods and services as payment for those goods and services and by creditors as payment for debts.

Money balances Synonymous with money, money stock, money holdings.

Money illusion Reacting to changes in money prices rather than relative prices. If a worker whose wages double when the price level also doubles thinks he or she is better off, that worker is suffering from money illusion.

Money multiplier A number that, when multiplied by a change in reserves in the banking system, yields the resulting change in the money supply.

Money price The price expressed in today's dollars; also called the *absolute* or *nominal price*.

Money supply The amount of money in circulation.

Monopolist The single supplier of a good or service for which there is no close substitute. The monopolist therefore constitutes its entire industry.

Monopolistic competition A market situation in which a large number of firms produce similar but not identical products. Entry into the industry is relatively easy.

Monopolization The possession of monopoly power in the relevant market and the willful acquisition or maintenance of that power, as distinguished from growth or development as a consequence of a superior product, business acumen, or historical accident.

Monopoly A firm that can determine the market price of a good. In the extreme case, a monopoly is the only seller of a good or service.

Monopsonist The only buyer in a market.

Monopsonistic exploitation Paying a price for the variable input that is less than its marginal revenue product; the difference between marginal revenue product and the wage rate.

Moral hazard The possibility that a borrower might engage in riskier behavior after a loan has been obtained.

Multiplier The ratio of the change in the equilibrium level of real GDP to the change in autonomous real expenditures. The number by which a change in autonomous real investment or autonomous real consumption, for example, is multiplied to get the change in equilibrium real GDP.

N

National income (NI) The total of all factor payments to resource owners. It can be obtained from net domestic product (NDP) by subtracting indirect business taxes and transfers and adding net U.S. income earned abroad and other business income adjustments.

National income accounting A measurement system used to estimate national income and its components. One approach to measuring an economy's aggregate performance.

Natural monopoly A monopoly that arises from the peculiar production characteristics in an industry. It usually arises when there are large economies of scale relative to the industry's demand such that one firm can produce at a lower average cost than can be achieved by multiple firms.

Natural rate of unemployment The rate of unemployment that is estimated to prevail in long-run macroeconomic equilibrium, when all workers and employers have fully adjusted to any changes in the economy.

Negative market feedback A tendency for a good or service to fall out of favor with more consumers because other consumers have stopped purchasing the item.

Negative-sum game A game in which players as a group lose during the process of the game.

Net domestic product (NDP) GDP minus depreciation.

Net investment Gross private domestic investment minus an estimate of the wear and tear on the existing capital stock. Net investment therefore measures the change in the capital stock over a one-year period.

Net public debt Gross public debt minus all government interagency borrowing.

Net wealth The stock of assets owned by a person, household, firm, or nation (net of any debts owed). For a household, net wealth can consist of a house, cars, personal belongings, stocks, bonds, bank accounts, and cash (minus any debts owed).

Network effect A situation in which a consumer's willingness to purchase a good or service is influenced by how many others also buy or have bought the item.

New entrant An individual who has never held a full-time job lasting two weeks or longer but is now seeking employment.

New growth theory A theory of economic growth that examines the factors that determine why technology, research, innovation, and the like are undertaken and how they interact.

New Keynesian inflation dynamics In new Keynesian theory, the pattern of inflation exhibited by an economy with growing aggregate demand—initial sluggish adjustment of the price level in response to increased aggregate demand followed by higher inflation later.

Nominal rate of interest The market rate of interest observed in contracts expressed in today's dollars.

Nominal values The values of variables such as GDP and investment expressed in current dollars, also called *money values;* measurement in terms of the actual market prices at which goods and services are sold.

Noncontrollable expenditures Government spending that changes automatically without action by Congress.

Noncooperative game A game in which the players neither negotiate nor cooperate in any way. As applied to firms in an industry, this is the common situation in which there are relatively few firms and each has some ability to change price.

Nondurable consumer goods Consumer goods that are used up within three years.

Nonincome expense items The total of indirect business taxes and depreciation.

Nonprice rationing devices All methods used to ration scarce goods that are price-controlled. Whenever the price system is not allowed to work, nonprice rationing devices will evolve to ration the affected goods and services.

Normal goods Goods for which demand rises as income rises. Most goods are normal goods.

Normal rate of return The amount that must be paid to an investor to induce investment in a business. Also known as the *opportunity cost of capital*.

Normative economics Analysis involving value judgments about economic policies; relates to whether outcomes are good or bad. A statement of *what ought to be*.

Number line A line that can be divided into segments of equal length, each associated with a number.

O

Oligopoly A market structure in which there are very few sellers. Each seller knows that the other sellers will react to its changes in prices, quantities, and qualities.

Open economy effect One of the reasons that the aggregate demand curve slopes downward: Higher price levels result in foreign residents desiring to buy fewer U.S.-made goods, while U.S. residents now desire more foreign-made goods, thereby reducing net exports. This is equivalent to a reduction in the amount of real goods and services purchased in the United States.

Open market operations The purchase and sale of existing U.S. government securities (such as bonds) in the open private market by the Federal Reserve System.

Opportunistic behavior Actions that focus solely on short-run gains because long-run benefits of cooperation are perceived to be smaller.

Opportunity cost The highest-valued, next-best alternative that must be sacrificed to obtain something or to satisfy a want.

Opportunity cost of capital The normal rate of return, or the available return on the next-best alternative investment. Economists consider this a cost of production, and it is included in our cost examples.

Optimal quantity of pollution The level of pollution for which the marginal benefit of one additional unit of pollution abatement just equals the marginal cost of that additional unit of pollution abatement.

Origin The intersection of the *y* axis and the *x* axis in a graph.

Outsourcing A firm's employment of labor outside the country in which the firm is located.

P

Par value The officially determined value of a currency.

Partnership A business owned by two or more joint owners, or partners, who share the responsibilities and the profits of the firm and are individually liable for all the debts of the partnership.

Passive (nondiscretionary) policy-making Policymaking that is carried out in response to a rule. It is therefore not in response to an actual or potential change in overall economic activity.

Patent A government protection that gives an inventor the exclusive right to make, use, or sell an invention for a limited period of time (currently, 20 years).

Payoff matrix A matrix of outcomes, or consequences, of the strategies available to the players in a game.

Perfect competition A market structure in which the decisions of *individual* buyers and sellers have no effect on market price.

Perfectly competitive firm A firm that is such a small part of the total *industry* that it cannot affect the price of the product it sells.

Perfectly elastic demand A demand that has the characteristic that even the slightest increase in price will lead to zero quantity demanded.

Perfectly elastic supply A supply characterized by a reduction in quantity supplied to zero when there is the slightest decrease in price.

Perfectly inelastic demand A demand that exhibits zero responsiveness to price changes. No matter what the price is, the quantity demanded remains the same.

Perfectly inelastic supply A supply for which quantity supplied remains constant, no matter what happens to price.

Permanent income hypothesis A theory of consumption in which an individual determines current consumption based on anticipated average lifetime income.

Personal Consumption Expenditure (PCE) Index A statistical measure of average prices that uses annually updated weights based on surveys of consumer spending.

Personal income (PI) The amount of income that households actually receive before they pay personal income taxes.

Persuasive advertising Advertising that is intended to induce a consumer to purchase a particular product and discover a previously unknown taste for the item.

Phillips curve A curve showing the relationship between unemployment and changes in wages or prices. It was long thought to reflect a trade-off between unemployment and inflation.

Physical capital All manufactured resources, including buildings, equipment, machines, and improvements to land that are used for production.

Planning curve The long-run average cost curve.

Planning horizon The long run, during which all inputs are variable.

Plant size The physical size of the factories that a firm owns and operates to produce its output. Plant size can be defined by square footage, maximum physical capacity, and other physical measures.

Policy irrelevance proposition The conclusion that policy actions have no real effects in the short run if the policy actions are anticipated and none in the long run even if the policy actions are unanticipated.

Portfolio investment The purchase of less than 10 percent of the shares of ownership in a company in another nation.

Positive economics Analysis that is *strictly* limited to making either purely descriptive statements or scientific predictions; for example, "If A, then B." A statement of *what is*.

Positive market feedback A tendency for a good or service to come into favor with additional consumers because other consumers have chosen to buy the item.

Positive-sum game A game in which players as a group are better off at the end of the game.

Potential money multiplier The reciprocal of the reserve ratio, assuming no leakages into currency. It is equal to 1 divided by the reserve ratio.

Precautionary demand Holding money to meet unplanned expenditures and emergencies.

Present value The value of a future amount expressed in today's dollars; the most that someone would pay today to receive a certain sum at some point in the future.

Price ceiling A legal maximum price that may be charged for a particular good or service.

Price controls Government-mandated minimum or maximum prices that may be charged for goods and services.

Price differentiation Establishing different prices for similar products to reflect differences in marginal cost in providing those commodities to different groups of buyers.

Price discrimination Selling a given product at more than one price, with the price difference being unrelated to differences in marginal cost.

Price elasticity of demand (E_p) The responsiveness of the quantity demanded of a commodity to changes in its price; defined as the percentage change in quantity demanded divided by the percentage change in price.

Price elasticity of supply (E_s) The responsiveness of the quantity supplied of a commodity to a change in its price—the percentage change in quantity supplied divided by the percentage change in price.

Price floor A legal minimum price below which a good or service may not be sold. Legal minimum wages are an example.

Price index The cost of today's market basket of goods expressed as a percentage of the cost of the same market basket during a base year.

Price searcher A firm that must determine the price-output combination that maximizes profit because it faces a downward-sloping demand curve.

Price system An economic system in which relative prices are constantly changing to reflect changes in supply and demand for different commodities. The prices of those commodities are signals to everyone within the system as to what is relatively scarce and what is relatively abundant.

Price taker A perfectly competitive firm that must take the price of its product as given because the firm cannot influence its price.

Principle of rival consumption The recognition that individuals are rivals in consuming private goods because one person's consumption reduces the amount available for others to consume.

Principle of substitution The principle that consumers shift away from goods and services that become priced relatively higher in favor of goods and services that are now priced relatively lower.

Prisoners' dilemma A famous strategic game in which two prisoners have a choice between confessing and not confessing to a crime. If neither confesses, they serve a minimum sentence. If both confess, they serve a longer sentence. If one confesses and the other doesn't, the one who confesses goes free. The dominant strategy is always to confess.

Private costs Costs borne solely by the individuals who incur them. Also called *internal costs*.

Private goods Goods that can be consumed by only one individual at a time. Private goods are subject to the principle of rival consumption.

Private property rights Exclusive rights of ownership that allow the use, transfer, and exchange of property.

Producer durables, or capital goods Durable goods having an expected service life of more than three years that are used by businesses to produce other goods and services.

Producer Price Index (PPI) A statistical measure of a weighted average of prices of goods and services that firms produce and sell.

Producer surplus The difference between the total amount that producers actually receive for an item and the total amount that they would have been willing to accept for supplying that item.

Product differentiation The distinguishing of products by brand name, color, and other minor attributes. Product differentiation occurs in other than perfectly competitive markets in which products are, in theory, homogeneous, such as wheat or corn.

Production Any activity that results in the conversion of resources into products that can be used in consumption.

Production function The relationship between inputs and maximum physical output. A production function is a technological, not an economic, relationship.

Production possibilities curve (PPC) A curve representing all possible combinations of maximum outputs that could be produced, assuming a fixed amount of productive resources of a given quality.

Profit-maximizing rate of production The rate of production that maximizes total profits, or the difference between total revenues and total costs. Also, it is the rate of production at which marginal revenue equals marginal cost.

Progressive taxation A tax system in which, as income increases, a higher percentage of the additional income is paid as taxes. The marginal tax rate exceeds the average tax rate as income rises.

Property rights The rights of an owner to use and to exchange property.

Proportional rule A decision-making system in which actions are based on the proportion of the "votes" cast and are in proportion to them. In a market system, if 10 percent of the "dollar votes" are cast for blue cars, 10 percent of automobile output will be blue cars.

Proportional taxation A tax system in which, regardless of an individual's income, the tax bill comprises exactly the same proportion.

Proprietorship A business owned by one individual who makes the business decisions, receives all the profits, and is legally responsible for the debts of the firm.

Public debt The total value of all outstanding federal government securities.

Public goods Goods for which the principle of rival consumption does not apply and for which exclusion of non-paying consumers is too costly to be feasible. They can be jointly consumed by many individuals simultaneously at no additional cost and with no reduction in quality or quantity. Furthermore, no one who fails to help pay for the good can be denied the benefit of the good.

Purchasing power The value of money for buying goods and services. If your money income stays the same but the price of one good that you are buying goes up, your effective purchasing power falls.

Purchasing power parity Adjustment in exchange rate conversions that takes into account differences in the true cost of living across countries.

Q

Quantitative easing Federal Reserve open market purchases intended to generate an increase in bank reserves at a nearly zero interest rate.

Quantity theory of money and prices The hypothesis that changes in the money supply lead to equiproportional changes in the price level.

Quota subscription A nation's account with the International Monetary Fund, denominated in special drawing rights.

Quota system A government-imposed restriction on the quantity of a specific good that another country is allowed to sell in the United States. In other words, quotas are restrictions on imports. These restrictions are usually applied to one or several specific countries.

R

Random walk theory The theory that there are no predictable trends in securities prices that can be used to "get rich quick."

Rate of discount The rate of interest used to discount future sums back to present value.

Rate-of-return regulation Regulation that seeks to keep the rate of return in an industry at a competitive level by not allowing prices that would produce economic profits.

Rational expectations hypothesis A theory stating that people combine the effects of past policy changes on important economic variables with their own judgment about the future effects of current and future policy changes.

Rationality assumption The assumption that people do not intentionally make decisions that would leave them worse off.

Reaction function The manner in which one oligopolist reacts to a change in price, output, or quality made by another oligopolist in the industry.

Real disposable income Real GDP minus net taxes, or after-tax real income.

Real rate of interest The nominal rate of interest minus the anticipated rate of inflation.

Real values Measurement of economic values after adjustments have been made for changes in the average of prices between years.

Real-balance effect The change in expenditures resulting from a change in the real value of money balances when the price level changes, all other things held constant; also called the *wealth effect*.

Real-income effect The change in people's purchasing power that occurs when, other things being constant, the price of one good that they purchase changes. When that price goes up, real income, or purchasing power, falls, and when that price goes down, real income increases.

Recession A period of time during which the rate of growth of business activity is consistently less than its long-term trend or is negative.

Recessionary gap The gap that exists whenever equilibrium real GDP per year is less than full-employment real GDP as shown by the position of the long-run aggregate supply curve.

Recognition time lag The time required to gather information about the current state of the economy.

Reentrant An individual who used to work full-time but left the labor force and has now reentered it looking for a job.

Regional trade bloc A group of nations that grants members special trade privileges.

Regressive taxation A tax system in which as more dollars are earned, the percentage of tax paid on them falls. The marginal tax rate is less than the average tax rate as income rises.

Reinvestment Profits (or depreciation reserves) used to purchase new capital equipment.

Relative price The money price of one commodity divided by the money price of another commodity; the number of units of one commodity that must be sacrificed to purchase one unit of another commodity.

Relevant market A group of firms' products that are closely substitutable and available to consumers within a geographic area.

Rent control Price ceilings on rents.

Repricing, or menu, cost of inflation The cost associated with recalculating prices and printing new price lists when there is inflation.

Reserve ratio The fraction of transactions deposits that banks hold as reserves.

Reserves In the U.S. Federal Reserve System, deposits held by Federal Reserve district banks for depository institutions, plus depository institutions' vault cash.

Resources Things used to produce goods and services to satisfy people's wants.

Retained earnings Earnings that a corporation saves, or retains, for investment in other productive activities; earnings that are not distributed to stockholders.

Ricardian equivalence theorem The proposition that an increase in the government budget deficit has no effect on aggregate demand.

Right-to-work laws Laws that make it illegal to require union membership as a condition of continuing employment in a particular firm.

Rule of 70 A rule stating that the approximate number of years required for per capita real GDP to double is equal to 70 divided by the average rate of economic growth.

Rules of origin Regulations that nations in regional trade blocs establish to delineate product categories eligible for trading preferences.

S

Sales taxes Taxes assessed on the prices paid on most goods and services.

Saving The act of not consuming all of one's current income. Whatever is not consumed out of spendable income is, by definition, saved. *Saving* is an action measured over time (a flow), whereas *savings* are a stock, an accumulation resulting from the act of saving in the past.

Say's law A dictum of economist J. B. Say that supply creates its own demand. Producing goods and services generates the means and the willingness to purchase other goods and services.

Scarcity A situation in which the ingredients for producing the things that people desire are insufficient to satisfy all wants at a zero price.

Search good A product with characteristics that enable an individual to evaluate the product's quality in advance of a purchase.

Seasonal unemployment Unemployment resulting from the seasonal pattern of work in specific industries. It is usually due to seasonal fluctuations in demand or to changing weather conditions that render work difficult, if not impossible, as in the agriculture, construction, and tourist industries.

Secondary boycott A refusal to deal with companies or purchase products sold by companies that are dealing with a company being struck.

Secular deflation A persistent decline in prices resulting from economic

growth in the presence of stable aggregate demand.

Securities Stocks and bonds.

Services Mental or physical labor or assistance purchased by consumers. Examples are the assistance of physicians, lawyers, dentists, repair personnel, housecleaners, educators, retailers, and wholesalers; items purchased or used by consumers that do not have physical characteristics.

Share of stock A legal claim to a share of a corporation's future profits. If it is *common stock*, it incorporates certain voting rights regarding major policy decisions of the corporation. If it is *preferred stock*, its owners are accorded preferential treatment in the payment of dividends but do not have any voting rights.

Share-the-gains, share-the-pains theory A theory of regulatory behavior that holds that regulators must take account of the demands of three groups: legislators, who established and oversee the regulatory agency; firms in the regulated industry; and consumers of the regulated industry's products.

Short run The time period during which at least one input, such as plant size, cannot be changed.

Shortage A situation in which quantity demanded is greater than quantity supplied at a price below the market clearing price.

Short-run aggregate supply curve The relationship between total planned economywide production and the price level in the short run, all other things held constant. If prices adjust incompletely in the short run, the curve is positively sloped.

Short-run break-even price The price at which a firm's total revenues equal its total costs. At the break-even price, the firm is just making a normal rate of return on its capital investment. (It is covering its explicit and implicit costs.)

Short-run economies of operation A distinguishing characteristic of an information product arising from declining short-run average total cost as more units of the product are sold.

Short-run shutdown price The price that covers average variable costs. It occurs just below the intersection of the marginal cost curve and the average variable cost curve.

Signals Compact ways of conveying to economic decision makers information needed to make decisions. An effective signal not only conveys information but also provides the incentive to react appropriately. Economic profits and economic losses are such signals.

Slope The change in the y value divided by the corresponding change in the x

value of a curve; the "incline" of the curve.

Small menu costs Costs that deter firms from changing prices in response to demand changes–for example, the costs of renegotiating contracts or printing new price lists.

Social costs The full costs borne by society whenever a resource use occurs. Social costs can be measured by adding external costs to private, or internal, costs.

Special drawing rights (SDRs) Reserve assets created by the International Monetary Fund for countries to use in settling international payment obligations.

Specialization The organization of economic activity so that what each person (or region) consumes is not identical to what that person (or region) produces. An individual may specialize, for example, in law or medicine. A nation may specialize in the production of coffee, e-book readers, or digital cameras.

Stagflation A situation characterized by lower real GDP, lower employment, and a higher unemployment rate during the same period that the rate of inflation increases.

Standard of deferred payment A property of an item that makes it desirable for use as a means of settling debts maturing in the future; an essential property of money.

Static tax analysis Economic evaluation of the effects of tax rate changes under the assumption that there is no effect on the tax base, meaning that there is an unambiguous positive relationship between tax rates and tax revenues.

Stock The quantity of something, measured at a given point in time—for example, an inventory of goods or a bank account. Stocks are defined independently of time, although they are assessed at a point in time.

Store of value The ability to hold value over time; a necessary property of money.

Strategic dependence A situation in which one firm's actions with respect to price, quality, advertising, and related changes may be strategically countered by the reactions of one or more other firms in the industry. Such dependence can exist only when there are a limited number of major firms in an industry.

Strategy Any rule that is used to make a choice, such as "Always pick heads."

Strikebreakers Temporary or permanent workers hired by a company to replace union members who are striking.

Structural unemployment Unemployment of workers over lengthy intervals resulting from skill mismatches with position requirements of employers and from fewer jobs being offered by employers constrained by governmental business regulations and labor market policies.

Subsidy A negative tax; a payment to a producer from the government, usually in the form of a cash grant per unit.

Substitutes Two goods are substitutes when a change in the price of one causes a shift in demand for the other in the same direction as the price change.

Substitution effect The tendency of people to substitute cheaper commodities for more expensive commodities.

Supply A schedule showing the relationship between price and quantity supplied for a specified period of time, other things being equal.

Supply curve The graphical representation of the supply schedule; a line (curve) showing the supply schedule, which generally slopes upward (has a positive slope), other things being equal.

Supply-side economics The suggestion that creating incentives for individuals and firms to increase productivity will cause the aggregate supply curve to shift outward.

Surplus A situation in which quantity supplied is greater than quantity demanded at a price above the market clearing price.

Sympathy strike A work stoppage by a union in sympathy with another union's strike or cause.

T

Tariffs Taxes on imported goods.

Tax base The value of goods, services, wealth, or incomes subject to taxation.

Tax bracket A specified interval of income to which a specific and unique marginal tax rate is applied.

Tax incidence The distribution of tax burdens among various groups in society.

Tax rate The proportion of a tax base that must be paid to a government as taxes.

Taylor rule An equation that specifies a federal funds rate target based on an estimated long-run real interest rate, the current deviation of the actual inflation rate from the Federal Reserve's inflation objective, and the gap between actual real GDP per year and a measure of potential real GDP per year.

Technology The total pool of applied knowledge concerning how goods and services can be produced.

The Fed The Federal Reserve System; the central bank of the United States.

Theory of public choice The study of collective decision making.

Third parties Parties who are not directly involved in a given activity or transaction. For example, in the relationship between caregivers and patients, fees may be paid by third parties (insurance companies, government).

Thrift institutions Financial institutions that receive most of their funds from the savings of the public. They include savings banks, savings and loan associations, and credit unions.

Tie-in sales Purchases of one product that are permitted by the seller only if the consumer buys another good or service from the same firm.

Tit-for-tat strategic behavior In game theory, cooperation that continues as long as the other players continue to cooperate.

Total costs The sum of total fixed costs and total variable costs.

Total income The yearly amount earned by the nation's resources (factors of production). Total income therefore includes wages, rent, interest payments, and profits that are received by workers, landowners, capital owners, and entrepreneurs, respectively.

Total revenues The price per unit times the total quantity sold.

Trade deflection Moving partially assembled products into a member nation of a regional trade bloc, completing assembly, and then exporting them to other nations within the bloc, so as to benefit from preferences granted by the trade bloc.

Trade diversion Shifting existing international trade from countries outside a regional trade bloc to nations within the bloc.

Trading Desk An office at the Federal Reserve Bank of New York charged with implementing monetary policy strategies developed by the Federal Open Market Committee.

Transaction costs All of the costs associated with exchange, including the informational costs of finding out the price and quality, service record, and durability of a product, plus the cost of contracting and enforcing that contract.

Transactions approach A method of measuring the money supply by looking at money as a medium of exchange.

Transactions demand Holding money as a medium of exchange to make payments. The level varies directly with nominal GDP.

Transactions deposits Checkable and debitable account balances in commercial banks and other types of financial institutions, such as credit unions and savings banks. Any accounts in financial institutions from which you can easily transmit debit-card and check payments without many restrictions.

Transfer payments Money payments made by governments to individuals for which no services or goods are rendered in return. Examples are Social Security old-age and disability benefits and unemployment insurance benefits.

Transfers in kind Payments that are in the form of actual goods and services, such as food stamps, subsidized public housing, and medical care, and for which no goods or services are rendered in return.

Traveler's checks Financial instruments obtained from a bank or a nonbanking organization and signed during purchase that can be used in payment upon a second signature by the purchaser.

Two-sided market A market in which an intermediary firm provides services that link groups of producers and consumers.

U

Unanticipated inflation Inflation at a rate that comes as a surprise, either higher or lower than the rate anticipated.

Unemployment The total number of adults (aged 16 years or older) who are willing and able to work and who are actively looking for work but have not found a job.

Union shop A business enterprise that may hire nonunion members, conditional on their joining the union by some specified date after employment begins.

Unit elasticity of demand A demand relationship in which the quantity demanded changes exactly in proportion to the change in price.

Unit of accounting A measure by which prices are expressed; the common denominator of the price system; a central property of money.

Unit tax A constant tax assessed on each unit of a good that consumers purchase.

Unlimited liability A legal concept whereby the personal assets of the owner of a firm can be seized to pay off the firm's debts.

Util A representative unit by which utility is measured.

Utility The want-satisfying power of a good or service.

Utility analysis The analysis of consumer decision making based on utility maximization.

V

Value added The dollar value of an industry's sales minus the value of intermediate goods (for example, raw materials and parts) used in production.

Variable costs Costs that vary with the rate of production. They include wages paid to workers and purchases of materials.

Versioning Selling a product in slightly altered forms to different groups of consumers.

Vertical merger The joining of a firm with another to which it sells an output or from which it buys an input.

Voluntary exchange An act of trading, done on an elective basis, in which both

parties to the trade expect to be better off after the exchange.

Voluntary import expansion (VIE) An official agreement with another country in which it agrees to import more from the United States.

Voluntary restraint agreement (VRA) An official agreement with another country that "voluntarily" restricts the quantity of its exports to the United States.

W

Wants What people would buy if their incomes were unlimited.

World Bank A multinational agency that specializes in making loans to about 100 developing nations in an effort to promote their long-term development and growth.

World Trade Organization (WTO) The successor organization to the GATT that handles trade disputes among its member nations.

X

x **axis** The horizontal axis in a graph.

Y

y **axis** The vertical axis in a graph.

Z

Zero-sum game A game in which any gains within the group are exactly offset by equal losses by the end of the game.

Index

A

Absolute advantage, 39
Absolute poverty, 672
Absolute (money) price, 49–50, 69
Absolute price elasticity of demand, 416
Accounting identities, 726–27
Accounting profit, 468–69
Accounting services, outsourcing to
    Canada, 629–30, 631
Additional cost, law of increasing, 34–35
Ad valorem taxation, 129, 132
Advantage, absolute, 39
Advantage, comparative. *See* Comparative
    advantage
Advertising, 557, 562–64
AFC (average fixed costs), 491, 565
AFL-CIO, 643, 645
Africa, region trade blocs, 718
African Americans, income differences, 670
African Growth and Opportunity Act
    (2000), 713
Age, income differences, 668
Age-earnings cycle, 668, 682–83
Aggregate, defined, 3
Agriculture, 64, 85–87
Airlines
    block times, 26, 42–43
    boarding lotteries, 81
    cap-and-trade program, 696–97
    diseconomies of scale, 500
    Ex-Im Bank loans to foreign carriers, 713
    fees, 542
    price elasticity of demand for, 420, 424
    regulation of, 596
    subsidies, 116
Air pollution, 687–89, 695–99. *See also*
    Pollution
Alcoa (Aluminum Company of America), 533
Allocation of capital, 521
Allocation of resources
    command and control economies, 4
    economic rent and, 465
    interest and, 471–72
    market clearing price, 519
    oligopolies, 578
Allowances, emissions, 695
Aluminum industry, 533, 575
American Airlines, 81, 500
Amidi, Saeed, 526
Amtrak, 544
Andean Community, 718
Antitrust legislation, 106, 606–11
Appreciation, 733
Apps. *See* Digital apps
Army, U.S., 491
Artificial intelligence (AI), 476
Association of Southeast Asian Nations,
    718
Assumptions
    bounded rationality, 9–10

ceteris paribus, 8
    defined, 8
Asymmetric information, 601–2
ATC. *See* Average total costs (ATC)
AT&T, 610
Attorneys, wages of, 627–28
Audience-seeking markets, 585
Auten, Gerald, 666
Automobile industry
    cash for clunkers program, 90–91
    electric cars, 50, 502
    four-firm concentration ratio, 577
    fragrance, 568
    gas mileage standards, 688
    Japanese imports, 714, 716
    lemons problem, 601–2
    as oligopoly, 574
    used car prices, 90–91
    U.S. government's command-and-control
        authority, 5
AVC. *See* Average variable costs (AVC)
Average cost pricing, 599
Average costs
    average physical product and, 496–97
    calculation, 491
    defined, 492
    information products, 565, 566
    marginal costs and, 493
Average fixed costs (AFC), 491, 565
Average physical product, 486, 496–97
Average tax rate, 124, 134–35
Average total costs (ATC)
    average physical product and, 496–97
    calculation, 491
    defined, 492
    information products, 565, 566
    marginal costs and, 493
Average variable costs (AVC)
    average physical product and, 496–97
    calculation, 491
    defined, 492
    information products, 565
    marginal costs and, 493

B

Bads, 28
Balance of payments, 726–31, 742–43
Balance of trade, 726
Balint, Frankie, 636
Banks, 6, 596, 602–3
Barriers to entry, 533–36, 548–49, 575
Basker, Emek, 426
Behavior
    models of, 9
    opportunistic behavior, 580–81
    tit-for-tat strategic behavior, 581
Behavioral economics, 9–10, 445–46, 447
Bentham, Jeremy, 435
Bilateral monopoly, 655

Birth rates, 12
Black market, 82–83
Blockbuster, 607
Block times, airline industry, 42–43
Bonds, 474–77
Books, 568–69, 603, 623, 720
Borrowing
    by corporations, 474
    by government, 123
Bounded rationality, 9–10, 447
Boycotts, 644
Brand names, 561–62
Brazil, real exchange rate against dollar, 741
Break-even price in short run, 515–16
Bretton Woods Agreement (1945), 739
Britain. *See* United Kingdom
Budget constraint, 456–57
Budget constraint, government, 123, 135
Budget share, price elasticity of demand
    and, 422
Bundling, 611
Businesses. *See* Firms

C

California
    cap-and-trade program, 696
    flower growers, 720–21
    hen housing regulation, 595
    high-speed rail project, 4
Canada
    outsourcing accounting services to,
        629–30, 631
    public employee unionization, 651
Cap-and-trade programs, 687, 695–99
Capital. *See also* Human capital
    allocation in competitive situation, 521
    financial, 470
    opportunity cost of, 468–69
    physical, 28
Capital account, 729–30
Capital flight, 731
Capital gains, 127
Capital gains tax, 127, 131
Capital goods, 36, 37–38
Capital loss, 127
Capital stock, defined, 667
Cappuccinos, consumer optimum, 439–41
Capture hypothesis, 604
Cartels, 581–83
Cash for clunkers program, 90–91
Caskets, demand for, 69
Caveat emptor, 601
Celebrities, 464
Cell phones. *See* Phones
Central planning, 4
Century bonds, 475
CEO pay, 670
Certificates of convenience and public
    necessity, 534–35

Ceteris paribus assumption, 8
Ceteris paribus conditions
  defined, 54
  of demand, 49, 54, 57
  industry supply curve, 519
  of supply, 62, 64
Chamberlin, Edward, 556, 561
Change in demand, 57
Change in quantity demanded, 57
Change in quantity supply, 64
Change in supply, 64
Change to Win, 645
Charitable donations, 9
Chevron, 488
Chicago, trash removal, 698
China
  child birth in Hong Kong, 1, 12
  electricity rationing, 83
  housing demand price elasticities, 429
  new factory and road trade-off, 33
  outsourcing to, 630
  trade deficit with, 742–43
Choice. *See also* Consumer choice
  economics as study of, 2–3
  rules of thumb, 10
  scarcity and, 29–30
  theory of public choice, 114–16
Chow, Gregory, 429
Chu, Steven, 446
CIO (Congress of Industrial
    Organizations), 643
Clayton Act (1914), 607
Closed shop, 644
Clothing, cotton prices, 63
Coffee, 76
Colbert, Jean-Baptiste, 123
Collective bargaining, 643, 657–58
Collective decision making, 114–16
College education
  economics major, 2
  employment prospects, 619
  marriage and, 664
  prices, 49, 69–70
  return on investment, 669
  student loans, 463
  textbooks, 588–89, 603
  tuition rates, 124, 545
Collusion, 556, 581–83
Colombia, cut flowers from, 720–21
Command-and-control economic system, 4
Commerce Department, U.S., 27
Commercial banks, 6, 596, 602–3
Common property, 693–95, 697
Common stock, 474
Community of East and Southern Africa, 718
Comparative advantage. *See also*
    Specialization
  among nations, 40–41, 631, 706–11
  defined, 38–39, 706
  linen production, 711
Competition. *See also* Monopolistic
    competition; Perfect competition
  government's role in promotion, 106
  international competitiveness, 712
  public vs. private sector, 114
Complementary inputs, 626–27
Complements, 56, 425
Computers

Japanese-made laptop tariff, 716, 717
  technical support services, 629, 631
Concentration ratio, 576, 588–89
Congress. *See also* Laws and legislation
  agricultural subsidies, 86
  capital gains tax, 127
  double taxation, 128
  health care, 111
  luxury tax, 129
  Social Security, 673
Congress of Industrial Organizations
    (CIO), 643
Constant-cost industry, 523
Constant returns to scale, 498
Construction, rent control impact, 83
Consumer choice, 434–61
  behavioral economics, 445–46
  consumer optimum, 439–43
  demand curve and, 444–45
  diamond-water paradox, 444–45
  healthful foods, 447–48
  indifference, 452–59
  utility analysis, 435–39, 445–46
Consumer expectations, demand curve
    shifts, 56
Consumer expenditures. *See* Consumption
Consumer optimum, 439–43, 447–48, 457–58
Consumer Price Index (CPI), 671
Consumer Product Safety Commission
    (CPSC), 597
Consumer protection regulations, 601–3
Consumers, taxation from point of view of,
    132–34
Consumer surplus, 96–97, 99, 553–54
Consumption
  defined, 36
  non-essential items, 27
  trade-offs between present and future,
    36–38
Consumption goods, 37–38
Consumption possibilities curve, 456–57
Contracting, 694
Cooperative game, 579, 581–83
Cork wine stoppers, 56
Corporations
  advantages and disadvantages of, 467
  CEO pay, 670
  decline in number of, 477–78
  defined, 467
  financing methods, 474–75
  income tax, 127–28
  incorporation outside U.S., 11, 478
  tax rate, 11
Cost(s). *See also* Average costs; Opportunity
    cost; Social costs
  explicit, 468
  external, 101–4, 688
  fixed, 489
  health care, 674–76
  implicit, 468
  internal, 688
  law of increasing additional, 34–35
  marginal, 492–96, 512–13, 691–92
  private, 688, 698–99
  short-run, 489–94
  total, 489, 510
  transaction, 76, 694
  variable, 489–91

Cost and output determination for firms,
    483–506
  long-run costs, 497–500
  minimum efficient scale, 500–501
  output-input relationship, 485–87
  short-run costs, 489–97
  short run vs. long run, 484
Cost curves
  long-run average, 497–500, 502, 534
  marginal, 534, 558–59
  short-run average, 491–92
Cost minimization, 634–35, 636–37
Cost-of-service regulation, 599
Cotton prices, 63
Coupons, rationing by, 81
CPI (Consumer Price Index), 671
CPSC (Consumer Product Safety
    Commission), 597
Craft unions, 643
Creative response, 603
Credence goods, 563, 602
Credit. *See also* Loans
  government extension to favored indus-
    tries, 473
  interest and, 470–71
Credit card industry, 586
Credit unions, 596
Cremations, 69
Cross price elasticity of demand (E_{xy}),
    424–25
Crowd funding, 467
Cuba, mixed economic system, 5
Currency market, 726, 732. *See also*
    Foreign exchange rates
Current account, 728–29

D

Deadweight loss, 554
Debit cards, 415, 586
Decision making
  collective, 114–16
  self-interest in, 2
Decreasing-cost industry, 523–24, 526–27
Delta (Δ), 416
Demand. *See also* Price elasticity of
    demand (E_p)
  changes in, 57, 77–80
  defined, 49
  derived, 622–23, 636–37, 733
  determinants of, 54–57
  for euros, 735–36
  for foreign currency, 732
  for health care, 676–77
  income elasticity of demand, 425–27
  for labor, 619–25, 632–34, 649–50
  law of, 49
  market, 52
  schedule, 51–52
  supply and, 64–68
Demand curve
  consumer choice, 444–45, 458–59
  defined, 52
  health care, 676–77
  horizontal summation, 53
  individual vs. market, 52
  labor, 623–25, 626, 633
  monopolistic competition, 558–59

monopolists, 536–38
perfect competitors, 509, 537
price-quantity relationship, 444–45
shifts in, 52–58, 77–79
Demand schedule, 51–52. *See also* Demand curve
Departments, U.S. *See under* United States
Dependent variables, 17
Depository institutions, regulation of, 596
Depreciation, 733
Depression. *See* Great Depression
Deregulation, 645
Derived demand, 622–23, 636–37, 733
Detroit Symphony strike, 646–47
Diamond-water paradox, 444–45
Digital apps
business-related apps, 484
consumer optimum, 439–41
human labor replaced by, 636–37
income elasticity of demand, 426
price-comparison apps, 446
utility analysis, 436–37, 442, 443
Diminishing marginal product, 487–89, 494–97
Diminishing marginal utility, 438–39
Direct marketing, 562
Direct relationship, 17
Dirty floating exchange rate, 739
Discounting, 473
Discrimination, 670
Diseconomies of scale, 498, 499–500
Distribution of income. *See also* Transfer payments
defined, 664
determinants of income differences, 667–70
gender wage gap, 670, 682–83
measurement of, 664–66
theories of, 670–71
U.S. trends, 666
Dividends, 128, 467
Division of labor, 40, 499
Dollar (U.S.)
exchange rates, 738
present value of, 472–73
trading, 737
Dominant strategies, 579
Donations, charitable, 9
Double taxation, 128
Dumping, 713–14
Dutch East India Company, 474
Dynamic tax analysis, 130–31

E

Earned Income Tax Credit (EITC), 673
Earnings, of superstars, 464. *See also* Wage(s)
Earnings, retained, 128
EBay, 584
e-books, 568–69, 623, 720
e-cigarettes, 604
e-commerce, 130
Economic analysis, power of, 2
Economic Community of West African States, 718
Economic goods, 28
Economic growth, production possibilities curve and, 36

Economic profits
accounting profits vs., 469
maximization, 470
monopolistic competition, 559–60
oligopolies, 582
perfect competition, 514, 515–16, 521–22
Economic regulation, 596, 612–13
Economic rent, 463–65
Economics
behavioral, 9–10, 445–46, 447
defined, 2–3
nature of, 1–25
normative analysis, 10–11
positive analysis, 10–11
as science, 7–10
systematic pursuit of self-motivated interest, 5–7
Economics of Imperfect Competition (Robinson), 556
Economic stability, foreign exchange rates and, 738
Economic stabilization policy, 107–8
Economic system, 3, 4–5
Economies of scale
electric car production, 502
monopolies, 534
monopolistic competition, 566
oligopolies, 575
reasons for, 498–99
Education, 112–13. *See also* College education
EEOC (Equal Employment Opportunity Commission), 597
Efficiency, 34, 578, 712
Efficient markets theory, 475–76
Effluent fee, 103
Egalitarian principle, 670–71
EITC (Earned Income Tax Credit), 673
Elastic demand, 417, 420
Elderly Americans, 674. *See also* Medicare; Social Security
Electric cars, 50, 502
Electricity, 599, 600
Electronic billboards, 563
Emanuel, Rahm, 698
Emissions Trading Scheme (EU), 695–96
Empirical science, 9
Employee benefits, 651
Employment
college education and, 619
minimum wage laws and, 88
in public sector, 612–13, 651
public vs. private sector employee similarity, 114–15
EMU (European Monetary Union), 731
Endangered Species Act (1973), 697
Energy conservation, 501
England. *See* United Kingdom
Entrepreneurs and entrepreneurship, 28, 465
Entry
barriers to, 533–36, 575
labor union limits, 649
monopolistically competitive firms, 558
oligopolies, 575
perfectly competitive firms, 521–22
Environmental economics, 687–703
appropriate pollution amount, 691–93

cap-and-trade programs, 687, 695–99
common property problem, 693–95, 697
endangered species protection, 697
externalities, 689–90
private vs. social costs, 688–90
Environmental Protection Agency (EPA), 597, 688
Equal Employment Opportunity Commission (EEOC), 597
Equality, income distribution theory based on, 670–71
Equilibrium
defined, 65
economic units, 727
foreign exchange rate, 732–37
in labor market, 625–26
market, 520–21
monopolistic competition, 559–60
perfect competition, 520, 524
Equilibrium foreign exchange rate, 732–37
Equilibrium price, 65, 78–79
Equilibrium quantity, 78, 133
Equipment, 499
Euro, 732–37
European Monetary Union (EMU), 731
European Union (EU)
antitrust policy, 608–9
cap-and-trade program, 695–96
international trade, 718
Exchange, voluntary, 76
Exchange rate. *See* Foreign exchange rates
Excise taxes, 132
Ex-Im Bank, 713
Exit of firms, 521–22
Experience, work, 669
Experience goods, 563
Explicit costs, 468
Export-Import (Ex-Im) Bank, 713
Exports, 711–12, 728. *See also* International trade
Expropriation, 115
External benefits, 103, 104–5
External costs, 101–4, 688
Externalities
defined, 101, 689
government tools to correct, 103–5
graphical representation, 102–3
pollution, 689–90, 698–99
resource misallocations, 103
Extreme elasticities, 417–18, 428

F

FAA (Federal Aviation Administration), 596, 601
Facebook, 574
Factors of production, 27, 634–35
Factor utilization, 634–35
Farming, 64, 85–87
Farm Security Act (2002), 86
FCC (Federal Communications Commission), 596, 600
FDA (Food and Drug Administration), 597, 604
FDIC (Federal Deposit Insurance Corporation), 596
Featherbedding, 650
Fed, the, 596

Federal Aviation Administration (FAA), 596, 601
Federal Communications Commission (FCC), 596, 600
Federal Deposit Insurance Corporation (FDIC), 596
Federal employees, 612–13
Federal government. *See* Government
Federal income tax, 126–27
Federal Insurance Contributions Act (FICA) (1935), 128
Federal Motor Carrier Safety Administration, 596
Federal Reserve System (the Fed), 596
Federal taxes, 125–29, 134–35
Federal Trade Commission (FTC)
    antitrust enforcement, 106, 609–11
    consumer protection, 601, 602
    establishment, 597, 608
        Hollywood Video-Blockbuster merger block, 607
        regulatory functions, 597
Federal Trade Commission Act (1914), 607, 608
Feedback effect, 603
Fees, user charges, 123
FICA (Federal Insurance Contributions Act) (1935), 128
Financial capital, 470
Financing
    of corporations, 467, 474–75
    health care, 675–76
    positive externalities of government, 104
    public sector, 123
Firms. *See also* Corporations
    change in number of and supply curve shifts, 63
    cost and output determination, 483–506
    crowd funding, 467
    decline in number of, 477–78
    defined, 465
    number in monopolistically competitive industry, 556–57
    number in oligopolies, 574
    organizational forms, 465–67, 477
    profits, 468–70
    short-run costs, 489–94
First come, first serve, 80
Fixed costs, 489, 491, 565
Fixed exchange rate, 739–41
Flexible exchange rates, 732
Floating exchange rate, 739, 741
Flowers, imports of, 720–21
Food, Conservation, and Energy Act (2008), 86–87
Food and Drug Administration (FDA), 597, 604
Food stamps, 673
Forbes, 464
Ford Motor Company, 564, 568
Foreign exchange market, 726, 732
Foreign exchange rates
    determination of, 732–38
    dirty, 739
    fixed, 739–41
    flexible, 732
    floating, 739, 741
    history of, 738–39
    interest rates and, 738

Foreign exchange risk, 740–41
Foreign trade. *See* International trade
Forgone alternatives, value of, 29–30
Fossil fuels, 705
Four-firm concentration ratio, 576–77
France, book imports, 720
Franchises, 534–35
Freely floating exchange rate, 739, 741
Free-rider problem, 107
Free trade, 712–14
Friedman, Nick, 477
Frito-Lay, 558
FTC. *See* Federal Trade Commission (FTC)
Full-Employment Act (1946), 107–8
Future, trade-off with present, 36–38

G

Gains, capital, 127
Gains from trade, 98–99
Game theory, 579–81
GAO (Government Accountability Office), 673
Gas mileage standards, 688
Gasoline prices, 63, 132–34
Gasoline taxes, 124, 132–34
GATT (General Agreement on Tariffs and Trade), 718
Gee, Geoffrey, 666
Genachowski, Julius, 600
Gender wage gap, 663, 670, 682–83
General Agreement on Tariffs and Trade (GATT), 718
Genetically modified products, 714
Gibson Guitars, 716
Gifford, Ted, 501
Gift cards, 39
Gifts, perceived value of, 7
Gold
    as official reserve asset, 730
    quantity restrictions, 89
Gold standard, 738–39
Goods
    capital, 36
    consumption, 37–38
    credence, 563, 602
    defined, 28
    economic, 28
    experience, 563
    government, 115
    government-inhibited, 108
    government-sponsored, 108, 116–17
    inferior, 55
    intangible, 28
    normal, 55
    political, 115
    private, 106
    public, 106–7
    related, 55–56
    search, 563
Gould, David, 714
Government. *See also* Local government; Public spending; Regulation; State government; Taxation
    bans of certain products, 446
    borrowing by, 123
    decision making, 114–16
    economic functions, 101–8
    political functions, 108–9

    price controls, 81–89
    quantity restrictions, 89
Government Accountability Office (GAO), 673
Government budget constraint, 123, 135
Government employees, 612–13, 651
Government (political) goods, 115
Government-inhibited goods, 108
Government spending. *See* Public spending
Government-sponsored goods, 108, 116–17
Grades, production possibilities curve for, 30–31
Graphs and graphical analysis
    externalities, 102–3
    marginal product of, 488
    maximum of short-run profits, 514
    minimization of short-run losses, 514
    monopoly profits, 542, 543
    price elasticity of demand and total revenues, 419, 420
    reading and working with, 17–24
    trade-offs, 30–31
    utility, 436–37
Great Depression
    agricultural price supports, 85
    government stabilization policy, 107–8
    public spending during, 109
    unions, 643
Greece, health care, 680
Greenhouse gases, cap-and-trade programs, 687, 695–99
Green products, 34
Growth, economic, 36

H

Hambrick, Stanley, 548
Hamburgers, 521
Hansen, David, 612
Happiness, 28, 435
Health care. *See also* Medicaid; Medicare
    Affordable Care Act (2010), 678–81
    cost increases, 674–76
    in Greece, 680
    price elasticity of demand for, 421
    public spending on, 110–12, 674, 675, 680, 681
Healthful food choices, 447–48
Health insurance, government mandate, 678
Health insurance exchanges, 679
Hedge, 741
Herfindahl-Hirschman Index (HHI), 577–78, 588–89, 609–10
Higher education. *See* College education
Higher Education Opportunity Act, 603
Hindenburg Omen, 476–77
Hiring, general rule for, 621
Holiday gifts, perceived value of, 7
Hong Kong, Chinese tourists giving birth in, 12
Horizontal merger, 575, 588
Hospitals, 533, 677. *See also* Health care
Household budget, price elasticity of demand and, 422
Housing
    in China, 429
    public, 108
    rent control effects on supply, 83–84

Human capital
  defined, 28
  investment in, 669, 681, 682–83
Hungary, taxes on prepackaged snacks in, 104
Hyundai, 588

I

Ideas, 711
Identities, accounting, 726–27
IMF (International Monetary Fund), 730, 739
Immigration, 645
Implicit costs, 468
Import quotas, 89
Imports. *See also* International trade
  balance of payments current account, 728
  exports and, 711–12
  flowers, 720–21
  unemployment rate and, 714
Incentives
  defined, 2
  Medicare, 110–11
  public education, 113
  public vs. private sector employees, 114–15
  responding to, 6
Income. *See also* Distribution of income
  college education and, 669
  demand curve shifts, 55
  distribution of, 664–71
  redistribution, 108
Income elasticity of demand (E_i), 425–27
Income in kind, 664–65
Income taxes, 126–28
Increasing additional cost, law of, 34–35
Increasing-cost industry, 523
Independent contractors, 635
Independent variables, 17
Indexes
  Consumer Price Index (CPI), 671
  Herfindahl-Hirschman Index (HHI), 577–78, 588–89, 609–10
India
  outsourcing of computer technical support services to, 629, 631
  specialization, 706–10
Indifference, consumer choice theory, 452–59
Indifference curve, 453–56
Industrial unions, 643
Industries. *See specific industries*
Industry concentration, 576–78, 584, 588–89, 609–10
Industry demand curve, 520, 536
Industry supply curve, 518–19, 520, 522–24
Inefficient point, 34
Inelastic demand, 417, 420
Inelastic supply, 427
Infant industry argument, 713
Inferior goods, 55
Inflation, interest rates and, 471
Informal advertising, 563
Information, asymmetric, 601–2
Information, inside, 476
Information products, 564–69
Inheritance, 669

In-kind benefits, 664–65
Input prices, supply curve shifts, 62–63
Inputs
  outputs and, 485–87
  price elasticity of demand for, 624–25
  short run vs. long run, 484
An Inquiry into the Nature and Causes of the Wealth of Nations, Smith, 5, 40
Inside information, 476
Institute for International Economics, 714
Institute for Management Development, 712
Insurance companies, 596, 675–76
Intangible goods, 28
Intellectual property, 535
Interactive marketing, 563
Interdependence, in oligopolies, 574
Interest
  allocative role of, 471–72
  credit and, 470–71
  defined, 470
Interest rates
  foreign exchange rates and, 738
  inflation and, 471
  present value and, 472–73
  real vs. nominal, 471
Internal costs, 688
International competitiveness, 712
International issues. *See also specific countries*
  antitrust policy, 608–9
  cap-and-trade programs, 695–97
  defense burden, 107
  marginal utility from oil change, 441
  outsourcing, 628–31
  shipping-container prices, 79
  unionization, 651
International Monetary Fund (IMF), 730, 739
International outsourcing, 628–31, 636
International trade
  arguments against free trade, 712–14
  balance of payments, 726–31
  balance of trade, 726
  benefits of, 706–11
  comparative advantage, 40–41, 631, 706–11
  deficits, 742–43
  defined, 40
  flows, 710
  fossil fuels, 705
  growth of, 705–6
  import quotas, 89
  organizations, 718–20
  restrictions, 711–12, 714, 715–18
Internet
  auction services, 584
  browsers, 578
  daily deals, 522
  dating sites, 586–87
  online services, 526
  phone service, 599
  sales tax, 130
  service providers, 600
Interstate trade, defined, 40
Inverse relationship, 17
Ireland, public employee unionization, 651

J

Japan
  air conditioning restrictions, 28

automobile imports from, 714, 716
  electronic billboards, 563
  laptop computer tariff, 716, 717
  tsunami (2011), 91
Jeans, consumer optimum, 440
Job flexibility, 627
Jobs. *See* Employment
Job search, 636
Junk food, taxes on, 104
Jurisdictional dispute, 644
Justice Department, U.S., 106, 609–11

K

Krafcik, John, 588
Kyoto Protocol, 695

L

Labor
  defined, 27
  division of, 40, 499
  economic rent to, 464
  marginal product of, 488
  opportunity cost of 17 minutes of, 30
  productivity, 626–27, 650
Labor demand, 619–25, 632–34, 649–50
Labor demand curve, 623–25, 626, 633
Labor Management Relations Act (1947), 643–44
Labor market, 618–41
  cost minimization, 634–35
  demand, 619–25, 632–34, 646–50
  equilibrium in, 625–26
  human labor replace by robotic devices, 636–37
  monopoly and, 632–34
  monopsonies, 651–56
  national health care program impact, 680
  outsourcing, 628–31, 636
  perfect competition, 619–23, 625–28
  price floors, 87–88
  regulation of, 597
  wage determination, 625–28
Labor productivity, 626–27, 650
Labor supply, 627, 649
Labor supply curve, 627
Labor unions
  antitrust law exemption, 608
  congressional control over, 643–44
  current status of, 644–45
  defined, 643
  economic effects, 650–51
  goals and strategies, 646–50
  history, 643
  strikes, 644, 646–47, 657–58
  ten largest, 645
  wages and, 647, 648–50
Land, defined, 27
Land rent, 463–64
Law (economic)
  of demand, 49
  of diminishing marginal product, 487–88
  of diminishing marginal utility, 438–39
  of increasing additional cost, 34–35
  of substitution, 455
  of supply, 58–59

Laws and legislation. *See also specific legislative acts*
  antitrust, 106, 606–11
  minimum wage, 87–88, 654–55
  right-to-work, 644
Least-cost rule, 634–35
Legal system, 105
Lemonade stands, 535
Lemons problem, 601–2
Liability, legal, 466, 467, 602
Licenses, 534–35, 548–49, 602
Light bulbs, 446
Limited liability, 467
Linear curve, slope of, 21–22
Linen production, 711
Lithium, 526–27
Living wage laws, 87
Loans
  marketing loans for farmers, 86–87
  student, 463
  U.S. Export-Import (Ex-Im) Bank, 713
Lobbying, 605, 720–21
Local government
  public spending, 109–10, 112–13
  taxes, 129–32
Locke, John, 555
Long run
  defined, 484
  firm cost and output determination, 484, 497–500
  perfect competition in, 520–24
  price elasticity of demand in, 423–24
  price elasticity of supply in, 428
Long-run average cost curve, 497–500, 502, 534
Long-run equilibrium
  information product industry, 567
  monopolistic competition, 559–60
  perfect competition, 524
  price level, 520
  zero economic profits, 522
Long-run industry supply curve, 522–24, 526–27
Long-run marginal cost curve, 534
Lorenz curve, 664–66
Luxury tax, 129

M

Macroeconomics, defined, 3
Majority rule, 115
Major League Baseball, antitrust law exemption, 608
Managed floating exchange rate, 739
Mandates, health insurance, 678
Manufacturing, 645
Marginal cost(s)
  average costs and, 493
  defined, 492–93
  marginal physical product and, 494–96
  of pollution abatement, 691–92
  profit maximization, 512–13
Marginal cost curve, 534, 558–59
Marginal cost pricing, 524–25, 566–67, 599
Marginal factor cost (MFC), 621, 652
Marginal factor cost (MFC) curve, 652
Marginal physical product (MPP)
  defined, 487

  diminishing marginal product and, 487–88, 493, 494–96
  of drilling, 488
  of labor, 488, 619–20, 622–23
Marginal product, 486–88, 492–97
Marginal productivity, 668–69
Marginal rate of substitution, 455
Marginal revenue, 512, 536–38, 632
Marginal revenue curve
  monopolies, 546, 598, 632
  monopolistic competitors, 558–59
  perfectly competitive market, 512, 524
Marginal revenue-marginal cost approach to profit maximization, 539–41
Marginal revenue product (MRP)
  calculation, 626
  defined, 621
  digital apps, 636–37
  income differences and, 668–69
  monopolies, 632–33
  perfectly competitive firm, 632
  profit maximization, 635
Marginal revenue product (MRP) curve, 621–23
Marginal tax rate
  2012, 126
  defined, 124
  progressive tax systems, 125
  proportional tax systems, 124
  regressive tax systems, 125
  top U.S. marginal tax rate, 125
Marginal utility
  calculation, 436
  defined, 436
  diamond-water paradox, 444–45
  diminishing marginal utility, 438–39
  graphical representation, 436–37
  healthful food, 447–48
Market(s). *See also* Labor market
  black (underground), 82–83
  defined, 49, 76
  foreign exchange, 726, 732
  product, 597, 619
  relevant, 609
  stock, 475–76
  two-sided, 584–86
  for uranium, 57
Market clearing price, 65, 519–20
Market demand, defined, 52
Market demand for labor, 623–25, 626
Market equilibrium, 520
Market failure, 101, 525, 601
Market feedback, 583–84
Marketing loan programs, 86–87
Market size, 57
Market supply curve, 60–61, 132
Market system. *See* Price system
Marriage, 664
Mass marketing, 562
Matchmaking markets, 585
Maximization of profits. *See* Profit maximization
Medicaid
  Affordable Care Act impact, 678
  dual-coverage, 678
  public spending, 111, 112
  purpose, 675
  third-party payments, 675–76

Medical care. *See* Health care
Medicare
  dual-coverage, 678
  payroll tax, 128
  public spending, 110–12, 677
  third-party payments, 675–76
Mercosur, 718
Mergers, 575, 588–89
MES (minimum efficient scale), 500–501, 502
MFC (marginal factor cost), 621, 652
MFC (marginal factor cost) curve, 652
Michigan, Item Pricing Law, 612
Microeconomics, defined, 3
Microsoft, 586
Middlemen, 77
Mileage taxes, 124
Miller, Larry, 548
Minimum cost points, 493–94
Minimum efficient scale (MES), 500–501, 502
Minimum wage, 87–88, 654–55
Mining Enforcement and Safety Administration, 597
Mixed economic systems, 5
Mobility, income, 666
Models
  assumptions, 8
  of behavior, 9
  defined, 7
  realism and, 7–8
  usefulness, 9
Money price, 49–50, 69
Monopolist, defined, 533. *See also* Monopoly
Monopolistic competition, 555–72
  advertising, 557, 562–64
  brand names, 561–62
  comparison with other market structures, 588
  defined, 556
  e-books, 568–69
  features of, 556–58
  information products, 564–68
  perfect competition vs., 560–61
  price and output, 558–60
Monopolization, defined, 609
Monopoly, 532–54
  antitrust policy, 106, 606–11
  barriers to entry, 533–36, 548–49
  bilateral, 655
  comparison with other market structures, 588
  consumer surplus, 553–54
  deadweight loss, 554
  defined, 106
  demand curve, 536–38
  elasticity of demand, 538
  perfect competition vs., 546–47
  price determination, 541–42
  price discrimination, 544–45
  in product market, 632–34
  profits, 536–37, 539–40
  regulation of, 596, 598–600
  social cost of, 546–47
  unions as, 651
Monopsonist, defined, 652
Monopsonistic exploitation, 654
Monopsony, 651–56

Moral hazard, health care, 677–78, 680
MPP. *See* Marginal physical product (MPP)
MRP. *See* Marginal revenue product (MRP)

N

NAFTA (North American Free Trade
    Agreement), 718
NASDAQ (National Association of
    Securities Dealers Automated
    Quotations), 475
National Credit Union Administration, 596
National health care program, 678–81
National Industrial Recovery Act (1933), 643
National Labor Relations Act (NLRA)
    (1935), 643
National security, 714
Natural gas, 599, 600
Natural monopoly, 534, 596, 598–600
Needs, wants vs., 29
Negative externalities, government
    correction of, 103–4
Negative market feedback, 583–84
Negative-sum game, 579
Network effect, 583–86
Newspapers, 104
New York Bond Exchange, 475
New York City rent controls, 83–85
New York Stock Exchange (NYSE), 475
Niu, Linlin, 429
NLRA (National Labor Relations Act)
    (1935), 643
Nominal (money) price, 49–50, 69
Nominal rate of interest, 471
Noncooperative game, 579
Non-essential items, 27
Nonlinear curve, slope of, 22–23
Nonprice rationing devices, 82
Normal goods, 55
Normal rate of return, 468
Normative economics, 10–11
North American Free Trade Agreement
    (NAFTA), 718
Number line, 18
NYSE (New York Stock Exchange), 475

O

Obama administration, Affordable Care
    Act (2010), 678–81
Occupational barriers to entry, 548–49
Occupational Safety and Health
    Administration (OSHA), 597
Office of Management and Budget, 605
Office of the Comptroller of the Currency,
    596
Oil drilling, 488, 492, 597
Old-age, survivors', and disability insur-
    ance (OASDI). *See* Social Security
Oligopoly, 573–93
    cartels, 581–83
    characteristics of, 574
    comparison with other market
        structures, 588
    defined, 574
    industry concentration measures,
        576–78
    network effects, 583–86

price and output determination, 579–81
    reasons for, 575
    textbook publishers, 588–89
    two-sided markets, 584–86
Online activity. *See* Internet
Opportunistic behavior, 580–81
Opportunity cost. *See also* Trade-offs
    of airlines' block times, 42–43
    of college education, 669
    comparative advantage and, 38–39
    defined, 30
    of labor in U.S., 30
    law of increasing additional cost, 34–35
    public vs. private sector, 114
    of regulatory compliance, 605
    scarcity and, 29–30
    of vacation time in South Korea, 41
Opportunity cost of capital, 468–69
Optimal quantity of pollution, 692–93,
    698–99
Ordered set of points, 18
Organization, forms of business, 465–67
Origin, 19
OSHA (Occupational Safety and Health
    Administration), 597
Outputs. *See also* Cost and output
    determination for firms
    inputs and, 485–87
    monopolistic competitors, 558–60
    oligopolies, 579–81
Outsourcing, 628–31, 636
Overallocation of resources, 103
Ownership
    command-and-control economic system, 4
    private property rights, 693–94
    of resources as barrier to entry, 533
    separation from control in corporations, 467

P

Paired observations of variables, 19–20
Partnerships, 466–67, 477–78
Par value, 739
Patent and Trademark Office, 561–62
Patents, 535
Patient Protection and Affordable Care
    Act (2010), 678–81
Payoff matrix, 579–80
Perfect competition, 507–31
    break-even price, 515–16
    characteristics of, 508
    comparison with other market
        structures, 588
    consumer surplus, 553–54
    defined, 508
    demand curve, 509, 537
    equilibrium, 520
    labor market, 619–23, 625–28
    lithium market, 526–27
    in long run, 520–24
    marginal cost pricing, 524–25
    marginal revenue, 512, 536
    monopolistic competition vs., 560–61
    monopoly vs., 546–47
    price determination under, 519–20
    production decision, 509–10
    profit-maximizing rate of production,
        510–14

profits, 513–14
    in short run, 513–19
    shutdown price, 515–16
    supply curve, 517–19
Perfectly competitive firms, 508
Perfectly elastic demand, 417–18
Perfectly elastic supply, 427
Perfectly inelastic demand, 417–18
Perfectly inelastic supply, 427
Personal income tax, 126–27
Persuasive advertising, 563
Pharmaceutical industry, 67, 89
Phones
    demand for reconditioned phones, 55
    Internet service, 599
    price-comparison apps, 446
    price elasticity of demand-total revenues
        for service relationship, 418–21
    trade-off with tablet devices, 32–33
Physical capital, 28
Physical force, rationing method, 80
Physicians, 677. *See also* Health care
Picketing, 656
Pilot projects, 501
Planning curve, 497
Planning horizon, 497
Plant size, 484, 497–98
PlentyOfFish, 586–87
Point of saturation, 488
Poland, floating exchange rate, 741
Policy issues
    gasoline vs. mileage taxes, 124
    top marginal tax rate, 125
    uranium, 57
Political functions of government, 108–9
Political (government) goods, 115
Political power, rationing method, 80
Political system, 115
Pollution
    abatement of, 691–92, 693
    assessment of appropriate amount,
        691–92
    costs of, 688–90
    defined, 691
    externalities, 689–90, 698–99
    optimal quantity of, 692–93, 698–99
Portugal, human capital investment, 681
Positive economics, 10–11
Positive externalities, 104
Positive market feedback, 583
Positive-sum game, 579
Poultry production, 64
Poverty
    absolute, 672
    anti-poverty programs, 672–74
    defined, 671
    relative, 672
    scarcity vs., 27
Poverty rate, 671, 672, 673–74
PPC. *See* Production possibilities curve (PPC)
Preferred stock, 474
Present, trade-off with future, 36–38
Present value, 472–73
Price(s)
    absolute (money), 49–50, 69
    break-even in short run, 515–16
    of college education, 49, 69–70
    demand and, 49–50, 52–54

Price(s) (*continued*)
equilibrium, 65, 78–79
of gasoline, 63, 132–34
of higher education, 69–70
input, 62–63
market clearing, 65, 519–20
rationing function of, 80–81
relative price, 49–50, 69–70
shutdown price in short run, 515–16
supply and, 58–59, 61–62
of used cars, 75, 90–91
Price ceilings, 81–85
Price changes
consumer optimum impact, 442–43
labor demand and, 627
price elasticity of demand and, 422–24
price elasticity of supply and, 427–29
Price controls
defined, 81
gains from trade and, 98–99
price ceilings, 81–85
price floors, 82, 85–89
Price determination
average cost pricing, 599
game theory and, 580–81
marginal cost pricing, 524–25, 566–67, 599
monopolies, 541–44
monopolistic competition, 558–60
oligopolies, 578–83
under perfect competition, 519–20
Price differentiation, 544
Price discrimination, 544–45, 610–11
Price elasticity of demand (E_p)
calculation of, 416–17
cross price elasticity of demand, 424–25
defined, 415–16
determinants of, 421–24
for health care services, 421
for labor, 624–25
monopolies, 538
ranges, 417–18
real-world examples, 424
for rock music, 429–30
total revenues and, 418–21
Price elasticity of supply (E_s), 427–29
Price expectations, and supply curve shifts, 63
Price flexibility, adjustment speed and, 79–80
Price floors, 82, 85–88
Price per constant-quality unit, 50
Price searcher, 539
Price supports, 85–87
Price system
defined, 76
features of, 4–5, 76–77
gains from trade within, 98
limitations of, 101
public sector vs., 114–16
Price tags, 612
Price taker, 508
Pricing. *See* Price determination
Principle of rival consumption, 106
Principle of substitution, 443
Prisoners' Dilemma, 579–80
Private costs, 688, 698–99
Private goods, 106
Private property rights, 693–94
Producers, taxation from point of view of,

132–34
Producer surplus, 97–98, 99
Product bundling, 611
Product differentiation, 557
Production
defined, 27, 485
economic system choice, 3
factors of, 27, 634–35
perfect competitors, 509–10
profit-maximizing rate of, 510–14
Production function, 485–87
Production possibilities curve (PPC)
assumptions underlying, 33
being outside, 34
defined, 31
economic growth and, 36
efficiency and, 34
grades, 30–31
law of increasing additional cost, 34–35
present and future consumption
trade-off, 36–38
smartphone and tablet device trade-off,
32–33
Productivity
income distribution theory based on, 670
of labor, 626–27, 650
specialization and, 38–40
Product markets, 597, 619
Product packaging, 610–11
Product quality, 601–2
Profit(s). *See also* Economic profits
accounting, 468–69
monopolists, 536–37, 539–44
reinvestment of, 475
in short run, 513–14
Profit maximization
factors of production, 635
as goal of firm, 470, 510
labor demand and, 635
monopolies, 539–42
monopolistic competitors, 557–58, 561
oligopolies, 582
perfectly competitive firms, 510–14
wage rates, 654
Profit-maximizing rate of production, 510–14
Progressive taxation, 125
Property rights
defined, 102, 693
environmental resources, 693–95
legal system's role in protection, 105
Proportional rule, 115
Proportional taxation, 124–25
Proprietorships, 466, 468–69, 477–78
Public choice, theory of, 114–16
Public education, public spending on,
112–13
Public goods, 106–7
Public housing, 108
Public spending
allocation, 109–10
education, 112–13
federal regulation, 605
health care, 110–12, 674, 675, 677, 680,
681
as percentage of national income, 135
price system limitations, 101
trends, 109, 122
on U.S. Postal Service, 100, 116–17

Publishing, 568–69, 588–89, 603, 623, 720
Purchasing power, 443
Pure monopoly. *See* Monopoly

Q

Quantity demanded, changes in, 57
Quantity restrictions, 89
Queues, rationing by, 80
Quick-response (QR) apps, 77
Quota system, 89, 715–16

R

Railroads, 544
Random assignment, 81
Random walk theory, 476
Rate of discount, 473
Rate-of-return regulation, 599, 612–13
Rate regulation, 596
Rationality, bounded, 9–10, 447
Rationality assumption, 506
Rationing, 80–81. *See also* Price controls
Rationing function of prices, 80–81
Raye, Billy, 656
Reaction function, 578
Real-income effect of price change, 443
Realism, models and, 7–8
Real rate of interest, 471
Recessions, dumping during, 713–14
Redistribution of income, 108
Regional trade blocs, 718–19, 720
Regressive taxation, 125
Regulation
advertising, 564
as barrier to entry, 535
consumer protection, 601–3
cost-of-service, 599
costs of, 605–6
creative response to, 603
economic, 596, 612–13
federal employee trends, 612–13
labor unions, 643–44
of natural monopolies, 596, 598–600
negative externality correction, 104
of nonmonopolistic industries, 596,
600–603
positive externality correction, 105
rate, 596
rate-of-return, 599, 612–13
regulators' behavior, 604–5
social, 597, 612–13
trends, 595
types of, 595–97
Reinvestment, 475
Related goods, 55–56
Relative poverty, 672
Relative price, 49–50, 69–70
Relevant market, 609
Rent, economic, 463–65
Rent control, 83–85
Reserve account transactions, 730–31
Resources
allocation of, 4, 465, 471–72, 519, 578
defined, 2
overallocation of, 103
scarcity and, 27–28
underallocation of, 103

Restraint of trade, 606. *See also* Monopoly
Retail industry, 547, 586
Retained earnings, 128
Revenues
    marginal, 512, 536–38, 632
    total, 418–21, 429–30, 510
Ricardo, David, 463–64
Right-to-work laws, 644
Robberies of banks, 6
Robinson, Joan, 556
Robinson-Patman Act (1936), 607, 608
Robotic devices, 636–37
Rock music, price elasticities of demand, 429–30
Ruffin, Roy, 714
Rules of origin, 719
Rules of thumb, 10

S
Sales promotion, 557
Sales taxes, 129–32
Saturation point, 488
Scaling, 18
Scalping, 68
Scarcity, 26–47. *See also* Trade-offs
    choice and, 29–30
    defined, 27
    goods vs. economic goods, 28
    opportunity cost and, 29–30
    resources and, 27–28
    specialization, 38–41
    wants vs. needs, 29
Schmalz, Linda, 568
Schneider National, 501
Science, economics as, 7–10
SDRs (special drawing rights), 730
Search goods, 563
Secondary boycott, 644
Securities
    bonds, 474–77
    defined, 475
    regulation of, 596
    stock, 474–77
Securities and Exchange Commission (SEC), 467, 596
Self-interest
    decision making role, 2
    defined, 6–7
    scarcity and, 39–40
Services
    balance of payment current account, 728
    defined, 28
Shared-input markets, 585, 586
Shared office space, 526
Share of stock, 474–77
Share-the-gains, share-the-pains theory, 604–5
Sherman Antitrust Act (1890), 606–7
Shipping-container prices, 79
Shock absorber, exchange rate as, 741
Shocks, supply and demand system effects, 77
Shortages
    defined, 67
    demand and supply, 65, 66–67
    drugs, 67, 89
    scarcity vs., 27, 67
    sports tickets, 68

Short run
    defined, 484
    firm cost and output determination, 484, 489–97
    perfect competition in, 513–19
    price elasticity of demand in, 423–24
    price elasticity of supply in, 428
Short-run average cost curve, 491–92
Short-run break-even price, 515–16
Short-run costs, 489–94
Short-run economies of operation, 566, 568–69
Short-run equilibrium, monopolistic competition, 559
Short-run profits, 513–14
Short-run shutdown price, 515–16
Short-run supply curve, 517–19
Shutdown price in short run, 515–16
Signals, 4, 76, 521, 563–64
Simulations, 491, 501
Slope, 21–23
Smartphones. *See* Phones
Smith, Adam, 5, 40, 444, 581
Smoot-Hawley Tariff, 716
SNAP (Supplemental Nutrition Assistance Program), 673
Social costs
    labor unions, 651
    monopolies, 546–47
    pollution, 688, 698–99
    regulation, 604–5
Social regulation, 597, 612–13
Social Security
    benefits, 672–73
    crisis, 134
    as government transfer payment, 108
    public spending on, 109, 110
    tax, 125, 128
Solar energy, 492, 697
Sole proprietorships, 466, 468–69, 477–78
Soliman, Omar, 477
South Korea, vacation time, 41
Space travel, 107
Special drawing rights (SDRs), 730
Specialization. *See also* Comparative advantage
    among nations, 706–11
    defined, 38
    division of labor, 40
    firms, 499
    linen production, 711
    output gains from, 706
    reasons for, 38–39
    self-interest and, 39–40
Spending. *See* Consumption; Public spending
Sports, scalping, 68
SSI (Supplemental Security Income), 673
Stabilization, policy goals, 107–8
Standard Oil Trust, 606
State government
    public spending, 109–10, 112–13
    taxes, 129–32
Static tax analysis, 129–30
Steel production, 59
Stock, share of, 474–77
Stockholders, 128, 467
Stock market, 475–77

Straight-line production possibilities curve, 31
Strategic dependence, 574
Strategy, 579
Strikebreakers, 646
Strikes, 644, 646–47, 657–58
Student loans, 463
Subsidies
    agriculture, 86–87
    airline industry, 116
    defined, 63
    by foreign governments, 713
    health care, 110–12, 678
    negative externality correction, 104
    supply curve shifts, 63
Substitutes
    cross price elasticity of demand and, 425
    defined, 56
    ownership of resources without, 533
    price elasticity of demand and, 422
Substitution
    law of, 455
    marginal rate of, 455
    principle of, 443
Substitution effect, 442–43
Sulfur dioxide cap-and-trade program, 698–99
Supermarkets, consumer choice, 435
Supplemental Nutrition Assistance Program (SNAP), 673
Supplemental Security Income (SSI), 673
Supply
    changes in, 64, 77–80
    defined, 58
    demand and, 64–68
    determinants of, 62–64
    of euros, 733–35, 737
    of foreign currency, 732
    of labor, 627, 649
    law of, 58–59
    price elasticity of, 427–29
    schedule, 59–61
Supply curve
    defined, 60
    horizontal summation, 60
    individual vs. market, 60–61
    labor, 627
    perfect competitors, 517–19
    shifts in, 61–64, 77–79
Supply schedule, 59–61. *See also* Supply curve
Surplus
    consumer surplus, 96–97, 99, 553–54
    defined, 65, 67
    producer surplus, 97–98, 99
Sympathy strike, 644

T
Tables, graphing number in, 19–20
Tablet devices, 32–33, 417
Taft-Hartley Act (1947), 643–44
Talent, 669
TANF (Temporary Assistance to Needy Families), 673
Tariffs, 535, 716–18, 720–21
Tastes and preferences, demand curve shifts, 55

Taxation. *See also* Marginal tax rate
  on capital gains, 127, 131
  of corporations, 127–28
  double, 128
  federal taxes, 125–29, 134–35
  income tax, 126–28
  of luxury goods, 129
  national health care program, 679, 681
  negative externality correction, 103
  of pollution, 690
  from producers' and consumers' point
    of view, 132–34
  revenues from, 129–32
  sales tax, 129–32
  supply curve shifts, 63
  systems of, 123–25
  unemployment, 128–29
  uniform tax, 690
  unit tax, 132
Tax base, 124
Tax bracket, 124
Tax credits, 673
Tax incidence, 128
Tax rate. *See also* Marginal tax rate
  average, 124, 134–35
  corporate, 11
  defined, 124
  setting for desired revenues, 129–32
Tax return preparation, 127
Tax subsidies, 678
Technology
  defined, 33
  supply curve shifts, 63
  trade-offs, 32–33
Teenagers, minimum wage and
    employment rate, 88
Telecommunications industry, 584, 596,
    599, 600, 610
Temporary Assistance to Needy Families
    (TANF), 673
Textbook-publishing industry, 588–89, 603
Textile industry, 715
Theories
  assumptions, 8
  defined, 7
  game theory, 579–81
Theory of Monopolistic Competition
    (Chamberlin), 556
Theory of public choice, 114–16
Third parties, 101, 676, 680
Three-dimensional (3D) printers, 485
Tie-in sales, 611
Tit-for-tat strategic behavior, 581
T-Mobile, 610
Tobacco bonds, 123
Tobacco products regulation, 604
Total costs, 489, 510
Total revenues, 418–21, 429–30, 510
Total revenue-total costs approach to
    profit maximization, 539
Total utility, 436, 437, 444–45
Trade. *See also* International trade
  among regions, 40
  gains from, 98–99
Trade and Tariff Act (1984), 716
Trade deficit, 742–43
Trade deflection, 719
Trade diversion, 719

Trade Expansion Act (1962), 716
Trademarks, 561–62
Trade-offs. *See also* Production possibilities
    curve (PPC)
  defined, 30
  present and future, 36–38
  smartphones and tablets, 32–33
Trade Reform Act (1974), 716
Training, 669
Transaction-based markets, 585, 586
Transaction costs, 76, 694
Transfer payments
  defined, 108
  to foreign residents, 725, 729
  government budget constraint, 123
  poverty reduction, 671, 672–74
  public spending and, 109–13
Transfers in kind, 108. *See also* Medicaid;
    Medicare
Transportation Department, U.S., 4
Transportation industry, 49, 79
Trash removal, 698
Trucking industry, 596
Two-country, two-good world example of
    specialization, 706–7
Two-good examples, of choice, 32, 439–40
Two-sided markets, 584–86

U

Underallocation of resources, 103
Underground transactions, 82–83
Unemployment, imports and, 714
Unemployment compensation, 128–29
Uniform tax, 690
Unilateral transfers, 729
Unions. *See* Labor unions
Union shop, 644
United Kingdom
  labor unions, 643
  public employee unionization, 651
United States. *See also specific index*
    headings
  economic system, 5
  minimum wage, 87–88
  opportunity cost of 17 minutes of labor, 30
  regional trade, 40
U.S. Army, 491
U.S. Congress. *See* Congress
U.S. Department of Commerce, 27
U.S. Department of Justice, 106, 609–11
U.S. Department of Transportation, 4
U.S. dollar. *See* Dollar (U.S.)
U.S. Export-Import (Ex-Im) Bank, 713
U.S. Patent and Trademark Office, 561–62
U.S. Postal Service (USPS), 100, 114,
    116–17
Unit elasticity of demand, 417, 420
Unit tax, 132
Unlimited liability, 466, 467
Uranium market, 57
Used car prices, 75, 90–91
User charges, 123
Util, 435
Utilitarianism, 435
Utilities, rate regulation, 596
Utility, defined, 436
Utility analysis, 435–39, 445–46

V

Value
  of forgone alternatives, 29–30
  of gifts, 7
  par, 739
  present, 472–73
Variable costs, 489–91
Variable factors of production, 484
Variable inputs, 484
Variables, 17
Vending machines, 438–39
Venezuela, coffee shortage, 76
Versioning, 610–11
Vertical merger, 575, 588
Veterinarians, 518
Video-rental stores, 607
VIE (voluntary import expansion), 716
Voluntary contracting, 694
Voluntary exchange, 76
Voluntary import expansion (VIE), 716
Voluntary restraint agreement (VRA), 716
Voting system, 115
VRA (voluntary restraint agreement), 716

W

Wage(s)
  attorneys, 626–27
  gender wage gap, 670, 682–83
  labor unions and, 647, 648–50
  under monopsony, 652–55
  national health care program impact,
    680
  outsourcing impact, 631
Wage determination, 625–28
Walmart, 426, 547
Wants, 2, 29
War games, 491
Wealth and wealthy people
  distribution of, 667
  marginal tax rate, 125
  scarcity and, 27
Wealth of Nations (Smith), 5, 40
Welfare, 108, 673, 674
Welfare Reform Act (1996), 674
Wild species, 697
Wine, cork vs. plastic stoppers, 56
Women, gender wage gap, 663, 670,
    682–83
Woodbridge, G. L., 714
Work. *See* Employment
Work experience, 669
Working conditions, 627
World Trade Organization (WTO), 713
WTO (World Trade Organization), 713

X

X axis, 19

Y

Y axis, 19

Z

Zero economic profits, 515–16, 559–60
Zero-sum game, 579